1995
THE COMPLETE HANDBOOK OF BASEBALL

① SIGNET SPORTS (0451)

FOR THE SPORTS FAN...

☐ **THE COMPLETE HANDBOOK OF PRO BASKETBALL: 1995 EDITION, edited by Zander Hollander.** Features Hakeem Olajuwon, Reggie Miller, John Starks and Bill Walton. Twenty-seven team yearbooks in one, including more than 300 profiles, 300 photos and year-by-year player and all-time records.
(177940—$5.99)

☐ **THE COMPLETE HANDBOOK OF PRO FOOTBALL: 1994 EDITION, edited by Zander Hollander. 20th anniversary celebration!** The ideal TV guide, with 300 profiles, 28 scouting reports and 300 photos. Plus features on John Madden, Deion Sanders, Emmitt Smith and Buddy Ryan. (177657—$5.99)

☐ **THE ILLUSTRATED SPORTS RECORD BOOK: Third Edition, by Zander Hollander and David Schulz.** 400 historic records recreated in stories with rare photos. Included are Joe Montana's Super Bowl marks, Michael Jordan's NBA playoff feat, Jack Nicklaus' Masters triumphs, Wayne Gretzky's scoring standards, Nolan Ryan's strikeout and no-hit plateaus, Martina Navratilova's Wimbledon crowns, Mark Spitz's Olympic gold medals, Joe DiMaggio's hitting streak, Bill Hartack's Kentucky Derby winners, and much more!
(171179—$5.99)

☐ **THE COMPLETE HANDBOOK OF BASEBALL: 25th Anniversary Edition, 1995, edited by Zander Hollander.** Features 10 great moments of the past 25 years, Bob Costas, David Cone, and Reggie Jackson on the Maris chase. Plus 28 team yearbooks in one, with 350 player, prospect and manager profiles, stats and records. (183894—$5.99)

Prices slightly higher in Canada

Buy them at your local bookstore or use this convenient coupon for ordering.

PENGUIN USA
P.O. Box 999 — Dept. #17109
Bergenfield, New Jersey 07621

Please send me the books I have checked above.
I am enclosing $_____ (please add $2.00 to cover postage and handling). Send check or money order (no cash or C.O.D.'s) or charge by Mastercard or VISA (with a $15.00 minimum). Prices and numbers are subject to change without notice.

Card # _____ Exp. Date _____
Signature_____
Name_____
Address_____
City _____ State _____ Zip Code _____

For faster service when ordering by credit card call **1-800-253-6476**

Allow a minimum of 4-6 weeks for delivery. This offer is subject to change without notice.

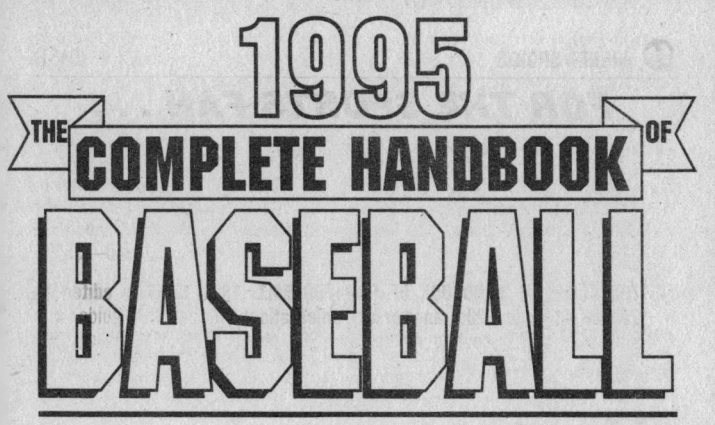

THE 1995 COMPLETE HANDBOOK OF BASEBALL

EDITED BY
ZANDER HOLLANDER

AN ASSOCIATED FEATURES BOOK

A SIGNET BOOK

ACKNOWLEDGMENTS

We unhappily went to press without resolution of the baseball strike. We trust that the impasse that marked the dawning of '95 will have been broken in time for the return of the game that may never be the same.

For this 25th edition, we thank associate editor Howard Blatt, contributing editor Eric Compton, art director Dot Gordineer of Libra Graphics, Lee Stowbridge, the writers and Seymour Siwoff and Bob Rosen of Elias Sports Bureau, Jerry Todd, Linda Spain, Deb Brody, Phyllis Hollander, Katy Feeney, Phyllis Merhige, Joe Fitzgerald, Ricky Clemons, MLB-IBM Information System, Bill Foley, Shā Lee-Carmichael and the crew at Westchester Book Composition.

Zander Hollander

PHOTO CREDITS: Cover—Focus on Sports. Inside Photos—George Gojkovich, Vic Milton, Rosemary Rahn, Mitch Reibel, Sports Photo Source, Wide World, UPI, NBC-TV, Topps and the major league team photographers.

SIGNET
Published by the Penguin Group
Penguin Books USA Inc., 375 Hudson Street,
New York, New York 10014, U.S.A.
Penguin Books Ltd, 27 Wrights Lane,
London W8 5TZ, England
Penguin Books Australia Ltd, Ringwood,
Victoria, Australia
Penguin Books Canada Ltd, 10 Alcorn Ave.,
Toronto, Ontario, Canada M4V 3B2
Penguin Books (N.Z.) Ltd, 182-190 Wairau Road,
Auckland 10, New Zealand

Penguin Books Ltd, Registered Offices:
Hamondsworth, Middlesex, England

First Signet Printing, March 1995
10 9 8 7 6 5 4 3 2 1

Copyright © 1995 Associated Features Inc.
All rights reserved.

 REGISTERED TRADEMARK—MARCA REGISTRADA

Printed in the United States of America

Without limiting the rights under copyright reserved above, no part of this publication may be reproduced, stored in or introduced into a retrieval system, or transmitted, in any form, or by any means (electronic, mechanical, photocopying, recording, or otherwise), without the prior written permission of both the copyright owner and the above publisher of this book.

BOOKS ARE AVAILABLE AT QUANTITY DISCOUNTS WHEN USED TO PROMOTE PRODUCTS OR SERVICES. FOR INFORMATION PLEASE WRITE TO PREMIUM MARKETING DIVISION, PENGUIN BOOKS USA INC., 375 HUDSON STREET, NEW YORK, NEW YORK 10014.

CONTENTS

TOP 10 GREAT MOMENTS OF PAST 25 YEARS
- By Joe Gergen... 8

REGGIE JACKSON HANDICAPS THE MARIS CHASE
- By Phil Pepe... 28

COVERING THE BASES WITH BOB COSTAS
- By Stan Isaacs... 38

THE REBIRTH OF DAVID CONE
- By Bob Klapisch.. 48

INSIDE THE AL - By Jon Heyman and Tony DeMarco..... 56

Baltimore Orioles	58	Kansas City Royals	134
Boston Red Sox	69	Milwaukee Brewers	145
Detroit Tigers	79	Minnesota Twins	154
New York Yankees	90	California Angels	164
Toronto Blue Jays	102	Oakland Athletics	174
Chicago White Sox	113	Seattle Mariners	186
Cleveland Indians	124	Texas Rangers	196

INSIDE THE NL - By Frank Isola and Kevin Kernan........204

Atlanta Braves	206	Houston Astros	283
Florida Marlins	217	Pittsburgh Pirates	293
Montreal Expos	227	St. Louis Cardinals	302
New York Mets	238	Colorado Rockies	312
Philadelphia Phillies	249	Los Angeles Dodgers	323
Chicago Cubs	260	San Diego Padres	333
Cincinnati Reds	272	San Francisco Giants	343

YEAR-BY-YEAR LEADERS................................... 354
ALL-TIME RECORDS.. 372
WORLD SERIES WINNERS................................... 374
OFFICIAL 1994 NATIONAL LEAGUE STATS................ 376
OFFICIAL 1994 AMERICAN LEAGUE STATS............... 404
ALL-TIME LEADERS.. 428

Editor's Note: The material herein includes trades and signings up to final printing deadline.

From The Editor

It was March 1971 and Johnny Bench was the cover boy on the first edition of *The Complete Handbook of Baseball* ($1.25). And now marks the 25th anniversary.

Contributors to the inaugural included Joe Gergen of *Newsday* and Lee Stowbridge of the *New York Daily News*. Both are still in the lineup—Gergen with "Top 10 Great Moments of Past 25 Years" (page 8) and Stowbridge as a peerless source of stats.

This is a silver salute to them, to associate editor Howard Blatt and to all the others who, despite impossible deadlines, late trades and strikes, have helped sustain the Handbook.

As editor, I've had the good fortune to meet some of baseball's immortals—and a few who were merely mortal. Each provided a special memory.

● There was this Sunday in late January one year when I spotted an aging Jackie Robinson on line for the shuttle to Washington at LaGuardia Airport. We'd met a few times before and I greeted him with a query: "Leaving town? Aren't you going to be at the New York baseball writers' dinner tonight?"

"I couldn't care less," snapped Jackie.

● The scene is Cincinnati's Riverfront Stadium at midnight after a night game and an interview I had with Pete Rose. The parking attendant brings Pete's car, Pete pulls out a wad of $100 bills, turns to me and says, "I've got nothing smaller. Can you spare a five?"

● Bob Feller came to the office one snowy, winter day. He wanted to do another book. It had been a long time since his *Strikeout Story*. A photographer from the *New York Daily News* showed up, seeking a shot of Feller throwing a snowball. On a Park Avenue sidewalk, Feller pitched. I caught. Picture made the paper next day. Catcher was cropped out.

● Needed some instructional pitching photos of Bob Gibson. Set up a shoot in his room at the Warwick Hotel. Only problem was that we'd forgotten to bring a baseball. So backup photographer Bob Brown hopped over to the nearby toy store, FAO Schwarz, and all they had was an official American League ball. The National Leaguer made sure to hold it so nobody could tell.

● It's 7 A.M. at New York's Americana Hotel. A limousine comes to pick up Ron (*Breakout: From Prison to the Big Leagues*) LeFlore for an appearance with David Hartman on ABC's "Good Morning America." No answer in LeFlore's room. No LeFlore. Seconds before he's to go on the tube, he shows up. "Out all night," he says with a grin.

● A baseball card collectors' show at the Armenian Church in Manhattan. Joe DiMaggio is giving his autograph for $40 a pop (this was a few years before the price soared to its current $150). A friend called to say he was shut out because 500 fans (the limit imposed by DiMaggio) had already paid in advance. I interceded with the show manager, telling him I knew DiMaggio. Which was the truth. My friend got his autograph.

For the record, I've only asked one athlete for his autograph—Joe DiMaggio. This was on a priceless photo of him coming down the gangplank of a transport ship at Pearl Harbor in 1944. That's when I first met Staff Sergeant DiMaggio.

This is a time for what boxing publicist Irving Rudd calls *nostaglia*. My favorite Handbook stories? Here are a few:

1973—*The Spitball: How Gaylord Perry Won the Cy Young Award* by Russ Schneider

1974—*Nolan Ryan Says "No More Strikeout Records for Me"* by Bill Libby

1975—*Who Will Break Joe DiMaggio's Hitting Streak?* by Leonard Koppett

1976—*Bill Lee: Baseball's Spaceman* by Peter Gammons

1977—*Life With the Bird: Mark Fidrych* by Jim Hawkins

1980—*Would Joe DiMaggio Make It as a Manager?* by Steve Jacobson

1981—*Jim Palmer: Master of Mound, Mike & Modeling* by Peter Pascarelli

1983—*BULLETIN: George Steinbrenner to Manage the Yankees* by Joe Gergen
Rickey Henderson: License to Steal by Dave Newhouse

1984—*Whatever Became of Jim Bouton?* by Phil Pepe
Playing Ball with Robert Redford in "The Natural" by Joe Castellano with Rick Wolff

1986—*How to Hit Dwight Gooden* by Marty Noble

1987—*Mike Schmidt Bats Down His Critics* by Peter Pascarelli

1989—*Orel & Kirk: The Dodgers' Odd Couple* by Ken Gurnick

1990—*Jim Abbott's Amazing Story* by Peter Schmuck

1990—*Tim McCarver, Voice of the '90s* by Howard Blatt

1991—*The Vindication of Nails Dykstra* by George King

1992—*Stephen King's Field of Dreams* by Bob Haskell

1993—*The Two Barry Bonds* by Bob Hertzel

1994—*Frank Thomas Conquers Chicago* by Alan Solomon

Over the years, readers have voiced the usual complaints. But one letter from a reader in Milwaukee stands over all:

"You made four errors. I want my money back.

"I received the book as a birthday present."

Favorite cover? Upside-down Ozzie Smith, 1976.

Best kiss? Morganna planting one on George Brett, 1979.

Zander Hollander

TOP 10 GREAT MOMENTS OF PAST 25 YEARS

By JOE GERGEN

In the grave new world of baseball, only salaries are guaranteed. As the business continued its hostile takeover of the game last year, the role of commissioner was reduced to apologist and the World Series, an annual rite of autumn for nine decades, was cancelled. There was no joy in Mudville or any of the cities that had faithfully supported the national pastime through most of the 20th century.

Baseball has been shaken, embarrassed and endangered by developments in the quarter-century since The Complete Handbook of Baseball *made its debut in 1971. It has endured drug scandals, a gambling investigation that precipitated the banishment of a major star and tawdry commercialism in the form of players hawking memorabilia on television shopping networks and attaching a price to their autographs. Meanwhile, management decided that the sport's ills would be remedied by a salary cap, one size fits all.*

The result was the latest, the longest and the most painful of eight work stoppages that have afflicted the major leagues since 1972. The hostility between a unified and undefeated union and a group of owners determined to regain control of the sport and exorcise their suicidal financial tendencies produced an unfinished season and lingering uncertainty. Some brilliant individual accomplishments were short-circuited.

Newsday *sports columnist Joe Gergen, who has seen it all, contributed to the first edition of* The Complete Handbook of Baseball *in 1971 and has been a mainstay ever since.*

GREAT MOMENTS • 9

Hank Aaron blasts history-making No. 715 in 1974.

Instead of an expanded playoff system to highlight a major realignment, October marked the first time since 1904 there was no Fall Classic. The World Series, an American experience that had endured two world wars and a massive earthquake, was expunged from the sports calendar.

Franchises no longer were defined by their leagues and respective divisions, but by the size of their markets, as determined by a Milwaukee automobile dealer and his cohorts. Bud Selig, the principal owner of the Brewers, continued to collect a $1-million salary as an office temp. He began his third year as interim commissioner last September.

Despite its labor troubles and its overemphasis on finance at

Kirk Gibson's HR ignited Dodgers in 1988 World Series.

the expense of sport, baseball provided no shortage of thrills in the last 25 years. Some of the game's most memorable moments and some of its greatest deeds occurred on our watch.

Herewith one person's Top 10, in inverse order of significance:

(10) KIRK GIBSON, ALIAS ROY HOBBLED, RIDES AGAIN

Few World Series are decided in the opening game, but that was the case in 1988 in Los Angeles. And the man who determined the outcome was Gibson, who had been so instrumental in the Dodgers' rise to the pennant that he was honored as the NL MVP despite modest statistics (.290 batting average, 25 home runs, 76 RBI).

Leg injuries, however, hampered him throughout the playoffs

and threatened to sideline him for the Series against the heavily favored Athletics. Oakland had romped to a division title behind Jose Canseco's unprecedented 40-40 achievement (42 home runs and 40 stolen bases) and appeared poised to take command in Game 1, following the slugger's grand slam off a television camera high above the fence in center field at Dodger Stadium. Leading, 4-3, entering the ninth inning, the Athletics turned the ball over to Dennis Eckersley.

All the Eck had done in 1988 was become the dominant closer in baseball. After compiling an AL-leading 45 saves during the regular season, he saved all four of Oakland's victories in the ALCS triumph over Boston and earned series MVP honors. He was as sharp as ever against the Dodgers in World Series Game 1, quickly retiring the first two batters. Then, much to his chagrin, the control artist walked Mike Davis, a pinch-hitter with a sub-.200 batting average.

Late in the game, a TV camera had panned the Dodger dugout and broadcaster Vince Scully had interpreted Gibson's absence to mean that he would be unavailable to pinch-hit. Listening to the broadcast in the clubhouse while he iced his legs, Gibson decided otherwise and sent word to manager Tom Lasorda that he was ready if needed. When Davis reached base, Gibson limped to the plate.

He was unable to run, but he could jog. And that was all that was required when, after Davis stole second, Gibson drove a full-count, back-door slider deep into the right-field pavilion. It marked the first time in World Series history that a trailing team had won on a homer in the last at-bat of a game and the scene was every bit as theatrical as the crashing blow by Roy Hobbs in the film *The Natural*. "I don't believe what I've just seen," veteran announcer Jack Buck intoned.

Neither did the Athletics, who wilted thereafter, winning only one game. Despite the absence of Gibson and several other Dodger regulars from the lineup, Los Angeles breezed to the championship behind the pitching and hitting of Orel Hershiser, who won both his starts and batted a nifty 1.000.

(9) LAST STOP FOR THE EXPRESS

By the time Nolan Ryan began the 1991 season, he already held two of the most prestigious pitching records in history. Two years earlier, he had surpassed 5,000 career strikeouts, a figure that dwarfed the numbers compiled by the legendary Walter Johnson. During the 1990 campaign, he had posted his sixth no-hitter, distancing himself from the great Sandy Koufax.

The man also had succeeded in providing the Rangers franchise with a identity, something the team had sorely lacked since it was transferred from Washington to Texas by owner Bob Short two decades earlier. A native Texan who had balked at the Astros' attempt to cut his salary by 20 percent after the 1988 season, Ryan left Houston and signed as a free agent with the Rangers. He instantly transformed that club into a popular attraction, despite its inadequate home, Arlington Stadium, erected on the foundation of a minor league ballpark. In short order, Ryan's face was on billboards throughout the Dallas area and there were lines at the turnstiles.

Each time Ryan went to the mound, there was a chance history might be made. On Aug. 22, 1989, he made Rickey Henderson his 5,000th strikeout victim, the pitch setting off flashbulbs throughout the packed stadium. On June 11, 1990, he became the oldest pitcher ever to throw a no-hitter, besting the Athletics, 5-0, in Oakland. One month later, he became the 20th major league pitcher to win 300 games, by beating the Brewers in Milwaukee.

Still, Nolan couldn't go on indefinitely. Or could he? On May 1, 1991, Ryan blew away the Blue Jays for his seventh no-hitter. The batter Ryan retired for the 27th out was Roberto Alomar. Alomar's father, Sandy, had made the initial out in Ryan's first gem, 18 years earlier.

Although Ryan pitched through 1993, he was beset by injuries in his final two seasons. He retired at 46 with 324 victories and the incredible total of 5,714 strikeouts in 5,387 innings. The Rangers franchise was sufficiently strengthened to command construction of a beautiful new ballpark, reached by a road known as the Nolan Ryan Expressway.

(8) A FRIGHTENING DELAY OF GAME

For the first time, the Battle of the Bay was a national event in 1989. Decades earlier, when both San Francisco and Oakland fielded teams in the Pacific Coast League, the Seals and the Oaks would play the first game of a doubleheader on one side of San Francisco Bay and take a ferry to the other side for the nightcap. But the initial meeting of the Giants and Athletics in the '89 World Series posed no logistical hardships, thanks to the luxury of a travel day between the second and third games and the presence of the Bay Bridge.

The Athletics, determined to atone for their surprising loss to the Dodgers the previous year, handily won the first two games

GREAT MOMENTS · 13

Nolan Ryan after recording 5,000th strikeout in 1989.

Rickey Henderson starred in earthquake Series in 1989.

at the Oakland Coliseum, 5-0 and 5-1. Two days later, with the Series set to resume at Candlestick Park, an earthquake shook the Bay Area at precisely 5:04 P.M. With Game 3 set to begin in approximately a half-hour, Candlestick was almost filled to its capacity of 62,000. The upper deck and light towers swayed for 15 to 20 seconds and electricity was interrupted, but the cold, cheerless and unloved Stick held fast.

Alas, the rest of the region was not so fortunate. Houses collapsed in San Francisco's Marina district, setting off fires. A portion of the bridge connecting San Francisco to Oakland collapsed and a section of the bi-level Nimitz Freeway in the East Bay pancaked in the middle of rush hour. Because ABC already was telecasting live from the ballpark, it became the primary news source of the devastation caused by the tremblor that killed 67 persons and wreaked millions of dollars in property damage. By association, this became baseball's earthquake.

On the following day, commissioner Fay Vincent appeared at a press conference in a hotel ballroom lit by candlepower and pledged that "our modest little sporting event" was secondary to the region's efforts to save lives and rebuild. But he declined to cancel the remainder of the Series or make plans to move games to a neutral site, as many in the media suggested. Vincent said he thought the continuation of the Fall Classic would contribute to the healing process and pledged to resume play in a week.

The delay was extended for another three days at the insistence of San Francisco's mayor and Game 3 was staged 10 days after the 7.1 quake. Remarkably, the fans came back in waves, some of them toasting themselves with champagne in the parking lot, others bearing signs that spoke of renewal and hope. In a moving pregame ceremony, ordinary citizens who had reacted with bravery to the crisis ("the real heroes," Vincent called them) were honored and the crowd sang several verses of "San Francisco," the song from the celebrated movie about the 1906 quake that leveled the city.

By comparison, the baseball was not nearly so uplifting. The A's rolled to a 13-3 lead en route to a 13-7 victory, then closed out the Series on the following night as Rickey Henderson's leadoff home run sparked a 9-6 triumph. Henderson led all hitters with a .474 batting average, but acclaim for the man and his great team was muted as a result of the tragic circumstances.

(7) A HOT DOG WITH RELISH

Thurman Munson, the man who conferred the title "Mr. October" on Reggie Jackson, did not intend it as a compliment.

Reggie Jackson hit three HRs in Game 6 of 1977 Series.

Munson was a Yankee teammate, but not a friend. Actually, Jackson made few friends among his teammates during his first season in New York, in 1977. He had been a cornerstone of three World Series champions in Oakland, where the players grew up with him and were not offended by his showmanship, best described by pitcher Darold Knowles' observation, "There's not enough mustard in the world to cover Reggie Jackson."

Some Yankee players and the manager, Billy Martin, took an instant dislike to Jackson when he signed a lucrative free-agent contract and proclaimed himself "the straw that stirs the drink." He said his presence guaranteed his new team would not suffer the same fate as it had the previous season, when the Yanks were swept by the Reds in the World Series. Jackson endured a turbulent season that included a nasty and public confrontation with Martin in the dugout at Fenway Park. Still, Jax hit 32 home runs and the team won 100 games and the AL East title.

When Jackson slumped in the ALCS, Martin announced he was benching the slugger for the climactic fifth game. Rather than pout, Reggie delivered a pinch-hit during the winning rally. However, it was in the World Series that he shined, fully living up to Munson's derisive nickname. He doubled to start a three-run inning and then hit a monstrous home run in Game 4, as the Yankees assumed a 3-1 lead over the Dodgers, and he homered in his last at-bat of Game 5, won by Los Angeles.

But Jackson really gilded the legend in Game 6, at Yankee Stadium. Walked on four pitches by Burt Hooton in the second inning, he took only three swings that night. Each resulted in a first-pitch home run, off Hooton in the fourth, Elias Sosa in the fifth and Charlie Hough in the eighth. Jackson's three home runs in one game tied a World Series record set by Babe Ruth. Hitting three in succession was unprecedented, as was his total of five in the Series.

The Yankees' 8-4 victory earned the franchise its first World Series championship since 1962, but, at the time, it seemed less significant than Jackson's performance. Steve Garvey, the Dodgers' first baseman, was so impressed he silently applauded into his glove as the star rounded the bases for the third time. "It's the greatest thing ever in a Championship Series, an All-Star Game or a World Series," Garvey said. "The last line in the history books will say, 'Semicolon, the Dodgers and the Yankees also played.'"

(6) A GAME FOR OUR TIME

By 1978, it had been more than a generation since Bobby Thomson's home run produced the most exciting conclusion to a regular season in history. In 1951, when the Brooklyn Dodgers and the New York Giants were the fiercest antagonists in pro sports, New York had rallied from a staggering 13½-game deficit to force a three-game playoff, then came from behind one last time to erase a 4-1 deficit in the ninth inning of the concluding game at the Polo Grounds. Brooklyn mourned.

The script seemed very familiar in 1978, when the Yankees, who trailed the Red Sox by 14 games in mid-July, made a blazing second-half run. The rivalry between the two teams had emerged as the closest thing to the old Dodger-Giant wars. Unlike the '51 Giants, the Yankees moved out to a considerable lead of their own

(3½ games) in September, but Boston won 11 of its last 13 games and caught New York on the final day of the regular season, forcing a one-game playoff for the AL East title the following afternoon at Fenway Park.

Fathers ordered their sons to skip school in order to witness such an historic event and tickets quickly were snapped up on the morning of the game. Old Red Sox hero Carl Yastrzemski homered in the first inning, off 25-game winner Ron Guidry, and later singled in a run to stake Mike Torrez to a 2-0 cushion. The former Yankee right-hander nursed the lead into the seventh when, with two out and two on, light-hitting shortstop Bucky Dent lifted a fly ball over the Green Monster and into the net. New York added two more runs in the eighth, the second on Jackson's home run, to increase its lead to 5-2 before the Sox rallied for a pair in the bottom of the inning to make it 5-4.

Rick Burleson drew a one-out walk from Yankee relief ace Rich Gossage in the ninth and advanced only one base when Jerry Remy followed with a line single to right, because a sun-blinded Lou Piniella deked Burleson into thinking he had a play on the ball. Both runners moved up as Jim Rice hit a long drive to right-center. The last batter was Yastrzemski. As usual, the weight of a franchise balanced on his shoulders.

The tension was excruciating. People in the stands stood and peered at the scene through their fingers, because they were afraid to watch. Gossage threw, Yaz swung and third baseman Graig Nettles caught the foul pop. The final score, as it had been in 1951, was 5-4. The team with the "B" on its caps had lost again. Boston mourned.

(5) A HIT FOR THE AGES

Not only was Pete Rose baseball's most accomplished hitter, he was its greatest ambassador. He played with gusto, running out walks and barrelling into catchers even during All-Star Games, and talked about the game with similar enthusiasm. For public relations value, there couldn't have been a man better suited to breaking the all-time record of the gruff Ty Cobb.

Rose, a self-made player who had vowed to become baseball's first $100,000 singles hitter and overachieved by a few million dollars, set the modern NL record for batting safely in 44 consecutive games at age 37 in 1978, three months after becoming the youngest player to reach the 3,000-hit plateau. As a free agent, he left Cincinnati to sign with the Phillies the following season and helped them secure their first World Series championship, in

GREAT MOMENTS • 19

Pete Rose acknowledges Ty-breaking No. 4,192 in 1985.

1980. Released in 1983, he surfaced briefly in Montreal and eventually was re-acquired by the Reds, his original team. They appointed him player-manager.

During the 1985 season, which served as a countdown to the record, Rose spoke freely about the man whose ghost he chased. "I feel like I know Ty Cobb," he said. On Sept. 11, at Riverfront Stadium, Rose lined a pitch by Eric Show of the San Diego Padres into left field for hit No. 4,192, surpassing Cobb's time-honored standard. While fireworks erupted and a blimp overhead flashed the news, the new hit king shared a hug with his son, Petey, who doubled as the Reds' batboy. "And then," Rose recalled, "I cried real hard."

Had the man removed his uniform on the spot, it would have been a smashing finish to an exemplary career. Rose did retire as an active player the following season with 4,256 hits, but he remained with the club as manager. The gambling problems that led to his eventual "permanently ineligible" status and KO'ed him from Hall of Fame consideration did not erase the capping moment of Rose's great career.

(4) THE BUCKNER STOPS HERE

It was a topper, a harmless grounder certain to find its way into a waiting glove. Or so all of Boston thought. To the Red Sox, however, it turned into a snake in the grass and a prime exhibit in that franchise's museum of broken dreams.

The 1986 postseason already had produced moments that strained credulity by the time the Red Sox and Mets opened the World Series. Within one strike of elimination in the ALCS, Boston had rallied to salvage Game 5 in extra innings, then swept the final two games at Fenway Park, denying the Angels their first pennant. Meanwhile, the Mets—the most dominant team in baseball during the regular season—struggled to erase a 3-0 deficit in the ninth inning of NLCS Game 6 and outlasted the Astros in the epic 16-inning struggle which decided that series.

Though the Mets were favored to overpower their AL opponents, the Red Sox won the first two games at Shea Stadium and returned to New York the following weekend with a 3-2 lead. When Dave Henderson homered leading off the 10th inning of Game 6 and Boston pushed across a second run to take a 5-3 lead, it appeared the Red Sox were prepared to wash away almost seven decades of frustration. Calvin Schiraldi, a former Met, retired the first two batters in the bottom half of the 10th inning and the home team's outlook was so bleak that captain Keith Hernandez repaired

Bill Buckner after blowing it in 1986 World Series.

to the clubhouse, removed his uniform top and walked into the manager's office to watch the final out on television.

But, at that point, the inning, the game and the Series took one of those unfortunate hops that always seem to bedevil the Red Sox. Schiraldi got two strikes on Gary Carter, but the catcher lined a single. Then Kevin Mitchell singled. Ray Knight followed with another hit, cutting the deficit to 5-4 and signalling Schiraldi's departure. New reliever Bob Stanley also came within a strike of closing out the World Series, but Stanley threw a pitch low and inside and Mookie Wilson jacknifed out of the way and the wild pitch accounted for the tying run.

The Red Sox barely had time to wipe the stunned expressions off their faces before Wilson hit his grass-cutter at Bill Buckner. The Boston first baseman, playing on damaged legs, reached down, but not far enough. The ball squirted through the wickets as Knight danced across home plate with the winner. Outside the visiting locker room, former pitcher Mike Torrez—the man who had yielded the homer to Bucky Dent in the classic playoff game of 1978—crowed, "I'm off the hook."

Of course, the same was not true of the Red Sox. After a one-day delay caused by heavy rain, this star-crossed team blew a 3-0 lead in Game 7 en route to a demoralizing 8-5 defeat.

(3) A BIG BLOW FOR THE HAMMER

The very worst that could be said about Henry Aaron was that he lacked flamboyance. He may have been the most efficient player of his generation, more akin in style to Joe DiMaggio than any of his peers. Never was this more evident than in the final stages of his monumental chase to surpass baseball's supreme record, the career home-run standard established by Babe Ruth.

Aaron began the 1974 season with 713 homers, one shy of the great Bambino's total. Before the first inning of the first game was over, before thousands in the sellout crowd at Cincinnati's Riverfront Stadium had even settled in their seats, Aaron hit No. 714 off the Reds' Jack Billingham. He sat out the second game of the series, because the Braves wanted him to set the record in Atlanta, where the quest was sure to help business at the box office. After stiff-necked commissioner Bowie Kuhn, prodded by some righteous members of the press, ordered Aaron to start in the series finale on Sunday, Hank failed to get the ball out of the infield.

On the following night at Fulton County Stadium, before a packed house and a national television audience, "The Hammer" once again drained the suspense from the occasion as early as possible. A nervous Al Downing walked Aaron without a swing in his first at-bat, but in the fourth inning, with a runner on and the Dodgers holding a 3-1 lead, the left-hander threw a pitch in the strike zone and Aaron deposited it over the left-field fence and into the Braves' bullpen. Tom House, the wired relief pitcher, speared the ball and rushed it to home plate, where Aaron's family joined teammates and a representative of the commissioner's office for a brief ceremony.

Aaron was more relieved than overjoyed. Most of the Atlanta fans, content with having witnessed history, promptly got up and left. The stadium was at least two-thirds empty when the game concluded. It was only many years later that Aaron revealed the full extent of the threats and hate mail he had received as he drew close to Ruth's record. It also disturbed him to think his home-run total would overshadow his other hitting and fielding skills, which made him a complete player. But, thanks to "The Hammer," the new number that symbolized slugging excellence became 755.

(2) FOR WHOM THE BELL TOLLS

In the 11th inning of Game 6 of the 1975 World Series, Pete Rose stepped into the batter's box at Fenway Park. A garrulous sort who wore his love for baseball on the sleeve of his Cincinnati uniform, he was exhilarated by the thought of participating in such a remarkable contest. Turning to Carlton Fisk, the Red Sox catcher, he said, "Isn't this fun?"

And it was. It also was a shining moment for baseball, a beacon in the night, a reminder of how enthralling the sport could be when played at such a high level of skill. Three days of rain in Boston, as well as the Reds' 3-2 Series lead, had dampened the sense of anticipation before the contest, but it was renewed almost immediately when the Red Sox scored three runs in the first inning.

When the Big Red Machine responded with three runs in the fifth and drove out Boston ace Luis Tiant with two runs in the seventh and one in the eighth, the crowd in the old ballpark prepared for the inevitable. But, in the bottom of the eighth, pinch-hitter Bernie Carbo, an erstwhile member of the Reds, slammed a game-tying, three-run drive into the center-field seats.

The Red Sox loaded the bases with none out in the ninth, but George Foster threw out Denny Doyle at the plate as he tried to score on a short fly ball, and the game went into extra innings. Cincinnati threatened in the 11th, but, in the aftermath of their conversation, Fisk made a fine play to force Rose at second on a bunt and right fielder Dwight Evans made a sensational twisting catch of a line drive by Joe Morgan to prevent a home run.

It was past midnight when the final twist unfolded. Fisk, the only native New Englander on the region's favorite team, led off the 12th by driving Pat Darcy's pitch toward the left-field corner. It was hit well enough to end the game, but was pulled sharply and appeared headed for foul territory. A few steps down the first-base line, Fisk began waving and willing it fair with exaggerated body motions. At the instant it struck the foul pole, Fisk leaped into the air and bounded around the bases. In Charlestown, N.H., where the catcher was raised, a man climbed to the top of the Episcopal church and rang the bells.

"Fisk did what everybody wanted to do, what everybody who jumped out on the field wanted to do," said Johnny Bench, the Reds' catcher. "He drove in the winning run in the World Series. He hit a home run. The only thing bigger could be doing that in the seventh game."

The winning hit in Game 7, it developed, was not a blast, but a bloop. Morgan singled to center off rookie left-hander Jim Burton in the ninth and the Reds, who had trailed 3-0, at one stage, completed a 4-3 victory.

But Fisk will always have Game 6.

(1) SAY IT'S SO, JOE

Baseball needed this. It needed it more than anyone could imagine at the time. It was as if some greater power ordained that the 1993 Fall Classic should be a great show, because there might not be another for a long time.

The participants were the defending champion Blue Jays, who truly made the World Series an international affair the previous year by squeezing past Atlanta in six games, and the unlikely Phillies, occupants of the NL East basement in 1992. Philadelphia had spoiled a rematch of the Blue Jays and Braves by surprising Atlanta, in six games.

Pitchers suffered a lot of abuse in this World Series, particularly in Game 4. It lasted four hours and 14 minutes, longer than any previous game in the annals of the event, and produced a record-tying 32 hits and an unprecedented 29 runs. The calls for relief were so frequent that the phones in the Toronto bullpen were short-circuited. Philadelphia carried a 14-9 lead into the eighth, but Mitch Williams—the notorious "Wild Thing" who made every trip to the mound an adventure—was ripped for a two-run single

GREAT MOMENTS • 25

Carlton Fisk slams 12th-inning HR in Game 6 in 1975.

by Rickey Henderson and a two-run triple by Devon White and the Blue Jays rallied for a stunning 15-14 triumph.

That made what happened in Game 5 all the more remarkable. NLCS MVP Curt Schilling threw a five-hit shutout and the Phillies stayed alive with a 2-0 triumph. Matters returned to normal in Game 6 at the SkyDome, however. Toronto jumped to a 3-0 lead in the first inning and increased the margin to 5-1 entering the seventh. Then, the Phillies made a final stand with a five-run outburst, featuring Lenny Dykstra's fourth home run of the Series.

Just when the Phillies thought it was safe to begin planning for a Game 7, manager Jim Fregosi summoned Williams from the bullpen to start the ninth. The erratic left-hander promptly walked the leadoff hitter and, one out later, World Series MVP Paul Molitor singled to center field. The next batter was Joe Carter,

Joe Carter ends it all with three-run belt in '93 Series.

baseball's most dependable run producer for the better part of a decade but a man often overlooked among the sport's stars. He swung at a 2-2 pitch and did what only one other man in history—Bill Mazeroski of the 1960 Pirates—had accomplished: he terminated a World Series with a home run.

His drive deep into the left-field seats not only lifted the Jays to an 8-6 triumph, but marked the first time a trailing team had ever clinched the World Series with a game-turning homer.

While Toronto became the first repeat champion since the 1978 Yankees, Williams gained a reputation he could not shed. The Phillies, saying irate fans' threats against the pitcher created an impossible situation, traded him to Houston. The Astros released the veteran early in the 1994 season and he retired to his Texas ranch long before his former teammates and peers walked out on strike.

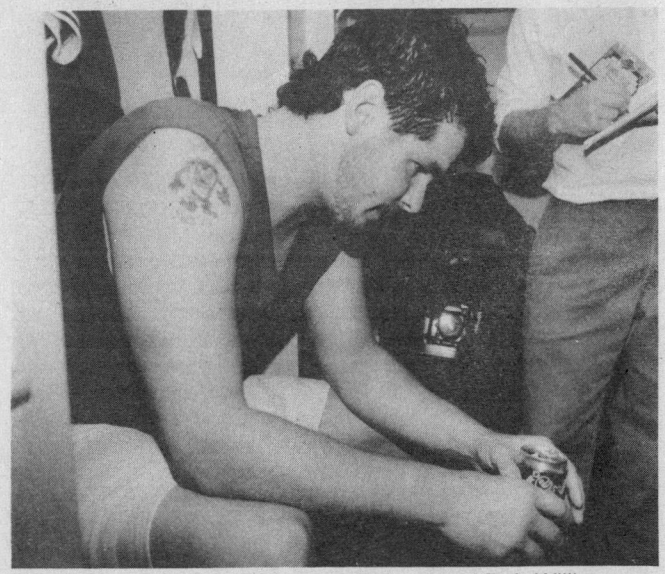

Nobody on the Phillies was sadder than Mitch Williams.

Griffey, Williams, Thomas, Bonds, Belle Stalk Roger

REGGIE JACKSON HANDICAPS THE MARIS CHASE

Reggie

Roger

By PHIL PEPE

"In 1969, Reggie Jackson went from being a fledgling Oakland celebrity on a coming ballclub to a national celebrity. That was the year I took a run at the mythical lady I called 'Ruth Maris.' I hit 47 home runs in 1969, and I hit 45 of them before the first of September, before the pressure of the fans and the media and the whole damn country caught up with me. I started fast and never let up until I just burned out at the end. I was 23 years old

---

Phil Pepe, sports director of WCBS-FM and longtime sports columnist, has followed the home run trail for more than three decades.

Matt Williams led 'em all with 43 HRs in short season.

and, all of a sudden, that burning spotlight was on me...

"I just wasn't ready. I would be ready for the pressure and the glare and the heat in all the seasons that would come—for the rest of my life, really—but I just wasn't ready for it in the summer of 1969."

—Reggie Jackson, from "Reggie" By Reggie Jackson with Mike Lupica.

On Aug. 12, when they pulled the plug on the 1994 baseball season—and what a season it was going to be—Matt Williams of the Giants had 43 home runs, Ken Griffey Jr. of the Mariners had 40, Frank Thomas of the White Sox had 38, Barry Bonds of the Giants had 37 and Albert Belle of the Indians had 36.

Never before had so many sluggers flirted at one time with the grand lady whom Reggie Jackson called "Ruth Maris." Never had the lady been so avidly pursued. Never had she been so seductive. Never was she so vulnerable.

Projected over a full season, Williams was on pace to hit 61 homers, Griffey 58, Thomas 54, Bonds and Belle 53 each. Not

Frank Thomas owns White Sox season record with 41 HRs.

figured in this mix is Houston's Jeff Bagwell, who had 39 homers, but was sidelined just before the strike with a fractured wrist.

It strains credulity to think of five hitters bashing 50 or more homers in the same season when you consider that, in the previous 93 seasons, the 50-home run mark had been reached only 18 times. And in only three seasons (1938, 1949 and 1961) had two hitters belted 50 or more in the same year.

What brought about this rash of home runs in 1994? Was it the lively ball? Inferior pitching? The smaller strike zone? The fact that today's athletes are bigger and stronger than their predecessors? All of the above?

For insight into the phenomenon, *The Complete Handbook of Baseball* called upon the thinking man's slugger, Reggie Jackson, 25 years after he flirted with "Ruth Maris."

"The popular thing is to say the ball is juiced up and let it go at that," Jackson said. "I don't buy into that theory, and I don't think Jose Canseco, Cecil Fielder and Juan Gonzalez would,

FIFTY OR MORE HOME RUNS IN A SEASON

Player	Season	No.	Age	The Competition
Roger Maris	1961	61	26	Mantle, 54
Babe Ruth	1927	60	32	Gehrig, 47
Babe Ruth	1921	59	26	K. Williams, 24
Jimmie Foxx	1932	58	24	Ruth, 41
Hank Greenberg	1938	58	27	Foxx, 50
Hack Wilson	1930	56	30	Klein, 40
Babe Ruth	1920	54	25	Sisler, 19
Babe Ruth	1928	54	33	Gehrig, 27
Ralph Kiner	1949	54	26	Musial, 36
Mickey Mantle	1961	54	29	Maris, 61
Mickey Mantle	1956	52	24	Wertz, 32
Willie Mays	1965	52	34	McCovey, 39
George Foster	1977	52	28	Burroughs, 41
Ralph Kiner	1947	51	24	Mize, 51
Johnny Mize	1947	51	34	Kiner, 51
Willie Mays	1955	51	24	Kluszewski, 47
Cecil Fielder	1990	51	26	Canseco, 44
Jimmie Foxx	1938	50	30	Greenberg, 58

either. I don't like to belittle ability. If you say it's the lively ball, that tends to belittle people.

"The lively ball may be part of it, but there are so many circumstances. Players of today are in better shape. They're bigger and stronger. There are better athletes in sports, no matter what the sport. They take better care of themselves. They work out all year, they're more diet-conscious and their preparation is better.

"I think you can make the case that the pitching is not as good. It's watered down by expansion. Working in the Yankees' front office, I've seen it. There just aren't as many hard throwers around as there were even 20 years ago. There used to be an abundance of pitchers who could throw 95 miles per hour and above. Now it's rare."

Probably the single most significant reason for the widespread power surge, Jackson says, is what he calls "the contagion factor."

"One guy gets rolling and he pulls others along with him. It

Barry Bonds has 259 HRs, 73 less than father Bobby.

becomes contagious," said Reggie. "Add to that watered-down pitching because of expansion and you have a year when a lot of guys hit a lot of home runs. I don't know if anyone ever will hit 60 homers again, but if someone does, it will probably come soon after an expansion year and when a lot of guys are hitting a lot of home runs."

Those are factors that prevailed in 1994 and maybe only the strike kept Maris' famous record of 61 in 1961 from being toppled.

When he hit 47 in 1969, Jackson points out, baseball had just expanded from 20 major league teams to 24. That meant watered-down pitching, which resulted in a home run explosion. Jackson's 47 didn't even lead the American League. Harmon Killebrew hit 49, Frank Howard 48 and Rico Petrocelli and Carl Yastrzemski each hit 40 for the Red Sox. In the National League, Willie McCovey belted 45 and Hank Aaron 44. In 1968, the previous season, only one hitter, Frank Howard, reached 40, with 44, while McCovey led the National League with 36.

Roger Maris, when he hit his 61 homers, benefitted both from expansion (the American League went from eight teams to 10 that year) and the contagion factor. Maris was pushed by his teammate, Mickey Mantle, who belted 54. In 1938, when Hank Greenberg hit 58 homers, Jimmie Foxx dogged him all season and finished with 50. And, in 1947, a home run race pushed Ralph Kiner and Johnny Mize, who finished tied with 51 each (check accompanying chart).

Even Babe Ruth, when he hit 60 in 1927, had competition from teammate Lou Gehrig, who smashed 47. Ruth, however, usually didn't need any impetus from outside forces. In three other 50-plus seasons, he had no competition. Ruth's 59 homers in 1921 were 35 more than runnerup, Ken Williams. In 1920, The Babe led the American League with 54 homers. George Sisler was second with 19. In 1928, Ruth again belted 54 homers and Gehrig was runnerup with 27.

Jackson's self-analysis that, at 23, he was too young and too immature to handle the pressure of the chase also is borne out by precedent. The average age of the 18 50-home run hitters is 28. Maris was 26 when he hit 61 and Ruth was 32 when he hit 60.

If Reggie had hit just three more home runs in 1969, he would have been the youngest player to reach the 50 level. Foxx in 1938, Kiner in 1947, Mantle in 1956 and Mays in 1955 all were 24 when they first reached the 50 plateau. Mays is the youngest to hit 50 as he reached age 24 on May 6 in '55, when he smashed 51 homers.

Griffey, who turned 25 in November, is the youngest of the

five current Maris challengers being considered. Bonds, who turns 31 in June, is the oldest. Williams turned 30 in November, Belle will be 29 in August and Thomas 27 in May. All five are in the prime years for a slugger.

"Of the five," said Jackson, "the guy who has the most ability with the bat is Griffey. You can make a strong argument that he has the best chance to hit 60. He or Bonds, but I'd have to go with Griffey, because of his age and because of his overall talent with the bat. He still hasn't reached his full maturity. Bonds has and he may have reached his peak

"Thomas may have had his career year this year. He may not hit .360 again (actually .353) or 50 homers. He might fall off to 40. Williams is strictly a slugger who is more prone to slumps than the other four, so that probably gives him less of a chance. On the other hand, he's a great home run hitter, a lot like Killebrew, and because he has the home run stroke, he may be the guy. I've seen less of Belle than the others, but he strikes me as the guy who most resembles me: strong, overpowering."

To break the record, Jackson said, a player has to be a little selfish. Selectivity as a hitter hurts Thomas' chances, for instance. He walks too often, 109 times in 113 games last season. Williams strikes out too much, 87 times in 112 games.

"I can say this now, because it's after the fact," Jackson said, "but I had several conversations with Griffey Jr. about going for the record. I tried to tell him about the pressure, what it would be like if he got close; if, say, he had 50 in September. The press wouldn't leave him alone. Everybody would want a piece of him and that can wear you down.

"I told him if he had 50 in September, and his team was not in the race, he would have to be selfish to break the record. He'd have to be willing to drop from .280, say, to .260, swing at some balls he wouldn't normally swing at, forget about the single and wait for the pitch he can hit out of the park."

The unknown factor in the equation, Jackson said, is how any hitter who comes close to the record reacts under the pressure and the unbelievable scrutiny that will be brought upon him. Press coverage in Maris' day wasn't what it is today, yet the pressure was so enormous, it caused Maris' hair to fall out in patches during his stretch run at Ruth.

Maris, however, was a trailblazer for all other record pursuers. He was trying to beat the record of an icon and doing it in a season that had expanded from 154 games in Ruth's day to 162 games. Maris had to endure the slurs of oldtimers who revered Ruth, including commissioner Ford Frick, who decreed that, if Maris

Reggie says Ken Griffey has best shot at the mark.

Albert Belle has slugged his way into the elite.

broke Ruth's record with the aid of additional games, his record would be listed separately, with an asterisk. Having obliterated Ruth's mark, Maris made it easy for future generations of sluggers—or at least easier. Maris is not revered quite as much as The Babe.

Greenberg and Foxx both were ahead of Ruth's 60 pace in September, but succumbed to the pressure of the chase and fell short. Ruth never had that kind of pressure because he wasn't chasing anybody, merely improving on the standards he had already set.

"The pressure was more than I expected at my age in 1969," Jackson said. "And I never even got to 50, but the pressure was there and it was too much for me to handle. I was immature. The attention, the scrutiny. It can overwhelm you if you're not prepared for it. It was difficult for me to handle it and put it into perspective."

When you're 23 and you hit 47 home runs, Jackson reasoned, you figure you're going to get another chance and you'll be prepared for it. But, although he would lead the league in homers four times and finish with 563 to rank sixth on the all-time list when he retired, Jackson would reach the 40 mark only once more—when he hit 41 with the Yankees in 1980, at age 34.

His one shot at the record had come and gone in 1969 and never would come again. And it had come when he was too young to appreciate it and deal with it.

"If I was 30," he said, "or 28 or 32, I think I would have come close. I might not have broken the record, but I think I would have been in the 50s. I would have been better prepared to handle the pressure and I would have given it a shot. And you know I would have had fun with it."

Covering The Bases With Bob Costas

By STAN ISAACS

It was shocking, outrageous and entirely inappropriate. But there was Bob Costas, serving as host of *Sports Illustrated's* TV celebration of the 40 most significant sports figures in the last four decades and failing to invoke the name of Mickey Mantle.

Costas, widely known as a devoted Mantle fan who has carried a Mantle baseball card in his wallet since he was a pup, snubbing "The Mick"? Even though Bob made it clear he had played no role in the selection process, one could almost envision him walking off the television set and being met by an urchin looking up at him with anguish and saying, "Say it ain't so, Robert."

Well, the extenuating circumstances suggested by his lack of input let Costas off the hook, somewhat. As *Sports Illustrated* explained in the magazine's anniversary edition, "Host Bob Costas nearly choked when he discovered that neither Willie Mays nor Mickey Mantle had made the list."

Should Costas have excused himself from the affair? Hardly. He had contracted much earlier to do the show; he is a professional and professionals don't walk away from commitments.

He has admitted, however, that it would be appropriate for him to do some penance for his lamentable appearance. He even came up with a fitting act of contrition. He agreed that if somebody would produce a 1965 Ross Moschitto baseball card, he would take the Mantle card out of his wallet for a season and replace it with the Moschitto card.

Stan Isaacs, former Newsday *TV sports columnist, has followed Bob Costas from his NBC beginnings in 1980.*

Bob Costas (c.) makes lineup at charity game with boyhood idol Mickey Mantle and comedian Robert Klein. (l.)

"I loved Ross Moschitto," he said. "He was Mickey's caddy for the 1965 season who had one home run for his big league career."

Any reader who has a 1965 Moschitto card can send it to Costas at NBC Sports, 30 Rockefeller Plaza, New York, N.Y. 10020.

It is typical of Costas that he good-naturedly accepted the barbs for hosting SI's questionable top 40. This 43-year-old sports broadcasting heavyweight can enjoy a joke on himself because he is a witty fellow, quick with a bon mot or a riposte, with an irreverent sense of humor that dovetails neatly with his depth and intelligence as a broadcaster. He has news smarts and is a sharp interviewer and an eloquent commentator.

His eloquence is evident in the sound bites used by Ken Burns in the monumental "Baseball" series. Costas exalted baseball without falling into the trap that befell some of Burns' other panelists. He didn't elevate baseball into a religion or a metaphor for all of life. Costas detailed some fascinating behind-the-scenes drama of his waits from the corner of a dugout and the clubhouse during the closing moments of World Series.

He talked about his first visits to Yankee Stadium with his father and how he had believed as a youth that Yankee greats Babe Ruth and Lou Gehrig were actually buried under their outfield monuments. More than a few viewers could relate only too well when Costas said, "Baseball is the only thing my father and I had in common."

Costas, born in Queens and raised in Commack on Long Island, was hooked at first by the Yankee broadcasts of Mel Allen and Red Barber. When the Yankees and Mets weren't playing, he would sit in the car on the driveway to listen to out-of-town games "because the reception was better outside. I would flip on the ignition and the radio and go up and down on the dial to get, say, Chuck Thompson on WBAL in Baltimore or Bob Prince on KDKA in Pittsburgh. You would fiddle with the slightest calibration to get through static and into a good pocket where you'd hear Harry Caray clear as a bell on KMOX in St. Louis. I could pick up Red Sox games from their WTIX affiliate in Hartford. I wasn't sneaking out of the house to do this. My father was betting on games, so sometimes I'd be on assignment from him to get scores."

Costas attended Syracuse, the powerhouse school for broadcasters whose distinguished alumni list starts with Marty Glickman and includes Hank Greenwald, Marv Albert, Dick Stockton and Len Berman as well as newsman Ted Koppel. He announced a number of sports for the campus radio and cable outlets, went on to radio and TV gigs at commercial stations there and didn't stay long enough to graduate because of an offer to go to KMOX in St. Louis to broadcast the games of the Spirits, an American Basketball Association franchise.

He free-lanced NBA basketball and pro football for CBS and joined NBC in 1980. He quickly established himself as a versatile, reliable announcer who, in Marty Glickman's words, "was born to be a sportscaster." He has done play-by-play, hosted studio shows, done significant interviews with sports and entertainment personalities and has displayed a keen journalistic sense in all his endeavors. He is a serious, funny fellow and a funny, serious fellow.

From 1983-89, he teamed with Tony Kubek on NBC's "Game of the Week" telecasts. Consider one particular raffish moment between the pair: while they were doing a telecast from Toronto they got to talking about veteran Tommy John, who was making a comeback with Oakland and would be getting into shape pitching for the Athletics' minor league team. Costas said, "John will be pissing in Appleton on Sunday." When Kubek said nothing and

Tony Kubek was Costas' Game of the Week partner.

suppressed a guffaw, Costas came back with, "Come to think of it he'll probably do both if he stays in Appleton."

Costas started winning Emmy awards in 1987.

"The first time I won was thrilling because I was relatively new and there were people like Al Michaels, Dick Enberg, Jim McKay and Jack Whitaker among the nominees. I am proud of the one I won for 1992, because I took that to signify my work as host for the Barcelona Olympics," he said.

Costas broke a string of rocky Olympics performances by hosts. McKay, generally esteemed for his Olympics work, had a difficult

Richard Dent (l.) and William Perry flank Costas at Super Bowl.

time at Calgary in his last Olympics; Bryant Gumbel was criticized for being too grim at Seoul in 1988; and Paula Zahn and Tim McCarver were ripped for presiding over a poorly-conceived CBS presentation of the Winter Olympics in 1992.

But it is baseball that has been a Costas passion since before he began carrying Mantle's baseball card in his wallet at age 12. "Every right-thinking American should carry a religious artifact on his person at all times," he would say. And Costas chose Mantle to be his presenter in 1985, the first of the five times he was voted "Sportscaster of the Year" by a Salisbury, N.C., group.

The friendship between the men flourished, and it was through talking with somebody like Costas that Mantle could appreciate the hold he had on a generation of Yankee fans. There was the time Costas and comedian Billy Crystal, who also grew up on Long Island as a Yankee fan, were sitting with Mickey in the restaurant of the hotel in Manhattan where Costas and Mantle stayed.

"Billy and I talked about Mickey and the Yankees and about 1961. He remembered none of it. But he was appreciative and he smiled," said Costas. "I had the impression that he was gratified to be able to put faces and names to people who thought of him that way. We weren't much different from the millions and millions of the fans who thought of him so, but this was relaxed and human; he was comfortable with us, we weren't coming at him in waves."

When Mantle went into the Betty Ford Institute for rehabilitation as an alcoholic, he called Costas beforehand, because he didn't want his friend to find this out in the newspaper. After he got out, Costas called Mantle and advised him about how to deal with the public.

"I told him, 'Being who you are, there will be a demand on you to tell your story. I strongly suggest you tell it in one place on national TV and in one place in a print medium. Pick the place carefully, don't let it be told in piecemeal by people with different agendas and different degrees of competence. Get maximum exposure, so you don't have to do it over and over again.' I hoped he would believe I would be the one, but there were others like "60 Minutes" who could be counted on to do it right."

Mantle chose to have his story come out in *Sports Illustrated*—after first going public in an interview with Costas on NBC's "Dateline" news magazine. It was a poignant, heart-rending interview sensitively handled over 18 minutes by Costas and one of the memorable moments of the 1994 television year. A few of the crew members broke up during the taping. "I would have also if I hadn't had dinner with him and played golf with him the day before. That helped me to have a sense of what to expect," said Costas.

Costas has made more sense than most in his comments about the baseball strike. In a nutshell, he said, it all came down to trust. "Despite all the complicated issues, people of reasonable intelligence and good will would have devised a fair system if they trusted each other. Instead they were like two people wrestling toward the cliff and tumbling off it together," he said.

He is unhappy about many aspects of baseball. He laments the way the game's caretakers realigned the divisions, destroying the competitive integrity of the game with wild cards and endless expansion. He said people who insist that the strike killed baseball's greatest season are wrong.

"It was a great season only in terms of individual achievement.

It would have been interesting to see Tony Gwynn chase .400 or Matt Williams and Ken Griffey Jr. pursue the home run record. But what really distinguishes a great season is great pennant races. There can't be a great pennant race like 1967 and 1978 when you have so many divisions and wild cards. The fact that the owners devised the new system and the players acquiesced gives you a good sense of the quality of the thinking that goes into the sport now."

If this sounds to you like the thinking of a man who might like to be the baseball commissioner, forget it. "When I hear people say that, I'm pleased, because they think I am making sense," he said. "But I'm not qualified. I don't have the business acumen, administrative experience or the temperament to do the job day to day. I'm not qualified—but if qualified means I could do better than these people, then I'm overqualified."

Costas has evolved into a troubleshooter for NBC, appearing as a panelist on "Meet the Press" about the baseball strike, popping up on the Charlie Rose show and "Nightline." He works on breaking sports stories and does pieces in prime time for the nightly news. His interviews last year with Bobby Knight, Barry Switzer, Ray Charles and Chevy Chase were of a piece with the interviews he did when he hosted the Emmy-winning interview program, "Later with Bob Costas." He recalls fondly his three shows with Paul McCartney, two with Elie Wiesel and one with comedian Jerry Seinfeld "in which we talked about the craft of comedy. We had less guffaws, but more insight into what he does."

On the other hand, he took some critical heat for the foul-shooting competition between him and Pat Riley when Riley worked for NBC between coaching gigs. Costas broke a tie at the end to win and the slickly groomed Riley had to wear his hair blow-dry style a la Costas. Some critics thought this was out of place on the NBA pregame telecasts.

"We never interfered with the games and if there were ever any pressing newsworthy developments on a weekend, we dropped the shootout," said Costas. "The whole thing took 30 seconds; it replaced only the credits. I never got so much attention. During the season, I must have been asked about it 50 times a day. Even today, somebody asks me about it a few times a month.

"I don't think there has been any network sportscaster who has pursued news with more serious purpose than I have. But life is a variety show. It's 'Here comes the senator and here comes the juggler.' "

Foul-shooting escapades aside, Costas strikes a chord in viewers, particularly those who share his love of baseball. "I get a lot

Jerry Seinfield was a guest on "Later with Bob Costas."

of thoughtful mail," he said. "A lot of it is appreciative from people who are aware, I think, of my attempt to do something different and not be in the cookie-cutter mold of sportscaster."

He has baseballs autographed by Babe Ruth, Ted Williams and Joe DiMaggio, but he is not a particular collector of memorabilia. Yet, people frequently send him baseball trinkets they think he ought to have. "I've always had an affinity to older fans," he said, "and I get letters from people saying that their fathers who had died would have wanted some of their old scorecards and the like to be sent to me."

He made it to the Topps.

Assuming baseball gets its act together by 1995, Costas will be presiding over NBC's "Game of the Week" telecasts as play-by-play host. He also continues to host the NBA pregame show and his nationally syndicated Sunday night radio show, "Costas Coast-to-Coast," ably backed up by two intelligent presences in Bruce Cornblatt, his personal producer, and Steve Horn. By the end of this year, he'll start his preparation to host NBC's 1996 Olympic telecasts from Atlanta.

Costas' contract with NBC runs through 1996. He has talked about "finding forums where you could talk about sports in greater depth than network programming would allow, whether through documentaries or magazine pieces." He sees that being achieved on the Public Broadcasting System (PBS) or HBO.

"I would still like to do baseball play-by-play on the network, but I am not optimistic about the future of the game or the future of network TV for baseball. A national Game of the Week would be wonderful if you could concentrate on the game and have time to broadcast in a leisurely fashion worthy of baseball rather than the MTV approach, with a million cut-ins and an appeal to the short-attention-span ninnies," he said.

Costas had a highly satisfactory stint substituting for vacationing Bryant Gumbel on the "Today" show in 1988. Co-host Jane Pauley said, "He's like a likeable boy who sat in front of you in home room, a boy who is well-prepared."

Though there is no question he would be suited for the job, Costas does not envision himself settling into a role as a host on a "Today" show or the like. For one thing, he would not like to be tied to a show that meant living in New York. He currently lives in a suburb of St. Louis with his wife Randy, whom he met when he spoke in front of her third-grade class in St. Louis. Costas and Randy Krummenancher were married in 1984, with Chubby Checker singing at the wedding. They have a five-year-old daughter, Taylor, and an eight-year-old son, Michael Kirby (named after Kirby Puckett).

"I'm not interested in that kind of inventory, because I don't think I'm at my best cranking out an effort five days a week," he said. "I have great respect for Bryant Gumbel and Katie Couric being able to handle that workload. I feel I could do it, but I would be screaming. I'd rather pick my spots and be on less often."

THE REBIRTH OF DAVID CONE

By BOB KLAPISCH

The clubhouse was empty, which wasn't unusual since it was 5 P.M. and the Royals were taking batting practice. The room had a clean, corporate feel, just like the organization itself. Any New Yorker could sense the Royals' middle America sensibilities, even in the way the equipment man smiled at the outsider's question.

"Dave Cone? Not here yet. Any minute, I guess," he said casually. One more look at the clock, and the internal alarms went off. Here it was, two hours before game time, and Cone, the starting pitcher, hadn't arrived. Imagine the tabloid frenzy such an absence would've caused in New York: there would have been phone calls to police, hospitals and the front office. Observation posts would be set up in the stadium parking lots and at the entrances, and Cone would become the media's prey. The first to get him, of course, would ask with back-page ferocity: **"WHERE WERE YOU?"**

But that was then, back when Cone was both a player and a prisoner in New York's baseball zoo. Cone was in his twenties then, a perfect age for the '80s, and perfectly suited for the Mets in an era when there were no restraints. The rules are loose and comfortable in Kansas City, too, but without the frenzy. That is why Cone could stroll into the Royals' clubhouse a few minutes before six, nod at teammates as if nothing was wrong, and then conduct an interview without feeling like a felon.

Bob Klapisch, a contributing national baseball writer for The Sporting News, *has covered baseball for the* New York Post *and* New York Daily News. *His newest book is* The Braves—A History of America's Team.

David Cone gives sweat off his brow to hometown Royals.

"Obviously, the situation here is a lot different than in New York," Cone said. "I used to think I needed all the excitement that you get there and, for a long time, it was great for me. But I've come to realize there's another way to live and, in the long run, a quieter existence has helped my career."

He says this without ego, without any "take that" resentment towards the Mets, although it'd be understandable if Cone were gloating. Two seasons after being traded by the Mets—exiled to the Blue Jays, actually, for Jeff Kent and Ryan Thompson—Cone took the AL Cy Young Award, edging former Toronto teammate and friend Jimmy Key of the Yankees. Cone garnered 108 total points to Key's 96 in balloting conducted by the Baseball Writers Association of America, and there was some low-level grumbling that Key should've won.

After all, Key won more games than Cone at 17-4, and his Yankees were 6½ games ahead of the pack in the AL East before the strike. But there's no denying Cone had more dominant overall numbers, going 16-4 with a 2.94 ERA. The question wasn't whether Cone would have won 20 games last season with another eight or nine starts in a strike-free pennant run, but rather would he have won 23 or 24?

Like so many other midsummer fantasies—Tony Gwynn chasing Ted Williams and .400 or Matt Williams and others taking on Roger Maris and his 61 home runs—Cone's '94 season will forever remain frozen by the Aug. 12 walkout. At least Cone's numbers didn't go unrecognized, as he won the first Cy Young Award of his nine-year career. What is interesting, though, is the way that Cone's stats reflected a change in pitching philosophy, one that fits with his overall maturation.

Cone came to the Mets from the Royals, in the spring of 1987, blessed with an arm that could turn a fastball into a weapon. For three straight seasons as a Met, from 1990-92, Cone surpassed 200 strikeouts, averaging more than one K per inning. He led the NL with 233 strikeouts in 1990 and 241 in '91, and there were days at Shea when he was the best pitcher in either league.

But Cone also maxed out on every pitch and, with that intensity, came a surcharge: the first time Cone would get in trouble, his inner demons went wild and that meant overthrowing that heater, choking the slider or bouncing the splitter in the dirt. It was said that Cone had the deepest arsenal of any power pitcher around, but his anxiety was stronger than his skill. When Cone panicked, he sought the strikeout as an elixir—and maybe that was why he never cloned his 20-3, 2.22 season of 1988.

Maybe it was New York itself that made Cone so overzealous.

As a Met in 1990, Cone argues a call with ump Charlie Williams.

Maybe he was eternally too pumped up by a baseball atmosphere overheated with tabloid wars and 24-hour sports talk on the radio. Or perhaps it was his friendly rivalry with Ron Darling, or trying to earn a big contract from then-Mets' GM Al Harazin, or attempting to prove to manager Jeff Torborg you didn't have to be a company man to succeed. Whatever the reason, the energy that Cone loved in New York was also sabotaging him on the mound, all of which takes Cone back to his original thesis: Kansas City's quiet is exactly what this excitable boy needed all along.

After being dealt in August 1992, after leaving the Mets with so much bitterness and helping the Blue Jays to their first World Series, Cone was baseball's most sought-after free agent. Who wouldn't want a 29-year-old with an explosive fastball, slider, curve and splitter? No matter what the Mets were whispering behind Cone's back—to this day, he swears they tried to sabotage his efforts to land with the Yankees—most GMs recognized Cone had enough talent to create a breakthrough season for any team. The only variable was Cone himself and where he wanted to play.

The Yankees, of course, were the most obvious choice, since he could remain in his familiar New York environment and teach the Mets a lesson as well. But late fall '92 was a time when owner-in-exile George Steinbrenner was still serving his suspension from

Fay Vincent and the Yankees' front office was unable to engineer a successful negotiation with Cone. He waited and waited, phone calls went unreturned and, by the winter meetings, it had occurred to him that his dream of going crosstown was evaporating. As he now says, "I don't think the Yankees had any idea what they wanted to do or who they wanted to sign. There was no real game plan over there."

If Steinbrenner had already returned to power, who knows? Cone and Key might've been on the same team and that would've ensured the Yankees of having the premier pitching staff in baseball. The power pitcher and the strike-zone scientist might've been reunited after a brief partnership in Toronto. Although Cone never did wear the same uniform as Key again following the '92 World Series, he learned from him. The lesson was: Not every fastball has to be an act of war and not every at-bat has to be a miniature apocalypse.

Watch Key and you will begin to understand that even-tempered, less-is-more philosophy. He teases hitters on the outside corner, gets them to lean over the plate and then slips an 87-mph fastball on the inside corner. Without this setup, Key's fastball would be vulnerable, almost suicidally so. At 87 mph, he's not quick enough to challenge anyone. But Key knows the importance of location and, even more critically, controlling a hitter's bat speed. Make the man at the plate hesitate, even for a fraction of a second, and he's yours. Any indecision will make an 87-mph heater look like Nolan Ryan's and, while Key never amassed strikeouts like body counts, he got hitters out. He had plenty of easy innings, comfortable at-bats and low pitch counts. And he almost always won.

"It was Jimmy who taught me how to be a smart pitcher, not just one with great stuff," said Cone, whose K total was a modest 132 in 171⅔ innings last season. "Watching him showed me that a ground ball on the first pitch of an at-bat is just as satisfying, if not more so, than blowing a guy away with a great fastball."

Cone would've never been able to embrace that philosophy in the '80s, at least not as a member of the ego-rich Mets. How could anyone who threw as hard as Cone think about finessing a hitter when, on the same staff, there was Dwight Gooden unleashing 94-mph gas? Power pitchers play the same macho mind games as long-ball hitters: Who can hit the ball farther and who can throw it harder?

But here was Cone in Kansas City in '94, six years after his 20-3 season at Shea, smoking a cigarette and thinking about how harnessed his energy had become. The room was still quiet. There was not another reporter in sight. Cone has always respected the media, but he welcomed the peace.

"That's another one of the nice things about playing here—not so much press," Cone said. "In New York, the scrutiny is very, very intense, and there's nothing wrong with that. But here, you get two or three guys covering the team and, a lot of times, it just feels more normal. You're able to play baseball without having to worry about everything you do or say ending up on the gossip pages. It's hard not to find that appealing."

He had plans for later that night—simple ones, like meeting his brother for a bite to eat after the game, then returning home to Leawood, a suburb of Kansas City. There used to be a time when Cone ran a hard night life, but those partying days are over, too. Cone was planning to marry his long-time girl friend, Lynn, last winter and Cone's brother Chris was only understating the truth when he said, "Getting married is definitely a good thing for Dave. He's very, very happy." Cone himself merely says, "Lynn and I have been through a lot together. It was time."

He didn't need to elaborate. There was a false sexual assault accusation against him in Philadelphia in 1991—the police never pressed charges—and a peripheral linking of Cone to the Florida rape investigation that targeted Dwight Gooden, Vince Coleman and Daryl Boston in the spring of 1992. Cone never did anything wrong, but somehow his name surfaced. And then there was the lawsuit from three New York women who claimed he exposed himself in the Met bullpen several years ago. Again, no charges were ever brought and no lawsuit was initiated, but Cone's reputation suffered.

A particularly outrageous *New York Post* cartoon of Cone flashing outraged so many Mets they staged a one-week boycott of the press. Cone did his best to take the publicity in stride, but deep inside, he knew the front office wouldn't allow him to remain in New York beyond the final season on his contract.

Maybe the prospect of a more peaceful existence was one reason that Royals owner Ewing Kauffman sounded so persuasive when he courted Cone as a free agent in the offseason following '92. Of course, it didn't hurt that Kauffman offered $18 million for three years, $9 million of which was a signing bonus. Cone's salary has fluctuated during the course of the contract, but he'll top out at $5 million for 1995.

Kauffman's money was great, and Cone, a conservative investor, is secure for life. But he could've made an ocean of cash almost anywhere. The Phillies were ready to sign him, as were the Blue Jays. But only the Royals offered Cone, born in Kansas

Cone fires away in ALCS against A's in 1992.

City and drafted by the Royals in the third round in 1981, a chance to come home again and to play baseball in an environment where sanity ruled.

"Mr. Kauffman is the one who made me understand the importance of roots, of coming back to where you started. I know it sounds corny, but once I got home I knew what he was talking about. I only wish he were still around to see how his message finally paid off for me and for the organization," Cone said.

Kauffman died in the summer of '93, after a long battle with bone-marrow cancer, and that was the year Cone struggled with the enormity of his contract. Kauffman had been subjected to intense criticism by other owners for overpaying Cone, and the pitcher desperately wanted to make the aging owner look good. That could've accounted for his 0-5 start with the Royals in '93, a humble beginning which allowed the Met front office to snicker in private.

Cone pressed and continued to search for the unhittable fastball. Cone's inner doubts remained until a May morning when the phone rang in his home. He was hoping it wasn't another reporter from

New York, wondering if Harazin was working long-distance voodoo on him. It wasn't. The voice on the other end belonged to Kauffman. As Cone recalled, "He wanted to tell me he didn't regret the move (to sign him). That had a profound impact on me."

Cone went 11-9 the rest of the way—not a great summer, but hardly the disaster towards which he had been heading. Still, it was the first losing season of Cone's career and, even though he was still regarded as an opposing hitter's nightmare, there was some question whether he'd ever have the career hinted at by his 1988 tour de force. The problem, Cone now says, was similar to the pressure he inflicted upon himself as a Met. Kauffman's assurances took time to sink in. As Cone admitted, "The whole idea of local boy comes home, makes good, was a little overwhelming to live up to."

Like most big-contract free agents, Cone simply needed time to find his peace. One year later, an AL Cy Young Award says Cone's inner wars are behind him.

Still, it was a hectic winter for Cone, despite the success. Getting married consumed most of the fall and, after that, Cone was an out-front figure in the Players Association's efforts to end the strike. He spent much of October and November shuttling between New York, where his wedding took place, and Washington, where Congress listened to the union's argument for stripping the owners of their antitrust exemption.

If it had been any other offseason, Cone would've spent the time working out with weights, playing basketball, reading—he's a newspaper/magazine junkie—or spending time with his family. Cone is especially close to his father, Ed, who raised Dave while working in the meat-packing industry in Kansas City. For as long as Cone could remember, his father has suffered from arthritis, a condition that has only worsened as Ed Cone grew older. That's one reason Dave bought his parents a home in Florida and it is why he devotes time and money to the Arthritis Foundation.

"Obviously, this is a disease I can relate to personally and I always felt I wanted to be a part of the effort to cure it," Cone said. "I've seen how it affected my father and, because it's a genetic thing, it's very possible I'll be dealing with the same problems later on in my life. So finding a cure is something I feel strongly about."

Priorities is another word for maturity. Doing charity work, building a family, returning to his roots have consumed Cone. No wonder he has found tranquility on the mound. Dave Cone, at 31, has finally stopped being James Dean.

INSIDE THE
AMERICAN LEAGUE

By JON HEYMAN and TONY DeMARCO
Newsday *Denver Post*

PREDICTED ORDER OF FINISH

East	*Central*	*West*
N.Y. Yankees	Chicago	Texas
Baltimore	Cleveland	Oakland
Toronto	Kansas City	Seattle
Boston	Minnesota	California
Detroit	Milwaukee	

Wild Card: Cleveland
Playoffs Winner: N.Y. Yankees

EAST DIVISION

		Owner		Morning Line / Manager
1	**YANKEES** Resume '94 pace	George Steinbrenner III / Navy blue pinstripes	1994 W 70 L 43	8-5 Buck Showalter
2	**ORIOLES** Photo finish under new jockey	Peter Angelos / Black & orange	1994 W 63 L 49	9-5 Phil Regan
3	**BLUE JAYS** Still laden with stars	P.N.T. Widdrington / Blue & white	1994 W 55 L 60	3-1 Cito Gaston
4	**RED SOX** Jose adds to Mo	John Harrington / Red, white & blue	1994 W 54 L 61	15-1 Kevin Kennedy
5	**TIGERS** Call for transfusion	Michael Ilitch / Navy, orange & white	1994 W 53 L 62	30-1 Sparky Anderson

INSIDE THE AL • 57

Big Apple Classic

95th Running. American League Race. Distance: 162 games plus playoffs. Payoff (based on '93, the strike having cancelled '94): $127,920 per winning player, World Series; $91,227 per losing player, World Series. A field of 14 entered in three divisions.

Track Record: 111 wins—Cleveland, 1954

CENTRAL DIVISION	Owner		Morning Line Manager
1 WHITE SOX No doubting Thomas & Co.	J. Reinsdorf/E. Einhorn Navy, white & scarlet	1994 W 67 L 46	3-1 Gene Lamont
2 INDIANS Ready to turn the corner	Richard Jacobs Black & orange	1994 W 66 L 47	5-1 Mike Hargrove
3 ROYALS New jockey helps	David D. Glass Royal blue & white	1994 W 64 L 51	10-1 Bob Boone
4 TWINS Kirby can't do it alone	Carl Pohlad Scarlet, white & black	1994 W 53 L 60	20-1 Tom Kelly
5 BREWERS Short on too many counts	Allan (Bud) Selig Blue, gold & white	1994 W 53 L 62	25-1 Phil Garner

WEST DIVISION	Owner		Morning Line Manager
1 TEXAS Starting over . . . once again	G. Bush/E. Rose Red, white & blue	1994 W 52 L 62	4-1 Johnny Oates
2 ATHLETICS La Russa keeps 'em close	Walter J. Haas Forest green, gold & white	1994 W 51 L 63	6-1 Tony La Russa
3 MARINERS Still adrift	John Ellis Blue, gold & white	1994 W 49 L 63	10-1 Lou Piniella
4 ANGELS Heaven can wait	Gene Autry Red, white & navy	1994 W 47 L 68	20-1 Marcel Lachemann

BALTIMORE ORIOLES

TEAM DIRECTORY: Managing. Gen. Partner: Peter Angelos; Vice Chairman/Bus.-Fin.: Joe Foss; GM: Roland Hemond; Asst. GM: Frank Robinson; Dir. Player Dev.: Syd Thrift; Dir. Pub. Rel.: Charles Steinberg; Trav. Sec.: Phil Itzoe; Mgr.: Phil Regan; Coaches: Steve Boros, Al Bumry, Chuck Cottier, Mike Flanagan, Elrod Hendricks, Lee May. Home: Oriole Park at Camden Yards (48,000). Field distances: 335, l.f. line; 410, l.c.; 400, c.f.; 386, r.c.; 318, r.f. line. Spring training: Sarasota and St. Petersburg, Fla.

SCOUTING REPORT

Even if they fail to meet owner Peter Angelos' great expectations again, this should be a memorable season for the Orioles. Cal Ripken Jr. is only 121 games from tying the remarkable record of 2,130 straight games, set by Lou Gehrig. Since Ripken plays through everything except strikes, it's a good bet he'll get there.

Actually, the Orioles have a whole lot more than the Gehrig chase going for them. Really, it's quite surprising they went just 63-49 last season, after management went to all that trouble and expense. The Orioles have a nice lineup, a potent one-two punch in the rotation and the AL's best group of fielders.

Their league-low 57 errors were 18 fewer than the next-best fielding team, the Twins. There is a lot of spectacular glove work seen in Camden Yards—and it's not all by the irrepressible Ripken at short. Brady Anderson is about as good as they come in center. Mark McLemore is handy around second, Leo Gomez solid at third and Rafael Palmeiro slick at first.

Palmeiro (.319, 23, 76) proved to be worth that $30.35-million contract he got as a free agent. However, not all of Angelos' free-agent investments were money well-spent.

Chris Sabo (.256, 11, 42) did quite a bit of sitting and sulking for his money and lots of Sid Fernandez's $9-million deal has already been spent on late-night pizza. In 115⅓ innings, the ever-expanding Fernandez (6-6, 5.15) surrendered 27 home runs.

Ripken (.315, 13, 75) is still the Al's most dangerous hitting shortstop. Chris Hoiles (.247, 19, 53) is one of the better hitting catchers, if not the best. And for backup, the Orioles signed free-agent Yankee catcher Matt Nokes (.291, 7, 19). Anderson (.263, 12, 48, 31 steals in 32 attempts) is one of the best leadoff hitters around. Jeffrey Hammonds (.296, 8, 31) overcame injuries and just might be the league's next superstar. DH Harold Baines

Caging Rafael Palmeiro to be big Bird was sweet stroke.

(.294,16, 54) re-signed as a free agent. And Barberie (.301, 5, 31) adds something at the plate.

New manager Phil Regan also likes what he sees on the mound. The Orioles' one-two pitching punch is among baseball's best as Mike Mussina (16-5, 3.06) and Ben McDonald (14-7, 4.06) are threats to win 20 games. If the Orioles can reach the postseason, such a potent one-two combination could make them dangerous. Arthur Rhodes (3-5, 5.81) has vast talent and could make the difference, particularly if Fernandez doesn't pan out.

There is also a lot of talent in the bullpen, although the Orioles need to re-sign free agent Lee Smith (1-4, 3.29, 33 saves) or find someone to assume his closer's role. The top candidates are Alan Mills (3-3, 5.16) or rookie Armando Benitez (0-0, 0.90 ERA, 14 Ks in 10 innings).

Angelos is expecting a lot from his expensive athletes. Last season, he made life impossible for manager Johnny Oates, floating rumors about Oates' impending demise. Soon after the season was called off, those rumors proved true.

There is a lot to watch here. There's Palmeiro. There's Ripken. There's all that talent. There's rookie manager Regan. But it's best to keep an eye on Angelos. That's where the action is.

was called off, those rumors proved true.

There is a lot to watch here. There's Palmeiro. There's Ripken. There's all that talent. There's rookie manager Regan. But it's best to keep an eye on Angelos. That's where the action is.

ORIOLE PROFILES

CAL RIPKEN Jr. 34 6-4 220   Bats R Throws R

Now just 121 games short of tying Lou Gehrig's thought-to-be-unbeatable streak of 2,130 straight games played... Has played 18,139 innings out of possible 18,287 during streak (99.2 percent)... Has played through major pains to keep streak alive... Said during strike that he would not consider crossing a picket line to keep streak going if the owners should employ replacement players... Missed just 12 innings during strike-shortened '94, with Tim Hulett subbing for him each time ... Without strike, he would have been on pace to break record at home against Yankees in 1995, but now big date is up in the air... Already a certain Hall of Famer... Bounced back from off year in '93, raising his average 68 points to .315... Still isn't taking advantage of short dimensions at Camden Yards... Only Oriole to receive two AL MVP awards (1983, 1991)... Named AL Rookie of the Year in '82... Sure-handed at shortstop, he makes up for so-so range by knowing the hitters... Born Aug. 24, 1960, in Havre de Grace, Md.... Would have made $5.4 million in '94... Signed five-year, $30.5-million contract before '93 season... Orioles' second-round pick in 1978... Son of former Baltimore coach and manager Cal Sr.

Year	Club	Pos.	G	AB	R	H	2B	3B	HR	RBI	SB	Avg.
1981	Baltimore	SS-3B	23	39	1	5	0	0	0	0	0	.128
1982	Baltimore	SS-3B	160	598	90	158	32	5	28	93	3	.264
1983	Baltimore	SS	162	663	121	211	47	2	27	102	0	.318
1984	Baltimore	SS	162	641	103	195	37	7	27	86	2	.304
1985	Baltimore	SS	161	642	116	181	32	5	26	110	2	.282
1986	Baltimore	SS	162	627	98	177	35	1	25	81	4	.282
1987	Baltimore	SS	162	624	97	157	28	3	27	98	3	.252
1988	Baltimore	SS	161	575	87	152	25	1	23	81	2	.264
1989	Baltimore	SS	162	646	80	166	30	0	21	93	3	.257
1990	Baltimore	SS	161	600	78	150	28	4	21	84	3	.250
1991	Baltimore	SS	162	650	99	210	46	5	34	114	6	.323
1992	Baltimore	SS	162	637	73	160	29	1	14	72	4	.251
1993	Baltimore	SS	162	641	87	165	26	3	24	90	1	.257
1994	Baltimore	SS	112	444	71	140	19	3	13	75	1	.315
	Totals		2074	8027	1201	2227	414	40	310	1179	34	.277

RAFAEL PALMEIRO 30 6-0 195 Bats L Throws L

A hit in his first year in Baltimore, he was on his way to a typically big year... Provided power the Orioles needed at first base... His five-year, $30.35-million deal, signed as free agent, was slightly more than what his former Mississippi State teammate and current rival Will Clark got from Rangers, this guy's former team... Outspoken critic of Clark and Rangers management, he wound up hitting 10 more homers than Clark (23), but knocked in four fewer runs (76) and batted 10 points less (.319)... Homered in first Orioles intrasquad game, first exhibition game, first game at Camden Yards and first two regular season games... Has had four straight 20-plus-homer seasons after averaging 11 homers over first four full years... Would have made $5,406,603 in '94... Acquired by Texas in nine-player deal in which Cubs received Mitch Williams after '88 season... Born Sept. 24, 1964, in Havana, Cuba, and migrated with family to Miami a few years later... Cubs drafted him 22nd overall in 1985.

Year	Club	Pos.	G	AB	R	H	2B	3B	HR	RBI	SB	Avg.
1986	Chicago (NL)	OF	22	73	9	18	4	0	3	12	1	.247
1987	Chicago (NL)	OF-1B	84	221	32	61	15	1	14	30	2	.276
1988	Chicago (NL)	OF-1B	152	580	75	178	41	5	8	53	12	.307
1989	Texas	1B	156	559	76	154	23	4	8	64	4	.275
1990	Texas	1B	154	598	72	191	35	6	14	89	3	.319
1991	Texas	1B	159	631	115	203	49	3	26	88	4	.322
1992	Texas	1B	159	608	84	163	27	4	22	85	2	.268
1993	Texas	1B	160	597	124	176	40	2	37	105	22	.295
1994	Baltimore	1B	111	436	82	139	32	0	23	76	7	.319
Totals			1157	4303	669	1283	266	25	155	602	57	.298

LEO GOMEZ 28 6-0 208 Bats R Throws R

Bounced back from horrendous '93 season to have quality season... Regained his job at third base by playing well after free-agent addition Chris Sabo went on DL early in the year... Orioles tried to dump him in several deals, but nobody wanted him after brutal '93 season... A solid third baseman, he made only five errors last season... Deadly slow, he has gone two straight seasons with zero stolen bases... Would have made $500,000 in '94... Born March 2, 1967, in Canovanas, P.R....

62 • THE COMPLETE HANDBOOK OF BASEBALL

Signed by Orioles as undrafted free agent in December 1985.

Year	Club	Pos.	G	AB	R	H	2B	3B	HR	RBI	SB	Avg.
1990	Baltimore	3B	12	39	3	9	0	0	0	1	0	.231
1991	Baltimore	3B-1B	118	391	40	91	17	2	16	45	1	.233
1992	Baltimore	3B	137	468	62	124	24	0	17	64	2	.265
1993	Baltimore	3B	71	244	30	48	7	0	10	25	0	.197
1994	Baltimore	3B-1B	84	285	46	78	20	0	15	56	0	.274
	Totals		422	1427	181	350	68	2	58	191	3	.245

BRADY ANDERSON 31 6-1 190   Bats L Throws L

Speed and stealing ability make this center fielder potent leadoff man... Swiped 31 bases in 32 attempts in '94, the best percentage in history for a player with at least 25 steals... His .969 steal percentage beat old mark of .962 by Max Carey (51-of-53 with 1922 Pirates)... His current string of 27 straight steals without being caught is only five off AL record, held by Willie Wilson and Julio Cruz... Has decent power for leadoff man (12 homers), but also whiffs a lot (75 strikeouts)... Breakthrough year was '92 and that is still his best all-around season ... Famous for wide sideburns, like Luke Perry of Beverly Hills 90210 fame... Red Sox' 10th-round choice in '85, out of UC-Irvine... Born Jan. 18, 1964, in Silver Spring, Md.... Acquired from Boston with Curt Schilling for veteran pitcher Mike Boddicker, July 30, 1988... Would have made $3,083,333 in '94.

Year	Club	Pos.	G	AB	R	H	2B	3B	HR	RBI	SB	Avg.
1988	Bos.-Balt.	OF	94	225	31	69	13	5	1	21	10	.212
1989	Baltimore	OF	94	266	44	55	12	2	4	16	16	.207
1990	Baltimore	OF	89	234	24	54	5	2	3	24	15	.231
1991	Baltimore	OF	113	256	40	59	12	3	2	27	12	.230
1992	Baltimore	OF	159	623	100	169	28	10	21	80	53	.271
1993	Baltimore	OF	142	560	87	147	36	8	13	66	24	.263
1994	Baltimore	OF	111	453	78	119	25	5	12	48	31	.263
	Totals		802	2717	404	672	131	34	56	282	161	.247

CHRIS HOILES 30 6-0 213   Bats R Throws R

Salvaged decent season after slow start... Still did not come close to matching big breakthrough year of '93... Even with hot finish, he saw batting average fall off 63 points to .247 ... Became one of five catchers in AL history to have 25 homers and hit .300 in '93, joining Bill Dickey (1937 and '38), Yogi Berra (1950), Carlton Fisk (1977) and Mike Stanley (1993)

... Also set club record for RBI by a catcher with 82, surpassing Gus Triandos' 78 (1958)... Also started slow in '93... Hit .291 in his last 42 games of '94... His homer swing is made for Camden Yards... Missed 51 games in '92, when he fractured right wrist when hit by a pitch from Tim Leary, who was accused of scuffing balls in that game... Born March 20, 1965, in Bowling Green, Ohio... Would have made $2 million in '94... Tigers' 19th pick overall in 1986 draft came to Orioles along with Robinson Garces and Cesar Mejia in deal for Fred Lynn, Aug. 31, 1988... Attended Eastern Michigan.

Year Club	Pos.	G	AB	R	H	2B	3B	HR	RBI	SB	Avg.
1989 Baltimore	C	6	9	0	1	1	0	0	1	0	.111
1990 Baltimore	C-1B	23	63	7	12	3	0	1	6	0	.190
1991 Baltimore	C-1B	107	341	36	83	15	0	11	31	0	.243
1992 Baltimore	C	96	310	49	85	10	1	20	40	0	.274
1993 Baltimore	C	126	419	80	130	28	0	29	82	1	.310
1994 Baltimore	C	99	332	45	82	10	0	19	53	2	.247
Totals		457	1474	217	393	67	1	80	213	3	.267

JEFFREY HAMMONDS 24 6-0 195   Bats R Throws R

Superb talent with superstar potential... Only question concerns bum knees he hurt as high school football star in New Jersey... Had surgery on anterior cruciate ligament Oct. 11, but remains one of top outfield prospects in baseball... Knee trouble had him in and out of lineup in 1994... If knees hold up, he will be starting right fielder for years to come... Easy-going, fun-loving kid... Born March 5, 1971, in Plainfield, N.J.... Would have made $150,000 in '94... Didn't play in Orioles' system in 1992 due to Olympic obligation... Selected fourth overall by Baltimore in '92, out of Stanford... Brother Reggie played in Pirates' system.

Year Club	Pos.	G	AB	R	H	2B	3B	HR	RBI	SB	Avg.
1993 Baltimore	OF	33	105	10	32	8	0	3	19	4	.305
1994 Baltimore	OF	68	250	45	74	18	2	8	31	5	.296
Totals		101	355	55	106	26	2	11	50	9	.299

HAROLD BAINES 36 6-2 195   Bats L Throws L

Quiet slugger had typical year... Consistent hitter has belted exactly 16 homers in four of last six years and he had 20 the other two... Bad knees forced him to become strictly DH ... Last played in outfield Oct. 4, 1992... Would have made $1.8 million in '94... Born March 15, 1959, in Easton, Md.... Acquired by hometown team from Athletics for two minor leaguers before 1993 season... Was chosen No. 1 overall in '77 draft by then-White Sox owner Bill Veeck, who admired him as a Little Leaguer... White Sox received Wilson Alvarez, Scott Fletcher and Sammy Sosa when they traded their best all-around hitter plus Fred Manrique to Texas in '89... Re-signed one-year contract as free agent in December.

Year	Club	Pos.	G	AB	R	H	2B	3B	HR	RBI	SB	Avg.
1980	Chicago (AL)	OF	141	491	55	125	23	6	13	49	2	.255
1981	Chicago (AL)	OF	82	280	42	80	11	7	10	41	6	.286
1982	Chicago (AL)	OF	161	608	89	165	29	8	25	105	10	.271
1983	Chicago (AL)	OF	156	596	76	167	33	2	20	99	7	.280
1984	Chicago (AL)	OF	147	569	72	173	28	10	29	94	1	.304
1985	Chicago (AL)	OF	160	640	86	198	29	3	22	113	1	.309
1986	Chicago (AL)	OF	145	570	72	169	29	2	21	88	2	.296
1987	Chicago (AL)	OF	132	505	59	148	26	4	20	93	0	.293
1988	Chicago (AL)	OF	158	599	55	166	39	1	13	81	0	.277
1989	Chi. (AL)-Tex.	OF	146	505	73	156	29	1	16	72	0	.309
1990	Tex.-Oak.	OF	135	415	52	118	15	1	16	65	0	.284
1991	Oakland	OF	141	488	76	144	25	1	20	90	0	.295
1992	Oakland	OF	140	478	58	121	18	0	16	76	1	.253
1993	Baltimore	DH	118	416	64	130	22	0	20	78	0	.313
1994	Baltimore	DH	94	326	44	96	12	1	16	54	0	.294
	Totals		2056	7486	973	2156	368	47	277	1198	30	.288

MIKE MUSSINA 26 6-2 185   Bats R Throws R

Has established himself as staff ace in short time... Was tied for second in AL in wins (16) ... Ranked fourth in ERA (3.06) and fifth in innings (176⅓)... His .712 mark is best lifetime winning percentage in Orioles' history (minimum 50 decisions)... His ability to remain healthy was major boon to O's one year after he had suffered shoulder and back pain ... Named to three straight All-Star teams, but did not pitch in '93, upsetting Camden Yards fans... Born Dec. 8, 1968, in Williamsport, Pa.... Another Stanford product... Orioles' first-round choice and 20th player drafted in '90... Earned economics degree in 3½ years... Would have made $750,000 in '94.

Year	Club	G	IP	W	L	Pct.	SO	BB	H	ERA
1991	Baltimore	12	87⅔	4	5	.444	52	21	77	2.87
1992	Baltimore	32	241	18	5	.783	130	48	212	2.54
1993	Baltimore	25	167⅔	14	6	.700	117	44	163	4.46
1994	Baltimore	24	176⅓	16	5	.762	99	42	163	3.06
	Totals	93	672⅔	52	21	.712	398	155	615	3.20

SID FERNANDEZ 32 6-1 225   Bats L Throws L

A bust after Orioles signed him to three-year, $9-million, free-agent deal... Listed weight is a joke... Big fan of midnight snacks... So overweight last year that he had trouble fielding his position... Once again limited opposing batters to low average (.248), but he was done in by allowing 27 homers as he tied for second-most in AL... Was risky investment after missing half of '93 season as a Met with cartilage tear in left knee ... Orioles management put all their free-agent signees through extensive medical exam, but apparently they forgot to put this big guy from Hawaii on a scale... Born Oct. 12, 1962, in Honolulu ... Mets got him from Dodgers in deal for Carlos Diaz and Bob Bailor before 1984 season... Was NL All-Star in '86 and '87... Would have made $3,333,333 in '94.

Year	Club	G	IP	W	L	Pct.	SO	BB	H	ERA
1983	Los Angeles	2	6	0	1	.000	9	7	7	6.00
1984	New York (NL)	15	90	6	6	.500	62	34	74	3.50
1985	New York (NL)	26	170⅓	9	9	.500	180	80	108	2.80
1986	New York (NL)	32	204⅓	16	6	.727	200	91	161	3.52
1987	New York (NL)	28	156	12	8	.600	134	67	130	3.81
1988	New York (NL)	31	187	12	10	.545	189	70	127	3.03
1989	New York (NL)	35	219⅓	14	5	.737	198	75	157	2.83
1990	New York (NL)	30	179⅓	9	14	.391	181	67	130	3.46
1991	New York (NL)	8	44	1	3	.250	31	9	36	2.86
1992	New York (NL)	32	214⅔	14	11	.560	193	67	162	2.73
1993	New York (NL)	18	119⅔	5	6	.455	81	36	82	2.93
1994	Baltimore	19	115⅓	6	6	.500	95	46	109	5.15
	Totals	276	1706	104	85	.550	1553	649	1283	3.29

BEN McDONALD 27 6-7 213   Bats R Throws R

Turned in best season of career while establishing himself as a fine No. 2 starter in 1994 ... Has yet to become the superstar many predicted he would be... Orioles made him No. 1 overall pick in '89 draft, after huge career at LSU... Has shown durability, not missing a single start in last three years... Tied for eighth in AL with five complete games... Free spirit who likes to wear army fatigues, in stark contrast to studious staff

ace Mike Mussina... Would have made $2.675 million in '94
... Born Nov. 24, 1967, in Baton Rouge, La.

Year	Club	G	IP	W	L	Pct.	SO	BB	H	ERA
1989	Baltimore	6	7⅓	1	0	1.000	3	4	8	8.59
1990	Baltimore	21	118⅔	8	5	.615	65	35	88	2.43
1991	Baltimore	21	126⅓	6	8	.429	85	43	126	4.84
1992	Baltimore	35	227	13	13	.500	158	74	213	4.24
1993	Baltimore	34	220⅓	13	14	.481	171	86	185	3.39
1994	Baltimore	24	157⅓	14	7	.667	94	54	151	4.06
	Totals.	141	857	55	47	.539	576	296	771	3.86

TOP PROSPECTS

CURTIS GOODWIN 22 5-11 180   **Bats L Throws L**
Fleet outfielder keeps progressing... Stole 59 bases in 69 attempts for Bowie (AA) in '94, the most steals of any player in Orioles' organization... Hit .286, but lacks power, as evidenced by homer total of two... Expected to play for Rochester (AAA) in '94... Orioles' 12th-round pick in '91... Born Sept. 30, 1972, in Oakland.

ALEX OCHOA 23 6-0 185   **Bats R Throws R**
Speedy outfielder in Jeffrey Hammonds mold... Good speed-power combination... Hit .301 with 14 home runs and 82 RBI for Bowie (AA) last season... Has one of strongest outfield arms in minors... Played shortstop in high school... Orioles drafted him third overall in '91 draft... Born March 29, 1972, in Miami Lakes, Fla.

ARMANDO BENITEZ 22 6-4 220   **Bats R Throws R**
Reliever made strong, quick impression following callup to Orioles last season... In 10 innings with O's, he had 0.90 ERA and struck out 14... Went 8-4, 3.14 with 16 saves for Bowie (AA), notching 106 strikeouts in 71⅔ innings... In '93 for Albany (A) and Frederick (A), he had 8-1 record and combined 1.34 ERA, winning Palmer Prize for top minor league pitcher... Signed as undrafted free agent in '90... Born Nov. 3, 1972, in Ramon Santana, D.R.

JIMMY HAYNES 22 6-4 185   **Bats R Throws R**
Showed strikeout stuff with Bowie (AA) in 1994 by whiffing 177

Cal Ripken Jr.'s date with Lou Gehrig is 121 games away.

batters in 173⅔ innings... In 51 pro starts, he has enjoyed 35 games in which he allowed two runs or fewer... Orioles' seventh-round pick in '91... Went 13-8 with 2.90 ERA for Bowie and 1-0, 6.75 for Rochester (AAA) in 1994... Born Sept. 5, 1972, in LaGrange, Ga.

MANAGER PHIL REGAN:  One of nine candidates interviewed by the Orioles, he was snapped up quickly when owner Peter Angelos realized that Texas GM Doug Melvin was about to interview him for Rangers' job... Ironically, Melvin was the one who recommended him to Angelos in the first place... Realized lifetime dream when he was hired Oct. 17... Was Indians' pitching coach in '94... Had been viewed as a potential successor to Tommy Lasorda in LA a few years earlier... Spent seven years as a major league scout with Dodgers... Managed in winter ball for 10 years in Venezuela and the Dominican Republic... Coached at Grand Valley State in Michigan from 1973-82, working with a few future big leaguers, including Greg Cadaret... Reliever was known as "The Vulture" during playing days for his ability to pick up victories with short stints... In 1966, he went 14-1 with 1.62 ERA and 21 saves for Dodgers... Lifetime, he was 96-81 in 13 seasons with Tigers, Dodgers, Cubs and White Sox... Born April 6, 1937, in Otsego, Mich.

ALL-TIME ORIOLE SEASON RECORDS

BATTING: Ken Singleton, .328, 1977
HRs: Frank Robinson, 49, 1966
RBI: Jim Gentile, 141, 1961
STEALS: Luis Aparicio, 57, 1964
WINS: Steve Stone, 25, 1980
STRIKEOUTS: Dave McNally, 202, 1968

BOSTON RED SOX

TEAM DIRECTORY: Gen. Partners: Jean Yawkey Trust; Trustees: John Harrington, William Gutfarb; CEO: John Harrington; VP-Baseball Oper.: Lou Gorman; Exec. VP-GM: Daniel Duquette; Exec. VP-Adm.: John Buckley; VP-Baseball: Ed Kasko; Dir. Scouting: Wayne Britton; Dir. Player Dev. and Adm.: Ed Kenney; VP-Pub. Rel.: Dick Bresciani; Pub. Mgr.: Kevin Shea; Trav. Sec.: Steve August; Mgr.: Kevin Kennedy; Coaches: Mike Easler, Tim Johnson, Dave Oliver, Herm Starrette. Home: Fenway Park (34,171). Field distances: 315, l.f. line; 379, l.c.; 390, c.f.; 420, deep c.f.; 380, deep r.f.; 302, r.f. line. Spring training: Fort Myers, Fla.

SCOUTING REPORT

The Red Sox did what lots of teams do after a 54-61 season: they fired their manager. Now, they're going to find out whether it will make a difference. Out went Butch Hobson, whose tenure was marked by a close relationship with players and questionable

Mo Vaughn is on the verge of superstardom.

game strategies. Hobson's successor is Kevin Kennedy, who did little to distinguish himself as the Rangers' manager, but must have done something to impress Red Sox GM Dan Duquette.

The Red Sox needed a thumper to go with Mo Vaughn (.310, 26, 82, Al-leading 20 intentional walks). So they traded for Rangers designated hitter Jose Canseco (.282, 31, 90), who came to Fenway in the December deal for center fielder Otis Nixon (.274,0,24,42 steals) and minor league third baseman Luis Ortiz. Left fielder Mike Greenwell (.269, 11, 45) shortstop John Valentin (.316, 9, 49), third baseman Scott Cooper (.282, 13, 53) and infielder Tim Naehring (.276, 7, 42) are key contributors. Duquette brought in Wes Chamberlain (.256, 4, 20) from Philadelphia in the hope that he could help, but that didn't work. After 19 seasons, free agent Andre Dawson (.240, 16, 48) appeared unlikely to be re-signed.

Nixon had given the Red Sox their first legitimate base-stealing threat in two decades (since Tommy Harper), but it didn't help all that much. The Red Sox produced just 552 runs—only nine more than the league-worst Angels—in '94. Also, their .264 team batting average bettered only Milwaukee and Oakland.

The best thing that happened to the Red Sox during their mostly dismal '94 season was the return to form by Roger Clemens (9-7, 2.85). His excellent pitching wasn't aided by significant offensive support, but don't let the record fool you. Clemens bounced back completely from an alarmingly poor 1993 season, limiting opposing batters to a league-low .204 batting average.

With Clemens and Aaron Sele (8-7, 3.83), the Red Sox can match just about any one-two pitching punch in the AL. Sele slumped late in the year, but his curve, poise and overall talent are so strong that he has the potential to be a co-ace one day.

The Red Sox have been relying for too many years on aging pitchers like likely free-agent defector Danny Darwin (7-5, 6.30) and the probably finished Frank Viola, and will need some fortification from their prospects. Frankie Rodriguez, a converted shortstop, is one possibility, perhaps the best. Gar Finnvold (0-4, 5.94) and Nate Minchey (2-3, 8.61) failed to show much potential in short stays with the Red Sox last year. Ken Ryan (2-3, 2.44, 13 saves) emerged as the closer last season, after Jeff Russell was traded.

Despite a number of flaws, there is some hope in Boston. There is always hope when you have a burgeoning star like Vaughn, a power swinger like Canseco and a great pitcher like Clemens. Those hopes are increased tenfold in the minds of rabid Red Sox fans, who have been dreaming about winning a World Series since

1918. Despite a new manager and relatively new management, it's likely they'll still be dreaming come next year.

RED SOX PROFILES

MO VAUGHN 27 6-1 225   Bats L Throws R

Posted second straight big season and was on his way to career highs in everything when strike hit... Despite fine numbers, he still has yet to make an All-Star Game, the result of a stockpile of big-hitting first basemen in AL... Played through nagging hamstring problems ...His .310 average, 26 homers and 82 RBI were all the more impressive considering he was practically a lone threat in limp Red Sox lineup... Was intentionally walked 20 times to lead league, once more than Ken Griffey Jr.... Had four multi-homer games... His 10 HBPs reflect inside pitching style that most employ against this large man ... Improving at first base, but he still made 10 errors... Would have earned $675,000 in '94... Ranked third in league with 112 whiffs... Born Dec. 15, 1967, in Norwalk, Conn.... A product of Seton Hall, like Red Sox shortstop John Valentin... Red Sox' second-round pick in 1989.

Year Club	Pos.	G	AB	R	H	2B	3B	HR	RBI	SB	Avg.
1991 Boston	1B	74	219	21	57	12	0	4	32	2	.260
1992 Boston	1B	113	355	42	83	16	2	13	57	3	.234
1993 Boston	1B	152	539	86	160	34	1	29	101	4	.297
1994 Boston	1B	111	394	65	122	25	1	26	82	4	.310
Totals		450	1507	214	422	87	4	72	272	13	.280

MIKE GREENWELL 31 6-0 205   Bats L Throws R

His season was marred when he crashed into the left field wall Opening Day, hurting his left shoulder... Still played into early August, although he wasn't his usual productive self... Finally had arthroscopic surgery in August... Ten of his 11 home runs came at Fenway Park ...Sixth-hardest to fan in AL (once per 14.4 at-bats), just behind former teammate Wade Boggs... Below-average defensive left fielder... Has made up for fielding weakness with clutch hitting in past... Club's vocal player rep during strike season... Would have made $3.325 million in '94... Born July 18, 1963, in Louisville, Ky.... Second in 1988 AL MVP voting to Jose Canseco... Boston's sixth-round pick in 1982.

Year	Club	Pos.	G	AB	R	H	2B	3B	HR	RBI	SB	Avg.
1985	Boston	OF	17	31	7	10	1	0	4	8	1	.323
1986	Boston	OF	31	35	4	11	2	0	0	4	0	.314
1987	Boston	OF-C	125	412	71	135	31	6	19	89	5	.328
1988	Boston	OF	158	590	86	192	39	8	22	119	16	.325
1989	Boston	OF	145	578	87	178	36	0	14	95	13	.308
1990	Boston	OF	159	610	71	181	30	6	14	73	8	.297
1991	Boston	OF	147	544	76	163	26	6	9	83	15	.300
1992	Boston	OF	49	180	16	42	2	0	2	18	2	.233
1993	Boston	OF	146	540	77	170	38	6	13	72	5	.315
1994	Boston	OF	95	327	60	88	25	1	11	45	2	.269
	Totals		1072	3847	555	1170	230	33	108	606	67	.304

SCOTT COOPER 27 6-3 205   Bats L Throws R

Started big before tailing off each of past two years... By having nice first halves, he made the All-Star team both years without putting up big overall numbers... Hit .342 with six homers and 23 RBI last April... Reached high of .350 one game into May before downturn began... Made 16 errors, but possesses perhaps the strongest third-base arm in AL... May forever be known as the guy who replaced Wade Boggs or the guy the Red Sox kept when they traded Jeff Bagwell... Would have made $475,000 in '94... Born Oct. 13, 1967, in St. Louis ... Third-round draft choice in 1986.

Year	Club	Pos.	G	AB	R	H	2B	3B	HR	RBI	SB	Avg.
1990	Boston	PH-PR	2	1	0	0	0	0	0	0	0	.000
1991	Boston	3B	14	35	6	16	4	2	0	7	0	.457
1992	Boston	INF	123	337	34	93	21	0	5	33	1	.276
1993	Boston	3B-SS	156	526	67	147	29	3	9	63	5	.279
1994	Boston	3B	104	369	49	104	16	4	13	53	0	.282
	Totals		399	1268	156	360	70	9	27	156	6	.284

JOSE CANSECO 30 6-4 240   Bats R Throws R

Slugging DH came to Red Sox from Texas in December trade for center fielder Otis Nixon and minor league third baseman Luis Ortiz... Was AL Comeback Player of the Year after hitting .282 with 31 homers and 90 RBI in 111 games... Used solely as a designated hitter... His 1993 season ended due to torn ulnar collateral ligament in right elbow suffered in the most infamous one-inning mop-up relief appearance in history... Also had fly ball bounce off his head and over the fence for a home run in Cleveland in '93... Would have earned $5.1 million in 1994, on fourth year of a five-year, $23.8-million deal he signed in Oakland... Remains the only 40-homer, 40-steal man in history... Born July 2, 1964, in Havana... Drafted by Oakland in 15th round in 1982... Acquired from Athletics for Jeff Russell, Ruben Sierra and Bobby Witt, Aug. 31, 1992... Twin brother Ozzie still bouncing around in Triple-A.

Year	Club	Pos.	G	AB	R	H	2B	3B	HR	RBI	SB	Avg.
1985	Oakland	OF	29	96	16	29	3	0	5	13	1	.302
1986	Oakland	OF	157	600	85	144	29	1	33	117	15	.240
1987	Oakland	OF	159	630	81	162	35	3	31	113	15	.257
1988	Oakland	OF	158	610	120	187	34	0	42	124	40	.307
1989	Oakland	OF	65	227	40	61	9	1	17	57	6	.269
1990	Oakland	OF	131	481	83	132	14	2	37	101	19	.274
1991	Oakland	OF	154	572	115	152	32	1	44	122	26	.266
1992	Oak-Tex	OF	119	439	74	107	15	0	26	87	6	.244
1993	Texas	OF-P	60	231	30	59	14	1	10	46	6	.255
1994	Texas	DH	111	429	88	121	19	2	31	90	15	.282
	Totals		1143	4315	732	1154	204	11	276	870	149	.267

JOHN VALENTIN 28 6-0 185　　　　Bats R Throws R

Had superb offensive season, improving on impressive '93 campaign by hitting team-leading .316... Injured his knee May 3 and returned June 6, after arthroscopic surgery... Finished big, batting .333 in June and .348 in July... Made 10th unassisted triple play in major league history, July 8 vs. Seattle... Caught liner off the bat of Mariners' Marc Newfield, stepped on second and tagged the runner coming from first... Dependable shortstop made just eight errors... Teammate of Mo Vaughn at Seton Hall was drafted in fifth round in 1988... Born Feb. 18, 1967, in Mineola, N.Y.... Would have made $370,000 in '94.

Year	Club	Pos.	G	AB	R	H	2B	3B	HR	RBI	SB	Avg.
1992	Boston	SS	58	185	21	51	13	0	5	25	1	.276
1993	Boston	SS	144	468	50	130	40	3	11	66	3	.278
1994	Boston	SS	84	301	53	95	26	2	9	49	3	.316
	Totals		286	954	124	276	79	5	25	140	7	.289

The Rocket named Roger showed his after-burners.

TIM NAEHRING 28 6-2 205 Bats R Throws R

Nice talent has battled injuries problems throughout career... Top candidate for starting job at second base, if he stays healthy... Missed a month with a right ankle sprain, derailing decent offensive year... Versatile player manned all four infield positions in '94 ... Had four-hit, two-homer game vs. Oakland April 19... Plagued by back and shoulder trou-

ble in the past... Steady fielder with a decent arm... Would have made $300,000 in '94... Born Feb. 1, 1967, in Cincinnati... Red Sox' eighth-round pick in 1988 draft.

Year	Club	Pos.	G	AB	R	H	2B	3B	HR	RBI	SB	Avg.
1990	Boston	SS-3B-2B	24	85	10	23	6	0	2	12	0	.271
1991	Boston	SS-3B-2B	20	55	1	6	1	0	0	3	0	.109
1992	Boston	SS-2B-3B-OF	72	186	12	43	8	0	3	14	0	.231
1993	Boston	2B-3B-SS	39	127	14	42	10	0	1	17	1	.331
1994	Boston	INF	80	297	41	82	18	1	7	42	1	.276
	Totals		235	750	78	196	43	1	13	88	2	.261

WES CHAMBERLAIN 28 6-2 218   Bats R Throws R

Did not provide the pop Red Sox were seeking after his May 31 acquisition from the Phillies... Good news is that all they gave up for him was Paul Quantrill and Billy Hatcher... Heard it from Fenway crowd when he did not live up to his billing... Plagued by questionable baseball instincts and a weight problem, not necessarily in that order... Shuttled in and out of lineup... Hit .327 vs. left-handers, but only .231 vs. right-handers... Hit grand slam Aug. 2 off Dave Stewart... Possesses strong arm, notching five outfield assists in limited action... Born April 13, 1966, in Chicago... Would have made $350,000 in '94, but was still overpaid... Pirates' fifth-round pick in '87.

Year	Club	Pos.	G	AB	R	H	2B	3B	HR	RBI	SB	Avg.
1990	Philadelphia	OF	18	46	9	13	3	0	2	4	4	.283
1991	Philadelphia	OF	101	383	51	92	16	3	13	50	9	.240
1992	Philadelphia	OF	76	275	26	71	18	0	9	41	4	.258
1993	Philadelphia	OF	96	284	34	80	20	2	12	45	2	.282
1994	Philadelphia	OF	24	69	7	19	5	0	2	6	0	.275
1994	Boston	OF	51	164	13	42	9	1	4	20	0	.256
	Totals		366	1221	140	317	71	6	42	166	19	.260

ROGER CLEMENS 32 6-4 220   Bats R Throws R

Came back after poor 1993 season to pitch brilliantly... Final record of 9-7 does not reflect his performance... Held opposing batters to a league-low .204 batting average... Red Sox scored two or fewer runs 13 times in 24 games while he was still on the mound... Back on Hall of Fame path, though he still needs a few more good years... Still throws 95-mph-plus... Questions abounded when he finished the '93 season by going 6-12 with 5.78 ERA over final 21 starts... Won back-to-back Cy Youngs in 1986 and 1987, becoming one of only four pitchers to do so (Sandy Koufax, Jim Palmer and Greg Maddux)... Added third Cy Young in '91... Became only pitcher to win league MVP, Cy Young and All-Star Game MVP in same season (1986) ... Born Aug. 4, 1962, in Dayton, Ohio... Starred at University of Texas... Was Red Sox' first-round pick and 19th player selected overall in 1983... Would have made $5,155,250 in '94.

Year	Club	G	IP	W	L	Pct.	SO	BB	H	ERA
1984	Boston	21	133⅓	9	4	.692	126	29	146	4.32
1985	Boston	15	98⅓	7	5	.583	74	37	83	3.29
1986	Boston	33	254	24	4	.857	238	67	179	2.48
1987	Boston	36	281⅔	20	9	.690	256	83	248	2.97
1988	Boston	35	264	18	12	.600	291	62	217	2.93
1989	Boston	35	253⅓	17	11	.607	230	93	215	3.13
1990	Boston	31	228⅓	21	6	.778	209	54	193	1.93
1991	Boston	35	271⅓	18	10	.643	241	65	219	2.62
1992	Boston	32	246⅔	18	11	.621	208	62	203	2.41
1993	Boston	29	191⅓	11	14	.440	160	67	175	4.46
1994	Boston	24	170⅔	9	7	.563	168	71	124	2.85
	Totals	326	2393⅓	172	93	.649	2201	690	2002	2.93

KEN RYAN 26 6-3 230   Bats R Throws R

Took over closer role from struggling Jeff Russell... One of the league's hardest throwers, he has been clocked at 98 mph... His name frequently came up in trade talks, but Red Sox were wise to hold onto him... Allowed just one run in 21 road appearances... Surrendered just one home run, to Baltimore's Chris Sabo June 10... Would have made $150,000 in '94 ... Born Oct. 24, 1968, in Pawtucket, R.I., coincidentally the current home of the Red Sox' Triple-A team... Signed as undrafted free agent in June 1986.

Year	Club	G	IP	W	L	Pct.	SO	BB	H	ERA
1992	Boston	7	7	0	0	.000	5	5	4	6.43
1993	Boston	47	50	7	2	.778	49	29	43	3.60
1994	Boston	42	48	2	3	.400	32	17	46	2.44
	Totals	96	105	9	5	.643	86	51	93	3.26

AARON SELE 24 6-5 205   Bats R Throws R

One of most promising young pitchers in game ... Big curve means big potential... Struggled some after starting 5-1 with 2.29 ERA in first eight starts... Tied Scott Erickson and Mark Leiter for league lead by hitting nine batters... Sophomore year did not quite match quick rookie start that included victories in his first six decisions... His 6-0 big-league start in

1993 matched Red Sox record held by George Winter (1901) and Dave "Boo" Ferriss (1945)... Born June 25, 1970, in Golden Valley, Minn.... Red Sox' first-round pick and 23rd player chosen in 1991... Went to Washington State... Would have made $190,000 in '94 and was still quite the bargain.

Year	Club	G	IP	W	L	Pct.	SO	BB	H	ERA
1993	Boston	18	111⅔	7	2	.778	93	48	100	2.74
1994	Boston	22	143⅓	8	7	.533	105	60	140	3.83
	Totals	40	255	15	9	.625	198	108	240	3.35

TOP PROSPECTS

TROT NIXON 20 6-2 196   Bats L Throws L
Back pains ended his season prematurely in 1994... Only question about this Len Dykstra type is health... Considered to have outstanding potential as a hitter... Center fielder batted .246 with 12 home runs, 43 RBI and 10 steals in 71 games for Lynchburg (A) before being sidelined with back trouble... Red Sox' first-round choice and seventh pick overall in '93... Born April 11, 1974, in Durham, N.C.... First name is Chris... Hit .519 with 12 homers and posted 12-0, 0.40 mark as pitcher for New Hanover H.S. in 1993 and was named High School Player of the Year by *Baseball America*.

FRANKIE RODRIGUEZ 22 6-0 175   Bats R Throws R
Hard thrower is working on a changeup and curve... Velocity is in mid-90s... Was 8-13 with 3.92 ERA for Pawtucket (AAA) and had 160 strikeouts in 186 innings... Went only 7-11 with 3.74 ERA for New Britain (AA) in '92... Born Dec. 11, 1972, in Brooklyn, N.Y.... Agreed to sign after Red Sox allowed him to play shortstop his first year, for Elmira (A), where he hit .271 with six home runs in 1991... Taken in second round of 1990 draft, with compensation pick from Braves for free agent Nick Esasky.

JEFF SUPPAN 20 6-2 210   Bats R Throws R
Led Florida State League in strikeouts with 174 in 173 innings ... Throws about 90 mph, but is considered to offer complete package as a pitcher... Red Sox view him as "the next Greg Maddux"... Very poised for age... Second-round draft pick in '93... Was 13-7 with 3.26 ERA for Sarasota (A)... Born Feb. 2, 1975, in Oklahoma City, Okla.

JOSE MALAVE 23 6-2 195 Bats R Throws R

Had big year in big ballpark at New Britain (AA)... Had 37 doubles, seven triples and 24 home runs... Batted .299 with 92 RBI... Pure hitter... Reminds some of a young Tony Armas... So-so defensive outfielder... Born May 31, 1971, in Cumana, Venezuela... Signed as undrafted free agent in August 1989.

MANAGER KEVIN KENNEDY: Hired Oct. 18 to replace the fired Butch Hobson following 54-61 finish... Had been fired only six days earlier by new Rangers GM Doug Melvin... It's not often a manager gets dismissed after guiding club to first-place finish, but Rangers were only 52-62 when players struck... In 10 seasons of managing, he still has never finished with less than second-best overall record... Another of those managing catchers, he never advanced beyond Triple-A as a player, thanks to career .238 batting average... Confident, honest and chatty, he often criticized his young players in Texas but never his stars... Biggest mistake occurred in Fenway Park in 1993, when he let Jose Canseco pitch in fiasco that became prelude to Canseco's elbow surgery... Knew Red Sox boss Dan Duquette from his Montreal tenure, which included serving as bench coach for Felipe Alou in 1992... Had 533-373 record as minor league manager in Dodgers' chain, but path was blocked by Tommy Lasorda... A rarity as an unmarried manager... Was Robin Yount's high school teammate in Woodland Hills, Cal.... Born May 26, 1954, in Los Angeles.

ALL-TIME RED SOX SEASON RECORDS

BATTING: Ted Williams, .406, 1941
HRs: Jimmie Foxx, 50, 1938
RBI: Jimmie Foxx, 175, 1938
STEALS: Tommy Harper, 54, 1973
WINS: Joe Wood, 34, 1912
STRIKEOUTS: Roger Clemens, 291, 1988

DETROIT TIGERS

TEAM DIRECTORY: Owner: Michael Ilitch; Chief Fin. Off.: Jerry Pasternak; GM: Joe Klein; Asst. GM: Gary Vitto; Sr. Dir. Pub. Rel.: Dan Ewald; Trav. Sec.: Bill Brown; Mgr.: Sparky Anderson; Coaches: Billy Consolo, Larry Herndon, Jeff Jones, Gene Roof, Dick Tracewski, Ralph Treuel. Home: Tiger Stadium (52,416). Field distances: 340, l.f. line; 365, l.c.; 440, c.f.; 370, r.c.; 325, r.f. line. Spring training: Lakeland, Fla.

SCOUTING REPORT

The Tigers keep hitting homers, but somehow it doesn't much matter. The more homers they hit (161 in '94) and the more runs they score (652), the more homers (94) and runs (671) their pitchers allow. As usual, there were more runs scored in Tiger games than anyone else's. They were exciting, but their average atten-

Fielder's 188 Tiger HRs suggest wonders will never Cec.

dance of 20,786 was lowest in the AL and they didn't win a heck of a lot, either, at 53-62. It is hard to tell, but last year probably aged wrinkled manager Sparky Anderson quite a bit.

While this Tiger team will contain many familiar elements and attributes, there are signs of change. Detroit will again be older and slower than most teams and will depend upon the home run more than just about anyone else. However, there are finally a few fast fellows in the minors and there are signs that one day there may be more to the Tiger arsenal than a Cecil Fielder three-run home run.

Of course, for now, Fielder (.259, 28, 90) will again be the biggest force in the Tigers' musclebound lineup, though far from the only one. Travis Fryman (.263, 18, 85) led the AL in at-bats and strikeouts, but has yet to post really big numbers in the more important categories.

One bad sign is that two of the Tigers' best players last season were Kirk Gibson, who retired a couple years ago and then came back, and Alan Trammell, who has thought about retiring a lot lately. Gibson (.276, 23, 72) had a huge year, but was a free agent unsigned at press time. Trammell (.267, 8, 26), also unsigned at press time, graciously abdicated his shortstop job in '94, but still showed he still has something left. Mickey Tettleton (.248, 17, 51) was a free agent at press time.

Trammell's longtime double-play partner, Lou Whitaker (.301, 12, 43), keeps on hitting and the same goes for leadoff man extraordinaire Tony Phillips (.281, 19, 61). Chris Gomez (.257, 8, 53) showed more pop than expected and may become a fine fielding shortstop.

As long as they don't all grow old at once, the Tigers should still score some runs. Whether they will score more than they allow is open to debate. When Mike Moore (11-10, 5.42) is one of your top pitchers, your fingers had better be crossed. John Doherty (6-7, 6.48) will have to improve and left-hander David Wells (5-7, 3.96) will have to show he was worthy of the $7.5-million, three-year deal he received.

The pitching isn't pretty. Nor is it deep. If there's anything more questionable than the Tigers' rotation, it's their bullpen. Even closer Mike Henneman (1-3, 5.19, 8 saves) had his worst year.

If things don't get better in the Motor City, Anderson himself may be on the way out. There were rumors late last year that the Tigers were going to replace the winningest active manager in the majors. Ultimately, upper management decided to give him one more year. Very likely, that's all it will be—one more year—if the Tigers don't show vast improvement.

TIGER PROFILES

CECIL FIELDER 31 6-3 250   Bats R Throws R

Shortened season killed his hopes for fifth successive 30-homer, 100-RBI year... Only other Tiger to have four straight 100-RBI years was Hank Greenberg, who did it from 1937-40... Despite playing just five seasons in Detroit, this burly first baseman is already 10th on Tigers' all-time homer list with 188... Caught Tigers' attention by hitting 38 home runs in 1989 for Hanshin Tigers, the Japanese League team that bought him from Blue Jays, and was signed as free agent prior to 1990 season... Still immensely popular in Japan, where he is called "Wild Bear"... Had been a part-time player in Toronto, splitting first base with Fred McGriff... Had his own candy bar sold in Tiger Stadium... Would have made $4,237,500 in '94... Signed a five-year, $36-million deal before '93 season... Born Sept. 21, 1963, in Los Angeles... Royals' fourth-round pick in 1982 draft.

Year	Club	Pos.	G	AB	R	H	2B	3B	HR	RBI	SB	Avg.
1985	Toronto	1B	30	74	6	23	4	0	4	16	0	.311
1986	Toronto	1B-3B-OF	34	83	7	13	2	0	4	13	0	.157
1987	Toronto	1B-3B	82	175	30	47	7	1	14	32	0	.269
1988	Toronto	1B-3B-2B	74	174	24	40	6	1	9	23	0	.230
1990	Detroit	1B	159	573	104	159	25	1	51	132	0	.277
1991	Detroit	1B	162	624	102	163	25	0	44	133	0	.261
1992	Detroit	1B	155	594	80	145	22	0	35	124	0	.244
1993	Detroit	1B	154	573	80	153	23	0	30	117	0	.267
1994	Detroit	1B	109	425	67	110	16	2	28	90	0	.259
	Totals		949	3295	500	853	130	5	219	680	0	.259

TRAVIS FRYMAN 26 6-1 194   Bats R Throws R

Always appears to be on the cusp of breaking through to superstardom... Actually regressed last season, with batting average falling (.263) and strikeouts rising... Accomplished rare feat by leading AL in both strikeouts (128) and at-bats (464) in 1994... Also tied for the lead league in sacrifice flies... Has one of strongest arms of any third baseman in baseball... Sullen star previously played some shortstop... Tigers' third-round pick in 1987 signed five-year, $25-million deal two winters ago

... Would have made $2.4 million in '94... Born March 25, 1969, in Lexington, Ky.

Year	Club	Pos.	G	AB	R	H	2B	3B	HR	RBI	SB	Avg.
1990	Detroit	3B-SS	66	232	32	69	11	1	9	27	3	.297
1991	Detroit	3B-SS	149	557	65	144	36	3	21	91	12	.259
1992	Detroit	SS-3B	161	659	87	175	31	4	20	96	8	.266
1993	Detroit	SS-3B	151	607	98	182	37	5	22	97	9	.300
1994	Detroit	3B	114	464	66	122	34	5	18	85	2	.263
	Totals		641	2519	348	692	149	18	90	396	34	.275

KIRK GIBSON 37 6-3 225   Bats L Throws L

Stunned folks by having his best year since 1989... Had actually retired in 1992 after short and dismal stints with Kansas City and Pittsburgh... His signing as free agent by Tigers owner Mike Ilitch prior to 1993 season was viewed as purely sentimental at the time, but this former force regained his touch back in his old home park... Had seven-RBI game June 11 at California... Of course, he's not quite as fast as in his youth, when he was a wide receiver at Michigan State... Outfielder is still best remembered for hitting one of history's most dramatic World Series home runs, the pinch-hit shot off Dennis Eckersley that won Game 1 of 1988 World Series for Los Angeles... One of Sparky Anderson's all-time favorites, because of his 1950s gung-ho style... Would have made $1.5 million in '94... Born May 28, 1957, in Pontiac, Mich.... Began career as Tigers' first-round pick in 1978 and was ALCS MVP for Detroit in 1984... Won NL MVP honors with Dodgers in 1988... **Free agent at press time.**

Year	Club	Pos.	G	AB	R	H	2B	3B	HR	RBI	SB	Avg.
1979	Detroit	OF	12	38	3	9	3	0	1	4	3	.237
1980	Detroit	OF	51	175	23	46	2	1	9	16	4	.263
1981	Detroit	OF	83	290	41	95	11	3	9	40	17	.328
1982	Detroit	OF	69	266	34	74	16	2	8	35	9	.278
1983	Detroit	OF	128	401	60	91	12	9	15	51	14	.227
1984	Detroit	OF	149	531	92	150	23	10	27	91	29	.282
1985	Detroit	OF	154	581	96	167	37	5	29	97	30	.287
1986	Detroit	OF	119	441	84	118	11	2	28	86	34	.268
1987	Detroit	OF	128	487	95	135	25	3	24	79	26	.277
1988	Los Angeles	OF	150	542	106	157	28	1	25	76	31	.290
1989	Los Angeles	OF	71	253	35	54	8	2	9	28	12	.213
1990	Los Angeles	OF	89	315	59	82	20	0	8	38	26	.260
1991	Kansas City	OF	132	462	81	109	17	6	16	55	18	.236
1992	Pittsburgh	OF	16	56	6	11	0	0	2	5	3	.196
1993	Detroit	OF	116	403	62	105	18	6	13	62	15	.261
1994	Detroit	OF	98	330	71	91	17	2	23	72	4	.276
	Totals		1565	5571	948	1494	248	52	246	835	275	.268

DETROIT TIGERS • 83

TONY PHILLIPS 35 5-10 175   Bats S Throws R

One of game's most versatile players and one of its best leadoff hitters, too... In 1993, he reached base 313 times, the first Tiger to surpass 300 since Norm Cash in 1961... His 95 walks were third-best in AL in '94... An all-around nice guy in clubhouse, his one drawback is tendency to occasionally berate official scorer ... Has played every position except pitcher and catcher, though he's below average in the outfield, where the Tigers have used him most... One of three Tigers to strike out at least 100 times (105) in 1994. Travis Fryman and Cecil Fielder were the others... Only Tiger to reach double figures in steals last year with 13... Would have made $2,366,667 last year... Born April 25, 1959, in Atlanta... Expos' first-round pick in secondary phase in January 1978 was signed by Tigers as free agent prior to 1990 season.

Year	Club	Pos.	G	AB	R	H	2B	3B	HR	RBI	SB	Avg.
1982	Oakland	SS	40	81	11	17	2	2	0	8	2	.210
1983	Oakland	SS-2B-3B	148	412	54	102	12	3	4	35	16	.248
1984	Oakland	SS-2B-OF	154	451	62	120	24	3	4	37	10	.266
1985	Oakland	3B-2B	42	161	23	45	12	2	4	17	3	.280
1986	Oakland	SS-2B-3B	118	441	76	113	14	5	5	52	15	.256
1987	Oakland	2B-3B-SS-OF	111	379	48	91	20	0	10	46	7	.240
1988	Oakland	INF-OF	79	212	32	43	8	4	2	17	0	.203
1989	Oakland	INF-OF	143	451	48	118	15	6	4	47	3	.262
1990	Detroit	3B-2B-SS-OF	152	573	97	144	23	5	8	55	19	.251
1991	Detroit	OF-3B-2B-SS	146	564	87	160	28	4	17	72	10	.284
1992	Detroit	OF-2B-3B-SS	159	606	114	167	32	3	10	64	12	.276
1993	Detroit	OF-2B-3B	151	566	113	177	27	0	7	57	16	.313
1994	Detroit	OF-2B	114	438	91	123	19	3	19	61	13	.281
	Totals		1557	5335	856	1420	236	40	94	568	126	.266

LOU WHITAKER 37 5-11 180   Bats L Throws R

Still one of game's best-hitting second basemen, he surpassed .300 for first time in 11 years, at .301... May or may not need a few more good years to make Hall of Fame... Was platooned last year... "Sweet Lou" has lost some range at second, but he remains fairly sure-handed... Created a stir in September when he showed up at a players union meeting in a stretch limousine with tinted glass... One of only two players in Tigers history to have logged at least 2,000 games, 2,000 hits and 200 homers, the other being Al Kaline... Detroit's fifth-round draft choice in 1975... He and shortstop Alan Trammell have formed one of best DP combos in history... Would have made $2,783,333 in '94... Born May 12, 1957, in Brooklyn, N.Y.

Year Club	Pos.	G	AB	R	H	2B	3B	HR	RBI	SB	Avg.
1977 Detroit........	2B	11	32	5	8	1	0	0	2	2	.250
1978 Detroit........	2B	139	484	71	138	12	7	3	58	7	.285
1979 Detroit........	2B	127	423	75	121	14	8	3	42	20	.286
1980 Detroit........	2B	145	477	68	111	19	1	1	45	8	.233
1981 Detroit........	2B	109	335	48	88	14	4	5	36	5	.263
1982 Detroit........	2B	152	560	76	160	22	8	15	65	11	.286
1983 Detroit........	2B	161	643	94	206	40	6	12	72	17	.320
1984 Detroit........	2B	143	558	90	161	25	1	13	56	6	.289
1985 Detroit........	2B	152	609	102	170	29	8	21	73	6	.279
1986 Detroit........	2B	144	584	95	157	26	6	20	73	13	.269
1987 Detroit........	2B	149	604	110	160	38	6	16	59	13	.265
1988 Detroit........	2B	115	403	54	111	18	2	12	55	2	.275
1989 Detroit........	2B	148	509	77	128	21	1	28	85	6	.251
1990 Detroit........	2B	132	472	75	112	22	2	18	60	8	.237
1991 Detroit........	2B	138	470	94	131	26	2	23	78	4	.279
1992 Detroit........	2B	130	453	77	126	26	0	19	71	6	.278
1993 Detroit........	2B	119	383	72	111	32	1	9	67	3	.290
1994 Detroit........	2B	92	322	67	97	21	2	12	43	2	.301
Totals		2306	8321	1350	2296	406	65	230	1040	139	.276

CHRIS GOMEZ 23 6-1 183   Bats R Throws R

Tigers' surprise of 1994 was this guy wresting starting shortstop job from long-time hero Alan Trammell on May 10... Wound up knocking in 26 runs in May, fourth-most in majors and more than Trammell had driven home in any month of his career... Showed surprising power, hitting more homers (8) than in any of his minor league seasons... Was given the job in rare youth move by aging Tigers... Would have made $140,000 in '94... Another Long Beach State product—and he wasn't a power threat there, either... Made just eight errors in 1994... Born June 16, 1971, in Los Angeles... Tigers' third-round pick in 1992.

Year Club	Pos.	G	AB	R	H	2B	3B	HR	RBI	SB	Avg.
1993 Detroit........	SS-2B	46	128	11	32	7	1	0	11	2	.250
1994 Detroit........	SS-2B	84	296	32	76	19	0	8	53	5	.257
Totals		130	424	43	108	26	1	8	64	7	.255

Lou Whitaker has been second-to-none Tiger since '77.

DAVID WELLS 31 6-4 225   Bats L Throws L

Suffered injury-marred 1994 season after signing three-year, $7.5-million, free-agent contract to return to Detroit... Underwent surgery to remove bone chips from his elbow April 20 ... Also has cleaned up his image somewhat in Detroit after being known as a late-night guy while with Blue Jays... Split time between bullpen and rotation in his unhappy Toronto years, but has become a staple of Tigers' weak rotation... Despite elbow trouble, he was still among AL leaders with five complete games... Also posted fine strikeout-to-walk ratio (71-24)... Born May 20, 1963, in Torrance, Cal. ... Would have made $2.5 million in '94... Blue Jays' second-round pick in 1982 draft left that organization via free agency prior to 1993 season.

Year	Club	G	IP	W	L	Pct.	SO	BB	H	ERA
1987	Toronto	18	29⅓	4	3	.571	32	12	37	3.99
1988	Toronto	41	64⅓	3	5	.375	56	31	65	4.62
1989	Toronto	54	86⅓	7	4	.636	78	28	66	2.40
1990	Toronto	43	189	11	6	.647	115	45	165	3.14
1991	Toronto	40	198⅓	15	10	.600	106	49	188	3.72
1992	Toronto	41	120	7	9	.438	62	36	138	5.40
1993	Detroit	32	187	11	9	.550	139	42	183	4.19
1994	Detroit	16	111⅓	5	7	.417	71	24	113	3.96
	Totals	285	985⅔	63	53	.543	659	267	955	3.88

MIKE MOORE 35 6-4 205   Bats R Throws R

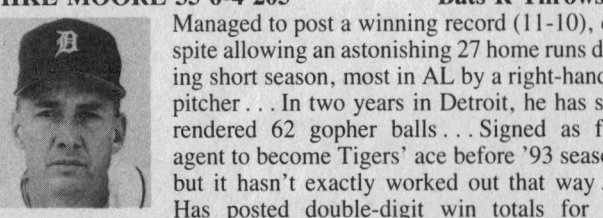

Managed to post a winning record (11-10), despite allowing an astonishing 27 home runs during short season, most in AL by a right-handed pitcher... In two years in Detroit, he has surrendered 62 gopher balls... Signed as free agent to become Tigers' ace before '93 season, but it hasn't exactly worked out that way... Has posted double-digit win totals for six straight years. If not for nine-win seasons in '87 and '88, that streak would be 10 years... Seattle's first-round selection in 1981 draft... Nice guy, but he is exceptionally dull interview subject

DETROIT TIGERS • 87

... Would have made $3,333,334 in '94... Born Nov. 26, 1959, in Eakly, Okla., the birthplace of Johnny Bench.

Year	Club	G	IP	W	L	Pct.	SO	BB	H	ERA
1982	Seattle	28	144⅓	7	14	.333	73	79	159	5.36
1983	Seattle	22	128	6	8	.429	108	60	130	4.71
1984	Seattle	34	212	7	17	.292	158	85	236	4.97
1985	Seattle	35	247	17	10	.630	155	70	230	3.46
1986	Seattle	38	266	11	13	.458	146	94	279	4.30
1987	Seattle	33	231	9	19	.321	115	84	268	4.71
1988	Seattle	37	228⅔	9	15	.375	182	63	196	3.78
1989	Oakland	35	241⅔	19	11	.633	172	83	193	2.61
1990	Oakland	33	199⅓	13	15	.464	73	84	204	4.65
1991	Oakland	33	210	17	8	.680	153	105	176	2.96
1992	Oakland	36	223	17	12	.586	117	103	229	4.12
1993	Detroit	36	213⅔	13	9	.591	89	89	227	5.22
1994	Detroit	25	154⅓	11	10	.524	62	89	152	5.42
	Totals	425	2699	156	161	.492	1603	1088	2679	4.23

MIKE HENNEMAN 33 6-4 205   Bats R Throws R

Closer suffered rough year, seeing his ERA balloon to 5.19... Not as happy as he once was in Detroit, probably because they have begun booing him... Said he might consider quitting in midseason... Heading into final year on three-year, $10.5-million deal... Tigers' all-time save leader with 136, supplanting John Hiller (125) in 1993... After four straight years with at least 20 saves, he picked up only eight last year... Born Dec. 11, 1961, in St. Charles, Mo.... Would have made $1,333,333 in '94, as he had foresight to take relatively low salary in strike year... Tigers' third-round pick in 1984, out of Oklahoma State.

Year	Club	G	IP	W	L	Pct.	SO	BB	H	ERA
1987	Detroit	55	96⅔	11	3	.786	75	30	86	2.98
1988	Detroit	65	91⅓	9	6	.600	58	24	72	1.87
1989	Detroit	60	90	11	4	.733	69	51	84	3.70
1990	Detroit	69	94⅓	8	6	.571	50	33	90	3.05
1991	Detroit	60	84⅓	10	2	.833	61	34	81	2.88
1992	Detroit	60	77⅓	2	6	.250	58	20	75	3.96
1993	Detroit	63	71⅓	5	3	.625	58	32	69	2.64
1994	Detroit	30	34⅔	1	3	.250	27	17	43	5.19
	Totals	462	640⅓	57	33	.633	456	241	600	3.12

TOP PROSPECTS

JUSTIN THOMPSON 22 6-3 175　　　　**Bats L Throws L**
Did not throw a pitch in '94... Spent entire year rehabbing sore elbow, but is still viewed as organization's top pitching prospect ... Already tabbed "Comeback Kid" for '95 by GM Joe Klein ... Hard thrower was hurt throwing in a big league spring training game in '94... Is expected to start '95 with Toledo (AAA)... Tigers' first-round choice in '91 draft... Was only 3-6 with 4.09 ERA for London (AA) in '93... Born March 8, 1973, in San Antonio.

MATT BRUNSON 20 5-10 160　　　　**Bats S Throws R**
Speedy shortstop is one of several youngsters who could potentially change Tigers' all-power, no-speed image... Hit just .216 for Fayetteville (A), but stole 50 bases... Hit .179 with three steals for Lakeland (A)... Tigers' first-round pick in '93 draft... Born Sept. 2, 1974, in Denver.

JOSE LIMA 22 6-2 170　　　　**Bats R Throws R**
A late-season callup, he was 0-1 with 13.50 ERA in 6⅔ innings with Tigers... Pitched no-hitter to beat Pawtucket, 3-0, Aug. 17 for Toledo (AAA), a well-timed victory because that was the day Tiger manager Sparky Anderson came to view youngsters... Threw 24 consecutive scoreless innings in August... Went 7-9 with 3.60 ERA overall for Toledo... Born Sept. 30, 1972, in Santiago, D.R. ... Has never posted winning record during five years in organization.

SEAN BERGMAN 24 6-4 230　　　　**Bats R Throws R**
Went 2-1 with 5.60 ERA in quick stint with Tigers, marking the second year in which he has seen some big league action... No relation to long-time Tiger Dave Bergman... Did attend the same Joliet, Ill., high school as Tigers' Bill Gullickson, though... Was 11-8 with 3.72 ERA for Toledo (AAA) and was third in the International League with 145 strikeouts... Born April 11, 1970, in Joliet, Ill... Tigers' sixth-round pick in 1991 draft, out of Southern Illinois.

MANAGER SPARKY ANDERSON:  There was much speculation that he would not be brought back for 17th season in Detroit after 53-62 finish in '94, but he's still here... Does not enjoy absolute support of management that he had for years in Detroit... Became Tigers' manager June 12, 1979, making him dean of AL managers... One year remains on a contract that pays him a reported $1 million annually... With lifetime mark of 2,134-1,750, he needs 26 victories to overtake Bucky Harris and move into third place on all-time victory list... First manager to win World Series in both leagues... Strategy never questioned, despite fact he eschews modern advantages like computers... Finally relented and hired an advance scout (Jerry Don Gleaton) last year... With Cincinnati from 1970-78, he won four NL West titles, four pennants and two World Series... His lone year as active player in big leagues was 1959, when he batted .218 with zero home runs and 34 RBI for Phils... Born Feb. 22, 1934, in Bridgewater, S.D., but grew up in Los Angeles... Tigers' all-time winningest manager with 1,271-1,164 mark.

ALL-TIME TIGER SEASON RECORDS

BATTING: Ty Cobb, .420, 1911
HRs: Hank Greenberg, 58, 1938
RBI: Hank Greenberg, 183, 1937
STEALS: Ty Cobb, 96, 1915
WINS: Denny McLain, 31, 1968
STRIKEOUTS: Mickey Lolich, 308, 1971

NEW YORK YANKEES

TEAM DIRECTORY: Principal Owner: George Steinbrenner III; General Partner: Joseph Malloy; VP/GM: Gene Michael; VP-Player Dev. and Scouting: Bill Livesey; Dir. Minor League Oper.: Mitch Lukevics; Scouting Coordinator: Kevin Elfering; Sr. Administrator: Arthur Richman; Dir. Media Rel.: Rob Butcher; Trav. Sec.: David Szen; Mgr.: Buck Showalter; Coaches: Clete Boyer, Brian Butterfield, Tony Cloninger, Billy Connors, Rick Down, Willie Randolph, Glenn Sherlock. Home: Yankee Stadium (57,545). Field distances: 312, l.f. line; 379, l.f.; 411, l.c.; 410, c.f.; 385, r.c.; 310, r.f. line. Spring training: Fort Lauderdale, Fla.

SCOUTING REPORT

The Yankees showed great patience at the plate, leading the AL with 530 walks in '94. As for their pennantless plight despite a 70-43 finish, they have no choice but to be patient. Before the strike struck, Buck Showalter's Yankees had positioned themselves for their first postseason appearance since 1981. While they were unfortunate to have saved their best for an aborted season, there is good reason to believe they can repeat that performance in '95.

For two straight seasons, the Yankees have led the AL in batting and their .290 average last year was the best since Red Sox hit .302 in 1950. While they lack a bonafide superstar, the Yankees compensate with an attack that is productive, top to bottom, and a roster deep in talent. The leader last year was AL batting champ Paul O'Neill (.359, 21, 83), but he had plenty of help. Wade Boggs (.342, 11, 55), Mike Stanley (.300, 17, 57), Jim Leyritz (.265, 17, 58), Don Mattingly (.304, 6, 51), Bernie Williams (.289, 12, 57), Luis Polonia (.311, 1, 36) and Danny Tartabull (.256, 19, 67) form a lineup that just doesn't quit.

The Yanks' only real weakness is a lack of speed. The club's top base-stealer was Polonia, but his 20 steals were somewhat offset by the 12 times he was caught.

While Mattingly is no longer the offensive threat he once was, he leads a splendid defense with few real holes. Mattingly, still the best first baseman around, and second baseman Pat Kelly cover the right side of the infield like few other tandems. O'Neill is one of the best in right, Williams is improving in center and Polonia has made gigantic strides in left. Third baseman Boggs, coming

Jimmy Key's corner-hugging recalls Ford named Whitey.

off his first Gold Glove, and catcher Stanley are no slouches defensively.

AL Cy Young runnerup Jimmy Key (17-4, 3.27) leads a solid pitching staff augmented by the winter acquisition of the White Sox' Jack McDowell (10-9, 3.73), who was, however, still unsigned at press time. Key has been the ace the Yankees needed since coming over from rival Toronto as a free agent prior to the '93 season. Melido Perez (9-4, 4.10) made a remarkable turnaround after his injury-plagued 1993 and Scott Kamieniecki (8-6, 3.76) proved effective as a starter after starting last year in the bullpen. Jim Abbott (9-8, 4.55) didn't live up to his press clippings in his two years in New York and he became an unrestricted free agent when the Yankees made no offer. Brash, young left-hander Sterling Hitchcock (4-1, 4.20) will bid anew for a spot in the rotation.

Steve Howe (3-0, 1.80, 15 saves) showed he still can pitch, stepping into the role as the club's closer after the Yankee brass failed to trade for one. If Howe should falter, there is also Bob Wickman (5-4, 3.09), who showed major improvement last year in becoming an effective setup man.

The Yankees retain the ingredients to remain a formidable contender and appear ready to break through to the postseason. The big question with the Yankees is always about whether club owner George Steinbrenner can refrain from meddling. If he does, this team might be ready to bask in some deferred glory.

YANKEE PROFILES

PAUL O'NEILL 32 6-4 215   Bats L Throws L

Emerged as one of the top players in AL last season... Hovered around .400 mark into June... Changed fortunes after coming to Yanks from Reds with Joe DeBerry in a deal for Roberto Kelly prior to 1993... Has hit .311 and .359 as a Yankee, compared to .259 lifetime average as a Red... His .359 mark in 1994 was best by Yankee since Mickey Mantle hit .365 in 1957... Picked up tainted batting title... Hitting coach Rick Down is credited for suggesting an exaggerated leg kick, leading to the stark turnaround... Famous for his mini-tantrums. Despite his big year, he still led team in helmets thrown... Picked a good time to have his best year, since he used threat of free agency to get rewarded with four-year, $19-million contract that included $2.2-million signing bonus last winter... Began the season being benched against some tough left-handers, but eventually took coveted No. 3 slot in batting order from Don Mattingly... Possesses one of the game's best arms in right... Born Feb. 25, 1963, in Columbus, Ohio... Would have earned $3,833,334 in 1994... Reds' fourth-round pick in 1981.

Year	Club	Pos.	G	AB	R	H	2B	3B	HR	RBI	SB	Avg.
1985	Cincinnati	OF	5	12	1	4	1	0	0	1	0	.333
1986	Cincinnati	PH	3	2	0	0	0	0	0	0	0	.000
1987	Cincinnati	OF-1B-P	84	160	24	41	14	1	7	28	2	.256
1988	Cincinnati	OF-1B	145	485	58	122	25	3	16	73	8	.252
1989	Cincinnati	OF	117	428	49	118	24	2	15	74	20	.276
1990	Cincinnati	OF	145	503	59	136	28	0	16	78	13	.270
1991	Cincinnati	OF	152	532	71	136	36	0	28	91	12	.256
1992	Cincinnati	OF	148	496	59	122	19	1	14	66	6	.246
1993	New York (AL)	OF	141	498	71	155	34	1	20	75	2	.311
1994	New York (AL)	OF	103	368	68	132	25	1	21	83	5	.359
	Totals		1043	3484	460	966	206	9	137	569	68	.277

DON MATTINGLY 33 6-0 200   Bats L Throws L

Earned great local sympathy when strike cost him his first chance at postseason play... Has now played 1,657 games without appearing in postseason, one fewer than current major league leader Julio Franco... Hinted in midsummer that he may not play much longer, but asserted this winter that he will definitely return, no matter how long the strike lasts... Batted .304, his highest mark since 1988... Because congenitive back ailment has sapped power that once made him one of game's top players, he hit just six home runs in 1994 . . . Still is considered the game's top-fielding first baseman . . . Season highlight was his first career pinch-hit home run, as he won a game with blast off Joe Grahe July 24 at California . . . Third-hardest to fan in AL (one whiff per 18.2 at-bats) . . . The club's captain since 1991, he has asserted himself as the team's unquestioned leader since old friend Buck Showalter became manager in '92 . . . Born April 20, 1961, in Evansville, Ind., and he still lives there . . . Was 19th-round draft choice by Yanks in 1979, because folks figured he was going to college . . . Salary would've been $4.02 million in 1994 . . . Captured batting title at .343 in 1984 and was AL MVP when he drove in 145 runs in 1985. . . . Won ninth Gold Glove in '94.

Year	Club	Pos.	G	AB	R	H	2B	3B	HR	RBI	SB	Avg.
1982	New York (AL)	OF-1B	7	12	0	2	0	0	0	1	0	.167
1983	New York (AL)	OF-1B-2B	91	279	34	79	15	4	4	32	0	.283
1984	New York (AL)	1B-OF	153	603	91	207	44	2	23	110	1	.343
1985	New York (AL)	1B	159	652	107	211	48	3	35	145	2	.324
1986	New York (AL)	1B-3B	162	677	117	238	53	2	31	113	0	.352
1987	New York (AL)	1B	141	569	93	186	38	2	30	115	1	.327
1988	New York (AL)	1B-OF	144	599	94	186	37	0	18	88	1	.311
1989	New York (AL)	1B-OF	158	631	79	191	37	2	23	113	3	.303
1990	New York (AL)	1B-OF	102	394	40	101	16	0	5	42	1	.256
1991	New York (AL)	1B	152	587	64	169	35	0	9	68	2	.288
1992	New York (AL)	1B	157	640	89	184	40	0	14	86	3	.288
1993	New York (AL)	1B	134	530	78	154	27	2	17	86	0	.291
1994	New York (AL)	1B	97	372	62	113	20	1	6	51	0	.304
Totals			1657	6545	948	2021	410	18	215	1050	14	.309

WADE BOGGS 36 6-2 197   Bats L Throws R

Five-time batting champ returned to Hall of Fame form in 1994, batting .342 to push his lifetime mark to .335 . . . Credits turnaround to rising comfort level in New York after miserable 1992 final season in Boston . . . Calls it a "godsend" that he didn't accept the Red Sox' two-year, $9.2-million offer in spring of '92 and instead signed three-year, $11-million deal with the Yankees prior to 1993 . . . Despite reports that he was selfish in Boston, he has fit beautifully into the Yankees' low-key clubhouse . . . Still eats chicken every game day and has about a million other superstitions . . . Showed surprising power with 11 home runs last year, which he credited to a rib injury, oddly enough . . . Won first Gold Glove in '94 . . . Now with 2,392 hits, he is still hoping to become a 3,000-hit man . . . Wants to play at least another four years and he'll probably need every one to get to 3,000... Born June 15, 1958, in Omaha, Neb., but moved a lot since father was in the service... Salary would have been $3.1 million in '94... Red Sox' seventh-round pick in 1976.

Year	Club	Pos.	G	AB	R	H	2B	3B	HR	RBI	SB	Avg.
1982	Boston	1B-3B-OF	104	338	51	118	14	1	5	44	1	.349
1983	Boston	3B	153	582	100	210	44	7	5	74	3	.361
1984	Boston	3B	158	625	109	203	31	4	6	55	3	.325
1985	Boston	3B	161	653	107	240	42	3	8	78	2	.368
1986	Boston	3B	149	580	107	207	47	2	8	71	0	.357
1987	Boston	3B-1B	147	551	108	200	40	6	24	89	1	.363
1988	Boston	3B	155	584	128	214	45	6	5	58	2	.366
1989	Boston	3B	156	621	113	205	51	7	3	54	2	.330
1990	Boston	3B	155	619	89	187	44	5	6	63	0	.302
1991	Boston	3B	144	546	93	181	42	2	8	51	1	.332
1992	Boston	3B	143	514	62	133	22	4	7	50	1	.259
1993	New York (AL)	3B	143	560	83	169	26	1	2	59	0	.302
1994	New York (AL)	3B-1B	97	366	61	125	19	1	11	55	2	.342
	Totals		1865	7139	1211	2392	467	49	98	801	18	.335

BERNIE WILLIAMS 26 6-2 205 · Bats S Throws R

Took another step toward stardom in '94, overcoming a painfully slow start to have his best season... Base-running has improved dramatically, to point where he no longer appears lost... Scored 80 runs despite batting in No. 6 hole much of season... A quiet, thoughtful type, he testified before Congress about the antitrust bill... Upset in spring training last season when Yankees would pay him only $225,000 because he was not yet arbitration eligible... Injured right shoulder forced him to be DH all spring, but when the season started he was ready to play... Outfield instincts still somewhat questionable, but he overcomes mistakes with raw speed in center... Still a much better hitter right-handed (.366) than left-handed (.247) last season... Born Sept. 13, 1968, in San Juan, P.R.... Yanks signed him as undrafted free agent in September 1985.

Year	Club	Pos.	G	AB	R	H	2B	3B	HR	RBI	SB	Avg.
1991	New York (AL)	OF	85	320	43	76	19	4	3	34	10	.238
1992	New York (AL)	OF	62	261	39	73	14	2	5	26	7	.280
1993	New York (AL)	OF	139	567	67	152	31	4	12	68	9	.268
1994	New York (AL)	3B-1B	108	408	80	118	29	1	12	57	16	.289
	Totals		394	1556	229	419	93	11	32	185	42	.269

MIKE STANLEY 31 6-0 190   Bats R Throws R

Catcher proved big 1993 season was no fluke, practically matching that performance in 1994 by hitting .300 with 17 home runs in strike-shortened year... Started slowly while feeling the pressure of proving detractors wrong, but he batted .335 after returning from DL June 15 ... His salary still has yet to catch up to his skill ... Salary would have been $512,500 last year, making him one of league's best bargains... Shortly after he signed his deal as a backup, manager Buck Showalter gave him starting job over Matt Nokes... Used to be known as a weak thrower, but he is considered adequate now... Was career backup when he signed minor league contract with Yankees as Ranger reject before '92 season... Born June 25, 1963, in Fort Lauderdale, Fla.... Texas drafted him in 16th round in 1985, out of University of Florida.

Year	Club	Pos.	G	AB	R	H	2B	3B	HR	RBI	SB	Avg.
1986	Texas	3B-C-OF	15	30	4	10	3	0	1	1	1	.333
1987	Texas	C-1B-OF	78	216	34	59	8	1	6	37	3	.273
1988	Texas	C-1B-3B	94	249	21	57	8	0	3	27	0	.229
1989	Texas	C-1B-3B	67	122	9	30	3	1	1	11	0	.246
1990	Texas	C-1B-3B	103	189	21	47	8	1	2	19	1	.249
1991	Texas	C-1B-3B-OF	95	181	25	45	13	1	3	25	0	.249
1992	New York (AL)	C-1B	68	173	24	43	7	0	8	27	0	.249
1993	New York (AL)	C	130	423	70	129	17	1	26	84	1	.305
1994	New York (AL)	C-1B	82	290	54	87	20	0	17	57	0	.300
	Totals		732	1873	262	507	87	5	67	288	7	.271

LUIS POLONIA 30 5-8 160   Bats L Throws L

Became the leadoff hitter whom the Yankees had sought... By batting .311, he topped .300 for the first time since 1990, his last year of his first stay in New York... Yankees did well by signing him to a two-year, $3-million deal as free agent prior to last season... Complained when he wasn't used against left-handed pitching, although his comments were muffled because Yankees were winning... A wild base-runner, he was thrown out often... His steal percentage of 62.5 remained below average... With hard work, he has made himself into a decent left fielder with a surprisingly effective arm... Known in quiet Yankees clubhouse as among the most outspoken and honest quotes... Served time in a Milwaukee prison before '90 season after conviction for having sex with a minor... Likes to play in

the Bronx, where many of his cousins live . . . Born Dec. 10, 1964, in Santiago City, D.R. . . . Originally signed by Athletics as undrafted free agent in January 1984 . . . Would have made $1.5 million in 1994.

Year Club	Pos.	G	AB	R	H	2B	3B	HR	RBI	SB	Avg.
1987 Oakland	OF	125	435	78	125	16	10	4	49	29	.287
1988 Oakland	OF	84	288	51	84	11	4	2	27	24	.292
1989 Oak.-NY (AL)	OF	125	433	70	130	17	6	3	46	22	.300
1990 NY (AL)-Cal.	OF	120	403	52	135	7	9	2	35	21	.335
1991 California	OF	150	604	92	179	28	8	2	50	48	.296
1992 California	OF	149	577	83	165	17	4	0	35	51	.286
1993 California	OF	152	576	75	156	17	6	1	32	55	.271
1994 New York (AL)	OF	95	350	62	109	21	6	1	36	20	.311
Totals		1000	3666	563	1083	134	53	15	310	270	.295

TONY FERNANDEZ 32 6-2 175   Bats S Throws R

Baseball's eternal malcontent . . . Never happy, but he still knows how to play this game . . . And now ex-Red free agent is a Yankee with two-year, $3-million contract . . . Lifelong shortstop played mostly third last year, but will be back at short . . . His six triples tied him for sixth in NL . . . Batted .352 with runners in scoring position . . . Free agent signed with Reds prior to last season . . . Homered in four straight games from April 25-28 . . . Batted .333 during Blue Jays' 1993 World Series triumph over Phils, but wanted long-term contract with Toronto while Blue Jays wanted to give him one-year deal . . . Owns soft hands as result of learning to play the game with cardboard cutout glove . . . Born June 30, 1962, in San Pedro de Macoris, D.R. . . . Originally signed as undrafted free agent by Blue Jays in 1979 . . . Would have made $500,000 in 1994.

Year Club	Pos.	G	AB	R	H	2B	3B	HR	RBI	SB	Avg.
1983 Toronto	SS	15	34	5	9	1	1	0	2	0	.265
1984 Toronto	SS-3B	88	233	29	63	5	3	3	19	5	.270
1985 Toronto	SS	161	564	71	163	31	10	2	51	13	.289
1986 Toronto	SS	163	687	91	213	33	9	10	65	25	.310
1987 Toronto	SS	146	578	90	186	29	8	5	67	32	.322
1988 Toronto	SS	154	648	76	186	41	4	5	70	15	.287
1989 Toronto	SS	140	573	64	147	25	9	11	64	22	.257
1990 Toronto	SS	161	635	84	175	27	17	4	66	26	.276
1991 San Diego	SS	145	558	81	152	27	5	4	38	23	.272
1992 San Diego	SS	155	622	84	171	32	4	4	37	20	.275
1993 New York (NL)	SS	48	173	20	39	5	2	1	14	6	.225
1993 Toronto	SS	94	353	45	108	18	9	4	50	15	.306
1994 Cincinnati	3B-SS-2B	104	366	50	102	18	6	8	50	12	.279
Totals		1574	6024	790	1714	292	87	61	593	214	.285

JIMMY KEY 33 6-1 185　　　　　　　Bats R Throws L

That four-year, $17-million contract he signed with Yanks as free agent prior to 1993 must be considered a bargain... Has become Yankees' much-needed ace and one of top pitchers in AL during last two seasons... Underwent arthroscopic surgery to repair inflamed rotator cuff last offseason... Has benefitted from pitching in Yankee Stadium rather than his previous home parks, SkyDome and Exhibition Stadium... Wife Cindy is his agent and she was praised for getting him a four-year deal after so-so '92 season with Blue Jays in which he went 13-13... Considered to have one of the best pickoff moves in AL... Also has one of the best change-ups and perhaps the best control... Cy Young runnerup in '94 is considered one of the fiercest competitors in baseball... Started the '94 All-Star Game... Salary would have been $5.25 million in 1994... Born April 22, 1961, in Huntsville, Ala.... Blue Jays' third-round pick in 1982, out of Clemson.

Year	Club	G	IP	W	L	Pct.	SO	BB	H	ERA
1984	Toronto	63	62	4	5	.444	44	32	70	4.65
1985	Toronto	35	212⅔	14	6	.700	85	50	188	3.00
1986	Toronto	36	232	14	11	.560	141	74	222	3.57
1987	Toronto	36	261	17	8	.680	161	66	210	2.76
1988	Toronto	21	131⅓	12	5	.706	65	30	127	3.29
1989	Toronto	33	216	13	14	.481	118	27	226	3.88
1990	Toronto	27	154⅔	13	7	.650	88	22	169	4.25
1991	Toronto	33	209⅓	16	12	.571	125	44	207	3.05
1992	Toronto	33	216⅔	13	13	.500	117	59	205	3.53
1993	New York (AL)	34	236⅔	18	6	.750	173	43	219	3.00
1994	New York (AL)	25	168	17	4	.810	97	52	177	3.27
	Totals	376	2100⅓	151	91	.624	1214	499	2020	3.36

JACK McDOWELL 29 6-5 180　　　　　Bats R Throws R

Acquired from White Sox in December in trade for minor league pitcher Keith Heberling and a player to be named... Had worst season since rookie year of 1988, but he still figures to remain one of game's better pitchers... Strike cost him his fifth consecutive 200-plus-innings season—and that may be a blessing considering he had averaged 257 innings per season from 1991-93... Won AL Cy Young in 1993, going 22-10 and leading White Sox to division title... Still a big winner, he is now 91-58 in big leagues... Would have earned $5.2 million in 1994 and should make close to $6 million in '95... Had salary battles with White Sox owner Jerry Reinsdorf that assured his departure... White Sox drafted him fifth overall in 1987, out of Stanford... Born Jan. 16, 1966, in Van Nuys, Cal.... At press time he was restricted free agent.

Year	Club	G	IP	W	L	Pct.	SO	BB	H	ERA
1987	Chicago (AL)	4	28	3	0	1.000	15	6	16	1.93
1988	Chicago (AL)	26	158⅔	5	10	.333	84	68	147	3.97
1990	Chicago (AL)	33	205	14	9	.609	165	77	189	3.82
1991	Chicago (AL)	35	253⅔	17	10	.630	191	82	212	3.41
1992	Chicago (AL)	34	260⅔	20	10	.667	178	75	247	3.18
1993	Chicago (AL)	34	256⅔	22	10	.688	158	69	261	3.37
1994	Chicago (AL)	25	181	10	9	.526	127	42	186	3.73
	Totals	191	1343⅔	91	58	.611	918	419	1258	3.50

STEVE HOWE 37 6-2 198   Bats L Throws L

Re-emerged as closer in 1994, after Yankees failed in bids to trade for one... Posted brilliant season, during which opposing batters hit only .194... Known for great control, he walked only seven in 40 innings... Declined to talk to the press, except about the labor issue, because he was unhappy with what he perceived as critical treatment... A colorful quote and an emotional person, he targeted himself for criticism during labor talks by accusing the owners of "unethical" behavior... Has been suspended seven times for drug- or alcohol-related offenses... Yankees gave him a controversial two-year, $4.2-million deal after he was reinstated following the 1992 season and exercised their option to keep him last winter... Would have made $1.9 million in '94... Born March 10, 1958, in Pontiac, Mich.... Dodgers drafted him 16th overall in '79 and he was NL Rookie of the Year in 1980.

Year	Club	G	IP	W	L	Pct.	SO	BB	H	ERA
1980	Los Angeles	59	85	7	9	.438	39	22	83	2.65
1981	Los Angeles	41	54	5	3	.625	32	18	51	2.50
1982	Los Angeles	66	99⅓	7	5	.583	49	17	87	2.08
1983	Los Angeles	46	68⅔	4	7	.364	52	12	55	1.44
1984	Los Angeles					Suspended				
1985	Los Angeles	19	22	1	1	.500	11	5	30	4.91
1985	Minnesota	13	19	2	3	.400	10	7	28	6.16
1987	Texas	24	31⅓	3	3	.500	19	8	33	4.31
1991	New York (AL)	37	48⅓	3	1	.750	34	7	39	1.68
1992	New York (AL)	20	22	3	0	1.000	12	3	9	2.45
1993	New York (AL)	51	50⅔	3	5	.375	19	10	58	4.97
1994	New York (AL)	40	40	3	0	1.000	18	7	28	1.80
	Totals	416	540⅓	41	37	.526	295	116	501	2.75

MELIDO PEREZ 29 6-4 210   Bats R Throws R

Made tremendous comeback after offseason shoulder surgery prior to 1994 . . . Had a brutal campaign in '93 and it appears now that the problem was that he was in pain . . . Known for having one of the best split-finger fastballs in baseball . . . Brother Pascual was a teammate for a few days in spring training of '93 with Yanks before being suspended for failing a drug test . . . His won-loss percentage never has equalled his talent, but last year was his best season in this regard (9-4) . . . Signed four-year, $14-million deal after big '92 season during which he went 13-16 despite dominating stuff . . . Acquired from White Sox in one of the most lopsided trades of the past few years, as Yankees also received Bob Wickman plus prospect Domingo Jean for the overrated Steve Sax after the 1991 season . . . Would have made $3.45 million in '94 . . . Born Feb. 15, 1966, in San Cristobal, D.R. . . . Signed as undrafted free agent by Royals in July 1983.

Year	Club	G	IP	W	L	Pct.	SO	BB	H	ERA
1987	Kansas City	3	10⅓	1	1	.500	5	5	18	7.84
1988	Chicago (AL)	32	197	12	10	.545	138	72	186	3.79
1989	Chicago (AL)	31	183⅓	11	14	.440	141	90	187	5.01
1990	Chicago (AL)	35	197	13	14	.481	161	86	177	4.61
1991	Chicago (AL)	49	135⅔	8	7	.533	128	52	111	3.12
1992	New York (AL)	33	247⅔	13	16	.448	218	93	212	2.87
1993	New York (AL)	25	163	6	14	.300	148	64	173	5.19
1994	New York (AL)	22	151⅓	9	4	.692	109	58	134	4.10
	Totals	230	1285⅓	73	80	.477	1048	520	1198	4.09

TOP PROSPECTS

DEREK JETER 20 6-3 175   Bats R Throws R

Made huge strides . . . Started the year with Tampa (A) and hit .329 . . . Hit .377 for Albany (AA) to reach Columbus (AAA), where he hit .349 and played so well that he became favorite to win big league shortstop job in '95 . . . Named Minor League Player of the Year by almost everyone, including *Baseball America* . . . Was Yanks' first-round pick and sixth player taken overall in 1992, signing for $700,000 . . . Was homesick his first year and error-prone his first two years, but has steadied himself immensely. He made just 25 errors last year after making 50-plus in 1993 . . . Hit .344 overall . . . Blessed with excellent speed and strong arm but suffered shoulder injury in Arizona League play last fall... More power may come when he fills out... Stole 50 bases in 58 attempts overall in 1994... Born June 26, 1974, in Pequannock, N.J.

BRIEN TAYLOR 23 6-3 195 Bats L Throws L
Spent 1994 season rehabbing in Tampa, after Dr. Frank Jobe performed reconstructive shoulder surgery Dec. 28, 1993... Controversy has surrounded this talented lefty since before he received then-record $1.55-million bonus as No. 1 overall pick in 1991 draft... Tore capsule and labrum in his pitching shoulder during a fight in December 1993, near his North Carolina home... Flashed brilliant talent with Albany (AA) in '93, going 13-7 with 3.48 ERA and holding Eastern League batters to .215 mark... Before the injury, there were questions about his ability to field his position and hold runners close... Born Dec. 26, 1971, in Beaufort, N.C.

RUBEN RIVERA 21 6-3 170 Bats R Throws R
Outfielder established himself as a top prospect with big power year for Tampa (A) and Greensboro (A), hitting total of 33 home runs and driving in 101 runs... Batted .288 for Greensboro and .261 for Tampa... Reportedly signed for a paltry $3,000 as undrafted free agent, out of Chorrera, Panama in November 1990 ... All-around ability has led to comparisons with Roberto Clemente... Stole 48 bases last year... Only weakness is high strikeout total... Whiffed 163 times in 1994... Frequently requested in trade talks... Born Nov. 14, 1973, in Chorrera.

RUSS DAVIS 25 6-0 170 Bats R Throws R
Third baseman was rumored to be going almost everywhere in trades last season, including Minnesota, San Diego, the Cubs and Mets... Has been blocked by Wade Boggs... Broke wrist when hit by a pitch from Charlotte's John Farrell Aug. 24, but is expected to recover fully... Has a chance to make Yankees as a backup in '95, but he wouldn't mind a trade to give him a chance at full-time duties... Went 2-for-14 in short midseason callup... Big power threat hit 25 homers and had 69 RBI for Columbus (AAA) after a slow start and finished at .276... Still some question about his defense and he made 23 errors in 1994... Born Sept. 13, 1969, in Birmingham, Ala.... Yanks' 29th-round pick in 1988 ... Father played in Orioles' system.

MANAGER BUCK SHOWALTER: Establishing himself as  one of the best young managers in game... Won AL Manager of the Year honors in '94 ... Had team in first place by 6½ games when players struck Aug. 12 and appeared on the way to managing in his first postseason before season was cancelled... Yankees' 70-43 mark in 1994, best in the AL, gives him a career mark of 234-203... Was youngest manager in baseball when he got the job, Oct. 29, 1991, and still is... Three-year contract expires after the 1995 season... Was legendary contact hitter for years in Yankees' minor league system, but never played above Triple-A... Compiled 360-207 minor league managerial record and won three championships, earning rave reviews along the way... Became Yankees' "Eye in the Sky" to start the 1990 season and was promoted to third-base coach early that year ... Was momentarily let go, with rest of the coaching staff, when Stump Merrill was fired after 1991 season, and had been eliminated as a managerial candidate until GM Gene Michael was convinced by the partners that Showalter should be given a shot over Doug Rader and Hal Lanier... Born May 23, 1956, in DeFuniak Springs, Fla.

ALL-TIME YANKEE SEASON RECORDS

BATTING: Babe Ruth, .393, 1923
HRs: Roger Maris, 61, 1961
RBI: Lou Gehrig, 184, 1931
STEALS: Rickey Henderson, 93, 1988
WINS: Jack Chesbro, 41, 1904
STRIKEOUTS: Ron Guidry, 248, 1978

TORONTO BLUE JAYS

TEAM DIRECTORY: Chairman: P.N.T. Widdrington; CEO: Paul Beeston; Pres./VP-GM: Gord Ash; Exec. VP-Baseball: Pat Gillick; VP-Baseball: Al LaMacchia, Bob Mattick; Dir. Pub. Rel.: Howard Starkman; Trav. Sec.: John Brioux; Mgr.: Cito Gaston; Coaches: Bob Bailor, Galen Cisco, Larry Hisle, Dennis Holmberg, Nick Leyva, Gene Tenace. Home: SkyDome (50,300). Field distances: 330, l.f. line; 375, l.c.; 400, c.f.; 375, r.c.; 330, r.f. line. Spring training: Dunedin, Fla.

SCOUTING REPORT

Since nobody took home the trophy last season, the Blue Jays got to keep it as '93 world champs. However, after their awful 55-60 1994 season, they can't feel the honor is deserved. Cito Gaston's Blue Jays enter the '95 season determined to recapture their recent glory, which included 11 straight seasons of .500-plus baseball before the '94 disaster. And don't put it past them.

The Blue Jays return the core of their great teams—Joe Carter, Roberto Alomar, Paul Molitor, John Olerud and Devon White—and any team with stars like those must be considered a threat. Nobody can pin the disappointment of '94 on Carter (.271, 27, 103), Molitor (.341, 14, 75) or White (.270, 13, 49). And while Alomar (.306, 8, 38) and Olerud (.297, 12, 67) didn't play up to their usual standards, there weren't bad, either.

It is hard to believe that a team with this much talent could lose more games than it won, but it happened. It's unlikely to happen again. Carter and Molitor have shown no signs of aging; Gold Glove center fielder White is in his prime, and Gold Glove second baseman Alomar and Olerud are just approaching their vintage years.

The problem with the Blue Jays last year was that their supporting players didn't hold up their end of the bargain. They are going to need more out of the shortstop, third base and catching positions to compete with the Yankees and Orioles. One big hope to lengthen their top-heavy lineup rests with Carlos Delgado (.215, 9, 24), who scorched pitchers last April before disintegrating. The Blue Jays need Delgado, who may be ready to be the full-time catcher, and third baseman Ed Sprague (.240, 11, 44) to recover from their off years. Also on the horizon is outfielder Shawn Green, another sweet swinger in the Olerud mold.

Toronto will also need much, much more from Juan Guzman

No other Alomar wields two-way impact of Robbie.

(12-11, 5.68), the one-time ace who got lit up last year. Guzman was afflicted by too many walks (76) and too many gopher balls (20). Prior to his surprisingly poor '94 season, he had a 40-11 career mark. Pat Hentgen (13-8, 3.40) is solid, but the Blue Jays will need at least one of their young pitchers to emerge—even if they decide to re-sign Todd Stottlemyre (7-7, 4.22), a free agent at press time. Perhaps the best hopes rest with Brad Cornett (1-3, 6.68) and Paul Spoljaric (0-1, 38.57).

More than anything, the Blue Jays can't do without a return to health by closer Duane Ward, one of the top relievers in baseball until shoulder pain wiped out his '94 season and ultimately resulted in surgery. The one small benefit from Ward's injury was the discovery of a late bloomer in left-hander Darren Hall (2-3, 3.41, 17 saves). Danny Cox (1-1, 1.45, 3 saves) also returned from his own health problems and may be ready for a full year.

One big change in the Blue Jays occurred off the field, where longtime GM Pat Gillick retired and was replaced by his assistant Gord Ash. It remains to be seen whether Ash will be as adept at pulling off the kind of deals—e.g. Alomar and Carter from San Diego for Fred McGriff and Tony Fernandez—that once made the Blue Jays baseball's best team.

BLUE JAY PROFILES

ROBERTO ALOMAR 27 6-0 185   Bats S Throws R

Did nothing to detract from his reputation as one of the game's best players... On Hall of Fame path, having completed seven wonderful years before his 27th birthday... Became youngest to win ALCS MVP in '92, when he batted .423 and hit pivotal home run against Dennis Eckersley... Top fielding second baseman in game as his range is second to none... Made just four errors in '94, none in last 45 games... Batted only .229 with runners in scoring position in 1994, down from .320 the year before, and his RBI total dipped from 93 in '93 to 38 ... Broken right leg sustained while playing winter ball in Puerto Rico in December 1993 did not cause him to miss any regular-season action... Lives where he plays, staying at the SkyDome hotel during season... Father Sandy was major league infielder for 15 years and brother Sandy Jr. is catcher for Indians... Would have made $5,333,334 in '94... Born Feb. 5, 1968, in Ponce, P.R.... Signed as undrafted free agent by Padres in 1985... Dealt to Toronto with Joe Carter for Fred McGriff and Tony Fernandez prior to 1991 season.... Won fourth Gold Glove in '94.

Year Club	Pos.	G	AB	R	H	2B	3B	HR	RBI	SB	Avg.
1988 San Diego	2B	143	545	84	145	24	6	9	41	24	.266
1989 San Diego	2B	158	623	82	184	27	1	7	56	42	.295
1990 San Diego	2B-SS	147	586	80	168	27	5	6	60	24	.287
1991 Toronto	2B	161	637	88	188	41	11	9	69	53	.295
1992 Toronto	2B	152	571	105	177	27	8	8	76	49	.310
1993 Toronto	2B	153	589	109	192	35	6	17	93	55	.326
1994 Toronto	2B	107	392	78	120	25	4	8	38	19	.306
Totals		1021	3943	626	1174	206	41	64	433	266	.298

PAUL MOLITOR 38 6-0 185   Bats R Throws R

Games lost to strike may have put his bid for 3,000 hits in jeopardy... Total stands at 2,647 after he ranked second in AL with 155 in '94 ... Would have made $4 million in '94 on deal he signed as free agent after '92 season... Has shown remarkable improvement in his later years, batting .290 over his first nine seasons and .323 in his last eight... Won World Series MVP in 1993, batting .500... This DH played third base at Atlanta in '93 Series because Blue Jays couldn't afford to lose his bat... In '93, he became the oldest player to record his first 100-

TORONTO BLUE JAYS • 105

RBI season and also the oldest to have 20 homers and 20 steals in same year... Has more hits than any other AL player since the start of '91 season (777)... Born Aug. 22, 1956, in St. Paul, Minn.... Brewers' first-round draft choice in '77 spent 15 seasons in Milwaukee... His 39-game hitting streak in 1987 remains longest in AL since Joe DiMaggio's record 56-game streak in 1941.

Year	Club	Pos.	G	AB	R	H	2B	3B	HR	RBI	SB	Avg.
1978	Milwaukee	2B-SS-3B	125	521	73	142	26	4	6	45	30	.273
1979	Milwaukee	2B-SS	140	584	88	188	27	16	9	62	33	.322
1980	Milwaukee	2B-SS-3B	111	450	81	137	29	2	9	37	34	.304
1981	Milwaukee	OF	64	251	45	67	11	0	2	19	10	.267
1982	Milwaukee	3B-SS	160	666	136	201	26	8	19	71	41	.302
1983	Milwaukee	3B	152	608	95	164	28	6	15	47	41	.269
1984	Milwaukee	3B	13	46	3	10	1	0	0	6	1	.217
1985	Milwaukee	3B	140	576	93	171	28	3	10	48	21	.297
1986	Milwaukee	3B-OF	105	437	62	123	24	6	9	55	20	.281
1987	Milwaukee	3B-2B	118	465	114	164	41	5	16	75	45	.353
1988	Milwaukee	3B-2B	154	609	115	190	34	6	13	60	41	.312
1989	Milwaukee	3B-2B	155	615	84	194	35	4	11	56	27	.315
1990	Milwaukee	2B-1B-3B	103	418	64	119	27	6	12	45	18	.285
1991	Milwaukee	1B	158	665	133	216	32	13	17	75	19	.325
1992	Milwaukee	1B	158	609	89	195	36	7	12	89	31	.320
1993	Toronto	1B	160	636	121	211	37	5	22	111	22	.332
1994	Toronto	1B	115	454	86	155	30	4	14	75	20	.341
	Totals		2131	8610	1482	2647	472	95	196	976	454	.307

JOHN OLERUD 26 6-5 218   Bats L Throws L

Lost 66 points off his batting average from previous year's league-leading .363 mark, but still matched his career average... Lost the magic of '93, when he was hitting .402 as late as Aug. 2... Led Blue Jays in just two offensive categories in '94: walks (61) and intentional walks (12)... Owns one of baseball's sweetest swings... Run total dropped from 109 in 1993 to 47... Never played a day in the minors... Still slightly clumsy around first base... Wears helmet when fielding since life-saving surgery to relieve an aneurism at the base of his brain as a collegian in 1989... Would have made $3.75 million in '94, when his salary tripled... Born Aug. 5, 1968, in Seattle... Blue Jays picked him in third round in 1989 draft, out of Washington State.

Year	Club	Pos.	G	AB	R	H	2B	3B	HR	RBI	SB	Avg.
1989	Toronto	1B	6	8	2	3	0	0	0	0	0	.375
1990	Toronto	1B	111	358	43	95	15	1	14	48	0	.265
1991	Toronto	1B	139	454	64	116	30	1	17	68	0	.256
1992	Toronto	1B	138	458	68	130	28	0	16	66	1	.284
1993	Toronto	1B	158	551	109	200	54	2	24	107	0	.363
1994	Toronto	1B	108	384	47	114	29	2	12	67	1	.297
	Totals		660	2213	333	658	156	6	83	356	2	.297

JOE CARTER 35 6-3 225   Bats R Throws R

Shortening of season did not prevent him from posting his eighth 100-RBI season in nine years ... Outfielder set club mark with 69 RBI at home in 1994 ... Stole 200th base in '94 and also hit 300th home run, becoming 10th player in history to have reached both of those career plateaus ... Since 1984, he has 1,096 RBI, most in majors ... Has five three-homer games, most in AL history ... First player in history to have three successive 100-RBI seasons for three different teams ... Capped '93 World Series with game-winning Game 6 home run off Mitch Williams ... Came to Toronto from Padres with Roberto Alomar for Fred McGriff and Tony Fernandez in most star-studded trade of past decade prior to 1991 season ... Would have made $5.5 million in '94 ... Born March 7, 1960, in Oklahoma City, Okla.

Year	Club	Pos.	G	AB	R	H	2B	3B	HR	RBI	SB	Avg.
1983	Chicago (NL)	OF	23	51	6	9	1	1	0	1	1	.176
1984	Cleveland	OF-1B	66	244	32	67	6	1	13	41	2	.275
1985	Cleveland	OF-1B-2B-3B	143	489	64	128	27	0	15	59	24	.262
1986	Cleveland	OF-1B	162	663	108	200	36	9	29	121	29	.302
1987	Cleveland	OF-1B	149	588	83	155	27	2	32	106	31	.264
1988	Cleveland	OF	157	621	85	168	36	6	27	98	27	.271
1989	Cleveland	OF-1B	162	651	84	158	32	4	35	105	13	.243
1990	San Diego	OF-1B	162	634	79	147	27	1	24	115	22	.232
1991	Toronto	OF	162	638	89	174	42	3	33	108	20	.273
1992	Toronto	OF-1B	158	622	97	164	30	7	34	119	12	.264
1993	Toronto	OF	155	603	92	153	33	5	33	121	8	.254
1994	Toronto	OF	111	435	70	118	25	2	27	103	11	.271
	Totals			1610	6239	889	1641	322	41	302	1097	200	.263

DEVON WHITE 32 6-2 182   Bats S Throws R

Generally regarded as game's best defensive center fielder ... Makes the impossible look routine ... Will forever be remembered for spectacular grab in Game 3 of '92 World Series, turning fence-crashing catch into a near triple play ... Even before labor action, it was clear he wasn't going to post a fourth straight 30-steal year ... Has hit between 11 and 17 home runs in the seven seasons since he popped 24 as a rookie with Angels in '87 ... Did not get along with Doug Rader in California, but has thrived in Toronto ... Only weakness is that he walks too infrequently (21 in '94) and strikes out too often (80) ... Willingly stepped aside as leadoff man for Rickey Henderson late in '93 ... One of game's best base-runners ... Would have made $3,083,334 in '94 ... Born Dec. 29, 1962, in Kingston, Jamaica

TORONTO BLUE JAYS • 107

... Angels drafted him in sixth round in 1981 and dealt him to Toronto with Willie Frazer and Marcus Moore for Junior Felix, Luis Sojo and Ken Rivers prior to 1991 season.... Won sixth Gold Glove in '94.

Year	Club	Pos.	G	AB	R	H	2B	3B	HR	RBI	SB	Avg.
1985	California	OF	21	7	7	1	0	0	0	0	3	.143
1986	California	OF	29	51	8	12	1	1	1	3	6	.235
1987	California	OF	159	639	103	168	33	5	24	87	32	.263
1988	California	OF	122	455	76	118	22	2	11	51	17	.259
1989	California	OF	156	636	86	156	18	13	12	56	44	.245
1990	California	OF	125	443	57	96	17	3	11	44	21	.217
1991	Toronto	OF	156	642	110	181	40	10	17	60	33	.282
1992	Toronto	OF	153	641	98	159	26	7	17	60	37	.248
1993	Toronto	OF	146	598	116	163	42	6	15	52	34	.273
1994	Toronto	OF	100	403	67	109	24	6	13	49	11	.270
	Totals		1167	4515	728	1163	223	53	121	462	238	.258

ED SPRAGUE 27 6-2 210   Bats R Throws R

Third baseman slumped badly after nice 1993 season... Was hitting .312 May 20 when he lost his batting eye in 1994... Was 0-for-35 when he homered June 1 off Athletics' Todd Van Poppel... Finished in top 10 in AL in two categories, ranking ninth in whiffs (95) and second in HBPs (11)... His dramatic homer won Game 2 of '92 World Series against Atlanta... Born July 25, 1967, in Castro Valley, Cal.... Father Ed was big league pitcher from 1968-76... Blue Jays drafted him 25th overall in 1988, out of Stanford... His wife, Kristen, won Olympic gold medal for synchronized swimming in 1992... Would have made $500,000 in '94.

Year	Club	Pos.	G	AB	R	H	2B	3B	HR	RBI	SB	Avg.
1991	Toronto	3B-1B-C	61	160	17	44	7	0	4	20	0	.275
1992	Toronto	C-1B-3B	22	47	6	11	2	0	1	7	0	.234
1993	Toronto	3B	150	546	50	142	31	1	12	73	1	.260
1994	Toronto	3B-1B	109	405	38	97	19	1	11	44	1	.240
	Totals		342	1158	111	294	59	2	28	144	2	.254

JUAN GUZMAN 28 5-11 190   Bats R Throws R

Slumped badly in '94, equalling loss total of his previous three seasons combined with 11... Lifetime win percentage dipped from .784 to .703... Allowed more hits (165) than innings pitched (147⅓) for first time in his short career... Also allowed the fifth-most runs in AL (102) in nightmarish season... Possessor of one of the league's nastier split-finger fastballs, he set AL record for wild pitches in '93 with 26... Also tied for league lead with 13 wild pitches last season... Has 5-0 record and 2.27 ERA in five LCS starts... Born Oct. 28, 1966, in Santo Domingo, D.R.... Acquired from Dodgers for infielder Mike Sharperson Sept. 22, 1987, in another steal by Blue Jays ... Would have made $1 million in '94.

Year	Club	G	IP	W	L	Pct.	SO	BB	H	ERA
1991	Toronto	23	138⅔	10	3	.769	123	66	98	2.99
1992	Toronto	28	180⅔	16	5	.762	165	72	135	2.64
1993	Toronto	33	221	14	3	.824	194	110	211	3.99
1994	Toronto	25	147⅓	12	11	.522	124	76	165	5.68
	Totals	109	687⅔	52	22	.703	606	324	609	3.80

PAT HENTGEN 26 6-2 200 Bats R Throws R

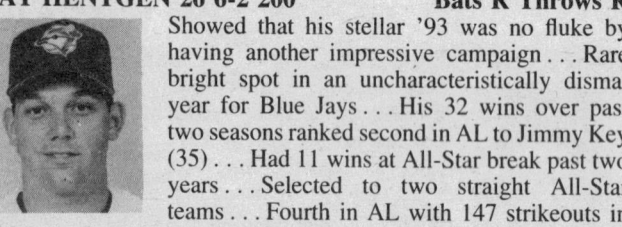

Showed that his stellar '93 was no fluke by having another impressive campaign... Rare bright spot in an uncharacteristically dismal year for Blue Jays... His 32 wins over past two seasons ranked second in AL to Jimmy Key (35)... Had 11 wins at All-Star break past two years... Selected to two straight All-Star teams... Fourth in AL with 147 strikeouts in 1994, up from 122 in full '93 season... Also tied for fourth in complete games (6), was seventh in ERA (3.40), tied for fifth in wins (13), tied for second in shutouts (3) and was sixth in innings (174⅔)... Would've made a bargain basement $500,000 in '94 ... Born Nov. 13, 1968, in Detroit... Fifth-round choice of Toronto in '86.

Year	Club	G	IP	W	L	Pct.	SO	BB	H	ERA
1991	Toronto	3	7⅓	0	0	.000	3	3	5	2.45
1992	Toronto	28	50⅓	5	2	.714	39	32	49	5.36
1993	Toronto	34	216⅓	19	9	.679	122	74	215	3.87
1994	Toronto	24	174⅔	13	8	.619	147	59	158	3.40
	Totals	89	448⅔	37	19	.661	311	168	427	3.83

DUANE WARD 30 6-4 215 Bats R Throws R

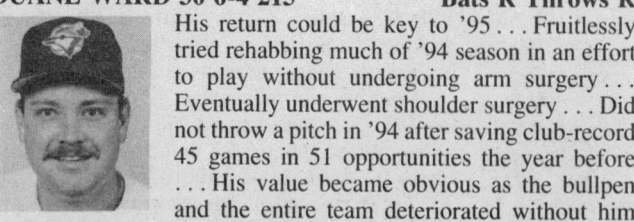

His return could be key to '95... Fruitlessly tried rehabbing much of '94 season in an effort to play without undergoing arm surgery... Eventually underwent shoulder surgery... Did not throw a pitch in '94 after saving club-record 45 games in 51 opportunities the year before ... His value became obvious as the bullpen and the entire team deteriorated without him ... Had been bullpen workhorse, logging 100-plus innings five straight years from 1988-92... Replaced Tom Henke as club's closer in 1992... Known for nasty fastball-forkball combination ... Has more career strikeouts than innings pitched... Acquired from Braves for Doyle Alexander, July 6, 1986... Born May 28, 1964, in Parkview, N.M.... Would have earned $4 million in '94... Braves drafted him ninth overall in 1982.

Year	Club	G	IP	W	L	Pct.	SO	BB	H	ERA
1986	Atlanta	10	16	0	1	.000	8	8	22	7.31
1986	Toronto	2	2	0	1	.000	1	4	2	13.50
1987	Toronto	12	11⅔	1	0	1.000	10	12	14	6.94
1988	Toronto	64	111⅔	9	3	.750	91	60	101	3.30
1989	Toronto	66	114⅔	4	10	.286	122	58	94	3.77
1990	Toronto	73	127⅔	8	2	.800	112	42	101	3.45
1991	Toronto	81	107⅓	7	6	.538	132	33	80	2.77
1992	Toronto	79	101⅓	7	4	.636	103	39	76	1.95
1993	Toronto	71	71⅔	2	3	.400	97	25	49	2.13
1994	Toronto					Injured				
	Totals	458	664	32	36	.471	676	281	540	3.19

TODD STOTTLEMYRE 29 6-3 195   Bats L Throws R

Pitched to .500 record at 7-7 last year, which seems to be the story of his so-so career... Started year in the bullpen, but proved incapable of replacing injured Duane Ward... Quickly returned to the rotation, where he settled into his usual mediocrity... Son of pitcher Mel Stottlemyre, who went 164-139 for the Yankees from 1964-74... Brother Mel Jr. pitched for Royals in 1990... Humiliated in Game 4 of the '93 Series, when he allowed six earned runs in two complete innings of Blue Jays' 15-14 victory and also bruised his chin sliding into third base... Day before that game, mayor of Philadelphia said he could hit Stott—and it didn't seem so far fetched after that game... Would have made $2.325 million in '94, the same as '93... Born May 20, 1965, in Yakima, Wash.... Blue Jays made him third player picked overall in '85 draft... **Free agent at press time.**

Year	Club	G	IP	W	L	Pct.	SO	BB	H	ERA
1988	Toronto	28	98	4	8	.333	67	46	109	5.69
1989	Toronto	27	127⅔	7	7	.500	63	44	137	3.88
1990	Toronto	33	203	13	17	.433	115	69	214	4.34
1991	Toronto	34	219	15	8	.652	116	75	194	3.78
1992	Toronto	28	174	12	11	.522	98	63	175	4.50
1993	Toronto	30	176⅔	11	12	.478	98	69	204	4.84
1994	Toronto	26	140⅔	7	7	.500	105	48	149	4.22
	Totals	206	1139	69	70	.496	662	414	1182	4.39

Paul Molitor stands 353 hits away from magic 3,000 club.

TOP PROSPECTS

CARLOS DELGADO 22 6-3 206   Bats L Throws R
Flashed tremendous ability during huge start to his rookie season in 1994, but fizzled quickly... Was leading majors in homers April 19, with eight... Hit only one more homer before a major slump caused his demotion to Syracuse (AAA)... Wound up batting .215 with nine homers and 24 RBI for Toronto in 43 games,

but he hit .319 with 19 homers and 58 RBI in 85 games for Syracuse... Played left field for Blue Jays, but was switched back to his old position, catcher, in minors... Seen as Jays' catcher of the future... Born June 25, 1972, in Aquadilla, P.R.... Signed as undrafted free agent in October 1988... Drove in 100 runs for Dunedin (A) in 1992 and 102 for Knoxville (AA) in 1993.

SHAWN GREEN 22 6-4 190   Bats L Throws L
Had huge year for Syracuse (AAA), winning league MVP honors after batting .344 with 13 homers and 61 RBI... Voted top prospect in International League... Also voted as having best outfield arm... Like Carlos Delgado, he struggled while with Blue Jays... But unlike Delgado, he did not even show flashes... Went 3-for-33 following late-season callup... Blue Jays' first-round pick in '91, when he was 16th choice overall... Born Nov. 10, 1972, in Des Plaines, Ill.

ALEX GONZALEZ 21 6-0 182   Bats R Throws R
Started the 1994 season as Blue Jays' shortstop, but struggled offensively and was quickly demoted... Batted .151 in 15 games with Jays... Was youngest player on any Opening Day roster last year... Hit .284 for Syracuse (AAA), with 12 home runs, 57 RBI and 23 stolen bases in 110 games... Viewed as quality defender with an excellent arm... Only a 14th-round choice in '91 draft... Born April 8, 1973, in Miami.

BRAD CORNETT 26 6-3 188   Bats R Throws R
Rose quickly through the system last year, performing well for Knoxville (AA) and Syracuse (AAA) before getting knocked around with Blue Jays... In nine games with Toronto, including four starts, he was 1-3 with 6.68 ERA... Allowed just one run in five innings of relief in his big league debut, June 8 vs. White Sox... Had sub-3.00 ERA for Knoxville (2-3, 2.41) and Syracuse (1-2, 1.42)... Signed as undrafted free agent in June 1992... Started '93 season with Class-A Hagerstown, the beginning of his sharp rise... Born Feb. 4, 1969, in La Mesa, Tex.

MANAGER CITO GASTON:  Hasn't received the respect and accolades normally accorded a two-time World Series-winning manager... Has expressed unhappiness over his lack of respect outside Blue Jays' organization... Even Toronto media is tough on him... Despite 55-60 season in '94, he has compiled a .562 winning percentage (481-375) since taking over as Toronto manager, May 31, 1989... Unemotional and softspoken, he is a '90s manager... Rarely made lots of moves in championship seasons, when he was blessed with talented, set lineup... Undermined by bullpen injuries last year... Hesitated before taking the managerial job... First African-American manager to guide his team into World Series... Made coaching debut as Braves' minor league batting instructor in '81... Known as Clarence Gaston during 12-year playing career for Atlanta, San Diego and Pittsburgh... Originally signed by the Milwaukee Braves, he went to San Diego in 1969 NL expansion draft... Was an outfielder with career .256 batting average... Represented Padres at 1970 All-Star Game.

ALL-TIME BLUE JAY SEASON RECORDS

BATTING: John Olerud, .363, 1993
HRs: George Bell, 47, 1987
RBI: George Bell, 134, 1987
STEALS: Dave Collins, 60, 1984
WINS: Jack Morris, 21, 1992
STRIKEOUTS: Dave Stieb, 198, 1984

CHICAGO WHITE SOX

TEAM DIRECTORY: Chairman: Jerry Reinsdorf; Vice Chairman: Eddie Einhorn; Exec. VP: Howard Pizer; Sr. VP-Baseball: Jack Gould; Sr. VP-Major League Oper.: Ron Schueler; VP-Free-Agent/Major League Scouting; Larry Monroe; Dir. Baseball Oper.: Dan Evans; Dir. Pub. Rel.: Doug Abel; Trav. Sec.: Glen Rosenbaum; Mgr.: Gene Lamont; Coaches: Terry Bevington, Jackie Brown, Walt Hriniak, Doug Mansolino, Noe Nossek, Rick Peterson. Home: Comiskey Park (44,321). Field distances: 347, l.f. line; 375, l.c.; 400, c.f.; 375, r.c., 347, r.f. line. Spring training: Sarasota, Fla.

SCOUTING REPORT

Only a strike kept the White Sox from postseason play for the second consecutive season and there is little reason to doubt they will get there this year.

For Gene Lamont's team, a 67-46 club in '94, it starts with

Wilson Alvarez rang up 15 Ws in a row over two years.

the best starting pitching this side of Atlanta. Jack McDowell's defection as a free agent will hurt. But, even without him, the White Sox boast three of the best young starting pitchers in the league in Alex Fernandez (11-7, 3.86), Jason Bere (12-2, 3.81) and Wilson Alvarez (12-8, 3.45).

All three are 25 or younger and possess outstanding stuff. And they represent only part of this organization's load of pitchers. Top prospects Scott Ruffcorn and James Baldwin certainly could fit in the rotation at some point this season.

Closer Roberto Hernandez (4-4, 4.91, 14 saves) had a down season, but he is young enough to rebound, and his surrounding cast in the bullpen is underrated. Free-agent veteran right-handers Kirk McCaskill (1-4, 3.42) and Scott Sanderson (8-4, 5.09) are dependable fifth-starter/middle reliever types. Left-hander Scott Radinsky is expected to return after missing last season while being treated for Hodgkin's Disease.

We've gone too long without mentioning two-time defending AL MVP, first baseman Frank Thomas. Most players would have trouble matching Thomas' 1994 numbers over a 162-game season, let alone in a strike-shortened one. Thomas hit .353 with 38 homers, 101 RBI, 109 walks and 106 runs in only 399 official at-bats and 113 games.

There is plenty of support for Thomas in a lineup that finished third in the AL in batting average (.287), fourth in runs (633) and fifth in slugging percentage (.444).

However, that was with Julio Franco setting career highs in home runs (20) and RBI (96) hitting behind Thomas and that will not be the case this season, as free-agent Franco has signed a two-year, $7-million contract to play in Japan. That will put more pressure on third baseman Robin Ventura (.282, 18, 78), a solid run producer, and right fielder Darrin Jackson (.312, 10, 51). Jackson, who enjoyed a strong comeback season in '94, was expected to re-sign as a free agent.

The rest of the lineup is filled with smurfs, from leadoff hitter Tim Raines (.266, 10, 52), still a threat at 35, to the underrated Lance Johnson (.277, 26 steals), to pesky Ozzie Guillen (.288) to speedy Joey Cora (.276).

Johnson in center, Guillen at shortstop and Ron Karkovice behind the plate make the White Sox strong defensively up the middle. Ventura has won three Gold Gloves, but Raines and Thomas are just adequate at left and first, respectively.

Lamont has almost everything a manager wants, except job security. He'll be working on a one-year deal again and that probably means the White Sox better reach postseason play or else.

WHITE SOX PROFILES

FRANK THOMAS 26 6-5 260   Bats R Throws R

Became AL's first back-to-back MVP choice since Roger Maris (1960-61) and 11th player in history to win award in consecutive seasons ... This big guy's numbers match up with those of all-time best in history ... Hit career-high .353 last season, raising career average to an amazing .326 ... Despite strike, he drove in 100-plus runs (101) and scored 100-plus runs (106) for fourth consecutive season ... Also hit 38 homers and had league-leading .729 slugging percentage and .487 on-base percentage ... No wonder his nickname is "Big Hurt" ... Would have earned $2.5 million in 1994, on first year of four-year, $29-million extension ... Unanimous AL MVP in 1993, when he set club record with 41 homers and finished in top 10 in 10 AL offensive categories ... Has improved defensively at first base, but he is still a liability ... Played season of football at Auburn, but made the right career choice ... Was seventh player picked in 1989 draft, after such non-notables as Paul Coleman and Donald Harris ... Born May 27, 1968, in Columbus, Ga.

Year	Club	Pos.	G	AB	R	H	2B	3B	HR	RBI	SB	Avg.
1990	Chicago (AL)	1B	60	191	39	63	11	3	7	31	0	.330
1991	Chicago (AL)	1B	158	559	104	178	31	2	32	109	1	.318
1992	Chicago (AL)	1B	160	573	108	185	46	2	24	115	6	.323
1993	Chicago (AL)	1B	153	549	106	174	36	0	41	128	4	.317
1994	Chicago (AL)	1B	113	399	106	141	34	1	38	101	2	.353
	Totals		644	2271	463	741	158	8	142	484	13	.326

ROBIN VENTURA 27 6-1 200   Bats L Throws R

Put together another standout season ... Pushed batting average back up to .282 after slipping to .262 in 1993 ... Has averaged 20 home runs and 91 RBI over last four seasons ... Missed four games before the strike, after playing in exactly 157 in each of three previous seasons ... Drew 61 walks, pushing on-base average to .373 ... Defense at third base fell off, however ... Committed 20 errors, high total for a three-time Gold Glove winner ... Would have earned $3.5 million in 1994 ... Got pounded by Nolan Ryan in memorable brawl, Aug. 4, 1993 ... Hard to believe he endured an 0-for-41 slump in 1990 rookie season...Member of 1988 U.S. Olympic Team... Starred at Oklahoma State and was drafted 10th overall in 1988 ...Born July 14, 1967, in Santa Monica, Cal.

Year	Club	Pos.	G	AB	R	H	2B	3B	HR	RBI	SB	Avg.
1989	Chicago (AL)	3B	16	45	5	8	3	0	0	7	0	.178
1990	Chicago (AL)	3B-1B	150	493	48	123	17	1	5	54	1	.249
1991	Chicago (AL)	3B-1B	157	606	92	172	25	1	23	100	2	.284
1992	Chicago (AL)	3B-1B	157	592	85	167	38	1	16	93	2	.282
1993	Chicago (AL)	3B-1B	157	554	85	145	27	1	22	94	1	.262
1994	Chicago (AL)	3B-1B-SS	109	401	57	113	15	1	18	78	3	.282
	Totals		746	2691	372	728	125	5	84	426	9	.271

Robin Ventura's BA jumped, fielding dipped.

OZZIE GUILLEN 31 5-11 165   Bats L Throws R

Posted a career-high batting average (.288) for second consecutive season... However, this free-swinging shortstop still draws walks about as often as he commits errors, which isn't very often... Drew 14 walks in 365 at-bats and committed 16 errors in 99 games... Would have earned $2.1 million in 1994... Made impressive comeback in 1993 after serious knee injury cost him almost all of 1992 season... Played only 12 games in 1992 before tearing up knee in collision with Tim Raines... Emotional spark in the clubhouse... Won Gold Glove in 1990... AL Rookie of the Year in 1985... Began career in Padres' chain... Acquired in deal with San Diego for LaMarr Hoyt after 1984 season... Follows Chico Carrasquel and Luis Aparicio in long line of quality White Sox shortstops from Venezuela... Born Jan. 20, 1964, in Oculare del Tuy, Venezuela.

Year	Club	Pos.	G	AB	R	H	2B	3B	HR	RBI	SB	Avg.
1985	Chicago (AL)	SS	150	491	71	134	21	9	1	33	7	.273
1986	Chicago (AL)	SS	159	547	58	137	19	4	2	47	8	.250
1987	Chicago (AL)	SS	149	560	64	156	22	7	2	51	25	.279
1988	Chicago (AL)	SS	156	566	58	148	16	7	0	39	25	.261
1989	Chicago (AL)	SS	155	597	63	151	20	8	1	54	36	.253
1990	Chicago (AL)	SS	160	516	61	144	21	4	1	58	13	.279
1991	Chicago (AL)	SS	154	524	52	143	20	3	3	49	21	.273
1992	Chicago (AL)	SS	12	40	5	8	4	0	0	7	1	.200
1993	Chicago (AL)	SS	134	457	44	128	23	4	4	50	5	.280
1994	Chicago (AL)	SS	100	365	46	105	9	5	1	39	5	.288
Totals			1329	4663	522	1254	175	51	15	427	146	.269

LANCE JOHNSON 31 5-11 160   Bats L Throws L

Little outfielder who often comes up big, especially with a glove on his right hand... Slap hitter who knows his limitations... Hit three home runs, tying a career high... Also drove in career-high 54 runs in only 106 games... Throw in a league-leading 14 triples and 26 stolen bases and you have a dangerous force at tail end of lineup... Didn't make an error in center and covered all kinds of ground... Arm is a bit weak, however... Would have earned $2,666,667 in 1994... White Sox got him and Ricky Horton from Cards for Jose DeLeon prior to 1988 season... Hasn't batted lower than .274 in any of last six seasons... Sixth-round pick of Cardinals in 1984 draft...

118 • THE COMPLETE HANDBOOK OF BASEBALL

Was Triton (Ill.) Junior College teammate of Kirby Puckett... Born July 6, 1963, in Cincinnati.

Year	Club	Pos.	G	AB	R	H	2B	3B	HR	RBI	SB	Avg.
1987	St. Louis	OF	33	59	4	13	2	1	0	7	6	.220
1988	Chicago (AL)	OF	33	124	11	23	4	1	0	6	6	.185
1989	Chicago (AL)	OF	50	180	28	54	8	2	0	16	16	.300
1990	Chicago (AL)	OF	151	541	76	154	18	9	1	51	36	.285
1991	Chicago (AL)	OF	159	588	72	161	14	13	0	49	26	.274
1992	Chicago (AL)	OF	157	567	67	158	15	12	3	47	41	.279
1993	Chicago (AL)	OF	147	540	75	168	18	14	0	47	35	.311
1994	Chicago (AL)	OF	106	412	56	114	11	14	3	54	26	.277
	Totals		836	3011	389	845	90	66	7	277	192	.281

TIM RAINES 35 5-8 185   Bats S Throws R

Isn't the player he used to be, but isn't exactly washed up, either... His .266 batting average last season was 32 points below previous career mark... But he scored 80 runs and drove in 52 in 101 games... Switch-hitter batted only .208 against left-handers... Outfield defense is slipping and arm is particularly weak... Would have earned $3,650,000 in 1994, on first year of three-year, $11-million deal... Had big ALCS in 1993, hitting .444 with 12 hits... Fourth on the all-time stolen-base list with 764 after swiping only 13 in '94... Nickname is "Rock"... He adopted nickname as his first name at start of 1991 season, only to drop it a few months later in midst of prolonged slump... Acquired from Expos with Jeff Carter and Mario Brito for Ivan Calderon and Barry Jones prior to 1991 season... Born Sept. 1, 1959, in Sanford, Fla.

Year	Club	Pos.	G	AB	R	H	2B	3B	HR	RBI	SB	Avg.
1979	Montreal	PR	6	0	3	0	0	0	0	0	2	.000
1980	Montreal	2B-OF	15	20	5	1	0	0	0	0	5	.050
1981	Montreal	OF-2B	88	313	61	95	13	7	5	37	71	.304
1982	Montreal	OF-2B	156	647	90	179	32	8	4	43	78	.277
1983	Montreal	OF-2B	156	615	133	183	32	8	11	71	90	.298
1984	Montreal	OF-2B	160	622	106	192	38	9	8	60	75	.309
1985	Montreal	OF	150	575	115	184	30	13	11	41	70	.320
1986	Montreal	OF	151	580	91	194	35	10	9	62	70	.334
1987	Montreal	OF	139	530	123	175	34	8	18	68	50	.330
1988	Montreal	OF	109	429	66	116	19	7	12	48	33	.270
1989	Montreal	OF	145	517	76	148	29	6	9	60	41	.286
1990	Montreal	OF	130	457	65	131	11	5	9	62	49	.287
1991	Chicago (AL)	OF	155	609	102	163	20	6	5	50	51	.268
1992	Chicago (AL)	OF	144	551	102	162	22	9	7	54	45	.294
1993	Chicago (AL)	OF	115	415	75	127	16	4	16	54	21	.306
1994	Chicago (AL)	OF	101	384	80	102	15	5	10	52	13	.266
	Totals		1920	7264	1293	2152	346	105	134	762	764	.296

CHICAGO WHITE SOX • 119

The Big Hurt aims for third straight AL MVP award.

WILSON ALVAREZ 25 6-1 235   Bats L Throws L

Emerging as league's most dominant lefthander this side of Randy Johnson . . : Won first eight decisions in 1994 before finishing 12-8 . . . Also won his last seven regular-season decisions in 1993, plus another in the ALCS, a complete-game effort . . . Tied for sixth in AL in wins and ninth in ERA (3.45) in 1994 and cut walks from 122 in 1993 to 62 . . . Finished second in AL in ERA in 1993, when he broke through to win 15

games... Allowed only 168 hits in 207⅔ innings... Would have earned $265,000 in 1994, but his day is coming... His development must haunt Rangers, who dealt him with Sammy Sosa and Scott Fletcher for Harold Baines and Fred Manrique, July 29, 1989... Was a phenom in native Venezuela, throwing 12 no-hitters and dominating older competition before signing contract with Texas as undrafted free agent at 16 in September 1986... Born March 24, 1970, in Maracaibo.

Year	Club	G	IP	W	L	Pct.	SO	BB	H	ERA
1989	Texas	1	0	0	1	.000	0	2	3	—
1991	Chicago (AL)	10	56⅓	3	2	.600	32	29	47	3.51
1992	Chicago (AL)	34	100⅓	5	3	.625	66	65	103	5.20
1993	Chicago (AL)	31	207⅔	15	8	.652	155	122	168	2.95
1994	Chicago (AL)	24	161⅔	12	8	.600	108	62	147	3.45
	Totals	100	526	35	22	.614	361	280	468	3.64

ALEX FERNANDEZ 25 6-1 215   Bats R Throws R

Fell back a bit from 18-victory season in 1993, but 27 other teams would love to have him... Still only 25 after four-plus big league seasons... Showed more flashes of brilliance, throwing three shutouts... But was too gopher-prone, allowing 25 home runs in 170⅓ innings... Has gone 29-16 in his last two seasons and is 51-45 in big leagues... Besides winning 18 in 1993, he finished fifth in AL in ERA and seventh in innings... Pitched two strong ALCS games, allowing three earned runs in 15 innings, but was 0-2... First-round pick of Brewers in 1988, but he decided to attend University of Miami... Stayed there only one season before transferring to junior college... White Sox picked him fourth overall in 1990 draft... Born Aug. 13, 1969, in Miami Beach... Would have earned $748,334 in 1994.

Year	Club	G	IP	W	L	Pct.	SO	BB	H	ERA
1990	Chicago (AL)	13	87⅔	5	5	.500	61	34	89	3.80
1991	Chicago (AL)	34	191⅔	9	13	.409	145	88	186	4.51
1992	Chicago (AL)	29	187⅔	8	11	.421	95	50	199	4.27
1993	Chicago (AL)	34	247⅓	18	9	.667	169	67	221	3.13
1994	Chicago (AL)	24	170⅓	11	7	.611	122	50	163	3.86
	Totals	134	884⅔	51	45	.531	592	289	858	3.88

JASON BERE 23 6-3 185 — Bats R Throws R

Yet another member of AL's best young staff ... Led AL in winning percentage (.857), was fifth in opponents' batting average (.229), tied for seventh with 12 victories and finished eighth in strikeouts with 127 ... Victory total wasn't hurt any by 6.13 runs per game worth of support from White Sox offense ... Allowed only 119 hits in 141⅔ innings ... Needs to hold runners more closely ... Allowed 25 stolen bases ... Has gone 24-7 in big league career ... Many regard his stuff as the best among talented White Sox starters ... Salary would have been $160,000 in 1994 ... Pitched in Single-A ball as recently as 1992 ... Lasted until the 36th round in 1990 draft ... Came out of high school throwing just over 80 mph, but blossomed after graduating ... Born May 26, 1971, in Cambridge, Mass.

Year	Club	G	IP	W	L	Pct.	SO	BB	H	ERA
1993	Chicago (AL)	24	142⅔	12	5	.706	129	81	109	3.47
1994	Chicago (AL)	24	141⅓	12	2	.857	127	80	119	3.81
	Totals	48	284⅓	24	7	.774	256	161	228	3.64

ROBERTO HERNANDEZ 30 6-4 235 — Bats R Throws R

Reliever struggled in 1994 after breakthrough season two years ago ... Saved only 14 in 20 opportunities and temporarily lost his closer's role ... His ERA jumped from 2.29 in 1993 to 4.91 ... Was tougher on lefties, allowing them only .217 batting average ... Heartwarming story ... Underwent surgery to relieve life-threatening blood-clotting problem in his right arm ... Took over closer's role from Bobby Thigpen late in 1992 season, when he saved 12 games ... Converted 38 of 44 save opportunities in 1993 ... White Sox got him from Angels for long-forgotten outfielder Mark Davis, Aug. 3, 1989 ... Angels' first-round pick and 16th overall choice in 1986 draft ... Would have earned $275,000 in 1994 ... Born Nov. 11, 1964, in Santurce, P.R., but grew up in New York City.

Year	Club	G	IP	W	L	Pct.	SO	BB	H	ERA
1991	Chicago (AL)	9	15	1	0	1.000	6	7	18	7.80
1992	Chicago (AL)	43	71	7	3	.700	68	20	45	1.65
1993	Chicago (AL)	70	78⅔	3	4	.429	71	20	66	2.29
1994	Chicago (AL)	45	47⅔	4	4	.500	50	19	44	4.91
	Totals	167	212⅓	15	11	.577	195	66	173	3.05

TOP PROSPECTS

SCOTT RUFFCORN 25 6-4 210   Bats R Throws R
Should stick with Chicago this time around... Finished 15-3 with 2.72 ERA for Nashville (AAA)... Struck out 144 and walked only 40 in 165⅔ innings... Went 0-2 with 12.79 ERA in two failed big league starts... White Sox' first-round pick and 25th player taken overall in 1991 draft, out of Baylor... Born Dec. 29, 1969, in New Braunfels, Tex.

JAMES BALDWIN 23 6-3 210   Bats R Throws R
Untouchable prospect who also could fit into rotation this year... Was 12-6 with 3.72 ERA for Nashville (AAA) in 1994... Power pitcher struck out 156 in 162 innings... Fanned 176 in total of 175⅓ innings for South Bend (A) and Sarasota (A) in 1992... White Sox' fourth-round pick in 1990... Born July 15, 1971, in South Pines, N.C.

RAY DURHAM 23 5-8 175   Bats S Throws R
Switch-hitting second baseman could win regular job in Chicago after hitting .296 with 16 homers, 66 RBI and 34 steals for Nashville (AAA)... Was second in Florida State League with 28 steals for Sarasota (A) in 1992... White Sox' fifth-round pick in 1990 ... Born Nov. 30, 1971, in Charlotte, N.C.

NORBERTO MARTIN 28 5-10 165   Bats R Throws R
Injuries helped him get into 45 games with White Sox last season, when he hit a respectable .275... A shortstop who can play other infield positions... Smurf-sized, in the Joey Cora mold... Nicknamed "Paco"... Signed by Chicago as undrafted free agent in March 1984... Born Dec. 10, 1966, in Santo Domingo, D.R.

MANAGER GENE LAMONT: Received a one-year extension last September, ending speculation that he would not be asked to return following 67-46 finish... Hasn't gotten due respect, considering his 247-190 record and the fact that he has won one division title and had another taken away by the strike... It's hard to manage with meddling ownership looking over your shoulder... Named AL Manager of the Year after

94-68 run to division title in 1993... It was an honor well-deserved, as clubhouse was a mine field, with Carlton Fisk, Bo Jackson and George Bell, and bench was very limited... Got criticized for being too low key, but last thing White Sox clubhouse needed was another forceful personality... Spent six years as Jim Leyland's third-base coach and right-hand man in Pittsburgh... Managed eight years in Royals' system, twice reaching Southern League (AA) Championship series... A former catcher, he hit .223 in 159 major league at-bats spread over five seasons with Detroit... Born Christmas Day, 1946, in Rockford, Ill.

ALL-TIME WHITE SOX SEASON RECORDS

BATTING: Luke Appling, .388, 1936
HRs: Frank Thomas, 41, 1993
RBI: Zeke Bonura, 138, 1936
STEALS: Rudy Law, 77, 1983
WINS: Ed Walsh, 40, 1908
STRIKEOUTS: Ed Walsh, 269, 1908

CLEVELAND INDIANS

TEAM DIRECTORY: Owner: Richard Jacobs; GM: John Hart; Dir. Baseball Oper./Asst. GM: Dan O'Dowd; VP-Pub. Rel: Bob DiBiasio: Dir. Med. Rel.: TBA; Trav. Sec.: Mike Seghi; Mgr.: Mike Hargrove; Coaches: Buddy Bell, Luis Isaac, Charles Manuel, Dave Nelson, Jeff Newman, Mark Wyley. Home: Jacobs Field (42,400). Field distances: 325, l.f. line; 368, l.c.; 400, c.f.; 375, r.c.; 320, r.f. line. Spring training: Winter Haven, Fla.

SCOUTING REPORT

The Indians got a new stadium last year and a new outlook with it. Cleveland's last postseason appearance came in 1954, but the Indians' next one may be just around the corner. When the season ended abruptly Aug. 12, the 66-47 Indians were in position to become the AL's first wild-card entry. Oh, well.

The good news is the Indians have so much young talent that it would be a major upset if they didn't reach the playoffs soon. The offense, downright dangerous, is led by a triumvirate of young stars—Albert Belle, Kenny Lofton and Carlos Baerga—likely to keep the Indians in contention for years.

Kenny Lofton was runaway AL leader in hits and steals.

Overall, the Indians' .290 batting average was just a hair behind the Yankees' major league-leading mark—and nobody hit more home runs than the Indians (167) or scored more runs (679). The Indians' potent offense was a perfect fit for Jacobs Field, helping them win 18 straight at home during one stretch last season.

The only thing that stopped cleanup hitter Belle (.357, 36, 101) was the bat-corking incident that cost him seven games. Leadoff man Lofton (.349, 12, 67, 60 steals) moved gracefully into superstardom. Baerga (.314, 19, 80) was just starting to get hot when the players struck. With those three, Eddie Murray (.254, 17, 76) and second-year man Manny Ramirez (.269, 17, 60), the Indians are hard to contain.

Their only offensive downfall is a vulnerability against left-handed pitching, because their switch hitters all hit much better from the left side. That's why they dealt for Dave Winfield (.252, 10, 43) during the strike and pondered re-signing him as a free agent last winter.

Defensively, the Indians are unusual: ultra-strong in some spots, ultra-weak in others. Lofton has established himself as one of the AL's best center fielders, in a class with fellow Gold Glovers Seattle's Ken Griffey Jr. and Toronto's Devon White. Gold Glove shortstop Omar Vizquel and catcher Sandy Alomar Jr. were two of the better players at their positions. However, the Indians closed their eyes and prayed when balls were hit to the corners. Third baseman Jim Thome needs work with the glove. Particularly butter-fingered are Belle, the left fielder, and right fielder Ramirez, who was better than advertised but still below-par.

For the first time since the days of Bob Lemon and Bob Feller, the Indians needn't be embarrassed about their pitching staff. Dennis Martinez (11-6, 3.52) proved worthy of the two-year, $9-million deal he signed. Charles Nagy (10-8, 3.45) returned strong from shoulder surgery and Mark Clark (11-3, 3.82) surprised folks with his big season. Even more impressive, the Indians have a stockpile of good, young arms like Albie Lopez, Julian Tavarez and Chad Ogea.

The big problem, in fact the only real problem, is the bullpen, where the Indians have been searching for a closer since the tragic death of Steve Olin in the spring of 1993. Jeff Russell (1-6, 5.09, 17 saves) imported from Boston, was less than awe-inspiring. In fact, Eric Plunk (7-2, 2.54) has been the club's best reliever the past couple years—and that is scary. How far the Indians go may depend upon their ability to find an effective closer. If they can do that, Mike Hargrove's Indians are a legitimate World Series threat.

INDIAN PROFILES

ALBERT BELLE 28 6-2 210   Bats R Throws R

Had spectacular offensive year in 1994 during which he batted .357, 87 points better than his previous career mark... Possessed outside shot at the Triple Crown before tail end of season was cancelled... Finished second in AL in batting, third in home runs (36) and tied for third in RBI (101)... Led league with 294 total bases and was second with .714 slugging average... Otherwise wonderful year was marred by six-game suspension for bat-corking incident against White Sox... Returned with a vengeance after suspension... Homered in 10 of 17 games heading into the strike... Became first Indian ever to hit 30-plus homers three straight seasons... Below-average defensive outfielder... Indians selected him in second round of 1987 draft, after big career at LSU... Would have made $2.6 million in '94 ... Born Aug. 25, 1966, in Shreveport, La.

Year	Club	Pos.	G	AB	R	H	2B	3B	HR	RBI	SB	Avg.
1989	Cleveland	OF	62	218	22	49	8	4	7	37	2	.225
1990	Cleveland	OF	9	23	1	4	0	0	1	3	0	.174
1991	Cleveland	OF	123	461	60	130	31	2	28	95	3	.282
1992	Cleveland	OF	153	585	81	152	23	1	34	112	8	.260
1993	Cleveland	OF	159	594	93	172	36	3	38	129	23	.290
1994	Cleveland	OF	106	412	90	147	35	2	36	101	9	.357
	Totals		612	2293	347	654	133	12	144	477	45	.285

CARLOS BAERGA 26 5-11 200   Bats S Throws R

Had typically wonderful offensive season, but was overshadowed by Albert Belle's much bigger numbers... Placed in top 10 in hits (tied for seventh with 139), total bases (ninth with 232) and doubles (tied for fifth with 32)... Batted .351 after All-Star break... Astoundingly, he walked just 10 times all year and he had to rally late to reach double figures... Batted .339 left-handed and just .269 right-handed... Erratic at second base... His 15 errors tied third baseman Jim Thome for most by an Indian... Would have made $2.2 million in '94... Came from San Diego, along with Sandy Alomar Jr. and Chris James, in Joe Carter trade prior to 1990 season... Born Nov. 4, 1968, in San Juan, P.R. ... Signed as undrafted free agent by Padres in November 1985.

Year	Club	Pos.	G	AB	R	H	2B	3B	HR	RBI	SB	Avg.
1990	Cleveland	3B-SS-2B	108	312	46	81	17	2	7	47	0	.260
1991	Cleveland	3B-2B-SS	158	593	80	171	28	2	11	69	3	.288
1992	Cleveland	2B	161	657	92	205	32	1	20	105	10	.312
1993	Cleveland	2B	154	624	105	200	28	6	21	114	15	.321
1994	Cleveland	2B	103	442	81	139	32	2	19	80	8	.314
	Totals		684	2628	404	796	137	13	78	415	36	.303

KENNY LOFTON 27 6-0 180   Bats L Throws L

Had huge all-around year, placing first in AL in hits (160), fourth in batting average (.349), second in runs (105) and first in stolen bases (60)... Has established himself as one of the game's finest defensive center fielders and won second Gold Glove in '94... Shocker was that he added power to his repertoire in '94, going from one homer in '93 to 12 last year... Reached base safely in all but nine games during '94... Had 18 games with at least three hits... Acquired from Houston in steal of a deal along with Dave Rohde for Ed Taubensee and Willie Blair prior to 1992 season... Would have made $875,000 in '94 ... Born May 31, 1967, in East Chicago, Ind.... Was basketball star at guard for University of Arizona... Did not play varsity baseball until junior year at Arizona... Astros' 17th-round pick in 1988.

Year	Club	Pos.	G	AB	R	H	2B	3B	HR	RBI	SB	Avg.
1991	Houston	OF	20	74	9	15	1	0	0	0	2	.203
1992	Cleveland	OF	148	576	96	164	15	8	5	42	66	.285
1993	Cleveland	OF	148	569	116	185	28	8	1	42	70	.325
1994	Cleveland	OF	112	459	105	160	32	9	12	57	60	.349
	Totals		428	1678	326	524	76	25	18	141	198	.312

EDDIE MURRAY 39 6-2 222   Bats S Throws R

Shortened season left him 70 hits short of 3,000, though chances are he'll still make it to magic number... Hit total places him in tie for 25th on all-time list, with Rogers Hornsby... Free-agent addition provided Indians with another big RBI man and lineup protection for cleanup man Albert Belle... Stretched his streak of seasons with at least 75 RBI to 18 by knocking home 76. Only Hank Aaron, who did it 19 straight years, has a longer streak... Would have made $3 million in '94...

Played much of last season with ligament damage in his right thumb... Batted .275 from left side, but just .216 from right side ... Fielding skills at first base have decreased more than batting skills in recent years... Born Feb. 24, 1956, in Los Angeles... Orioles' third-round choice in '73.

Year	Club	Pos.	G	AB	R	H	2B	3B	HR	RBI	SB	Avg.
1977	Baltimore	OF-1B	160	611	81	173	29	2	27	88	0	.283
1978	Baltimore	1B-3B	161	610	85	174	32	3	27	95	6	.285
1979	Baltimore	1B	159	606	90	179	30	2	25	99	10	.295
1980	Baltimore	1B	158	621	100	186	36	2	32	116	7	.300
1981	Baltimore	1B	99	378	57	111	21	2	22	78	2	.294
1982	Baltimore	1B	151	550	87	174	30	1	32	110	7	.316
1983	Baltimore	1B	156	582	115	178	30	3	33	111	5	.306
1984	Baltimore	1B	162	588	97	180	26	3	29	110	10	.306
1985	Baltimore	1B	156	583	111	173	37	1	31	124	5	.297
1986	Baltimore	1B	137	495	61	151	25	1	17	84	3	.305
1987	Baltimore	1B	160	618	89	171	28	3	30	91	1	.277
1988	Baltimore	1B	161	603	75	171	27	2	28	84	5	.284
1989	Los Angeles	1B-3B	160	594	66	147	29	1	20	88	7	.247
1990	Los Angeles	1B	155	558	96	184	22	3	26	95	8	.330
1991	Los Angeles	1B-3B	153	576	69	150	23	1	19	96	10	.260
1992	New York (NL)	1B	156	551	64	144	37	2	16	93	4	.261
1993	New York (NL)	1B	154	610	77	174	28	1	27	100	2	.285
1994	Cleveland	1B	108	433	57	110	21	1	17	76	8	.254
	Totals		2706	10167	1477	2930	511	34	458	1738	100	.288

DAVE WINFIELD 43 6-6 245   Bats R Throws R

Finally showed signs of age last year, posting career lows in most offensive categories... Has still hit .275 since turning 40... Hit .343 in '94 against lefthanded pitching, which was the reason the Indians acquired him from Twins on Aug. 31 trading deadline last season... Season cancellation killed his chance to exact revenge on Yankees owner George Steinbrenner in postseason... Tabbed "Mr. May" by Steinbrenner shortly after his 1-for-21 1981 World Series for Yankees... Showed clutch hitting ability with World Series-winning double off Braves' Charlie Leibrandt in Game 6 of '92 Series... Ranks 15th on all-time hit list with 3,088... Counting Cleveland, even though he never actually played for Indians in '94, he has been on rosters of five different organizations in past five years... Was selected in baseball, basketball and football drafts after starring in baseball and basketball at University of Minnesota... Padres picked him fourth overall in 1973... Born Oct. 3, 1951, in St. Paul, Minn.

...Would have made $2.725 million in '94... **Free agent at press time.**

Year	Club	Pos.	G	AB	R	H	2B	3B	HR	RBI	SB	Avg.
1973	San Diego....	OF-1B	56	141	9	39	4	1	3	12	0	.277
1974	San Diego....	OF	145	498	57	132	18	4	20	75	9	.265
1975	San Diego....	OF	143	509	74	136	20	2	15	76	23	.267
1976	San Diego....	OF	137	492	81	139	26	4	13	69	26	.283
1977	San Diego....	OF	157	615	104	169	29	7	25	92	16	.275
1978	San Diego....	OF-1B	158	587	88	181	30	5	24	97	21	.308
1979	San Diego....	OF	159	597	97	184	27	10	34	118	15	.308
1980	San Diego....	OF	162	558	89	154	25	6	20	87	23	.276
1981	New York (AL)	OF	105	388	52	114	25	1	13	68	11	.294
1982	New York (AL)	OF	140	539	84	151	24	8	37	106	5	.280
1983	New York (AL)	OF	152	598	99	169	26	8	32	116	15	.283
1984	New York (AL)	OF	141	567	106	193	34	4	19	100	6	.340
1985	New York (AL)	OF	155	633	105	174	34	6	26	114	19	.275
1986	New York (AL)	OF-3B	154	565	90	148	31	5	24	104	6	.262
1987	New York (AL)	OF	156	575	83	158	22	1	27	97	5	.275
1988	New York (AL)	OF	149	559	96	180	37	2	25	107	9	.322
1989	New York (AL)			Injured								
1990	NY (AL)-Cal....	OF	132	475	70	127	21	2	21	78	0	.267
1991	California.....	OF	150	568	75	149	27	4	28	86	7	.262
1992	Toronto.......	OF	156	583	92	169	33	3	26	108	2	.290
1993	Minnesota....	OF-1B	143	547	72	148	27	2	21	76	2	.271
1994	Minnesota....	OF	77	294	35	74	15	3	10	43	2	.252
	Totals.......		2927	10888	1658	3088	535	88	463	1829	222	.284

MANNY RAMIREZ 22 6-0 190   Bats R Throws R

Contributed mightily to Indians' strong attack with big rookie season... Exactly half of his 78 hits went for extra bases, accounting for impressive .521 slugging average... Compiled huge minor league numbers, leading to a quick ascension... Indians' first-round draft choice in 1991... Known for quick bat... Sometimes appears lost in right field, although he made just one error in '94... Born May 30, 1972, in Santo Domingo, D.R., but was raised in New York City... Sometimes, he seems even younger than 22... Once asked a sportswriter to lend him $70,000, so he could buy a motorcycle... Would have made $111,000 in '94... Indians selected him 13th overall in 1991 draft.

Year	Club	Pos.	G	AB	R	H	2B	3B	HR	RBI	SB	Avg.
1993	Cleveland.....	OF	22	53	5	9	1	0	2	5	0	.170
1994	Cleveland.....	OF	91	290	51	78	22	0	17	60	4	.269
	Totals.......		113	343	56	87	23	0	19	65	4	.254

SANDY ALOMAR Jr. 28 6-5 215　　　　Bats R Throws R

Catcher cried on TV the day the rest of 1994 season was cancelled, showing the Cleveland area how much he wanted it... Younger brother Roberto has played on Blue Jays' World Series champions in 1992 and 1993, but this was first winning team Sandy had played on in Cleveland... Father Sandy Sr. enjoyed 15-year big league career and is now a minor league manager in Cubs organization... Was on way to the best all-around offensive year of his injury-marred career... His 14 home runs were a career high... Came from Padres with Carlos Baerga and Chris James in Joe Carter trade before '90 season... When healthy, he is known for his strong arm... Would have made $2.2 million in '94... Born June 18, 1966, in Salinas, P.R. ... Padres signed him as undrafted free agent in October 1983.

Year	Club	Pos.	G	AB	R	H	2B	3B	HR	RBI	SB	Avg.
1988	San Diego	PH	1	1	0	0	0	0	0	0	0	.000
1989	San Diego	C	7	19	1	4	1	0	1	6	0	.211
1990	Cleveland	C	132	445	60	129	26	2	9	66	4	.290
1991	Cleveland	C	51	184	10	40	9	0	0	7	0	.217
1992	Cleveland	C	89	299	22	75	16	0	2	26	3	.251
1993	Cleveland	C	64	215	24	58	7	1	6	32	3	.270
1994	Cleveland	C	80	292	44	84	15	1	14	43	8	.288
	Totals		424	1455	161	390	74	4	32	180	18	.268

OMAR VIZQUEL 27 5-9 165　　　　Bats S Throws R

This spectacular defensive shortstop made just six errors in '94, his initial season in Cleveland ... Three of those errors came in one unusually sloppy game... Club record for fewest errors by a shortstop had been eight, by Lou Boudreau in 1949 and Frank Duffy in 1973... Missed out on the juiced-ball fun, hitting just one home run in 286 at-bats... Had career-high RBI game with six at Boston... Would have made $2.3 million in '94 ... Like rest of Indians' switch hitters, he hit much better from left side (.304) than right (.226)... Born April 24, 1967, in Caracas, Venezuela... Won second Gold Glove in '94... Was acquired from Seattle in trade for Felix Fermin, Reggie Jefferson and cash prior to last season, because Mariners were trying to save money... Mariners signed him as undrafted free agent in April 1984.

Year	Club	Pos.	G	AB	R	H	2B	3B	HR	RBI	SB	Avg.
1989	Seattle	SS	143	387	45	85	7	3	1	20	1	.220
1990	Seattle	SS	81	255	19	63	3	2	2	18	4	.247
1991	Seattle	SS-2B	142	426	42	98	16	4	1	41	7	.230
1992	Seattle	SS	136	483	49	142	20	4	0	21	15	.294
1993	Seattle	SS	158	560	68	143	14	2	2	31	12	.255
1994	Cleveland	SS	69	286	39	78	10	1	1	33	13	.273
	Totals		729	2397	262	609	70	16	7	164	52	.254

CHARLES NAGY 27 6-3 200   Bats L Throws R

Comeback season after shoulder surgery was mostly a success, although his impressive 3.45 ERA for this big-hitting club wasn't reflected in his so-so 10-8 record in 1994... Had big '92 season before injury-wrecked '93 ended with June 29 shoulder surgery... Led club with 108 strikeouts in '94 and has had better than a two-to-one strikeout-to-walk ratio past three seasons... Indians' first-round choice and 17th pick overall in '88 draft... Member of gold medal-winning '88 Olympic team... Would have made $1,241,667 in '94... Born May 5, 1967, in Fairfield, Conn.... Articulate and accessible to media, he was Indians' player rep.

Year	Club	G	IP	W	L	Pct.	SO	BB	H	ERA
1990	Cleveland	9	45⅔	2	4	.333	26	21	58	5.91
1991	Cleveland	33	211⅓	10	15	.400	109	66	228	4.13
1992	Cleveland	33	252	17	10	.630	169	57	245	2.96
1993	Cleveland	9	48⅔	2	6	.250	30	13	66	6.29
1994	Cleveland	23	169⅓	10	8	.556	108	48	175	3.45
	Totals	107	727	41	43	.488	442	205	772	3.83

DENNIS MARTINEZ 39 6-1 190   Bats R Throws R

Was proving to be worth every penny of two-year, $9-million deal that Indians gave this free agent, then the strike hit... Ranked fourth in AL in innings (176⅔) and tied for second in complete games (7)... Outspoken veteran irritated management with some hard-line comments during strike... Unafraid to upset management, he had done the same a year earlier when he vetoed Aug. 25, 1993 trade that would have sent him from Expos to Braves and enhanced his chances to pitch in the playoffs... Overcame alcohol problem in middle of career... Born May 14, 1955, in Granada, Nicaragua... Signed with

Orioles as undrafted free agent in '73, the same year current teammate Eddie Murray came to Baltimore... One of six pitchers to win at least 100 games in each league... Pitched perfect game against Dodgers, July 28, 1991... Would have made team-high $4.5 million in '94... Known as "El Presidente."

Year	Club	G	IP	W	L	Pct.	SO	BB	H	ERA
1976	Baltimore	4	28	1	2	.333	18	8	23	2.57
1977	Baltimore	42	167	14	7	.667	107	64	157	4.10
1978	Baltimore	40	276	16	11	.593	142	93	257	3.25
1979	Baltimore	40	292	15	16	.484	132	78	279	3.67
1980	Baltimore	25	100	6	4	.600	42	44	103	3.96
1981	Baltimore	25	179	14	5	.737	88	62	173	3.32
1982	Baltimore	40	252	16	12	.571	111	87	262	4.21
1983	Baltimore	32	153	7	16	.304	71	45	209	5.53
1984	Baltimore	34	141⅔	6	9	.400	77	37	145	5.02
1985	Baltimore	33	180	13	11	.542	68	63	203	5.15
1986	Baltimore	4	6⅔	0	0	.000	2	2	11	6.75
1986	Montreal	19	98	3	6	.333	63	28	103	4.59
1987	Montreal	22	144⅔	11	4	.733	84	40	133	3.30
1988	Montreal	34	235⅓	15	13	.536	120	55	215	2.72
1989	Montreal	34	232	16	7	.696	142	49	227	3.18
1990	Montreal	32	226	10	11	.476	156	49	191	2.95
1991	Montreal	31	222	14	11	.560	123	62	187	2.39
1992	Montreal	32	226⅓	16	11	.593	147	60	172	2.47
1993	Montreal	35	224⅔	15	9	.625	138	64	211	3.85
1994	Cleveland	24	176⅔	11	6	.647	92	44	166	3.52
	Totals	582	3561	219	171	.562	1923	1034	3427	3.63

TOP PROSPECTS

ALBIE LOPEZ 23 6-0 210   Bats R Throws R
Only real question about this talented right-hander is his head... Moped after his demotion to Charlotte (AAA)... Showed potential with complete-game shutout for Cleveland Aug. 4 in 2-0 victory over Tigers, but went 1-2, 4.24 as Indian in '94... Was 13-3 with 3.94 ERA for Charlotte last season... Has gone 4-3 with 5.54 ERA in stints over two seasons with Cleveland... Born Aug. 18, 1971, in Mesa, Ariz.... Indians' 20th-round pick in 1990 has career record of 39-16 in minors.

JULIAN TAVAREZ 21 6-2 165   Bats R Throws R
Considered to have best arm in system... Went 15-6 with 3.48 ERA for Charlotte (AAA) in 1994... Toughest thing for him now is keeping on the weight... Had one start for Cleveland and got

Carlos Baerga hit .339 from left side, .269 from right.

hammered, allowing six hits and eight runs (four earned) in 1⅔ innings... Also suffered shellacking after callup in '93, when he posted 13-6 combined mark for Kinston (A) and Canton-Akron (AA)... Born May 22, 1973, in Santiago, D.R.... Signed by Indians as undrafted free agent in March 1990.

DAVID BELL 22 5-10 180   **Bats R Throws R**
Son of former Indians and Rangers star Buddy Bell and grandson of Gus had nice season with Charlotte (AAA), hitting 18 home runs and knocking in 88 runs enroute to .293 average... When he reaches majors, Bells will become the second family with three generations of big leaguers, joining the Boones (Ray, Bob and Bret)... Has great hands at third base, like dad, but big question

is: Will he hit enough?... Born Sept. 14, 1972, in Cincinnati... Drafted by Indians in seventh round in 1990.

HERBERT PERRY 25 6-2 220 **Bats R Throws R**
First baseman had big offensive year, batting .327, hitting 13 homers and knocking in 70 runs for Charlotte (AAA)... His season was ended Aug. 9, when he broke his left wrist in collision at first... Quarterback at University of Florida... Born Sept. 15, 1969, in Live Oak, Fla.... Indians' second-round pick in 1991.

MANAGER MIKE HARGROVE: Earned contract extension  by guiding Indians to 66-47 record and second-place finish in AL Central... Had Indians in position for their first postseason appearance in 40 years before the season was aborted... Widely praised for his leadership during tragic 1993 season, when Indians relievers Steve Olin, Tim Crews and Cliff Young were killed in two separate accidents... Despite club's 76-86 mark in 1993, he finished sixth in balloting for Manager of the Year honors for his work with shell-shocked team... However, club reserved judgment on him until last season and eventually liked what they saw... Has 250-272 mark as Indians manager... Was Indians' first-base coach when he took over for John McNamara, July 6, 1991... Named Triple-A Manager of the Year in 1989, when he led Colorado Springs to first-half title in Pacific Coast League... Nicknamed "The Human Rain Delay" for his deliberate style of hitting during a 12-year playing career as a first baseman with Texas, San Diego and Cleveland... Born Oct. 26, 1949, in Perrytown, Tex.

ALL-TIME INDIAN SEASON RECORDS

BATTING: Joe Jackson, .408, 1911
HRs: Al Rosen, 43, 1953
RBI: Hal Trosky, 162, 1936
STEALS: Kenny Lofton, 70, 1993
WINS: Jim Bagby, 31, 1920
STRIKEOUTS: Bob Feller, 348, 1946

KANSAS CITY ROYALS

TEAM DIRECTORY: Chairman/CEO: David D. Glass; Exec. VP/GM: Herk Robinson; VP-Adm.: Dennis Cryder; Dir. Scouting: Art Stewart; Dir. Minor League Oper.: Bob Hegman; VP-Pub. Rel.: Dean Vogelaar; Trav. Sec.: Dave Witty; Mgr.: Bob Boone; Coaches: Jeff Cox, Bruce Kison, Mitchell Page, Jamie Quirk. Home: Kauffman Stadium (40,625). Field distances: 330, l.f. line; 385, l.c.; 410, c.f.; 385, r.c.; 330, r.f. line. Spring training: Baseball City Stadium, Orlando, Fla.

SCOUTING REPORT

The Royals have made no secret about their approach to '95, after a 64-51 finish last year. They have done the economically smart thing every small-market team must do these days, shaving their bloated payroll by several million dollars and turning to their talented farm system. That doesn't appear to be the way to finish ahead of the White Sox and the Indians in the tough AL Central,

Royal family welcomed Bob Hamelin, Rookie of the Year.

but so be it.

The shift in philosophy began in earnest with the firing of manager Hal McRae, whom the club thought was better suited to guiding a veteran team. New skipper Bob Boone has only two years of minor league managerial experience, but he has been pegged as a successful big league manager since his days as one of the game's headiest catchers.

What Boone can count on is a pair of aces in Cy Young Award winner David Cone (16-5, 2.94) and Kevin Appier (7-6, 3.83) and one of the league's best closers in Jeff Montgomery (2-3, 4.03, 27 saves). Cone got the run support he needed and turned in his best season since his 20-3 year in 1988. Right-hander Tom Gordon (11-7, 4.35) was second on the club in victories. Free-agent right-hander Mark Gubicza (7-9, 4.50) re-signed and will be a solid No. 4 starter. Top prospects Jeff Granger and Jose DeJesus (3-1, 4.73) will get a chance at the fifth spot.

Montgomery is surrounded by a solid bullpen cast, including former Pirates closer Stan Belinda (2-2, 5.14), Hipolito Pichardo (5-3, 4.92), Rusty Meacham (3-3, 3.73) and lefty Billy Brewer (4-1, 2.56).

The other big change around Kauffman Stadium is the installation of natural grass. How that will affect the Royals offensively and defensively remains to be seen. But they weren't built for turf, anyway.

AL Rookie of the Year Bob Hamelin (.282, 24, 65) was a desperately needed power source. The hefty designated hitter looms as the lone power threat if free-agent catcher Mike Macfarlane (.255, 14, 47) goes elsewhere. The Royals are a team that must manufacture runs. At least first baseman Wally Joyner (.311, 8, 57) and right fielder Felix Jose (.303, 11, 55) hit above .300 to compensate for their lack of long-ball pop. But Jose refused assignment and is gone as a free agent.

Vince Coleman (.240, 50 steals) still can steal bases, but he didn't get on base often enough at the top of the order and then departed via free agency. He figures to be replaced by rookies Michael Tucker and Dwayne Hosey. Center fielder Brian McRae (.273, 4, 40) stole 28 bases during the strike-shortened season and will hit in one of the first three spots in the lineup.

Another rookie, Joe Randa, might get an opportunity to replace re-signed free agent Gary Gaetti (.287, 12, 57) at third base. Randa is ready defensively, but there are questions about his bat. The middle-infield combination is Greg Gagne (.259, 7, 51) and Jose Lind (.269, 1, 31), whose high guaranteed salaries keep them in place for another year. But the days of free spending are over in Kansas City.

ROYAL PROFILES

WALLY JOYNER 32 6-2 205   Bats L Throws L

Professional hitter who can drive in runs, but doesn't hit for power, especially in Kauffman Stadium... Posted a career-high .311 average in 363 at-bats in 1994... Batted above .300 against both lefties and righties... Was bothered by injuries in each of two previous seasons with Royals... Committed eight errors in 86 games at first, a high figure for this slick fielder ... Would have earned $4.6 million in 1994, in third year of four-year deal he signed as free agent... Made emotional departure from Angels after 1991 season... Has never again approached his power numbers of 1987, when he hit 34 home runs and drove in 117 runs... Finished second to Jose Canseco for AL Rookie of the Year in 1986... Born June 16, 1962, in Atlanta... Angels' third-round pick in 1983, out of Brigham Young.

Year	Club	Pos.	G	AB	R	H	2B	3B	HR	RBI	SB	Avg.
1986	California	1B	154	593	82	172	27	3	22	100	5	.290
1987	California	1B	149	564	100	161	33	1	34	117	8	.285
1988	California	1B	158	597	81	176	31	2	13	85	8	.295
1989	California	1B	159	593	78	167	30	2	16	79	3	.282
1990	California	1B	83	310	35	83	15	0	8	41	2	.268
1991	California	1B	143	551	79	166	34	3	21	96	2	.301
1992	Kansas City	1B	149	572	66	154	36	2	9	66	11	.269
1993	Kansas City	1B	141	497	83	145	36	3	15	65	5	.292
1994	Kansas City	1B	97	363	52	113	20	3	8	57	3	.311
	Totals		1233	4640	656	1337	262	19	146	706	47	.288

GREG GAGNE 33 5-11 180   Bats R Throws R

Steady and dependable shortstop has held up nicely over the years... Put together a typical year in 1994... Needs to get more red lights on the basepaths... Was thrown out in 17 of 27 steal attempts last season... Had career year in 1993 after signing big free-agent deal with Royals... Set career highs in average, doubles and RBI... Doesn't come cheaply... Would have earned $2,966,667 in 1994... Hit game-winning homer in Game 2 of 1991 World Series for Minnesota... Spent all or part of 10 seasons with Twins before leaving because he felt unappre-

Wally Joyner reached career-high .311 in '94.

ciated... Twins got him from Yankees in deal involving Roy Smalley, April 10, 1982... Yanks' fourth-round pick in 1979... Born Nov. 12, 1961, in Fall River, Mass.

Year	Club	Pos.	G	AB	R	H	2B	3B	HR	RBI	SB	Avg.
1983	Minnesota	SS	10	27	2	3	1	0	0	3	0	.111
1984	Minnesota	PR-PH	2	1	0	0	0	0	0	0	0	.000
1985	Minnesota	SS	114	293	37	66	15	3	2	23	10	.225
1986	Minnesota	SS-2B	156	472	63	118	22	6	12	54	12	.250
1987	Minnesota	SS-OF-2B	137	437	68	116	28	7	10	40	6	.265
1988	Minnesota	SS-OF-2B-3B	149	461	70	109	20	6	14	48	15	.236
1989	Minnesota	SS-OF	149	460	69	125	29	7	9	48	11	.272
1990	Minnesota	SS-OF	138	388	38	91	22	3	7	38	8	.235
1991	Minnesota	SS-3B	139	408	52	108	23	3	8	42	11	.265
1992	Minnesota	SS	146	439	53	108	23	0	7	39	6	.246
1993	Kansas City	SS	159	540	66	151	32	3	10	57	10	.280
1994	Kansas City	SS	107	375	39	97	23	3	7	51	10	.259
	Totals		1406	4301	557	1092	238	41	86	443	99	.254

BRIAN McRAE 27 6-0 185   Bats S Throws R

No longer carries burden of being the manager's son now that father Hal was fired... Suffered a big power drop from 12 homers in 1993 to four during strike-shortened 1994, but set career high with 28 stolen bases... Batting average also fell, but he cut strikeouts from 105 in 1993 to 67 and raised on-base percentage to .359... Enjoyed breakthrough 1993 season, when he set full-season career highs in average, home runs and RBI... Entered that spring needing to recapture an everyday job... Struggled in 1992, when his average didn't get above .200 until June 5... One of the game's best and most acrobatic center fielders... Pulled off unassisted double play, Aug. 23, 1992, the first by an AL outfielder since 1974... Would have earned $1.9 million in 1994... Born Aug. 27, 1967, in Bradenton, Fla.... Royals drafted him 17th overall in 1985.

Year Club	Pos.	G	AB	R	H	2B	3B	HR	RBI	SB	Avg.
1990 Kansas City...	OF	46	168	21	48	8	3	2	23	4	.286
1991 Kansas City...	OF	152	629	86	164	28	9	8	64	20	.261
1992 Kansas City...	OF	149	533	63	119	23	5	4	52	18	.223
1993 Kansas City...	OF	153	627	78	177	28	9	12	69	23	.282
1994 Kansas City...	OF	114	436	71	119	22	6	4	40	28	.273
Totals.......		614	2393	319	627	109	32	30	248	93	.262

BOB HAMELIN 27 6-0 235   Bats L Throws L

Big guy broke in with a bang, winning AL Rookie of the Year honors... Hit 24 homers in only 312 at-bats... A whopping 50 of his 88 hits were for extra bases... Not just a slugger, as illustrated by his .282 batting average and .388 on-base percentage... Power and girth turned him into a cult hero of sorts... Nicknamed "The Hammer"... Played 24 games at first, but is best suited for designated hitter duties... Stole four bases despite hefty frame... Career was slowed by back trouble after the Royals picked him in second round in 1988... Underwent disc fusion surgery, June 28, 1991... Broke through in 1993, hitting .259 with 29 homers, 84 RBI and 82 walks for Omaha (AAA)... Attended UCLA... Born Nov. 29, 1967, in Elizabeth, N.J.... Would have earned $110,000 in 1994.

Year Club	Pos.	G	AB	R	H	2B	3B	HR	RBI	SB	Avg.
1993 Kansas City...	1B	16	49	2	11	3	0	2	5	0	.224
1994 Kansas City...	1B	101	312	64	88	25	1	24	65	4	.282
Totals.......		117	361	66	99	28	1	26	70	4	.274

JOSE LIND 30 5-11 175   Bats R Throws R

Did what was expected of him by hitting .269 and playing sparkling second base... Committed five errors in 84 games there... Free swinger walked only 16 times, leaving him with a very low .306 on-base percentage... On the plus side, he is one of the toughest to strike out ... Acquired from Pirates for pitchers Dennis Moeller and Joel Johnston prior to '93 season ... Salary dumping was at root of deal... Would have earned $2.35 million in 1994... Played with three division champions during five-plus seasons with Pirates... Unfortunately, his ninth-inning error in Game 7 of 1992 NLCS against Atlanta will be remembered more than his contributions... Signed by Pirates as undrafted free agent in 1982... Born May 1, 1964, in Toabaja, P.R.

Year	Club	Pos.	G	AB	R	H	2B	3B	HR	RBI	SB	Avg.
1987	Pittsburgh	2B	35	143	21	46	8	4	0	11	2	.322
1988	Pittsburgh	2B	154	611	82	160	24	4	2	49	15	.262
1989	Pittsburgh	2B	153	578	52	134	21	3	2	48	15	.232
1990	Pittsburgh	2B	152	514	46	134	28	5	1	48	8	.261
1991	Pittsburgh	2B	150	502	53	133	16	6	3	54	7	.265
1992	Pittsburgh	2B	135	468	38	110	14	1	0	39	3	.235
1993	Kansas City	2B	136	431	33	107	13	2	0	37	3	.248
1994	Kansas City	2B	85	290	34	78	16	2	1	31	9	.269
	Totals		1000	3537	359	902	140	27	9	317	62	.255

DAVID CONE 32 6-1 190   Bats R Throws R

Proved that you can come home again in second season back in KC... Edged Jimmy Key for his first Cy Young Award... Tied for second in league with 16 wins and finished third in ERA (2.94), sixth in innings (171⅔) and sixth in strikeouts (132)... Held opponents to .209 average, second-lowest mark in league... Returned to hometown and original organization when he accepted a three-year, $18-million deal as a free agent prior to 1993 season... His only luck that season was bad as he finished 11-14 despite 3.33 ERA... Received worst run support in league... Would have earned $5 million in 1994... Finished 17-10 with Mets and Blue Jays in 1992... Went from Mets to Blue Jays for Jeff Kent and Ryan Thompson, Aug. 27, 1992... Mets stole him from Royals for catcher Ed Hearn prior to 1987 season in one of the most lopsided trades in recent history... Royals' third-round pick in 1981 draft... Born Jan. 2, 1963, in Kansas City, Mo.

Year	Club	G	IP	W	L	Pct.	SO	BB	H	ERA
1986	Kansas City	11	22⅔	0	0	.000	21	13	29	5.56
1987	New York (NL)	21	99⅓	5	6	.455	68	44	87	3.71
1988	New York (NL)	35	231⅓	20	3	.870	213	80	178	2.22
1989	New York (NL)	34	219⅔	14	8	.636	190	74	183	3.52
1990	New York (NL)	31	211⅔	14	10	.583	233	65	177	3.23
1991	New York (NL)	34	232⅔	14	14	.500	241	73	204	3.29
1992	New York (NL)	27	196⅔	13	7	.650	214	82	162	2.88
1992	Toronto	8	53	4	3	.571	47	29	39	2.55
1993	Kansas City	34	254	11	14	.440	191	114	205	3.33
1994	Kansas City	23	171⅔	16	5	.762	132	54	130	2.94
	Totals	258	1692⅔	111	70	.613	1550	628	1394	3.12

JEFF MONTGOMERY 33 5-11 180   Bats R Throws R

Outstanding closer coming off what for him was an off year... Converted 27 of 32 save opportunities, notching second-highest save total in AL behind Orioles' Lee Smith... But his ERA rose to 4.03, a run and one-half higher than his previous sparkling career mark... Allowed more hits (48) than innings pitched (44⅔), but struck out 50, for an average of 10.07 per nine innings... Left-handers hit .302 against him... A very busy closer, he has pitched 491 innings in last six seasons... Tied Toronto's Duane Ward for AL save lead with 45 in 1993 and won Rolaids Relief Award that season by six points over Ward ... Would have earned $3,166,667 in 1994... A Royal steal, he was acquired from Cincinnati for outfielder Van Snider prior to 1988 season... Reds' ninth-round pick in 1983 draft... Born Jan. 7, 1962, in Wellston, Ohio.

Year	Club	G	IP	W	L	Pct.	SO	BB	H	ERA
1987	Cincinnati	14	19⅓	2	2	.500	13	9	25	6.52
1988	Kansas City	45	62⅔	7	2	.778	47	30	54	3.45
1989	Kansas City	63	92	7	3	.700	94	25	66	1.37
1990	Kansas City	73	94⅓	6	5	.545	94	34	81	2.39
1991	Kansas City	67	90	4	4	.500	77	28	83	2.90
1992	Kansas City	65	82⅔	1	6	.143	69	27	61	2.18
1993	Kansas City	69	87⅓	7	5	.583	66	23	65	2.27
1994	Kansas City	42	44⅔	2	3	.400	50	15	48	4.03
	Totals	438	573	36	30	.545	510	191	483	2.64

KEVIN APPIER 27 6-2 200   Bats R Throws R

His numbers were off in 1994, but he's still one of league's top pitchers... Got only 13 decisions (7-6) in 23 starts despite averaging 6.7 innings per start... His 3.83 ERA was highest of career, almost one run higher than previous career mark... Had averaged 210 innings per season until strike-shortened 1994, when he totalled 155... Definitely a winner, he has gone 66-44 in five-plus seasons... Increased victory total every year until 1994... Would have earned $3.8 million in 1994 ... Cy Young Award candidate in 1993, when he went 18-8 with 2.56 ERA and 186 strikeouts... His across-his-body delivery has some scouts predicting injury for him, but it hasn't happened... AL Rookie Pitcher of the Year in 1990... Royals' first-round pick and ninth player taken overall in 1987... Born Dec. 6, 1967, in Lancaster, Cal.

Year	Club	G	IP	W	L	Pct.	SO	BB	H	ERA
1989	Kansas City	6	21⅔	1	4	.200	10	12	34	9.14
1990	Kansas City	32	185⅔	12	8	.600	127	54	179	2.76
1991	Kansas City	34	207⅔	13	10	.565	158	61	205	3.42
1992	Kansas City	30	208⅓	15	8	.652	150	68	167	2.46
1993	Kansas City	34	238⅔	18	8	.692	186	81	183	2.56
1994	Kansas City	23	155	7	6	.538	145	63	137	3.83
	Totals	159	1017	66	44	.600	776	339	905	3.09

TOM GORDON 27 5-9 180   Bats R Throws R

Little guy finally appears to have developed some consistency... Nothing wrong with his stuff... Owns one of the game's best breaking balls... Posted second consecutive winning season... Is 67-59 in six-plus seasons, including 17-9 start in 1989... Allowed only 136 hits in 155⅓ innings, but walked 87 and threw 12 wild pitches... Size limits durability. He didn't complete any of his 24 starts... Doesn't hold runners well ... Allowed 32 stolen bases, 22 more than next-highest total by a Royals starter... Received average of only 4.75 runs of support per start, lowest figure in rotation... Would have earned $2,635,000 in 1994... Has averaged 8.3 strikeouts per nine innings over career... Royals' sixth-round pick in 1986 draft...

Born Nov. 18, 1967, in Sebring, Fla.... Strike kept him out of free-agent market last winter.

Year	Club	G	IP	W	L	Pct.	SO	BB	H	ERA
1988	Kansas City	5	15⅔	0	2	.000	18	7	16	5.17
1989	Kansas City	49	163	17	9	.654	153	86	122	3.64
1990	Kansas City	32	195⅓	12	11	.522	175	99	192	3.73
1991	Kansas City	45	158	9	14	.391	167	87	129	3.87
1992	Kansas City	40	117⅔	6	10	.375	98	55	116	4.59
1993	Kansas City	48	155⅔	12	6	.667	143	77	125	3.58
1994	Kansas City	24	155⅓	11	7	.611	126	87	136	4.35
	Totals	243	960⅔	67	59	.532	880	498	836	3.94

TOP PROSPECTS

DWAYNE HOSEY 28 5-10 175   Bats S Throws R
Made run at Triple Crown in American Association... Hit .333 with 27 homers, 80 RBI and 27 steals for Omaha (AAA)... Arm may limit him to left field in big leagues, but he is a good defensive outfielder... Has bounced around from White Sox to Athletics to Brewers to Padres to Royals organizations since being picked by White Sox in 13th round in 1987 draft... Born March 11, 1967, in Sharon, Pa.

MICHAEL TUCKER 23 6-2 185   Bats L Throws R
Could be in Royals' outfield this season... Power potential was realized with 21 homers and 77 RBI for Omaha (AAA)... Bounced between the infield and outfield before settling in the latter... Royals' top pick in 1992 draft and 10th overall selection... Played on U.S. Olympic Team in Barcelona... Born June 25, 1971, in South Boston, Va.... Hit .305 for Wilmington (A) and .279 for Memphis (AA) in 1993 with combined total of 15 homers and 79 RBI.

JOE VITIELLO 24 6-2 215   Bats R Throws R
Wally Joyner's replacement at first is just about ready... Had breakthrough season, hitting .344 with 10 homers and 61 RBI for Omaha (AAA)... Hit .288 with 15 homers and 66 RBI for Memphis (AA) in '93... Royals' first-round pick and seventh player taken overall in 1991 draft... Born April 11, 1970, in Cambridge, Mass.

PHIL HIATT 25 6-3 200   Bats R Throws R
Batted .218 with seven homers in 238 at-bats for Royals in 1993 as a third baseman... Was moved to outfield in minors last season

...Hit .300 with 17 homers for Memphis (AA)...Belted 27 homers for Memphis in 1992...Royals' eighth-round pick in 1990, out of Louisiana Tech...Born May 1, 1969, in Pensacola, Fla.

MANAGER BOB BOONE:  Named to replace Hal McRae on Oct. 7, after Royals finished at 64-51...Was bench coach for Davey Johnson in Cincinnati last season...Managed Tacoma, the Athletics' Triple-A farm club, in 1992...Middle third of game's first three-generation family. Father is Ray, former infielder. Son is Bret, Reds' second baseman. Another son, Aaron, is on the way...If he succeeds as a manager—and almost everybody thinks he will—he will buck trend of great players who didn't make good managers...Second all-time in games caught behind Carlton Fisk...Was behind the plate in 2,225 games over 18-year career that ended in Kansas City in 1990...Played nine years with Phillies and seven with Angels...One of game's best receivers in his day...Played in four NLCS with Phillies and two ALCS with Angels...A four-time All-Star...Born Nov. 19, 1947, in San Diego...Holds degree in psychology from Stanford, where sons also attended.

ALL-TIME ROYAL SEASON RECORDS

BATTING: George Brett, .390, 1980
HRs: Steve Balboni, 36, 1985
RBI: Hal McRae, 133, 1982
STEALS: Willie Wilson, 83, 1979
WINS: Bret Saberhagen, 23, 1989
STRIKEOUTS: Dennis Leonard, 244, 1977

MILWAUKEE BREWERS

TEAM DIRECTORY: Pres./CEO: Allan (Bud) Selig; Sr. VP-Baseball Oper.: Sal Bando; Dir. Player Dev.: Fred Stanley; VP-Corp. Affairs; Laurel Prieb; Dir. Media Rel.: Jon Greenberg; Dir. Publications: Mario Ziino; Trav. Sec.: Steve Ethier; Mgr.: Phil Garner; Coaches: Bill Castro, Duffy Dyer, Tim Foley, Don Rowe. Home: Milwaukee County Stadium (53,192). Field distances: 315, l.f. line; 362, l.f.; 392, l.c.; 402, c.f.; 392, r.c.; 362, r.f.; 315, r.f. line. Spring training: Chandler, Ariz.

SCOUTING REPORT

The small-market Brewers continue to be plagued by the same ills that have hurt them in most recent seasons. Not only is the market small, so is the payroll. The talent is thin, too, which explains last year's 53-62 finish.

It isn't hard to see why watching this team play the past few

Greg Vaughn has emerged as one-man Brew Crew of '90s.

seasons convinced owner Bud Selig that it's time for economic revolution. Because they've lacked the proper finances, the Brewers lost Paul Molitor to free agency and traded Gary Sheffield in recent seasons—and those two players have talent to dwarf anybody on the current roster.

In the Year of the Home Run, the Brewers were the only AL team that failed to hit 100 home runs (99). What's worse, their 59 steals were more than only three other teams. What happened to those theft-happy Brewers of 1992? It seems other teams have caught on to Phil Garner's game, depriving the Brewers of their one remaining weapon.

Almost as bad as the Brewers' lack of resources has been their lack of luck. Injuries curtailed or ruined the '94 seasons of Darryl Hamilton, B.J. Surhoff, Pat Listach, Kevin Seitzer, Jeff Bronkey and Brian Harper, and many questions remain. Greg Vaughn's second shoulder surgery in two years is likely to leave him as the designated hitter and center fielder Hamilton may have to move to left after reconstructive elbow surgery. Harper (.291, 4, 32), Surhoff (.261, 5, 22) and Jody Reed (.271, 2, 37) were free agents unsigned at press time.

Vaughn (.254, 19, 55) provides the only substantial power threat, although Australian Dave Nilsson (.275, 12, 69) may be on the verge of a real breakthrough. Beyond those two, the Brewers are mostly a collection of singles hitters like Seitzer (.314, 5, 49). Without power or speed, the Brewers need too many hits to survive. They can take some solace in the play of shortstop Jose Valentin (.239, 11, 46) and outfielder Matt Mieske (.259, 10, 38).

Ricky Bones (10-9, 3.43), had a big first month and managed to finish with a winning record, no small achievement considering the lack of offense. The ace is Cal Eldred (11-11, 4.68), who keeps piling up the innings. The great mystery remains Jaime Navarro (14-9, 6.62), who showed star potential a couple years ago, but has failed to live up to his ability, and the staple has been Bill Wegman (8-4, 4.10). The bullpen received a boost with the emergence of Mike Fetters (1-4, 2.54, 17 saves), although it is still less than deep. The pitching is far better than the hitting, but still no cause to begin printing playoff tickets.

Indeed, the Brewers have been hurt by a low payroll the past several seasons. However, they get no bonus points for several decisions. They gave big contracts to players who gave them precious little return, including Surhoff, Teddy Higuera and Franklin Stubbs. Then they foolishly claimed poverty when it came time to pay local legend Molitor. Selig can blame the tiny market for some of the Brewers' sorry predicament, but not all.

BREWER PROFILES

GREG VAUGHN 29 6-0 205   Bats R Throws R

Brewers' only real power source, he led the club in homers (19) for the fourth straight season... His power totals are all the more impressive considering he lacks real protection in batting order... Only one of his homers came after the All-Star break... Signed three-year, $12-million contract before '94 season... Would have made $3 million in '94... Born July 3, 1965, in Sacramento, Cal.... Has had five or more RBI in a game eight times... Underwent offseason shoulder surgery again last winter and outfielder could be relegated to DH duties in '95... Brewers' first-round pick in secondary phase in 1986, out of the University of Miami, where he earned a business degree.

Year Club	Pos.	G	AB	R	H	2B	3B	HR	RBI	SB	Avg.
1989 Milwaukee	OF	38	113	18	30	3	0	5	23	4	.265
1990 Milwaukee	OF	120	382	51	84	26	2	17	61	7	.220
1991 Milwaukee	OF	145	542	81	132	24	5	27	98	2	.244
1992 Milwaukee	OF	141	501	77	114	18	2	23	78	15	.228
1993 Milwaukee	OF	154	569	97	152	28	2	30	97	10	.267
1994 Milwaukee	OF	95	370	59	94	24	1	19	55	9	.254
Totals		693	2477	383	606	123	12	121	412	47	.245

DAVE NILSSON 25 6-3 215   Bats L Throws R

Made big step in '94, showing power and clutch hitting the Brewers so desperately need... Became first Brewers catcher to reach double digits in homers (12) since Bill Schroeder hit 14 in 1987... Hit well when it counted most, leading Brewers in RBI with 69... Hit the first ever home run at The Ballpark at Arlington... Had four four-hit games, the most by a Brewer since Paul Molitor had seven in '91... Needs work defensively behind the plate... Born Dec. 14, 1969, in Brisbane, Australia ... One of two Australian-born players on Brewers, along with reliever Graeme Lloyd... Would have made $182,500 in '94... Brewers signed him as undrafted free agent in January 1987.

Year Club	Pos.	G	AB	R	H	2B	3B	HR	RBI	SB	Avg.
1992 Milwaukee	C-1B	51	164	15	38	8	0	4	25	2	.232
1993 Milwaukee	C-1B	100	296	35	76	10	2	7	40	3	.257
1994 Milwaukee	C-1B	109	397	51	109	28	3	12	69	1	.275
Totals		260	857	101	223	46	5	23	134	6	.260

Kevin Seitzer relocated .300 stroke missing since '88.

KEVIN SEITZER 33 5-11 180 Bats R Throws R

Hit .300-plus for the fourth time in his career, but the first time since 1988... Showed why teammates call him "Psycho" when he returned to action two days after suffering multiple facial fractures when hit by a pitch from the Yankees' Melido Perez Aug. 1... Wore facemask on helmet after returning from beaning... Best year was 1987, when he had 207 hits and 105 runs... Owned the Brewers' longest hitting streak of last year, at 15 games... Hit .343 on road in '94, .280 at home... Younger brother Brad, also a third baseman, played for Brewers' Class-A Beloit club... Would have made $650,000 in '94... Born March 26, 1962, in Springfield, Ill.... Brewers signed him as free agent in July 1993, after he was dumped by Athletics... Royals' 11th-round pick in 1983 draft, out of Eastern Illinois.

Year	Club	Pos.	G	AB	R	H	2B	3B	HR	RBI	SB	Avg.
1986	Kansas City...	1B-OF-3B	28	96	16	31	4	1	2	11	0	.323
1987	Kansas City...	3B-OF-1B	161	641	105	207	33	8	15	83	12	.323
1988	Kansas City...	3B-OF	149	559	90	170	32	5	5	60	10	.304
1989	Kansas City...	3B-SS-OF-1B	160	597	78	168	17	2	4	48	17	.281
1990	Kansas City...	3B-2B	158	622	91	171	31	5	6	38	7	.275
1991	Kansas City...	3B	85	234	28	62	11	3	1	25	4	.265
1992	Milwaukee....	3B-2B-1B	148	540	74	146	35	1	5	71	13	.270
1993	Oak.-Mil......	INF-OF	120	417	45	112	16	2	11	57	7	.269
1994	Milwaukee....	3B-1B	80	309	44	97	24	2	5	49	2	.314
	Totals.......		1089	4015	571	1164	203	29	54	442	72	.290

JOSE VALENTIN 25 5-10 175 Bats S Throws R

Showed decent pop as rookie, hitting most homers (11) of any Brewers middle infielder since Dale Sveum hit 25 in 1987... Also became first Brewers shortstop to lead the league in errors (20) since Robin Yount made 44 miscues in 1975... Only Brewer to reach double digits in steals, with 12... Despite flawed year, he figures to be shortstop of future... Came from Padres with Matt Mieske and Ricky Bones in controversial trade for Gary Sheffield prior to 1992 season... Padres had signed him as undrafted free agent in October 1986... Born Oct. 12, 1969, in Manati, P.R.... Hit .262 left-handed and just .135 right-handed last year... Would have made $113,000 in '94.

Year	Club	Pos.	G	AB	R	H	2B	3B	HR	RBI	SB	Avg.
1992	Milwaukee....	SS-2B	4	3	1	0	0	0	0	1	0	.000
1993	Milwaukee....	SS	19	53	10	13	1	2	1	7	1	.245
1994	Milwaukee....	SS-2B-3B	97	285	47	68	19	0	11	46	12	.239
	Totals.......		120	341	58	81	20	2	12	54	13	.238

RICKY BONES 26 6-0 190   Bats R Throws R

Huge start was offset by mediocre ending and he wound up having only a slightly better season than his previous two... Posted league-leading 1.11 ERA in April, but finished at 3.43, eighth-best mark in AL... Became first Brewers starting pitcher to make the All-Star team since Ted Higuera in 1986... Was also the only AL player not to play in All-Star Game ... Main weakness is that he has yet to develop a strikeout pitch, as evidenced by just 57 whiffs in 170⅔ innings last year... Came from Padres as part of controversial Gary Sheffield trade before the '92 season... San Diego signed him as undrafted free agent in May 1986... Born April 7, 1969, in Salinas, P.R.... Would have made $325,000 in '94.

Year	Club	G	IP	W	L	Pct.	SO	BB	H	ERA
1991	San Diego	11	54	4	6	.400	31	18	57	4.83
1992	Milwaukee	31	163⅓	9	10	.474	65	48	169	4.57
1993	Milwaukee	32	203⅔	11	11	.500	63	63	222	4.86
1994	Milwaukee	24	170⅔	10	9	.526	57	45	166	3.43
	Totals	98	591⅔	34	36	.486	216	174	614	4.37

CAL ELDRED 27 6-4 235   Bats R Throws L

Workhorse of the staff finished third in AL in innings (179) and tied for fourth in complete games (6)... Posted second straight .500 season after big 11-2 rookie year, although Brewers' weak offense was mostly to blame... Limited opposing batters to .236 average in 1994... Won 10 in a row between Aug. 8-Sept. 29 in 1992... A bargain at $375,000 price tag in '94... Has only nine no-decisions in 78 big league starts... Gained 20th career win in just 30th appearance, tying big league mark of three others—Bob Ferris (1945), Russ Ford (1910) and Nick Maddox (1908)... Has allowed whopping 55 homers during past two seasons... Born Nov. 24, 1967, in Cedar Rapids, Iowa... Brewers' first-round selection in 1989.

Year	Club	G	IP	W	L	Pct.	SO	BB	H	ERA
1991	Milwaukee	3	16	2	0	1.000	10	6	20	4.50
1992	Milwaukee	14	100⅓	11	2	.846	62	23	76	1.79
1993	Milwaukee	36	258	16	16	.500	180	91	232	4.01
1994	Milwaukee	25	179	11	11	.500	98	84	158	4.68
	Totals	78	553⅓	40	29	.580	350	204	486	3.84

BILL WEGMAN 32 6-5 235   Bats R Throws R

Sputtered after starting off 6-0 last year... His burst out of gate was one victory off record for best start by a Brewer, held by Eddie Rodriguez ... Has not been the same since big '92 season during which he pitched 261⅔ innings... He came came up in trade talks with several contending clubs... Allowed opposing batters to hit astounding .303 last season... Brewers scored an average of 6.3 runs per game for him in '94, making up for a lack of support in past years... Suffered an abdomen strain, the official injury of the Brewers... Would have made $2,375,000 in '94... Born Dec. 19, 1962, in Cincinnati... Brewers drafted him in fifth round in 1981.

Year	Club	G	IP	W	L	Pct.	SO	BB	H	ERA
1985	Milwaukee	3	17⅔	2	0	1.000	6	3	17	3.57
1986	Milwaukee	35	198⅓	5	12	.294	82	43	217	5.13
1987	Milwaukee	34	225	12	11	.522	102	53	229	4.24
1988	Milwaukee	32	199	13	13	.500	84	50	207	4.12
1989	Milwaukee	11	51	2	6	.250	27	21	69	6.71
1990	Milwaukee	8	29⅔	2	2	.500	20	6	37	4.85
1991	Milwaukee	28	193⅓	5	7	.682	89	40	176	2.84
1992	Milwaukee	35	261⅔	13	14	.481	127	55	251	3.20
1993	Milwaukee	20	120⅔	4	14	.222	50	34	135	4.48
1994	Milwaukee	19	115⅔	8	4	.667	59	26	140	4.51
	Totals	225	1412	76	83	.478	646	331	1478	4.10

MIKE FETTERS 30 6-4 215   Bats R Throws R

Established himself as Brewers' best reliever after toiling in virtual obscurity for years... Saved 17 games in 20 tries as he took over closer role from Doug Henry, who had saved 17 in 1993... Acquired from Angels along with Glenn Carter in trade for Chuck Crim prior to 1992 season... Cited occasionally for vague resemblance to Babe Ruth... Has allowed no homers since July 30, 1993, a period covering 63⅓ innings...

Born Dec. 19, 1964, in Van Nuys, Cal.... Would have made $400,000 in '94... Angels' first-round pick in 1986.

Year	Club	G	IP	W	L	Pct.	SO	BB	H	ERA
1989	California	1	3⅓	0	0	.000	4	1	5	8.10
1990	California	26	67⅔	1	1	.500	35	20	77	4.12
1991	California	19	44⅔	2	5	.286	24	28	53	4.84
1992	Milwaukee	50	62⅔	5	1	.833	43	24	38	1.87
1993	Milwaukee	45	59⅓	3	3	.500	23	22	59	3.34
1994	Milwaukee	42	46	1	4	.200	31	27	41	2.54
	Totals	183	283⅔	12	14	.462	160	122	273	3.36

TOP PROSPECTS

JEFF CIRILLO 25 6-2 190   Bats R Throws R
An excellent defensive third baseman, he showed his skills following midseason callup to Brewers... Named Best Defensive Third Baseman in American Association... Batted .309 with 10 home runs and 46 RBI for New Orleans (AAA), but struggled offensively with the Brewers, hitting just .238 after his promotion ... Born Sept. 23, 1969, in Pasadena, Cal.... Brewers' 11th-round pick in 1991, out of USC.

SID ROBERSON 23 5-9 170   Bats L Throws L
This gem was nabbed in 29th round of 1992 draft... Was Texas League Pitcher of the Year in 1994, going 15-8 with 2.83 ERA for El Paso (AA)... Won top pitcher honors in California League in 1993, too, as he went 12-8 with 2.50 ERA for Stockton (A) ... Born Sept. 7, 1971, in Jacksonville, Fla.

TIM UNROE 24 6-3 200   Bats R Throws R
Has exceeded expectations after being selected in 28th round of '92 draft... Led Texas League in RBI (103) and several other offensive categories playing for El Paso (AA)... Plays third base as well as first base, a Brewers' weakness for years... Born Oct. 7, 1970, in Round Lake Beach, Ill.

DUANE SINGLETON 22 6-1 170   Bats L Throws R
Progressed through organization last year, starting with Stockton (A) and eventually spending a week with Brewers, although he did not bat for them... Hit .291 for Stockton, .288 for El Paso (AA) and .278 for New Orleans (AAA)... Has good speed and arm and is viewed as an excellent prospect in center field... Stole

total of 31 bases in '94... Lacks pop, as evidenced by just six homers and 51 RBI last season... Born Aug. 6, 1972, in Staten Island, N.Y.... Brewers' fifth-round pick in 1990.

MANAGER PHIL GARNER:  Has posted successive losing years after bursting onto scene with big debut in 1992, when he managed Brewers to a 92-70 record and had them challenging Blue Jays into season's final weekend... Last year's 53-62 mark must be considered impressive considering the Brewers' low payroll and amazing run of bad health... Known as "Scrap Iron" during his playing days for his aggressive, hard-nosed manner, he encourages his teams to play the same way... Played 14 years in the majors with Oakland, Pittsburgh, Houston and Los Angeles... Spent three seasons on Astros' coaching staff after his retirement from playing in 1988... Was choice of GM Sal Bando to succeed Tom Trebelhorn when almost everyone expected Bando to pick Don Baylor, then a Brewers coach... Born April 30, 1949, in Jefferson City, Tenn.... Career mark is 214-225.

ALL-TIME BREWER SEASON RECORDS

BATTING: Paul Molitor, .353, 1987
HRs: Gorman Thomas, 45, 1979
RBI: Cecil Cooper, 126, 1983
STEALS: Pat Listach, 54, 1992
WINS: Mike Caldwell, 22, 1978
STRIKEOUTS: Ted Higuera, 240, 1987

MINNESOTA TWINS

TEAM DIRECTORY: Owner: Carl Pohlad; Pres.: Jerry Bell; Exec. VP/GM: Andy MacPhail; VP-Player Pers.: Terry Ryan; Dir. Media Rel.: Rob Antony; Trav. Sec.: Remzi Kiratli; Mgr.: Tom Kelly; Coaches: Terry Crowley, Ron Gardenhire, Rick Stelmaszek, Dick Such, Scott Ullger. Home: Hubert H. Humphrey Metrodome (55,883). Field distances: 343, l.f. line; 408, c.f.; 327, r.f. line. Spring training: Fort Myers, Fla.

SCOUTING REPORT

Piece by piece, the components of one of the game's surprising success stories in recent history have gone away. Jack Morris, Dave Winfield, Kent Hrbek, and perhaps most importantly, GM Andy MacPhail all are gone from a team that won world championships in 1987 and 1991. What is left is a small-market franchise increasingly restricted by economic factors beyond its control and stuck in a rebuilding phase after a 53-60 finish.

Fortunately, local legend Kirby Puckett and manager Tom Kelly still are around. The former's smiling face and potent bat make him arguably the game's best leader. The latter won't win any popularity contests outside of his own clubhouse, but his nononsense, team-first concept gets the most out of his team.

Yes, Puckett (.317, 20, 112) has slowed a step and isn't the defensive player he used to be in the outfield. But he remains one of the league's best offensive players, despite little protection in a depleted lineup.

It used to be that Kelly could count on plenty of offense, but the Twins have fallen off to the middle of the AL pack in the major offensive categories. Take away Hrbek (retired) and Winfield (traded) and prospects for improvement aren't great, despite the development of Scott Leius (.246, 14, 49).

Shane Mack (.333, 15, 61), unsigned at press time, Alex Cole (.296, 4, 23, 29 steals) and Chuck Knoblauch (.312, 51 RBI, 35 steals) will presumably set the table for Puckett, but the Twins still are waiting for several of their young players to blossom. Pedro Munoz (.295, 11, 36) remains a platoon player, David McCarty (.260, 1, 12) couldn't stick with the big club and catcher Matt Walbeck hit .204.

More young players could break into the lineup this season,

Nine-time All-Star Kirby Puckett reigns as Minny legend.

as Steve Dunn has a chance to replace Hrbek at first (if one-time Yankee Kevin Maas doesn't make it) and Rich Becker could fit into the outfield picture.

The Twins' real problems lie with their pitching staff. The bullpen posted a cumulative 5.41 ERA—and the relievers were the better half of the staff. Even in a year of offense, the 5.84 ERA of the Twins' starting rotation was abominable.

Right-handers Kevin Tapani (11-7, 4.62) and Pat Mahomes (9-5, 4.73) were the only starters with winning records in 1994. Enigmatic Scott Erickson (8-11, 5.44) is durable if not effective. Beyond that, Kelly will have to suffer through the growing pains of Eddie Guardado (0-2, 8.47) and Carlos Pulido (3-7, 5.98).

As bad as the bullpen was in 1994, it could get worse if the rumored departure of high-priced closer Rick Aguilera (1-4, 3.36, 23 saves) comes to fruition. He probably would have been traded for pitching prospects down the stretch last season, but there was no stretch.

Lefty Mark Guthrie (4-2, 6.17) should be much better, right-hander Mike Trombley (2-0, 6.33) has good stuff and Dave Stevens (5-2, 6.80) figures to step in if Aguilera does eventually exit. No, this isn't a pretty picture.

TWIN PROFILES

KIRBY PUCKETT 34 5-8 220   Bats R Throws R

Mr. Twin... Ultimate franchise player... His popularity in Twin Cities is immense... Getting on in years, but remains one of game's best hitters... Batted above .300 for seventh time in nine years and was only one point off his career average of .318... Despite strike, he reached 20-homer mark for second year in row after going four years without doing so... His 112 RBI were second-highest total of his career, topped only by 121 in 1988... Passed 2,000-hit mark last April and finished year at 2,135... Autobiography is entitled "I Love This Game"... Would have earned $5.2 million in 1994, in second year of five-year, $30-million deal... Has made nine consecutive All-Star teams... Has six Gold Gloves, although he's not the center fielder he used to be... Twins' first-round pick as third player selected in January 1982 draft... Born March 14, 1961, in Chicago.

Year	Club	Pos.	G	AB	R	H	2B	3B	HR	RBI	SB	Avg.
1984	Minnesota	OF	128	557	63	165	12	5	0	31	14	.296
1985	Minnesota	OF	161	691	80	199	29	13	4	74	21	.288
1986	Minnesota	OF	161	680	119	223	37	6	31	96	20	.328
1987	Minnesota	OF	157	624	96	207	32	5	28	99	12	.332
1988	Minnesota	OF	158	657	109	234	42	5	24	121	6	.356
1989	Minnesota	OF	159	635	75	215	45	4	9	85	11	.339
1990	Minnesota	OF-2B-SS-3B	146	551	82	164	40	3	12	80	5	.298
1991	Minnesota	OF	152	611	92	195	29	6	15	89	11	.319
1992	Minnesota	OF-2B-3B-SS	160	639	104	210	38	4	19	110	17	.329
1993	Minnesota	OF	156	622	89	184	39	3	22	89	8	.296
1994	Minnesota	OF	108	439	79	139	32	3	20	112	6	.317
	Totals		1646	6706	988	2135	375	57	184	986	131	.318

CHUCK KNOBLAUCH 26 5-9 180   Bats R Throws R

Name a category and this scrappy, little second baseman was on his way to setting career high in it before strike... Hit above .300 for first time (.312) and had career-best 35 stolen bases... Hit .344 in Metrodome and .362 with runners in scoring position... Made only three errors in 478 chances in 109 games... Made second All-Star Game appearance... Capped AL Rookie of the Year season in 1991 with 15 postseason hits, a record for rookies... Averaged 153 games played in first three seasons and missed only four games before strike... Would have earned $1,550,000 in 1994... Twins' first pick and 25th player taken overall in 1989 draft, after stellar career as shortstop at Texas A&M ... Born July 7, 1968, in Houston.

Year	Club	Pos.	G	AB	R	H	2B	3B	HR	RBI	SB	Avg.
1991	Minnesota	2B-SS	151	565	78	159	24	6	1	50	25	.281
1992	Minnesota	2B-SS	155	600	104	178	19	6	2	56	34	.297
1993	Minnesota	2B-SS-OF	153	602	82	167	27	4	2	41	29	.277
1994	Minnesota	2B-SS	109	445	85	139	45	3	5	51	35	.312
	Totals		568	2212	349	643	115	19	10	198	123	.291

SHANE MACK 31 6-0 190 Bats R Throws R

Shoulder woes lingered from 1993, but once healthy, this outfielder was his usual productive self ... Hit over .300 for the fourth time in five seasons as Twin. Only Kirby Puckett also can say that ... Power numbers were better than in full season in 1993, despite 200 fewer at-bats in strike-shortened year ... Base-stealing took a big decline, from 15 in '93 to 4 ... Separated his shoulder in spring of 1993 and never fully recovered ... Hit only .276 with 10 homers ... Would have earned $3,250,000 in 1994 ... Had 22-game hitting streak in 1992, when he also established career highs in runs, home runs, RBI and steals ... Stolen by Twins from Padres in December 1989 minor league draft ... Padres made him 11th pick overall in 1984 draft ... Played for U.S. Olympic Team that summer ... Born Dec. 7, 1963, in Los Angeles ... Free agent at press time.

Year	Club	Pos.	G	AB	R	H	2B	3B	HR	RBI	SB	Avg.
1987	San Diego	OF	105	238	28	57	11	3	4	25	4	.239
1988	San Diego	OF	56	119	13	29	3	0	0	12	5	.244
1990	Minnesota	OF	125	313	50	102	10	4	8	44	13	.326
1991	Minnesota	OF	143	442	79	137	27	8	18	74	13	.310
1992	Minnesota	OF	156	600	101	189	31	6	16	75	26	.315
1993	Minnesota	OF	128	503	66	139	30	4	10	61	15	.276
1994	Minnesota	OF	81	303	55	101	21	2	15	61	4	.333
	Totals		894	2518	392	754	133	27	71	352	80	.299

PEDRO MUNOZ 26 5-10 210 Bats R Throws R

Continues to show he can hit, but doesn't bring much else to the party ... In spot duty, he batted .295 with .508 slugging percentage in 244 at-bats ... Role may have to increase on budget-conscious Twins ... Likely to do more designated hitting with Dave Winfield and Kent Hrbek gone ... Twenty-eight of his 72 hits went for extra bases ... Can't run and rates as liability in the outfield... Hit .301 against right-handers and .308 in the Metrodome, but only .150 in late-inning pressure situations... Would have earned $590,000 in 1994... Signed by Blue Jays as undrafted free agent in May 1985... Traded from Toronto to Twins with Nelson Liriano for John Candelaria, July 27, 1990... Born Sept. 19, 1968, in Ponce, P.R.

Year	Club	Pos.	G	AB	R	H	2B	3B	HR	RBI	SB	Avg.
1990	Minnesota	OF	22	85	13	23	4	1	0	5	3	.271
1991	Minnesota	OF	51	138	15	39	7	1	7	26	3	.283
1992	Minnesota	OF	127	418	44	113	16	3	12	71	4	.270
1993	Minnesota	OF	104	326	34	76	11	1	13	38	1	.233
1994	Minnesota	OF	75	244	35	72	15	2	11	36	0	.295
	Totals		379	1211	141	323	53	8	43	176	11	.267

SCOTT LEIUS 29 6-3 195   Bats R Throws R

Settled in at third base after lost 1993 season... Set career highs in virtually every offensive category... He's no Gary Gaetti, but he was third on club in homers (14) and fifth in RBI (49)... Hit only .212 with runners in scoring position and .216 in Metrodome... Committed eight errors in 95 games at third base... Injuries cost him most of 1993 season... Pushed into regular duty in 1992, he hit .249 in 409 at-bats... Hit .357 in 1991 World Series, with a home run and two RBI... Came up as a shortstop... Had never hit as many as 10 homers in a season until last year... Twins' 13th-round pick in 1986... Salary would have been $275,000 in 1994... Born Sept. 24, 1965, in Yonkers, N.Y.

Year	Club	Pos.	G	AB	R	H	2B	3B	HR	RBI	SB	Avg.
1990	Minnesota	SS-3B	14	25	4	6	1	0	1	4	0	.240
1991	Minnesota	3B-SS-OF	109	199	35	57	7	2	5	20	5	.286
1992	Minnesota	3B-SS	129	409	50	102	18	2	2	35	6	.249
1993	Minnesota	SS	10	18	4	3	0	0	0	2	0	.167
1994	Minnesota	3B-SS	97	350	57	86	16	1	14	49	2	.246
	Totals		359	1001	150	254	42	5	22	110	13	.254

ALEX COLE 29 6-0 175   Bats L Throws L

Talk about pleasant surprises... Outfielder had career year after being discarded by expansion Rockies, who tired of his fielding and baserunning flaws... Truly a journeyman... Twins are his sixth organization in 11 years... He and fundamentalist Tom Kelly didn't appear to be a good match, but it worked... Hit .296 and his four homers pushed his big league total to four... Stole 40 bases in second half of 1990 season with Cleveland... Swiped 29 in 37 tries last season... Would have earned $250,000 in 1994... Was 17th pick overall by Rockies in expansion draft... Selected by Cardinals in second round of 1985 draft... Traded to Padres with Steve Peters for Omar Olivares prior to 1990 season... Five months later, he went to Indians for Tom Lampkin and made major league debut... Born Aug. 17, 1965, in Fayetteville, N.C.

Year	Club	Pos.	G	AB	R	H	2B	3B	HR	RBI	SB	Avg.
1990	Cleveland	OF	63	227	43	68	5	4	0	13	40	.300
1991	Cleveland	OF	122	387	58	114	17	3	0	21	27	.295
1992	Cleveland	OF	41	97	11	20	1	0	0	5	9	.206
1992	Pittsburgh	OF	64	205	33	57	3	7	0	10	7	.278
1993	Colorado	OF	126	348	50	89	9	4	0	24	30	.256
1994	Minnesota	OF	105	345	68	102	15	5	4	23	29	.296
	Totals		521	1609	263	450	50	23	4	96	142	.280

KEVIN TAPANI 31 6-0 187   Bats R Throws R

Got back on winning track in '94, despite 4.62 ERA... Has had winning record in four of last five seasons... Has 69-52 record since coming to Twins from Mets with four other pitchers in Frank Viola trade, July 31, 1989, so he must be doing something right... Allowed 181 hits in 156 innings in 1994, including 62 for extra bases... Surrendered 243 hits in 225⅓ innings in 1993... ERA was above 4.00 for second consecutive season ... Loss of velocity is at root of problem... Has to have pinpoint control to succeed... Walked 39 in 156 innings, on high side for him... Would have earned $2,575,000 in 1994... Had back-to-back, 16-victory seasons in 1991 and 1992, with ERAs of 2.99 and 3.97... Won Game 2 of 1991 World Series after two poor ALCS outings... Athletics' second-round pick in 1986 draft... Born Feb. 18, 1964, in Des Moines, Iowa.

Year	Club	G	IP	W	L	Pct.	SO	BB	H	ERA
1989	New York (NL)	3	7⅓	0	0	.000	2	4	5	3.68
1989	Minnesota	5	32⅔	2	2	.500	21	8	34	3.86
1990	Minnesota	28	159⅓	12	8	.600	101	29	164	4.07
1991	Minnesota	34	244	16	9	.640	135	40	225	2.99
1992	Minnesota	34	220	16	11	.593	138	48	226	3.97
1993	Minnesota	36	225⅔	12	15	.444	150	57	243	4.43
1994	Minnesota	24	156	11	7	.611	91	39	181	4.62
	Totals	164	1045	69	52	.570	638	225	1078	3.94

SCOTT ERICKSON 27 6-4 225   Bats R Throws R

Take away his surprising no-hitter on April 27 of last season and it was another disappointing season for this enigmatic right-hander... Blanked Milwaukee, 6-0, in no-no, walking four and striking out five in 129-pitch effort... Was on disabled list with strained side a month later... Had second consecutive losing season ... Hasn't been the same since first half of 1991 season... Has gone 37-47 since 1991 All-Star break, at which point he was 12-3 for the season and 20-7 in his career... Doesn't click with manager Tom Kelly or pitching coach Dick Such... Had 30⅓ scoreless inning streak in 1991... Had 5.06 ERA and two no-decisions in 1991 World Series... Would have made $1,325,000 in '94... Twins' fourth-round pick in 1989 draft, out of University of Arizona... Born Feb. 2, 1968, in Long Beach, Cal.

Year	Club	G	IP	W	L	Pct.	SO	BB	H	ERA
1990	Minnesota	19	113	8	4	.667	53	51	108	2.87
1991	Minnesota	32	204	20	8	.714	108	71	189	3.18
1992	Minnesota	32	212	13	12	.520	101	83	197	3.40
1993	Minnesota	34	218⅔	8	19	.296	116	71	266	5.19
1994	Minnesota	23	144	8	11	.421	104	59	173	5.44
	Totals	140	891⅔	57	54	.514	482	335	933	4.05

PAT MAHOMES 24 6-4 210   Bats R Throws R

Started to fulfill enormous potential, but still has some rough edges... Stayed in rotation all season for first time... Second on staff in victories with nine... Got plenty of support, an average of 6.38 runs per game... Walked 62, nine more than he struck out, despite 90-plus-mph fastball... Left-handers batted .293 against him... Needs to be more consistent, especially with his breaking pitch... Flipped his truck in offseason accident on Minneapolis highway, but he escaped with only minor injuries... Would have earned $126,000 in 1994... Couldn't stick with Twins in 1993, when he went 1-5 with 7.71 ERA in 12 starts after winning job in spring training... Picked by Twins in sixth round of 1988 draft... Born Aug. 9, 1970, in Bryan, Tex.

Year	Club	G	IP	W	L	Pct.	SO	BB	H	ERA
1992	Minnesota	14	69⅔	3	4	.429	44	37	73	5.04
1993	Minnesota	12	37⅓	1	5	.167	23	16	47	7.71
1994	Minnesota	21	120	9	5	.643	53	62	121	4.73
	Totals	47	227	13	14	.481	120	115	241	5.31

RICK AGUILERA 33 6-5 205   Bats R Throws R

Quality closer slipped slightly in 1994... Had 23 saves, but six blown opportunities, and lost four of five decisions... Allowed alarming 57 hits in 44⅔ innings... Opponents hit .303 against him... His ERA (3.63) was highest since he moved from rotation to bullpen... Control and stuff was apparently still there, as 10 walks and 46 strikeouts indicated... Subject of trade rumors in second half of last season... Could be a luxury on rebuilding Twins... Saved two games and earned a victory in 1991 World Series... Another key part of five-player package Twins received from Mets for Frank Viola, July 31, 1989 ... Spent four-plus seasons with Mets, posting 37-27 record as starter and reliever... Mets' third-round pick in 1983... Born Dec. 31, 1961, in San Gabriel, Cal.... Has 179 career saves.

Year	Club	G	IP	W	L	Pct.	SO	BB	H	ERA
1985	New York (NL)	21	121⅓	10	7	.588	74	37	118	3.24
1986	New York (NL)	28	141⅔	10	7	.588	104	36	145	3.88
1987	New York (NL)	18	115	11	3	.786	77	33	124	3.60
1988	New York (NL)	11	24⅔	0	4	.000	16	10	29	6.93
1989	New York (NL)	36	69⅓	6	6	.500	80	21	59	2.34
1989	Minnesota	11	75⅔	3	5	.375	57	17	71	3.21
1990	Minnesota	56	65⅓	5	3	.625	61	19	55	2.76
1991	Minnesota	63	69	4	5	.444	61	30	44	2.35
1992	Minnesota	64	66⅔	2	6	.250	52	17	60	2.84
1993	Minnesota	65	72⅓	4	3	.571	59	14	60	3.11
1994	Minnesota	44	44⅔	1	4	.200	46	10	57	3.63
	Totals	417	866⅔	56	53	.514	687	244	822	3.29

TOP PROSPECTS

RICH BECKER 23 5-10 180   Bats S Throws R
Promising prospect... Viewed as center fielder of the future, which could arrive as soon as this season... Hit .265 with one homer and eight RBI in 98 at-bats with Twins and .316 with two homers and 38 RBI in 282 at-bats for Salt Lake (AAA)... Knee injury ended strong 1993 season, which concluded with promotion to Twins... Twins' third-round pick in 1990 draft... Born Feb. 1, 1972, in Aurora, Ill.

LaTROY HAWKINS 22 6-5 195   Bats R Throws R
Voted best prospect in Southern League (AA), where he went 9-2 with 2.33 ERA for Nashville (AA) in '94... Allowed only

50 hits in 73 innings there... Went 5-4 with 4.08 ERA for Salt Lake (AAA)... Started 1993 with Fort Myers (A), so his rise has been meteoric... Twins' seventh-round pick in 1991 draft... Born Dec. 21, 1972, in Gary, Ind.

DENNY HOCKING 25 5-10 180   Bats S Throws R
Pressing Pat Meares for regular shortstop job in Minnesota... Hit .323 in 31 at-bats and didn't commit an error in 10 games for Twins... Batted .279 with five homers, 57 RBI and 13 stolen bases for Salt Lake (AAA)... Late-round find went in 52nd round in 1989 draft... Born April 2, 1970, in Torrance, Cal.

STEVE DUNN 24 6-4 225   Bats L Throws L
Has chance to replace retired Kent Hrbek at first base... Hit .229 in 35 at-bats for Twins and .309 with 15 homers and 73 RBI for Salt Lake (AAA)... Had big year with Visalia (A) in 1992, amassing 26 homers and 113 RBI... Has power potential... Twins' fourth-round pick in 1988... Born April 18, 1970, in Champaign, Ill.

MANAGER TOM KELLY: It's been a tough stretch for one of game's best managers... His Twins have gone 101-125 since July 27, 1992, as key pitchers have struggled and nucleus of position players grew old... However, players swear by him and love to play for him... Gets the most out of his roster, particularly role players... Won't tolerate individualistic behavior by his players... Sports 651-619 overall record after eight-plus seasons, following 53-60 finish in '94... Named AL Manager of the Year in 1991, when his Twins gave him second World Series championship... Has lightened up with media in recent years, after challenging a Minnesota beat writer to a fight... Replaced Ray Miller as manager, Sept. 12, 1986... Had served as Twins' third-base coach since 1983... Three-time Manager of the Year in the minors from 1979-81... Spent all but 49 games of 11-year playing career in minors... Hit .181 in 127 at-bats for Twins at end of 1975 season, but he can say he got a hit off Nolan Ryan... Born Aug. 15, 1950, in Graceville, Minn.

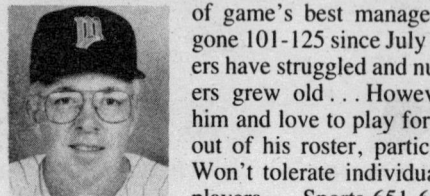

Chuck Knoblauch has no Twin when it comes to scrappy.

ALL-TIME TWIN SEASON RECORDS

BATTING: Rod Carew, .388, 1977
HRs: Harmon Killebrew, 49, 1964, 1969
RBI: Harmon Killebrew, 140, 1969
STEALS: Rod Carew, 49, 1976
WINS: Jim Kaat, 25, 1966
STRIKEOUTS: Bert Blyleven, 258, 1973

CALIFORNIA ANGELS

TEAM DIRECTORY: Chairman: Gene Autry; Pres./CEO: Richard Brown; Exec. VP: Jackie Autry; VP-Oper.: Kevin Uhlich; GM: Bill Bavasi; Dir. Minor League Oper.: Ken Forsch; VP-Civic Affairs: Tom Seeberg; VP-Media Relations: John Sevano; Dir. Baseball Inf.: Larry Babcock; Trav. Sec.: Frank Sims; Mgr.: Marcel Lachemann; Coaches: Mick Billmeyer, Rick Burleson, Rod Carew, Chuck Hernandez, Bobby Knoop, Bill Lachemann, Joe Maddon. Home: Anaheim Stadium (64,593). Field distances: 333, l.f. line; 386, l.c.; 404, c.f.; 386, r.c.; 333, r.f. line. Spring training: Tempe, Ariz.

SCOUTING REPORT

The strike might have been the best thing to happen to the Angels last season. When the players walked, nobody in the AL had a worse record than the Angels' 47-68 mark. They tried a philosophical change of direction and a managerial switch, but nothing worked.

The problems start right at the top, where Jackie Autry has hoodwinked owners around the game into believing that market forces—and not mismanagement—are behind the Angels' fall from grace. The Angels a small-market team? Don't buy it.

Nice guy Marcel Lachemann has the unenviable task of guiding a team that is young but not especially talented. Lachemann was brought in last May, primarily because his predecessor, Buck Rodgers, differed with the front office on evaluations of players. As soon as Lachemann took over, J.T. Snow was recalled from the minors—and proved Rodgers correct by hitting .220. Rodgers also wanted to make a third baseman out of Eduardo Perez, an idea that also has been scrapped.

Not even an unexpectedly good year from designated hitter Chili Davis (.311, 26, 84) could keep the Angels from sporting the league's weakest offense. They were 11th in batting average (.264), last in runs (543), tied for eighth in homers (120) and 10th in stolen bases (65). The only consistent threat besides Davis was right fielder Tim Salmon (.287, 23, 70), who overcame a slow start.

The Angels did get more than they expected from rookie Jim Edmonds (.273, 5, 37) and Bo Jackson (.279, 13, 43), who remained unsigned at press time. But center fielder Chad Curtis (.256, 11, 50, 25 steals) still isn't showing enough discipline at

Angels always relish having Tim Salmon at the dish.

the plate, infielder Damion Easley (.215, 6, 30) was another disappointment, and Lachemann got next to nothing offensively from catchers Greg Myers (.246, 2, 8) and Chris Turner (.242, 1, 12) and not much from shortstop Gary Di Sarcina (.260, 3, 33).

What the Angels do have is the best trio of left-handed starting pitchers in the league. Mark Langston's season was interrupted by surgery, but he figures to rebound from his 7-8, 4.68 numbers. Chuck Finley (10-10, 4.32) is another good one and Brian Anderson (7-5, 5.22) got his chance when Langston got hurt and proved he belongs. Rookie Andrew Lorraine could make it four good lefties in the rotation and right-hander Phil Leftwich (5-10, 5.68) is serviceable.

The bullpen wasn't quite as blessed. Joe Grahe (2-5, 6.65, 13 saves) lost his closer's job and was dumped, replaced now by ex-Oriole maestro Lee Smith (1-4, 3.29, 33 saves) and ex-Astro Mitch Williams (1-4, 7.65, 6 saves). Mike Butcher (2-1, 6.67) was too erratic in the late role. Rookie Troy Percival has to overcome injuries. Mark Leiter (4-7, 4.72, 2 saves) had to contend with the death of his infant child.

The only thing the Angels have established is that they won't figure in the 1995 AL West race.

ANGEL PROFILES

TIM SALMON 26 6-3 220   Bats R Throws R

Followed remarkable rookie season with another good one in 1994... It didn't start that way, however... Was struggling in low .200s with high strikeout ratio until he got hot in May... Belted seven homers during nine-game stretch... Still struck out 102 times in 373 at-bats... Forty-three of his 107 hits went for extra bases... Outfield defense dropped off, as he committed eight errors... Named AL Rookie of the Year in runaway in 1993, thanks to 31-homer, 95-RBI production... Numbers could have been even better if he hadn't missed final three weeks because of fractured ring finger... Was headed for PCL batting title with .347 mark for Edmonton (AAA) in 1992 when he was promoted Aug. 20... Struggled to .177 average with Angels that season, causing some to doubt him. But there's no doubt now... Would have earned $600,000 in 1994... Angels' third-round pick in 1989 draft... Born Aug. 24, 1968, in Long Beach, Cal.

Year Club	Pos.	G	AB	R	H	2B	3B	HR	RBI	SB	Avg.
1992 California	OF	23	79	8	14	1	0	2	6	1	.177
1993 California	OF	142	515	93	146	35	1	31	95	5	.283
1994 California	OF	100	373	67	107	18	2	23	70	1	.287
Totals		265	967	168	267	54	3	56	171	7	.276

CHAD CURTIS 26 5-9 175   Bats R Throws R

Little guy with big heart is overachiever... However, he couldn't get along with hitting instructor Rod Carew, who questioned his willingness to accept coaching... Struggled offensively, but he did set highs for home runs (11) and RBI (50)... Dropped out of leadoff spot after slow start... On-base percentage was just .317, as he drew only 37 walks in 453 at-bats... Outfielder slipped on basepaths, too, as he stole only 25, in 36 attempts, after swiping total of 91 in first two seasons... Would have made $600,000 in '94... MVP of 1991 Venezuelan Winter League... Picked by Angels in 45th round in 1989 draft, after being named NAIA All-American at Grand Canyon College... Born Nov. 6, 1968, in Marion, Ind.

Year Club	Pos.	G	AB	R	H	2B	3B	HR	RBI	SB	Avg.
1992 California	OF	139	441	59	114	16	2	10	46	43	.259
1993 California	OF-2B	152	583	94	166	25	3	6	59	48	.285
1994 California	OF	114	453	67	116	23	4	11	50	25	.256
Totals		405	1477	220	396	64	9	27	155	116	.268

CALIFORNIA ANGELS • 167

CHILI DAVIS 35 6-3 210 Bats S Throws R

Keeps on ticking... Hadn't batted as high as .311 since 1984 until last season... Made third All-Star Game appearance and his first since 1988... Won Angels' Triple Crown, leading club in average, home runs (26) and RBI (84) ... Has hit 53 homers and driven in 196 runs during last two seasons... Finally broke good-year, bad-year pattern that had persisted for five seasons... Strictly a designated hitter, he did not play the field in '93... Had big year during Twins' 1991 championship run... Tailed off badly in 1992, when most thought he was near the end of his career... Returned to Angels as free agent after 1992 season ... Played first six big league seasons with Giants... Real name is Charles Theodore... Would have earned $2.4 million in 1994 ... Giants' 11th-round pick in 1977 draft... Born Jan. 17, 1960, in Kingston, Jamaica.

Year	Club	Pos.	G	AB	R	H	2B	3B	HR	RBI	SB	Avg.
1981	San Francisco	OF	8	15	1	2	0	0	0	0	2	.133
1982	San Francisco	OF	154	641	86	167	27	6	19	76	24	.261
1983	San Francisco	OF	137	486	54	113	21	2	11	59	10	.233
1984	San Francisco	OF	137	499	87	157	21	6	21	81	12	.315
1985	San Francisco	OF	136	481	53	130	25	2	13	56	15	.270
1986	San Francisco	OF	153	526	71	146	28	3	13	70	16	.278
1987	San Francisco	OF	149	500	80	125	22	1	24	76	16	.250
1988	California	OF	158	600	81	161	29	3	21	93	9	.268
1989	California	OF	154	560	81	152	24	1	22	90	3	.271
1990	California	OF	113	412	58	109	17	1	12	58	1	.265
1991	Minnesota	OF	153	534	84	148	34	1	29	93	5	.277
1992	Minnesota	OF-1B	138	444	63	128	27	2	12	66	4	.288
1993	California	DH	153	573	74	139	32	0	27	112	4	.243
1994	California	OF-DH	108	392	72	122	18	1	26	84	3	.311
	Totals		1851	6663	945	1799	325	29	250	1014	124	.270

BO JACKSON 32 6-1 230 Bats R Throws R

So how many other players with artificial hips have you heard about?... Exceeded all expectations with .279 average, 13 homers and 43 RBI... Even played 46 games in the outfield, committing only three errors... Salary would have been $1 million in 1994, a pittance compared to his endorsement revenue... White Sox let him go after 1993 comeback season and Angels signed him as free agent prior to last season... Missed all of 1992 with well-documented hip-replacement surgery... Reached highs of 32 homers and 105 RBI with Royals in 1989 ... Extraordinary two-sport athlete with extraordinary willpower ... Heisman Trophy winner at Auburn in 1985... First overall pick in 1986 NFL draft, by Tampa Bay Bucs... Royals drafted him in fourth round of 1986 draft... Played in 1989 All-Star Game and 1990 Pro Bowl... Born Nov. 30, 1962, in Bessemer, Ala. ... Free agent at press time.

Year	Club	Pos.	G	AB	R	H	2B	3B	HR	RBI	SB	Avg.
1986	Kansas City	OF	25	82	9	17	2	1	2	9	3	.207
1987	Kansas City	OF	116	396	46	93	17	2	22	53	10	.235
1988	Kansas City	OF	124	439	63	108	16	4	25	68	27	.246
1989	Kansas City	OF	135	515	86	132	15	6	32	105	26	.256
1990	Kansas City	OF	111	405	74	110	16	1	28	78	15	.272
1991	Chicago (AL)	DH	23	71	8	16	4	0	3	14	0	.225
1992	Chicago (AL)					Injured						
1993	Chicago (AL)	OF	85	284	32	66	9	0	16	45	0	.232
1994	California	OF	75	201	23	56	7	0	13	43	1	.279
	Totals		694	2393	341	598	86	14	141	415	82	.250

JIM EDMONDS 24 6-1 190   Bats L Throws L

Made strong and somewhat unexpected showing in rookie season... Hit his way into regular duty as more highly regarded Angels prospects struggled... Nothing spectacular, but a solid and consistent player... Hit .289 against left-handers, proving he can play every day... Line-drive hitter, but does not have much power ... Hit only five homers and had 19 extra-base hits... Led club with .349 batting average with runners in scoring position... Can play first base, left field and right field... Would have earned $117,500 in 1994... Good hitter who was plagued by injuries in minors... Didn't hit below .290 in last four minor league seasons... Angels' seventh-round choice in 1988... Born June 27, 1970, in Fullerton, Cal.

Year	Club	Pos.	G	AB	R	H	2B	3B	HR	RBI	SB	Avg.
1993	California	OF	18	61	5	15	4	1	0	4	0	.246
1994	California	OF-1B	94	289	35	79	13	1	5	37	4	.273
	Totals		112	350	40	94	17	2	5	41	4	.269

GARY DiSARCINA 27 6-1 180   Bats R Throws R

Solid and dependable defensive shortstop... Committed only nine errors in 110 games there... Not much with the bat... On-base percentage was only .294... Drew only 18 walks in 389 at-bats... Had consecutive-game streak of 211 until Aug. 26, 1993, when he suffered a broken thumb when hit by a Ben McDonald pitch... Stole only three bases in 10 attempts last season... Would have made $400,000 in 1994... Has hit three home runs in each of his three full seasons... His .260 batting average in '94 was his best... Boyhood hero was Celtic great Larry Bird and he wears Bird's No. 33 to prove it... Angels' sixth-round pick in 1988 draft... Brother Glenn is infielder in White Sox chain... Born Nov. 19, 1967, in Malden, Mass.

Year	Club	Pos.	G	AB	R	H	2B	3B	HR	RBI	SB	Avg.
1990	California	SS–2B	18	57	8	8	1	0	0	0	1	.140
1991	California	SS–2B–3B	18	57	5	12	2	0	0	3	0	.211
1992	California	SS	157	518	48	128	19	0	3	42	9	.247
1993	California	SS	126	416	44	99	20	1	3	45	5	.238
1994	California	SS	112	389	53	101	14	2	3	33	3	.260
	Totals		431	1437	158	348	56	4	9	123	18	.242

J.T. SNOW 27 6-2 202   Bats S Throws L

Has experienced up-and-down first two seasons... Promoted and put in the starting lineup shortly after Marcel Lachemann took over as manager... Didn't do much to preserve that status... Hit just .220 with 12 extra-base hits in 223 at-bats... Hit .226 against left-handers, .216 against right-handers and only .162 on the road... Was among AL batting leaders for much of April 1993, but cooled considerably and was in the minors by July 26... Returned one month later and raised his average from .223 to .241... Great defensive first baseman who is already as smooth around the bag as anybody... Would have made $125,000 in 1994... Obtained from Yankees, along with Jerry Nielsen and Russ Springer, for Jim Abbott prior to 1993 season... Son of former NFL wide receiver Jack... Born Feb. 26, 1968, in Long Beach, Cal.

Year	Club	Pos.	G	AB	R	H	2B	3B	HR	RBI	SB	Avg.
1992	New York (AL)	1B	7	14	1	2	1	0	0	2	0	.143
1993	California	1B	129	419	60	101	18	2	16	57	3	.241
1994	California	1B	61	223	22	49	4	0	8	30	0	.220
	Totals		197	656	83	152	23	2	24	89	3	.232

DAMION EASLEY 25 5-11 185   Bats R Throws R

Coming off disappointing third season... Bounced between second base and third base and apparently will remain at the former position... Played 47 games at third and 40 at second... Stole only four bases in nine tries... Hit only .189 against lefties and .207 at home... His 1993 season was interrupted by painful shin splint condition... Hit .313 in 230 at-bats and showed base-stealing ability... Made impressive late-season 1992 showing, hitting .258 in 151 at-bats... Would have earned $170,000 in 1994... Angels' 30th-round pick in 1988, out of Long Beach City College... Born Nov. 11, 1969, in New York City.

Year	Club	Pos.	G	AB	R	H	2B	3B	HR	RBI	SB	Avg.
1992	California	3B-SS	47	151	14	39	5	0	1	12	9	.258
1993	California	2B-3B	73	230	33	72	13	2	2	22	6	.313
1994	California	3B-2B	88	316	41	68	16	1	6	30	4	.215
	Totals		208	697	88	179	34	3	9	64	19	.257

CHUCK FINLEY 32 6-6 215   Bats L Throws L

Fell off from strong 1993 season, as his ERA rose above 4.00 (4.32) for first time since 1988... Lost first three decisions before three-hit shutout of Oakland May 8... One of AL's most durable left-handed starters... Led AL with 183⅓ innings in '94... Tied for second in league with seven complete games... One of 10 pitchers who tied for AL lead with 25 starts... Led league in complete games (13) in 1993, when he bounced back for 16-win season... Went 7-12 in 1992, when he was plagued by elbow and toe problems... Strangely, he has less success against left-handers than right-handers... Has 85-63 mark in last six years... Two-time All-Star... Would have made $3,875,000 in 1994... Angels' first-round pick in January 1985 draft... Born Nov. 26, 1962, in Monroe, La.

Year	Club	G	IP	W	L	Pct.	SO	BB	H	ERA
1986	California	25	46⅓	3	1	.750	37	23	40	3.30
1987	California	35	90⅔	2	7	.222	63	43	102	4.67
1988	California	31	194⅓	9	15	.375	111	82	191	4.17
1989	California	29	199⅔	16	9	.640	156	82	171	2.57
1990	California	32	236	18	9	.667	177	81	210	2.40
1991	California	34	227⅓	18	9	.667	171	101	205	3.80
1992	California	31	204⅓	7	12	.368	124	98	212	3.96
1993	California	35	251⅓	16	14	.533	187	82	243	3.15
1994	California	25	183⅓	10	10	.500	148	71	178	4.32
	Totals	277	1633⅓	99	86	.535	1174	663	1552	3.50

MARK LANGSTON 34 6-2 185 Bats R Throws L

Had second losing season in last three, but he had a medical excuse... Underwent arthroscopic elbow surgery in mid-April and was back by mid-May... Missed only six starts, but probably rushed back too soon... His ERA was over 4.00 (4.68) for first time since 1990 ... Best start was three-hit shutout of Baltimore July 2... Worked out with pro soccer team during strike... His durability is hard to match... Prior to 1994, he had eight consecutive 200-plus-inning seasons... Made his first All-Star Game start in 1993 at Camden Yards... Has been named to four AL All-Star teams... Has never won 20 games, but he has averaged 14 over 11-year career... Also has won six Gold Gloves... Would have earned $3,550,000 in 1994... Angels signed him as free agent prior to 1990 season... Traded from Mariners to Expos for Randy Johnson, Gene Harris and Brian Holman, May 25, 1989... Spent five-plus seasons with Mariners, going 74-67... Born Aug. 20, 1960, in San Diego... Mariners' third-round pick in 1981.

Year	Club	G	IP	W	L	Pct.	SO	BB	H	ERA
1984	Seattle	35	225	17	10	.630	204	118	188	3.40
1985	Seattle	24	126⅔	7	14	.333	72	91	122	5.47
1986	Seattle	37	239⅓	12	14	.462	245	123	234	4.85
1987	Seattle	35	272	19	13	.594	262	114	242	3.84
1988	Seattle	35	261⅓	15	11	.577	235	110	222	3.34
1989	Seattle	10	73⅓	4	5	.444	60	19	60	3.56
1989	Montreal	24	176⅔	12	9	.571	175	93	138	2.39
1990	California	33	223	10	17	.370	195	104	215	4.40
1991	California	34	246⅓	19	8	.704	183	96	190	3.00
1992	California	32	229	13	14	.481	174	74	206	3.66
1993	California	35	256⅓	16	11	.593	196	85	220	3.20
1994	California	18	119⅓	7	8	.467	109	54	121	4.68
	Totals	352	2448⅓	151	134	.530	2110	1081	2158	3.74

LEE SMITH 37 6-6 258 Bats R Throws R

Oriole free agent signed two-year contract over the winter with Angels after leading majors with 33 saves in 39 tries in 1994... Also holds major league record for saves with 434... If he doesn't make the Hall of Fame, relievers all over will have a major gripe... Will have trouble picking cap for Cooperstown because he will have pitched for at least six teams... Notched total of 46 saves for Cardinals and Yankees in '93... Whispers his fastball had deserted him were unfounded, as he fanned 42 batters in 38⅓ innings in 1994... Almost unhittable early, he tailed off somewhat in July and August... Had 27 saves by July 1... Allowed game-tying home run to Fred McGriff, blowing save in 1994 All-Star Game... Would have made $1.5 million in '94... Born Dec. 4, 1957, in Jamestown, La.... Cubs' second-round pick in 1985.

Year	Club	G	IP	W	L	Pct.	SO	BB	H	ERA
1980	Chicago (NL)	18	22	2	0	1.000	17	14	21	2.86
1981	Chicago (NL)	40	67	3	6	.333	50	31	57	3.49
1982	Chicago (NL)	72	117	2	5	.286	99	37	105	2.69
1983	Chicago (NL)	66	103⅓	4	10	.286	91	41	70	1.65
1984	Chicago (NL)	69	101	9	7	.563	86	35	98	3.65
1985	Chicago (NL)	65	97⅔	7	4	.636	112	32	87	3.04
1986	Chicago (NL)	66	90⅓	9	9	.500	93	42	69	3.09
1987	Chicago (NL)	62	83⅔	4	10	.286	96	32	84	3.12
1988	Boston	64	83⅔	4	5	.444	96	37	72	2.80
1989	Boston	64	70⅔	6	1	.857	96	33	53	3.57
1990	Boston	11	14⅓	2	1	.667	17	9	13	1.88
1990	St. Louis	53	68⅔	3	4	.429	70	20	58	2.10
1991	St. Louis	67	73	6	3	.667	67	13	70	2.34
1992	St. Louis	70	75	4	9	.308	60	26	62	3.12
1993	St. Louis	55	50	2	4	.333	49	9	49	4.50
1993	New York (AL)	8	8	0	0	.000	11	5	4	0.00
1994	Baltimore	41	38⅓	1	4	.200	42	11	34	3.29
	Totals	891	1163⅔	68	82	.453	1152	427	1006	2.92

TOP PROSPECTS

GARRET ANDERSON 22 6-3 190   Bats L Throws L
Home-grown talent could fit in Angels' outfield soon... Tore up Pacific Coast League, hitting .321 with 12 homers and 102 RBI for Vancouver (AAA) last season... Had 27-game hitting streak, the longest in pro ball last season... Above-average defensively... Angels' fourth-round pick in 1990 draft... Born June 30, 1972, in Los Angeles... Hit .385 in 13 at-bats with Angels in '94.

ANDREW LORRAINE 22 6-3 195   Bats L Throws L
Fast-developing lefty made major league debut in second pro season... Was roughed up badly in two starts (0-2, 10.61 as an Angel), but he was voted best pitching prospect in Pacific Coast League... Was 12-4 with 3.42 ERA for Vancouver (AAA) in hitters' league... Angels' fourth-round pick in 1993 draft, out of Stanford... Born Aug. 11, 1972, in Los Angeles.

TROY PERCIVAL 25 6-3 200   Bats R Throws R

Hard-throwing closer got career back on track in second half of 1994 season... Went 2-6 with 4.13 ERA and 15 saves for Edmonton (AAA)... Struck out 73 in 61 innings... Bad spring cost him shot in 1993... Lost much of that season to elbow surgery... Started pro career as catcher... Angels' sixth-round pick in 1990 draft... Born Aug. 9, 1969, in Fontana, Cal.

MANAGER MARCEL LACHEMANN:

Long-time big league pitching coach finally got his chance to manage at age 52... Made debut May 19 of last season, two days after Buck Rodgers was fired... Club went 30-42 under him, after going 17-26 for Rodgers and interim manager Bobby Knoop... His hiring signalled club's renewed commitment to youth movement... Never managed in pro career before last year... Was pitching coach for younger brother Rene with Marlins... Now he and Rene are only brother combination managing in big leagues and the first since George and Harry Wright in 1879... Before going to Marlins, he spent 11 seasons in Angels' organization, including nine as major league pitching coach... Worked as pitching instructor in Montreal chain from 1973-75... Also served as an assistant coach at USC from 1977-81 before returning to pro ranks... Pitched parts of three seasons with Oakland, from 1969-71... Big league record was 7-4 with 3.44 ERA... Born June 13, 1941, in Los Angeles.

ALL-TIME ANGEL SEASON RECORDS

BATTING: Rod Carew, .339, 1983
HRs: Reggie Jackson, 39, 1982
RBI: Don Baylor, 139, 1979
STEALS: Mickey Rivers, 70, 1975
WINS: Clyde Wright, 22, 1970
       Nolan Ryan, 22, 1974
STRIKEOUTS: Nolan Ryan, 383, 1973

OAKLAND ATHLETICS

TEAM DIRECTORY: Chairman: Walter J. Haas; Pres./GM: Sandy Alderson; Exec. VP: Andy Dolich; Dir. Player Dev.: Keith Lieppman; Dir. Scouting: Grady Fuson; Dir. Baseball Inf.: Jay Alves; Trav. Sec.: Mickey Morabito; Mgr.: Tony La Russa; Coaches: Dave Duncan, Art Kusnyer, Jim Lefebvre, Dave McKay, Tommie Reynolds. Home: Oakland Coliseum (47,313). Field distances: 330, l.f. line; 375, l.c.; 400, c.f.; 375, r.c.; 330, r.l. line. Spring training: Phoenix, Ariz.

SCOUTING REPORT

With the Haas family trying to unload the ballclub, the Athletics are in a state of flux. But that doesn't mean that they can't sneak in another division title, especially in the pathetic American League West.

For starters, they retained Tony La Russa for at least another season and that certainly gives them a shot at winning. It was La Russa's will that kept the Athletics from totally falling off the face of the earth after a dreadful start in '94 as Oakland salvaged a 51-63 season.

When everybody is healthy, the Athletics still can assemble a lineup that scares people. Of course, the words Mark McGwire (.252, 9, 25 in 135 at-bats) and healthy haven't been in the same sentence often over the last two seasons. The big guy missed most of last year with heel trouble and will try to rebound after surgery.

If not, right fielder Ruben Sierra (.268, 23, 92) will have to carry too much of the load—and he hasn't responded well to that kind of pressure in the past. Second baseman Brent Gates (.283, 2, 24), an All-Star waiting to happen, also missed an extended period last season.

Rickey Henderson's skills are diminishing, but his numbers (.260, 6, 20, 22 steals) show he has something left and La Russa knows better than anybody how to get the best out of Rickey. Catcher Terry Steinbach (.285, 11, 57) remains rock-steady behind the plate and a leader in the clubhouse.

Third baseman Scott Brosius (.238, 14, 49) is about to blossom into a 20-25-home-run threat, Stan Javier (.272, 10, 44) proved he could play every day and McGwire's absence gave Geronimo Berroa (.306, 13, 65) a chance that was long overdue. Mike Bordick (.253, 2, 37) anchors the defense at shortstop.

Not long ago, pitching coach Dave Duncan was considered

Terry Steinbach's myriad skills make him huge catch.

to be a genius. But that reputation has taken it on the chin the last two seasons, a development that probably cost Duncan a chance to become a major league manager. Things don't look much better for Duncan and his staff this season.

No longer automatic closer Dennis Eckersley (5-4, 4.26 ERA, 19 saves) was unsigned at press time, along with durable if not always effective Bobby Witt (8-10, 5.04). Ron Darling (10-11, 4.50) is another year older, but he might be the most reliable starter the Athletics have if Todd Van Poppel (7-10, 6.09) can't reverse the trend that has seen him go from prep phenom to pro flop. Van Poppel does have the raw ability and he's still only 23.

The rest of the rotation likely will include free-agent Steve Ontiveros (6-4, 2.65), Steve Karsay (1-1, 2.57) and Miguel Jiminez (1-4, 7.41). Even if Eckersley is gone, there is potential for a solid bullpen with 6-8 closer-in-waiting Mark Acre (5-1, 3.41), Billy Taylor (1-3, 3.50), John Briscoe (4-2, 4.01), Mike Mohler (0-1, 7.71) and Vince Horsman (0-1, 4.91).

ATHLETIC PROFILES

MARK McGWIRE 31 6-5 250   Bats R Throws R

More Achilles troubles limited him to 47 games and 135 at-bats... That left him with total of only 219 at-bats in last two seasons... Dangerous when healthy... Hit 42 homers and drove in 104 runs in rebound 1992 season... Lost AL homer title that season when he missed final three weeks with rib-cage injury... Averaged 38 homers and 105 RBI from 1987-90 ... Would have earned $3 million in 1994... Signed five-year, $28-million deal after 1992 season... Bottomed out at .201 with 22 homers in 1991... Set major league rookie record with 49 homers in 1987... Outstanding defensive first baseman... Has spent extensive time in weight room, adding 25 pounds in recent years... Athletics drafted him 10th overall in 1984... Member of 1984 U.S. Olympic Team... Born Oct. 1, 1963, in Pomona, Cal.

Year Club	Pos.	G	AB	R	H	2B	3B	HR	RBI	SB	Avg.
1986 Oakland	3B	18	53	10	10	1	0	3	9	0	.189
1987 Oakland	1B-3B-OF	151	557	97	161	28	4	49	118	1	.289
1988 Oakland	1B-OF	155	550	87	143	22	1	32	99	0	.260
1989 Oakland	1B	143	490	74	113	17	0	33	95	1	.231
1990 Oakland	1B	156	523	87	123	16	0	39	108	2	.235
1991 Oakland	1B	154	483	62	97	22	0	22	75	2	.201
1992 Oakland	1B	139	467	87	125	22	0	42	104	0	.268
1993 Oakland	1B	27	84	16	28	6	0	9	24	0	.333
1994 Oakland	1B	47	135	26	34	3	0	9	25	0	.252
Totals		990	3342	546	834	137	5	238	657	6	.250

RUBEN SIERRA 29 6-1 210   Bats S Throws R

Got his batting average back out of embarrassing territory at .268, following .233 mark in 1993... Almost equalled his 1993 power numbers despite strike, with 23 homers and 92 RBI ... Stopped running, stealing only eight bases ... Wasn't in top 10 in any AL offensive category in sub-par 1993 season... Would have earned $4.7 million in 1994... Landed in Oakland along with Bobby Witt and Jeff Russell in deal with Texas for Jose Canseco, Aug. 31, 1992, shortly before becoming free agent... Re-signed with Athletics, who gave him five-year deal worth nearly $30 million... Outfielder left Rangers after six-plus seasons as club's all-time leader in six offensive categories...

Signed by Rangers as undrafted free agent in 1982 ... Born Oct. 6, 1965, in Rio Piedras, P.R.

Year	Club	Pos.	G	AB	R	H	2B	3B	HR	RBI	SB	Avg.
1986	Texas	OF	113	382	50	101	13	10	16	55	7	.264
1987	Texas	OF	158	643	97	169	35	4	30	109	16	.263
1988	Texas	OF	156	615	77	156	32	2	23	91	18	.254
1989	Texas	OF	162	634	101	194	35	14	29	119	8	.306
1990	Texas	OF	159	608	70	170	37	2	16	96	9	.280
1991	Texas	OF	161	661	110	203	44	5	25	116	16	.307
1992	Tex.-Oak.	OF	151	601	83	167	34	7	17	87	14	.278
1993	Oakland	OF	158	630	77	147	23	5	22	101	25	.233
1994	Oakland	OF	110	426	71	114	21	1	23	92	8	.268
	Totals		1328	5200	736	1421	274	50	201	866	121	.273

RICKEY HENDERSON 36 5-10 190 Bats R Throws L

Prime time is gone for this once-electrifying force ... Left fielder hit just .260 with only 19 extra-base hits ... All-time steals leader has total of 1,117 after he swiped only 22 in 1994, his lowest total in big leagues ... Has stolen at least 50 bases 12 times, including record 130 in 1982 ... Spectacular postseason in 1989 helped Athletics win World Series as he was ALCS MVP ... Won AL MVP in 1990, his best of many outstanding seasons ... Would have earned $4.8 million in '94, part of two-year, $8.6-million deal ... Athletics dealt him to Toronto for Steve Karsay, July 31, 1993, then re-signed him as free agent after that season ... Was fourth-round pick of Athletics in 1976 ... Signed with Yankees in 1985, then Athletics got him back 4½ seasons later for Greg Cadaret, Luis Polonia and Eric Plunk ... Born Christmas Day, 1958, in Chicago.

Year	Club	Pos.	G	AB	R	H	2B	3B	HR	RBI	SB	Avg.
1979	Oakland	OF	89	351	49	96	13	3	1	26	33	.274
1980	Oakland	OF	158	591	111	179	22	4	9	53	100	.303
1981	Oakland	OF	108	423	89	135	18	7	6	35	56	.319
1982	Oakland	OF	149	536	119	143	24	4	10	51	130	.267
1983	Oakland	OF	145	513	105	150	25	7	9	48	108	.292
1984	Oakland	OF	142	502	113	147	27	4	16	58	66	.293
1985	New York (AL)	OF	143	547	146	172	28	5	24	72	80	.314
1986	New York (AL)	OF	153	608	130	160	31	5	28	74	87	.263
1987	New York (AL)	OF	95	358	78	104	17	3	17	37	41	.291
1988	New York (AL)	OF	140	554	118	169	30	2	6	50	93	.305
1989	NY (AL)-Oak.	OF	150	541	113	148	26	3	12	57	77	.274
1990	Oakland	OF	136	489	119	159	33	3	28	61	65	.325
1991	Oakland	OF	134	470	105	126	17	1	18	57	58	.268
1992	Oakland	OF	117	396	77	112	18	3	15	46	48	.283
1993	Oak.-Tor.	OF	134	481	114	139	22	2	21	59	53	.289
1994	Oakland	OF	87	296	66	77	13	0	6	20	22	.260
	Totals		2080	7656	1652	2216	364	56	226	804	1117	.289

GERONIMO BERROA 30 6-0 195   Bats R Throws R

AL pitchers discovered in '94 what Triple-A pitchers have known for years—this guy can hit... Finally got an extended chance in majors and he proved he belonged... Got off to great start and finished with team-leading .306 batting average, 65 RBI and .485 slugging percentage... Hit .233 in 189 at-bats during four previous big league tries... Bounced around minors, hitting at every stop... Had 36 homers and 108 RBI for Knoxville (AA) in 1987... Batted .322, .328 and .327 at three different Triple-A stops from 1991-93... His fielding is a liability ... Played 42 games in outfield, nine at first and 45 as Athletics' designated hitter in '94... Signed by Blue Jays as undrafted free agent in 1984... Selected by Braves in Rule V draft prior to 1989 season... Athletics signed him prior to '94 season, after he was released by Marlins... Salary would have been $109,000 in 1994 ... Born March 18, 1965, in Santo Domingo, D.R.

Year	Club	Pos.	G	AB	R	H	2B	3B	HR	RBI	SB	Avg.
1989	Atlanta	OF	81	136	7	36	4	0	2	9	0	.265
1990	Atlanta	OF	7	4	0	0	0	0	0	0	0	.000
1992	Cincinnati	OF	13	15	2	4	1	0	0	0	0	.267
1993	Florida	OF	14	34	3	4	1	0	0	0	0	.118
1994	Oakland	OF-1B-DH	96	340	55	104	18	2	13	65	7	.306
	Totals		211	529	67	148	24	2	15	74	7	.280

TERRY STEINBACH 33 6-1 200   Bats R Throws R

Another solid season for this dependable veteran and team leader... Hit .285 for second year in a row... Power numbers (11 homers, 57 RBI) were better despite playing in one fewer game than in 1993, when his season ended in mid-August due to broken right wrist ... Player representative and clubhouse leader ... Type of player who will make a good manager some day... Hit .343 against left-handers and .315 with runners in scoring position... Catcher threw out league-leading 44 percent of would-be base-stealers... Has been above 40 percent each of last two seasons... Would have earned $2.8 million in 1994, on second year of four-year, $14-million deal... Oak-

OAKLAND ATHLETICS • 179

land's ninth-round pick in 1983 draft, out of University of Minnesota... Born March 2, 1962, in New Ulm, Minn.

Year	Club	Pos.	G	AB	R	H	2B	3B	HR	RBI	SB	Avg.
1986	Oakland	C	6	15	3	5	0	0	2	4	0	.333
1987	Oakland	C-3B-1B	122	391	66	111	16	3	16	56	1	.284
1988	Oakland	C-3B-1B-OF	104	351	42	93	19	1	9	51	3	.265
1989	Oakland	C-OF-1B-3B	130	454	37	124	13	1	7	42	1	.273
1990	Oakland	C-1B	114	379	32	95	15	2	9	57	0	.251
1991	Oakland	C-1B	129	456	50	125	31	1	6	67	2	.274
1992	Oakland	C-1B	128	438	48	122	20	1	12	53	2	.279
1993	Oakland	C-1B	104	389	47	111	19	1	10	43	3	.285
1994	Oakland	C-1B	103	369	51	105	21	2	11	57	2	.285
	Totals		940	3242	376	891	154	12	82	430	14	.275

BRENT GATES 25 6-1 180   Bats S Throws R

Second baseman played only 64 games due to injuries... When healthy, he proved his strong rookie showing in 1993 was only the beginning of a standout career... Hit .344 against lefties... Was recalled May 5, 1993, and led Athletics in hits, tied for first in batting average and was second in runs... Started 1993 season with Huntsville (AA) and finished it as solid AL Rookie of the Year candidate... His .290 average in 1993 is club record for switch-hitter... Would have earned $190,000 in 1994... Picked by Athletics as 26th overall choice in 1991 draft... Broke Oakland teammate Terry Steinbach's career batting average record at University of Minnesota... Named Big Ten Player of the Year in 1991... Born March 14, 1970, in Grand Rapids, Mich.

Year	Club	Pos.	G	AB	R	H	2B	3B	HR	RBI	SB	Avg.
1993	Oakland	2B	139	535	64	155	29	2	7	69	7	.290
1994	Oakland	2B-1B	64	233	29	66	11	1	2	24	3	.283
	Totals		203	768	93	221	40	3	9	93	10	.288

MIKE BORDICK 29 5-11 175   Bats R Throws R

Has settled in as solid defensive shortstop... Apparently was over his head when he hit .300 as a rookie in 1992... Has averaged .249 and .253 in last two seasons... Committed only 13 errors in 112 games at short and one error at second... Durable middle infielder led club in games (114) and at-bats (391)... Salary would have been $1,050,000 in 1994... Never hit higher than .270 in the minors before batting .300 in first full major league season... Was recalled in June 1991, when Walt

Weiss was injured, and started 81 of final 85 games... Athletics traded Weiss following 1992 season to open job for him... Signed by Oakland as undrafted free agent in July 1986, after career at University of Maine... Appeared in two College World Series ... Born July 21, 1965, in Marquette, Mich.

Year	Club	Pos.	G	AB	R	H	2B	3B	HR	RBI	SB	Avg.
1990	Oakland	3B-SS-2B	25	14	0	1	0	0	0	0	0	.071
1991	Oakland	SS-2B-3B	90	235	21	56	5	1	0	21	3	.238
1992	Oakland	2B-SS	154	504	62	151	19	4	3	48	12	.300
1993	Oakland	SS-2B	159	546	60	136	21	2	3	48	10	.249
1994	Oakland	SS-2B	114	391	38	99	18	4	2	37	7	.253
	Totals		542	1690	181	443	63	11	8	154	32	.262

TROY NEEL 29 6-4 215   Bats L Throws R

Left-handed hitter with power... Best years yet to come... Stint on the disabled list cost him 30 games and cut into power numbers... Designated hitter still hit 15 homers and drove in 48 runs in 278 at-bats in 1994... Batted .350 against lefties and .301 at Oakland Coliseum ... Made team out of spring training in 1993, but was sent back to minors... Returned June 17 and for the rest of the season he hit .326 with 15 homers and 50 RBI in 310 at-bats... Would have earned $225,000 in 1994 ... Won Pacific Coast League batting championship in 1992, when he batted .351 for Tacoma (AAA)... Oakland got him from Cleveland for infielder Larry Arndt prior to 1991 season... Earned football scholarship as linebacker to Texas A&M... Born Sept. 14, 1965, in Freeport, Tex.

Year	Club	Pos.	G	AB	R	H	2B	3B	HR	RBI	SB	Avg.
1992	Oakland	OF-1B	24	53	8	14	3	0	3	9	0	.264
1993	Oakland	1B	123	427	59	124	21	0	19	63	3	.290
1994	Oakland	1B	83	278	43	74	13	0	15	48	2	.266
	Totals		230	758	110	212	37	0	37	120	5	.280

DENNIS ECKERSLEY 40 6-2 195   Bats R Throws R

Star on the decline, but he is still a formidable closer... Converted 19 of 25 save opportunities... Allowed more hits (49) than innings pitched (44⅓)... ERA was above 4.00 (4.26) for second consecutive season... Was subject of trade rumors late last season... Five-year run from 1988-92 was greatest in history by a reliever... Won AL MVP and Cy Young Awards in 1992, when he saved 51 of 54 games... Only four

OAKLAND ATHLETICS • 181

relievers have won both awards in same year... Didn't blow a save in 1992 until Aug. 9... Since 1988, he has saved 275 of 316... Save total of 294 gives him AL record... Also has pitched a no-hitter, has been a 20-game winner, has posted 188 victories and has battled alcohol addiction during certain Hall of Fame career... Would have earned $3.75 million in '94... Stolen by Athletics from Cubs with Dan Rohn for Dave Wilder, Brian Guinn and Mark Leonette in deal prior to 1987 season... Born Oct. 3, 1954, in Oakland... **Free agent at press time.**

Year	Club	G	IP	W	L	Pct.	SO	BB	H	ERA
1975	Cleveland	34	187	13	7	.650	152	90	147	2.60
1976	Cleveland	36	199	13	12	.520	200	75	155	3.44
1977	Cleveland	33	247	14	13	.519	191	54	214	3.53
1978	Boston	35	268	20	8	.714	162	71	258	2.99
1979	Boston	33	247	17	10	.630	150	59	234	2.99
1980	Boston	30	198	12	14	.462	121	44	188	4.27
1981	Boston	23	154	9	8	.529	79	35	160	4.27
1982	Boston	33	224⅓	13	13	.500	127	43	228	3.73
1983	Boston	28	176⅓	9	13	.409	77	39	223	5.61
1984	Boston	9	64⅔	4	4	.500	33	13	71	5.01
1984	Chicago (NL)	24	160⅓	10	8	.556	81	36	152	3.03
1985	Chicago (NL)	25	169⅓	11	7	.611	117	19	145	3.08
1986	Chicago (NL)	33	201	6	11	.353	137	43	226	4.57
1987	Oakland	54	115⅔	6	8	.429	113	17	99	3.03
1988	Oakland	60	72⅔	4	2	.667	70	11	52	2.35
1989	Oakland	51	57⅔	4	0	1.000	55	3	32	1.56
1990	Oakland	63	73⅓	4	2	.667	73	4	41	0.61
1991	Oakland	67	76	5	4	.556	87	9	60	2.96
1992	Oakland	69	80	7	1	.875	93	11	62	1.91
1993	Oakland	64	67	2	4	.333	80	13	67	4.16
1994	Oakland	45	44⅓	5	4	.556	47	13	49	4.26
	Totals	849	3082⅔	188	153	.551	2245	705	2863	3.46

RON DARLING 34 6-3 200   Bats R Throws R

Led staff in wins, starts (25) and innings (160), but had a 10-11 record and 4.50 ERA... Getting by on guile these days... Rebounded to 15-10 with 3.66 ERA in 1992 after winning total of only 15 games in previous two seasons... Was 99-70 in seven-plus seasons with Mets, including five consecutive winning records from 1984-88... Would have earned $2.25 million in 1994... Another Athletics' steal... They sent Russ Cormier and Matt Grott to Expos for him, July 31, 1991... Rangers drafted him ninth overall in 1981, then dealt him to Mets in ill-fated trade for Lee Mazzilli... Yale product pitched in one of college baseball's greatest games against Frank Viola. He threw

11 no-hit innings, only to lose, 1-0, in 12 innings...Born Aug. 19, 1960, in Honolulu.

Year	Club	G	IP	W	L	Pct.	SO	BB	H	ERA
1983	New York (NL)	5	35⅓	1	3	.250	23	17	31	2.80
1984	New York (NL)	33	205⅔	12	9	.571	136	104	179	3.81
1985	New York (NL)	36	248	16	6	.727	167	114	214	2.90
1986	New York (NL)	34	237	15	6	.714	184	81	203	2.81
1987	New York (NL)	32	207⅔	12	8	.600	167	96	183	4.29
1988	New York (NL)	34	240⅔	17	9	.654	161	60	218	3.25
1989	New York (NL)	33	217⅓	14	14	.500	153	70	214	3.52
1990	New York (NL)	33	126	7	9	.438	99	44	135	4.50
1991	NY (NL)-Mont.	20	119⅓	5	8	.385	69	33	121	4.37
1991	Oakland	12	75	3	7	.300	60	38	64	4.08
1992	Oakland	33	206⅓	15	10	.600	99	72	198	3.66
1993	Oakland	31	178	5	9	.357	95	72	198	5.16
1994	Oakland	25	160	10	11	.476	108	59	162	4.50
	Totals	361	2256⅓	132	109	.548	1521	860	2120	3.77

BOBBY WITT 30 6-2 205   Bats R Throws R

Never has reached potential, but he is the best part of Athletics' rotation in transition... Pitched one-hitter and three consecutive shutouts during 1994 stretch, allowing only nine hits in 27 innings... But, otherwise, he wound up with disappointing 8-10 season... His ERA climbed back above 5.00 mark (5.04) for first time in three years... Walked 70 in 135⅔ innings... Posted a winning record (14-13) in 1993 on team that finished 26 games below .500... Would have earned $3,250,000 in 1994, when Athletics exercised option on him... Went to Oakland with Ruben Sierra and Jeff Russell from Texas for Jose Canseco in Aug. 31, 1992 blockbuster... Best year was 1990, when he won 12 in a row and finished 17-10... Rangers' first pick and third overall choice in 1984 draft... Member of 1984 U.S. Olympic Team... Born May 11, 1964, in Arlington, Va. ... **Free agent at press time.**

Year	Club	G	IP	W	L	Pct.	SO	BB	H	ERA
1986	Texas	31	157⅔	11	9	.550	174	143	130	5.48
1987	Texas	26	143	8	10	.444	160	140	114	4.91
1988	Texas	22	174⅓	8	10	.444	148	101	134	3.92
1989	Texas	31	194⅓	12	13	.480	166	114	182	5.14
1990	Texas	33	222	17	10	.630	221	110	197	3.36
1991	Texas	17	88⅔	3	7	.300	82	74	84	6.09
1992	Texas-Oak.	31	193	10	14	.417	125	114	183	4.29
1993	Oakland	35	220	14	13	.519	131	91	226	4.21
1994	Oakland	24	135⅔	8	10	.444	111	70	151	5.04
	Totals	250	1528⅔	91	96	.487	1318	957	1401	4.56

TODD VAN POPPEL 23 6-5 205　　　Bats R Throws R

Still struggling to establish himself... Should have spent more time in minors, but his agent's insistence on a major league contract when he first signed has left Athletics in Catch-22. They know he needs more seasoning, but can't send him down without having to put him on waivers, where he would be claimed... Walked more batters (89) than he struck out (83) and finished with 6.09 ERA... Still has two above-average major league pitches... Shoulder trouble forced him to shut down in '92, except for nine starts with Tacoma (AAA)... Made major league debut Sept. 11, 1991, only 15 months after graduating from high school... Struck out six White Sox hitters in 4⅔ innings, but was touched for five runs in fifth inning... Received then-record, $1.2-million deal after Athletics picked him No. 14 overall in 1990 draft and convinced him to turn his back on scholarship to University of Texas... Born Dec. 9, 1971, in Hinsdale, Ill.

Year	Club	G	IP	W	L	Pct.	SO	BB	H	ERA
1991	Oakland	1	4⅔	0	0	.000	6	2	7	9.64
1993	Oakland	16	84	6	6	.500	47	62	76	5.04
1994	Oakland	23	116⅔	7	10	.412	83	89	108	6.09
	Totals	40	205⅓	13	16	.448	136	153	191	5.74

TOP PROSPECTS

MARK ACRE 26 6-8 240　　　Bats R Throws R
This big right-hander is heir apparent to Dennis Eckersley in closer role... Went 5-1, 3.41 in 34 games with Athletics in 1994... Was 1-1 with 1.88 ERA in 29 innings for Tacoma (AAA)... Switched to relief in 1993, when he saved 30 games for Madison (A) and Huntsville (AA)... Played basketball for New Mexico State... Signed by Oakland as undrafted free agent in August 1991... Born Sept. 16, 1968, in Concord, Cal.

ERNIE YOUNG 25 6-1 190　　　Bats R Throws R
Hit .347 with 14 homers and 55 RBI for Huntsville (AA) to lead Southern League, but his stints in Oakland and Tacoma (AAA) left him without enough at-bats to win batting title... Boasts strong arm and is good enough to be a major league center fielder... Hit .284 with six homers and 16 RBI for Tacoma and .067 in 30 at-bats with Athletics... Hit 23 homers for Modesto (A) in

1993... Athletics' 10th-round pick in 1990 draft... Born July 8, 1969, in Chicago.

CRAIG PAQUETTE 26 6-0 190   Bats R Throws R
Hit .286 with 17 homers in 245 at-bats for Tacoma (AAA) and .143 in 49 at-bats with Oakland... Third baseman hit 12 homers with Athletics in 1993, but batted just .219... Will resurface in big leagues soon... Athletics' eighth-round choice in 1989 draft ... Born March 28, 1969, in Long Beach, Cal.

JOHN WASDIN 22 6-2 190   Bats R Throws R
May have been best pitcher in Southern League by end of last season... Finished 12-3 with 3.43 ERA and pitched well in playoffs as Huntsville (AA) won league title... Fastball and breaking pitch are already major league quality... Athletics' first-round pick in 1993 and 25th choice overall, out of Florida State University... Born Aug. 5, 1972, in Fort Belvoir, Va.

MANAGER TONY La RUSSA:
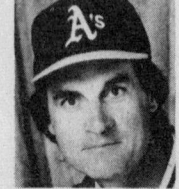
Subject of offseason managerial rumors in Boston, Baltimore and nearly everywhere else that a change was made, but he chose to remain in Oakland and signed three-year extension... Three-time AL Manager of the Year has 1,253-1,106 record, as losses continue to mount with this aging, retooling club ... Kept bottom from falling out after horrid start and kept team in sad AL West race... Victory total is third among active managers, behind Sparky Anderson and Tommy Lasorda... Winning percentage of .531 is fifth among active managers... During seven-plus seasons in Oakland, his record is 731-596... Hired by Athletics July 1, 1986, only two weeks after being dismissed as manager by White Sox owner Jerry Reinsdorf, who calls that decision his biggest mistake... Playing career went nowhere... Hit .199 with no homers and seven RBI in 176 major league at-bats... Was an Athletics bonus baby in 1962, when he was drafted out of high school ... One of five lawyer-managers in history—and other four are in the Hall of Fame... Passed bar exam in 1979, after graduating from Florida State University law school... Played youth baseball with Mariners manager Lou Piniella... Born Oct. 4, 1944, in Tampa.

Ron looks simply Darling in '55 Oaks uniform replica.

ALL-TIME A's SEASON RECORDS

BATTING: Napoleon Lajoie, .422, 1901
HRs: Jimmie Foxx, 58, 1932
RBI: Jimmie Foxx, 169, 1932
STEALS: Rickey Henderson, 130, 1982
WINS: John Coombs, 31, 1910
      Lefty Grove, 31, 1931
STRIKEOUTS: Rube Waddell, 349, 1904

SEATTLE MARINERS

TEAM DIRECTORY: Chairman: John Ellis; Pres.: Chuck Armstrong; VP-Baseball Oper.: Woody Woodward; VP-Scouting and Player Dev.: Roger Jongewaard; Dir. Baseball Adm.: Lee Pelekoudas; Dir. Player Dev.: Jim Beattie; Dir. Pub. Rel.: David Aust; Trav. Sec.: Craig Detwiler; Mgr.: Lou Piniella; Coaches: Bobby Cuellar, Lee Elia, John McLaren, Sam Mejias, Sam Perlozzo, Matt Sinatro. Home: Kingdome (59,166). Field distances: 331, l.f. line; 389, l.c.; 405, c.f.; 380, r.c.; 312, r.f. line. Spring training: Peoria, Ariz.

SCOUTING REPORT

Adrift at sea. That's where the Mariners find themselves once again after a 49-63 voyage in '94. Despite boasting two of the game's biggest stars in Ken Griffey Jr. and Randy Johnson, they couldn't even contend in the miserable AL West last season, a division many thought they would win.

Theirs is a dilemma typical of many small-market franchises. With a handful of stars grabbing a large share of the payroll, there isn't enough cash to spread around to fill out the roster with quality players. Last year, finances forced them to part with shortstop Omar Vizquel and their defense suffered as a result. Last winter, they faced a similarly tough decision about how high to go to retain free-agent right fielder Jay Buhner, and they resolved it by re-signing him to a three-year, $15.5-million contract.

What manager Lou Piniella has to hope for is a renaissance by his pitching staff, which was so dreadful in '94 that pitching coach Sammy Ellis was fired. Johnson (13-6, 3.19, 204 Ks) was his usual overpowering self, but injuries and ineffectiveness struck Greg Hibbard (1-5, 6.69), Chris Bosio (4-10, 4.32) and Dave Fleming (7-11, 6.46).

So much for a rotation many thought could carry the Mariners to the division title. But all three are young enough to rebound and it is reasonable to expect young right-hander Roger Salkeld (2-5, 7.17) to improve as he overcomes arm troubles.

Few bullpens can boast three hard-throwing right-handers such as closer Bobby Ayala (4-3, 2.86, 18 saves), Bill Risley (9-6, 3.44) and Jeff Nelson (0-0, 2.76).

But Piniella searched in vain to find a dependable left-hander from among John Cummings (2-4, 5.63), Jim Converse (0-5, 8.69) and Kevin King (0-2, 7.04).

Hitters get jelly-kneed at sight of Randy Johnson.

Griffey (.323, 40, 90) just keeps improving and arguably is the game's best player. But you knew that already. What of the supporting cast? Buhner (.279, 21, 68) is vital as protection behind Griffey. First baseman Tino Martinez (.261, 20, 61) has become more of a consistent power threat, first baseman-designated hitter Reggie Jefferson (.327, 8, 32) is a rare switch-hitter in the middle of the lineup and third baseman Edgar Martinez (.285, 13, 51) can hit when he's healthy.

But there are weaknesses behind the plate and at second base, left fielder Eric Anthony (.237, 10, 30) was a major disappointment (he was placed on waivers in December) and there is no consistent threat in the leadoff spot. Shortstop Felix Fermin (.317), who was a free agent before signing a two-year contract in November, had a career offensive year as Vizquel's replacement. Regardless, he faces strong opposition from phenom Alex Rodriguez, who made his major league debut just 13 months after his high school graduation.

The trouble is the Mariners don't have enough Rodriguez-caliber players in their system. And unless salary structures are dramatically reduced around the game, they will have trouble putting together a roster that can post the third winning record in franchise history.

MARINER PROFILES

KEN GRIFFEY Jr. 25 6-3 205   Bats L Throws L

As great as he is, he keeps getting better... May have wrestled top player in the game designation away from Barry Bonds... Led AL in home runs (40)... Was third in runs (94), total bases (292), extra-base hits (68) and slugging percentage (.674), eighth in batting average (.323) and ninth in RBI (90)... Also had 12 assists as one of game's best defensive center fielders... Has hit above .300 five consecutive seasons... Already has played in five All-Star Games... A bargain at the $5 million he would've earned in 1994, on four-year, $24-million deal he signed before 1993 season... Tied Don Mattingly and Dale Long for major league record by hitting home runs in eight consecutive games, July 20-28, 1993... Hit first ball off the warehouse at Oriole Park during homer hitting contest... Mariners wisely made him first overall pick in 1987 draft... Was part of first father-son active teammate combo with Ken Sr.... Born Nov. 21, 1969, in Donora, Pa.... Won fifth Gold Glove in '94.

Year	Club	Pos.	G	AB	R	H	2B	3B	HR	RBI	SB	Avg.
1989	Seattle	OF	127	455	61	120	23	0	16	61	16	.264
1990	Seattle	OF	155	597	91	179	28	7	22	80	16	.300
1991	Seattle	OF	154	548	76	179	42	1	22	100	18	.327
1992	Seattle	OF	142	565	83	174	39	4	27	103	10	.308
1993	Seattle	OF-1B	156	582	113	180	38	3	45	109	17	.309
1994	Seattle	OF	111	433	94	140	24	4	40	90	11	.323
	Totals		845	3180	518	972	194	19	172	543	88	.306

TINO MARTINEZ 27 6-2 210   Bats L Throws R

Continues to improve as a power source... Hit career-high 20 homers in 329 at-bats... Fell only five short of RBI high with 61... Has hit .257, .265 and .261 in last three years for .261 average... Hit lefties better than righties, ending his platoon-player status... Had 1993 season cut short Aug. 13, because of knee surgery... Supplanted Pete O'Brien as regular first baseman that season... Would have earned $500,000 in 1994... Mariners' first pick and 14th player taken in 1988 draft... Member of 1988 U.S. Olympic Team... Three-time Div. II All-American at University of Tampa... Born Dec. 7, 1967, in

Tampa, he is product of same high school that produced Fred McGriff.

Year	Club	Pos.	G	AB	R	H	2B	3B	HR	RBI	SB	Avg.
1990	Seattle	1B	24	68	4	15	4	0	0	5	0	.221
1991	Seattle	1B	36	112	11	23	2	0	4	9	0	.205
1992	Seattle	1B	136	460	53	118	19	2	16	66	2	.257
1993	Seattle	1B	109	408	48	108	25	1	17	60	0	.265
1994	Seattle	1B	97	329	42	86	21	0	20	61	1	.261
	Totals		402	1377	158	350	71	3	57	201	3	.254

EDGAR MARTINEZ 32 5-11 200   Bats R Throws R

Found a middle ground after up-and-down 1992 and 1993 seasons... After .285 season in 1994, his career batting average is .303... Total of 37 of his 93 hits went for extra bases... Hit .329 against lefties and .319 in the Kingdome... Made nine errors in 64 games at third base, a high total considering his lack of range ... Appeared in 23 games as designated hitter ... Batting average fell from league-leading .343 in 1992 to .237 in only 135 at-bats in 1993, the biggest dip ever by a defending batting champion... Nagged by hamstring trouble most of that season... Hit above .300 from 1990-92... Set career highs in home runs, RBI and runs in 1992... Would have earned $3,316,667 in 1994... Signed by Mariners as undrafted free agent in December 1982... Spent six seasons in minors before reaching majors to stay... Born Jan. 2, 1963, in New York.

Year	Club	Pos.	G	AB	R	H	2B	3B	HR	RBI	SB	Avg.
1987	Seattle	3B	13	43	6	16	5	2	0	5	0	.372
1988	Seattle	3B	14	32	0	9	4	0	0	5	0	.281
1989	Seattle	3B	65	171	20	41	5	0	2	20	2	.240
1990	Seattle	3B	144	487	71	147	27	2	11	49	1	.302
1991	Seattle	3B	150	544	98	167	35	1	14	52	0	.307
1992	Seattle	3B-1B	135	528	100	181	46	3	18	73	14	.343
1993	Seattle	3B	42	135	20	32	7	0	4	13	0	.237
1994	Seattle	3B	89	326	47	93	23	1	13	51	6	.285
	Totals		652	2266	362	686	142	9	62	268	23	.303

JAY BUHNER 30 6-3 205   Bats R Throws R

Has averaged 25 homers and 81 RBI last four seasons... Had 21 homers and 68 RBI when strike hit in 1994... Also posted career-high batting average (.279)... Hits them as far as anybody in the game... Outstanding right fielder possesses arguably the league's best throwing arm in the outfield... Had 11 assists, tying for fourth in AL, and everybody knows

Griffey known as Junior is five-time All-Star at 25.

not to run on him... For the first time as a major leaguer, he walked more often than he struck out (66-63)... Dramatically cut strikeout total, which generally has exceeded 100... Hit .336 against left-handers... Salary would have been $4.35 million in 1994... Mariners got him and two other minor leaguers from Yankees for Ken Phelps, July 21, 1988... Pirates' fourth-round pick in January 1984 draft... Traded to Yankees 11 months later in Steve Kemp deal... Born Aug. 13, 1964, in Louisville, Ky.

Year	Club	Pos.	G	AB	R	H	2B	3B	HR	RBI	SB	Avg.
1987	New York (AL)	OF	7	22	0	5	2	0	0	1	0	.227
1988	NY (AL)-Sea...	OF	85	261	36	56	13	1	13	38	1	.215
1989	Seattle.......	OF	58	204	27	56	15	1	9	33	1	.275
1990	Seattle.......	OF	51	163	16	45	12	0	7	33	2	.276
1991	Seattle.......	OF	137	406	64	99	14	4	27	77	0	.244
1992	Seattle.......	OF	152	543	69	132	16	3	25	79	0	.243
1993	Seattle.......	OF	158	563	91	153	28	3	27	98	2	.272
1994	Seattle.......	OF	101	358	74	100	23	4	21	68	0	.279
	Totals.......		749	2520	377	646	123	16	129	427	6	.256

FELIX FERMIN 31 5-11 170   Bats R Throws R

Career .256 hitter entering '94 went 61 points better, posting .317 batting average... You can't walk him or strike him out, either... Free swinger drew only 11 walks and struck out only 22 times in 379 at-bats... Expert bunter and handler of bat... Can do the little things, such as moving over runners... Shares major league record for sacrifices in game with four, Aug. 22, 1989... Led AL in sacrifice hits (32) that season... Very steady shortstop... Makes the play on nearly everything he reaches... Committed light errors in 77 games at short and two in 25 games at second last season... Would have earned $1,050,000 in 1994... Signed as undrafted free agent by Pirates in June 1983... Traded to Indians in Jay Bell deal prior to 1989 season... Born Oct. 9, 1963, in Mao Valverde, D.R.... Acquired by Mariners from Indians with Reggie Jefferson for Omar Vizquel prior to last season... Was free agent before signing two-year contract in November.

Year	Club	Pos.	G	AB	R	H	2B	3B	HR	RBI	SB	Avg.
1987	Pittsburgh	SS	23	68	6	17	0	0	0	4	0	.250
1988	Pittsburgh	SS	43	87	9	24	0	2	0	2	3	.276
1989	Cleveland	SS–2B	156	484	50	115	9	1	0	21	6	.238
1990	Cleveland	SS–2B	148	414	47	106	13	2	1	40	3	.256
1991	Cleveland	SS	129	424	30	111	13	2	0	31	5	.262
1992	Cleveland	INF	79	215	27	58	7	2	0	13	0	.270
1993	Cleveland	SS	140	480	48	126	16	2	2	45	4	.263
1994	Seattle	SS-SB	101	379	52	120	21	0	1	35	4	.317
	Totals		819	2551	269	677	79	11	4	191	25	.265

RANDY JOHNSON 31 6-10 225   Bats R Throws L

There is no more overpowering pitcher around when "Big Unit" is on... Led AL in strikeouts (204), complete games (9) and shutouts (4)... Also ranked fifth in ERA (3.19)... Allowed only 132 hits in 172 innings... Opponents hit just .216 against him... Won 19 and struck out 308 in 1993, his breakthrough season... Nolan Ryan annointed him the power pitcher of the 1990s and you won't get many arguments here... Rarely faces a left-handed hitter... Pitched no-hitter against Detroit, June 2, 1990... Tallest player in major league history... Went to USC on basketball scholarship... Listens to rock music and plays drums as part of his pre-start ritual... Mariners got him from Montreal with Brian Holman and Gene Harris for Mark Langston, May 25, 1989... Expos' second-round pick in 1985 draft... Would have earned $3,275,000 in '94... Born Sept. 10, 1963, in Walnut Creek, Cal.

Year	Club	G	IP	W	L	Pct.	SO	BB	H	ERA
1988	Montreal	4	26	3	0	1.000	25	7	23	2.42
1989	Montreal	7	29⅔	0	4	.000	26	26	29	6.67
1989	Seattle	22	131	7	9	.438	104	70	118	4.40
1990	Seattle	33	219⅔	14	11	.560	194	120	174	3.65
1991	Seattle	33	201⅓	13	10	.565	228	152	151	3.98
1992	Seattle	31	210⅓	12	14	.462	241	144	154	3.77
1993	Seattle	35	255⅓	19	8	.704	308	99	185	3.24
1994	Seattle	23	172	13	6	.684	204	72	132	3.19
	Totals	188	1245⅓	81	62	.566	1330	690	966	3.70

DAVE FLEMING 25 6-3 200   Bats L Throws L

Career is heading in wrong direction... Victory total has gone from 17 to 12 to 7 over last three seasons... Still is 37-26 in big league career... ERA has risen from 3.39 to 4.36 to 6.46... Lasted just more than five innings per start... Got plenty of run support last season, but still finished 7-11... Allowed 152 hits in 117 innings and walked 65... Right-handers hit .317 against him... Control pitcher who must be perfect with 85-mph fastball... Went 17-10 for 1992 team that finished 34 games below .500... Was 11-3 at All-Star break that season... Mariners' third-round pick in 1990 draft... Salary would have been $505,000 in '94... Saved Georgia's College World Series-clinching victory in 1990... Born Nov. 7, 1969, in Queens, N.Y.

Year	Club	G	IP	W	L	Pct.	SO	BB	H	ERA
1991	Seattle	9	17⅔	1	0	1.000	11	3	19	6.62
1992	Seattle	33	228⅓	17	10	.630	112	60	225	3.39
1993	Seattle	26	167⅓	12	5	.706	75	67	189	4.36
1994	Seattle	23	117	7	11	.389	65	65	152	6.46
	Totals	91	530⅓	37	26	.587	263	195	585	4.48

CHRIS BOSIO 32 6-3 235   Bats R Throws R

Injuries and lack of support led to tough season... Dropped to 4-10 in 1994 after going 39-25 from 1991-93... Received average of only 4.37 runs per game worth of backing from Mariners' offense... But his 4.32 ERA was his highest in seven seasons... Would be wise to watch his ballooning weight as he has become too injury-prone... Spent time on disabled list for second year in a row... Takes the ball whenever he can... Up-and-down 1993 season was highlighted by no-hitter, April 22 against Boston... One start later, he dislocated collarbone in collision at first base and missed a month... Underwent two knee operations in 1990... Salary would have been $4 million in 1994... Brewers' second-round pick in January 1982 draft... Born April 3, 1963, in Carmichael, Cal.

Year	Club	G	IP	W	L	Pct.	SO	BB	H	ERA
1986	Milwaukee	10	34⅔	0	4	.000	29	13	41	7.01
1987	Milwaukee	46	170	11	8	.579	150	50	187	5.24
1988	Milwaukee	38	182	7	15	.318	84	38	190	3.36
1989	Milwaukee	33	234⅔	15	10	.600	173	48	225	2.95
1990	Milwaukee	20	132⅔	4	9	.308	76	38	131	4.00
1991	Milwaukee	32	204⅔	14	10	.583	117	58	187	3.25
1992	Milwaukee	33	231⅓	16	6	.727	120	44	223	3.62
1993	Seattle	29	164⅓	9	9	.500	119	59	138	3.45
1994	Seattle	19	125	4	10	.286	67	40	137	4.32
	Totals	260	1479⅓	80	81	.497	935	388	1459	3.77

BOBBY AYALA 25 6-3 200   Bats R Throws R

Young, hard-throwing right-hander is about to emerge as one of AL's better closers... Converted 18 saves in 24 opportunities, but those weren't the best of his numbers... Had 2.86 ERA, allowed only 42 hits in 56⅔ innings and struck out 76... Allowed only two home runs... Opponents hit only .203, with right-handers at .183... Manager Lou Piniella engineered deal with Reds that brought him and catcher Dan Wilson for Erik Hanson and Bret Boone prior to last season... Would have earned $180,000 in 1994... Bounced between rotation and bullpen in Cincinnati, finishing 7-10 with 5.60 ERA in 1993... Saved three games that season... Signed by Reds as undrafted free agent in June 1988... Born July 8, 1969, in Ventura, Cal.

Year	Club	G	IP	W	L	Pct.	SO	BB	H	ERA
1992	Cincinnati	5	29	2	1	.667	23	13	33	4.34
1993	Cincinnati	43	98	7	10	.412	65	45	106	5.60
1994	Seattle	46	56⅔	4	3	.571	76	26	42	2.86
	Totals	94	183⅔	13	14	.481	164	84	181	4.56

GREG HIBBARD 30 6-0 185   Bats L Throws L

Will try to bounce back from lost 1994 season, when he went 1-5 with astronomical 6.69 ERA in 15 games before going on the disabled list... Allowed 115 hits in 80⅔ innings... Has pitched only one complete game since 1991... Crossed town from Comiskey Park to Wrigley Field in 1993 and won career-high 15 games... Won last five decisions that season... Issued two or fewer walks in 22 starts that year... Mariners spent $6.75 million to sign him to three-year deal as free agent after 1993 season... Would have earned $1,250,000 in 1994... Selected by Marlins from White Sox in expansion draft, then traded on same day to Cubs for Alex Arias and Gary Scott... Royals' 16th-round pick in 1986 draft... Born Sept. 13, 1964, in New Orleans.

Year	Club	G	IP	W	L	Pct.	SO	BB	H	ERA
1989	Chicago (AL)	23	137⅓	6	7	.462	55	41	142	3.21
1990	Chicago (AL)	33	211	14	9	.609	92	55	202	3.16
1991	Chicago (AL)	32	194	11	11	.500	71	57	196	4.31
1992	Chicago (AL)	31	176	10	7	.588	69	57	187	4.40
1993	Chicago (NL)	31	191	15	11	.577	82	47	209	3.96
1994	Seattle	15	80⅔	1	5	.167	39	31	115	6.69
	Totals	165	990	57	50	.533	408	288	1051	4.05

TOP PROSPECTS

ALEX RODRIGUEZ 19 6-3 190   Bats R Throws R
There is no better prospect in baseball than this shortstop phenom ... Made his major league debut at age 18 last July, in first pro season and only 13 months after his high school graduation... Has size, power and defensive ability... Can't miss... Hit .204 in 54 at-bats for Mariners before being sent back... Could be Mariners' starting shortstop this season... First overall pick in 1993 draft... Born July 27, 1975, in New York... Hit .319 with 14 homers and 55 RBI for Appleton (A), .288 with one homer and eight RBI for Jacksonville (AA) and .311 with six homers and 21 RBI for Calgary (AAA) in 1994.

MARC NEWFIELD 22 6-4 205   Bats R Throws R
Legitimate power prospect lit up Pacific Coast League in 1994 ... Outfielder batted .349 with 19 homers and 83 RBI for Calgary (AAA)... Hit .227 in 66 at-bats for Mariners in 1993 and .184 in 38 at-bats for them last year... Missed much of 1992 season with foot injury that required surgery... Mariners made him sixth pick overall in 1990 draft... Born Oct. 19, 1972, in Sacramento, Cal.

RON VILLONE 25 6-3 235   Bats L Throws L
A rare commodity: a hard-throwing left-hander... Struck out 94 in 79 innings for Jacksonville (AA)... Was 6-7 with 3.86 ERA ... Played with Team USA in 1992 Olympics... Baseball and football star at University of Massachusetts... Mariners' first-

round pick and 14th overall choice in 1992 draft... Born Jan. 16, 1970, in Englewood, N.J.

DARREN BRAGG 25 5-9 180 Bats L Throws R
Little outfielder has some pop... Hit .350 with 17 homers, 85 RBI, 112 runs scored and 28 stolen bases for Calgary (AAA) in 1994... Leadoff hitter draws plenty of walks (68 last year)... Overachieved after Mariners picked him in 22nd round of 1991 draft... Born Sept. 7, 1969, in Waterbury, Conn.

MANAGER LOU PINIELLA: Slipped back below .500 at 49-63 in 1994 after leading Mariners to second winning season in their history in 1993... Has 131-143 record in Seattle and 610-567 overall mark in managerial stops with Yankees, Reds and Mariners... Clashed with Mariners general manager Woody Woodward on player personnel decisions, but still received contract extension through 1996 season last winter... Has hard time dealing with realities of operating within a small-market budget... Tired of owner Marge Schott's unconventional methods, he left Reds after three seasons, including 1990 World Series sweep of Oakland... Frustration boiled over there later in 1992 season in form of clubhouse fight with Rob Dibble... Posted 179-145 record as Yankee manager in 1986 and 1987, but was kicked upstairs to GM job by George Steinbrenner... Was back as Yankee manager by June 1988, going 45-48 after replacing Billy Martin... Batted .291 in 16-plus seasons spent mostly as outfielder with Royals and Yankees... Taken from Indians in expansion draft by Seattle Pilots, then traded to Royals... Was AL Rookie of the Year in 1969... Born Aug. 28, 1943, in Tampa.

ALL-TIME MARINER SEASON RECORDS

BATTING: Edgar Martinez, .343, 1992
HRs: Ken Griffey Jr., 45, 1993
RBI: Alvin Davis, 116, 1984
STEALS: Harold Reynolds, 60, 1987
WINS: Mark Langston, 19, 1987
   Randy Johnson, 19, 1993
STRIKEOUTS: Randy Johnson, 308, 1993

TEXAS RANGERS

TEAM DIRECTORY: General Partners: George W. Bush, Edward W. (Rusty) Rose; Pres.: J. Thomas Schieffer; VP/GM: Doug Melvin; VP-Business Oper.: John McMichael; VP-Adm.: Charles Wangner; Asst. GM-Scouting: Sandy Johnson; VP-Pub. Rel.: John Blake; Trav. Sec.: Dan Schimek; Mgr.: Johnny Oates; Coaches: Dick Bosman, Bucky Dent, Larry Hardy, Rudy Jaramillo, Ed Napoleon, Jerry Narron. Home: The Ballpark in Arlington (49,292). Field distances: 332, l.f. line; 390, l.c.; 400, c.f.; 377-381, r.c.; 325, r.f. line. Spring training: Port Charlotte, Fla.

SCOUTING REPORT

The faces have changed once again in Texas and that could change the outlook for team that had enough offense but not enough pitching and defense.

New GM Doug Melvin replaced Tom Grieve after a 52-62 finish and 10 seasons without a division title and then brought with him manager Johnny Oates from Baltimore to replace Kevin Kennedy.

The Rangers' early offseason moves involved pitching losses. Kevin Brown filed for free agency and, after years of confrontation with management, said he wouldn't re-sign. After Brown's nightmarish '94 season (7-9, 4.82, 218 hits allowed in 170 innings), there wasn't much sentiment to bring him back, anyway.

The club didn't exercise its option on veteran closer Tom Henke (3-6, 3.79, 15 saves), who became a Cardinal.

Kenny Rogers, otherwise known as "Mr. Perfect", was denied free agency by the Player Relations Committee last winter and was expected to return. There wasn't much else to rely on in the rotation or the bullpen. Darren Oliver (4-0, 3.42), a hard-throwing left-hander coming off elbow surgery, figures to be Henke's successor. No other regular had an ERA under 5.00 in 1994, one of the reasons pitching coach Claude Osteen lost his job.

Besides Rogers (11-8, 4.46), young right-handers Roger Pavlik (2-5, 7.69), Hector Fajardo (5-7, 6.91) and Rick Helling (3-2, 5.88) are available. But the trade for John Burkett (6-8, 3.62 with the Giants) and signing of Dodger free agent Kevin Gross

Will Clark made himself at home on Rangers.

(9-7, 3.60) are major moves toward rebuilding the staff.

First baseman Will Clark (.329, 13, 80) had no trouble adjusting to the American League in a rebound season. His return to prominence was no more impressive than that of DH Jose Canseco (.282, 31, 90). But Canseco was traded to the Red Sox in the December deal that brought in leadoff hitter and center fielder Otis Nixon (.274, 0, 24, 42 steals).

It's a measure of just how dangerous left fielder Juan Gonzalez can be that his numbers last season (.275, 19, 85) were considered disappointing. He struggled for most of the first two months before getting untracked. Third baseman Dean Palmer (.246, 19, 59) also didn't have the year many expected of him, as he battled injuries.

Ivan Rodriguez (.298, 16, 57) is a three-time Gold Glove Award winner whose offense continues to improve. Rusty Greer (.314, 10, 46) also was a pleasant surprise with his strong showing in the AL Rookie of the Year balloting.

But there are questions concerning the middle infield defense, which should be aided by the signing of ex-Oriole third baseman Mark McLemore. Changes were definitely in order and the Melvin-Oates combo has made the Rangers into a prominent contender for No. 1 in the West.

RANGER PROFILES

WILL CLARK 31 6-1 190   Bats L Throws L

Bounced back from back-to-back sub-par, injury-filled seasons in first year as an American Leaguer... Finished with .329 batting average after blazing start and that pushed his career average back over .300... Hit over .300 against lefties and righties, as well as at home and on the road... Batted .365 with runners in scoring position... Quickly took leadership role in troubled Rangers clubhouse... Usually a slick fielder at first, he committed 10 errors... Would have earned $3,825,972 in first year of five-year, $30-million deal signed as free agent... Spent first eight seasons in San Francisco... Left Giants ranking fourth on all-time club hit list with 1,278... Batted .489 with 11 RBI in memorable 1989 NLCS... Born March 13, 1964, in New Orleans... Giants made him second player taken in 1985 draft, out of Mississippi State.

Year	Club	Pos.	G	AB	R	H	2B	3B	HR	RBI	SB	Avg.
1986	San Francisco	1B	111	408	66	117	27	2	11	41	4	.287
1987	San Francisco	1B	150	529	89	163	29	5	35	91	5	.308
1988	San Francisco	1B	162	575	102	162	31	6	29	109	9	.282
1989	San Francisco	1B	159	588	104	196	38	9	23	111	8	.333
1990	San Francisco	1B	154	600	91	177	25	5	19	95	8	.295
1991	San Francisco	1B	148	565	84	170	32	7	29	116	4	.301
1992	San Francisco	1B	144	513	69	154	40	1	16	73	12	.300
1993	San Francisco	1B	132	491	82	139	27	2	14	73	2	.283
1994	Texas	1B	110	389	73	128	24	2	13	80	5	.329
	Totals		1270	4658	760	1406	273	39	189	789	57	.302

JUAN GONZALEZ 25 6-3 220   Bats R Throws R

Superstar status suffered a bit in sub-par season ... In the Year of the Hitter, he managed only a .275 average, 19 homers and 85 RBI in 422 at-bats... Those are good numbers for most hitters, but can't compare with his breakthrough season of 1993... That year, he won second consecutive AL home run title with 46 and also set career highs in batting average (.310), RBI (118) and runs (105)... Still only 25, he has some growing up to do mentally, if not physically... Has upgraded his defense and now is considered an average left fielder with an above-average arm... Would have earned $3.4 million in 1994... Born Oct. 16, 1969, in Vega Baja, P.R.... Signed as an undrafted free agent in May 1986... Married to the sister of Braves' catcher Javier Lopez.

Year	Club	Pos.	G	AB	R	H	2B	3B	HR	RBI	SB	Avg.
1989	Texas	OF	24	60	6	9	3	0	1	7	0	.150
1990	Texas	OF	25	90	11	26	7	1	4	12	0	.289
1991	Texas	OF	142	545	78	144	34	1	27	102	4	.264
1992	Texas	OF	155	584	77	152	24	2	43	109	0	.260
1993	Texas	OF	140	536	105	166	33	1	46	118	4	.310
1994	Texas	OF	107	422	57	116	18	4	19	85	6	.275
	Totals		593	2237	334	613	119	9	140	433	14	.274

IVAN RODRIGUEZ 23 5-9 210   Bats R Throws R

Laser-armed catcher is perennial All-Star at age 23... Still has flaws, but still is getting better... Threw out 39 percent of would-be basestealers and improved in calling games and handling pitchers... Offense is steadily improving... Fell below .300 mark just before strike, but still set career high with .298 batting average... Also hit career-high 16 homers... Would have earned $500,000 in 1994, quite a bargain considering he has played in three All-Star Games... Should get big salary boost in arbitration... Nicknamed "Pudge" in minor leagues, because of stocky frame... Married at home plate in Drillers Stadium in Tulsa on the day he was called up to the majors, June 20, 1991... Born Nov. 30, 1971, in Vega Baja, P.R., the same town as Juan Gonzalez... Signed as undrafted free agent in July 1988.... Won Gold Glove in '94.

Year	Club	Pos.	G	AB	R	H	2B	3B	HR	RBI	SB	Avg.
1991	Texas	C	88	280	24	74	16	0	3	27	0	.264
1992	Texas	C	123	420	39	109	16	1	8	37	0	.260
1993	Texas	C	137	473	56	129	28	4	10	66	8	.273
1994	Texas	C	99	363	56	108	19	1	16	57	6	.298
	Totals		447	1536	175	420	79	6	37	187	14	.273

OTIS NIXON 36 6-2 180   Bats S Throws R

Became a Ranger in December when Red Sox traded him for Jose Canseco and minor league third baseman Luis Ortiz... His 42 steals were most by a Red Sox since Tommy Harper had 54 in 1973... Couldn't capitalize on juicedball year, however, stroking no homers, one fewer than previous year... But provided prototype center fielder Red Sox sought... Did not become a fulltime player until 1991, with Braves, when he was

32... Swiped 160 bases between 1991–93... Born Jan. 9, 1959, in Evergreen, N.C.... Would have made $3.25 million in '94 ... Brother Donell played with Mariners, Giants, and Orioles.

Year	Club	Pos.	G	AB	R	H	2B	3B	HR	RBI	SB	Avg.
1983	New York (AL)	OF	13	14	2	2	0	0	0	0	2	.143
1984	Cleveland	OF	49	91	16	14	0	0	0	1	12	.154
1985	Cleveland	OF	104	162	34	38	4	0	3	9	20	.235
1986	Cleveland	OF	105	95	33	25	4	1	0	8	23	.263
1987	Cleveland	OF	19	17	2	1	0	0	0	1	2	.059
1988	Montreal	OF	90	271	47	66	8	2	0	15	46	.244
1989	Montreal	OF	126	258	41	56	7	2	0	21	37	.217
1990	Montreal	OF-SS	119	231	46	58	6	2	1	20	50	.251
1991	Atlanta	OF	124	401	81	119	10	1	0	26	72	.297
1992	Atlanta	OF	120	456	79	134	14	2	2	22	41	.294
1993	Atlanta	OF	134	461	77	124	12	3	1	24	47	.269
1994	Boston	OF	103	398	60	109	15	1	0	25	42	.274
	Totals		1106	2855	518	746	80	14	7	172	394	.261

DEAN PALMER 26 6-1 195   Bats R Throws R

Still struggling to get the most out of his immense power potential... Treaded water offensively after solid 1993 season... Batting average rose only one point from 1993 to .246 ... Struck out once per 3.84 at-bats in 1994 ... Hit only .167 in late-inning pressure situations... Was nagged by injuries that kept him out of 23 games... Exploded for 33 homers and 96 RBI in 1993, when he, Juan Gonzalez and Rafael Palmeiro combined to hit 116 homers, most of any trio of teammates... Would have earned $475,000 in '94... Regular spot was cleared for him at third with Aug. 30, 1991 trade of Steve Buechele to Pittsburgh... But he's no Buechele with the glove... His 22 errors were most by AL third baseman in '94... Born Dec. 27, 1968, in Tallahassee, Fla.... Sleeper as Rangers' third-round pick in 1986 draft.

Year	Club	Pos.	G	AB	R	H	2B	3B	HR	RBI	SB	Avg.
1989	Texas	3B-SS-OF	16	19	0	2	2	0	0	1	0	.105
1991	Texas	3B-OF	81	268	38	50	9	2	15	37	0	.187
1992	Texas	3B	152	541	74	124	25	0	26	72	10	.229
1993	Texas	3B-SS	148	519	88	127	31	2	33	96	11	.245
1994	Texas	3B	93	342	50	84	14	2	19	59	3	.246
	Totals		490	1689	250	387	81	6	93	265	24	.229

KENNY ROGERS 30 6-1 205   Bats L Throws L

Mr. Perfect... Now known for something else besides sharing a name with famous country singer... Pitched 15th perfect game in history, first in AL since 1984 and first by a left-hander in AL history, against California July 28... Led staff in wins with 11 and pitched two shutouts... Had breakthrough 16-win season in 1993, when he finally established himself as a starter... One of few success stories in Texas for pitching coach Claude Osteen... Would have earned $2.3 million in 1994... Battled arm trouble in minors... Thirty-seven rounds passed in 1983 draft before Rangers selected him... Often played shortstop in high school, despite throwing left-handed... Grew up on a strawberry farm near Plant City, Fla.... Born Nov. 10, 1964, in Savannah, Ga.... Was denied free agency by Player Relations Committee ruling last winter.

Year	Club	G	IP	W	L	Pct.	SO	BB	H	ERA
1989	Texas	73	73⅔	3	4	.429	63	42	60	2.93
1990	Texas	69	97⅔	10	6	.625	74	42	93	3.13
1991	Texas	63	109⅔	10	10	.500	73	61	121	5.42
1992	Texas	81	78⅔	3	6	.333	70	26	80	3.09
1993	Texas	35	208⅓	16	10	.615	140	71	210	4.10
1994	Texas	24	167⅓	11	8	.579	120	52	169	4.46
	Totals	345	735⅓	53	44	.546	540	294	733	4.03

DARREN OLIVER 24 6-2 200   Bats R Throws L

Came from nowhere to become one of top left-handed setup men in AL... Does it with hard stuff all the way... Was 4-0 with two saves as Tom Henke's principal setup man... Should inherit Henke's closer role in very near future... Struck out 50 and allowed only 40 hits in 50 innings... Fastball is 90-mph plus and he also throws a hard breaking pitch... Opponents hit only .223 against him... Left-handers had no chance. The few that faced him hit just .119... Son of former major league infielder Bob... Development was slowed by arm troubles... Pitched only 55⅓ innings from 1990-92 and had elbow surgery in 1991... Broke through in 1993, when he posted 1.96 ERA and struck out 77 in 73⅓ innings for Tulsa (AA)... Rangers picked him in third round in 1988... Born Oct. 6, 1970, in Kansas City, Mo.

Year	Club	G	IP	W	L	Pct.	SO	BB	H	ERA
1993	Texas	2	3⅓	0	0	.000	4	1	2	2.70
1994	Texas	43	50	4	0	1.000	50	35	40	3.42
	Totals	45	53⅓	4	0	1.000	54	36	42	3.38

JOHN BURKETT 30 6-3 205   Bats R Throws R

Came in stunning winter trade that gave Giants two minor leaguers, infielder Rich Aurilia and outfielder Desi Wilson... Despite etching a better ERA (3.62) than during his 22-win season in 1993, he couldn't even win as many as he lost as a Giant last season... Allowed only two walks per nine innings... Allowed fourth-most hits (176) in league, though... Tied Tom Glavine for NL lead in wins with 22 in 1993, most wins by a Giant since Ron Bryant won 23 in 1973... Losing pitcher in 1993 All-Star Game... Won 14 games in his rookie year of 1990, after seven years in minors... Has bowled three perfect games, but has yet to pitch one... Would have earned $3.55 million last year... Born Nov. 28, 1964, in New Brighton, Pa.... Selected by Giants in sixth round of 1983 draft.

Year	Club	G	IP	W	L	Pct.	SO	BB	H	ERA
1987	San Francisco	3	6	0	0	.000	5	3	7	4.50
1990	San Francisco	33	204	14	7	.667	118	61	201	3.79
1991	San Francisco	36	206⅔	12	11	.522	131	60	223	4.18
1992	San Francisco	32	189⅔	13	9	.591	107	45	194	3.84
1993	San Francisco	34	231⅔	22	7	.759	145	40	224	3.65
1994	San Francisco	25	159⅓	6	8	.429	85	36	176	3.62
	Totals	163	997⅓	67	42	.615	591	245	1025	3.83

TOP PROSPECTS

BENJI GIL 22 6-2 185   Bats R Throws R
Shortstop of the future continues to struggle in the present, despite obvious big league skills... Hit .248 with 10 homers, 55 RBI and 120 strikeouts for Oklahoma City (AAA) in 1994... Injuries forced Rangers to use him for two stints in 1993, when he was overmatched and hit .123 in 57 at-bats... Drafted 19th overall in 1991, out of Castle Park High in Chula Vista, Cal.... Also was a promising pitching prospect... Born Oct. 6, 1972, in Tijuana, Mexico.

RICK HELLING 24 6-3 215 Bats R Throws R
Went 3-2 with 5.88 ERA in nine big league starts for Rangers before being sent back to minors last season... Should be back to stay this year, despite 4-12, 5.78 showing for Oklahoma City (AAA) in 1994... Had impressive first pro season, going 12-8 with a 3.60 ERA for Tulsa (AA), then 1-1 with 1.64 ERA for Oklahoma City in 1993... Was member of 1992 U.S. Olympic Team and Rangers' top draft choice that year... Attended Stanford for one season... Born Dec. 15, 1970, in Fargo, N.D.

MANAGER JOHNNY OATES: Followed new Rangers GM  Doug Melvin from Baltimore after he was fired by impetuous Orioles owner Pete Angelos... His crime? Not leading Orioles to first place in strike-shortened 1994 season... His Birds finished 63-49, third-best mark in AL... Went into last season under pressure after disappointing 85-77 finish in '93, which included 38-36 second half... His record in Baltimore was 291-270 in three-plus seasons and now he succeeds Kevin Kennedy in Texas... Was Orioles' first-base coach before replacing Frank Robinson as manager, May 24, 1991, and inheriting a 13-24 club... Was very successful minor league manager... Captured Southern League championship with Nashville (AA) in first managerial stop in 1982... Took regular-season title with Columbus (AAA) in 1983, his second season in Yankees' system ... Spent four years as major league coach with Cubs, then returned to Orioles' organization after 16-year absence to manage Rochester (AAA)... He took Red Wings to league championship and was named International League Manager of the Year... Began catching career as Orioles' first-round draft choice in 1967 ... Also played for Braves, Dodgers and Yankees in 10-year big league career... Born Jan. 21, 1946, in Sylva, Va.

ALL-TIME RANGER SEASON RECORDS

BATTING: Julio Franco, .341, 1991
HRs: Juan Gonzalez, 46, 1993
RBI: Ruben Sierra, 119, 1989
STEALS: Bump Wills, 52, 1987
WINS: Ferguson Jenkins, 25, 1974
STRIKEOUTS: Nolan Ryan, 301, 1989

INSIDE THE
NATIONAL LEAGUE

By FRANK ISOLA and KEVIN KERNAN
N.Y. Daily News   *San Diego Union*

PREDICTED ORDER OF FINISH

East	*Central*	*West*
Montreal	Houston	San Francisco
Atlanta	Cincinnati	San Diego
N. Y. Mets	St. Louis	Los Angeles
Philadelphia	Pittsburgh	Colorado
Florida	Chicago	

Wild Card: Atlanta
Playoffs Winner: Montreal

EAST DIVISION

#	Team	Colors	Owner	1994 Record	Morning Line / Manager
1	**EXPOS** — October is calling	Scarlet, white & royal blue	Claude Brochu	1994 W 74 L 40	2-1 Felipe Alou
2	**BRAVES** — A mound of might	Royal blue & white	Ted Turner	1994 W 68 L 46	4-1 Bobby Cox
3	**METS** — Time to climb	Orange, white & blue	N. Doubleday/F. Wilpon	1994 W 55 L 58	30-1 Dallas Green
4	**PHILLIES** — '93 is only a memory	Crimson & white	William Y. Giles	1994 W 54 L 61	40-1 Jim Fregosi
5	**MARLINS** — Too many holes	Blue, silver, orange & black	Wayne Huizenga	1994 W 51 L 64	100-1 Rene Lachemann

"O Canada" Derby

119th Running. National League Race. Distance 162 games plus playoffs. Payoff (based on '93, the strike having cancelled '94): $127,920 per winning player, World Series; $91,227 per losing player, World Series. A field of 14 entered in three divisions.

> Track Record: 116 wins—Chicago, 1906

CENTRAL DIVISION

		Owner		Morning Line Manager
1	**ASTROS** Orange & white *Bagging it with Bagwell*	Drayton McLane Jr.	1994 W 66 L 49	8-5 Terry Collins
2	**REDS** Red & white *Will go to the wire*	Marge Schott	1994 W 66 L 48	9-5 Davey Johnson
3	**CARDINALS** *New hope on the hill*	August A. Busch III Red & white	1994 W 53 L 61	20-1 Joe Torre
4	**PIRATES** Old gold, white & black *Not enough Bell-ringers*	Mark Sauer	1994 W 53 L 61	30-1 Jim Leyland
5	**CUBS** Royal blue & white *Lost in the distance*	Stanton Cook	1994 W 49 L 64	40-1 Jim Riggleman

WEST DIVISION

		Owner		Morning Line Manager
1	**GIANTS** White, orange & black *Cashing in with Bonds & Williams*	Peter Magowan	1994 W 55 L 60	8-5 Dusty Baker
2	**PADRES** Brown, gold & white *Up from the cellar*	John Moores	1994 W 47 L 70	15-1 Jim Riggleman
3	**DODGERS** Royal blue & white *Casting for pitching*	Peter O'Malley	1994 W 58 L 66	18-1 Tom Lasorda
4	**ROCKIES** Purple, silver & black *Still growing*	Jerry McMorris	1994 W 53 L 64	30-1 Don Baylor

ATLANTA BRAVES

TEAM DIRECTORY: Owner: Ted Turner; Chairman: Bill Bartholomay; Pres.: Stan Kasten; Sr. VP/Asst. to Pres.: Hank Aaron; Exec. VP/GM: John Schuerholz; Asst. GM/Dir. Player Pers.: Chuck LaMar; Dir. Pub. Rel.: Jim Schultz; Med. Rel. Mgr.: Glen Serra; Trav. Sec.: Bill Acree; Mgr.: Bobby Cox; Coaches: Jim Beauchamp, Pat Corrales, Clarence Jones, Leo Mazzone, Jimy Williams, Ned Yost. Home: Atlanta-Fulton County Stadium (52,709). Field distances: 330, l.f. line; 402, c.f.; 330, r.f. line. Spring training: West Palm Beach, Fla.

SCOUTING REPORT

The best team never to win a World Series is still the team to beat in the NL. As long as the pitching holds up, Atlanta's window of opportunity will remain wide open.

Yes, the Braves finished six games behind the Expos in the NL East last season, but Bobby Cox' club still finished 22 games over .500 at 68-46. Considering the Braves' recent history of late surges, the final six weeks of the '94 season would have been interesting. And let's not forget the Braves' lineup was handicapped by a first-year catcher (Javier Lopez) and first-year left fielder (Ryan Klesko).

Baseball's best pitching staff assures the Braves of staying competitive each season. The Atlanta staff ranked first in the NL in complete games (16), shutouts (8), and strikeouts (865) and ranked second overall in ERA (3.57). Greg Maddux (16-6, 1.56), with three Cy Young Awards in his pocket, is second to none and gearing to rewrite history. Tom Glavine, 13-9, 3.97 in 1994, is the best No. 2 starter in baseball.

Steve Avery is 26-9 over the last two seasons and only 24 years old. John Smoltz is coming off arthroscopic surgery and is eager to prove he's a better pitcher than his 6-10, 4.14 showing in 1994 indicates. Kent Mercker (9-4, 3.45) is the club's No. 5 starter until one of the Braves' Triple-A pitchers is ready to move up. All Mercker did last season was pitch a no-hitter.

Atlanta's bullpen is a cause for concern. Greg McMichael (4-6, 3.84, 21 saves) has saved 40 games in 52 opportunities, but faltered in the 1993 NLCS and was unreliable last year. Mark Wohlers (7-2, 4.59) throws hard but straight and Mike Stanton (3-1, 3.55) is an solid setup man. The Braves still need a dependable closer.

It was case of Maddux redux as Greg won third Cy.

The lineup remains lethal, despite the departure of free-agent Terry Pendleton. Fred McGriff (.318, 34, 94) and Dave Justice (.313, 19, 59) were the driving forces behind the Braves' NL-leading 137 home runs. Their supporting cast will be better this season.

Lopez (.245, 13, 35), now with a full season under his belt, is the best young catching prospect this side of Mike Piazza. Second baseman Mark Lemke (.294, 3, 31) is coming off his best year and shortstop Jeff Blauser (.258, 6, 45), a free agent unsigned at press time, is a sound defensive player and proven run producer. Jose Oliva and Chipper Jones, who missed the entire 1994 season following spring knee surgery, will compete for the third baseman's job, but replacing Pendleton's leadership and defense will be difficult.

Jones could conceivably be moved to outfield and share time with Klesko (.278, 17, 47). Roberto Kelly (.293, 9, 45, 19 steals) is not the leadoff hitter or distraction his predecessor Deion Sanders was, but he is a presence in the middle of the order.

The Braves, with a good blend of veterans and young stars, will be there in October. Maybe this time, they won't come up a little short.

BRAVE PROFILES

DAVE JUSTICE 28 6-3 197   Bats L Throws L

Great player who is finally showing leadership qualities... Strike halted his bid for five straight seasons with 20-plus home runs... All-Star led NL with .386 batting average with runners in scoring position in '94... Became first Braves right fielder to hit .300 (.313) since Hank Aaron in 1973... Batted .331 with 15 homers and 48 RBI after May 21... Had only two-homer game June 15 vs. Rockies... Tied club record by reaching base via hit or walk in 34 consecutive games from June 19-July 27... Ranked second in NL with 69 walks and fourth with .427 on-base percentage... Set career highs in home runs and RBI in 1993... Finished third in NL MVP voting in '93, behind Barry Bonds and Lenny Dykstra... Was NL Rookie of the Year in '90... Married to actress Halle Berry... Born April 14, 1966, in Cincinnati... Selected by Braves in fourth round of 1985 draft... Would have earned $3.2 million in 1994.

Year Club	Pos.	G	AB	R	H	2B	3B	HR	RBI	SB	Avg.
1989 Atlanta	OF	16	51	7	12	3	0	1	3	2	.235
1990 Atlanta	1B-OF	127	439	76	124	23	2	28	78	11	.282
1991 Atlanta	OF	109	396	67	109	25	1	21	87	8	.275
1992 Atlanta	OF	144	484	78	124	19	5	21	72	2	.256
1993 Atlanta	OF	157	585	90	158	15	4	40	120	3	.270
1994 Atlanta	OF	104	352	61	110	16	2	19	59	2	.313
Totals		657	2307	379	637	101	14	130	419	28	.276

RYAN KLESKO 23 6-3 220   Bats L Throws L

One of NL's top rookies... Appeared lost at times after being moved from first base to left field, but still produced offensively... Finished third in Rookie of the Year award balloting... Hit home run once per 14.4 at-bats... Held a .300-plus batting average through July 21... Collected 25 of his 47 RBI on home runs and 33 of his 68 hits were extra-base hits... Produced first two-homer game of his career June 26 vs. Phillies... Smacked four homers in four days from June 26-30... Had string of six straight games with at least one RBI from June 26-July 2... Batted .421 in June... All 17 of his homers came off right-handed pitching... Braves' sixth-round selection in 1989 draft... Born June 12, 1971, in Westminster, Cal.... Would have earned $111,500 in 1994.

Year Club	Pos.	G	AB	R	H	2B	3B	HR	RBI	SB	Avg.
1992 Atlanta	1B	13	14	0	0	0	0	0	1	0	.000
1993 Atlanta	1B-OF	22	17	3	6	1	0	2	5	0	.353
1994 Atlanta	OF-1B	92	245	42	68	13	3	17	47	1	.278
Totals		127	276	45	74	14	3	19	53	1	.268

JAVIER LOPEZ 24 6-3 185   Bats R Throws R

Within five years, he could become measuring stick for all catchers... Stepped right into Braves' potent lineup and made an immediate impact in first full season... Posted eight-game hitting streak from April 10-20... Had pair of two-homer games... Became only third player to reach upper deck of Joe Robbie Stadium April 26... Caught Kent Mercker's no-hitter April 6 vs. Dodgers, in just his 10th major league start, becoming youngest backstop in NL to catch a no-hitter since Ted Simmons caught Bob Gibson's in 1971... Threw out only 16 of 81 would-be base-stealers... Named an International League All-Star with Richmond (AAA) in 1993... Signed as undrafted free agent in 1987... Born Nov. 5, 1970, in Ponce, P.R.... Would have earned $115,000 in '94.

Year Club	Pos.	G	AB	R	H	2B	3B	HR	RBI	SB	Avg.
1992 Atlanta	C	9	16	3	6	2	0	0	2	0	.375
1993 Atlanta	C	8	16	1	6	1	1	1	2	0	.375
1994 Atlanta	C	80	277	27	68	9	0	13	35	0	.245
Totals		97	309	31	80	12	1	14	39	0	.259

FRED McGRIFF 31 6-3 216   Bats L Throws L

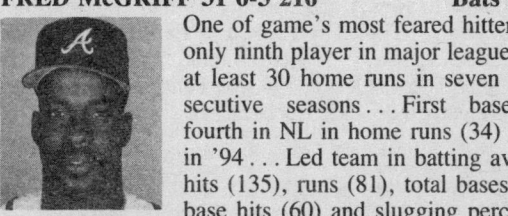

One of game's most feared hitters... Became only ninth player in major league history to hit at least 30 home runs in seven or more consecutive seasons... First baseman ranked fourth in NL in home runs (34) and RBI (94) in '94... Led team in batting average (.318), hits (135), runs (81), total bases (264), extra-base hits (60) and slugging percentage (.623) ... Hit 250th career home run July 3, off Florida's David Weathers ... Named All-Star MVP after hitting game-tying, ninth-inning homer off Orioles' Lee Smith... Acquired from Padres for Melvin Nieves, Donnie Elliott and Vince Moore, July 18, 1993... Sparked Braves to 51-17 finish from that point and NL West title

... Led majors in homers with 35 for San Diego in 1992, becoming second player in history to win homer titles in both leagues (he led AL with 36 for Blue Jays in 1989)... Traded from Blue Jays to Padres with Tony Fernandez for Roberto Alomar and Joe Carter prior to 1991 season... Yankees' ninth-round pick in 1981... Born Oct. 31, 1963, in Tampa, Fla. ... Would have earned $3.75 million in '94.

Year	Club	Pos.	G	AB	R	H	2B	3B	HR	RBI	SB	Avg.
1986	Toronto	1B	3	5	1	1	0	0	0	0	0	.200
1987	Toronto	1B	107	295	58	73	16	0	20	43	3	.247
1988	Toronto	1B	154	536	100	151	35	4	34	82	6	.282
1989	Toronto	1B	161	551	98	148	27	3	36	92	7	.269
1990	Toronto	1B	153	557	91	167	21	1	35	88	5	.300
1991	San Diego	1B	153	528	84	147	19	1	31	106	4	.278
1992	San Diego	1B	152	531	79	152	30	4	35	104	8	.286
1993	S.D.-Atl.	1B	151	557	111	162	29	2	37	101	5	.291
1994	Atlanta	1B	113	424	81	135	25	1	34	94	7	.318
	Totals		1147	3984	703	1136	202	16	262	710	45	.285

ROBERTO KELLY 30 6-2 194   Bats R Throws R

Baseball world is still trying to decide if this center fielder is a superstar or simply an above-average player... Caught fire following trade from Reds for Deion Sanders May 29... Batted .298 in leadoff spot... Led team with 37 multi-hit games and 19 stolen bases... Had two nine-game hitting streaks in June, hitting .330 for the month... Batted .360 (18-50) with runners in scoring position and less than two outs... Was leading NL in hits and steals before suffering season-ending shoulder injury in 1993... Named to second All-Star team in '93... Changed his name to Bobby and batted .319 and yet went back to Roberto last year... Traded by Yankees to Reds in Paul O'Neill deal prior to 1993 season... Signed as undrafted free agent by Yankees in 1982... Born Oct. 1, 1964, in Panama City, Panama ... Would have earned $3,133,333 last year.

Year	Club	Pos.	G	AB	R	H	2B	3B	HR	RBI	SB	Avg.
1987	New York (AL)	OF	23	52	12	14	3	0	1	7	9	.269
1988	New York (AL)	OF	38	77	9	19	4	1	1	7	5	.247
1989	New York (AL)	OF	137	441	65	133	18	3	9	48	35	.302
1990	New York (AL)	OF	162	641	85	183	32	4	15	61	42	.285
1991	New York (AL)	OF	126	486	68	130	22	2	20	69	32	.267
1992	New York (AL)	OF	152	580	81	158	31	2	10	66	28	.272
1993	Cincinnati	OF	78	320	44	102	17	3	9	35	21	.319
1994	Cin.-Atl.	OF	110	434	73	127	23	3	9	45	19	.293
	Totals		826	3031	437	866	150	18	74	338	191	.286

MARK LEMKE 29 5-9 167   Bats S Throws R

Perfect complimentary player on team loaded with stars... Set franchise record for highest fielding percentage by a second baseman (.994) last season... Committed three errors all season and finished year without a miscue in final 64 games... Batted .294 from both sides of the plate... Batted .352 in May... Registered career-high, 11-game hitting streak from June 22-July 3... Was 5-for-9 with 12 RBI with bases loaded... Set career highs in nearly every offensive category in '93, his first full season as Braves' second baseman... Owns lifetime .326 World Series batting average in 12 games, with 14 hits and three triples... Selected by Braves in 27th round of 1983 draft... Born Aug. 13, 1965, in Utica, N.Y.... Would have earned $1.1 million last year.

Year	Club	Pos.	G	AB	R	H	2B	3B	HR	RBI	SB	Avg.
1988	Atlanta	2B	16	58	8	13	4	0	0	2	0	.224
1989	Atlanta	2B	14	55	4	10	2	1	2	10	0	.182
1990	Atlanta	3B-2B-SS	102	239	22	54	13	0	0	21	0	.226
1991	Atlanta	2B-3B	136	269	36	63	11	2	2	23	1	.234
1992	Atlanta	2B-3B	155	427	38	97	7	4	6	26	0	.227
1993	Atlanta	2B	151	493	52	124	19	2	7	49	1	.252
1994	Atlanta	2B	104	350	40	103	15	0	3	31	0	.294
	Totals		678	1891	200	464	71	9	20	162	2	.245

JEFF BLAUSER 29 6-1 183   Bats R Throws R

Not ready to give up position to prospect Chipper Jones without a fight... Reliable shortstop with pop in his bat... Matched his own club record with .970 fielding percentage in '94... Batted .314 in May... Ended campaign with season-high, eight-game hitting streak and hit safely in 10 of last 11 games... Batted .319 from seventh inning on... Led team with four triples... Tied for ninth in NL with six sac flies... Disabled from May 2-20 with pulled stomach muscle and it marked first time in four seasons he went on DL... Posted career highs in average, home runs, RBI, hits, runs, walks and steals in '93, his first full season at shortstop... In '93, he became first Braves shortstop to hit over .300 (.305) since Alvin Dark batted .322 in 1948... Batted .280 with two homers vs. Phillies in 1993 NLCS... Braves' first selection in secondary phase of 1984 draft... Born

Nov. 8, 1965, in Los Gatos, Cal. . . . Would have earned $3.75 million last year . . . **Free agent at press time.**

Year	Club	Pos.	G	AB	R	H	2B	3B	HR	RBI	SB	Avg.
1987	Atlanta	SS	51	165	11	40	6	3	2	15	7	.242
1988	Atlanta	2B-SS	18	67	7	16	3	1	2	7	0	.239
1989	Atlanta	3B-2B-SS-OF	142	456	63	123	24	2	12	46	5	.270
1990	Atlanta	SS-2B-3B-OF	115	386	46	104	24	3	8	39	3	.269
1991	Atlanta	SS-2B-3B	129	352	49	91	14	3	11	54	5	.259
1992	Atlanta	SS-2B-3B	123	343	61	90	19	3	14	46	5	.262
1993	Atlanta	SS	161	597	110	182	29	2	15	73	16	.305
1994	Atlanta	SS	96	380	56	98	21	4	6	45	1	.258
	Totals		835	2746	403	744	140	21	70	325	42	.271

GREG MADDUX 28 6-0 175   Bats R Throws R

Simply the best pitcher in baseball . . . Won third straight Cy Young Award in '94 . . . Winningest pitcher in majors over last seven years (123) . . . Also ranks first in starts (237), complete games (58) and innings (1,724⅓) from 1988-94 . . . Led majors in ERA (1.56), innings (202) and complete games (10) in '94 . . . Set major league record by finishing with ERA 1.09 lower than next nearest big leaguer, Athletics' Steve Ontiveros, who posted 2.65 mark . . . Previous record spread was 0.48 margin set by Bob Gibson when he rang up 1.12 mark in 1968 . . . Set career high with 10 complete games, more than every other NL team except for Dodgers (13) . . . Set career high in strikeouts with 11 April 24 vs. Pirates . . . Tied Expos' Ken Hill for most victories (16) in NL . . . Most durable pitcher in majors, he has amassed 200-plus innings seven straight years . . . Signed five-year, $28-million contract with Braves as free agent prior to 1993 season . . . Born April 14, 1966, in San Angelo, Tex. . . . Cubs' second-round pick in 1984 draft . . . Would have earned $4 million in '94 . . . Won fifth Gold Glove in '94.

Year	Club	G	IP	W	L	Pct.	SO	BB	H	ERA
1986	Chicago (NL)	6	31	2	4	.333	20	11	44	5.52
1987	Chicago (NL)	30	155⅔	6	14	.300	101	74	181	5.61
1988	Chicago (NL)	34	249	18	8	.692	140	81	230	3.18
1989	Chicago (NL)	35	238⅓	19	12	.613	135	82	222	2.95
1990	Chicago (NL)	35	237	15	15	.500	144	71	242	3.46
1991	Chicago (NL)	37	263	15	11	.577	198	66	232	3.35
1992	Chicago (NL)	35	268	20	11	.645	199	70	201	2.18
1993	Atlanta	36	267	20	10	.667	197	52	228	2.36
1994	Atlanta	25	202	16	6	.727	156	31	150	1.56
	Totals	273	1911	131	91	.590	1290	538	1730	3.02

ATLANTA BRAVES • 213

STEVE AVERY 24 6-4 190   Bats L Throws L

Still young and already a star... His .727 winning percentage was fourth-best in NL... Held opposing batters to .227 average in '94... Began season by winning five of first six decisions with 2.49 ERA... Went 4-0 in May... From May 26-July 23, he posted 1-2 record and seven no-decisions... Finished 2-0 with 1.08 ERA in last three starts... Struck out career-high 11 batters Aug. 8 vs. Reds... Braves were 15-9 in games he started last season and are 41-13 in his last 54 outings dating back to May 2, 1993... Braves scored 139 runs in his 24 starts in '94 ... Won career-high eight straight games while matching career best with 18 wins in 1993... Youngest player in Braves' history to reach 50 career wins... Captured 1991 NLCS MVP honors vs. Pirates as he went 2-0 with 16⅓ shutout innings... Braves made him third overall pick in 1988 draft... Born April 14, 1970, in Trenton, Mich.... Would have earned $2.8 million in 1994.

Year	Club	G	IP	W	L	Pct.	SO	BB	H	ERA
1990	Atlanta	21	99	3	11	.214	75	45	121	5.64
1991	Atlanta	35	210⅓	18	8	.692	137	65	189	3.38
1992	Atlanta	35	233⅔	11	11	.500	129	71	216	3.20
1993	Atlanta	35	223⅓	18	6	.750	125	43	216	2.94
1994	Atlanta	24	151⅔	8	3	.727	122	55	127	4.04
	Totals.	150	918	58	39	.598	588	279	869	3.58

JOHN SMOLTZ 27 6-3 185   Bats R Throws R

Someone on Braves' incredible staff has to lose and, in 1994, it was him... Suffered his first losing season in six years... Underwent arthroscopic surgery to remove bone chips from right elbow Sept. 8... Averaged 7.6 strikeouts per nine innings, eighth-best in NL... Held opponents to .239 batting average... Closed out season 1-4 with 6.32 ERA in his final eight starts... Lost five straight games from April 22-May 19... Served eight-game suspension from June 20-28 for hitting Mets' John Cangelosi with pitch May 14... Selected to third All-Star team in 1993, when he matched career high with 15 wins and finished second in NL with 208 strikeouts... Led NL with 215 strikeouts in 1992... Impressive 5-1 record in 10 career postseason starts... Born May 15, 1967, in Warren, Mich.... Signed by Tigers as undrafted free agent in September 1985... Traded to Braves for Doyle Alexander, Aug. 12, 1987... Would have earned $3.25 million last season.

Year	Club	G	IP	W	L	Pct.	SO	BB	H	ERA
1988	Atlanta	12	64	2	7	.222	37	33	74	5.48
1989	Atlanta	29	208	12	11	.522	168	72	160	2.94
1990	Atlanta	34	211⅓	14	11	.560	170	90	206	3.85
1991	Atlanta	36	229⅔	14	13	.519	148	77	206	3.80
1992	Atlanta	35	246⅔	15	12	.556	215	80	206	2.85
1993	Atlanta	35	243⅔	15	11	.577	208	100	208	3.62
1994	Atlanta	21	134⅔	6	10	.375	113	48	120	4.14
	Totals	202	1358	78	75	.510	1059	500	1180	3.59

TOM GLAVINE 29 6-1 185   Bats L Throws L

Second-best pitcher on NL's top staff, which is saying something... Hit double figures in victories for sixth straight season... Ranked fifth in NL in wins (13) and sixth in strikeouts (140)... Also finished sixth in hits allowed (173) and second in walks (70)... Has 79-35 mark with 3.05 ERA since Sept. 4, 1990... Won six of last eight decisions last year... Allowed 18 of his 76 runs in first inning... In 1993, he became first NL pitcher to win 20 games three straight years since Ferguson Jenkins won 20 six years in a row from 1967-72... Recorded career-high five shutouts in 1992... Won NL Cy Young in 1991 ... Braves' second pick in 1984 draft and also fourth-round pick of NHL's Los Angeles Kings... Born March 25, 1966, in Concord, Mass.... Would have earned $4.75 million.

Year	Club	G	IP	W	L	Pct.	SO	BB	H	ERA
1987	Atlanta	9	50⅓	2	4	.333	20	33	55	5.54
1988	Atlanta	34	195⅓	7	17	.292	84	63	201	4.56
1989	Atlanta	29	186	14	8	.636	90	40	172	3.68
1990	Atlanta	33	214⅓	10	12	.455	129	78	232	4.28
1991	Atlanta	34	246⅔	20	11	.645	192	69	201	2.55
1992	Atlanta	33	225	20	8	.714	129	70	197	2.76
1993	Atlanta	36	239⅓	22	6	.786	120	90	236	3.20
1994	Atlanta	25	165⅓	13	9	.591	140	70	173	3.97
	Totals	233	1522⅓	108	75	.590	904	513	1467	3.58

TOP PROSPECTS

CHIPPER JONES 22 6-3 195   Bats S Throws R
Could be Braves' everyday shortstop or third baseman if he doesn't end up in outfield... Promising year ended before it began March

3, when he torn anterior cruciate ligament in his left knee running to first . . . Started working out with team Aug. 1 and all indications are that the knee is healthy again . . . In 1993, he led International League in hits (174), runs (97), total bases (268) and triples (12) in his first season with Richmond (AAA) . . . Made major league debut Sept. 10, 1993, vs. Reds . . . Collected single in first at-bat . . . Has dominated at every minor league level . . . Braves made him first overall selection in 1990 draft . . . Born April 24, 1972, in Deland, Fla.

MIKE KELLY 24 6-4 195   Bats R Throws R
Probably wondering when he'll get his chance, considering Braves are so loaded with talented outfielders . . . Spent three tours with Braves, batting .272 with two homers and nine RBI in 30 games . . . Had 15 homers, 45 RBI and .262 average for Richmond (AAA) . . . Made club out of spring training . . . Collected first big league hit, a double, April 7 vs. Padres . . . Optioned to minors May 5, when he was hitting .185 . . . Recalled again Aug. 1 . . . Braves made him second overall pick in 1991 draft . . . Three-time All-American at Arizona State . . . Born June 2, 1970, in Los Angeles.

JOSE OLIVA 24 6-3 215   Bats R Throws R
Leading candidate to replace Terry Pendleton at third . . . Batted .288 in 19 games with Braves and six of his 17 hits were home runs . . . He drove in 11 runs and struck out 10 times . . . Started '94 season with Richmond (AAA), where he batted .253 with 24 home runs and 64 RBI in 371 at-bats . . . Acquired from Rangers for Charlie Leibrandt and Pat Gomez prior to 1993 season . . . Originally signed by Texas as undrafted free agent in November 1987 . . . Born March 3, 1971, in San Pedro de Macoris, D.R.

BRAD WOODALL 25 6-0 175   Bats S Throws L
Competing for fifth spot in Braves' rotation . . . Went 15-6 with 2.38 ERA in 27 starts for Richmond (AAA) and led International League in victories . . . Led staff in innings (186) and ranked second in strikeouts (137) . . . Made one start for Braves, allowing three runs over six innings while picking up loss . . . Started 1993 season with Durham (A) and finished season with Richmond . . . Born June 25, 1969, in Atlanta . . . Signed by Braves as undrafted free agent in June 1991.

MANAGER BOBBY COX: Still searching for that evasive World Series championship... Did good job blending young players with veterans last season... His Braves teams have won more games in last four years (364) than any other team in baseball... Club finished 68-46 last season with rookie catcher and rookie left fielder... Ended season six games behind first-place Expos in NL East... Guided club to franchise-record 104 wins in 1993... Braves became first NL West team to win three straight titles in '93... Twice named NL Manager of the Year... He's only manager other than Sparky Anderson to win title in both leagues, earning award with Blue Jays in 1985 ... Joined Braves as GM in October 1985... Took over managerial reins from Russ Nixon during 1990 season... In 1991, Braves went from worst to first and lost to Twins in Game 7 of World Series... Managed Blue Jays from 1982-85... One year after Toronto had finished seventh, he took Blue Jays to within one game of the World Series in 1985... Compiled a 266-323 record from 1978-81 as Braves skipper... Played 12 professional seasons, including 10 in minors, before bad knees ended this third baseman's career... Born May 21, 1941, in Tulsa, Okla.... Overall major league managerial record is 1,025-908.

ALL-TIME BRAVE SEASON RECORDS

BATTING: Rogers Hornsby, .387, 1928
HRs: Eddie Mathews, 47, 1953
    Hank Aaron, 47, 1971
RBI: Eddie Mathews, 135, 1953
STEALS: Otis Nixon, 72, 1991
WINS: Vic Willis, 27, 1902
    Charles Pittinger, 27, 1902
    Dick Rudolph, 27, 1914
STRIKEOUTS: Phil Niekro, 262, 1977

FLORIDA MARLINS

TEAM DIRECTORY: Owner: H. Wayne Huizenga; Pres.: Don Smiley; Exec. VP/GM: David Dombrowski; VP-Business Oper.: Richard Andersen; VP-Broadcasting: Dean Jordan; Dir. Scouting: Gary Hughes; Dir. Player Dev.: John Boles; Dir. Media Rel.: Chuck Pool; Dir. Team Travel: Bill Beck; Mgr.: Rene Lachemann; Coaches: Rusty Kuntz, Jose Morales, Cookie Rojas, Larry Rothschild, Rick Williams. Home: Joe Robbie Stadium (47,226). Field distances: 335, l.f. line; 380, l.c.; 410, c.f.; 380, r.c.; 345, r.f. line. Spring training: Viera, Fla.

SCOUTING REPORT

Rene Lachemann's club finished in the NL East cellar at 51-64 last year, but ahead of the Padres and Cubs in the overall standings. That is not bad for a two-year-old baseball team.

But, make no mistake, the improving Marlins should still be classified as an expansion club. They have too many holes in their lineup and not enough quality arms to begin entertaining

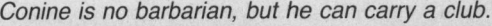

Conine is no barbarian, but he can carry a club.

thoughts of competing for a playoff spot. A year after finishing dead last in the majors in runs at 581, the Marlins ranked 13th in 1994 with 468 runs.

Gary Sheffield (.276, 27, 78), moved from third base to right field, was the Marlins' best offensive player, despite missing 28 games due to injuries. If—and this is a big if—Sheffield stays healthy for 162 games, he has a legitimate shot at winning the Triple Crown.

Jeff Conine (.319, 18, 82), a first-time All-Star who led the club in RBI, is the Marlins' only other threat. Benito Santiago (.273, 11, 41) is still one of the best catchers in baseball and has some pop in his bat, but was unlikely to return as a free agent.

Kurt Abbott (.249, 9, 33), with one full season at shortstop, may be Florida's most promising young player. Second baseman Bret Barberie (.301, 5, 31) is now an Oriole, but he'll be replaced by Quilvio Veras, the 23-year-old minor league star who came in a November trade from the Mets for outfielder Carl Everett. First baseman Greg Colbrunn (.303, 6, 31) is hoping to stay healthy long enough to reach 200 at-bats for the first time.

Center fielder Chuck Carr (.263, 2, 30, 32 steals) will wreak havoc on the basepaths and chase down any ball hit in his area code. Darrell Whitmore and Nigel Wilson will be given enough chances to prove they can play.

Florida's pitching staff experienced growing pains and physical pains last season. Chris Hammond (4-4, 3.07), Bryan Harvey (0-0, 5.23, 6 saves) and Jeremy Hernandez (3-3, 2.70, 9 saves) all missed most of the year due to injuries. Hammond, limited to 13 starts last season, is the Marlins' best starter.

Robb Nen (5-5, 2.95, 15 saves) replaced Hernandez, who replaced Harvey as Florida's closer last season. With Nen, Harvey, Hernandez and Yorkis Perez (3-0, 3.54), the Marlins should have a formidable bullpen to go with their suspect rotation.

David Weathers (8-12, 5.27) remains a highly rated prospect despite his struggles last season. Pat Rapp (7-8, 3.85) and Ryan Bowen (1-5, 4.94) are young and talented, but Bowen may miss the entire season after undergoing knee surgery in December. Jay Powell, a 23-year-old pitching prospect, joined the Marlins in the December trade for Barberie.

The Marlins ranked next-to-last in fielding last season, when youngsters Abbott and Barberie patrolled the middle infield and Sheffield was making the adjustment from third to the outfield.

The Marlins are improving. But, even if their pitching staff stays healthy and Sheffield challenges for an MVP award, a .500 record may still be out of the question.

MARLIN PROFILES

GARY SHEFFIELD 26 5-11 190   Bats R Throws R

Move from third base to right field did not affect his offensive production... Set club record with 27 home runs in '94 as he tied for seventh in NL... Missed 28 games with bruised muscle in rotator cuff... Made two trips to DL... Played 580 straight games in infield before switching to outfield... Recorded seven outfield assists in 87 games last season... Tied his personal best and set club record with 10 homers in April... Acquired from Padres with Rich Rodriguez for Trevor Hoffman, Andres Berumen and Jose Martinez, June 24, 1993... Youngest defending batting champ (.330 in 1992) ever traded... First expansion player to start All-Star Game in '93... Started his Marlins career with 12-game hitting streak... Became Marlins' first major star... Born Nov. 18, 1968, in Tampa, Fla.... Nephew of Mets' Dwight Gooden... Highest-paid Marlin, he would have made $4.65 million in 1994... Brewers' first pick in 1986 draft.

Year	Club	Pos.	G	AB	R	H	2B	3B	HR	RBI	SB	Avg.
1988	Milwaukee	SS	24	80	12	19	1	0	4	12	3	.238
1989	Milwaukee	SS–3B	95	368	34	91	18	0	5	32	10	.247
1990	Milwaukee	3B	125	487	67	143	30	1	10	67	25	.294
1991	Milwaukee	3B	50	175	25	34	12	2	2	22	5	.194
1992	San Diego	3B	146	557	87	184	34	3	33	100	5	.330
1993	S.D.-Fla.	3B	140	494	67	145	20	5	20	73	17	.294
1994	Florida	OF	87	322	61	89	16	1	27	78	12	.276
	Totals		667	2483	353	705	131	12	101	384	77	.284

CHUCK CARR 26 5-10 165   Bats S Throws R

One of game's most exciting players... Center fielder can outrun almost any ball hit to him... Solid leadoff hitter... Finished fourth in NL with 32 steals... Stole 30 bases in 32 attempts while playing on grass... Notched 100th career stolen base against Phillies July 26... Tied Gary Sheffield for club lead in runs (61)... Was hitting .353 May 20, after seven-game hitting streak... Set franchise mark with five hits (all singles) in five at-bats May 3 at Atlanta... Led NL with 58 steals in 1993... First rookie to win steals title since Vince Coleman in 1985... Collected 17 bunt base hits in '93... Missed 19 games with pulled rib-cage muscle, but had career-high, 15-game hitting streak from July 30-Aug. 14 in '93... Marlins' seventh pick in expansion draft... Originally selected by Reds in ninth round in 1986... Born Aug. 10, 1968, in San Bernardino, Cal.... Would have earned $230,000.

Year	Club	Pos.	G	AB	R	H	2B	3B	HR	RBI	SB	Avg.
1990	New York (NL)	OF	4	2	0	0	0	0	0	0	1	.000
1991	New York (NL)	OF	12	11	1	2	0	0	0	1	1	.182
1992	St. Louis	OF	22	64	8	14	3	0	0	3	10	.208
1993	Florida	OF	142	551	75	147	19	2	4	41	58	.267
1994	Florida	OF	106	433	61	114	19	2	2	30	32	.263
	Totals		286	1061	145	277	41	4	6	75	102	.261

JEFF CONINE 28 6-1 220 Bats R Throws R

Baseball's unknown superstar... May be moved from outfield to third base... Selected to All-Star team as he led Marlins in nearly every offensive category for second straight year... Finished 10th in NL in batting average (.319)... Ranked second in games played (115), tied for third in at-bats (451) and fifth in hits (144)... Did not go hitless in more than two consecutive starts all season... Average stayed above .300 after June 3... Has played in 277 consecutive games, the longest active streak in majors behind Cal Ripken Jr.... Set expansion record by appearing in all 162 games in 1993, when he was named to All-Rookie team... Marlins' 11th pick in expansion draft... Originally drafted by Royals in 58th round in 1987... Born June 27, 1966, in Tacoma, Wash.... Would have earned $230,000.

Year	Club	Pos.	G	AB	R	H	2B	3B	HR	RBI	SB	Avg.
1990	Kansas City	1B	9	20	3	5	2	0	0	2	0	.250
1992	Kansas City	OF-1B	28	91	10	23	5	2	0	9	0	.253
1993	Florida	OF-1B	162	595	75	174	24	3	12	79	2	.292
1994	Florida	OF-1B	115	451	60	144	27	6	18	82	1	.319
	Totals		314	1157	148	346	58	11	30	172	3	.299

KURT ABBOTT 25 6-0 185 Bats R Throws R

Inherited starting shortstop job from Walt Weiss and made immediate impact in rookie season... Raised his average by hitting safely in 13 of last 18 games, including four-hit performance against Mets Aug. 8... His 98 strikeouts were fourth-highest total in NL... Tied for NL lead with two grand slams... Set club record by homering in four consecutive games from June 14-17... Tied Jerry Browne for most errors on team with 15... Acquired by Marlins from Oakland for Kerwin Moore prior to last season... Started 14 games for Athletics in 1993 after being promoted to majors Sept. 7... In first major league start and second at-bat Sept. 9, he homered off Toronto's Jack Morris ... Was Pacific Coast League All-Star with Tacoma (AAA) in '93... Athletics selected him in 15th round of 1989 draft... Would have earned $109,000 in '94... Born June 2, 1969, in Zanesville, Ohio.

Year	Club	Pos.	G	AB	R	H	2B	3B	HR	RBI	SB	Avg.
1993	Oakland	OF-SS-2B	20	61	11	15	1	0	3	9	2	.246
1994	Florida	SS	101	345	41	86	17	3	9	33	3	.249
	Totals		121	406	52	101	18	3	12	42	5	.249

Marlins root for an injury-free Gary Sheffield.

ROBB NEN 25 6-4 190 Bats R Throws R

Emerged as closer following season-ending injuries to Bryan Harvey and Jeremy Hernandez... Converted first 15 save opportunities, longest streak in majors since blown saves were first tracked in 1988... Recorded first major league save May 18 vs. Mets by tossing two perfect innings... Allowed only one of 28 inherited runners to score... Retired first batter he faced 32 times in 44 chances... Held left-handed batters to .161 average... Pitched season-high four innings of relief May 21 against St. Louis... Made major league debut with Rangers in '93... Dealt to Marlins by Rangers with Kurt Miller for Cris Carpenter, July 17, 1993... Son of former major league first baseman Dick... Born Nov. 28, 1969, in San Pedro, Cal.... Would have earned $130,000 last season.

Year	Club	G	IP	W	L	Pct.	SO	BB	H	ERA
1993	Texas	9	22⅔	1	1	.500	12	26	28	6.35
1993	Florida	15	33⅓	1	0	1.000	27	20	35	7.02
1994	Florida	44	58	5	5	.500	60	17	46	2.95
	Totals	68	114	7	6	.538	99	63	109	4.82

CHRIS HAMMOND 29 6-1 195 Bats L Throws L

Promising season was ruined by injuries... Each of lefty's four wins were shutouts... Ranked among league leaders in ERA before suffering back strain June 11... Made three rehab starts in minors... Activated Aug. 3, but left start vs. Cubs in fourth inning after Derrick May line drive nailed him in left leg... Went 3-0 with 0.61 ERA in May... Held opponents scoreless for 24 innings in May... Gave up one homer in last 40 innings... Tossed Marlins' first shutout at Joe Robbie Stadium May 5 vs. Phillies... Acquired from Reds for Gary Scott and Hector Carrasco prior to 1993 season... Had career-high eight game winning streak from May 26-July 2 in '93... Went 6-0 with 2.53 ERA in June... Selected in sixth round by Reds in 1986 draft... Born Jan. 21, 1966, in Atlanta... Would have earned $925,000 last season.

Year	Club	G	IP	W	L	Pct.	SO	BB	H	ERA
1990	Cincinnati	3	11⅓	0	2	.000	4	12	13	6.35
1991	Cincinnati	20	99⅔	7	7	.500	50	48	92	4.06
1992	Cincinnati	28	147⅓	7	10	.412	79	55	149	4.21
1993	Florida	32	191	11	12	.478	108	66	207	4.66
1994	Florida	13	73⅓	4	4	.500	40	23	79	3.07
	Totals	96	522⅔	29	36	.446	291	204	540	4.26

BRYAN HARVEY 31 6-2 212   Bats R Throws R

Injury-riddled season limited him to 12 appearances... Served three stints on disabled list... Underwent season-ending abdominal surgery July 14... Was leading NL with six saves before straining flexor muscle in right elbow April 26... Activated May 26 for one day and placed back on DL until June 22 due to elbow soreness... Gave up four runs in 3⅔ innings (9.82 ERA) in four games after being activated June 22 ... Averaging 10.4 strikeouts per nine innings in his career... Veteran closer finished third in NL with 45 saves in 48 opportunities in 1993... Only player to save 45 games in a season in both leagues... Involved in 72 percent of Marlins' victories in '93, highest percentage by any reliever in history... Suffered season-ending groin injury Sept. 22 against Phillies... Marlins' 10th pick in expansion draft... Underwent elbow surgery in 1992 ... Set Angels' club record with 46 saves in 1991... Signed with Angels as undrafted free agent in 1984... Born June 2, 1963, in Chattanooga, Tenn.... Would have earned $3.375 million last season.

Year	Club	G	IP	W	L	Pct.	SO	BB	H	ERA
1987	California	3	5	0	0	.000	3	2	6	0.00
1988	California	50	76	7	5	.583	67	20	59	2.13
1989	California	51	55	3	3	.500	78	41	36	3.44
1990	California	54	64⅓	4	4	.500	82	35	45	3.22
1991	California	67	78⅔	2	4	.333	101	17	51	1.60
1992	California	25	28⅔	0	4	.000	34	11	22	2.83
1993	Florida	59	69	1	5	.167	73	13	45	1.70
1994	Florida	12	10⅓	0	0	.000	10	4	12	5.23
	Totals	321	387	17	25	.405	448	143	276	2.42

PAT RAPP 27 6-3 215   Bats R Throws R

Marlins' most consistent starter in his first full season in majors... Posted lowest ERA by Marlins starter in club history (3.85)... Also led staff in strikeouts (75), walks (69) and complete games (2)... Became first Marlin to toss back-to-back, nine-inning complete games, July 22 vs. Colorado and July 27 vs. Phillies ... Opened season with three straight wins in 11 appearances, but lost four straight starts from June 18-July 4 ... Was 3-6 in last 10 starts as Marlins scored 24 runs in those starts... Won first major league game July 21, 1993 vs. Colorado

... Tossed first career complete game Sept. 2, 1993 vs. Padres
... Allowed one home run in final 45 innings in '93 ... Marlins' fifth pick of expansion draft ... Selected by Giants in 15th round of 1989 draft ... Born July 13, 1967, in Jennings, La. ... Would have earned $136,000 last season.

Year	Club	G	IP	W	L	Pct.	SO	BB	H	ERA
1992	San Francisco	3	10	0	2	.000	3	6	8	7.20
1993	Florida	16	94	4	6	.400	57	39	101	4.02
1994	Florida	24	131⅓	7	8	.467	75	69	132	3.85
	Totals	43	237⅓	11	16	.407	135	114	241	4.06

DAVID WEATHERS 25 6-3 205   Bats R Throws R

Started strong, but finished the season by dropping last five starts ... Led club in wins (8), losses (12), innings (135) and starts (24) ... Ranked second in NL in losses behind Padres' Andy Benes (14) ... His 79 earned runs allowed were fifth-highest figure in NL ... Dropped first start of year, but won next five ... Went 4-1 with 2.10 ERA in April ... Has gone at least six innings in 18 of 30 career starts ... Gave up nine homers in his last 110⅔ innings after giving up four in first 24⅓ ... Split time between Florida and Edmonton (AAA) in 1993 ... Chosen 29th overall in second round of expansion draft ... Selected by Blue Jays in third round of 1988 draft ... Born Sept. 25, 1969, in Lawrenceburg, Tenn. ... Would have earned $135,000 in '94.

Year	Club	G	IP	W	L	Pct.	SO	BB	H	ERA
1991	Toronto	15	14⅔	1	0	1.000	13	17	15	4.91
1992	Toronto	2	3⅓	0	0	.000	3	2	5	8.10
1993	Florida	14	45⅔	2	3	.400	34	13	57	5.12
1994	Florida	24	135	8	12	.400	72	59	166	5.27
	Totals	55	198⅔	11	15	.423	122	91	243	5.26

TOP PROSPECTS

CHARLES JOHNSON 23 6-2 215   Bats R Throws R
One of best young catching prospects in baseball ... First player from Marlins' farm system to reach majors ... Third player from 1992 draft to reach majors, joining Jeffrey Hammonds and Rick

Helling... Started season with Portland (AA) and was called up to majors May 6... Collected a hit in all four games with Marlins... Returned to Portland on May 10... Tied for Double-A lead in home runs with 28 and had 80 RBI and .264 average... Florida's first-round pick and 28th choice overall in 1992... Born July 20, 1971, in Ft. Pierce, Fla.

NIGEL WILSON 25 6-1 185 **Bats L Throws L**
Speedy outfielder is ready to take next step... Spent 1994 season with Edmonton (AAA), hitting .309 with 12 home runs and 62 RBI in 87 games... Played seven games for Marlins after being promoted Sept. 7, 1993 and struck out 11 times in 16 at-bats... Marlins made him second overall pick in expansion draft... Originally signed by Blue Jays as undrafted free agent in 1987... Born Jan. 12, 1970, in Oshawa, Ontario.

JOSH BOOTY 19 6-3 210 **Bats R Throws R**
Two-sport star is now full-time shortstop after Marlins made him fifth overall pick of 1994 draft... Batted .222 (8-36) with one home run and five RBI for Melbourne in rookie league before promotion to Elmira (A), where he hit .250 in 16 at-bats... Season ended after six games due to mononucleosis... Accepted scholarship to play baseball and football at LSU... As a quarterback, he rewrote national high school record book for passing with 11,700 yards, 128 touchdowns and 1,400 completions... Named *Parade Magazine's* Player of the Year... Signed record $1.6-million signing bonus, July 10, 1994... Born April 29, 1975, in Starkville, Miss.

MANAGER RENE LACHEMANN: The job of building an expansion franchise became tougher in his second year... Marlins finished fifth in NL East with 51-64 record, third-worst mark in NL... Did respectable job juggling young pitching staff, which lost Chris Hammond and Bryan Harvey to injuries for much of season... Signed two-year extension in October through 1997 season... Named Marlins' first manager Oct. 23, 1992... Posted 64-98 record in club's inaugural season, fifth-best beginning in history for expansion team... Served as coach under Athletics' Tony La Russa from 1987-92... Became youngest manager in majors when he replaced Maury Wills in Seattle, May 6, 1981... Managed Mariners for three seasons, finishing with a 140-180 mark... Recorded 67-94 record as Brewers manager in 1984... Former catcher batted .210 during 118-game major league career... Former Dodgers' bat boy... Born May 4, 1945, in Los Angeles... Overall major league managerial record is 322-436.

ALL-TIME MARLIN SEASON RECORDS

BATTING: Jeff Conine, .319, 1994
HRs: Gary Sheffield, 27, 1994
RBI: Orestes Destrade, 87, 1993
STEALS: Chuck Carr, 58, 1993
WINS: Chris Hammond, 11, 1993
STRIKEOUTS: Charlie Hough, 126, 1993

MONTREAL EXPOS

TEAM DIRECTORY: Pres.-General Partner: Claude Brochu; VP-Baseball Oper.: Bill Stoneman; Dir. Player Pers.: Kevin Malone; Dir. Media Rel.: Richard Griffin; Dir. Media Services: Monique Giroux; Trav. Sec.: Erik Ostling; Mgr.: Felipe Alou; Coaches: Pierre Arsenault, Tommy Harper, Tim Johnson, Joe Kerrigan, Jerry Manuel, Luis Pujois. Home: Olympic Stadium (46,500). Field distances: 325, l.f. line; 375, l.c.; 404, c.f.; 375, r.c.; 325, r.f. line. Spring training: West Palm Beach, Fla.

SCOUTING REPORT

Once again, the baseball world is paying homage to the great white north. First, it was the Blue Jays and now it's the Expos who are setting the perfect example of how to build a winner.

Felipe Alou once again has a club that will battle the Braves for supremacy in the NL East. The Expos seem to have everything:

Moises is chip off Felipe when it comes to hitting.

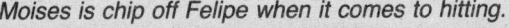

a solid pitching staff, a potent offense, speed and defense.

The Expos ranked third in the NL in batting average (.278), runs (585), hits (1,111) and on-base percentage (.343). Moises Alou, the manager's talented son, batted .339 with 22 home runs and 78 RBI last season and is a legitimate superstar. His supporting cast in equally impressive.

Restricted free agent Marquis Grissom (.288, 11, 45, 36 steals) combines power with speed and solid defense in center. Wil Cordero's defensive skills at shortstop will eventually match his offensive talents (.294, 15, 63) and Darrin Fletcher (.260, 10, 57) is an All-Star caliber catcher. Of course, if Larry Walker (.322, 19, 86) winds up splitting via free agency, the middle of the Expos' order will be damaged.

Montreal is counting on first baseman Cliff Floyd (.281, 4, 41) to develop into a big-time run producer. Floyd struggled in his rookie season, but is still regarded as one of the NL's top prospects. Rondell White (.278, 2, 13) is another talented youngster who will see plenty of action as a reserve outfielder. Prospect Shane Andrews may wind up starting at third base.

Montreal's pitching staff is again a formidable unit. Montreal led the NL in wins (74), ERA (3.56), shutouts (8) and saves (46) and ranked second in hits (970).

The ace of the staff is restricted free agent Ken Hill (16-5, 3.32), who tied Cy Young winner Greg Maddux for the NL lead in wins last season and is a threat to win 20. Pedro Martinez (11-5, 3.42) is an emerging star while Butch Henry (8-3, 2.43) and Jeff Fassero (8-6, 2.99) will be looking to repeat career years. Rookie Gabe White (1-1, 6.08) is a candidate for No. 5 starter.

No team has a one-two punch in the bullpen like the Expos. If restricted free agent John Wetteland (4-6, 2.83, 25 saves) does not shut you down, Mel Rojas (3-2, 3.32, 16 saves) is available.

Defensively, the Expos may have the best outfield in the majors, but their infield is not as solid. Floyd is agile, but inexperienced at first and Cordero needs to become more consistent at short. Third baseman Sean Berry and second baseman Mike Lansing are adequate.

Montreal had the best record in baseball at 74-40 last season before the strike interrupted its dream season. The Expos know they're good and fear no one, including the Braves. There's no reason to think that Hill and Martinez won't have good years again in '95 and the bullpen should be strong.

If the Expos' young players provide offense to go with Alou's numbers, Montreal may again post the best record in baseball—perhaps even 100 wins—and should win the NL East title.

EXPO PROFILES

MOISES ALOU 28 6-3 190   Bats R Throws R

Solidified himself as one of baseball's elite players last season . . . Produced game-winning double in 10th inning of his first All-Star Game . . . Finished third in NL in batting (.339), sixth in runs (81), hits (143), extra-base hits (58) and slugging percentage (.592) . . . His 45 multi-hit games was second-highest total in NL to Tony Gwynn's 54 . . . Had two homers and five RBI June 6 vs. Astros and repeated that feat three days later against Mets' Dwight Gooden . . . Had career-best, 14-game hitting streak snapped April 29 . . . Drove in 53 runs and scored 47 in final 54 games . . . Clubhouse leader in mold of father Felipe, now the Expos' manager . . . Suffered dislocated ankle, fractured fibula and ligament damage rounding first base in St. Louis, Sept. 16, 1993 . . . Runnerup to Dodgers' Eric Karros for NL Rookie of the Year honors in '92 . . . Missed entire 1991 season following right shoulder surgery . . . Acquired from Pirates with Scott Ruskin and Willie Greene for Zane Smith, Aug. 8, 1990 . . . Pirates' first pick and second player taken overall in 1986 draft . . . Cousin Mel Rojas is teammate . . . Born July 3, 1966, in Atlanta . . . Outfielder would have earned $1.4 million last season.

Year	Club	Pos.	G	AB	R	H	2B	3B	HR	RBI	SB	Avg.
1990	Pitt.-Mont.	OF	16	20	4	4	0	1	0	0	0	.200
1991	Montreal					Injured						
1992	Montreal	OF	115	341	53	96	28	2	9	56	16	.282
1993	Montreal	OF	136	482	70	138	29	6	18	85	17	.286
1994	Montreal	OF	107	422	81	143	31	5	22	78	7	.339
	Totals		374	1265	208	381	88	14	49	219	40	.301

WIL CORDERO 23 6-2 185   Bats R Throws R

Enjoyed breakthrough year in his second full season at shortstop . . . Led all NL shortstops in batting average (.294), home runs (15) and RBI (63) . . . Named to first All-Star team, replacing injured Barry Larkin . . . Set club season record for homers by shortstop July 25 vs. Braves . . . Batted .332 with nine homers and 20 doubles in final 51 games . . . Had career-high, 10-game hitting streak snapped June 24 . . . Homered in three straight games June 4-6 . . . Recorded team-record 36 errors as a rookie shortstop in 1993 . . . Became first Expos shortstop to hit 10-plus homers and steal 10-plus bases in season in '93 . . . Singled in first two

major league at-bats, off Dodgers' Ramon Martinez, July 24, 1992
. . . Signed by Expos as undrafted free agent in 1988 . . . Born Oct.
3, 1971, in Mayaguez, P.R. . . . Would have earned $200,000 last
year.

Year	Club	Pos.	G	AB	R	H	2B	3B	HR	RBI	SB	Avg.
1992	Montreal	SS-2B	45	126	17	38	4	1	2	8	0	.302
1993	Montreal	SS-3B	138	475	56	118	32	2	10	58	12	.248
1994	Montreal	SS	110	415	65	122	30	3	15	63	16	.294
	Totals		293	1016	138	278	66	6	27	129	28	.274

DARRIN FLETCHER 28 6-1 198   Bats L Throws R

Expos' best catcher since Gary Carter . . .
Strong defensively, he is just starting to blossom as an offensive player . . . Expos
were 52-27 in games he started last season . . . Since
June 1, 1993, he has hit 18 home runs and
collected 105 RBI in 581 at-bats . . . Had 48
RBI in last 61 games last season . . . Appeared
in first All-Star Game . . . Had career-high five
RBI May 24 vs. Marlins . . . Led NL with 12 sac flies . . . Started
105 games in 1993, his first full season in majors . . . Acquired
from Phillies for Barry Jones prior to 1992 season . . . Sixth-round
pick of Dodgers in 1987 . . . Father Tom pitched for Tigers in 1962
. . . Born Oct. 3, 1966, in Elmhurst, Ill. . . . Would have earned
$600,000 in '94.

Year	Club	Pos.	G	AB	R	H	2B	3B	HR	RBI	SB	Avg.
1989	Los Angeles	C	5	8	1	4	0	0	1	2	0	.500
1990	L.A.-Phil.	C	11	23	3	3	1	0	0	1	0	.130
1991	Philadelphia	C	46	136	5	31	8	0	1	12	0	.228
1992	Montreal	C	83	222	13	54	10	2	2	26	0	.243
1993	Montreal	C	133	396	33	101	20	1	9	60	0	.255
1994	Montreal	C	94	285	28	74	18	1	10	57	0	.260
	Totals		372	1070	83	267	57	4	23	158	0	.250

MARQUIS GRISSOM 27 5-11 190   Bats R Throws R

Centerpiece to baseball's best outfield . . .
Would be a major run producer if he didn't
have to bat leadoff . . . Expos went 48-22 in
games in which he batted in top spot in order
. . . Ranked second in NL in runs (96) and at-bats (475) and third in steals (36) . . . Hit first
career inside-the-park homer to win game in
10th inning, Aug. 1 vs. Cards . . . Batted .304
with 65 runs, 16 doubles, 27 walks and nine homers in final 67
games . . . Batted .287 with 16 RBI while hitting third in order for
36 games . . . Homered in three straight games from July 30-Aug.
1 . . . Homered off Randy Johnson in second All-Star Game ap-

pearance... Had 14-game hitting streak snapped June 12... Won Gold Glove in 1993 when he amassed 188 hits, fourth-highest total in club history... Led NL in stolen bases in 1991 and 1992 ... Expos' third-round pick in 1988... Born April 17, 1967, in Atlanta... Would have earned $3.5 million in '94... Won second Gold Glove in '94.

Year Club	Pos.	G	AB	R	H	2B	3B	HR	RBI	SB	Avg.
1989 Montreal	OF	26	74	16	19	2	0	1	2	1	.257
1990 Montreal	OF	98	288	42	74	14	2	3	29	22	.257
1991 Montreal	OF	148	558	73	149	23	9	6	39	76	.267
1992 Montreal	OF	159	653	99	180	39	6	14	66	78	.276
1993 Montreal	OF	157	630	104	188	27	2	19	95	53	.298
1994 Montreal	OF	110	475	96	137	25	4	11	45	36	.288
Totals		698	2678	430	747	130	23	54	276	266	.279

CLIFF FLOYD 22 6-4 220   Bats L Throws L

Limitless potential... Rated No. 1 prospect by *Baseball America* during first full season in majors... Started 63 games at first base and 16 in outfield... Team went 29-12 when he batted second in lineup... Batted .319 in final 16 games... Had career-high, eight-game hitting streak snapped June 22... Enjoyed first four-hit game July 24 vs. Dodgers... Power hitter with deceiving speed... Made his major league debut Sept. 18, 1993, after Moises Alou was disabled... Hit first big league homer Sept. 26 vs. Mets... Spent half of '93 season with Harrisburg (AA) and was named MVP of Eastern League after leading league with 26 homers, 101 RBI and .600 slugging percentage... Expos' first pick and 14th player chosen overall in 1991 draft... Born Dec. 5, 1972, in Chicago... Would have earned $109,500.

Year Club	Pos.	G	AB	R	H	2B	3B	HR	RBI	SB	Avg.
1993 Montreal	1B	10	31	3	7	0	0	1	2	0	.226
1994 Montreal	1B-OF	100	334	43	94	19	4	4	41	10	.281
Totals		110	365	46	101	19	4	5	43	10	.277

JEFF FASSERO 32 6-1 195   Bats L Throws L

Finished tied with Butch Henry for fourth on staff in wins with eight in first full season in starting rotation... Effective low-ball pitcher ... Posted fourth-best ERA (2.99) in NL... Came within one strike of tossing no-hitter June 13 before Pirates' Carlos Garcia singled off pitcher's glove... Suffered rib cage injury July 22 and returned on eve of strike... Made first major league start July 10, 1993 against the Padres, after 161 consecutive relief appearances... Amassed more victories than any left-handed reliever in majors in 1992... Selected by Cardinals in 22nd round of 1984 draft... Spent time in Cleveland system... Signed by Expos as minor league free agent in 1991... Born Jan. 5, 1963, in Springfield, Ill.... Would have earned $315,000 last year.

Year	Club	G	IP	W	L	Pct.	SO	BB	H	ERA
1991	Montreal	51	55⅔	2	5	.286	42	17	39	2.44
1992	Montreal	70	85⅔	8	7	.533	63	34	81	2.84
1993	Montreal	56	149⅔	12	5	.706	140	54	119	2.29
1994	Montreal	21	138⅔	8	6	.571	119	40	119	2.99
	Totals	198	429⅓	30	23	.566	364	145	358	2.64

BUTCH HENRY 26 6-1 195 Bats L Throws L

Unsung star of a quality pitching staff... Finished tied for third on staff in wins (8) with Jeff Fassero... Fell 6⅔ innings short of qualifying for ERA title. He would have finished second to Braves' Greg Maddux at 2.43... Finished sixth in NL with .727 winning percentage... Won his first four starts... Started season with Ottawa (AAA), but was promoted April 18 after tossing 14 shutout innings in two minor league starts... In 1993, he split time between Ottawa and Montreal after being acquired from Colorado July 16... Between July 10-20, he was a member of four different teams without appearing in a game... Optioned to Colorado Springs (AAA) July 11 and traded to Expos five days later for Kent Bottenfield. He joined Ottawa before being recalled by Montreal... Finished second on the Astros in starts and innings pitched in 1992... Originally drafted by Reds in 15th round of 1987 draft... Was Colorado's fifth choice in expansion draft prior to '93... Born Oct. 7, 1968, in El Paso, Tex.... Would have earned $180,000 in '94.

Year	Club	G	IP	W	L	Pct.	SO	BB	H	ERA
1992	Houston	28	165⅔	6	9	.400	96	41	185	4.02
1993	Col.-Mont.	30	103	3	9	.250	47	28	135	6.12
1994	Montreal	24	107⅓	8	3	.727	70	20	97	2.43
	Totals	82	376	17	21	.447	213	89	419	4.14

KEN HILL 29 6-2 195 — Bats R Throws R

Ace of one of majors' best pitching staffs... Tied Cy Young winner Greg Maddux for league lead in wins with 16... Appeared in first All-Star Game, hurling two no-hit innings with a walk... Reached 15 wins faster than any other pitcher in club history... His .762 winning percentage was third-best in NL... Won five straight decisions from June 10-July 7... Shut out Padres on five hits July 7... Pitched at least six innings in 20 of 22 starts... Tied for NL lead with 16 sac bunts... Had 6-0 mark in 1993 before suffering groin injury... Acquired from Cardinals for Andres Galarraga prior to 1992 season... Signed by Tigers as undrafted free agent in 1985... Born Dec. 14, 1965, in Lynn, Mass.... Would have earned $2.25 million in '94.

Year	Club	G	IP	W	L	Pct.	SO	BB	H	ERA
1988	St. Louis	4	14	0	1	.000	6	6	16	5.14
1989	St. Louis	33	196⅔	7	15	.318	112	99	186	3.80
1990	St. Louis	17	78⅔	5	6	.455	58	33	79	5.49
1991	St. Louis	30	181⅓	11	10	.524	121	67	147	3.57
1992	Montreal	33	218	16	9	.640	150	75	187	2.68
1993	Montreal	28	183⅔	9	7	.563	90	74	163	3.23
1994	Montreal	23	154⅔	16	5	.762	85	44	145	3.32
	Totals	168	1027	64	53	.547	622	398	923	3.50

PEDRO MARTINEZ 23 5-11 170 — Bats R Throws R

Baby-faced right-hander became NL public enemy No. 1 for challenging opposing batters high and in tight... Led majors with 11 hit batsmen... Had perfect game in late innings April 13 before plunking Reds' Reggie Sanders, who charged the mound... Younger brother of Dodgers' Ramon ignited another bench-clearing brawl April 29 vs. San Diego after grooving fastball under Derek Bell's chin... Held opponents to .220 batting average, second-best in NL... Ranked fifth in NL in strikeouts with 142... Traded by Dodgers for Delino DeShields after 1993 season... Started 1993 with Albuquerque (AAA), but was promoted to Los Angeles after one start... Broke Steve Howe's rookie record for most games (65) in '93... Underwent 1992 postseason reconstructive surgery on non-pitching shoulder... Signed by Dodgers as undrafted free agent in 1988... Born

July 25, 1971, in Santo Domingo, D.R. . . . Would have earned $200,000 last year.

Year	Club	G	IP	W	L	Pct.	SO	BB	H	ERA
1992	Los Angeles	2	8	0	1	.000	8	1	6	2.25
1993	Los Angeles	65	107	10	5	.667	119	57	76	2.61
1994	Montreal	24	144⅔	11	5	.688	142	45	115	3.42
	Totals	91	259⅔	21	11	.656	269	103	197	3.05

MEL ROJAS 28 5-11 195   Bats R Throws R

First-rate finisher on team with two quality late-inning relievers . . . Has made no bones about wanting to be traded, because he wants to be No. 1 finisher . . . Subject of persistent trade rumors . . . Recorded career-high 16 saves . . . Ranked second in NL in games (58) . . . Only setup man to record 10-plus saves in each of last three seasons (36 total) . . . Recorded a save in eight straight appearances from April 20-May 2 . . . Led majors with 84 relief innings last season . . . Converted 10 of 11 save opportunities and stranded 48 of 58 inherited runners in 1992 . . . Signed by Expos scout Jesus Alou, his uncle, as undrafted free agent in 1985 . . . Born Dec. 10, 1966, in Haina, D.R. . . . Would have earned $850,000 last season.

Year	Club	G	IP	W	L	Pct.	SO	BB	H	ERA
1990	Montreal	23	40	3	1	.750	26	24	34	3.60
1991	Montreal	37	48	3	3	.500	37	13	42	3.75
1992	Montreal	68	100⅔	7	1	.875	70	34	71	1.43
1993	Montreal	66	88⅓	5	8	.385	48	30	80	2.95
1994	Montreal	58	84	3	2	.600	84	21	71	3.32
	Totals	252	361	21	15	.583	265	122	298	2.79

JOHN WETTELAND 28 6-2 210   Bats R Throws R

Dominant closer is still underrated in some respects . . . His 25 saves ranked fourth in NL . . . Blew 10 save chances . . . Placed second behind Giants' Rod Beck in games finished with 43 . . . Recorded his 100th save as Expo July 26 vs. Braves . . . Placed on 15-day disabled list with strained right hamstring April 18 . . . Did not record first save until May 8 vs. Braves . . . Had two wins and 11 saves in final 15 appearances . . . Blown save Aug. 6 at Philly was second straight via homer in ninth inning (John Kruk) . . . Cashed in 13 of his last 16 save opportunities . . . Broke Jeff Reardon's club record for saves (41 in 1985) with 43 in 1993, despite missing first three weeks with broken big right toe... Acquired from Reds with Bill Risley for Scott Ruskin, Dave Martinez and Willie Greene prior to 1992 season... Selected in second round by Dodgers in 1985... Born Aug. 21, 1966, in San Mateo, Cal.... Would have earned $2.2 million last year... Has 106 career saves.

Year	Club	G	IP	W	L	Pct.	SO	BB	H	ERA
1989	Los Angeles	31	102⅔	5	8	.385	96	34	81	3.77
1990	Los Angeles	22	43	2	4	.333	36	17	44	4.81
1991	Los Angeles	6	9	1	0	1.000	9	3	5	0.00
1992	Montreal	67	83⅓	4	4	.500	99	36	64	2.92
1993	Montreal	70	85⅓	9	3	.750	113	28	58	1.37
1994	Montreal	52	63⅔	4	6	.400	68	21	46	2.83
	Totals	248	387	25	25	.500	421	138	298	2.93

TOP PROSPECTS

SHANE ANDREWS 23 6-1 215   Bats R Throws R
Competing for starting third baseman's job... Will be big league run producer, but needs to cut down on strikeouts... Struck out 126 times in 460 at-bats in first full season with Ottawa (AAA) in 1994... Led team in homers (16) and RBI (85) while batting .254... Ranked sixth in home runs (18) and fifth in doubles (29) in Eastern League with Harrisburg (AA) in '93... In 1992, he led Expos' minor league system in home runs (25) and was second in RBI with 87 for Albany (A)... Montreal's first-round pick and 11th choice overall in 1990 draft... Turned down football scholarship to be punter and placekicker for University of Miami... Born Aug. 28, 1971, in Dallas.

CARLOS PEREZ 24 6-2 168   Bats L Throws L
Yes, it's another Perez brother... Younger sibling of Pascual and Melido is vying for a spot in Expos' rotation following strong minor league season in '94... Went 7-2 with 1.94 ERA in 12 games for Harrisburg (AA) before being promoted to Ottawa (AAA), where he finished with 7-5 record and 3.33 ERA in 17 starts... Has career 28-18 mark in six minor league seasons... Signed as undrafted free agent in 1988... Born Jan. 14, 1971, in Nigua, D.R.

GABE WHITE 23 6-2 200   Bats L Throws L
In the hunt for spot in rotation... Went 1-1 with 6.08 ERA in seven games with Expos... Spent most of season with Ottawa (AAA), finishing with 8-3 record and 5.05 ERA in 14 starts... Struck out 63 in 73 innings... Was leading Eastern League in

ERA (2.16) for Harrisburg (AA) before being promoted to Ottawa in 1993... Was Expos' extra pick in 1990 draft as compensation for Angels signing free agent Mark Langston... Born Nov. 20, 1971, in Sebring, Fla.

RONDELL WHITE 23 6-1 205   **Bats R Throws R**
Prize of Expos' talent-laden system... Outfielder is being compared to former Expo Andre Dawson for his hitting style and quiet demeanor... Split time between Montreal and Ottawa (AAA) in '94... Hit .278 with two homers in 97 at-bats for Expos... Hit .272 with seven homers and 18 RBI in 169 at-bats for Ottawa... Enjoyed best day July 24 vs. Dodgers, collecting home run among career-high four hits and seven RBI... Finished third in balloting for *USA Today's* Minor League Player of the Year award in '93, behind teammate Cliff Floyd and Manny Ramirez... Expos' second first-round pick and 24th overall choice in 1990 draft... Born Feb. 23, 1972, in Milledgeville, Ga.

MANAGER FELIPE ALOU: Finally has some hardware to show for two-plus seasons of exceptional managing... Was named NL Manager of the Year in '94... Received 27 of 28 first-place votes... Guided club to major league-best 74-40 record last season. Expos were six games in front of heavily favored Atlanta when strike hit... His teams have finished no lower than second last three seasons... Expos won 94 games, second-highest total in club history, in his first full season as skipper in '93... Became ninth manager in club history May 22, 1992... Took over team that had started 17-20 under Tom Runnells and Expos finished 87-75 and battled the Pirates up to next-to-last weekend of season... First Dominican-born manager in major league history... Has served in Expos' organization for 19 years... Paid his dues by managing 12 seasons in minors and 12 in winter leagues... Outfielder enjoyed impressive 17-year playing career, batting .286 with 206 home runs and 852 RBI... Born May 12, 1935, in Haina, D.R.... Overall major league managerial record is 238-163.

Butch Henry came out of nowhere to post 2.43 ERA.

ALL-TIME EXPO SEASON RECORDS

BATTING: Moises Alou, .339, 1994
HRs: Andre Dawson, 32, 1983
RBI: Tim Wallach, 123, 1987
STEALS: Ron LeFlore, 97, 1980
WINS: Ross Grimsley, 20, 1978
STRIKEOUTS: Bill Stoneman, 251, 1971

NEW YORK METS

TEAM DIRECTORY: Chairman: Nelson Doubleday; Pres./CEO: Fred Wilpon; Sr. VP-Consultant: Frank Cashen; Exec. VP-Baseball Oper.: Joe McIlvaine; VP-Business Affairs: Dave Howard; VP-Baseball Oper.: Gerry Hunsicker; Dir. Minor Leagues: Steve Phillips; Dir. Scouting: John Barr; Dir. Media Rel.: Jay Horwitz; Coaches: Mike Cubbage, Frank Howard, Tom McCraw, Greg Pavlick, Bobby Wine; Mgr.: Dallas Green. Home: Shea Stadium (55,601). Field distances: 338, l.f. line; 371, l.c.; 410, c.f.; 371, r.c.; 388, r.f. line. Spring training: Port St. Lucie, Fla.

SCOUTING REPORT

Baseball's greatest reclamation project continues in Flushing, N.Y. The Mets finished under .500 last season (55-58) for the fourth consecutive year, but finally started showing progress. Dallas Green's club improved 20 1/2 games from the nightmare that was its 1993 season and acted more responsibly off the field.

GM Joe McIlvaine is building a club that may be ready to compete for a wild card and possibly a division title in 1996. As for 1995, New Yorkers are once again being asked to exercise patience, especially with the young pitchers.

The Mets are developing a solid staff, led by undisputed ace Bret Saberhagen (14-4, 2.74). Sinkerballer Bobby Jones (12-7, 3.15) is the perfect complement to Saberhagen and left-hander Jason Jacome (4-3, 2.67) pitched himself into the rotation in '95.

Replacing fallen phenom Dwight Gooden's arm and presence will be a difficult chore, although the Mets were preparing for life after Gooden even before baseball suspended him for violating his drug aftercare program. The Mets were hoping to sign ex-Astro Pete Harnisch (8-5, 5.40), an unrestricted free agent, to provide quality innings until minor league prospects Bill Pulsipher, Chris Roberts, Juan Castillo and Jason Isringhausen are ready to make the jump.

The possible defection of free-agent John Franco (1-4, 2.70), who led the NL with 30 saves, might lead to Josias Manzanillo (3-2, 2.66), ex-Brewer Doug Henry (2-3, 4.60) or ex-Indian Jerry DiPoto (0-0, 8.04) becoming the club's closer.

The Mets ranked next-to-last in the NL last season in batting average (.250) and hits (966) and ninth in RBI (477), so this is a team in need of another big bopper in the lineup.

Bobby Bonilla (.290, 20, 67) is the Mets' most dangerous

Bret Saberhagen struck out 143 and walked only 13.

hitter, but needs someone to hit behind him. First baseman Rico Brogna (.351, 7, 20), who feasted on NL pitching and unseated David Segui after being promoted to the majors June 20, could be that man. The Mets still believe that Jeff Kent (.292, 14, 68), one of baseball's best-hitting second basemen, will hit 30 home runs in some season. Center fielder Ryan Thompson (.225, 18, 59, 94 Ks) has the potential, but lacks the patience to become a true slugger.

Jose Vizcaino (.256, 3, 33) is a quality No. 2 hitter masquerading as a leadoff hitter. The Mets ranked last in the NL in stolen bases with 25 in '94, underscored by Vizcaino's ludicrous one steal in 11 attempts.

Vizcaino helped solidify the Mets' infield at short. But third baseman Bonilla and second baseman Kent committed more errors than any other NL players at their respective positions and Bonilla appears headed back to the outfield. Brogna is smooth at first. Thompson can chase down any flyball, but could be moved to left if young switch-hitting Carl Everett, acquired from the Marlins, proves himself as a center fielder and leadoff hitter.

There's no reason the Mets cannot finish at 81-81. An above- .500 mark is attainable, but only if the Mets add speed and power to their lineup.

MET PROFILES

BOBBY BONILLA 32 6-3 240　　　　　Bats S Throws R

Still the most feared bat in Mets' lineup... Volunteered to leave outfield and return to third base for first time since 1989 and committed league-high 18 errors in '94... May be headed back to right field... Lost $31,148 per day during strike, most of any player in baseball... Led team in RBI with 67... Set club record rith at least one RBI in nine straight games as he collected 13 from May 20-29... Put together 12-game hitting streak from May 17-30, raising average from .279 to .329... Missed one week in April after injuring surgically repaired left shoulder diving for ball... Hit career-high 34 homers in 1993 before suffering season-ending shoulder injury... Originally signed by Pirates as undrafted free agent in July 1981... Born Feb. 23, 1963, in New York... Would have earned $6.3 million last season on third year of five-year, $29-million deal he signed with Mets as free agent prior to 1992 season.

Year	Club	Pos.	G	AB	R	H	2B	3B	HR	RBI	SB	Avg.
1986	Chicago (AL)...	OF-1B	75	234	27	63	10	2	2	26	4	.269
1986	Pittsburgh.....	OF-1B-3B	63	192	28	46	6	2	1	17	4	.240
1987	Pittsburgh.....	3B-OF-1B	141	466	58	140	33	3	15	77	3	.300
1988	Pittsburgh.....	3B	159	584	87	160	32	7	24	100	3	.274
1989	Pittsburgh.....	3B-1B-OF	163	616	96	173	37	10	24	86	8	.281
1990	Pittsburgh.....	OF-3B-1B	160	625	112	175	39	7	32	120	4	.280
1991	Pittsburgh.....	OF-3B-1B	157	577	102	174	44	6	18	100	2	.302
1992	New York (NL)	OF-1B	128	438	62	109	23	0	19	70	4	.249
1993	New York (NL)	OF-3B-1B	139	502	81	133	21	3	34	87	3	.265
1994	New York (NL)	3B	108	403	60	117	24	1	20	67	1	.290
	Totals.......		1293	4637	713	1290	269	41	189	750	36	.278

TODD HUNDLEY 25 5-11 185　　　　　Bats S Throws R

Rebounded from disastrous 1993 campaign last season, but Mets are still waiting for the son of former major league catcher to blossom into solid everyday player... Lost starting job to rookie Kelly Stinnett during spring training, but regained No. 1 status with strong start... Belted career-high 16 home runs... Threw out 20 of 63 would-be base-stealers (32 percent), including four in one game... Became fourth Met in history to homer from both sides of the plate in same game, June 18 at Florida... Struggled with throwing mechanics in 1993... In one stretch, he threw out only one of 22 would-be base-stealers... Established record for Met catchers by playing 113 consecutive errorless games, a streak that ended June 18, 1993 in Pittsburgh ... Made major league debut May 18, 1990 as 20-year-old... Mets' second-round pick in 1987... Father Randy played with Giants, Cubs, Twins and Padres and also wore No. 9... Born May 27, 1969, in Martinsville, Va.... Would have earned $290,000 last season.

Year Club	Pos.	G	AB	R	H	2B	3B	HR	RBI	SB	Avg.
1990 New York (NL)	C	36	67	8	14	6	0	0	2	0	.209
1991 New York (NL)	C	21	60	5	8	0	1	1	7	0	.133
1992 New York (NL)	C	123	358	32	75	17	0	7	32	3	.209
1993 New York (NL)	C	130	417	40	95	17	2	11	53	1	.228
1994 New York (NL)	C	91	291	45	69	10	1	16	42	2	.237
Totals		401	1193	130	261	50	4	35	136	6	.219

JEFF KENT 27 6-1 185   Bats R Throws R

Okay, so he'll probably never win a Gold Glove at second, but his defense improved dramatically in '94... Was baseball's MVP for first month of season... Hit .375 with eight home runs and 26 RBI in 22 April games... Had a pair of nine-game hitting streaks... Batted .385 with runners in scoring position... Played in 107 games last season, despite playing with sore right foot... One of the most intense players in Mets' clubhouse... In 1993, he set club records for homers and RBI by a second baseman and batted .303 with 16 home runs and 55 RBI in final 82 games... Made jump from Double-A to majors with Blue Jays in 1992... Traded by Toronto to Mets with Ryan Thompson for David Cone, Aug. 27, 1992... Born March 7, 1968, in Bellflower, Cal.... Blue Jays' 21st-round pick in 1989 ... Played shortstop at Cal-Berkeley... Built a home in Austin, Tex.... Would have earned $437,500 in '94.

Year Club	Pos.	G	AB	R	H	2B	3B	HR	RBI	SB	Avg.
1992 Toronto	3B–2B–1B	65	192	36	46	13	1	8	35	2	.240
1992 New York (NL)	2B–3B–SS	37	113	16	27	8	1	3	15	0	.239
1993 New York (NL)	2B-3B-SS	140	496	65	134	24	0	21	80	4	.270
1994 New York (NL)	2B	107	415	53	121	24	5	14	68	1	.292
Totals		349	1216	170	328	69	7	46	198	7	.270

JOE ORSULAK 32 6-1 205   Bats L Throws L

A favorite of his teammates and coaching staff for his dedication and professionalism in face of wife's serious illness in '94... Excels as part-time player, who added limited first-base duties to his resume the last two seasons... Started 67 games in outfield and tied for fifth in NL with eight outfield assists... Collected his 1,000 hit July 18... Batted .361 in final 16 games... Started 94 games in outfield in 1993, when he also hit .333 as a pinch- hitter... Signed free-agent contract with Mets prior to 1993 season... Led Orioles in hitting at .289 in 1992... Led majors with 22 outfield assists for Baltimore in 1991... Had career-best 21-game hitting streak in '91... Selected by Pirates in sixth round of 1980 draft... Traded to Orioles for Terry Crowley and Rico Rossy prior to 1988 season... Born May 31, 1962, in Glen Ridge, N.J.... Would have earned $850,000 in '94.

Year	Club	Pos.	G	AB	R	H	2B	3B	HR	RBI	SB	Avg.
1983	Pittsburgh	OF	7	11	0	2	0	0	0	1	0	.182
1984	Pittsburgh	OF	32	67	12	17	1	2	0	3	3	.254
1985	Pittsburgh	OF	121	397	54	119	14	6	0	21	24	.300
1986	Pittsburgh	OF	138	401	60	100	19	6	2	19	24	.249
1988	Baltimore	OF	125	379	48	109	21	3	8	27	9	.288
1989	Baltimore	OF	123	390	59	111	22	5	7	55	5	.285
1990	Baltimore	OF	124	413	49	111	14	3	11	57	6	.269
1991	Baltimore	OF	143	486	57	135	22	1	5	43	6	.278
1992	Baltimore	OF	117	391	45	113	18	3	4	39	5	.289
1993	New York (NL)	OF-1B	134	409	59	116	15	4	8	35	5	.284
1994	New York (NL)	OF-1B	96	292	39	76	3	0	8	42	4	.260
	Totals		1160	3636	482	1009	149	33	53	342	91	.278

RYAN THOMPSON 27 6-3 200   Bats R Throws R

Gifted center fielder continues to struggle at the plate... Set career highs in home runs (18) and RBI (59), but struck out 94 times... Hit .305 with 13 homers and 37 RBI on road... Batted in eighth spot for majority of season... Established career best with three four-RBI games... Had career-high seven-game hitting streak from June 1-8... Underwent arthroscopic right knee surgery Sept. 20... Split time between majors and Norfolk

(AAA) in 1993... Hit .270 with 11 home runs and 25 RBI in final 64 games with Mets... Came to Mets from Blue Jays with Jeff Kent as player to be named later in David Cone deal, Sept. 1, 1992... Made 27 starts following trade... Recruited to play football at Maryland... Blue Jays' 13th-round pick in 1987... Born Nov. 4, 1967, in Chestertown, Md.... Would have earned $175,000 in '94.

Year	Club	Pos.	G	AB	R	H	2B	3B	HR	RBI	SB	Avg.
1992	New York (NL)	OF	30	108	15	24	7	1	3	10	2	.222
1993	New York (NL)	OF	80	288	34	72	19	2	11	26	2	.250
1994	New York (NL)	OF	98	334	39	75	14	1	18	59	1	.225
	Totals.......		208	730	88	171	40	4	32	95	5	.234

JOSE VIZCAINO 27 6-1 180   Bats R Throws R

Steady, but unspectacular shortstop failed to provide much-needed speed at top of lineup... Stole only one base in 11 tries last season... Best suited to be No. 2 hitter... Committed 13 errors in 99 starts at short... Matched career-best, 16-game hitting streak from May 20-June 9... Acquired from Cubs for Anthony Young and Ottis Smith just before start of last season... Smacked solo home run against Mike Morgan in his second at-bat for Mets, Opening Day in Wrigley Field... Batted .280 from left side of plate... In 1993, he set career highs in nearly every major offensive category... Signed as undrafted free agent by Dodgers in February 1986 and traded to Cubs for Greg Smith four years later... Born March 26, 1968, in Palenque de San Cristobal, D.R.... Would have earned $850,000 in '94.

Year	Club	Pos.	G	AB	R	H	2B	3B	HR	RBI	SB	Avg.
1989	Los Angeles...	SS	7	10	2	2	0	0	0	0	0	.200
1990	Los Angeles...	SS-2B	37	51	3	14	1	1	0	2	1	.275
1991	Chicago (NL)..	3B-SS-2B	93	145	7	38	5	0	0	10	2	.262
1992	Chicago (NL)..	SS-3B-2B	86	285	25	64	10	4	1	17	3	.225
1993	Chicago (NL)..	SS-3B-2B	151	551	74	158	19	4	4	54	12	.287
1994	New York (NL)	SS	103	410	47	105	13	3	3	33	1	.256
	Totals.......		477	1452	158	381	48	12	8	116	19	.262

BOBBY JONES 25 6-4 225   Bats R Throws R

Quickly established himself as No. 2 starter, behind Bret Saberhagen, in his first full season in majors... Fearless competitor... Finished eighth in NL in ERA (3.15)... Tied for sixth in victories (12)... Was 8-1 with 1.77 ERA in 10 road starts... Tossed first career shutout and complete game May 7 in St. Louis... Posted 5-0 record in last eight starts... Won his major league debut Aug. 14, 1993, at Philadelphia... Tossed 10 shutout innings against St. Louis in 17-inning Met victory, Sept. 29, 1993 ... Selected as compensation pick in 1991 draft for losing free agent Darryl Strawberry to Dodgers... Attended Fresno High School, same school that produced Hall of Famer Tom Seaver... Born Feb. 10, 1970, in Fresno, Cal.... Would have earned $130,000 last season.

Year	Club	G	IP	W	L	Pct.	SO	BB	H	ERA
1993	New York (NL)	9	61²/₃	2	4	.333	35	22	61	3.65
1994	New York (NL)	24	160	12	7	.632	80	56	157	3.15
	Totals	33	221²/₃	14	11	.560	15	78	218	3.29

BRET SABERHAGEN 30 6-1 190   Bats R Throws R

Re-established himself as one of game's elite pitchers... Two-time Cy Young winner (1985 and 1989) was selected to his third All-Star Game... Ranked second in NL in ERA (2.74) and tied for third in victories (14)... Had seven-game winning streak from June 20-Aug. 10... Set modern-day record by allowing just 0.7 walks per nine innings in '94... Set club record by not allowing a walk for 47⅓ innings... Became fourth pitcher since 1900 to have more victories than walks (13) in a season with a minimum of 150 innings... Named NL Pitcher of the Month for July, when he went 4-0 with 1.43 ERA... Pitched 10 innings against Padres July 15 and got no-decision despite giving up no runs, no walks and just five hits and striking out 11 ... Pitched seven or more innings in 19 of 24 starts... Injured left knee Aug. 7, 1993 and missed remainder of season... Made only 15 starts in 1992 due to inflammation of right index finger ... Royals' 19th-round pick in 1982... Acquired from Royals with Bill Pecota for Gregg Jefferies, Keith Miller and Kevin McReynolds prior to 1992 season... World Series MVP for Kansas City in 1985... Born April 11, 1964, in Chicago Heights, Ill.

... Would have earned $4.36 million last year, not counting incentive bonuses that became unreachable because of strike.

Year	Club	G	IP	W	L	Pct.	SO	BB	H	ERA
1984	Kansas City	38	157⅔	10	11	.476	73	36	138	3.48
1985	Kansas City	32	235⅓	20	6	.769	158	38	211	2.87
1986	Kansas City	30	156	7	12	.368	112	29	165	4.15
1987	Kansas City	33	257	18	10	.643	163	53	246	3.36
1988	Kansas City	35	260⅔	14	16	.467	171	59	271	3.80
1989	Kansas City	36	262⅓	23	6	.793	193	43	209	2.16
1990	Kansas City	20	135	5	9	.357	87	28	146	3.27
1991	Kansas City	28	196⅓	13	8	.619	136	45	165	3.07
1992	New York (NL)	17	97⅔	3	5	.375	81	27	84	3.50
1993	New York (NL)	19	139⅓	7	7	.500	93	17	131	3.29
1994	New York (NL)	24	177⅓	14	4	.778	143	13	169	2.74
	Totals	312	2074⅔	134	94	.588	1410	388	1935	3.19

JOHN FRANCO 34 5-10 185   Bats L Throws L

Fiery closer rescued his career by producing one of his best seasons in final year of two-year, $8-million extension... Led NL in saves (30) for third time in career and ranked second in baseball to Orioles' Lee Smith (33) last season... His 266 lifetime saves are most by left-handed pitcher and eighth on all-time list... Mets' all-time saves leader with 118... Surgically repaired left elbow forced him to go to DL twice during 1993 season, when he converted just 10 of 17 save opportunities ... In 1992, he was disabled twice and eventually underwent surgery Sept. 29 to repair a torn flexor tendon in his elbow... Best season was in 1988, when he cashed in 39 of 42 save opportunities for Reds... Acquired from Reds with Don Brown for Randy Myers and Kip Gross prior to 1990 season... Dodgers' fifth-round pick in 1981, out of St. John's... Born Sept. 17, 1960, in Brooklyn, N.Y.... Would have earned $4 million in 1994... **Free agent at press time.**

Year	Club	G	IP	W	L	Pct.	SO	BB	H	ERA
1984	Cincinnati	54	79⅓	6	2	.750	55	36	74	2.61
1985	Cincinnati	67	99	12	3	.800	61	40	83	2.18
1986	Cincinnati	74	101	6	6	.500	84	44	90	2.94
1987	Cincinnati	68	82	8	5	.615	61	27	76	2.52
1988	Cincinnati	70	86	6	6	.500	46	27	60	1.57
1989	Cincinnati	60	80⅔	4	8	.333	60	36	77	3.12
1990	New York (NL)	55	67⅔	5	3	.625	56	21	66	2.53
1991	New York (NL)	52	55⅓	5	9	.357	45	18	61	2.93
1992	New York (NL)	31	33	6	2	.750	20	11	24	1.64
1993	New York (NL)	35	36⅓	4	3	.571	29	19	46	5.20
1994	New York (NL)	47	50	1	4	.200	42	19	47	2.70
	Totals	613	770⅓	63	51	.553	559	298	704	2.63

PETE HARNISCH 28 6-0 198   Bats R Throws R

Acquired in November by Mets from Astros for pitchers Andy Beckerman and Juan Castillo, but became unrestricted free agent after Mets didn't tender qualifying offer... Struggled physically last year, coming off 16-win season in 1993, when he led NL with four shutouts and held opponents to lowest batting average in league at .214... In his first nine starts of '94, he was 2-4 with 7.15 ERA before landing on disabled list May 27 with partially torn right biceps tendon... Showed toughness by coming back only one month later and went 4-0 in July ... Owns 28-16 lifetime record with 2.94 ERA at Astrodome... Acquired by Astros from Orioles with Steve Finley and Curt Schilling for Glenn Davis prior to 1991 season... Born Sept. 23, 1966, in Commack, N.Y.... Selected by Orioles with compensation pick between the first and second rounds in 1987 draft... Would have earned $3.205 million last year.

Year	Club	G	IP	W	L	Pct.	SO	BB	H	ERA
1988	Baltimore	2	13	0	2	.000	10	9	13	5.54
1989	Baltimore	18	103⅓	5	9	.357	70	64	97	4.62
1990	Baltimore	31	188⅔	11	11	.500	122	86	189	4.34
1991	Houston	33	216⅔	12	9	.571	172	83	169	2.70
1992	Houston	34	206⅔	9	10	.474	164	64	182	3.70
1993	Houston	33	217⅔	16	9	.640	185	79	171	2.98
1994	Houston	17	95	8	5	.615	62	39	100	5.40
	Totals	168	1041	61	55	.526	785	424	921	3.73

TOP PROSPECTS

CARL EVERETT 23 6-0 190   Bats S Throws R

Switch-hitting outfielder came to Mets from Marlins in November trade for infielder Quilvio Veras... Enjoyed best pro season in 1994... Hit career-best .336 with 11 home runs and 47 RBI for Edmonton (AAA)... Recalled to majors twice last season, hitting .216 in 51 at-bats... Belted first major league homer May 22, off Cards' Allen Watson... Selected to Triple-A All-Star team last year... Started 1993 season with High Desert (A), but made major league debut July 1, 1993 vs. Mets... Marlins' made him 27th choice overall in second round of expansion draft... Yanks' first-round pick and 10th player taken overall in 1990... Born June 3, 1971, in Tampa, Fla.

RICO BROGNA 24 6-2 205   Bats L Throws L

Achieved cult hero status in New York after being promoted June

20 . . . Began his Met career 0-for-7 and later went on 15-game hitting streak . . . Hit safely in 23 starts from July 22-Aug. 7 . . . Forced club to shift incumbent first baseman David Segui to left field to make room for his smooth glove and blazing bat . . . Homered in three consecutive games, June 28-July 2 . . . Acquired from Tigers for Alan Zinter just before start of 1994 season in deal of former No. 1 picks . . . Born April 18, 1970, in Turner Falls, Mass. . . . Hit .244 with 12 homers and 37 RBI for Norfolk (AAA) in '94 . . . Hit .351 with seven homers and 20 RBI as a Met.

REY ORDONEZ 23 5-10 170　　　　　**Bats R Throws R**
Mets' shortstop of the future . . . Defensive prowess has drawn comparisons to Ozzie Smith . . . Improving offensive player . . . Batted .262 in 48 games for Eastern League champion Binghamton (AA), notching 20 RBI and committing eight errors . . . Hit .309 with two homers and 40 RBI for St. Lucie (A) in early part of '94 . . . In 1992, he defected from Cuba during World University Games in Buffalo by scaling a 10-foot fence . . . Became a Met through weighted lottery in October 1993 . . . Born Jan. 11, 1972, in Havana, Cuba.

JASON JACOME 24 6-3 160　　　　　**Bats L Throws L**
Skinny left-hander opened eyes during his two-month stint with the Mets . . . Recalled June 29 to replace suspended Dwight Gooden in rotation . . . Made his major league debut July 2 at San Diego . . . Had a streak of 19 scoreless innings from July 2-16 . . . Returned to Norfolk (AAA) on eve of strike and made four more starts . . . Led International League in ERA (2.84) while going 8-6 for Norfolk . . . Was 4-3 with 2.67 ERA in eight starts for Mets . . . Tucson native was selected in 12th round of 1991 draft . . . Born Nov. 24, 1970, in Tulsa, Okla.

BILL PULSIPHER 21 6-3 208　　　　　**Bats L Throws L**
"Pulse" has hearts of Mets' front-office honchos beating faster following terrific season with Binghamton (AA) . . . Hard-throwing lefty went 14-9 with a 3.22 ERA in 28 starts with league-leading 171 strikeouts . . . Tossed first no-hitter in Eastern League playoff game since 1937, against Harrisburg . . . Pitched 14-strikeout, four-hitter against New Haven in start preceding no-hitter . . . Mets' second-round pick in 1991 . . . Born Oct. 9, 1973, in Fort Benning, Ga.

MANAGER DALLAS GREEN:  This self-proclaimed "dinosaur" performed one of best managing jobs in majors last season, turning Mets from laughing stocks into respectable outfit... Rebuilding process began in spring training as he ran his players into ground... Club finished 55-58 in '94, despite having Dwight Gooden for only seven starts... Finished fourth in NL Manager of the Year voting... Turned 60 last year, but he has hinted he may want to manage beyond 1995... Inherited club from Jeff Torborg, May 21, 1993. Mets were 13-25 when he took over and finished with worst record (59-103) in baseball ... Team was regarded as one of worst in history... Managed Phillies from 1979-81, winning World Series in 1980... Served as Cubs' GM from 1982-87 and he was named Executive of the Year when Cubs won divisional title in 1984... Managed Yankees for 121 games in 1989 and spent most of those days fighting with owner George Steinbrenner... Right-handed pitcher compiled lifetime 20-22 record during eight seasons with Phillies, Senators and Mets... Born Aug. 4, 1934, in Newport, Del.... Lives on farm in Chester County, Pa.... Overall major league managerial record is 326-331.

ALL-TIME MET SEASON RECORDS

BATTING: Cleon Jones, .340, 1969
HRs: Darryl Strawberry, 39, 1987, 1988, 1990
RBI: Howard Johnson, 117, 1991
STEALS: Mookie Wilson, 58, 1982
WINS: Tom Seaver, 25, 1969
STRIKEOUTS: Tom Seaver, 289, 1971

PHILADELPHIA PHILLIES

TEAM DIRECTORY: Pres.: William Y. Giles; Exec. VP/COO: David Montgomery; VP/GM: Lee Thomas; Player Pers. Adm.: Ed Wade; VP-Pub. Rel.: Larry Shenk; Mgr. Media Rel.: Gene Dias; Trav. Sec.: Eddie Ferenz; Mgr.: Jim Fregosi; Coaches: Larry Bowa, Denis Menke, Johnny Podres, Mel Roberts, Mike Ryan, John Vukovich. Home: Veterans Stadium (64,538). Field distances: 330, l.f. line; 408, c.f.; 330, r.f. line. Spring training: Clearwater, Fla.

Darren Daulton's 15 homers and 56 RBI led Phillies.

SCOUTING REPORT

As bad as the Phillies were in finishing 54-61 last season, they'll still begin 1995 as the defending NL champs. But are they good enough to hold the title for three straight years?

Injuries to Darren Daulton, John Kruk, Dave Hollins, Lenny Dykstra and Curt Schilling ruined the Phillies in 1994 as Jim Fregosi's club finished 20 1/2 games behind the Expos in the NL East.

Offensively, the Phillies are capable of duplicating the outrageous numbers they produced in 1993, when they scored a league-leading 877 runs. Their team batting average dipped from .274 in '93 to .262 as most of the Phillies' power brokers were nursing injuries.

Daulton (.300, 15, 56), one of the best-hitting catchers in the league, figures to benefit greatly from the strike-induced extended break. His body needed the rest. Dave Hollins (.222, 4, 26), Philadelphia's best third baseman since Mike Schmidt, is capable of producing big numbers if he stays healthy.

Dykstra (.273, 5, 24, 15 steals) is the NL's best leadoff hitter and the undisputed leader of the Phillies. Kruk (.302, 5, 38), a free agent at press time, will be replaced at first base by ex-Cardinal Gregg Jeffries (.325, 12, 55), who was one of the most sought-after free agents. Free agent Mariano Duncan (.268, 8, 48) is coming off an All-Star season, Kevin Stocker (.273, 2, 28) is a solid, but unspectacular shortstop and second baseman Mickey Morandini batted .292 last season. Jim Eisenreich (.300, 4, 43) is a quality platoon player.

The Phillies lost Schilling (2-8, 4.48), Tommy Greene (2-0, 4.54) and Ben Rivera (3-4, 6.87) for most of the season but still finished with the fourth-best ERA in the NL at 3.85. However, Danny Jackson (14-6, 3.26), signed as a free agent with the Cardinals. Schilling's fall from grace was probably an aberration. Greene's right arm may never throw 95-mph fastballs again, but he's still a threat to win 12-15 games.

Rivera, David West (4-10, 3.55) and Bobby Munoz (7-5, 2.67) will compete for the remaining spots in the rotation. In the bullpen, All-Star closer Doug Jones (2-4, 2.17, 27 saves) still has some life left in his arm, but was unsigned at press time. Heathcliff Slocumb, who posted a 5-1 record and 2.86 ERA in 52 appearances, is emerging as a decent setup man.

Defensively, the Phillies continue to resemble the Keystone Cops. Philadelphia was the third-worst defensive team in the NL in '94, although the additions of Billy Hatcher and Tony Longmire

PHILLIE PROFILES

LENNY DYKSTRA 32 5-10 185   Bats L Throws L

Phillies' diminutive sparkplug... Center fielder led club in runs (68), on-base percentage (.404), walks (68), steals (15) and doubles (26), despite missing 30 games from June 18-July 23 after undergoing surgery for appendicitis... Finished tied for third in NL in walks... Voted an All-Star starter for second time in career, but he did not play due to injury... Scored at least one run in 10 consecutive games from April 18-29... Hit safely in seven straight at-bats from May 1-3... Shared NL Player of the Month honors in May with Dodgers' Mike Piazza. He batted .392 with 26 runs, 40 hits and 23 walks that month... Hit three leadoff home runs, giving him 18 for his career and 11 for Phillies ... Finished last season ranked eighth on Phillies' all-time stolen-base list with 156... Scored 143 runs in 1993, most in NL since Chuck Klein's 152 in 1932... In '93, he became first player in NL history to lead league in walks and at-bats in same season. His 733 plate appearances set all-time record... Finished second in NL MVP voting in '93... A career .320 hitter with six homers and 11 RBI in 13 World Series games... Mets' 12th-round pick in 1981 draft... Acquired from Mets with Roger McDowell for Tom Edens and Juan Samuel, June 18, 1989... Born Feb. 10, 1963, in Santa Ana, Cal.... Would have earned $2.6 million last year on four-year contract extension signed prior to last season.

Year	Club	Pos.	G	AB	R	H	2B	3B	HR	RBI	SB	Avg.
1985	New York (NL)	OF	83	236	40	60	9	3	1	19	15	.254
1986	New York (NL)	OF	147	431	77	127	27	7	8	45	31	.295
1987	New York (NL)	OF	132	431	86	123	37	3	10	43	27	.285
1988	New York (NL)	OF	126	429	57	116	19	3	8	33	30	.270
1989	N.Y.(NL)-Phil.	OF	146	511	66	121	32	4	7	32	30	.237
1990	Philadelphia...	OF	149	590	106	192	35	3	9	60	33	.325
1991	Philadelphia...	OF	63	246	48	73	13	5	3	12	24	.297
1992	Philadelphia...	OF	85	345	53	104	18	0	6	39	30	.301
1993	Philadelphia...	OF	161	637	143	194	44	6	19	66	37	.305
1994	Philadelphia...	OF	84	315	68	86	26	5	5	24	15	.273
	Totals........		1176	4171	744	1196	260	39	76	373	272	.287

DARREN DAULTON 33 6-2 202   Bats L Throws R

Phillies' catcher was on pace to set career highs in several offensive categories before fracturing his right clavicle June 28... Missed final 38 games... Was among NL leaders in RBI (56) and RBI-per-at-bats ratio (one per 4.6) at time of injury... Reliable backstop started 67 of Phils' first 76 games... Batted .457 with 11 RBI in last nine games prior to injury... Hit 100th career homer April 7 vs. Rockies... Had three homers and 10 RBI in three-game span April 10-13... Had two four-RBI games and six three-RBI games... Hit .325 with runners in scoring position in '94... Led team in RBI for second straight season in 1993, when he was named to All-Star team for second time... Phillies' 25th-round pick in 1980 draft... Born Jan. 3, 1962, in Arkansas City, Kan.... Would have earned $2.225 million last season.

Year Club	Pos.	G	AB	R	H	2B	3B	HR	RBI	SB	Avg.
1983 Philadelphia...	C	2	3	1	1	0	0	0	0	0	.333
1985 Philadelphia...	C	36	103	14	21	3	1	4	11	3	.204
1986 Philadelphia...	C	49	138	18	31	4	0	8	21	2	.225
1987 Philadelphia...	C–1B	53	129	10	25	6	0	3	13	0	.194
1988 Philadelphia...	C–1B	58	144	13	30	6	0	1	12	2	.208
1989 Philadelphia...	C	131	368	29	74	12	2	8	44	2	.201
1990 Philadelphia...	C	143	459	62	123	30	1	12	57	7	.268
1991 Philadelphia...	C	89	285	36	56	12	0	12	42	5	.196
1992 Philadelphia...	C	145	485	80	131	32	5	27	109	11	.270
1993 Philadelphia...	C	147	510	90	131	35	4	24	105	5	.257
1994 Philadelphia...	C	69	257	43	77	17	1	15	56	4	.300
Totals.......		922	2881	396	700	157	14	114	470	41	.243

JOHN KRUK 34 5-10 214   Bats L Throws L

Sweet-swinging first baseman with the softball player's physique was symbol of courage last season... Underwent surgery for removal of a cancerous testicle March 8 and missed Phillies' first six games... Returned for home opener April 11 vs. Rockies and hit double in his emotional first at-bat, the first of his three hits that day... Hit .370 in his first 17 games... Was disabled from May 12-June 6 after undergoing arthroscopic surgery on his right knee May 13... Collected 10 RBI in nine-game span from June 12-24... Batted .335 vs. right-handers...

Reached safely via a hit or walk in 65 of his 75 games... Reached career highs in runs, doubles and walks in 1993, when he also hit .348 in World Series... Acquired by Phils from Padres with Randy Ready for Chris James, June 3, 1989... Padres' third-round pick in 1981... Born Feb. 9, 1961, in Charleston, W. Va. ... Would have earned $2.45 million last year... **Free agent at press time.**

Year	Club	Pos.	G	AB	R	H	2B	3B	HR	RBI	SB	Avg.
1986	San Diego	OF-1B	122	278	33	86	16	2	4	38	2	.309
1987	San Diego	OF-1B	138	447	72	140	14	2	20	91	18	.313
1988	San Diego	1B-OF	120	378	54	91	17	1	9	44	5	.241
1989	S.D.-Phil.	OF-1B	112	357	53	107	13	6	8	44	3	.300
1990	Philadelphia	OF-1B	142	443	52	129	25	8	7	67	10	.291
1991	Philadelphia	1B-OF	152	538	84	158	27	6	21	92	7	.294
1992	Philadelphia	1B-OF	144	507	86	164	30	4	10	70	3	.323
1993	Philadelphia	1B	150	535	100	169	33	5	14	85	6	.316
1994	Philadelphia	1B	75	255	35	77	17	0	5	38	4	.302
	Totals		1155	3738	569	1121	192	34	98	569	58	.300

DAVE HOLLINS 28 6-1 207   Bats S Throws R

Managers always warn players about sliding head-first into first base... He tried it anyway and the dive essentially cost him his '94 season ... Missed 53 games after breaking bone in left hand May 22 vs. Mets... Activated from DL July 23, but fractured hook of hamate bone in his left hand that same day vs. Padres... Underwent season-ending hand surgery July 28 ... Third baseman appeared in his first All-Star Game in 1993, when he set career highs in runs, doubles, walks and matched career high in RBI, despite missing 16 games with broken hand ... In '92 and '93, he became first Phillie with back-to-back 100-run seasons (104 each year) since Juan Samuel in 1984-85... Set club record for homers (27) and RBI (93) for switch-hitter in 1992 ... San Diego's sixth-round pick in 1987... Selected out of Padres organization in 1989 Rule V draft... Born May 25, 1966, in Buffalo, N.Y.... Would have earned $2 million last season.

Year	Club	Pos.	G	AB	R	H	2B	3B	HR	RBI	SB	Avg.
1990	Philadelphia	3B-1B	72	114	14	21	0	0	5	15	0	.184
1991	Philadelphia	3B-1B	56	151	18	45	10	2	6	21	1	.298
1992	Philadelphia	3B-1B	156	586	104	158	28	4	27	93	9	.270
1993	Philadelphia	3B	143	543	104	148	30	4	18	93	2	.273
1994	Philadelphia	3B-OF	44	162	28	36	7	1	4	26	1	.222
	Totals		471	1556	268	408	75	11	60	248	13	.262

MICKEY MORANDINI 28 5-11 171   Bats L Throws R

Steady second baseman hit career-best .292 in 87 games (70 starts)... Was batting .220 May 13 and hit .312 the rest of season... His 10-game hitting streak from May 15-29 was longest by a Phillie in '94... Did not strikeout until 51st plate appearance... Has made just two errors in last 103 games, dating back to June 1, 1993... Ranked fourth in NL with .985 fielding percentage... Tied for ninth in NL with five triples... Batted .345 in July... Matched career high with four hits July 31 vs. Braves... Batted .313 with runners in scoring position... Finished second among NL second basemen with .990 fielding percentage in 1993... Had 66-game errorless streak snapped Sept. 25, 1993 vs. Braves... Phillies' fifth-round pick in 1988 draft... Born April 22, 1966, in Leechburg, Pa.... Would have earned $750,000 last season.

Year	Club	Pos.	G	AB	R	H	2B	3B	HR	RBI	SB	Avg.
1990	Philadelphia...	2B	25	79	9	19	4	0	1	3	3	.241
1991	Philadelphia...	2B	98	325	38	81	11	4	1	20	13	.249
1992	Philadelphia...	2B-SS	127	422	47	112	8	8	3	30	8	.265
1993	Philadelphia...	2B	120	425	57	105	19	9	3	33	13	.247
1994	Philadelphia...	2B	87	274	40	80	16	5	2	26	10	.292
	Totals.......		457	1525	191	397	58	26	10	112	47	.260

KEVIN STOCKER 25 6-1 178   Bats S Throws R

His first full season in majors was interrupted by wrist injury... Missed 27 games following wrist surgery May 5... Hit .308 in four-game rehab assignment with Scranton-Wilkes-Barre (AAA)... Tied career high with three hits April 26 vs. Dodgers... Posted career-best eight-game hitting streak from July 18-25, during which he batted .414... Reached base via hit or walk in 25 straight games from July 1-29... His .383 on-base percentage was third on club... Batted .301 at Vet... Began 1993 season in Triple-A and became Phillies' everyday shortstop July 7... Made major league debut by playing all 20 innings of Phils' 7-6 victory over Dodgers... Phillies' second-round pick in 1991 draft... Born Feb. 13, 1970, in Spokane, Wash.... Would have earned $190,000 last season.

Year	Club	Pos.	G	AB	R	H	2B	3B	HR	RBI	SB	Avg.
1993	Philadelphia...	SS	70	259	46	84	12	3	2	31	5	.324
1994	Philadelphia...	SS	82	271	38	74	11	2	2	28	2	.273
	Totals.......		152	530	84	158	23	5	4	59	7	.298

JIM EISENREICH 35 6-11 200   Bats L Throws R

Veteran outfielder batted team-high .372 at home, .342 after All-Star break and .341 with runners in scoring position... Has made only three errors in last 320 games... Best season was in 1993, when he joined Phillies as free agent and led team in hitting with career-high .318... Memorable moment came in Game 2 of 1993 World Series when he hit third-inning, three-run homer off Toronto's Dave Stewart to give Phillies 5-0 lead... Born April 18, 1959, in St. Cloud, Minn.... Selected by Twins in 16th round of 1980 draft... Has had to overcome neurological disorder, Tourette's Syndrome, which forced him out of baseball from 1984-86... Royals claimed him on waivers before 1987 season... Would have earned $1.4 million in '94... Valuable as platoon player.

Year	Club	Pos.	G	AB	R	H	2B	3B	HR	RBI	SB	Avg.
1982	Minnesota	OF	34	99	10	30	6	0	2	9	0	.303
1983	Minnesota	OF	2	7	1	2	1	0	0	0	0	.286
1984	Minnesota	OF	12	32	1	7	1	0	0	3	2	.219
1987	Kansas City	DH	44	105	10	25	8	2	4	21	1	.238
1988	Kansas City	OF	82	202	26	44	8	1	1	19	9	.218
1989	Kansas City	OF	134	475	64	139	33	7	9	59	27	.293
1990	Kansas City	OF	142	496	61	139	29	7	5	51	12	.280
1991	Kansas City	OF-1B	135	375	47	113	22	3	2	47	5	.301
1992	Kansas City	OF	113	353	31	95	13	3	2	28	11	.269
1993	Philadelphia	OF-1B	153	362	51	115	17	4	7	54	5	.318
1994	Philadelphia	OF	104	290	42	87	15	4	4	43	6	.300
	Totals		955	2796	344	796	153	31	36	334	78	.285

GREGG JEFFERIES 27 5-10 185   Bats S Throws R

Born to play baseball... That is what his father thought and he polished his son into sparkling diamond... After five years of heartache in New York and one season in Kansas City, he put together brilliant back-to-back years with Cardinals... But free agent signed four-year, $20-million contract with Phillies in December ... First baseman led Cards in hitting (.325), but suffered 17-point dropoff from 1993... Was second-hardest in NL to fan, striking out once per 17.2 at-bats... Batted .336 vs. right-handers... Mets chose him 20th overall in 1985 draft ... Named *Baseball America's* Minor League Player of the Decade for 1980s... Arrived in New York carrying expectations of a city desperate for a hero... Couldn't handle load and fell to pieces... Acquired by Cards from Royals with Ed Gerald for Felix Jose and Craig Wilson prior to 1993 season... Would have earned $4.6 million... Born Aug. 1, 1967, in Burlingame, Cal.

Year	Club	Pos.	G	AB	R	H	2B	3B	HR	RBI	SB	Avg.
1987	New York (NL)	PH	6	6	0	3	1	0	0	2	0	.500
1988	New York (NL)	3B-2B	29	109	19	35	8	2	6	17	5	.321
1989	New York (NL)	2B-3B	141	508	72	131	28	2	12	56	21	.258
1990	New York (NL)	2B-3B	153	604	96	171	40	3	15	68	11	.283
1991	New York (NL)	2B-3B	136	486	59	132	19	2	9	62	26	.272
1992	Kansas City...	3B-2B	152	604	66	172	36	3	10	75	19	.285
1993	St. Louis	1B-2B	142	544	89	186	24	3	16	83	46	.342
1994	St. Louis	1B	103	397	52	129	27	1	12	55	12	.325
	Totals		862	3258	453	959	183	16	80	418	140	.294

CURT SCHILLING 28 6-4 225   Bats R Throws R

This big talent was nearly shut out in win column... Started season with 0-7 mark in nine starts... Won first game July 25 vs. Marlins... Tossed complete-game shutout vs. Mets Aug. 9 at Vet. That victory was his first at Vet since pitching a complete-game shutout against Blue Jays in Game 5 of 1993 World Series... Placed on DL for first time in career May 17 with tender right elbow... Underwent elbow surgery May 20 and knee surgery June 10... Made three minor league rehab starts... Phillies scored 25 runs in his last 12 starts while he was still in game... In '93, he finished tied for second in NL in complete games (7), tied for third in shutouts (2) and fourth in strikeouts (186)... Acquired from Astros for Jason Grimsley prior to 1992 season... Born Nov. 14, 1966, in Anchorage, Alaska... Would have earned $2.3 million in '94.

Year	Club	G	IP	W	L	Pct.	SO	BB	H	ERA
1988	Baltimore	4	14⅔	0	3	.000	4	10	22	9.82
1989	Baltimore	5	8⅔	0	1	.000	6	3	10	6.23
1990	Baltimore	35	46	1	2	.333	32	19	38	2.54
1991	Houston	56	75⅔	3	5	.375	71	39	79	3.81
1992	Philadelphia	42	226⅓	14	11	.560	147	59	165	2.35
1993	Philadelphia	34	235⅓	16	7	.696	186	57	234	4.02
1994	Philadelphia	13	82⅓	2	8	.200	58	28	87	4.48
	Totals	189	689	36	37	.493	504	215	635	3.55

TOMMY GREENE 27 6-5 222   Bats R Throws R

Best season of career was followed by disappointing, injury-plagued 1994 campaign... Limited to seven starts due to arm problems... Left his first start with right shoulder tendinitis April 7... Placed on DL from April 8-26... Made six starts before returning to DL May 23 with small tear in his right rotator cuff... Underwent shoulder surgery May 27... Finished 2-0 in four '94 games at the Vet to extend his home streak to 14-0 in his last 24 games... Set career highs in victories and strikeouts in 1993, when he began season 8-0... Tossed no-hitter vs. Expos, May 23, 1991... Braves made him 14th player selected overall in 1985 draft... Acquired from Braves with Dale Murphy for Jeff Parrett, Jim Vatcher and Victor Rosario, Aug. 3, 1990... Born April 6, 1967, in Lumberton, N.C.... Would have earned $2 million in '94.

Year	Club	G	IP	W	L	Pct.	SO	BB	H	ERA
1989	Atlanta	4	26⅓	1	2	.333	17	6	22	4.10
1990	Atl.-Phil.	15	51⅓	3	3	.500	21	26	50	5.08
1991	Philadelphia	36	207⅔	13	7	.650	154	66	177	3.38
1992	Philadelphia	13	64⅓	3	3	.500	39	34	75	5.32
1993	Philadelphia	31	200	16	4	.800	167	62	175	3.42
1994	Philadelphia	7	35⅔	2	0	1.000	28	22	37	4.54
	Totals	106	585⅓	38	19	.667	426	216	536	3.86

TOP PROSPECTS

TYLER GREEN 25 6-5 192   Bats R Throws R

Took significant step backwards last season... Finished a dismal 7-16 with 5.56 ERA for Scranton-Wilkes Barre (AAA)... Second straight losing season for Phillies' top pick in 1991 draft as 10th player chosen overall... Gave up 179 hits in 162 innings in '94... Went 6-10 with 3.95 ERA for Scranton-Wilkes Barre in 1993... Appeared in three games for Phillies in '93, compiling 7.36 ERA and striking out seven in 7⅓ innings... Born Feb. 18, 1970, in Springfield, Ohio.

MIKE LIEBERTHAL 23 6-0 185   Bats R Throws R

Recalled from Triple-A June 29, when Darren Daulton went on disabled list... Started 21 games at catcher for Phils... Batted

.266 with one homer and five RBI in 24 games in majors... Collected first major league hit in first game June 30 vs. Dodgers... Smacked first homer July 16, off Dodgers' Ramon Martinez... Batted .233 with one homer and 32 RBI for Scranton-Wilkes Barre in '94... Phils made him third overall pick in 1990 draft... Born Jan. 18, 1972, in Glendale, Cal.

TONY LONGMIRE 26 6-1 195   Bats L Throws R
Outfielder spent first full season with Phillies... Used mostly as a reserve... Batted .237 with 17 RBI in 139 at-bats... Led club in pinch-hits (8) and pinch at-bats (30)... Had eight hits in last 22 pinch at-bats... Collected career-high three hits July 4 vs. Padres... Drove in career-best three runs June 19 vs. Expos... Was 6-for-10 with five doubles and six RBI with a runner on third and two outs... Missed entire 1992 season due to shin splints... Pirates' eighth-round pick in 1986... Acquired by Phils from Pirates with Wes Chamberlain and Julio Peguero for Carmelo Martinez, Aug. 30, 1990... Born Aug. 12, 1968, in Vallejo, Cal.

GENE SCHALL 24 6-3 190   Bats R Throws R
Phillies' Minor League Player of Year... Possible successor to John Kruk at first base... Led Scranton-Wilkes Barre with 16 home runs and 89 RBI and hit .285 in first full season in Triple-A... Split time between Reading (AA) and Scranton in 1993, when he hit total of 19 home runs and drove in 76 runs... Attended Villanova University... Phillies' fourth-round pick in 1991 draft... Born June 5, 1970, in Abington, Pa.

MANAGER JIM FREGOSI: Phils' bid to repeat as NL East champs was undermined by injuries to key personnel... He lost Darren Daulton, Dave Hollins, Curt Schilling and Tommy Greene for most of season and Philadelphia finished 54-61, 20½ games behind Expos in NL East... Year was eerily reminiscent to 1992, when Phillies were devastated by injuries and finished 70-92... GM Lee Thomas stuck with him after 1992 and it paid off... Was credited with turning last-place club in 1992 into first-place unit in 1993... Phillies finished 97-65 in 1993 and upset heavily favored Braves in NLCS before losing

World Series to Blue Jays in six games... Runs a loose clubhouse, but gets his players to produce on field... Replaced Nick Leyva as Phillies' manager, April 23, 1991, and guided team to third-place finish, Phils' best since 1986... Managed Angels from 1978-81, winning divisional title in 1979... Skipper of Louisville (AAA) from 1983-86, winning two divisional crowns and being named American Association's Manager of the Year twice... Returned to majors to manage White Sox from 1986-88... Infielder enjoyed 18-year playing career with Angels, Mets, Rangers and Pirates... Batted .265 with 151 homers... Went to six All-Star Games as AL shortstop... Overall major league managerial record is 725-768.

ALL-TIME PHILLIE SEASON RECORDS

BATTING: Frank O'Doul, .398, 1929
HRs: Mike Schmidt, 48, 1980
RBI: Chuck Klein, 170, 1930
STEALS: Juan Samuel, 72, 1984
WINS: Grover Alexander, 33, 1916
STRIKEOUTS: Steve Carlton, 310, 1972

CHICAGO CUBS

TEAM DIRECTORY: Chairman: Stanton Cook; Pres./CEO: Andy MacPhail; GM: Ed Lynch; Dir. Player Development: Jim Hendry; Dir. Media Rel.: Sharon Pannozzo; Media Inf. Coordinator: Chuck Wasserstrom; Trav. Sec.: Jimmy Bank; Mgr.: Jim Riggleman; Coaches: Billy Williams, Tony Muser, Dan Radison, Dave Bialas, Ferguson Jenkins, Max Oliveras. Home: Wrigley Field (38,712). Field distances: 355, l.f. line; 400, c.f.; 353, r.f. line. Spring training: Mesa, Ariz.

SCOUTING REPORT

Here's a news flash: The Cubs are rebuilding. This is baseball's equivalent to dog bites man.

At least they are starting with a solid foundation after hiring Andy MacPhail last September. MacPhail, the team's new president and CEO, owns two World Series rings from his days in Minnesota and is an astute talent evaluator. But he and new GM Ed Lynch have their work cut out for them with the Cubs.

Sammy Sosa serves as living legacy of ex-GM Larry Himes.

That also applies to new manager Jim Riggleman, who spent the last two-plus seasons as the Padres' skipper and now inherits a club that finished 49-64 under Tom Trebelhorn.

Riggleman's first order of business is restoring a starting staff that was decimated by injuries last season, when the Cubs finished 10th in the NL with a 4.47 ERA. Steve Trachsel and Willie Banks provide reasons for optimism. Trachsel went 9-7, 3.21 in his rookie year and Banks, despite finishing at 8-12, 5.40, showed flashes of brilliance.

What the Cubs desperately need is for Jose Guzman (2-2, 9.15) and Mike Morgan (2-10, 6.69) to provide leadership and wins. Morgan, who suffered arm and back injuries in '94, has now lost 25 games the last two seasons. Anthony Young (4-6, 3.92), who knows a lot about losing, could spend much of the season on the sidelines following major elbow surgery last August. Frank Castillo (2-1, 4.30) and Turk Wendell (0-1, 11.93) are competing for the fifth spot in the rotation.

At least when the Cubs get to the ninth inning with a lead, they are in good hands. Randy Myers (1-5, 3.79, 21 saves) is still one of the best closers around.

The Cubs should be a better offensive team than the one which ranked 11th in the NL in batting average (.259), hits (1,015) and on-base percentage (.325) last season. First baseman Mark Grace (.298, 6, 44) is still a quality hitter and outstanding fielder, but was pondering an exit via free agency at press time. Rey Sanchez (.285, 0, 24) obviously is not the run producer or the fielder Ryne Sandberg was, but he'll hit for average. Shawon Dunston (.278, 11, 35) is healthy again and anticipating a big season.

Rick Wilkins (.227, 7, 39) returned to reality following a fabulous rookie season in '93 and will have an opportunity to prove which year was a fluke. Sammy Sosa (.300, 25, 70) is definitely the real deal. Sosa has hit 58 home runs the last two seasons and is still just 26 years old. Left fielder Derrick May (.284, 8, 51) is perhaps the Cubs' top left-handed hitter and Glenallen Hill (.297, 10, 38) is the top reserve outfielder.

Even after the sudden loss of second baseman Sandberg to retirement during last season, the Cubs remain one of the top defensive clubs in baseball with Grace at first and Dunston at short. The Cubs' 80 errors in 1994 was the fourth-lowest total in the NL.

Pitching, not defense, is the Cubs' greatest weakness and, unless Morgan and Guzman reach double figures in wins, Chicago will finish on the wrong side of .500 again.

CUB PROFILES

MARK GRACE 30 6-2 190   Bats L Throws L

Slick-fielding first baseman enjoyed another strong season... Played in club-high 106 games... Has batted .296 or better in six of his seven major league seasons... Was seventh-hardest batter in NL to strike out last year, fanning once per 11.1 at-bats... Struggled early, but caught fire in May, hitting .356 in that month... Hit just one home run prior to July 4... Batted .378 in final 22 games... Hit safely in season-high 12 straight games from July 14-26... It was 12th double-digit hitting streak of his career... His .994 career fielding percentage is highest in club history for first baseman (minimum 500 games)... Two-time Gold Glove winner... Born June 28, 1964, in Winston-Salem, N.C.... Cubs' 24th-round selection in 1985 draft... Would have earned $4.4 million last season... **Free agent at press time.**

Year Club	Pos.	G	AB	R	H	2B	3B	HR	RBI	SB	Avg.
1988 Chicago (NL)	1B	134	486	65	144	23	4	7	57	3	.296
1989 Chicago (NL)	1B	142	510	74	160	28	3	13	79	14	.314
1990 Chicago (NL)	1B	157	589	72	182	32	1	9	82	15	.309
1991 Chicago (NL)	1B	160	619	87	169	28	5	8	58	3	.273
1992 Chicago (NL)	1B	158	603	72	185	37	5	9	79	6	.307
1993 Chicago (NL)	1B	155	594	86	193	39	4	14	98	8	.325
1994 Chicago (NL)	1B	106	403	55	120	23	3	6	44	0	.298
Totals		1012	3804	511	1153	210	25	66	497	49	.303

STEVE BUECHELE 33 6-2 200   Bats R Throws R

Reliable third baseman ranked second on club in home runs (14) and RBI (52)... Made 95 starts at third base... His .974 fielding percentage was second-best mark among NL third basemen... Batted .281 with four homers and 12 RBI in April... Homered in three straight games from April 11-15... Mired in miserable slump from May 2-June 16 as he hit .168 (19 for 113) over 38-game stretch... Enjoyed 11-game hitting streak from June 27-July 7... Recorded his 1,000th career hit July 6 off Colorado's Curt Leskanic... Posted career-high batting average in 1993 . . . Rangers' fifth-round pick in 1982 . . . Traded to Cubs from Pirates for Danny Jackson, July 11, 1992 . . . Born Sept. 26, 1961, in Lancaster, Cal. . . . Would have earned $2.55 million last year.

Year	Club	Pos.	G	AB	R	H	2B	3B	HR	RBI	SB	Avg.
1985	Texas	3B-2B	69	219	22	48	6	3	6	21	3	.219
1986	Texas	3B-2B-OF	153	461	54	112	19	2	18	54	5	.243
1987	Texas	3B-2B-OF	136	363	45	86	20	0	13	50	2	.237
1988	Texas	3B-2B	155	503	68	126	21	4	16	58	2	.250
1989	Texas	3B-2B	155	486	60	114	22	2	16	59	1	.235
1990	Texas	3B-2B	91	251	30	54	10	0	7	30	1	.215
1991	Texas	3B-2B-SS	121	416	58	111	17	2	18	66	0	.267
1991	Pittsburgh	3B	31	114	16	28	5	1	4	19	0	.246
1992	Pitt-Chi (NL)	3B	145	524	52	137	23	4	9	64	1	.261
1993	Chicago (NL)	3B-1B	133	460	53	125	27	2	15	65	1	.272
1994	Chicago (NL)	3B-1B-2B	104	339	33	82	11	1	14	52	1	.242
	Totals		1293	4136	491	1023	181	21	136	538	17	.247

SHAWON DUNSTON 32 6-1 180   Bats R Throws R

Made inspiring and successful return to baseball after missing nearly two seasons with back injury . . . Reclaimed starting shortstop job . . . Had .966 fielding percentage in 84 games at short . . . Was batting .294 through July before finishing season with 1-for-21 slide . . . After appearing in only 18 games over previous two years, he began season with six-game hitting streak . . . His home run off Expos' Mel Rojas April 8 was his first since 1991 . . . Went 7-for-48 (.146) from April 15-May 8 . . . Batted leadoff 33 times and hit .333 . . . Played in 1,000th major league game July 17 at Cincinnati . . . Had surgery to remove a herniated disc, May 13, 1992 . . . Cubs made him first overall pick in 1982 draft . . . Born March 21, 1963, in Brooklyn, N.Y. . . . Would have earned $2.375 million last year.

Year	Club	Pos.	G	AB	R	H	2B	3B	HR	RBI	SB	Avg.
1985	Chicago (NL)	SS	74	250	40	65	12	4	4	18	11	.260
1986	Chicago (NL)	SS	150	581	66	145	36	3	17	68	13	.250
1987	Chicago (NL)	SS	95	346	40	85	18	3	5	22	12	.246
1988	Chicago (NL)	SS	155	575	69	143	23	6	9	56	30	.249
1989	Chicago (NL)	SS	138	471	52	131	20	6	9	60	19	.278
1990	Chicago (NL)	SS	146	545	73	143	22	8	17	66	25	.262
1991	Chicago (NL)	SS	142	492	59	128	22	7	12	50	21	.260
1992	Chicago (NL)	SS	18	73	8	23	3	1	0	2	2	.315
1993	Chicago (NL)	SS	7	10	3	4	2	0	0	2	0	.400
1994	Chicago (NL)	SS	88	331	38	92	19	0	11	35	3	.278
	Totals		1013	3674	448	959	177	38	84	379	136	.261

DERRICK MAY 26 6-4 225   Bats L Throws R

Emerged as one of Cubs' top left-handed bats in his second full big league season... Got off to a blistering start, batting .317 in April and .357 in May... Had 30 RBI in first two months... Went 16-for-94 (.170) from June 1-July 3... Starting with four-hit game against Colorado July 4, he batted .314 for rest of season... Made first career Opening Day start... Batted .392 with three homers, 10 RBI and 12 runs in final 14 games... Averaged strikeout per 11.1 plate appearances, sixth-best ratio in NL... Outfielder underwent surgery on right shoulder prior to 1993 season... Cubs' top pick and ninth player chosen in 1986 draft... Born July 14, 1968, in Rochester, N.Y.... Would have earned $300,000 last season.

Year	Club	Pos.	G	AB	R	H	2B	3B	HR	RBI	SB	Avg.
1990	Chicago (NL)	OF	17	61	8	15	3	0	1	11	1	.246
1991	Chicago (NL)	OF	15	22	4	5	2	0	1	3	0	.227
1992	Chicago (NL)	OF	124	351	33	96	11	0	8	45	5	.274
1993	Chicago (NL)	OF	128	465	62	137	25	2	10	77	10	.295
1994	Chicago (NL)	OF	100	345	43	98	19	2	8	51	3	.284
	Totals		384	1244	150	351	60	4	28	187	19	.282

SAMMY SOSA 26 6-0 185   Bats R Throws R

Sammy is still the bull in Cubs' lineup... Club's Triple Crown winner... First player to lead Cubs in batting average (.300), homers (25) and RBI (70) since Bill Buckner in 1981... Outfielder ranked ninth in NL in homers... Established career-high batting average... Had four two-homer games, giving him 11 for his career... Homered in three consecutive games from July 19-22... On April 22, he became the first player to clear 30-foot-high center-field fence at Mile High Stadium when he crushed a 461-foot homer off Mike Munoz... Tied for sixth in NL with six triples... Posted career-high, 10-game hitting streak from June 7-24... Batted .339 in final 53 games with 12 homers and 38 RBI... Became first 30-30 player in team history in 1993... Acquired by Cubs from White Sox for Ken Patterson and George Bell prior to 1992 season... Rangers signed him as undrafted free agent in July 1985... Born Nov. 12, 1968, in San

Pedro de Macoris, D.R. . . . Would have earned $2.95 million last season.

Year Club	Pos.	G	AB	R	H	2B	3B	HR	RBI	SB	Avg.
1989 Tex.-Chi. (AL)	OF	58	183	27	47	8	0	4	13	7	.257
1990 Chicago (AL)	OF	153	532	72	124	26	10	15	70	32	.233
1991 Chicago (AL)	OF	116	316	39	64	10	1	10	33	13	.203
1992 Chicago (NL)	OF	67	262	41	68	7	2	8	25	15	.260
1993 Chicago (NL)	OF	159	598	92	156	25	5	33	93	36	.261
1994 Chicago (NL)	OF	105	426	59	128	17	6	25	70	22	.300
Totals		658	2317	330	587	93	24	95	304	125	.253

GLENALLEN HILL 30 6-2 220   Bats R Throws R

Late surge helped him salvage 1994 season... Started at all three outfield positions, appearing in 89 games overall... Did not have an RBI until he smacked two homers May 6 against the Pirates, including 11th upper-deck blast in history of Three Rivers... Used primarily as a pinch-hitter until June 18... On that day, he started in right field against the Giants and went 2-for-3 with homer and career-high five RBI... Was Cubs' starting center fielder in 42 of final 48 games... From June 18 through end of season, he batted .316 with eight homers, 30 RBI, 35 runs and 11 doubles... Recorded career-high 19 steals... Blue Jays' ninth-round pick in 1983... Acquired by Cubs from Indians for Candy Maldonado, Aug. 20, 1993... Born March 22, 1965, in Santa Cruz, Cal.... Would have earned $1 million last year.

Year Club	Pos.	G	AB	R	H	2B	3B	HR	RBI	SB	Avg.
1989 Toronto	OF	19	52	4	15	0	0	1	7	2	.288
1990 Toronto	OF	84	260	47	60	11	3	12	32	8	.231
1991 Tor.-Clev.	OF	72	221	29	57	8	2	8	25	6	.258
1992 Cleveland	OF	102	369	38	89	16	1	18	49	9	.241
1993 Cleveland	OF	66	174	19	39	7	2	5	25	7	.224
1993 Chicago (NL)	OF	31	87	14	30	7	0	10	22	1	.345
1994 Chicago (NL)	OF	89	269	48	80	12	1	10	38	19	.297
Totals		463	1432	199	370	61	9	64	198	52	.258

RICK WILKINS 27 6-2 210   Bats L Throws R

Production decreased dramatically following breakthrough season in 1993... Was hitting .198 May 16... Thirty-four of his 71 hits were extra-base hits... Led club with career-high 25 doubles... Had 17 multi-hit games... Threw out 27 of 78 would-be base-stealers (34.6 percent)... Had a fielding percentage of .993, committing four errors in 601 chances...

Cubs' Opening Day catcher for second straight season... In 1993, he became one of six catchers in major league history to hit 30 homers and bat .300 and he ranked 10th in NL in homers... Selected by Cubs in 23rd round of 1986 draft... Born June 4, 1967, in Jacksonville, Fla.... Would have earned $350,000 last season.

Year Club	Pos.	G	AB	R	H	2B	3B	HR	RBI	SB	Avg.
1991 Chicago (NL) ..	C	86	203	21	45	9	0	6	22	3	.222
1992 Chicago (NL) ..	C	83	244	20	66	9	1	8	22	0	.270
1993 Chicago (NL) ..	C	136	446	78	135	23	1	30	73	2	.303
1994 Chicago (NL) ..	C	100	313	44	71	25	2	7	39	4	.227
Totals		405	1206	163	317	66	4	51	156	9	.263

WILLIE BANKS 26 6-1 195 Bats R Throws R

Potential is still there, but inconsistency continues to undermine his development... In his first season in NL, he led team in losses (12), but ranked second in wins (8) behind Steve Trachsel... Recorded his first NL win April 11 vs. New York... Went 4-0 with 1.48 ERA from May 13-30... Tossed first complete game and shutout May 24 against the Dodgers, allowing just four hits... Took a no-hitter into eighth inning May 30 against Phillies before giving up a one-out single to Kim Batiste... Had 17-inning scoreless stretch from May 24-30, longest by a Cub since Greg Maddux' 19 scoreless innings in 1992... Went 0-6 in last eight starts. Cubs scored nine runs in those six losses while he was still in the game... Set career highs in wins and losses in 1993... Acquired by Cubs from Twins for Dave Stevens and Matt Walbeck prior to last season... Twins made him third overall pick in 1987 draft... Born Feb. 27, 1969, in Jersey City, N.J.... Would have earned $190,000 last season.

Year Club	G	IP	W	L	Pct.	SO	BB	H	ERA
1991 Minnesota.........	5	17⅓	1	1	.500	16	12	21	5.71
1992 Minnesota.........	16	71	4	4	.500	37	37	80	5.70
1993 Minnesota.........	31	171⅓	11	12	.478	138	78	186	4.04
1994 Chicago (NL).......	23	138⅓	8	12	.400	91	56	139	5.40
Totals............	75	398	24	29	.453	282	183	426	4.88

CHICAGO CUBS • 267

MIKE MORGAN 35 6-2 220 Bats R Throws R

Experienced worst season of long career... Was disabled three times and was limited to career-low 15 starts... Pitched six or more innings in only four of his starts... Lost Opening Day outing against Mets and started out 0-7... No Cub pitcher in 20th century has opened with 0-8 slide... Ended his winless woes June 23 at Florida, pitching six innings in 9-3 victory and snapping personal nine-game losing streak... Disabled from May 9-27 with right elbow inflammation... Made two starts and returned to DL from June 2-22, due to emotional stress... Placed on DL with lower back spasms July 26 and missed remainder of season... Signed by Cubs as free agent prior to 1992 season... Athletics drafted him fourth overall in 1978... Born Oct. 8, 1959, in Tulare, Cal.... Would have earned $3.375 million last year.

Year	Club	G	IP	W	L	Pct.	SO	BB	H	ERA
1978	Oakland	3	12	0	3	.000	0	8	19	7.50
1979	Oakland	13	77	2	10	.167	17	50	102	5.96
1982	New York (AL)	30	150⅓	7	11	.389	71	67	167	4.37
1983	Toronto	16	45⅓	0	3	.000	22	21	48	5.16
1985	Seattle	2	6	1	1	.500	2	5	11	12.00
1986	Seattle	37	216⅓	11	17	.393	116	86	243	4.53
1987	Seattle	34	207	12	17	.414	85	53	245	4.65
1988	Baltimore	22	71⅓	1	6	.143	29	23	70	5.43
1989	Los Angeles	40	152⅔	8	11	.421	72	33	130	2.53
1990	Los Angeles	33	211	11	15	.423	106	60	216	3.75
1991	Los Angeles	34	236⅓	14	10	.583	140	61	197	2.78
1992	Chicago (NL)	34	240	16	8	.667	123	79	203	2.55
1993	Chicago (NL)	32	207⅔	10	15	.400	111	74	206	4.03
1994	Chicago (NL)	15	80⅔	2	10	.167	57	35	111	6.69
	Totals	345	1913⅔	95	137	.409	951	655	1968	4.01

JOSE GUZMAN 31 6-3 195 Bats R Throws R

His poor health was one of main reasons Cubs had one of the worst pitching staffs in baseball in '94... Underwent arthroscopic surgery on right shoulder June 1... His loss crippled an already weakened Cubs staff... Opened season as Cubs' No. 2 starter... Went 0-2 with 16.43 ERA in first two starts before being sidelined with tendinitis in shoulder... Made one injury rehab start for Orlando (AA)... Earned first win May 17 vs. Padres, allowing three runs over six innings... Matched that performance six days later in beating Dodgers... Scratched from May 29 start at Atlanta due to shoulder stiffness, he had surgery three days later... Led Cubs in strikeouts and innings in 1993

...Tossed 8⅔ innings of no-hit ball in NL debut, April 6 vs. Braves... Signed by Cubs as free agent prior to 1993 season... Originally signed as undrafted free agent by Rangers in February 1981... Born April 9, 1963, in Santa Isabel, P.R.... Would have earned $3.5 million in '94.

Year	Club	G	IP	W	L	Pct.	SO	BB	H	ERA
1985	Texas	5	32⅔	3	2	.600	24	14	27	2.76
1986	Texas	29	172⅓	9	15	.375	87	60	199	4.54
1987	Texas	37	208⅓	14	14	.500	143	82	196	4.67
1988	Texas	30	206⅔	11	13	.458	157	82	180	3.70
1989	Texas					Injured				
1991	Texas	25	169⅔	13	7	.650	125	84	152	3.08
1992	Texas	33	224	16	11	.593	179	73	229	3.66
1993	Chicago (NL)	30	191	12	10	.545	163	74	188	4.34
1994	Chicago (NL)	4	19⅔	2	2	.500	11	13	22	9.15
	Totals	193	1224⅓	80	74	.519	889	482	1193	4.05

RANDY MYERS 32 6-1 230   Bats L Throws L

Somehow managed to save 21 games for lowly Cubs... Selected to All-Star team for second time in career... Name was mentioned in every trade rumor... Tied for fifth in NL in saves... In 26 opportunities, he allowed only seven earned runs... Stranded 11 of 18 inherited runners... Retired first batter he faced in 28 of 38 outings... Holds club record with 20 straight converted saves... Cashed in 10 straight save opportunities from April 28-May 30... Ranks 15th on all-time saves list with 205... Became fourth left-handed reliever to reach 200-saves mark June 27 vs. Pirates... Third on Cubs' all-time list with 74, behind Lee Smith (180) and Bruce Sutter (133)... Set NL record with 53 saves for Cubs in 1993, as he fell four short of Bobby Thigpen's major league mark... Signed by Cubs as free agent prior to 1993 season... Mets made him ninth player chosen in secondary phase of 1982 draft... Born Sept. 19, 1962, in Vancouver, Wash.... Would have earned $3,583,330 last season.

Year	Club	G	IP	W	L	Pct.	SO	BB	H	ERA
1985	New York (NL)	1	2	0	0	.000	2	1	0	0.00
1986	New York (NL)	10	10⅔	0	0	.000	13	9	11	4.22
1987	New York (NL)	54	75	3	6	.333	92	30	61	3.96
1988	New York (NL)	55	68	7	3	.700	69	17	45	1.72
1989	New York (NL)	65	84⅓	7	4	.636	88	40	62	2.35
1990	Cincinnati	66	86⅔	4	6	.400	98	38	59	2.08
1991	Cincinnati	58	132	6	13	.316	108	80	116	3.55
1992	San Diego	66	79⅔	3	6	.333	66	34	84	4.29
1993	Chicago (NL)	73	75⅓	2	4	.333	86	26	65	3.11
1994	Chicago (NL)	38	40⅓	1	5	.167	32	16	40	3.79
	Totals	486	654	33	47	.413	654	291	543	3.11

STEVE TRACHSEL 24 6-4 205 — Bats R Throws R

Talented right-hander emerged as ace of Cubs' staff in his rookie year... Ranked eighth in NL in ERA (3.21)... Held opponents to .242 batting average, ninth-lowest mark in league... Led major league rookies in victories (9) and innings (146)... Ranked second among rookies in ERA and strikeouts (108)... Worked at least seven innings in 12 of his 22 starts... Earned first major league win April 8 vs. Expos by working 7⅓ scoreless innings... Tossed first complete game April 24 at Orlando... Went 8-0 with 2.79 ERA in 10 road starts... Went 5-4 with 1.88 ERA in his final 10 starts... Was on 15-day DL from July 20-Aug. 4 with blister on middle right finger... Optioned to Iowa (AAA) the day of strike, he went 0-2 with 10.00 ERA there... Cubs' eighth-round pick in 1991 draft... Born Oct. 31, 1970, in Oxnard, Cal.... Would have earned $112,000 in '94.

Year	Club	G	IP	W	L	Pct.	SO	BB	H	ERA
1993	Chicago (NL)	3	19⅔	0	2	.000	14	3	16	4.58
1994	Chicago (NL)	22	146	9	7	.563	108	54	133	3.21
	Totals	25	165⅔	9	9	.500	122	57	149	3.37

TOP PROSPECTS

KEVIN FOSTER 26 6-1 160 — Bats R Throws R
One of the few positive developments for Cubs last season... Finished 3-4 with 2.89 ERA in 13 starts for them... Acquired from Phillies for Shawn Boskie, April 12, 1994... Started three games for Orlando (AA), going 1-0, 0.95, and six games for Iowa (AAA), going 3-1, 4.28, before being promoted April 30... Won first major league game and collected first hit June 19 at San Francisco... Had consecutive 10-strikeout outings against Reds July 17 and 23... Expos' 31st-round pick in 1987... Born Jan. 13, 1969, in Evanston, Ill.

KEVIN ROBERSON 27 6-4 210 — Bats S Throws R
Opened 1994 season with Iowa (AAA) and was recalled by Cubs May 2... Batted .313 in 19 games in minors... Outfielder appeared in 44 games for Cubs, batting .218 with four homers and nine RBI... Went 9-for-35 (.257) with three homers and seven RBI as pinch-hitter... Has four career pinch-hit homers... Suffered season-ending right hand injury July 5... Appeared in 62

games for Cubs in 1993, batting .189 with three home runs and 17 RBI in 62 games... Selected by Cubs in 16th round of 1988 draft... Born Jan. 29, 1968, in Decatur, Ill.

TURK WENDELL 27 6-2 190   **Bats R Throws R**
Ready to assume role with big league club... Spent most of 1994 with Iowa (AAA), going 11-6 with 2.95 ERA in 23 starts... Pitched six complete games, including three shutouts... Ranked fifth in American Association in ERA and fourth in strikeouts (118)... Had two stints with Cubs, going 0-1, 11.93 in six games... Went 1-2 with 4.37 ERA in seven appearances for Cubs in 1993... Has combined 23-14 mark in his last three years at Iowa... Braves' fifth-round pick in 1988... Born May 19, 1967, in Pittsfield, Mass.... Cubs got him from Atlanta with Yorkis Perez for Damon Berryhill and Mike Bielecki, Sept. 29, 1991.

EDDIE ZAMBRANO 29 6-3 200   **Bats R Throws R**
Utility player appeared in 67 games in his first full season with Cubs... Batted .259 with six home runs and 18 RBI... Saw action at first, third and outfield... Was 7-for-26 (.269) as pinch-hitter... Smacked first major league home run April 9 at Montreal, off Jeff Fassero... Posted first career two-homer game and career-high four RBI May 9 vs. Cardinals... Batted .303 with 32 homers and 115 RBI for Iowa (AAA) in 1993... Signed as six-year minor league free agent prior to 1993 season... Originally signed as undrafted free agent by Red Sox in December 1984... Born Feb. 1, 1966, in Maracaibo, Venezuela.

MANAGER JIM RIGGLEMAN: Talk about your lateral moves... Switched from lowly Padres to hapless Cubs... Named Chicago's 12th manager in 12 years last Oct. 20... Took over team from Tom Trebelhorn, who was fired Oct. 17 following 49-64 season as skipper... This guy was only man new GM Ed Lynch interviewed. They had worked together as recently as two years ago in San Diego... Padres finished 47-70 and in last place in NL West in 1994, his second full season at helm... Replaced Greg Riddoch, Sept. 28, 1992... Padres went 61-101 under him in 1993... A Whitey Herzog disciple... Spent nine years in Cardinals organization as a coach, including

two seasons as first-base coach under Herzog... Managed Las Vegas (AAA) for two years before moving to majors... Began managerial career with St. Petersburg (A) from 1982-84 before moving on to Arkansas (AA) for three years... Named Cards' director of player development in 1988... Played eight seasons in St. Louis organization as infielder-outfielder... Fourth-round pick of Dodgers in 1976 never made it to majors... Born Nov. 9, 1952, in Fort Dix, N.J.... Overall major league managerial record is 112-179.

ALL-TIME CUB SEASON RECORDS

BATTING: Rogers Hornsby, .380, 1929
HRs: Hack Wilson, 56, 1930
RBI: Hack Wilson, 190, 1930
STEALS: Frank Chance, 67, 1903
WINS: Mordecai Brown, 29, 1908
STRIKEOUTS: Ferguson Jenkins, 274, 1970

CINCINNATI REDS

TEAM DIRECTORY: Principal Owner/Pres.: Marge Schott; GM: James Bowden IV; Dir. Scouting: Julian Mock; Dir. Player Development: Sheldon (Chief) Bender; Publicity Dir.: TBA; Trav. Sec.: Joel Pieper; Mgr.: Davey Johnson; Coaches: Bob Boone, Mike Griffin, Don Gullett, Grant Jackson, Ray Knight, Joel Youngblood. Home: Riverfront Stadium (52,952). Field distances: 330, l.f. line; 404, c.f.; 330, r.f. line. Spring training: Plant City, Fla.

SCOUTING REPORT

Who's laughing now? The establishment howled at the Reds when Jim Bowden took over as GM. But in just his second year, Bowden's unorthodox moves had the rest of baseball jealous—and the Reds sitting atop a 66-48 record. His method of success has been simple. Take other teams' talented but troublesome players like Kevin Mitchell, a free agent unsigned at press time, and Deion Sanders, arguably the most gifted athlete in the game.

Mitchell (.326, 30, 77) murdered opposing pitchers, but may not figure in the future, because Ron Gant is being counted on to come back from a broken leg that sidelined him in '94. Sanders, last season's other pickup from the Braves, finished second in the NL in stolen bases with 38 and batted .283 with four homers and 28 RBI. Reggie Sanders (.263, 17, 62) is a great talent and gives the Reds a tremendous outfield. Bret Boone (.320, 12, 68), who came over from the Mariners before last season, shocked everyone with his sterling play at second.

Hal Morris (.335, 10, 78) rebounded from two injury-plagued seasons to solidify the batting order last year. Barry Larkin (.279, 9, 52) had another good season at short, although it wasn't up to his normal standards. Catcher Ed Taubensee (.283, 8, 21) was a pleasant surprise and will be helped by the addition of ex-Red Sox receiver Damon Berryhill (.263, 6, 34). Youngster Willie Greene (.216, 1, 5) will finally get his shot at third.

As a team, the Reds easily led the NL in hitting with a .286 mark. They also finished first in runs (609), total bases (1,797) and slugging percentage (.449).

A big part of the credit for the Reds' success has to go to manager Davey Johnson, another baseball castoff picked up by Bowden. Johnson did a masterful job handling the pitching staff as the Reds finished third in the NL with a 3.78 ERA. Anchor

Hal Morris, whose bat was cat-quick, led Reds at .335.

Jose Rijo (9-6, 3.08) finished second in the NL in strikeouts (171). Tom Browning (3-1, 4.20) broke his arm before becoming a free agent and his future is in doubt, but John Smiley (11-10, 3.86) bounced back, thanks to some big batting support. John Roper (6-2, 4.50) is developing while Pete Schourek (7-2, 4.09) was a valuable addition. And the Reds signed 39-year-old Jack Morris (10-6, 5.60 with the Indians) in December.

In the bullpen, Hector Carrasco (5-6, 2.24, 6 saves) possesses a blistering fastball and should be even more of a presence in his second season. Veteran Jeff Brantley (6-6, 2.48, 15 saves) is a major part of the save committee, along with Chuck McElroy (1-2, 2.34, 6 saves).

Johnson uses his speed wisely as the Reds finished third in stolen bases (119) and compiled an excellent 46-30 mark on artificial turf, a sign of good speed and good defense. Last year, the Reds finished second in the league with a .983 fielding percentage, which is amazing considering that Mitchell, a born DH, had to play left field in the NL. The Reds like any great team, are also strong up the middle with Gold Glover Larkin, Boone and Sanders.

RED PROFILES

DEION SANDERS 27 6-1 195 Bats L Throws L

Baseball's biggest talker and football's too... Batted .277 after coming to Reds from Braves in May 29 trade for Roberto Kelly and Roger Etheridge... Finished second in NL in stolen bases (38), only one behind Astros' Craig Biggio... No Red has led league in stolen bases since 1970, when Bobby Tolan did it... Made history with appearance in Game 5 of 1992 NLCS, becoming first player to suit up for teams in two pro sports on the same day (Braves and Falcons)... Center fielder gave glimpse of what he's capable of doing with .533 average in '92 World Series... Played for NFL San Francisco 49ers as defensive back last season... Born Aug. 9, 1967, in Ft. Myers, Fla.... Signed by Atlanta as minor league free agent in January 1991... Yanks chose him in the 30th round of 1988 draft, out of Florida State... Would have earned $3 million for baseball in '94.

Year	Club	Pos.	G	AB	R	H	2B	3B	HR	RBI	SB	Avg.
1989	New York (AL)	OF	14	47	7	11	2	0	2	7	1	.234
1990	New York (AL)	OF	57	133	24	21	2	2	3	9	8	.158
1991	Atlanta	OF	54	110	16	21	1	2	4	13	11	.191
1992	Atlanta	OF	97	303	54	92	6	14	8	28	26	.304
1993	Atlanta	OF	95	272	42	75	18	6	6	28	19	.276
1994	Atl.-Cin.	OF	92	375	58	106	17	4	4	28	38	.283
	Totals		409	1240	201	326	46	28	27	113	103	.263

BARRY LARKIN 30 6-0 185 Bats R Throws R

Age may be catching up to this shortstop... For the first time in six seasons, he did not hit .300 (.279)... Managed to put together 19-game hitting streak from June 4-26... Played in pain for most of '93 season because of damaged left thumb... Ended Ozzie Smith's record string of 10 straight All-Star starts when fans voted him No. 1 that year... His five straight seasons of .300-plus average (1989-93) marked first time in 40 years an NL shortstop has accomplished that feat... Batted .358 vs. lefties in '93, but only .284 against them last year... Sparkled in 1990 World Series, hitting .353... Was named Big 10 MVP twice at Michigan... Reds' first-round selection and

Gold Glover Barry Larkin aims to return to .300.

fourth player chosen overall in 1985 draft... Born April 29, 1964, in Cincinnati... Would have earned $4.3 million last season... Won first Gold Glove in '94.

Year	Club	Pos.	G	AB	R	H	2B	3B	HR	RBI	SB	Avg.
1986	Cincinnati	SS-2B	41	159	27	45	4	3	3	19	8	.283
1987	Cincinnati	SS	125	439	64	107	16	2	12	43	21	.244
1988	Cincinnati	SS	151	588	91	174	32	5	12	56	40	.296
1989	Cincinnati	SS	97	325	47	111	14	4	4	36	10	.342
1990	Cincinnati	SS	158	614	85	185	25	6	7	67	30	.301
1991	Cincinnati	SS	123	464	88	140	27	4	20	69	24	.302
1992	Cincinnati	SS	140	533	76	162	32	6	12	78	15	.304
1993	Cincinnati	SS	100	384	57	121	20	3	8	51	14	.315
1994	Cininnati	SS	110	427	78	119	23	5	9	52	26	.279
	Totals		1045	3933	613	1164	193	38	87	471	188	.296

REGGIE SANDERS 27 6-1 183   Bats R Throws R

All-around solid player... Finished tied for second in NL in triples (8)... Also finished second in outfield assists, behind Dodgers' Raul Mondesi, with 12... Bashed 17 homers and stole 21 bases... Should be a fixture in 20-20 club for years to come... Ex-shortstop continues to improve in center... Born Dec. 1, 1967, in Florence, S.C.... Reds are counting on him for future and proved it by signing him to four-year, $6.75-million deal that runs through 1996 season... Seventh-round draft choice of Reds in 1987... In 1993, he led Reds in batting (.274), runs (90), RBI (83) and stolen bases (27)... Kind of athlete any winning team needs... Would have earned $925,000 in '94.

Year	Club	Pos.	G	AB	R	H	2B	3B	HR	RBI	SB	Avg.
1991	Cincinnati	OF	9	40	6	8	0	0	1	3	1	.200
1992	Cincinnati	OF	116	385	62	104	26	6	12	36	16	.270
1993	Cincinnati	OF	138	496	90	136	16	4	20	83	27	.274
1994	Cincinnati	OF	107	400	66	105	20	8	17	62	21	.263
	Totals		370	1321	224	353	62	18	50	184	65	.267

HAL MORRIS 29 6-4 215   Bats L Throws L

Overcame shoulder injury that sidelined him much of '93 and a variety of 1992 injuries... That shoulder injury occurred in spring training fight with Cleveland pitcher Jose Mesa... First baseman fought back on the field last year, leading Reds in average with .335 mark, fourth-best in NL... Also led the club in RBI (78) and hits (146)... Owns one of the smoothest swings in baseball... In '91, he came within one hit of winning NL batting title... Reds stole him from Yankees along with Rodney Imes for Tim Leary and Van Snider prior to 1990 season... Hit .417 in 1990 NLCS vs. Pirates, but posted .071 mark in World Series... Born April 9, 1965, in Fort Rucker, Ala.... Eighth-round selection of Yankees in 1986... Barry Larkin's teammate at Michigan... Would have earned $2.1 million last season.

Year	Club	Pos.	G	AB	R	H	2B	3B	HR	RBI	SB	Avg.
1988	New York (AL)	OF	15	20	1	2	0	0	0	0	0	.100
1989	New York (AL)	OF-1B	15	18	2	5	0	0	0	4	0	.278
1990	Cincinnati	1B-OF	107	309	50	105	22	3	7	36	9	.340
1991	Cincinnati	1B-OF	136	478	72	152	33	1	14	59	10	.318
1992	Cincinnati	1B	115	395	41	107	21	3	6	53	6	.271
1993	Cincinnati	1B	101	379	48	120	18	0	7	49	2	.317
1994	Cincinnati	1B	112	436	60	146	30	4	10	78	6	.335
	Totals		601	2035	274	637	124	11	44	279	33	.313

CINCINNATI REDS • 277

BRET BOONE 25 5-10 180   Bats R Throws R

Fiery competitor kick-started Reds' offense... What else would you expect with all the baseball in his bloodlines?... Second baseman finished third on team in batting (.320) and second in doubles (25)... Ended season by hitting safely in 14 of his last 17 games... Father Bob is now manager of Royals, after 19-year career as big league catcher... Grandfather Ray was an All-Star infielder during 13-year major league career and is scout for Red Sox... Brother Aaron, a third baseman, is on his way to bigs, too... Acquired by Reds from Seattle with Erik Hanson for Bobby Ayala and Dan Wilson prior to 1994 season ... Was Mariners' fifth-round selection in 1990 draft... Would have made $175,000 in '94, making him one of the best bargains around... Born April 6, 1969, in El Cajon, Cal.

Year	Club	Pos.	G	AB	R	H	2B	3B	HR	RBI	SB	Avg.
1992	Seattle	2B-3B	33	129	15	25	4	0	4	15	1	.194
1993	Seattle	2B	76	271	31	68	12	2	12	38	2	.251
1994	Cincinnati	2B-3B	108	381	59	122	25	2	12	68	3	.320
	Totals		217	781	105	215	41	4	28	121	6	.275

JOSE RIJO 29 6-2 200   Bats R Throws R

When you watch him throw that nasty slider, you think he should be best pitcher in league ... Maybe he is too nice a guy... Won seven of his last 10 decisions to finish at 9-6 in '94 ... Ended season second in NL in strikeouts (171) and sixth in ERA (3.08)... Has struck out 10 or more batters 23 times in his career ... Had banner year in '93, leading NL in strikeouts (227), tying for lead in starts (36), ranking second in ERA (2.48) and innings (257⅓)... Opponents hit only .230 against him in '93, the third-lowest mark in league, and he became first Red to lead league in strikeouts since Ewell Blackwell in 1947 ... Originally signed as undrafted free agent by Yankees in August 1980, but was traded to Athletics in seven-player deal for Rickey Henderson prior to 1985 season... A's sent him to Reds with Tim Birtsas for Dave Parker following 1987 season... Born May

13, 1965, in San Cristobal, D.R.... Would have earned $4.875 million last season.

Year	Club	G	IP	W	L	Pct.	SO	BB	H	ERA
1984	New York (AL)	24	62⅓	2	8	.200	47	33	74	4.76
1985	Oakland	12	63⅔	6	4	.600	65	28	57	3.53
1986	Oakland	39	193⅔	9	11	.450	176	108	172	4.65
1987	Oakland	21	82⅓	2	7	.222	67	41	106	5.90
1988	Cincinnati	49	162	13	8	.619	160	63	120	2.39
1989	Cincinnati	19	111	7	6	.538	86	48	101	2.84
1990	Cincinnati	29	197	14	8	.636	152	78	151	2.70
1991	Cincinnati	30	204⅓	15	6	.714	172	55	165	2.51
1992	Cincinnati	33	211	15	10	.600	171	44	185	2.56
1993	Cincinnati	36	257⅓	14	9	.609	227	62	218	2.48
1994	Cincinnati	26	172⅓	9	6	.600	171	52	177	3.08
	Totals	318	1717	106	83	.561	1494	612	1526	3.12

TOM BROWNING 34 6-1 200   Bats L Throws L

Gutsy competitor had '94 season shattered when he broke his left arm as he threw a pitch in game against Padres May 10... Freak injury came as a result of putting too much stress on arm... At the time, he was off to solid start, winning three of his first four decisions... Did surrender eight homers in his 40⅔ innings...

His body is slowly falling apart... Suffered major injury each of last three seasons, including ruptured knee ligaments and fractured finger on pitching hand... On Sept. 16, 1988, he pitched first perfect game in Reds' history, against Dodgers... Has posted only one losing record in 11 major league seasons... Born April 28, 1960, in Casper, Wy.... Reds selected him in ninth round of 1982 draft... Would have earned $3.75 million last season... **Free agent at press time.**

Year	Club	G	IP	W	L	Pct.	SO	BB	H	ERA
1984	Cincinnati	3	23⅓	1	0	1.000	14	5	27	1.54
1985	Cincinnati	38	261⅓	20	9	.690	155	73	242	3.55
1986	Cincinnati	39	243⅓	14	13	.519	147	70	225	3.81
1987	Cincinnati	32	183	10	13	.435	117	61	201	5.02
1988	Cincinnati	36	250⅔	18	5	.783	124	64	205	3.41
1989	Cincinnati	37	249⅔	15	12	.556	118	64	241	3.39
1990	Cincinnati	35	227⅔	15	9	.625	99	52	235	3.80
1991	Cincinnati	36	230⅓	14	14	.500	115	56	241	4.18
1992	Cincinnati	16	87	6	5	.545	33	28	108	5.07
1993	Cincinnati	21	114	7	7	.500	53	20	159	4.74
1994	Cincinnati	7	40⅔	3	1	.750	22	13	34	4.20
	Totals	300	1911	123	88	.583	997	506	1918	3.92

Jose Rijo ranked second in NL strikeouts with 171.

JOHN SMILEY 30 6-4 217 **Bats L Throws L**

Bounced back from being biggest free-agent bust of 1993 to post respectable 11-10 mark last year... Still embarrassingly overpaid at what would've been $4.975 million in '94... So, how did this left-hander turn it around?... Teammates took care of him by giving him average support of 6.18 runs per nine innings, third-highest mark in NL, behind Phils' Danny Jackson (6.62) and Expos' Ken Hill (6.40)... Opponents hit sturdy .275 against him and he surrendered team-high 18 homers

... Reds have gotten only 14 wins in two years for the nearly $10 million they have forked over to him ... Pirates' 12th-round pick in '83 ... Pirates traded him to Twins for Denny Neagle and Midre Cummings before 1992 season ... Won 20 games for Bucs in 1991, but collapsed in postseason, lasting less than total of three innings in two starts ... Born March 17, 1965, in Phoenixville, Pa.

Year	Club	G	IP	W	L	Pct.	SO	BB	H	ERA
1986	Pittsburgh	12	11⅔	1	0	1.000	9	4	4	3.86
1987	Pittsburgh	63	75	5	5	.500	58	50	69	5.76
1988	Pittsburgh	34	205	13	11	.542	129	46	185	3.25
1989	Pittsburgh	28	205⅓	12	8	.600	123	49	174	2.81
1990	Pittsburgh	26	149⅓	9	10	.474	86	36	161	4.64
1991	Pittsburgh	33	207⅔	20	8	.714	129	44	194	3.08
1992	Minnesota	34	241	16	9	.640	163	65	205	3.21
1993	Cincinnati	18	105⅔	3	9	.250	60	31	117	5.62
1994	Cincinnati	24	158⅔	11	10	.524	112	37	169	3.86
	Totals	272	1359⅓	90	70	.563	869	362	1278	3.70

TOP PROSPECTS

POKEY REESE 21 5-11 180   **Bats R Throws R**
Best prospect in Reds' organization, by far ... Feeling is that this shortstop will be able to take over for Barry Larkin in a couple of years ... Batted .269 for Chattanooga (AA) and showed good power with 12 homers, 23 doubles and 49 RBI ... Had hit only 12 homers in three previous pro seasons ... Born June 10, 1973, in Columbia, S.C. ... Reds' No. 1 pick in 1991 draft ... Real name is Calvin.

BEN VanRYN 23 6-5 185   **Bats L Throws L**
In exchange of southpaws, he was traded by Dodgers to Reds for William Brunson in December ... Continued climb up ladder last season, posting combined 12-4 record for Albuquerque (AAA) and San Antonio (AA) ... Was 4-1, 6.39 for Albuquerque and 8-3, 2.99 for San Antonio ... Named to Texas League All-Star team in 1993 and was tabbed league's Pitcher of the Year as he compiled 14-4 record with 2.21 ERA for San Antonio ... Acquired by Dodgers from Expos for Mark Griffin prior to 1992 season ... Born Aug. 9, 1971, in Fort Wayne, Ind. ... Expos' 37th-round pick in 1990 draft.

SCOTT SULLIVAN 24 6-4 210   Bats R Throws R
Best closer in organization... His first year in pro ball, he finished 5-0 with 1.67 ERA for Billings (Rookie) in '93... Followed that with an 11-7 mark, 3.41 ERA and seven saves for Chattanooga (AA) last season... Struck out 111 batters in 121⅓ innings... Born March 13, 1971, in Tuscaloosa, Ala.... Drafted by Reds in second round in 1993, out of Auburn.

C.J. NITKOWSKI 22 6-2 190   Bats L Throws L
Team's No. 1 pick last year, out of St. John's University, which has produced other great left-handers like Frank Viola and John Franco... Ninth player selected overall in '94... Moved from the Big East to Chattanooga (AA) and produced 6-3 mark with 3.50 ERA in 14 games in '94... Opponents hit just .227 against him... Born March 3, 1973, in Suffern, N.Y.

CHAD FOX 24 6-3 175   Bats R Throws R
After two mediocre seasons, he blossomed with Winston-Salem (A) last year, posting 12-5 record with 3.86 ERA in 25 starts... In 156⅓ innings, he struck out 137 batters... Went 9-12 for Charleston (A) in '93... Born Sept. 3, 1970, in Conroe, Tex. ... Taken by Reds in 23rd round of 1992 draft, out of Tarleton State.

MANAGER DAVEY JOHNSON: Replaced much-beloved Tony Perez amid swarm of controversy, May 25, 1993, and team went down the tubes after All-Star break, going 28-44 and finishing fifth... At that point, everyone thought former Met manager had lost his touch... Everyone was wrong... Led Reds to 66-48 mark last year and first-place finish in NL Central... Received one-year extension as manager last fall and will move to front office in 1996, when coach Ray Knight will probably take over as field boss... Had problems with owner Marge Schott, but managed to survive them... Could find himself out of a job at any time because Marge is reportedly not a big fan of his... Owns impressive 714-530 career mark as major league manager... When Mets went 100-60 in 1988, he became first NL manager to win 90 or more games in each of his first five seasons... Under his guidance, Mets captured division titles in 1986 and 1988 and one World Series ('86)... As a player, this second baseman was selected to four All-Star teams and played in four World Series with the Orioles... Born Jan. 30, 1943, in Orlando, Fla.

ALL-TIME RED SEASON RECORDS

BATTING: Cy Seymour, .377, 1905
HRs: George Foster, 52, 1977
RBI: George Foster, 149, 1977
STEALS: Bob Bescher, 81, 1911
WINS: Adolfo Luque, 27, 1923
      Bucky Walters, 27, 1939
STRIKEOUTS: Mario Soto, 274, 1982

HOUSTON ASTROS

TEAM DIRECTORY: Owner: Drayton McLane Jr.; GM: Bob Watson; Dir. Pub. Rel.: Rob Matwick; Trav. Sec.: Barry Waters; Mgr.: Terry Collins; Coaches: Jesse Barfield, Matt Galante, Steve Henderson, Julio Linares, Mel Stottlemyre. Home: Astrodome (54,313). Field distances: 325, l.f. line; 375, l.c.; 400, c.f.; 375, r.c.; 325, r.f. line. Spring training: Kissimmee, Fla.

SCOUTING REPORT

All the ingredients are in place for the Astros to win the NL Central. They have the pitching, the hitting and the defense. And Terry Collins proved in his rookie year, they also have the managing as the Astros finished at 66-49, just a half-game behind the

Jeff Bagwell's MVP numbers were simply Astro-nomical.

Reds last season.

Any championship team needs a cornerstone to build on and carry the weight of winning. The Astros have that in NL MVP Jeff Bagwell (.368, 39, 116). The first baseman has become one of the most feared hitters in the game and was a big reason the Astros finished second in the NL in hitting with a .278 mark. The only NL team to hit for a higher average was Cincinnati (.286). That .278 average marked the sixth straight season the team batting average has improved for the Astros. And to think the Dome used to be known only as the home of great pitchers.

Besides Bagwell, the Astros will be counting on another bang-up year from third baseman Ken Caminiti (.283, 18, 75) and second baseman Craig Biggio (.318, 6, 56). Biggio also led the team in steals with 39 as the Astros finished second in the NL in stolen bases with 124, 13 fewer than the Expos. James Mouton (.245, 2, 16) swiped 24 bases.

Speedy outfielders Steve Finley (.276, 11, 33) and Luis Gonzalez (.273, 8, 67) are major contributors offensively and had a combined total of 28 stolen bases.

Overall, the Astros are an excellent defensive team. They tied the Reds for second in fielding percentage in the NL with a .983 mark last season and figure to improve this year with another season of Collins accenting the fundamentals. Electric young shortstop Andujar Cedeno (.263, 9, 49) needs to cut down on his errors after committing 23 in '94.

Pitching, it always seems, is an Astros' strength. Even though the Astrodome is a bit friendlier to hitters than it had been in the past, the Astros finished fifth in the league with a 3.97 ERA. Opponents only batted .262 against Houston, the fourth-best mark in the NL.

As long as Doug Drabek (12-6, 2.84) is there, the Astros have their go-to guy. Drabek bounced back from a poor 1993 to finish among the league leaders in wins, ERA and complete games (6).

With Pete Harnisch exiled to the Mets, Darryl Kile (9-6, 4.57), Greg Swindell (8-9, 4.37) and Shane Reynolds (8-5, 3.05) round out a solid rotation. The hefty Swindell rounds out more than a rotation and needs to get in better shape. To make things even more interesting, the Astros did the almost impossible, picking up a closer—John Hudek (0-2, 2.97, 16 saves)—off the scrap heap.

As long as Bagwell doesn't break his hand again and Drabek stays healthy, this is one of the NL's class teams. Big things happen in Texas. Expect big things from the Astros.

ASTRO PROFILES

JEFF BAGWELL 26 6-0 200   Bats R Throws R

Unanimous choice as NL MVP in 1994 became first player to finish first or second in his league in average (.368), runs (104), RBI (116) and homers (39) since Carl Yastrzemski in 1967... Kind of fitting it was Yaz, considering it was Red Sox who dealt this first baseman to Astros for Larry Andersen, Aug. 31, 1990. That deal ranks up there with Babe Ruth giveaway... Last NL player to finish first or second in all those categories was Willie Mays in 1955... Homers, RBI and extra-base hits (73) were club records, despite fact he played just 110 games... Season came to an end Aug. 10, when he broke his left hand as result of being hit by Andy Benes pitch... Named to All-Star team for the first time... Destroyed left-handers, batting .457 with 18 homers... Became first Astro to win Rookie of the Year honors in 1991... Born May 27, 1968, in Boston... Chosen by Red Sox in fourth round of 1989 draft... Would have earned $2.4 million last year... Won first Gold Glove in '94... Signed record four-year, $27.5-million extension through 2001 season last winter.

Year	Club	Pos.	G	AB	R	H	2B	3B	HR	RBI	SB	Avg.
1991	Houston	1B	156	554	79	163	26	4	15	82	7	.294
1992	Houston	1B	162	586	87	160	34	6	18	96	10	.273
1993	Houston	1B	142	535	76	171	37	4	20	88	13	.320
1994	Houston	1B-OF	110	400	104	147	32	2	39	116	15	.368
	Totals		570	2075	346	641	129	16	92	382	45	.309

CRAIG BIGGIO 29 5-11 180   Bats R Throws R

Homer production dropped from 21 in '93 to six, but he tied for NL lead with 44 doubles ... That also tied a franchise record... Moving him from catcher to second allowed him to become all-around player... Led NL with career-high 39 stolen bases... Tied a club record by scoring four runs April 20... Has been selected to All-Star team three times in last four years... Batted .330 with runners in scoring position... Became first player in history to make All-Star team at catcher (1991) and second base (1992)... Born Dec. 14, 1965, in Smithtown, N.Y. ... Attended Seton Hall... Chosen by Astros in first round of

1987 draft... Would have earned $3.35 million in '94... Won first Gold Glove in '94.

Year Club	Pos.	G	AB	R	H	2B	3B	HR	RBI	SB	Avg.
1988 Houston	C	50	123	14	26	6	1	3	5	6	.211
1989 Houston	C-OF	134	443	64	114	21	2	13	60	21	.257
1990 Houston	C-OF	150	555	53	153	24	2	4	42	25	.276
1991 Houston	C-3B-OF	149	546	79	161	23	4	4	46	19	.295
1992 Houston	2B	162	613	96	170	32	3	6	39	38	.277
1993 Houston	2B	155	610	98	175	41	5	21	64	15	.287
1994 Houston	2B	114	437	88	139	44	5	6	56	39	.318
Totals		914	3327	492	938	191	22	57	312	163	.282

KEN CAMINITI 31 6-0 200   Bats S Throws R

Finally got away from unlucky 13... After three straight years of hitting 13 homers, he clubbed career-high 18... Became fourth Astro in history to homer from both sides of the plate in a game July 3 against Cubs... Was May masher, hitting .372 with six homers and 21 RBI... Jim Leyland respected him. He tied major league mark with three intentional walks against Pirates July 16... No third baseman since Brooks Robinson dives, gets up quicker and puts more juice on the throw than him... Would have earned $3.2 million last season... Born April 21, 1963, in Hanford, Cal.... Astros' third-round selection in 1984 draft, out of San Jose State.

Year Club	Pos.	G	AB	R	H	2B	3B	HR	RBI	SB	Avg.
1987 Houston	3B	63	203	10	50	7	1	3	23	0	.246
1988 Houston	3B	30	83	5	15	2	0	1	7	0	.181
1989 Houston	3B	161	585	71	149	31	3	10	72	4	.255
1990 Houston	3B	153	541	52	131	20	2	4	51	9	.242
1991 Houston	3B	152	574	65	145	30	3	13	80	4	.253
1992 Houston	3B	135	506	68	149	31	2	13	62	10	.294
1993 Houston	3B	143	543	75	142	31	0	13	75	8	.262
1994 Houston	3B	111	406	63	115	28	2	18	75	4	.283
Totals		948	3441	409	896	180	13	75	445	39	.260

LUIS GONZALEZ 27 6-2 180   Bats L Throws R

After he got a four-fold boost in salary, his production went down... Established career highs in all major offensive categories in '93... His average dropped 27 points to .273 in '94... Did manage a career-high 49 walks... Was coming on strong when strike hit, batting .331 with 15 doubles and 35 RBI in his final 41 games... Made the switch from infield to outfield in 1991... Committed just two errors in left field last year... Would have made $1.63 million in '94... Selected by Astros in fourth round of 1988 draft... Born Sept. 3, 1967, in Tampa, Fla.... Attended South Alabama University... In 1990, he tied for Southern League in home runs with 24 for Columbus (AA)... Owns a bright, bright future.

Year	Club	Pos.	G	AB	R	H	2B	3B	HR	RBI	SB	Avg.
1990	Houston	3B-1B	12	21	1	4	2	0	0	0	0	.190
1991	Houston	OF	137	473	51	120	28	9	13	69	10	.254
1992	Houston	OF	122	387	40	94	19	3	10	55	7	.243
1993	Houston	OF	154	540	82	162	34	3	15	72	20	.300
1994	Houston	OF	112	392	57	107	29	4	8	67	15	.273
	Totals		537	1813	231	487	112	19	46	263	52	.269

STEVE FINLEY 30 6-2 180   Bats L Throws L

Rocked by injuries last two years... Center fielder got off to electric start, batting .323 with seven homers and 16 RBI in April... Broke bone in his right hand June 8 in Montreal... Broke his wrist in '93... Was back in the lineup by July 3 last season and managed to hit career-high 11 homers... Got off to difficult start in 1993, when he was hampered by Bell's Palsy in spring training... Viral infection in his upper neck caused numbness and made it impossible to close his left eye... Came to Houston from Orioles with Pete Harnisch and Curt Schilling in deal for Glenn Davis prior to 1991 season... Another steal... Selected by Orioles in 14th round of 1987 draft... Born March 12, 1965, in Union City, Tenn.... Would have made $3.05 million last season.

Year	Club	Pos.	G	AB	R	H	2B	3B	HR	RBI	SB	Avg.
1989	Baltimore	OF	81	217	35	54	5	2	2	25	17	.249
1990	Baltimore	OF	142	464	46	119	16	4	3	37	22	.256
1991	Houston	OF	159	596	84	170	28	10	8	54	34	.285
1992	Houston	OF	162	607	84	177	29	13	5	55	44	.292
1993	Houston	OF	142	545	69	145	15	13	8	44	19	.266
1994	Houston	OF	94	373	64	103	16	5	11	33	13	.276
	Totals		780	2802	382	768	109	47	37	248	149	.274

JAMES MOUTON 26 5-9 175   Bats R Throws R

On the fast track, although he did hit a few speed bumps his first season in bigs... Reached base four times in his first big league game April 4 against Expos, but he hit only .200 in April... Produced four-hit game May 24 in Atlanta... Former second baseman is learning to play outfield... First major league homer was a grand slam, off Vincente Palacios

April 23 in St. Louis... In 1993, he made jump to Tucson (AAA) from Osceola (A) and responded in a big way. He was named PCL MVP after batting .315, scoring 126 runs, knocking in 92 and amassing 42 doubles, 12 triples and 16 homers in 134 games... Born Dec. 29, 1968, in Denver... Astros' seventh-round selection in 1991 draft... Would have made $109,000 last year.

Year Club	Pos.	G	AB	R	H	2B	3B	HR	RBI	SB	Avg.
1994 Houston	OF	99	310	43	76	11	0	2	16	24	.245

DOUG DRABEK 32 6-1 185   Bats R Throws R

The master still has it... Finished among top 10 in NL in wins (12), ERA (2.84), complete games (6), shutouts (2), innings (164⅔) and winning percentage (.667) after horrible 1993 ... Left Pirates to sign four-year, $19.5-million contract with Astros as free agent prior to '93 season and had the most losses (18) of his career in Houston debut... Fanned 10 batters, one short of his career high, May 18 of last season vs. Giants... Matched longest winning streak of his career when he captured seven in a row from April 10-May 24... Compiled 1.97 ERA during that streak... Would have earned $4.25 million last season ... Named NL Cy Young winner in 1990... Born July 25, 1962, in Victoria, Tex.... Has posted double figures in wins seven times in his eight full seasons... A true winner.

Year	Club	G	IP	W	L	Pct.	SO	BB	H	ERA
1986	New York (AL)	27	131⅔	7	8	.467	76	50	126	4.10
1987	Pittsburgh	29	176⅓	11	12	.478	120	46	165	3.88
1988	Pittsburgh	33	219⅓	15	7	.682	127	50	194	3.08
1989	Pittsburgh	35	244⅓	14	12	.538	123	69	215	2.80
1990	Pittsburgh	33	231⅓	22	6	.786	131	56	190	2.76
1991	Pittsburgh	35	234⅔	15	14	.517	142	62	245	3.07
1992	Pittsburgh	34	256⅔	15	11	.577	177	54	218	2.77
1993	Houston	34	237⅔	9	18	.333	157	60	242	3.79
1994	Houston	23	164⅔	12	6	.667	121	45	132	2.84
	Totals	283	1896⅔	120	94	.561	1174	492	1727	3.17

SHANE REYNOLDS 27 6-3 210   Bats R Throws R

A real comer... In his first full major league season, he ranked fifth in NL in ERA (3.05) ... Brings it with power, averaging 8.0 strikeouts per nine innings, which tied him for fourth-best in NL... Here's the best part, though... Also finished fourth in fewest walks per nine innings at 1.5... Did all this great work despite splitting season between bullpen and rotation

... His first 11 appearances were in relief... Retired first 15 batters he faced as a starter, striking out eight Dodgers May 11 at Los Angeles... Finished second in PCL in ERA (3.62) for Tucson (AAA) in 1993 and allowed just 1.4 walks per nine innings... Born March 26, 1968, in Bastrop, La.... Selected by Astros in third round of 1989 draft... Would have made $117,500 last season.

Year	Club	G	IP	W	L	Pct.	SO	BB	H	ERA
1992	Houston	8	25⅓	1	3	.250	10	6	42	7.11
1993	Houston	5	11	0	0	.000	10	6	11	0.82
1994	Houston	33	124	8	5	.615	110	21	128	3.05
	Totals	46	160⅓	9	8	.529	130	33	181	3.54

DARRYL KILE 26 6-5 190   Bats R Throws R

Who needs Mitch Williams when this right-hander is around?... Scares batters with his wild stuff... Led NL in walks (82), tied for league lead in wild pitches (10) and ranked third in hit batsmen (9)... Did not walk a batter his final 13 innings... Ranked second on staff with nine wins and struck out 10 Cubs April 28, one short of matching career high... Received fifth-highest run support in NL at 5.67 per game... Fired ninth no-hitter in club history, Sept. 8, 1993 against Mets in Houston. Faced just 28 batters in 7-1 win, allowing only a fourth-inning walk to Jeff McKnight... Won 11 of his first 12 decisions that year... Born Dec. 2, 1968, in Garden Grove, Cal.... Would have earned $477,500 last season... Good scouting pays off... Astros selected him in 30th round of 1987 draft.

Year	Club	G	IP	W	L	Pct.	SO	BB	H	ERA
1991	Houston	37	153⅔	7	11	.389	100	84	144	3.69
1992	Houston	22	125⅓	5	10	.333	90	63	124	3.95
1993	Houston	32	171⅔	15	8	.652	141	69	152	3.51
1994	Houston	24	147⅔	9	6	.600	105	82	153	4.57
	Totals	115	598⅓	36	35	.507	436	298	573	3.91

JOHN HUDEK 28 6-1 200   Bats S Throws R

This kind of story makes up for all the spoiled brats in baseball... Right-hander just loves the game and was rewarded for his tenacity by making the All-Star team... Became just fifth player in major league history who began a season in minors and made it to midsummer classic. Others were Don Newcombe (1949), Don Schwall (1961), Bill Dawley (1983) and

Alvin Davis (1984)... Registered eight saves in his first 19 appearances and finished with 16 after being called up from Tucson (AAA), where he had two in six games... Succeeded in 16 of 18 save opportunities with Astros, limiting opposing batters to .174 average... Claimed off waivers from Tigers, June 29, 1993 ... Born Aug. 8, 1966, in Tampa, Fla.... Would have made $109,000.

Year	Club	G	IP	W	L	Pct.	SO	BB	H	ERA
1994	Houston	42	39⅓	0	2	.000	39	18	24	2.97

TOP PROSPECTS

ORLANDO MILLER 26 6-1 180 Bats R Throws R
Shortstop of the future batted .257 with 10 homers and 55 RBI for Tucson (AAA) and hit .325 during 16-game, fill-in stint for Astros in July... Batted .304 for Tucson with 86 runs, 29 doubles, 16 triples and 16 homers in 1993... Named to South Atlantic League All-Star team with Ashville (A) in 1990 and was selected 10th-best prospect in circuit... Born Jan. 13, 1969, in Changuinola, Panama... Acquired by Astros from Yankees for Dave Silvestri prior to 1990 season... Signed as undrafted free agent by Yankees in 1987.

ROBERTO PETAGINE 23 6-1 172 Bats L Throws L
Young first baseman had pair of short stints with Astros in '94, going hitless in just seven at-bats, but he hit .316 with 10 homers and 44 RBI for Tucson (AAA)... Batted Texas League-leading .334 for Jackson (AA) in 1993... Born June 7, 1971, in Nueva Esparita, Venezuela... Signed by Astros as undrafted free agent in February 1990.

PHIL NEVIN 24 6-2 180 Bats R Throws R
A lot is expected from this third baseman, whom Astros made No. 1 pick overall in 1992 draft, out of Cal State-Fullerton... Posted 15-game hitting streak for Tucson (AAA) from April 2-May 6 last season... Finished with 12 homers and 79 RBI, third-highest RBI total on club, but hit only .263 and made an astounding 32 errors... Born Jan. 19, 1971, in Fullerton, Cal.... Drove in 93 runs for Tucson in 1993.

Doug Drabek recaptured grand old days as Pirate.

BOB ABREU 21 6-0 165 **Bats L Throws R**
Outfielder was one of the youngest players in Texas League, but he batted .303 with 16 homers and 73 RBI for Jackson (AA)... Hit .363 over second half of last season... Knocked in 32 runs in his final 50 games... Hit 17 triples for Osceola (A) in Florida State League in '93... Born March 11, 1974, in Aragua, Venezuela... Signed as undrafted free agent in August 1990.

MANAGER TERRY COLLINS: Pirates manager Jim Leyland knew what he was talking about when he said his former bullpen coach was best man to manage the Astros... That recommendation was right on the mark as rookie skipper led Houston to 66-49 record and second-place finish, only a half-game behind Reds in NL Central... That finish at 17 games over .500 marked club's highest finish over .500 since 1986 West Division champs posted 96-66 record... This man paid his dues... Worked his way up by managing in minors, where he posted Triple-A record of 634-578... Overall minor league managerial mark is 824-736... Posted three straight 80-win seasons in Pirates' system with Buffalo (1989-1991)... Born May 27, 1949, in Midland, Mich.... Prior to managing at Buffalo, he managed in Dodgers' system for eight years... In 1988, he was named PCL Manager of the Year after leading Albuquerque to league-best 85-56 mark... Dodgers let a good one get away... Spent 10 years as a middle infielder in minors, beginning his professional career in 1971 in Pirate organization at Niagara Falls.

ALL-TIME ASTRO SEASON RECORDS

BATTING: Jeff Bagwell, .368, 1994
HRs: Jeff Bagwell, 39, 1994
RBI: Jeff Bagwell, 116, 1994
STEALS: Gerald Young, 65, 1988
WINS: Joe Niekro, 21, 1979
STRIKEOUTS: J. R. Richards, 313, 1979

PITTSBURGH PIRATES

TEAM DIRECTORY: Pres./CEO: Mark Sauer; GM: Cam Bonifay; Dir. Media Rel.: Jim Trdinich; Trav. Sec.: Greg Johnson; Mgr.: Jim Leyland; Coaches: Rich Donnelly, Milt May, Ray Miller, Tommy Sandt, Spin Williams, Bill Virdon. Home: Three Rivers Stadium (49,972). Field distances: 335, l.f. line; 375, l.c.; 400, c.f.; 375, r.c.; 335, r.f. line. Spring training: Bradenton, Fla.

SCOUTING REPORT

The Pirates' pennant-winning teams of the late '80s and early '90s are but a distant memory. Jay Bell, possibly Zane Smith, Jeff King and manager Jim Leyland are still around, but the buzzword in Pittsburgh these days is rebuilding.

There is a lot of work to be done. The Pirates, who finished tied for third place in the NL Central at 53-61, are one of the weakest offensive teams in the league and their pitching staff is at least two quality arms short of solid.

Steady SS Jay Bell is link to Pirate glory.

What do the Pirates need? It's easier to come up with a list of what they don't need.

The Pirates ranked 12th in the NL with a .259 batting average and were last in runs (466), total bases (1,485), RBI (435) and slugging percentage (.384). They'll have a hard time manufacturing runs and an even harder time hitting home runs, judging from the 80 they managed last season.

Bell (.276, 9, 45), an outstanding defensive shortstop, will take on an greater leadership role now that long-time center fielder Andy Van Slyke (.246, 6, 30) is gone via free agency. The Pirates also need Bell to hit a little bit more than he did last season. All-Star second baseman Carlos Garcia (.277, 6, 28, 18 steals) provides speed and sound defense while King (.263, 5, 42) is a fine third baseman, but not the run producer the Pirates had hoped he would be. Orlando Merced (.272, 9, 51), the Pirates' best pure hitter, will share time at first with prospect Kevin Young (.205, 1, 11).

Midre Cummings (.244, 1, 12), another highly touted prospect, or ex-Red Jacob Brumfield (.311, 4, 11) could become Van Slyke's permanent replacement in center. Merced, Al Martin (.286, 9, 33) and Dave Clark (.296, 10, 46) make up the rest of the Pirates outfield, which underscores the club's need for a big-time run producer. Too bad the Pirates don't have another Barry Bonds in their system.

The Pirates do have a few prospects in the minors, but they are not expected to make much of an impact this season. Somehow, respected pitching coach Ray Miller will have to improve a staff that compiled a 4.64 ERA and a league-worst .289 batting average against. The Pirates' pitchers also struck out an NL-low 632 batters.

Smith (10-8, 3.27) has been called upon to hold together a suspect staff, but he was unsigned at press time. Randy Tomlin (0-3, 3.92) is a proven starter who suffered a disturbing career setback last season and this may be a make-or-break year for him. Scouts say Steve Cooke (4-11, 5.02) has good stuff, but the lefty starter has been unable to transfer his talent into wins.

Denny Neagle (9-10, 5.12) was used exclusively as a starter for the first time in four years in '94, but may split time between the bullpen and the rotation this season. Free-agent addition Dan Plesac (2-3, 4.61, 1 save with Cubs), Paul Wagner (7-8, 4.59), Rick White (4-5, 3.82), Mike Dyer (1-1, 5.87) and Ravelo Manzanillo (4-2, 4.14) make up the Pirates' bullpen by committee.

Because Leyland is one of the game's top managers, the Pirates will stay competitive. But they won't have the talent to challenge in the division.

PIRATE PROFILES

JAY BELL 29 6-0 181   Bats R Throws R

Anchor of Pirates' infield and their inspirational leader... Made 108 starts and led major league shortstops with 547 total chances... Has led NL shortstops in chances for five straight seasons... Led club in hits (117) for second straight year... Ranked third in NL with 35 doubles... Was batting only .203 on June 4, but hit .313 in June, .314 during July and .357 in August... Seven of his nine homers were solo shots... Won first Gold Glove in 1993, snapping Ozzie Smith's 13-year reign ... Batted career-high .310 in '93 and also set career highs in runs, hits, triples, walks and stolen bases... Owns lifetime .282 batting average in three NLCS... Acquired from Indians for Felix Fermin prior to 1989 season... Twins' first-round draft pick and eighth player taken overall in 1984... Born Dec. 11, 1965, at Eglin AFB, Fla.... Would have earned $3 million in '94.

Year Club	Pos.	G	AB	R	H	2B	3B	HR	RBI	SB	Avg.
1986 Cleveland	2B	5	14	3	5	2	0	1	4	0	.357
1987 Cleveland	SS	38	125	14	27	9	1	2	13	2	.216
1988 Cleveland	SS	73	211	23	46	5	1	2	21	4	.218
1989 Pittsburgh	SS	78	271	33	70	13	3	2	27	5	.258
1990 Pittsburgh	SS	159	583	93	148	28	7	7	52	10	.254
1991 Pittsburgh	SS	157	608	96	164	32	8	16	67	10	.270
1992 Pittsburgh	SS	159	632	87	167	36	6	9	55	7	.264
1993 Pittsburgh	SS	154	604	102	187	32	9	9	51	16	.310
1994 Pittsburgh	SS	110	424	68	117	35	4	9	45	2	.276
Totals		933	3472	519	931	192	39	57	335	56	.268

JEFF KING 30 6-1 187   Bats R Throws R

Solid third baseman who struggled offensively for much of season... Homered for first time May 21, in his 136th at-bat... Placed on DL with back strain from May 25-June 9... Hit safely in 11 of last 13 games... Made 89 starts at third... Ranked sixth in NL with seven sacrifice flies... Batted every place in order except second and ninth... In 1993, he led club in games, doubles and RBI... Smacked career-high 14 home runs in 1992... Demoted to Buffalo (AAA) for seven games in 1992 ... Set career records in homers and RBI at University of Arkansas

... Top overall pick in 1986 draft ... Born Nov. 26, 1964, in Marion, Ind. ... Would have earned $2.4 million last season.

Year	Club	Pos.	G	AB	R	H	2B	3B	HR	RBI	SB	Avg.
1989	Pittsburgh	1B-3B-2B-SS	75	215	31	42	13	1	5	19	4	.195
1990	Pittsburgh	3B-1B	127	371	46	91	17	1	14	53	3	.245
1991	Pittsburgh	3B	33	109	16	26	1	1	4	18	3	.239
1992	Pittsburgh	3B-2B-1B-SS-OF	130	480	56	111	21	2	14	65	4	.231
1993	Pittsburgh	3B-2B-SS	158	611	82	180	35	3	9	98	8	.295
1994	Pittsburgh	3B-2B	94	339	36	89	23	0	5	42	3	.263
	Totals		617	2125	267	539	110	8	51	295	25	.254

CARLOS GARCIA 27 6-1 193   Bats R Throws R

Slick-fielding second baseman became an All-Star in his second big league season ... His 10 assists vs. Rockies June 5 fell two shy of major league record for second baseman ... Made 98 starts at second ... Led Pirates in stolen bases (18) for second straight season ... Hit safely in 15 of his first 19 games and batted .304 in April ... Was batting .326 on May 20 before producing just 23 hits in 102 at-bats in June ... Set career high with four RBI June 15 vs. Houston ... Led club with 36 multi-hit games and 19 infield hits ... Made 132 starts at second base and ranked fifth among second baseman with .983 fielding percentage in '93 ... Signed as undrafted free agent in January 1987 ... Born Oct. 15, 1967, in Tachira, Venezuela ... Would have earned $192,500 in '94 ... Wears No. 13 in honor of countryman Dave Concepcion, former Reds All-Star.

Year	Club	Pos.	G	AB	R	H	2B	3B	HR	RBI	SB	Avg.
1990	Pittsburgh	SS	4	4	1	2	0	0	0	0	0	.500
1991	Pittsburgh	SS-3B-2B	12	24	2	6	0	2	0	1	0	.250
1992	Pittsburgh	2B-SS	22	39	4	8	1	0	0	4	0	.205
1993	Pittsburgh	2B-SS	141	546	77	147	25	5	12	47	18	.269
1994	Pittsburgh	2B	98	412	49	114	15	2	6	28	18	.277
	Totals		277	1025	133	277	41	9	18	80	36	.270

AL MARTIN 27 6-2 215   Bats L Throws L

Promising season ended abruptly July 11 when young outfielder suffered wrist injury ... Underwent surgery to repair ligament and cartilage damage to his left wrist Aug. 2 ... Started season with 1-for-16 downer, then hit safely in 13 of next 18 games ... Batted .310 in month of May ... Tied career best with four hits and four RBI May 26 vs. New York ... Stole 15 bases in 21 attempts ... Led all NL rookies in runs (85) in 1993 ... Ranked second among NL rookies in home runs (18)

behind Dodgers' Mike Piazza... Led club in home runs in '93, collecting the most by a Pirates rookie since Ralph Kiner hit 23 in 1946... Uncle Rod played with NFL Raiders for 12 seasons ... Braves' eighth-round pick in 1985... Nicknamed "Little Hurt"... Signed as minor league free agent prior to 1992 season ... Born Nov. 24, 1967, in West Covina, Cal.... Would have earned $192,5000 last season.

Year	Club	Pos.	G	AB	R	H	2B	3B	HR	RBI	SB	Avg.
1992	Pittsburgh	OF	12	12	1	2	0	1	0	2	0	.167
1993	Pittsburgh	OF	143	480	85	135	26	8	18	64	16	.281
1994	Pittsburgh	OF	82	276	48	79	12	4	9	33	15	.286
	Totals		237	768	134	216	38	13	27	99	31	.281

KEVIN YOUNG 25 6-2 219   Bats R Throws R

Young first baseman took a step backwards following strong 1993 season... Started 1994 season in Pittsburgh and batted .192 with three RBI in first 21 games... Was optioned to Buffalo (AAA) May 10... Batted .327 for Bisons before being recalled May 25... In next 38 games as a Pirate, in '93, he went 5-for-70 (.214)... Extended errorless streak at first base to 115 games... Demoted to Buffalo July 11... Batted .213 in next 27 games with Bisons, but hit .338 in final 19 games to push final Triple-A numbers to .276 with five homers and 27 RBI in 228 at-bats... Recalled to Pirates Sept. 7... Spent entire 1993 season with Pirates, making 121 starts at first base... Led all NL first basemen with a .998 fielding percentage while committing a league-low three errors in '93... Pirates' seventh-round pick in 1990... Born June 16, 1969, in Alpena, Mich.... Would have earned $160,000 in '94.

Year	Club	Pos.	G	AB	R	H	2B	3B	HR	RBI	SB	Avg.
1992	Pittsburgh	3B-1B	10	7	2	4	0	0	0	4	1	.571
1993	Pittsburgh	1B-3B	141	449	38	106	24	3	6	47	2	.236
1994	Pittsburgh	1B-3B-OF	59	122	15	25	7	2	1	11	0	.205
	Totals		210	578	55	135	31	5	7	62	3	.234

ORLANDO MERCED 28 5-11 191   Bats L Throws R

One of Pirates' most consistent performers... Led club in RBI with 51... Made 55 starts in right and 47 at first base... Hit first career homer off a left-handed pitcher when he connected off Montreal's Denis Boucher May 21... Reached base via a hit or walk in 17 of his first 19 games... Hit safely in career-best 16 straight games from June 14-July 1...

Smacked five home runs and knocked in 17 runs during streak
... Grounded into 17 double plays, second-highest total in NL
behind Padres' Tony Gwynn (20)... Set career highs in average,
games, hits, RBI and walks in 1993, when he finished ninth in
NL in batting average and ranked fourth with .414 on-base percentage... Signed as undrafted free agent in February 1985...
Born Nov. 2, 1966, in San Juan, P.R.... Would have earned
$1.485 million in '94.

Year	Club	Pos.	G	AB	R	H	2B	3B	HR	RBI	SB	Avg.
1990	Pittsburgh	OF-C	25	24	3	5	1	0	0	0	0	.208
1991	Pittsburgh	1B-OF	120	411	83	113	17	2	10	50	8	.275
1992	Pittsburgh	1B-OF	134	405	50	100	28	5	6	60	5	.247
1993	Pittsburgh	OF-1B	137	447	68	140	26	4	8	70	3	.313
1994	Pittsburgh	OF-1B	108	386	48	105	21	3	9	51	4	.272
	Totals		524	1673	252	463	93	14	33	231	20	.277

STEVE COOKE 25 6-6 232   Bats R Throws L

The promise that he exhibited in 1993 was nowhere to be found last season... Tall lefthander led Bucs' staff in losses (11) and ranked third in NL with 21 home runs allowed... Was charged with 75 earned runs, seventh-most in NL... Started season by dropping first three decisions... Surrendered just two earned runs in first two starts... Went 0-5 with 8.57 ERA in last five starts... Tossed complete game in losing effort May 14 vs. Phillies... Beat Phillies June 21, his final win of season
... In 1993, he led all major league rookies in starts, innings and
strikeouts... Became first rookie pitcher to lead Pirates in strikeouts since Bill Werle in 1949... Born Jan. 14, 1970, in Kauai,
Hawaii... Selected by Pirates in 35th round of 1989 draft...
Would have earned $187,500 last season.

Year	Club	G	IP	W	L	Pct.	SO	BB	H	ERA
1992	Pittsburgh	11	23	2	0	1.000	10	4	22	3.52
1993	Pittsburgh	32	210⅔	10	10	.500	132	59	207	3.89
1994	Pittsburgh	25	134⅓	4	11	.267	74	46	157	5.02
	Totals	68	368	16	21	.432	216	109	386	4.28

DENNY NEAGLE 26 6-2 216   Bats L Throws L

Was used exclusively as a starter for first time since 1990 season... Ranked second on club in wins (9) behind Zane Smith... Led club in strikeouts (122)... Averaged 8.0 strikeouts per nine innings and ranked fourth in NL in that category... Charged with 78 earned runs, sixth-highest total in NL... Held the Giants hitless for five innings before dropping 4-2 decision in season debut April 6... Collected single off Expos' Pedro Martinez May 22 after going hitless in first 40 career at-bats, third-longest career-starting drought in history... Tossed first complete game and struck out career-high nine batters June 8 vs. Giants... Minnesota's third-round pick in 1989... Acquired from Twins with Midre Cummings for John Smiley prior to 1992 season... Born Sept. 13, 1968, in Gambrills, Md.... Would have earned $220,000 last year.

Year	Club	G	IP	W	L	Pct.	SO	BB	H	ERA
1991	Minnesota	7	20	0	1	.000	14	7	28	4.05
1992	Pittsburgh	55	86⅓	4	6	.400	77	43	82	4.48
1993	Pittsburgh	50	81⅓	3	5	.375	73	37	82	5.31
1994	Pittsburgh	24	137	9	10	.474	122	49	135	5.12
	Totals	136	324⅔	16	22	.473	286	136	325	4.93

ZANE SMITH 34 6-1 207　　　　Bats L Throws L

Ace of a mediocre Pirates staff... Led club in victories (10) and innings (157)... Ranked 10th in NL in ERA (3.27)... Was 3-1 with 3.16 ERA in five April starts... Tossed complete game April 27 vs. Reds in his 300th career game... Won four of five decisions in June... Made lone relief appearance July 9 against Cincinnati... Went 0-2 with 4.45 ERA in first five starts after the All-Star break before tossing five-hit shutout in final start of the season, Aug. 11 against Expos... Limited left-handed batters to .217 average... Began 1993 season on disabled list following arthroscopic surgery on throwing shoulder... Braves' third-round pick in 1982... Acquired from Expos by Pirates for Scott Ruskin, Willie Greene and Moises Alou, Aug. 8, 1990... Born Dec. 28, 1960, in Madison, Wis.... Would have earned $3.125 million last season... **Free agent at press time.**

Year	Club	G	IP	W	L	Pct.	SO	BB	H	ERA
1984	Atlanta	3	20	1	0	1.000	16	13	16	2.25
1985	Atlanta	42	147	9	10	.474	85	80	135	3.80
1986	Atlanta	38	204⅔	8	16	.333	139	105	209	4.05
1987	Atlanta	36	242	15	10	.600	130	91	245	4.09
1988	Atlanta	23	140⅓	5	10	.333	59	44	159	4.30
1989	Atl.-Mont.	48	147	1	13	.071	93	52	141	3.49
1990	Mont.-Pitt.	33	215⅓	12	9	.571	130	50	196	2.55
1991	Pittsburgh	35	228	16	10	.615	120	29	234	3.20
1992	Pittsburgh	23	141	8	8	.500	56	19	138	3.06
1993	Pittsburgh	14	83	3	7	.300	32	22	97	4.55
1994	Pittsburgh	25	157	10	8	.556	57	34	162	3.27
	Totals	320	1725⅓	88	101	.466	917	539	1732	3.56

TOP PROSPECTS

RICH AUDE 23 6-5 209   Bats R Throws R
Power-hitting first baseman took major step forward in his first full season in Triple-A... Led Buffalo with 15 home runs and 79 RBI and batted .281... Started 1993 season with Carolina (AA), but was promoted to Bisons after belting 18 home runs and driving in 73 runs in 120 games... Made major league debut Sept. 9, 1993 vs. Colorado... Pirates' second-round pick in 1989... Born July 13, 1971, in Van Nuys, Cal.

DANNY CLYBURN 20 6-3 220   Bats R Throws R
Rising star in Pirates' farm system... Power-hitting outfielder batted .273 with team-high 20 home runs and 90 RBI for Salem (A)... Belted nine homers and had 66 RBI for Augusta (A) in 1993... Pirates' second-round pick in 1992... In first season of pro ball in 1992, he batted .342 in 39 games for Bradenton (R) in Gulf Coast League... Born April 6, 1974, in Lancaster, S.C.

MIDRE CUMMINGS 23 6-0 199   Bats L Throws R
Speedy outfielder could become Andy Van Slyke's successor in center... Started last season with Buffalo (AAA) and made 48 starts in center... Recalled to majors July 15... Blasted first major league homer July 31, off Mets' Juan Castillo... Hit .244 with one homer and 12 RBI as Pirate and .311 with two homers and 22 RBI for Buffalo... Started 1993 season with Carolina (AA), but spent most of year with Buffalo... Minnesota's supplemental first-round pick in 1990 draft... Acquired from Twins with Denny Neagle for pitcher John Smiley prior to 1992 season... Born Oct. 14, 1971, in St. Croix, V.I.

JOHN HOPE 24 6-3 195   Bats R Throws R
Struggled in first Triple-A season, going 4-9 with 3.87 ERA in 18 games for Buffalo... Appeared in nine games for Pirates, compiling 0-0 record and 5.79 ERA... Began 1993 season with Carolina (AA) and led staff with nine wins... Appeared in seven games with Pirates, finishing 0-2 with 4.03 ERA... Pirates' second-round pick in 1989 draft... Born Dec. 21, 1970, in Ft. Lauderdale, Fla.

MANAGER JIM LEYLAND:  The epitome of a players' manager... One of most respected and sought-after managers in baseball... In his 10th season as Pittsburgh's skipper, he guided Pirates to respectable 53-61 record in '94, despite not having a single superstar... Team finished tied for third, 13 games behind Reds in NL Central... Passed Chuck Tanner (711) to become third-winningest manager in Pirate history with 795, behind Fred Clarke (1,422) and Danny Murtaugh (1,115)... Named NL Manager of the Year in 1990 and 1992 as Pirates won three straight division crowns from 1990-92... Spent entire playing career as minor league catcher... Started managing in Tigers' system in 1971... Became Pirates' manager in 1986, after serving four seasons as White Sox coach under Tony La Russa... Born Dec. 15, 1944, in Toledo, Ohio... Overall major league managerial record is 719-686.

ALL-TIME PIRATE SEASON RECORDS

BATTING: Arky Vaughan, .385, 1935
HRs: Ralph Kiner, 54, 1949
RBI: Paul Waner, 131, 1927
STEALS: Omar Moreno, 96, 1980
WINS: Jack Chesbro, 28, 1902
STRIKEOUTS: Bob Veale, 276, 1965

ST. LOUIS CARDINALS

TEAM DIRECTORY: Chairman: August A. Busch III; Vice Chairmen: Fred L. Kuhlmann, Stuart F. Meyer; Pres.: Mark Lamping; GM: Walt Jocketty; Dir. Player Pers.: Mike Jorgensen; Mgr. Pub. Rel.: Brian Bartow; Trav. Sec.: C.J. Cherre; Mgr.: Joe Torre; Coaches: Jose Cardenal, Chris Chambliss, Bob Gibson, Gaylen Pitts, Mark Riggins, Red Schoendienst. Home: Busch Stadium (57,000). Field distances: 330, l.f. line; 402, c.f.; 330, r.f. line. Spring training: St. Petersburg, Fla.

SCOUTING REPORT

This is an underachieving franchise and that is why Dal Maxvill was replaced as GM by Walt Jocketty after a 53-61 finish. For years, the Cardinals were known for their pitching, and maybe they will be again—with the addition over the winter of free agents Danny Jackson and Tom Henke. Last year, the staff was a mess, finishing with the NL's second-worst ERA at 5.14.

Manager Joe Torre brought in a new pitching coach, Mark Riggins, and brought back one of the all-time great Cardinal pitchers, Bob Gibson, as an assistant coach to give the pichers a sense of what toughness is all about. Even though they play at spacious Busch Stadium, the Cardinals surrendered the most homers in the NL (134) and struck out the fewest hitters (632) as their lack of a power pitcher was a major problem.

Jackson (14-6, 3.26 with the Phillies last year) will lead a lefty rotation that includes Allen Watson (6-5, 5.52) and Rheal Cormier (3-2, 5.45). Tom Urbani (3-7, 5.15). Donovan Osborne (if he can come back from shoulder surgery) and youngster Alan Benes, who posted 17 wins in the minors last season, add to the cast. Bob Tewksbury (12-10, 5.32) was a free agent at press time after compiling the highest ERA of his career. No NL pitcher surrendered more hits than Tewksbury (190, including 19 homers).

Henke (3-6, 3.79, 15 saves) assumes the closer's role, with Rene Arocha (4-4, 4.01, 11 saves) the setup man. Mike Perez (2-3, 8.71, 12 saves) is coming off shoulder surgery.

The Cardinals' offense in '94 revolved around first baseman Gregg Jefferies (.325, 12, 55), but he signed as a free agent with the Phillies. Even with Jefferies, the Cardinals ranked fifth in the NL in runs (535) and ninth in home runs (108) last season. Those

Wizard of Oz can still motor on other side of 40.

numbers would've been more modest if not for top long-ball threat, Todd Zeile (.267, 19, 75).

As for team speed, most of it is in the outfield now that living legend Ozzie Smith (.262, 3, 30) has lost a step. Start with exciting Ray Lankford (.267, 19, 57, 11 steals), whose biggest problem is making contact (113 Ks). Potential superstar Mark Whiten (.293, 14, 53, 10 steals) is still raw. Bernard Gilkey (.253, 22 doubles, 15 steals) is another speed merchant.

Torre got the defense to come around after a miserable 1993, when the Cardinals finished with the NL's third-most errors (159). Last year, the Cards finished with the league's fourth-best fielding percentage at .982 and committed just 80 errors. Once again, third baseman Zeile led the club in errors with 12, but that was a big improvement from the 33 he made in 1993. Shortstop Smith is finally beginning to show signs of age, but he still is as a wizard. Gold Glove catcher Tom Pagnozzi threw out an incredible 51 percent of the runners who tried to steal on him.

The bottom line with this team is that, unless the pitching improves, the Cardinals will be battling the woeful Cubs and Pirates for last place in the Central. Torre has some good new coaches, but what he really needs is some new stud pitchers who can throw like Gibson once could.

CARDINAL PROFILES

MARK WHITEN 28 6-3 215   Bats S Throws R

Right fielder has best outfield arm in baseball, bar none... Threw out nine runners, only fifth-best in NL, but that's because no one would run on him... Pulled rib-cage muscles early in season and that was reason for slow start... Batted .322 in his last 48 games, when he amassed 38 of his 53 RBI... From July 16 to end of the year, he raised his average from .263 to .293... Had game of his life and one for the ages, Sept. 7, 1993, in second game of doubleheader against Reds, when he homered four times and drove in 12 runs to tie all-time single-game records... Born Nov. 25, 1966, in Pensacola, Fla.... Blue Jays' fifth-round pick in 1986 draft... Traded from Indians to Cards for Mark Clark and Juan Andujar prior to 1993 season... Would have earned $1.008 million last season.

Year Club	Pos.	G	AB	R	H	2B	3B	HR	RBI	SB	Avg.
1990 Toronto	OF	33	88	12	24	1	1	2	7	2	.273
1991 Tor.-Clev.	OF	116	407	46	99	18	7	9	45	4	.243
1992 Cleveland	OF	148	508	73	129	19	4	9	43	16	.254
1993 St. Louis	OF	152	562	81	142	13	4	25	99	15	.253
1994 St Louis	OF	92	334	57	98	18	2	14	53	10	.293
Totals		541	1899	269	492	69	18	59	247	47	.259

OZZIE SMITH 40 5-10 169   Bats S Throws R

One of the most consistent and artistic players to ever wear a uniform... In Cards' last game of '94 season he picked up his 100th hit, giving him 17 straight seasons with 100 or more... Wizard of Oz has performed 100 defensive gems in each of those years, too... The finest-fielding shortstop of his era... Passed Luis Aparicio July 14 and became baseball's all-time assist leader among shortstops. His 8,084 career assists make him one of only four players with more than 8,000... Has made 2,040 consecutive starts (dating back to May 22, 1980) without striking out three times in game, the longest current streak in majors... Named to All-Star team for 13th time... Finished last year by hitting safely in 20 of last 22 games, raising his batting average from .231 to .262... Collected 19 of his 24 extra-base hits after June 1... Born Dec. 26, 1954, in Mobile, Ala.... Padres' fourth-round pick in 1977... Traded to Cards for shortstop Garry Templeton prior to 1982 season, after falling out of favor with Padres' ownership... Cardinal fans have done backflips over that deal... Would have earned $3 million last year.

Year	Club	Pos.	G	AB	R	H	2B	3B	HR	RBI	SB	Avg.
1978	San Diego	SS	159	590	69	152	17	6	1	46	40	.258
1979	San Diego	SS	156	587	77	124	18	6	0	27	28	.211
1980	San Diego	SS	158	609	67	140	18	5	0	35	57	.230
1981	San Diego	SS	110	450	53	100	11	2	0	21	22	.222
1982	St. Louis	SS	140	488	58	121	24	1	2	43	25	.248
1983	St. Louis	SS	159	552	69	134	30	6	3	50	34	.243
1984	St. Louis	SS	124	412	53	106	20	5	1	44	35	.257
1985	St. Louis	SS	158	537	70	148	22	3	6	54	31	.276
1986	St. Louis	SS	153	514	67	144	19	4	0	54	31	.280
1987	St. Louis	SS	158	600	104	182	40	4	0	75	43	.303
1988	St. Louis	SS	153	575	80	155	27	1	3	51	57	.270
1989	St. Louis	SS	155	593	82	162	30	8	2	50	29	.273
1990	St. Louis	SS	143	512	61	130	21	1	1	50	32	.254
1991	St. Louis	SS	150	550	96	157	30	3	3	50	35	.285
1992	St. Louis	SS	132	518	73	153	20	2	0	31	43	.295
1993	St. Louis	SS	141	545	75	157	22	6	1	53	21	.288
1994	St. Louis	SS	98	381	51	100	18	3	3	30	6	.262
Totals			2447	9013	1205	2365	387	66	26	764	569	.262

RAY LANKFORD 27 5-11 198   Bats L Throws L

If he could ever cut down on his strikeouts, the speedy center fielder would be one of best all-around players in majors... Whiffed 113 times in '94, one short of league leader Reggie Sanders of Reds... Take away his Ks from his at-bat total and he would've batted .366... Bounced back from injury-plagued 1993 to lead club with 49 extra-base hits, including homer in his first 1994 at-bat... Tied for team league in doubles (25) and homers (19) with Todd Zeile... Still learning how to steal a base... Stole 11 in '94, but was caught 10 times... Came to bat 416 times and never grounded into double play... Born June 5, 1967, in Los Angeles... Cards' third-round pick in 1987 draft

...Led club in 13 offensive categories in 1992...Would have earned $1.65 million in '94.

Year	Club	Pos.	G	AB	R	H	2B	3B	HR	RBI	SB	Avg.
1990	St. Louis	OF	39	126	12	36	10	1	3	12	8	.286
1991	St. Louis	OF	151	566	83	142	23	15	9	69	44	.251
1992	St. Louis	OF	153	598	87	175	40	6	20	86	42	.293
1993	St. Louis	OF	127	407	64	97	17	3	7	45	14	.238
1994	St Louis	OF	109	416	89	111	25	5	19	57	11	.267
	Totals		579	2113	335	561	115	30	58	269	119	.265

TODD ZEILE 29 6-1 190　　　　Bats R Throws R

Strike came at a bad time for third baseman... Hit .328 with 11 doubles, one triple, nine homers and 38 RBI after July 1...Batted .299 vs. right-handers...Led club in RBI (75) and tied Ray Lankford for team lead in homers (19) and doubles (25)...Vastly improved his fielding, making just 12 errors in '94 after committing 33 previous season...Slow starter... Sixteen of his 17 homers in '93 came after June 1...Opposite of speedy Ray Lankford, he grounded into 13 double plays, sixth-most in NL...Finished fifth in sacrifice flies with seven...Born Sept. 9, 1965, in Van Nuys, Cal....Cards' third-round pick in 1986 draft...Began rookie year as starting catcher, but that was a mistake and he was switched to third...Would have earned $2.7 million last year.

Year	Club	Pos.	G	AB	R	H	2B	3B	HR	RBI	SB	Avg.
1989	St. Louis	C	28	82	7	21	3	1	1	8	0	.256
1990	St. Louis	C-3B-1B-OF	144	495	62	121	25	3	15	57	2	.244
1991	St. Louis	3B	155	565	76	158	36	3	11	81	17	.280
1992	St. Louis	3B	126	439	51	113	18	4	7	48	7	.257
1993	St. Louis	3B	157	571	82	158	36	1	17	103	5	.277
1994	St. Louis	3B	113	415	62	111	25	1	19	75	1	.267
	Totals		723	2567	340	682	143	13	70	372	32	.266

BERNARD GILKEY 28 6-0 190　　　Bats R Throws R

Just when you think this left fielder is going to put it together, he collapses...His average dropped 52 points from '93 to .253...Managed only eight multi-hit games all season at home...Season was shorter, but extra-base hits fell off from 61 in '93 to 29...Runs plunged from 99 in '93 to 52...Get the picture?...Tied for third in NL in hit by pitches

with 10... Signed by Cardinals as undrafted free agent in 1984
... Suffered through injury-riddled rookie year in 1991... Born
Sept. 24, 1966, in St. Louis... Graduated from St. Louis' University City High in 1984... Salary would have zoomed from
$175,000 in '93 to $1.635 million last season.

Year Club	Pos.	G	AB	R	H	2B	3B	HR	RBI	SB	Avg.
1990 St. Louis	OF	18	64	11	19	5	2	1	3	6	.297
1991 St. Louis	OF	81	268	28	58	7	2	5	20	14	.216
1992 St. Louis	OF	131	384	56	116	19	4	7	43	18	.302
1993 St. Louis	OF-1B	137	557	99	170	40	5	16	70	15	.305
1994 St. Louis	OF	105	380	52	96	22	1	6	45	15	.253
Totals		472	1653	246	459	93	14	35	181	68	.278

TOM PAGNOZZI 32 6-1 190 — Bats R Throws R

Had his problem with injuries, too, hurting his knee in spring training... Played in just 70 games... Homered in each of last three games of '94 season to give him seven, matching his career high... Catching skills earned him third Gold Glove in '94... Made just one error to give him .998 fielding percentage for '94... Also threw out 51 percent of would-be basestealers (23 of 45)... Threw out 35 percent in '93... Born July 30, 1962, in Tucson, Ariz.... Selected by Cards in eighth round of 1983 draft... Would have earned $2.575 million last year... Last year was his second straight year of knee problems... Brother Mike played in Orioles' organization and brother Tim was in Phils' organization... Former third baseman attended Arkansas.

Year Club	Pos.	G	AB	R	H	2B	3B	HR	RBI	SB	Avg.
1987 St. Louis	C-1B	27	48	8	9	1	0	2	9	1	.188
1988 St. Louis	1B-C-3B	81	195	17	55	9	0	0	15	0	.282
1989 St. Louis	C-1B-3B	52	80	3	12	2	0	0	3	0	.150
1990 St. Louis	C-1B	69	220	20	61	15	0	2	23	1	.277
1991 St. Louis	C-1B	140	459	38	121	24	5	2	57	9	.264
1992 St. Louis	C	139	485	33	121	26	3	7	44	2	.249
1993 St. Louis	C	92	330	31	85	15	1	7	41	1	.258
1994 St Louis	C-1B	70	243	21	66	12	1	7	40	0	.272
Totals		670	2060	171	530	104	10	27	232	14	.257

DANNY JACKSON 33 6-0 220   Bats R Throws L

Seemed destined to be imported to aid someone's pennant push until strike ended season ... And now Phillies' top starter in 1994 has turned his free agency into three-year, $11-million pact with Cardinals ... Named to All-Star team for second time ... Finished tied for third in NL in wins (14) ... Ranked second in NL in innings (179⅓), tied for second in starts (25) and seventh in strikeouts (129) ... His 14 wins were tops among all NL lefties and his most since 1988 ... Recorded his 1,000th career strikeout, vs. Reds' Brian Dorsett April 6 ... Won his 100th career game June 2 vs. Cubs ... Drove in career-high and team-high five runs June 18 vs. Expos ... Won career-high 23 games with Reds in 1988 and finished second in race for Cy Young Award ... Owns lifetime 3-1 record with 2.35 ERA in six LCS appearances ... Came to Phils from Marlins for Matt Whisenant and Joel Adamson prior to '93 season ... Born Jan. 5, 1962, in San Antonio, Tex. ... Would have earned $2.265 million in '94.

Year	Club	G	IP	W	L	Pct.	SO	BB	H	ERA
1983	Kansas City	4	19	1	1	.500	9	6	26	5.21
1984	Kansas City	15	76	2	6	.250	40	35	84	4.26
1985	Kansas City	32	208	14	12	.538	114	76	209	3.42
1986	Kansas City	32	185⅔	11	12	.478	115	79	177	3.20
1987	Kansas City	36	224	9	18	.333	152	109	219	4.02
1988	Cincinnati	35	260⅔	23	8	.742	161	71	206	2.73
1989	Cincinnati	20	115⅔	6	11	.353	70	57	122	5.60
1990	Cincinnati	22	117⅓	6	6	.500	76	40	119	3.61
1991	Chicago (NL)	17	70⅔	1	5	.167	31	48	89	6.75
1992	Chi (NL)-Pitt.	34	201⅓	8	13	.381	97	77	211	3.84
1993	Philadelphia	32	210⅓	12	11	.522	120	80	214	3.77
1994	Philadelphia	25	179⅓	14	6	.700	129	46	183	3.26
	Totals	304	1868	107	109	.495	1114	724	1859	3.77

TOM HENKE 37 6-5 230   Bats R Throws R

Cardinals signed Ranger free agent to one-year, $1-million pact plus bonus after season of injuries and ineffectiveness ... Finished with 15 saves, his lowest total in nine years ... Blew six save opportunities and lost six games ... Otherwise, his hits (33) and walks (12) per innings pitched (38) were quite good ... Had saved 30 or more games five times and more than 20 in previous eight seasons ... Sub-par year followed big success upon his return to Texas in 1993, when he saved club-record 40 games...Career save total is 275...Would have earned $3,752,625 in 1994, on second year of two-year, $8-million deal...Rangers' fourth-round pick in 1980...Blue Jays selected him from Rangers as compensation for loss of Cliff Johnson to free agency prior to 1985 season...Blue Jays' all-time save leader with 217...Born Dec. 21, 1957, in Kansas City, Mo.

Year	Club	G	IP	W	L	Pct.	SO	BB	H	ERA
1982	Texas	8	15⅔	1	0	1.000	9	8	14	1.15
1983	Texas	8	16	1	0	1.000	17	4	16	3.38
1984	Texas	25	28⅓	1	1	.500	25	20	36	6.35
1985	Toronto	28	40	3	3	.500	42	8	29	2.03
1986	Toronto	63	91⅓	9	5	.643	118	32	63	3.35
1987	Toronto	72	94	0	6	.000	128	25	62	2.49
1988	Toronto	52	68	4	4	.500	66	24	60	2.91
1989	Toronto	64	89	8	3	.727	116	25	66	1.92
1990	Toronto	61	74⅔	2	4	.333	75	19	58	2.17
1991	Toronto	49	50⅓	0	2	.000	53	11	33	2.32
1992	Toronto	57	55⅔	3	2	.600	46	22	40	2.26
1993	Texas	66	74⅓	5	5	.500	79	27	55	2.91
1994	Texas	37	38	3	6	.333	39	12	33	3.79
	Totals	590	735⅓	40	41	.494	813	237	565	2.73

ALLEN WATSON 24 6-3 190   Bats L Throws L

Rocketed through Cardinals' system and made it to big leagues in 1993, just his second full professional season...But his stock dropped last year, when he lost his control...His 53 walks were most on the club...He also hit eight batters and surrendered 15 homers...Put together 2.91 ERA for Louisville (AAA) in 1993 to earn rapid promotion in July...Won first six big league decisions in '93, then lost his next seven...Owns sharp slider and decent fastball...Born Nov. 18, 1970, in Jamaica, N.Y....Selected by Cards in first round as 21st player taken overall in 1991 draft...Pitched at three levels in 1992, posting combined 14-9 mark and 1.99 ERA...Would have earned $130,000 last season...Grew up idolizing Ron Guidry ...Played one year of high school ball at Christ the King and was named New York City Player of the Year.

Year	Club	G	IP	W	L	Pct.	SO	BB	H	ERA
1993	St. Louis	16	86	6	7	.462	49	28	90	4.60
1994	St. Louis	22	115⅔	6	5	.545	74	53	130	5.52
	Totals	38	201⅔	12	12	.500	123	81	220	5.13

RENE AROCHA 29 6-0 180   Bats R Throws R

Escaped Cuba to find a home in Cards' bullpen ... Moved from starter to reliever last season and found niche as a closer, coming up with 11 saves ... Wound up with elbow problems and had to undergo arthroscopic surgery to remove bone spurs after '94 season ... Moved to bullpen on May 10 and had just one blown save ... Allowed just eight earned runs in his 35 games (46⅓ innings) for 1.55 ERA ... In his rookie year, he went 3-0 with 1.66 ERA before going on disabled list in April with broken finger ... Went 8-8 the rest of the way in '93 ... Born Feb. 24, 1966, in Havana ... Defected to U.S. July 10, 1991 and Cards won his rights in lottery ... Named to American Association All-Star team in '92, when he went 12-7 with 2.70 ERA for Louisville ... Would have earned $140,000 in '94.

Year	Club	G	IP	W	L	Pct.	SO	BB	H	ERA
1993	St. Louis	32	188	11	8	.579	96	31	197	3.78
1994	St. Louis	45	83	4	4	.500	62	21	94	4.01
	Totals	77	271	15	12	.556	158	52	291	3.85

TOP PROSPECTS

JOHN MABRY 24 6-4 195   Bats Left Throws R
Another Cardinal right fielder with a cannon for an arm ... Batted .262 with 15 homers, 30 doubles and 68 RBI for Louisville (AAA) ... Named to Texas League All-Star team in 1993, when he batted .290 and had 15 assists for Arkansas (AA) ... Cards' sixth-round selection in 1991 draft ... Born Oct. 17, 1970, in Wilmington, Del.

ALAN BENES 23 6-5 215   Bats R Throws R
Younger brother of Padres' Andy ... Is top pitching prospect in organization ... Blistered through four levels of minor league ball and is on fast track to majors ... Compiled overall 17-3 mark for Savannah (A), St. Petersburg (A), Arkansas (AA) and Louisville (AAA), where he was 1-0 with 2.93 ERA ... Cardinals' first-round selection in 1993 draft ... Born Jan. 21, 1972, in Evansville, Ind.

ALLEN BATTLE 26 6-0 172   Bats R Throws R
Selected by White Sox out of Cardinals organization in Rule V draft in winter of 1993, but was returned to St. Louis last spring

... Speedy outfielder put together solid all-around season in '94, batting .313 with 44 doubles, 63 RBI and 23 steals for Louisville (AAA) ... Born Nov. 29, 1968, in Grantham, N.C. ... Picked by Cards in 10th round of 1991 draft.

TERRY BRADSHAW 26 6-1 181   Bats L Throws R
Outfielder split time between Arkansas (AA) and Louisville (AAA) in '94 ... Batted .250 with four homers and eight RBI for Louisville after hitting .280 with 10 homers, 52 RBI and 25 doubles for Arkansas ... Injured his knee in 1992, but has come back strong ... Born Feb. 3, 1969, in Franklin, Va. ... Cards' ninth-round selection in 1990 draft.

MANAGER JOE TORRE: If you don't like this guy, you don't like baseball ... One of game's top entertainers behind the batting cage, he is storyteller in uniform ... That doesn't win games, however ... His Cards finished fourth in NL Central with 53-61 record in '94 ... Invited back for fifth year as Cards' manager, he must produce a winner ... Owns 331-327 record with Cards ... Will try to rebuild pitching this year with help of Bob Gibson, Cardinals' new bullpen coach, and Mark Riggins, new pitching coach ... In 1993, he figured life would be easier for Gregg Jefferies if he moved to first base, a brilliant stroke ... Born July 18, 1940, in Brooklyn, N.Y. ... Catcher-third baseman had splendid 18-year career with Braves, Cards and Mets, batting .297 with 252 homers and 1,185 RBI ... Was NL MVP in 1971 with Cardinals and also won batting title (.363) ... Of his 230 hits in '71, there wasn't a single cheap one ... Nine-time All-Star ... Managed Mets from 1977-81 and Braves from 1982-84 ... Won divisional title in 1982 ... Left Angels' broadcast booth to become Cards' manager, Aug. 1, 1990 ... Overall major league managerial record is 874-976.

ALL-TIME CARDINAL SEASON RECORDS

BATTING: Rogers Hornsby, .424, 1924
HRs: Johnny Mize, 43, 1940
RBI: Joe Medwick, 154, 1937
STEALS: Lou Brock, 118, 1974
WINS: Dizzy Dean, 30, 1934
STRIKEOUTS: Bob Gibson, 274, 1970

COLORADO ROCKIES

TEAM DIRECTORY: Chairman/CEO: Jerry McMorris; Exec. VP-Oper.: John McHale Jr.; Sr. VP/GM: Bob Gebhard; VP-Player Pers.: Dick Balderson: Dir. Scouting: Pat Daugherty; Asst. GM: Tony Siegle; Pub. Rel.: Mike Swanson; Trav. Sec.: Peter Durso; Mgr.: Don Baylor; Coaches: Larry Bearnarth, Ron Hassey, Art Howe, Rick Mathews, Don Zimmer. Home: Coors Field (50,000). Field Distances: 347, l.f. line; 415, c.; 350, r.f. line. Spring training: Tucson, Ariz.

SCOUTING REPORT

If nothing else, give the Rockies credit for making the games exciting for their record-breaking legion of fans. The Rockies averaged 58,598 fans last year and put on a fireworks show that didn't disappoint as they finished fifth in NL hitting with a .274 mark.

No expansion team ever has come so fast so quickly, but there's still a long way to go. The most important thing the Rockies have to do this season is find a way to keep the Big Cat purring. Andres Galarraga (.319, 31, 85) finished fifth in the NL in homers and seventh in RBI, but played in only 103 games because of a fractured hand.

Dante Bichette (.304, 27, 95) put together an amazing year, finishing third in the NL in RBI. Bichette, just now maturing as a power hitter, could be one of the game's brightest starts for years to come. The Rockies did not offer a 1995 contract to Charlie Hayes (.288, 10, 50), making him an unrestricted free agent. The team hopes for the healthy return of Ellis Burks (.322, 13, 24 in 42 games).

The Rockies also deserve credit for coming up with a player off the scrap heap, Mike Kingery, who hit a career-high .349. Kingery actually hit higher on the road (.362) than in the rarefied air of home (.333). As a team, the Rockies hit .298 at home and .251 on the road, but actually hit more homers (66) away than they did at home (59).

Hitting, obviously, is not the problem for this team, which finished 53-64 in '94. All their problems start on the mound and they could've been worse if Marvin Freeman (10-2, 2.80) hadn't been denied free agency by the Player Relations Committee last winter. Freeman was the pitching surprise of last year, when he led the NL with an .833 winning percentage.

Workhorse Steve Reed (3-2, 3.94) led the NL in appearances

Andres Galarraga's broken hand shattered Rockies.

with 61 while Bruce Ruffin (4-5, 4.04) found a home in the bullpen and was tied for eighth in the NL with 16 saves. Young David Nied (9-7, 4.80) is beginning to hit his stride as a starter and figures to be the rock of this rocky Rockie rotation. Kevin Ritz (5-6, 5.62) has battled back from reconstructive elbow surgery and will be used as a starter. No pitcher was in worse shape than Greg Harris (3-13, 6.65), who allowed the most runs in the NL (99 in 130 innings).

Defensively, the Rockies are getting better. After finishing last in NL defense in 1993 with a .973 fielding percentage, they improved to seventh last season at .981. They turned the third-most double plays with 117 and, with Joe Girardi (.276, 4, 34) behind the plate most of the time, their catchers only allowed a league-low five passed balls. Bichette is making a habit of finishing among the NL leaders in outfield assists and Walt Weiss (.251, 1, 32) is an above-average shortstop.

Overall, this franchise could be as breathtaking as a Rocky Mountain view once all the pieces come together, because the Rockies have money, fans, a brilliant new stadium on the way and a no-nonsense leader in manager Don Baylor. All these things promise a bright future. This will be the model franchise in the majors in a few years, once the pitching comes around. Until then, every game at least figures to be exciting.

ROCKIE PROFILES

ANDRES GALARRAGA 33 6-3 245   Bats R Throws R

"Big Cat" proved to be top cat again... Rockies had climbed to within a half-game of first-place Dodgers when first baseman fractured his right hand July 28. Without him, Rockies finished 3-10... Paced club with career-high 31 homers, fifth-best mark in NL... Had two homers in a game four times... Has made the most of expansion... Signed a four-year, $16.4-million contract to remain in Colorado after 1993 season, when his .370 average led NL... That was highest average by a right-handed hitter in NL since Ducky Medwick batted .374 for Cards in 1937... Signed with Rockies as free agent prior to '93, after rocky year with Cards in '92, and Don Baylor resurrected his batting stroke... Went to Cards from Expos for Ken Hill following 1991 season... Born June 18, 1961, in Caracas, Venezuela... Signed by Expos as undrafted free agent in 1979... Would have earned $3.85 million in '94.

Year	Club	Pos.	G	AB	R	H	2B	3B	HR	RBI	SB	Avg.
1985	Montreal	1B	24	75	9	14	1	0	2	4	1	.187
1986	Montreal	1B	105	321	39	87	13	0	10	42	6	.271
1987	Montreal	1B	147	551	72	168	40	3	13	90	7	.305
1988	Montreal	1B	157	609	99	184	42	8	29	92	13	.302
1989	Montreal	1B	152	572	76	147	30	1	23	85	12	.257
1990	Montreal	1B	155	579	65	148	29	0	20	87	10	.256
1991	Montreal	1B	107	375	34	82	13	2	9	33	5	.219
1992	St. Louis	1B	95	325	38	79	14	2	10	39	5	.243
1993	Colorado	1B	120	470	71	174	35	4	22	98	2	.370
1994	Colorado	1B	103	417	77	133	21	0	31	85	8	.319
	Totals		1165	4294	580	1216	238	20	169	655	69	.283

DANTE BICHETTE 31 6-3 235   Bats R Throws R

His hero is Ted Williams... Received congratulatory call from Williams after being named Rockies' only All-Star representative in '94... Set career highs in homers (27) and RBI (95)... Led majors in at-bats (484) and games (116) and finished tied for second in NL in hits (147)... Owns gun for an arm... Right fielder tied for third in NL with 10 assists... Even led Rockies in stolen bases (21)... Compiled club-record 16-game

The boom in Dante Bichetti's bat says he's blooming.

hitting streak from April 6-24... Only Astros' Jeff Bagwell and Giants' Matt Williams had more total bases than his 265 in '94 ... Born Nov. 18, 1963, in West Palm Beach, Fla.... Angels took him in 17th round of 1984 draft, but didn't have the patience to let him bloom... Traded by California to Milwaukee for Dave Parker prior to 1991 season... Brewers lost faith in him and made terrible trade on day of expansion draft prior to '93 season, sending him to Rockies for Kevin Reimer... Would have earned $2.8 million in '94.

Year	Club	Pos.	G	AB	R	H	2B	3B	HR	RBI	SB	Avg.
1988	California	OF	21	46	1	12	2	0	0	8	0	.261
1989	California	OF	48	138	13	29	7	0	3	15	3	.210
1990	California	OF	109	349	40	89	15	1	15	53	5	.255
1991	Milwaukee	OF-3B	134	445	53	106	18	3	15	59	14	.238
1992	Milwaukee	OF	112	387	37	111	27	2	5	41	18	.287
1993	Colorado	OF	141	538	93	167	43	5	21	89	14	.310
1994	Colorado	OF	116	484	74	147	33	2	27	95	21	.304
	Totals		681	2387	311	661	145	13	86	360	75	.277

ELLIS BURKS 30 6-2 205   Bats R Throws R

Outfielder seemed to be on his way to a terrific season in '94, when he severely sprained his left wrist May 17... Injury knocked him out of next 70 games... Blasted homer in his first at-bat of 1994... Named NL Player of the Month in April, when he hit .413 with seven doubles, two triples, nine homers, 17 RBI and 24 runs... Hit club's first inside-the-park homer, April 15 off Montreal's Jeff Fassero... Signed by Rockies as free agent prior to last season... Signed with White Sox as free agent prior to 1993 season, after knee injuries had plagued him in his final season with Red Sox... Missed 96 games with knee woes in '92... Red Sox' first-round pick in January 1983 draft... Born Sept. 11, 1964, in Vicksburg, Miss.... Would have earned $3 million last season.

Year	Club	Pos.	G	AB	R	H	2B	3B	HR	RBI	SB	Avg.
1987	Boston	OF	133	558	94	152	30	2	20	59	27	.272
1988	Boston	OF	144	540	93	159	37	5	18	92	25	.294
1989	Boston	OF	97	399	73	121	19	6	12	61	21	.303
1990	Boston	OF	152	588	89	174	33	8	21	89	9	.296
1991	Boston	OF	130	474	56	119	33	3	14	56	6	.251
1992	Boston	OF	66	235	35	60	8	3	8	30	5	.255
1993	Chicago (AL)	OF	146	499	75	137	24	4	17	74	6	.275
1994	Colorado	OF	42	149	33	48	8	3	13	24	3	.322
	Totals		910	3442	548	970	192	34	123	485	102	.282

JOE GIRARDI 30 5-11 200   Bats R Throws R

Smart catcher gave young pitching staff much-needed guidance... Landed on DL July 11 with knee problems... Returned July 26 and hit homer in first at-bat... That was his career-best fourth homer... Hit into 13 double plays, four less than teammate Dante Bichette, to finish among NL's top 10 in that category... Underwent surgery to remove hamate bone from his left hand in June 1993... Taken from Cubs by Rockies with 10th pick of expansion draft prior to '93 season... Another example of poor planning by Cubs... Owns an industrial engineering degree from Northwestern University, where he earned Academic All-American honors three times... Born Oct. 14, 1964, in Peoria, Ill.... Selected by Cubs in fifth round of 1986 draft... Would have earned $1 million last year.

Year	Club	Pos.	G	AB	R	H	2B	3B	HR	RBI	SB	Avg.
1989	Chicago (NL)	C	59	157	15	39	10	0	1	14	2	.248
1990	Chicago (NL)	C	133	419	36	113	24	2	1	38	8	.270
1991	Chicago (NL)	C	21	47	3	9	2	0	0	6	0	.191
1992	Chicago (NL)	C	91	270	19	73	3	1	1	12	0	.270
1993	Colorado	C	86	310	35	90	14	5	3	31	6	.290
1994	Colorado	C	93	330	47	91	9	4	4	34	3	.276
	Totals		483	1533	155	415	62	12	10	135	19	.271

MIKE KINGERY 34 6-0 185   Bats L Throws L

You never know in this game... Entering his 15th year of pro ball, this journeyman outfielder made the Rockies out of spring training as a non-roster invitee... Established career bests in average (.349), runs (56), hits (105), doubles (27) and triples (8)... Tied for third in NL in triples... His homer off Mets' Eric Hillman May 30 was his first off a left-hander in seven seasons... Also produced his first four-hit game in eight seasons, Aug. 1 against Astros... Batted .406 on artificial turf and .380 at night... Born March 29, 1961, in St. James, Minn.... Would have earned $175,000 last season, making him one of best bargains in game... Colorado is his fifth major-league stop... Also played in Kansas City, Seattle, San Francisco and Oakland... Originally signed by Royals as undrafted free agent in August 1979.

Year	Club	Pos.	G	AB	R	H	2B	3B	HR	RBI	SB	Avg.
1986	Kansas City	OF	62	209	25	54	8	5	3	14	7	.258
1987	Seattle	OF	120	354	38	99	25	4	9	52	7	.280
1988	Seattle	OF-1B	57	123	21	25	6	0	1	9	3	.203
1989	Seattle	OF	31	76	14	17	3	0	2	6	1	.224
1990	San Francisco	OF	105	207	24	61	7	1	0	24	6	.295
1991	San Francisco	OF-1B	91	110	13	20	2	2	0	8	1	.182
1992	Oakland	OF	12	28	3	3	0	0	0	1	0	.107
1994	Colorado	OF-1B	105	301	56	105	27	8	4	41	5	.349
	Totals		583	1408	194	384	78	20	19	155	30	.273

WALT WEISS 31 6-0 175   Bats S Throws R

Just call him "Mr. Expansion"... Jumped from Marlins to Rockies before start of last season, when free-agent shortstop signed two-year, $2.2-million contract... Managed to hit first homer of his career from right side of the plate, off Cubs' Blaise Ilsley April 23. That was his only homer of the year... Hit only .104 from July 23 until end of season... Collected season-high four hits May 24 vs. Reds... Was AL Rookie of the Year with Athletics in 1988, when he had 58-game errorless streak and batted .333 in ALCS against Red Sox... Acquired by Marlins from Oakland for Eric Helfand and Scott Baker before 1993 season... Born Nov. 28, 1963, in Tuxedo, N.Y.... Would have earned $550,000 last season... Athletics drafted him first overall in 1985.

Year	Club	Pos.	G	AB	R	H	2B	3B	HR	RBI	SB	Avg.
1987	Oakland	SS	16	26	3	12	4	0	0	1	1	.462
1988	Oakland	SS	147	452	44	113	17	3	3	39	4	.250
1989	Oakland	SS	84	236	30	55	11	0	3	21	6	.233
1990	Oakland	SS	138	445	50	118	17	1	2	35	9	.265
1991	Oakland	SS	40	133	15	30	6	1	0	13	6	.226
1992	Oakland	SS	103	316	36	67	5	2	0	21	6	.212
1993	Florida	SS	158	500	50	133	14	2	1	39	7	.266
1994	Colorado	SS	110	423	58	106	11	4	1	32	12	.251
	Totals		796	2531	286	634	85	13	10	201	51	.250

MARVIN FREEMAN 31 6-7 223   Bats R Throws R

In high school, he had unique job of making quality violin bows... After 10 years of pro ball, he finally made beautiful music as a pitcher... Shocked everyone by leading NL with .833 winning percentage... Was slated for bullpen duty, but rash of injuries gave him his opportunity... Finished '94 season with three-game winning streak and 1.63 ERA over that four-game stretch as he led club in wins (10)... Signed by Rockies as free agent prior to last season, after four years with pitching-rich Braves... Now has 25-12 mark as major leaguer... Tied career high with seven strikeouts May 13 at Houston and suffered his first loss... Eight of the 10 homers he allowed in '94 came with the bases empty... Phils' second-round selection in 1984 draft... Traded to Braves for Joe Boever, July 23, 1990... Born April 10, 1963, in Chicago... Would have earned $500,000 last season... Denied free agency by Player Relations Committee last winter.

Year	Club	G	IP	W	L	Pct.	SO	BB	H	ERA
1986	Philadelphia	3	16	2	0	1.000	8	10	6	2.25
1988	Philadelphia	11	51⅔	2	3	.400	37	43	55	6.10
1989	Philadelphia	1	3	0	0	.000	0	5	2	6.00
1990	Phil.-Atl.	25	48	1	2	.333	38	17	41	4.31
1991	Atlanta	34	48	1	0	1.000	34	13	37	3.00
1992	Atlanta	58	64⅓	7	5	.583	41	29	61	3.22
1993	Atlanta	21	23⅔	2	0	1.000	25	10	24	6.08
1994	Colorado	19	112⅔	10	2	.833	67	23	113	2.80
	Totals	172	367⅓	25	12	.676	250	150	339	3.77

BRUCE RUFFIN 31 6-2 213   Bats S Throws R

A baseball rarity: a pitcher who likes to work at Mile High Stadium... Was 2-0 with seven saves in 27 outings at Mile High... Came into last year with five career saves and only two in last five years, but he wound up with club-high 16 in '94, tying for eighth-best total in NL... Began '94 season as left-handed setup man, but was handed the stopper's role by Don Baylor the first week of May... After blowing save May 7 in San Diego, he converted his next nine opportunities... In 1993, he made Rockies as non-roster invitee and he wound up leading the club in strikeouts with career-best 126... Born Oct. 4, 1963, in Lubbock, Tex.... Taken by Phils in second round of 1985 draft... Was college teammate of Roger Clemens on University of Texas team that won 1983 College World Series.

Year	Club	G	IP	W	L	Pct.	SO	BB	H	ERA
1986	Philadelphia	21	146⅓	9	4	.692	70	44	138	2.46
1987	Philadelphia	35	204⅔	11	14	.440	93	73	236	4.35
1988	Philadelphia	55	144⅓	6	10	.375	82	80	151	4.43
1989	Philadelphia	24	125⅔	6	10	.375	70	62	152	4.44
1990	Philadelphia	32	149	6	13	.316	79	62	178	5.38
1991	Philadelphia	31	119	4	7	.364	85	38	125	3.78
1992	Milwaukee	25	58	1	6	.143	45	41	66	6.67
1993	Colorado	59	139⅔	6	5	.545	126	69	145	3.87
1994	Colorado	56	55⅔	4	5	.444	65	30	55	4.04
	Totals	338	1142⅓	53	74	.417	715	499	1246	4.25

DAVID NIED 26 6-2 188   Bats R Throws R

His claim to fame will always be that he was the first player selected in expansion draft, from Braves prior to '93 season... After difficult first year, he showed much progress last season, finishing second on club in victories (9) behind Marvin Freeman... Was starting pitcher in three of the Rockies' five shutouts... He'll also be answer to question: Which Rockies pitcher threw the first complete-game shutout?... Blanked Astros at Mile High Stadium June 21... Had difficult year off the field... Because of four months premature birth of son Tanner June 4 in New York, his wife spent the next two months there to be with infant... Child finally gained enough strength to move into the family home Oct. 8... Born Dec. 22, 1968, in Dallas... Selected by Braves in 14th round of 1987 draft... Would have earned

$190,000 in '94... Braves protected Deion Sanders instead of this right-hander.

Year	Club	G	IP	W	L	Pct.	SO	BB	H	ERA
1992	Atlanta	6	23	3	0	1.000	19	5	10	1.17
1993	Colorado	16	87	5	9	.357	46	42	99	5.17
1994	Colorado	22	122	9	7	.563	74	47	137	4.80
	Totals	44	232	17	16	.515	139	94	246	4.58

TOP PROSPECTS

MARK THOMPSON 23 6-2 205   Bats R Throws R
Path to majors was slowed by arthroscopic shoulder surgery in 1993... Came back to go 8-9 with 4.49 ERA for Colorado Springs (AAA) last season... Born April 7, 1971, in Russellville, Ky. ... Rockies' second-round selection in 1992 draft... Started first game in the organization's history, June 16, 1992 in Bend, Ore. He was not the pitcher of record that night, but won his first three pro starts.

ROD PEDRAZA 25 6-2 210   Bats R Throws R
Started last year with 11-0 burst for New Haven (AA)... Was promoted to Colorado Springs (AAA)... Went 1-3, 9.27 in Triple A and was sent back to New Haven, where he finished 13-3 with 3.24 ERA, seventh-lowest mark in Eastern League... Born Dec. 28, 1969, in San Antonio, Tex.... Acquired from Expos with Ivan Arteaga for Freddie Benavides prior to last season... Attended University of Texas.

JUAN ACEVEDO 24 6-2 195   Bats R Throws R
Ace of staff at New Haven (AA), where he compiled impressive 17-6 record with 2.37 ERA... Led Eastern League in both wins and ERA and finished third in strikeouts, fanning 161 in 174⅔ innings... Named Pitcher of the Year in the organization and was Eastern League's Rookie of the Year... Born May 5, 1970, in Juarez, Mexico... Selected by Rockies in 14th round of 1992 draft.

JASON BATES 24 5-11 170   Bats S Throws R
Shortstop hit .286 with 76 RBI, 10 homers, 19 doubles and 60 walks for Colorado Springs (AAA)... Named to PCL All-Star team... Born Jan. 5, 1971, in Downey, Cal.... Selected by Rockies in seventh round of 1992 draft... Batted .267 with 13 homers and 62 RBI for Colorado Springs in '93.

Rockies unearthed jewel in journeyman Mike Kingery.

MANAGER DON BAYLOR: Natural-born leader helped Rockies become the expansion club to reach the 100-victory mark the fastest... When they won their 33rd game last season, it put them at 100 in their 233rd game, six games faster than the Los Angeles Angels in '62... Thanks to Padres, they avoided NL West cellar for second straight year as they finished 53-64... Winning percentage jumped from .414 to .453...

Owns 120-159 major league record... Key to Rockies' success is that he does not panic... A very good listener, he takes a lot of advice from coach Don Zimmer... As a player, he showed he had potential to be a great manager... Participated in three World Series and seven AL playoffs... Former outfielder, first baseman and designated hitter... His major league playing career spanned 1970-88 with Orioles, Athletics, Angels, Yankees, Red Sox, Twins and Athletics again.... Blasted 338 home runs... Was named AL MVP as Angel in 1979... Owned .260 career average and 1,276 RBI... This is all you really need to know: He was hit by pitches a record 255 times... His managerial idols were Earl Weaver and Gene Mauch... Prior to being named manager, he spent four years as major league hitting instructor, two years each with Brewers and Cardinals... Born June 28, 1949, in Austin, Tex.

ALL-TIME ROCKIE SEASON RECORDS

BATTING: Andres Galarraga, .370, 1993
HRs: Andres Galarraga, 31, 1994
RBI: Andres Galarraga, 98, 1993
    Charlie Hayes, 98, 1993
STEALS: Eric Young, 42, 1993
WINS: Armando Reynoso, 12, 1993
STRIKEOUTS: Bruce Ruffin, 126, 1993

LOS ANGELES DODGERS

TEAM DIRECTORY: Pres.: Peter O'Malley; Exec. VP-Player Pers.: Fred Claire; VP-Marketing: Barry Stockhamer; VP-Communications: Tommy Hawkins; Dir. Minor League Oper.: Charlie Blaney; Dir. Scouting: Terry Reynolds; Publicity Dir.: Jay Lucas; Trav. Sec.: Billy DeLury; Mgr.: Tom Lasorda; Coaches: Joe Amalfitano, Mark Cresse, Manny Mota, Bill Russell, Reggie Smith, Dave Wallace. Home: Dodger Stadium (56,000). Field distances: 330, l.f. line; 370, l.c.; 395, c.f.; 370, r.c.; 330, r.f. line. Spring training: Vero Beach, Fla.

SCOUTING REPORT

Youth is being served by the Dodgers, who came up with their third straight NL Rookie of the Year in outfielder Raul Mondesi

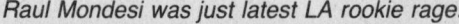

Raul Mondesi was just latest LA rookie rage.

can build around as he has speed (8 triples, 11 steals) and a great arm (an NL-leading 16 assists). The two previous rookie winners were catcher Mike Piazza (.319, 24, 92) and first baseman Eric Karros (.266, .14, 46). Piazza is getting stronger every year and is one of the best power threats in the majors, hitting one homer per 16.9 at-bats last season.

The Dodgers finished a solid sixth in NL batting with a .270 mark, but may say goodbye to leadoff man Brett Butler (.314, 8, 33), a free agent unsigned at press time. Butler tied for the NL lead in triples (9) and was eighth in the league in runs (79). If he leaves, Mondesi will move to center. Another veteran, Tim Wallach (.280, 23, 78), had his best year in five seasons, but became a free agent and then re-signed. To pick up the offense, the Dodgers need stronger years out of Delino DeShields (.250, 2, 33, 27 steals) and Jose Offerman (.210, 1, 25).

Pitching has been a Dodger strength forever, but the team did slip to ninth in the NL in ERA with a 4.17 mark in '94, compared to a 3.50 mark in '93. GM Fred Claire's trading of Pedro Martinez to the Expos backfired. Claire's other big move of two winters ago, the signing of free agent Todd Worrell, also blew up in his face as Worrell (6-5, 4.29) managed just 11 saves. Compound that with the elbow woes of reliever Darren Dreifort (0-5, 6.21) and you have big bullpen problems. The Dodgers were dead last in the NL with only 20 saves.

Ramon Martinez (12-7, 3.97) was back to his old form while Kevin Gross (9-7, 3.60) surprised everyone before exploring free agency, and then signed with the Rangers. Knuckleballer Tom Candiotti (7-7, 4.12) still hasn't had a season with more wins than losses in three years with the Dodgers and Orel Hersheiser (6-6, 3.79) was a free agent unsigned at press time. He wasn't the only disappointment as youngster Pedro Astacio (6-8, 4.29) slipped after winning 14 games in 1993. Pitching coach Ron Perranoski, one of the best in the game, was made the scapegoat for the Dodgers' pitching troubles and was fired. He'll be missed. The fact that the Dodgers were ninth in the NL in fielding percentage (.980) didn't help the pitchers, either.

Over the years, Tommy Lasorda has been one of the great motivators in major league history and that kind of ability can never be underestimated with young players. Lasorda had the Dodgers in first at 58-56 when the '94 season ended, but he needs more pitching help this season to turn the trick again.

DODGER PROFILES

MIKE PIAZZA 26 6-3 210   Bats R Throws R

Squashed so-called sophomore jinx... Catcher's average (.319), homers (24) and RBI (92) put him ahead of pace he set in '93, when he was unanimous NL Rookie of the Year selection... Paced team in homers and RBI last season... Posted one RBI per 4.4 at-bats and one homer per 16.9 at-bats... His first grand slam was 477-foot shot off Florida's Mark Gardner June 6, the longest homer in Joe Robbie Stadium history... Batted .367 with runners in scoring position... Everybody is always looking for catching, but nobody looked to him... Taken by Dodgers in 62nd round of 1988 draft as 1,389th player chosen ... His rookie average of .318 was highest by any NL Rookie of the Year since the award began in 1947 and he was the first winner to drive in 100 runs (112)... Frank Robinson was only NL rookie to hit more homers than his 35, with 38 in 1956... Born Sept. 4, 1968, in Norristown, Pa.... Would have earned $600,000 last season.

Year Club	Pos.	G	AB	R	H	2B	3B	HR	RBI	SB	Avg.
1992 Los Angeles...	C	21	69	5	16	3	0	1	7	0	.232
1993 Los Angeles...	C-1B	149	547	81	174	24	2	35	112	3	.318
1994 Los Angeles...	C	107	405	64	129	18	0	24	92	1	.319
Totals.......		277	1021	150	319	45	2	60	211	4	.312

BRETT BUTLER 37 5-10 160   Bats L Throws L

Baseball's version of the Energizer Bunny... Keeps going and going and getting better... Posted career-high average (.314) in '94... Collected 10 more bunt hits, giving him 261 in his career, 98 with Dodgers... Center fielder batted .409 (9-for-22) with two outs and a runner on third... Managed to hit homers in back-to-back games for first time in his career, June 25 off Houston's Doug Drabek and June 26 off Mitch Williams ... Tied Delino DeShields for club lead in stolen bases (27)... Would have earned $3.5 million last season... Born June 15, 1957, in Los Angeles... Traded by Braves to Indians with Brook

Jacoby and Rick Behenna for Len Barker following the 1983 season... Left Giants to sign with Dodgers as free agent prior to 1991 season... Bravges' 23rd-round pick in 1979 draft... **Free agent at press time**.

Year	Club	Pos.	G	AB	R	H	2B	3B	HR	RBI	SB	Avg.
1981	Atlanta	OF	40	126	17	32	2	3	0	4	9	.254
1982	Atlanta	OF	89	240	35	52	2	0	0	7	21	.217
1983	Atlanta	OF	151	549	84	154	21	13	5	37	39	.281
1984	Cleveland	OF	159	602	108	162	25	9	3	49	52	.269
1985	Cleveland	OF	152	591	106	184	28	14	5	50	47	.311
1986	Cleveland	OF	161	587	92	163	17	14	4	51	32	.278
1987	Cleveland	OF	137	522	91	154	25	8	9	41	33	.295
1988	San Francisco	OF	157	568	109	163	27	9	6	43	43	.287
1989	San Francisco	OF	154	594	100	168	22	4	4	36	31	.283
1990	San Francisco	OF	160	622	108	192	20	9	3	44	51	.309
1991	Los Angeles	OF	161	615	112	182	13	5	2	38	38	.296
1992	Los Angeles	OF	157	553	86	171	14	11	3	39	41	.309
1993	Los Angeles	OF	156	607	80	181	21	10	1	42	39	.298
1994	Los Angeles	OF	111	417	79	131	13	9	8	33	27	.314
	Totals		1945	7193	1207	2089	250	118	53	514	503	.290

DELINO DeSHIELDS 26 6-1 175   Bats L Throws R

Second baseman was too rich for Montreal's tastes, so he was dealt to Dodgers for Pedro Martinez after 1993 season, even though he was most popular Expo... Responded to that deal by having worst season of his career, although he tied Brett Butler for team lead in steals (27) ... Big reason for all his '94 problems were injuries that included fractured cheekbone and a finger laceration... His .986 fielding percentage at second ranked third in NL, behind Braves' Mark Lemke and Astros' Craig Biggio... Stole his 200th career base May 19 at Colorado... Dodgers went 25-15 in games in which he scored... Born Jan. 15, 1969, in Seaford, Del.... Expos' first-round draft choice in 1987, out of Tennessee... Would have earned 2.7 million last season and will make $3 million on a one-year deal this season.

Year	Club	Pos.	G	AB	R	H	2B	3B	HR	RBI	SB	Avg.
1990	Montreal	2B	129	499	69	144	28	6	4	45	42	.289
1991	Montreal	2B	151	563	83	134	15	4	10	51	56	.238
1992	Montreal	2B	135	530	82	155	19	8	7	56	46	.292
1993	Montreal	2B	123	481	75	142	17	7	2	29	43	.295
1994	Los Angeles	2B-SS	89	320	51	80	11	3	2	33	27	.250
	Totals		627	2393	360	655	90	28	25	214	214	.274

RAUL MONDESI 24 5-11 210   Bats R Throws R

Maybe they should just call it the Dodgers' Rookie of the Year award... This right fielder became third straight Dodger to win NL rookie award in '94—and he did it in unanimous fashion... Had at least one hit in 84 of his 112 games, drove in at least one run in 42 games and scored at least one run in 50 games... Went hitless his first four games and then never went more than two straight games without collecting hit... Struck out rarely in second half of the season... Batted .512 against Rockies... Not only can he hit, he led all major league outfielders with 16 assists... Spent his first full year with Albuquerque (AAA) in 1993 and batted .280 with 22 doubles, seven triples and 65 RBI... Born March 12, 1971, in San Cristobal, D.R.... Signed by Dodgers as undrafted free agent in June 1988 ... Would have earned $126,000 in '94.

Year Club	Pos.	G	AB	R	H	2B	3B	HR	RBI	SB	Avg.
1993 Los Angeles...	OF	42	86	13	25	3	1	4	10	4	.291
1994 Los Angeles...	OF	112	434	63	133	27	8	16	56	11	.306
Totals.......		154	520	76	158	30	9	20	66	15	.304

ERIC KARROS 27 6-4 205   Bats R Throws R

Some people considered it a fluke when he won NL Rookie of the Year award in 1992, but he has strung together three solid seasons... Owns LA personality and is camera friendly ... First baseman has hit 78 doubles in last three years... Ten of his 14 homers came against right-handers... Went from June 5-July 24 without a homer... Finished second in league with 11 sacrifice flies, one behind Montreal's Darrin Fletcher, last season... Became first Dodger to hit 20 or more homers in first two seasons... Born Nov. 4, 1967, in Hackensack, N.J.... Played at UCLA, where he earned All-American honors after joining club as a walk-on... Dodgers' sixth-round pick in 1988 would have earned $650,000 last season.

Year Club	Pos.	G	AB	R	H	2B	3B	HR	RBI	SB	Avg.
1991 Los Angeles...	1B	14	14	0	1	1	0	0	1	0	.071
1992 Los Angeles...	1B	149	545	63	140	30	1	20	88	2	.257
1993 Los Angeles...	1B	158	619	74	153	27	2	23	80	0	.247
1994 Los Angeles...	1B	111	406	51	108	21	1	14	46	2	.266
Totals.......		432	1584	188	402	79	4	57	215	4	.254

TIM WALLACH 37 6-3 205   Bats R Throws R

Just when you thought his career was over, this old warhorse responded with his best season since 1990... His 23 homers in '94 were the most he has hit since 1987, when he had 26... If not for the strike, he most likely would have established career high... Way back in 1982, he hit 28 for Expos... Played the most games on team... Comeback kid raised his average 58 points from '93, to .280... Finished strong, batting .417 in August and .375 after All-Star break... Collected 1,000th RBI of his career off Kent Bottenfield May 16 in Colorado... Born Sept. 14, 1957, in Huntington Park, Cal.... Acquired by Dodgers from Expos for infielder Tim Barker prior to 1993 season... Would have earned $3.412 million last season... Third baseman was drafted 10th overall by Expos in 1979... As free agent, re-signed one-year, $1.5-million pact for '95.

Year	Club	Pos.	G	AB	R	H	2B	3B	HR	RBI	SB	Avg.
1980	Montreal	OF-1B	5	11	1	2	0	0	1	2	0	.182
1981	Montreal	OF-1B-3B	71	212	19	50	9	1	4	13	0	.236
1982	Montreal	3B-OF-1B	158	596	89	160	31	3	28	97	6	.268
1983	Montreal	3B	156	581	54	156	33	3	19	70	0	.269
1984	Montreal	3B-SS	160	582	55	143	25	4	18	72	3	.246
1985	Montreal	3B	155	569	70	148	36	3	22	81	9	.260
1986	Montreal	3B	134	480	50	112	22	1	18	71	8	.233
1987	Montreal	3B-P	153	593	89	177	42	4	26	123	9	.298
1988	Montreal	3B-2B	159	592	52	152	32	5	12	69	2	.257
1989	Montreal	3B-P	154	573	76	159	42	0	13	77	3	.277
1990	Montreal	3B	161	626	69	185	37	5	21	98	6	.296
1991	Montreal	3B	151	577	60	130	22	1	13	73	2	.225
1992	Montreal	3B-1B	150	537	53	120	29	1	9	59	2	.223
1993	Los Angeles	3B-1B	133	477	42	106	19	1	12	62	0	.222
1994	Los Angeles	3B	113	414	68	116	21	1	23	78	0	.280
	Totals		2013	7420	847	1916	400	33	239	1045	50	.258

JOSE OFFERMAN 26 6-0 160   Bats S Throws R

What happened to this guy?... Average plummeted 59 points from '93, to .210... Shortstop committed 11 errors in only 72 games, giving him 90 errors in last three years... Dodgers became so disgusted with his play that he was sent to Albuquerque (AAA) June 27... Regained his stroke there and batted .330 in 56 games... His 62 RBI in 1993 were most by a Dodger shortstop since Bill Russell set LA record with 65 in 1974 and 1976... Born Nov. 8, 1968, in San Pedro de Macoris, D.R.

...Signed by Dodgers as undrafted free agent in July 1986...Would have earned $515,000 last season...Named *Sporting News'* Minor League Player of the Year in 1990 and tabbed the best shortstop prospect by *Baseball America* from 1989-91...Needs to turn around his career quickly.

Year	Club	Pos.	G	AB	R	H	2B	3B	HR	RBI	SB	Avg.
1990	Los Angeles...	SS	29	58	7	9	0	0	1	7	1	.155
1991	Los Angeles...	SS	52	113	10	22	2	0	0	3	3	.195
1992	Los Angeles...	SS	149	534	67	139	20	8	1	30	23	.260
1993	Los Angeles...	SS	158	590	77	159	21	6	1	62	30	.269
1994	Los Angeles...	SS	72	243	27	51	8	4	1	25	2	.210
	Totals.......		460	1538	188	380	51	18	4	127	59	.246

RAMON MARTINEZ 27 6-5 171   Bats R Throws R

Tommy Lasorda didn't burn him out after all ...After two sub-par years, he rebounded to win his most games since 1991 (12)...Tied for team high in victories as only five other NL pitchers won more...Finished fourth in NL with four complete games and his three shutouts were tops in league...Dodgers went 15-9 in games he pitched in '94...Has reached seventh inning in 100 of his 168 career starts...Elbow problems caused him to shut it down last month of 1992 season...Started 1991 by going 15-6, but is just 32-37 since that point...On June 4, 1990, he tied Sandy Koufax' all-time Dodger single-game strikeout record with 18...In 1990, he became youngest Dodger to win 20 since Ralph Branca won 21 at 21 in 1947...Born March 22, 1968, in Santo Domingo, D.R....Signed by Dodgers as undrafted free agent at 16 in September 1984...Would have earned $2.687 million last season...Expos' Pedro is his younger brother.

Year	Club	G	IP	W	L	Pct.	SO	BB	H	ERA
1988	Los Angeles........	9	35⅔	1	3	.250	23	22	27	3.79
1989	Los Angeles........	15	98⅔	6	4	.600	89	41	79	3.19
1990	Los Angeles........	33	234⅓	20	6	.769	223	67	191	2.92
1991	Los Angeles........	33	220⅓	17	13	.567	150	69	190	3.27
1992	Los Angeles........	25	150⅔	8	11	.421	101	69	141	4.00
1993	Los Angeles........	32	211⅔	10	12	.455	127	104	202	3.44
1994	Los Angeles........	24	170	12	7	632	119	56	160	3.97
	Totals............	171	1121⅔	74	56	.569	832	428	990	3.44

TOM CANDIOTTI 37 6-2 210   Bats R Throws R

Another free-agent nightmare... Cost more than $15 million when he signed four-year contract with Dodgers before 1992 season, but has yet to post a winning record in three years... Knuckleballer should stick to daylight hours, because he was 4-0 with 1.82 ERA in games under sun last year... Led team with five complete games... Allowed just two homers in his last 64⅔ innings... After finishing second in AL with 2.65 ERA in 1991, he jumped to 3.00 in 1992, but posted just 11 wins because of lack of offensive and defensive support... Acquired by Blue Jays from Indians with Turner Ward for Mark Whiten, Glenallen Hill and Denis Boucher, June 27, 1991... Would have earned $3.65 million last year, making him Dodgers' highest-paid player... Born Aug. 31, 1957, in Walnut Creek, Cal.... Originally signed as undrafted free agent by Royals in January 1980, after making pro debut with independent Victoria in '79.

Year	Club	G	IP	W	L	Pct.	SO	BB	H	ERA
1983	Milwaukee	10	55⅔	4	4	.500	21	16	62	3.23
1984	Milwaukee	8	32⅓	2	2	.500	23	10	38	5.29
1986	Cleveland	36	252½	16	12	.571	167	106	234	3.57
1987	Cleveland	32	201⅔	7	18	.280	111	93	193	4.78
1988	Cleveland	31	216⅔	14	8	.636	137	53	225	3.28
1989	Cleveland	31	206	13	10	.565	124	55	188	3.10
1990	Cleveland	31	202	15	11	.577	128	55	207	3.65
1991	Clev.-Tor.	34	238	13	13	.500	167	73	202	2.65
1992	Los Angeles	32	203⅔	11	15	.423	152	63	177	3.00
1993	Los Angeles	33	213⅔	8	10	.444	155	71	192	3.12
1994	Los Angeles	23	153	7	7	.500	102	54	149	4.12
	Totals	301	1975	110	110	.500	1287	649	1867	3.46

PEDRO ASTACIO 25 6-2 190   Bats R Throws R

After leading club in wins (14) in 1993, he slumped to 6-8 mark in '94... Best stretch was May 11-22, when he was 2-0 with 0.72 ERA and 18 strikeouts in 25 innings... His first start of last season was complete-game victory against Houston... Did not strike out a batter, making it first game pitched without a strikeout by a Dodger since Sept. 13, 1990... Following Dodger pattern of young pitchers running out of gas in second and third seasons... Finished 1993 with 7-3 record and 1.02 ERA in last 11 starts and he held opponents to two runs or fewer in eight of final nine starts... Born Nov. 28, 1969, in Hato Mayor,

D.R. . . . Signed by Dodgers as undrafted free agent in November 1987 . . . Would have earned $325,000 in '94.

Year	Club	G	IP	W	L	Pct.	SO	BB	H	ERA
1992	Los Angeles	11	82	5	5	.500	43	20	80	1.98
1993	Los Angeles	31	186⅓	14	9	.609	122	68	165	3.57
1994	Los Angeles	23	149	6	8	.429	108	47	142	4.29
	Totals	65	417⅓	25	22	.532	273	135	387	3.52

TOP PROSPECTS

BILLY ASHLEY 24 6-7 220   **Bats R Throws R**
Dodgers must find a spot for this outfielder . . . Could keep club's Rookie of the Year streak alive . . . Named PCL Player of the Year and Minor League Player of the Year by *USA Today* after hitting .345 with 37 homers and 105 RBI for Albuquerque (AAA) . . . Named to PCL All-Star team two straight years . . . Played in two games with Dodgers and hit .333 in six at-bats before being optioned out April 14 . . . Born July 11, 1970, in Taylor, Mich. . . . Dodgers' third-round selection in 1988 draft.

PAUL KONERKO 19 6-3 205   **Bats R Throws R**
Dodgers' first-round draft choice showed why he was first catcher taken in 1994 draft and 13th choice overall . . . Batted .288 with 15 doubles, six homers and 58 RBI in 257 at-bats for Yakima (A) . . . Walked 36 times and struck out 52 times . . . Ranked second-best prospect in Northwest League by *Baseball America* . . . Born March 5, 1976, in Providence, R.I.

MANAGER TOM LASORDA: World's greatest baseball salesman continues to make his mark . . . With 2-0 win over Reds Aug. 11, he moved into tie with Earl Weaver for 15th on all-time managerial list with 1,480 victories. Clark Griffith is next with 1,491 victories . . . Dodgers led NL West with 58-56 mark in '94. Dodgers also were in first place for only other major work stoppage, in 1981 . . . This will be his 46th year in Dodgers' organization and his 19th as manager . . . His overall major league record is 1,480-1,336... Has won seven division titles, three pennants and two World Series since replacing Walter Alston in 1977... Only Alston has won more games as Dodger manager (2,042) and Sparky Anderson is only active manager with more victories (2,134)... Had short-lived major league career as left-handed pitcher (1954 with Dodgers and 1955 with Dodgers and Kansas City)... Appeared in 26 games and had 0-4 record... If you get to the park early enough, you can still catch him throwing batting practice... Born Sept. 22, 1927, in Norristown, Pa.... Walking into his office at Dodgers Stadium is like walking into a photo gallery of rich and famous... A true baseball character.

ALL-TIME DODGER SEASON RECORDS

BATTING: Babe Herman, .393, 1930
HRs: Duke Snider, 43, 1956
RBI: Tommy Davis, 153, 1962
STEALS: Maury Wills, 104, 1962
WINS: Joe McGinnity, 29, 1900
STRIKEOUTS: Sandy Koufax, 382, 1965

SAN DIEGO PADRES

TEAM DIRECTORY: Principal Owner: John Moores; Exec. VP/GM: Randy Smith; Asst. GM: Reggie Waller; Dir. Scouting: Kevin Towers: Dir. Minor League Adm.: Priscilla Oppenheimer; Dir. Media Rel. and Team Travel: Roger Riley; Mgr.: Bruce Bochy; Coaches: Rob Picciolo, Marv Rettenmund, Sonny Siebert. Home: San Diego Jack Murphy Stadium (59,700). Field distances: 327, l.f. line; 405, c.f.; 327, r.f. line. Spring training: Peoria, Ariz.

SCOUTING REPORT

Don't laugh, but the Padres just may not be the biggest joke in baseball this season. For the first time since sitcom king Tom Werner dismantled the franchise in a money-saving purge, and now with new ownership, the Padres have a fighting chance to be respectable. Ironically, their one big need is a big bat in the middle of the lineup, someone like Fred McGriff or Gary Sheffield, who were dumped along with their salaries a couple of years ago.

We'll never know if Tony Gwynn would've done .400.

The strength of this team is young pitching. There are some golden-armed talents who began to establish themselves while the Padres registered a 37-38 mark after May 21 in '94. The Padres finished with a 4.07 ERA to rank seventh in the NL and, after the All-Star break, they were even more impressive, posting a 3.52 ERA. The Padres finished second in the NL in strikeouts (862), led by Andy Benes, who paced the league with 189.

Benes (6-14, 3.86) needs to not think about the strikeout so much and concentrate instead on not making the bad pitch that continues to cost him games. In short, he has to re-learn how to win. Rookie Joey Hamilton (9-6, 2.98) had no such problem and is regarded as the best pitcher on the staff by management, ahead of Benes. Andy Ashby (6-11, 3.40) has the most movement on his ball, but still makes the crucial mistake. Scott Sanders (4-8, 4.78) rounds out the rotation.

The bullpen is in great shape with closer Trevor Hoffman (4-4, 2.57, 20 saves) and prospect Dustin Hermanson, who flew through the system last year and is expected to be in the majors Opening Day.

NL batting champ Tony Gwynn (.394, 12, 64) continues to be a marvel and gets better with age. New manager Bruce Bochy, well-liked and respected by the players, might even be able to get through to the talented, but sometimes troubled Bip Roberts (.320, 2, 31, 21 steals), who re-signed as a free agent.

Phil Plantier (.220, 18, 41) suffered through an injury-plagued year, but first baseman Eddie Williams (.331, 11, 42) was one of the biggest surprises in baseball and Brad Ausmus (.251, 7, 24) helped stabilize the club behind the plate. Derek Bell (.311, 14, 54) shocked everyone by showing he could play center and do more than just swing for the fences.

The biggest hole continues to be third base, which had been a major trouble spot until Sheffield plugged the gap. The answer may have to come from the free-agent market.

If you're going to build with pitching, you have to have defense, too, and that's a serious problem for the Padres, who finished dead last in NL fielding with a .975 percentage and committed a major league-high 111 errors. Shortstop could fall into the hands of Craig Shipley (.333, 4, 30) because Ricky Gutierrez (.240, 1, 28, 22 errors) slipped so badly. Gutierrez' problems gave Luis Lopez (.277, 2, 20) the chance to play.

With Bochy in charge, there figures to be more discipline and a tighter defense and that should produce an improvement over last year's 47-70 finish. One more consistent bat in the lineup could work wonders for this team.

PADRE PROFILES

TONY GWYNN 34 5-11 222   Bats L Throws L

One of strike tragedies was that we'll never know if this bat magician would have hit .400 in '94. That magic number still belongs to Ted Williams, who hit .406 in 1941... His .394 mark in '94 was highest in NL since Bill Terry of New York Giants batted .401 in 1930... Despite the disappointment of no .400 chase, he picked up his fifth batting title... Batted an incredible .397 with two strikes... Dedicated last season to his father, who died the previous November... Once again, he was hardest to strike out in majors, fanning just once per 25 at-bats... Previous three seasons ended prematurely with knee injury... Finished second in NL with .358 mark in '93... Some critics maintain his weight is more of a problem than opposing pitchers... Picky, picky, picky... The man can flat out hit... Right fielder has batted .300 or more for past 12 years, longest streak since Stan Musial hit .300 for 16 straight seasons... Padres' third-round pick in 1981 draft, out of San Diego State, where he starred in basketball... Would have made $4 million last year and should make same amount this year... Born May 9, 1960, in Los Angeles.

Year	Club	Pos.	G	AB	R	H	2B	3B	HR	RBI	SB	Avg.
1982	San Diego	OF	54	190	33	55	12	2	1	17	8	.289
1983	San Diego	OF	86	304	34	94	12	2	1	37	7	.309
1984	San Diego	OF	158	606	88	213	21	10	5	71	33	.351
1985	San Diego	OF	154	622	90	197	29	5	6	46	14	.317
1986	San Diego	OF	160	642	107	211	33	7	14	59	37	.329
1987	San Diego	OF	157	589	119	218	36	13	7	54	56	.370
1988	San Diego	OF	133	521	64	163	22	5	7	70	26	.313
1989	San Diego	OF	158	604	82	203	27	7	4	62	40	.336
1990	San Diego	OF	141	573	79	177	29	10	4	72	17	.309
1991	San Diego	OF	134	530	69	168	27	11	4	62	8	.317
1992	San Diego	OF	128	520	77	165	27	3	6	41	3	.317
1993	San Diego	OF	122	489	70	175	41	3	7	59	14	.358
1994	San Diego	OF	110	419	79	165	35	1	12	64	5	.394
	Totals		1695	6609	991	2204	351	79	78	714	268	.333

PHIL PLANTIER 26 5-11 195   Bats L Throws R

Sometimes you hurt yourself in this game... Left fielder swings the bat so hard that he often hits himself on left hip and that was one of big reasons for down season... Started wearing a pad to protect himself, but would not stick with it... Led club with 18 homers in '94, but hit just .220... Twelve of his homers were solo shots... Acquired by Padres from Boston for

Jose Melendez prior to 1993 season... Shocked everyone in first full major league season in '93 by tying for seventh in NL in homers (34) and tying for ninth in RBI (100)... Matched Dave Winfield's 1979 mark for most homers by a Padres outfielder in '93... Lives in San Diego year-round... Red Sox' 11th-round selection in 1987... Would have made $500,000 last season... Born Jan. 27, 1969, in Manchester, N.H.

Year	Club	Pos.	G	AB	R	H	2B	3B	HR	RBI	SB	Avg.
1990	Boston	OF	14	15	1	2	1	0	0	3	0	.133
1991	Boston	OF	53	148	27	49	7	1	11	35	1	.331
1992	Boston	OF	108	349	46	86	19	0	7	30	2	.246
1993	San Diego	OF	138	462	67	111	20	1	34	100	4	.240
1994	San Diego	OF	96	341	44	75	21	0	18	41	3	.220
	Totals		409	1315	185	323	68	2	70	209	10	.246

BIP ROBERTS 31 5-7 167   Bats S Throws R

Is he worth the trouble?... That's the question GM Randy Smith had to ask after this guy batted .320, second-highest mark of his career... Second baseman left team for several days in May because of pressure-related problems, which he later insisted were sinus-related... Came back strong to post 23-game hitting streak, longest in NL since Jerome Walton hit in 30 straight for Cubs in 1989... Nagging injuries continue to be a major problem... Injuries wore him down early and he quickly wore out his welcome with Reds in '93, after banner 1992 season... Padres traded him to Reds for Randy Myers prior to 1992 season and he became club's MVP... Born Oct. 27, 1963, in Berkeley, Cal.... Signed by Pirates, who took him in first round of secondary phase of 1982 draft, but he was left unprotected and was taken by Padres... Took major pay cut last season, going from $3.9 million to scheduled salary of $1.5 million... Free agent re-signed two-year, $4.8-million contract in December.

Year	Club	Pos.	G	AB	R	H	2B	3B	HR	RBI	SB	Avg.
1986	San Diego	2B	101	241	34	61	5	2	1	12	14	.253
1988	San Diego	2B-3B	5	9	1	3	0	0	0	0	0	.333
1989	San Diego	OF-3B-SS-2B	117	329	81	99	15	8	3	25	21	.301
1990	San Diego	OF-3B-SS-2B	149	556	104	172	36	3	9	44	46	.309
1991	San Diego	2B-OF	117	424	66	119	13	3	3	32	26	.281
1992	Cincinnati	OF-2B-3B	147	532	92	172	34	6	4	45	44	.323
1993	Cincinnati	2B-OF-3B-SS	83	292	46	70	13	0	1	18	26	.240
1994	San Diego	2B-OF	105	403	52	129	15	5	2	31	21	.320
	Totals		824	2786	476	825	131	27	23	207	198	.296

DEREK BELL 26 6-2 202 Bats R Throws R

Management was scared to death he wouldn't go along with the program, but he turned out to be a model citizen... Finished with highest batting average of his career (.311) and turned into terrific center fielder... Was on trading block much of previous winter, but no one wanted him... Led team with 24 stolen bases and ranked second with 54 RBI in '94... Batted .458 vs. Rockies... Thought he had found heaven when Blue Jays traded him to Padres with Stoney Briggs for Darrin Jackson prior to '93 season... Joined best friend and former Little League teammate Gary Sheffield and mentor Fred McGriff in San Diego, but soon they were gone... Puts on one of baseball's best batting practice shows... Born Dec. 11, 1968, in Tampa, Fla.... Signed by Blue Jays as second-round selection in 1987 draft... Another Padres' bargain, he would've made $385,000 in '94.

Year	Club	Pos.	G	AB	R	H	2B	3B	HR	RBI	SB	Avg.
1991	Toronto	OF	18	28	5	4	0	0	0	1	3	.143
1992	Toronto	OF	61	161	23	39	6	3	2	15	7	.242
1993	San Diego	OF-3B	150	542	73	142	19	1	21	72	26	.262
1994	San Diego	OF	108	434	54	135	20	0	14	54	24	.311
	Totals		337	1165	155	320	45	4	37	142	60	.275

BRAD AUSMUS 25 5-11 185 Bats R Throws R

If only every team could be the Cardinals... Batted .444 against St. Louis... Also likes to hit at Jack Murphy Stadium, where he batted .283 in '94 and has hit 10 of his 12 career homers... Gifted with great physical tools, but sometimes he becomes lackadaisical... Part of his problem is that he was rushed to majors and didn't have enough experience dealing with unique catching situations... In time, he could turn out to be one of the top catchers in the game... Born April 14, 1969, in New Haven, Conn.... Yanks' 47th-round pick in 1987... Rockies claimed him in third round of expansion draft prior to '93 season... Acquired by Padres with Andy Ashby and Doug Bochtler for Greg Harris and Bruce Hurst, July 26, 1993... Would have earned $133,500 in '94.

Year	Club	Pos.	G	AB	R	H	2B	3B	HR	RBI	SB	Avg.
1993	San Diego	C	49	160	18	41	8	1	5	12	2	.256
1994	San Diego	C-1B	101	327	45	82	12	1	7	24	5	.251
	Totals		150	487	63	123	20	2	12	36	7	.253

EDDIE WILLIAMS 30 6-0 175   Bats R Throws R

One of 1994's great stories... First baseman was washed up and out of professional baseball when he was signed by Padres prior to start of last season... Had been playing for a semi-pro team in San Diego... Would have made $109,000 in '94... Loved every minute of return to game... Started with Las Vegas (AAA) and batted .352 with 20 homers and 54 RBI in 75 games... Batted .331 with 42 RBI in 49 games with Padres... First start was June 17 vs. Houston, when he homered in his first at-bat. It was his first in majors since July 23, 1990, when he was in first go-round with Padres... Blasted one homer per 15.9 at-bats... Road to majors included 12 minor league stops and short stints with Indians and White Sox... Born Nov. 1, 1964, in Shreveport, La.... Mets made him fourth player chosen overall in 1983 draft.

Year	Club	Pos.	G	AB	R	H	2B	3B	HR	RBI	SB	Avg.
1986	Cleveland	OF	5	7	2	1	0	0	0	1	0	.143
1987	Cleveland	3B	22	64	9	11	4	0	1	4	0	.172
1988	Cleveland	3B	10	21	3	4	0	0	0	1	0	.190
1989	Chicago (AL)	3B	66	201	25	55	8	0	3	10	1	.274
1990	San Diego	3B	14	42	5	12	3	0	3	4	0	.286
1994	San Diego	1B-3B	49	175	32	58	11	1	11	42	0	.331
	Totals		166	510	76	141	26	1	18	62	1	.276

LUIS LOPEZ 24 5-11 175   Bats S Throws R

By time strike hit, he had completely won over club management after overcoming horrible start... Pulled hamstring in spring training... Went to Las Vegas (AAA) and batted just .204 being called up to Padres... His first career homer was grand slam May 22 against Giants' Mark Portugal... He became only second Padre to turn that trick, joining Mike Corkins, who did it Sept. 4, 1970. That just happened to be the day this guy was born, in Cidra, P.R.... Was inserted as team's starting shortstop after All-Star break and remained there for rest of season... Batted .333 vs. left-handers... Would have made $109,000 in '94... Signed as undrafted free agent in September 1987.

Year	Club	Pos.	G	AB	R	H	2B	3B	HR	RBI	SB	Avg.
1993	San Diego	2B	17	43	1	5	1	0	0	1	0	.116
1994	San Diego	SS-2B-3B	77	235	29	65	16	1	2	20	3	.277
	Totals		94	278	30	70	17	1	2	21	3	.252

RICKY GUTIERREZ 24 6-1 175 Bats R Throws R

Talented player needs to boost his enthusiasm level to stay in majors... Slick infielder has great range, but tends to get careless... Made most errors on club with 22... Raised average from .147 to .257 before cooling off... Future may be at second, not short, the position he lost to Luis Lopez... Came to Padres from Orioles with Erik Schullstrom for Craig Lefferts, Sept. 4, 1992. That was beginning of owner Tom Werner's great fire sale... Led club in runs with 76 in 1993... Born May 23, 1970, in Miami... Second-round selection of Orioles in 1988 draft... Would have earned $187,500 last year... Father Roberto is one of the most respected umpires in South America.

Year	Club	Pos.	G	AB	R	H	2B	3B	HR	RBI	SB	Avg.
1993	San Diego	SS-2B-3B-OF	133	438	76	110	10	5	5	26	4	.251
1994	San Diego	SS-2B	90	275	27	66	11	2	1	28	2	.240
	Totals		223	713	103	176	21	7	6	54	6	.247

ANDY BENES 27 6-6 240 Bats R Throws R

Has great stuff, but sometimes appears to lack will to win... Led NL in strikeouts (189), becoming first Padre to lead league... Has gone 8-22 over his last 35 starts... When he gets serious, hitters don't stand a chance... Perhaps life with Padres has beaten him down... Fanned career-high 14 against Mets in first start after All-Star break... Lost his first four decisions of year and his last four... In 1993, he was leading league in ERA as late as Aug. 6, but then collapsed... Born Aug. 20, 1967, in Evansville, Ind.... Padres made him first player selected in 1988 draft, two slots ahead of Steve Avery... Would have earned $3.05 million last season... Enters walk year this season and could wind up being traded... Bottom line is that he's too talented to have 6-14 record like he did in '94.

Year	Club	G	IP	W	L	Pct.	SO	BB	H	ERA
1989	San Diego	10	66⅔	6	3	.667	66	31	51	3.51
1990	San Diego	32	192⅓	10	11	.476	140	69	177	3.60
1991	San Diego	33	223	15	11	.577	167	59	194	3.03
1992	San Diego	34	231⅓	13	14	.481	169	61	230	3.35
1993	San Diego	34	230⅔	15	15	.500	179	86	200	3.78
1994	San Diego	25	172⅓	6	14	.300	189	51	155	3.86
	Totals	168	1116⅓	65	68	.489	910	357	1007	3.51

TREVOR HOFFMAN 27 6-0 200   Bats R Throws R

Owns one of NL's best arms... One-time shortstop was handed closer's reins at start of last season and allowed just one earned run in first 17⅓ innings... Finished seventh in NL with 20 saves in 23 opportunities... Held opponents to .193 average... So good that former manager Jim Riggleman had tendency to overuse him... Came to Padres with Jose Martinez and Andres Berumen in deal with Marlins for Gary Sheffield and Rich Rodriguez, June 24, 1993... After arriving, he did not allow any of his first 17 inherited runners to score... Finished '93 with Padres having allowed just one of 29 inherited runners to cross the plate... Comes from talented stock... Brother Glenn played infield for Red Sox, Dodgers and Angels... Father was a professional singer—known as the Singing Usher in Anaheim Stadium—and mother was a ballet star... Born Oct. 13, 1967, in Bellflower, Cal.... Would have earned $180,000 last year... Reds' 11th-round pick in 1989 was chosen by Marlins in expansion draft prior to 1993 season.

Year	Club	G	IP	W	L	Pct.	SO	BB	H	ERA
1993	Fla.-S.D.	67	90	4	6	.400	79	39	80	3.90
1994	San Diego	47	56	4	4	.500	68	20	39	2.57
	Totals	114	146	8	10	.444	147	59	119	3.39

JOEY HAMILTON 24 6-4 221   Bats R Throws R

May have brighter future with Padres than Andy Benes... Knows how to win... Opened last season in Las Vegas (AAA) and went 3-5 with 2.73 ERA... Won three times as many games in majors to lead Padres after being called up May 24... Won first two starts, becoming first Padres rookie to do that since Dave Freisleben in 1974... Would have made $109,000 last season... Padres' first-round pick in '91 draft, as eighth player taken overall... Surrendered one earned run or fewer in seven of his 16 starts... Starred at Georgia Southern University... Born Sept. 9, 1970, in Statesboro, Ga.... Never gets flustered and that is a big reason for his success.

Year	Club	G	IP	W	L	Pct.	SO	BB	H	ERA
1994	San Diego	16	108⅔	9	6	.600	61	29	98	2.98

TOP PROSPECTS

RAY McDAVID 23 6-2 190   Bats L Throws R
Center fielder of future and maybe present... Some scouts believe he has Barry Bonds-type potential... Made most of his first Triple-A season, hitting .271 with 13 homers, 62 RBI and 24 stolen bases for Las Vegas and earning promotion... Hit .250 with no homers and two RBI in 28 at-bats for Padres... In 1993, he finished second in Texas League with 33 steals, batted .270 and had 11 home runs, but struck out 104 times in 441 at-bats for Wichita (AA)... Didn't play much baseball in high school and is still learning the game... Born July 20, 1971, in San Diego ... Selected by Padres in ninth round of 1989 draft.

MELVIN NIEVES 23 6-2 195   Bats S Throws R
Unless this outfielder makes major impact, the Fred McGriff deal will be forever remembered as one of worst trades in history... Came to Padres from Braves with Donnie Elliott and Vince Moore for McGriff in fire sale, July 18, 1993... Needed to get his head on straight early last year, but was a monster the rest of the season ... Bashed 25 homers, hit .308 and posted .564 slugging percentage, the best mark in entire organization, for Las Vegas (AAA) ... Did strike out 138 times in 111 games... Appears ready to make the jump to majors... Born Dec. 28, 1971, in San Juan, P.R. ... Signed by Braves as undrafted free agent in May 1988.

GLENN DISHMAN 24 6-1 195   Bats R Throws L
Continued to impress in just his second pro season, striking out 165 batters in 169 innings for Wichita (AA) to lead Texas League ... Was leading Wichita in wins at 11-8, 2.82 before being promoted to Las Vegas (AAA), where he went 1-1, 3.46... Named to Texas League's All-Star squad... Threw no-hitter for Spokane in 1993... Born Nov. 5, 1970, in Baltimore... Signed by Padres as undrafted free agent in June 1993.

DUSTIN HERMANSON 22 6-2 195   Bats R Throws R
Club's top pick in 1994 draft and third player chosen overall... Right-hander, out of Kent University, paid immediate dividends and could wind up sharing closing duties with Trevor Hoffman ... Was dominant for Wichita (AA), going 1-0 and picking up eight saves before moved to Las Vegas (AAA)... Struck out 30 batters in 21 innings and posted 0.43 ERA for Wichita... Moved

up to Las Vegas where he picked up three saves in seven games despite 6.14 ERA... Born Dec. 21, 1972, in Hamilton, Ohio.

MANAGER BRUCE BOCHY:  GM Randy Smith wasted no time in naming him as Jim Riggleman's replacement after Riggleman jumped to Cubs Oct. 21, 1994... Hours later, former Padres catcher was named skipper... Third-base coach in 1994... Should do better than Riggleman, who posted 112-179 managerial record in San Diego... Won three minor league championships during four years of managing in Padres' system.... At 39, he becomes youngest manager in NL ... Bottom line is he is Smith's guy and should feel comfortable even with one-year contract... Became 15th manager in Padres' 26-year history and fourth in last five years... Born April 16, 1955, in Landes de Boussac, France... Attended Brevard Community College and Florida State before beginning pro career in 1975... Drafted by Astros in first round of 1975 draft... Made his major league debut in 1978... Joined Padres in 1983... Hit .239 in 333 major league games... Won titles in Padres' system while managing Spokane (A), High Desert (A) and Wichita (AA) before joining Riggleman's staff in 1993.

ALL-TIME PADRE SEASON RECORDS

BATTING: Tony Gwynn, .394, 1994
HRs: Fred McGriff, 35, 1992
RBI: Dave Winfield, 118, 1979
STEALS: Alan Wiggins, 70, 1984
WINS: Randy Jones, 22, 1976
STRIKEOUTS: Clay Kirby, 231, 1971

SAN FRANCISCO GIANTS

TEAM DIRECTORY: Pres./Managing General Partner: Peter Magowan; Sr. VP/Gen. Mgr.: Bob Quinn; Exec. VP: Larry Baer; Sr. VP-Business Oper.: Pat Gallagher; VP-Scouting and Player Pers.: Brian Sabean; Dir. Pub. Rel.: Bob Rose; Trav. Sec.: Dirk Smith; Mgr.: Dusty Baker; Coaches: Bobby Bonds, Bob Brenly, Wendell Kim, Bob Lillis, Dick Pole, Denny Sommers. Home: Candlestick Park (62,000). Field distances: 335, l.f. line; 365, l.c.; 400, c.f.; 365, l.c.; 328, r.f. line. Spring training: Scottsdale, Ariz.

SCOUTING REPORT

Perhaps this will be the year the Giants get their timing right. Thanks to the addition of Dodger reject Darryl Strawberry, they

Roger Maris was spared Giant footsteps of Matt Williams.

finished with a flourish last season. On July 7, the Giants were in last place, but they won 20 of their final 30 games to finish at 55-60, only 3 1/2 games behind the Dodgers in the watered-down NL West.

Strawberry (.239, 4, 17) doesn't have the sweet swing he once had, but he gives enough protection to Barry Bonds (.312, 37, 81) and Matt Williams (.267, 43, 96) to help make them the most powerful back-to-back hitters since the glory days of the M&M Boys, Willie Mays and Willie McCovey. Of course, the key to this unique group is Strawberry and Bonds keeping their heads screwed on straight. Manager Dusty Baker should have taken some advanced psychology courses in all the down time he had as a result of the strike.

If the Giants don't bury you with their big bats, they'll steal the game from under your nose. With Darren Lewis (.257, 4, 29, 30 steals), Bonds (29 steals) and Royce Clayton (.236, 3, 30, 23 steals) each stealing at least 20 bases last year, the '94 edition became the first Giants team to feature a trio of 20 stolen-base producers since 1919, when George Burns (40), Ross Youngs (24) and Benny Kauff (21) turned the trick.

Defense also continues to be a trademark of this club, even though reliable second baseman Robby Thompson (.209, 2, 7) was saddled with injuries last season. For the second straight year, the Giants led the NL in fielding, with a .985 percentage, and Lewis is simply brilliant in center.

The most impressive aspect of this team, though, may be closer Rod Beck (2-4, 2.77, 28 saves). Forty-six times last season, the Giants went into the ninth with the lead and each time they came out a winner. Even more amazing is the fact that the Giants have won the last 165 games in which they have entered the ninth with a lead. As for overall pitching, the Giants finished sixth in the NL with a 3.99 ERA.

So why can't this power-packed club win a division title? For one thing, the Giants have to stay healthy. Eleven players wound up on the disabled list, including key free-agent acquisition Mark Portugal (10-8, 3.93) in '94. Uncertainty revolves around the rotation. The Giants traded John Burkett (6-8, 3.61) to Texas and Billy Swift (8-7, 3.38) was a free agent at press time. Portugal and Bill Van Lindingham (8-2, 3.54) lead a lean list of starters.

The Giants finished dead last in the majors in batting with a .249 average. That translated into a lot of losses, because they were 8-45 when outhit by their opponents. More consistent bats would work wonders. And so would an added arm or two.

GIANT PROFILES

MATT WILLIAMS 29 6-2 205   Bats R Throws R

Third baseman could have been the new Babe, but the 1994 season struck out... Had launched 43 homers when strike hit and was making run at Roger Maris' single-season record of 61... Amazingly, shortened season was no bitter pill to swallow for him. "There's no reason to drive yourself nuts over something you can't control," he said... Has averaged 33.6 homers over last five seasons... On fire at the end, he batted .354 with eight doubles, nine homers and 21 RBI in last 20 games ... His 40 homers through July set NL mark... Third baseman ranked fourth in fielding percentage at .963... Finished among league leaders in six offensive categories in 1993... Attended Nevada-Las Vegas and Giants made him third player taken overall in 1986 draft... Born Nov. 28, 1965, in Bishop, Cal.... Would have earned $4.050 million last season... Won first Gold Glove in '94.

Year	Club	Pos.	G	AB	R	H	2B	3B	HR	RBI	SB	Avg.
1987	San Francisco	SS-3B	84	245	28	46	9	2	8	21	4	.188
1988	San Francisco	3B-SS	52	156	17	32	6	1	8	19	0	.205
1989	San Francisco	3B-SS	84	292	31	59	18	1	18	50	1	.202
1990	San Francisco	3B	159	617	87	171	27	2	33	122	7	.277
1991	San Francisco	3B-SS	157	589	72	158	24	5	34	98	5	.268
1992	San Francisco	3B	146	529	58	120	13	5	20	66	7	.227
1993	San Francisco	3B	145	579	105	170	33	4	38	110	1	.294
1994	San Francisco	3B	112	445	74	119	16	3	43	96	1	.267
Totals			939	3452	472	875	146	23	202	582	26	.253

BARRY BONDS 30 6-1 190   Bats L Throws L

Four-time All-Star and five-time Gold Glover didn't win NL MVP for a change, but that doesn't mean he didn't have an MVP-like season in '94... Despite fact he was playing with bone spur in his right elbow after early May, his projected numbers would have been better than his results in '93, when he won third MVP ... Was on pace to slam 52 homers and drive in 114 runs in '94... Brilliant left fielder benefitted greatly from Darryl Strawberry's signing... Batted .388 with 14 homers and 28 RBI in 27 games with Straw in lineup... Has proven to be worth every penny of six-year, $43.75-million contract he signed with Giants as free agent after 1992 season... Ranked near the top in nearly every offensive category in 1993... He and father Bobby, now Giants hitting coach, hold all-time father-son homer record with 591 (Bobby had 332 and Barry has 259)... Would have earned $4.984 million last season... Pirates drafted him sixth overall in 1985... Has .191 mark with one homer and three RBI in 68 at-bats in NLCS play... Born July 24, 1964, in Riverside, Cal.... Won first Gold Glove in '94.

Year	Club	Pos.	G	AB	R	H	2B	3B	HR	RBI	SB	Avg.
1986	Pittsburgh	OF	113	413	72	92	26	3	16	48	36	.223
1987	Pittsburgh	OF	150	551	99	144	34	9	25	59	32	.261
1988	Pittsburgh	OF	144	538	97	152	30	5	24	58	17	.283
1989	Pittsburgh	OF	159	580	96	144	34	6	19	58	32	.248
1990	Pittsburgh	OF	151	519	104	156	32	3	33	114	52	.301
1991	Pittsburgh	OF	153	510	95	149	28	5	25	116	43	.292
1992	Pittsburgh	OF	140	473	109	147	36	5	34	103	39	.311
1993	San Francisco	OF	159	539	129	181	38	4	46	123	29	.336
1994	San Francisco	OF	112	391	89	122	18	1	37	81	29	.312
	Totals		1281	4514	890	1287	276	41	259	760	309	.285

ROBBY THOMPSON 32 5-11 170   Bats R Throws R

His body is slowly falling apart... Tremendously underrated second baseman had worst year of his career... Spent two stints on DL because of shoulder problems... Finally underwent arthroscopic rotator cuff surgery July 8, ending his nightmare season... In 1993, he overcame back problems to produce finest year by San Francisco second baseman with career highs in average, home runs and RBI... His 65 RBI in '93 were most ever by San Francisco second baseman, eclipsing Tito Fuentes' mark of 63 in 1973 and his 19 homers matched his own 1991 mark... Beaned by Padres' Trevor Hoffman, Sept. 24, 1993, and he suffered broken left cheekbone... Came back to start the last game of '93 season... Born May 10, 1962, in West Palm Beach, Fla.... Giants' first-round selection in secondary phase of 1983 draft, out of Florida... Would have earned $3.333 million last season.

Year	Club	Pos.	G	AB	R	H	2B	3B	HR	RBI	SB	Avg.
1986	San Francisco	2B-SS	149	549	73	149	27	3	7	47	12	.271
1987	San Francisco	2B	132	420	62	110	26	5	10	44	16	.262
1988	San Francisco	2B	138	477	66	126	24	6	7	48	14	.264
1989	San Francisco	2B	148	547	91	132	26	11	13	50	12	.241
1990	San Francisco	2B	144	498	67	122	22	3	15	56	14	.245
1991	San Francisco	2B	144	492	74	129	24	5	19	48	14	.262
1992	San Francisco	2B	128	443	54	115	25	1	14	49	5	.260
1993	San Francisco	2B	128	494	85	154	30	2	19	65	10	.312
1994	San Francisco	2B	35	129	13	27	8	2	2	7	3	.209
	Totals		1146	4049	585	1064	212	38	106	414	100	.263

DARRYL STRAWBERRY 34 6-6 200 Bats L Throws L

May be most physically gifted player in game and has nearly thrown all that talent down the drain... Has played in only 104 games total in last three seasons due to back woes and substance abuse problems... Dodgers got tired of right fielder's act and cut him loose... Signed with LA's archrivals June 19 last season... Giants went 20-10 with him... By batting fifth, he enabled Matt Williams and Barry Bonds to see better pitches... Hit career homer No. 293 at Montreal July 17, passing Rusty Staub for 68th on all-time list... Dodgers gave him five-year, $20.25-million contract as free agent prior to 1991 season... Made $3.3 million-plus last year... Left New York as Mets' all-time leader in home runs (252), RBI (733), extra-base hits (469) and runs (662)... Born March 12, 1962, in Los Angeles... Mets made him first player chosen in 1980 draft... Faces federal indictment charging failure to report to IRS $500,000 in income from memorabilia shows.

Year	Club	Pos.	G	AB	R	H	2B	3B	HR	RBI	SB	Avg.
1983	New York (NL)	OF	122	420	63	108	15	7	26	74	19	.257
1984	New York (NL)	OF	147	522	75	131	27	4	26	97	27	.251
1985	New York (NL)	OF	111	393	78	109	15	4	29	79	26	.277
1986	New York (NL)	OF	136	475	76	123	27	5	27	93	28	.259
1987	New York (NL)	OF	154	532	108	151	32	5	39	104	36	.284
1988	New York (NL)	OF	153	543	101	146	27	3	39	101	29	.269
1989	New York (NL)	OF	134	476	69	107	26	1	29	77	11	.225
1990	New York (NL)	OF	152	542	92	150	18	1	37	108	15	.277
1991	Los Angeles...	OF	139	505	86	134	22	4	28	99	10	.265
1992	Los Angeles...	OF	43	156	20	37	8	0	5	25	3	.237
1993	Los Angeles...	OF	32	100	12	14	2	0	5	12	1	.140
1994	San Francisco	OF	29	92	13	22	3	1	4	17	0	.239
Totals			1352	4756	793	1232	222	35	294	886	205	.259

ROYCE CLAYTON 25 6-0 185 Bats R Throws R

Growing up as a player... Made just 14 errors, almost slicing his 1993 total of 27 in half... Finished fourth in fielding percentage among NL shortstops with .973 mark... Offensive numbers took a big dip, dropping 46 points in average from '93 to .236 and seeing RBI total plummet by 40... Finished sixth in NL in stolen bases (23) and was caught stealing just three times... Tied for sixth in triples (6)... Batted only .176 vs. lefties and hit .202 over final 34 games... In his first full major league season in 1993, he tied Chris Speier's record for RBI (70) by San Francisco shortstop... Born Jan. 2, 1970, in Burbank,

Cal. ... Giants made him 15th player selected overall in 1988 draft ... In 1991, he was named top prospect in minors by *The Sporting News* ... Would have earned $325,000 last season.

Year	Club	Pos.	G	AB	R	H	2B	3B	HR	RBI	SB	Avg.
1991	San Francisco	SS	9	26	0	3	1	0	0	2	0	.115
1992	San Francisco	SS-3B	98	321	31	72	7	4	4	24	8	.224
1993	San Francisco	SS	153	549	54	155	21	5	6	70	11	.282
1994	San Francisco	SS	108	385	38	91	14	6	3	30	23	.236
	Totals		368	1281	123	321	43	15	13	126	42	.251

DARREN LEWIS 27 6-0 190   Bats R Throws R

Center fielder is human after all ... His major league consecutive errorless streak came to end at 392 games and 938 chances when he booted Cliff Floyd's single June 30 vs. Expos at Candlestick ... That was his first major league error ... Shame, shame ... On July 9, he misplayed Mickey Morandini's single, too ... Leadoff man hit a career-high .257 ... Has stolen 76 bases in past two years ... Born Aug. 28, 1967, in Berkeley, Cal. ... Oakland's 18th-round pick in 1988 ... Acquired from cross-Bay rival Athletics for Ernest Riles prior to 1991 season ... Would have earned $350,000 last season ... Attended University of California-Berkeley ... Awarded first Gold Glove in '94.

Year	Club	Pos.	G	AB	R	H	2B	3B	HR	RBI	SB	Avg.
1990	Oakland	OF	25	35	4	8	0	0	0	1	2	.229
1991	San Francisco	OF	72	222	41	55	5	3	1	15	13	.248
1992	San Francisco	OF	100	320	38	74	8	1	1	18	28	.231
1993	San Francisco	OF	136	522	84	132	17	7	2	48	46	.253
1994	San Francisco	OF	114	451	70	116	15	9	4	29	30	.257
	Totals		447	1550	237	385	45	20	8	111	119	.248

ROD BECK 26 6-1 240   Bats R Throws R

Looks and pitches like Goose Gossage in his prime ... Was successful in all 28 save opportunities, leaving him two saves behind league leader John Franco of Mets ... It marked second straight year that he has finished second in NL in saves ... Owns 40 straight converted save opportunities, dating back to 1993, equaling major league mark set by Oakland's Dennis Eckersley in 1991 and '92 ... Unhittable at night, when he posted

2-0 mark with 13 saves and a 0.39 ERA...Only blemish on record was 10 homers he surrendered, leading to 14 of his 15 earned runs allowed...All this success was achieved despite breaking bone in his left foot Opening Day...In 1992, he ranked second in NL in relief ERA with 1.76 mark...Was converted into reliever in 1991...Would have earned $700,000 in '94... Acquired from Athletics for Charlie Corbell before 1988 season, he knocked around minors until 1991...Born Aug. 3, 1968, in Burbank, Cal....Oakland chose him in 13th round of 1986 draft.

Year	Club	G	IP	W	L	Pct.	SO	BB	H	ERA
1991	San Francisco	31	52⅓	1	1	.500	38	13	53	3.78
1992	San Francisco	65	92	3	3	.500	87	15	62	1.76
1993	San Francisco	76	79⅓	3	1	.750	86	13	57	2.16
1994	San Francisco	48	48⅔	2	4	.333	39	13	49	2.77
	Totals	220	272⅓	9	9	.500	250	54	221	2.45

MARK PORTUGAL 32 6-0 200   Bats R Throws R

After coming aboard as free agent prior to last season, he was rolling along when he tore anterior cruciate ligament Aug. 5 in his old home, the Astrodome...Still managed to be club's winningest pitcher with 10...Also bothered by groin injury that landed him on DL... Teammates averaged 7.5 runs in his victories and only 2.1 in his losses...Batted .354, the highest mark by Giants pitcher since Joe Genewich batted .375 for 1929 New York Giants...Loved Astrodome in 1993, running up 10-1 record with 2.37 ERA there...Underwent elbow surgery July 24, 1992 to remove bone chips and bone spur...Born Oct. 30, 1962, in Los Angeles...Originally signed with Twins as undrafted free agent in 1980...Traded by Minnesota to Astros for Todd McClure before 1989 season...Would have earned $2.333 million last season.

Year	Club	G	IP	W	L	Pct.	SO	BB	H	ERA
1985	Minnesota	6	24⅓	1	3	.250	12	14	24	5.55
1986	Minnesota	27	112⅔	6	10	.375	67	50	112	4.31
1987	Minnesota	13	44	1	3	.250	28	24	58	7.77
1988	Minnesota	26	57⅔	3	3	.500	31	17	60	4.53
1989	Houston	20	108	7	1	.875	86	37	91	2.75
1990	Houston	32	196⅔	11	10	.524	136	67	187	3.62
1991	Houston	32	168⅓	10	12	.455	120	59	163	4.49
1992	Houston	18	101⅓	6	3	.667	62	41	76	2.66
1993	Houston	33	208	18	4	.818	131	77	194	2.77
1994	San Francisco	21	137⅓	10	8	.556	87	45	135	3.93
	Totals	228	1158⅓	73	57	.562	760	431	1100	3.78

Despite injuries, Mark Portugal led in club wins.

TOP PROSPECTS

J.R. PHILLIPS 24 6-1 185   Bats L Throws L
Will Clark's eventual replacement at first... Power prospect hammered 27 homers for second straight season with Phoenix (AAA) ... Also drove in 79 runs and hit .300 in '94... Acquired by Giants on waiver claim from Angels prior to 1993 season... Born April 29, 1970, in West Covina, Cal.... Selected by Angels in third round of 1988 draft... Played in only 15 games for Giants (.132 with one homer and 13 RBI), because Dusty Baker didn't want all the pressure of replacing Clark thrust upon him.

DAN CARLSON 25 6-1 185   Bats R Throws R
Promising right-hander has finished with double-digit victories the last four seasons... Led Phoenix (AAA) with 13-6 mark in '94, posting 4.64 ERA in hitters' league... Won total of 12 games for Shreveport (AA) and Phoenix in '93... Giants' 33rd-round selection in 1989 draft... Born Jan. 26, 1970, in Portland, Ore. ... Won 16 games for Clinton (A) in 1991.

CHAD FONVILLE 24 5-6 155   Bats S Throws R
Little shortstop makes things happen... Batted .307 with 22 steals for San Jose (A)... Second straight year with plus-.300 average ... Hit .306 and swiped 52 bases for Clinton (A) in 1993... Born March 5, 1971, in Jacksonville, N.C.... Giants' 11th-round selection in 1992 draft.

JEFF MARTIN 22 6-2 180   Bats L Throws R
Switched to bullpen in 1991... Finished 5-5 with club-leading 20 saves and 2.83 ERA for Clinton (A) last season... Struck out 104 batters in 89 innings in '94... Giants' 10th-round selection in 1991 draft... Born March 28, 1973, in Renton, Wash.... Played in Netherlands during 1993 summer tour put on by major league baseball.

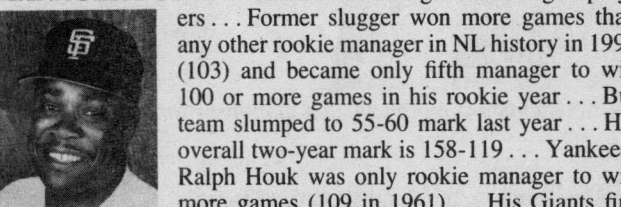

MANAGER DUSTY BAKER: His strength is relating to players... Former slugger won more games than any other rookie manager in NL history in 1993 (103) and became only fifth manager to win 100 or more games in his rookie year... But team slumped to 55-60 mark last year... His overall two-year mark is 158-119... Yankees' Ralph Houk was only rookie manager to win more games (109 in 1961)... His Giants finished one game out in 1993 and 3½ behind last season... Named NL Manager of the Year in 1993 for his efforts... Was named Giants' field boss Dec. 16, 1992, replacing the fired Roger Craig

No Bonds are more valuable than three-time MVP Barry.

and becoming sixth minority manager in majors... Spent nearly 16 years as a player with Braves, Dodgers, Giants and Athletics, compiling .278 average, 242 home runs and 1,013 RBI before retiring after 1986 season... Hit .320 in 1981, helping the Dodgers to World Series championship... After retiring, he stayed away from game for just one year. During that time, he worked as an investment broker... Before becoming manager, he spent four years as Giants' hitting instructor... Believes communication is key to success... Born June 15, 1949, in Riverside, Cal.... Boyhood friend of current Giants hitting coach Bobby Bonds.

ALL-TIME GIANT SEASON RECORDS

BATTING: Bill Terry, .401, 1930
HRs: Willie Mays, 52, 1965
RBI: Mel Ott, 151, 1929
STEALS: George Burns, 62, 1914
WINS: Christy Mathewson, 37, 1908
STRIKEOUTS: Christy Mathewson, 267, 1903

MAJOR LEAGUE YEAR-BY-YEAR LEADERS

NATIONAL LEAGUE MVP

Year Player, Club
1931 Frank Frisch, St. Louis Cardinals
1932 Chuck Klein, Philadelphia Phillies
1933 Carl Hubbell, New York Giants
1934 Dizzy Dean, St. Louis Cardinals
1935 Gabby Hartnett, Chicago Cubs
1936 Carl Hubbell, New York Giants
1937 Joe Medwick, St. Louis Cardinals
1938 Ernie Lombardi, Cincinnati Reds
1939 Bucky Walters, Cincinnati Reds
1940 Frank McCormick, Cincinnati Reds
1941 Dolph Camilli, Brooklyn Dodgers
1942 Mort Cooper, St. Louis Cardinals
1943 Stan Musial, St. Louis Cardinals
1944 Marty Marion, St. Louis Cardinals
1945 Phil Cavarretta, Chicago Cubs
1946 Stan Musial, St. Louis Cardinals
1947 Bob Elliott, Boston Braves
1948 Stan Musial, St. Louis Cardinals
1949 Jackie Robinson, Brooklyn Dodgers
1950 Jim Konstanty, Philadelphia Phillies
1951 Roy Campanella, Brooklyn Dodgers
1952 Hank Sauer, Chicago Cubs
1953 Roy Campanella, Brooklyn Dodgers
1954 Willie Mays, New York Giants
1955 Roy Campanella, Brooklyn Dodgers
1956 Don Newcombe, Brooklyn Dodgers
1957 Hank Aaron, Milwaukee Braves
1958 Ernie Banks, Chicago Cubs
1959 Ernie Banks, Chicago Cubs
1960 Dick Groat, Pittsburgh Pirates

Year Player, Club
1961 Frank Robinson, Cincinnati Reds
1962 Maury Wills, Los Angeles Dodgers
1963 Sandy Koufax, Los Angeles Dodgers
1964 Ken Boyer, St. Louis Cardinals
1965 Willie Mays, San Francisco Giants
1966 Roberto Clemente, Pittsburgh Pirates
1967 Orlando Cepeda, St. Louis Cardinals
1968 Bob Gibson, St. Louis Cardinals
1969 Willie McCovey, San Francisco Giants
1970 Johnny Bench, Cincinnati Reds
1971 Joe Torre, St. Louis Cardinals
1972 Johnny Bench, Cincinnati Reds
1973 Pete Rose, Cincinnati Reds
1974 Steve Garvey, Los Angeles Dodgers
1975 Joe Morgan, Cincinnati Reds
1976 Joe Morgan, Cincinnati Reds
1977 George Foster, Cincinnati Reds
1978 Dave Parker, Pittsburgh Pirates
1979 Keith Hernandez, St. Louis Cardinals
     Willie Stargell, Pittsburgh Pirates
1980 Mike Schmidt, Philadelphia Phillies
1981 Mike Schmidt, Philadelphia Phillies
1982 Dale Murphy, Atlanta Braves
1983 Dale Murphy, Atlanta Braves
1984 Ryne Sandberg, Chicaco Cubs
1985 Willie McGee, St. Louis Cardinals
1986 Mike Schmidt, Philadelphia Phillies
1987 Andre Dawson, Chicago Cubs
1988 Kirk Gibson, Los Angeles Dodgers
1989 Kevin Mitchell, San Francisco Giants
1990 Barry Bonds, Pittsburgh Pirates
1991 Terry Pendleton, Atlanta Braves
1992 Barry Bonds, Pittsburgh Pirates
1993 Barry Bonds, San Francisco Giants
1994 Jeff Bagwell, Houston Astros

AMERICAN LEAGUE MVP

Year Player, Club
1931 Lefty Grove, Philadelphia Athletics
1932 Jimmy Foxx, Philadelphia Athletics
1933 Jimmy Foxx, Philadelphia Athletics
1934 Mickey Cochrane, Detroit Tigers

Year	Player, Club
1935	Hank Greenberg, Detroit Tigers
1936	Lou Gehrig, New York Yankees
1937	Charley Gehringer, Detroit Tigers
1938	Jimmy Foxx, Boston Red Sox
1939	Joe DiMaggio, New York Yankees
1940	Hank Greenberg, Detroit Tigers
1941	Joe DiMaggio, New York Yankees
1942	Joe Gordon, New York Yankees
1943	Spud Chandler, New York Yankees
1944	Hal Newhouser, Detroit Tigers
1945	Hal Newhouser, Detroit Tigers
1946	Ted Williams, Boston Red Sox
1947	Joe DiMaggio, New York Yankees
1948	Lou Boudreau, Cleveland Indians
1949	Ted Williams, Boston Red Sox
1950	Phil Rizzuto, New York Yankees
1951	Yogi Berra, New York Yankees
1952	Bobby Shantz, Philadelphia Athletics
1953	Al Rosen, Cleveland Indians
1954	Yogi Berra, New York Yankees
1955	Yogi Berra, New York Yankees
1956	Mickey Mantle, New York Yankees
1957	Mickey Mantle, New York Yankees
1958	Jackie Jensen, Boston Red Sox
1959	Nellie Fox, Chicago White Sox
1960	Roger Maris, New York Yankees
1961	Roger Maris, New York Yankees
1962	Mickey Mantle, New York Yankees
1963	Elston Howard, New York Yankees
1964	Brooks Robinson, Baltimore Orioles
1965	Zoilo Versalles, Minnesota Twins
1966	Frank Robinson, Baltimore Orioles
1967	Carl Yastrzemski, Boston Red Sox
1968	Dennis McLain, Detroit Tigers
1969	Harmon Killebrew, Minnesota Twins
1970	Boog Powell, Baltimore Orioles
1971	Vida Blue, Oakland A's
1972	Dick Allen, Chicago White Sox
1973	Reggie Jackson, Oakland A's
1974	Jeff Burroughs, Texas Rangers
1975	Fred Lynn, Boston Red Sox
1976	Thurman Munson, New York Yankees
1977	Rod Carew, Minnesota Twins

Year	Player, Club
1978	Jim Rice, Boston Red Sox
1979	Don Baylor, California Angels
1980	George Brett, Kansas City Royals
1981	Rollie Fingers, Milwaukee Brewers
1982	Robin Yount, Milwaukee Brewers
1983	Cal Ripken Jr., Baltimore Orioles
1984	Willie Hernandez, Detroit Tigers
1985	Don Mattingly, New York Yankees
1986	Roger Clemens, Boston Red Sox
1987	George Bell, Toronto Blue Jays
1988	Jose Canseco, Oakland A's
1989	Robin Yount, Milwaukee Brewers
1990	Rickey Henderson, Oakland A's
1991	Cal Ripken Jr., Baltimore Orioles
1992	Dennis Eckersley, Oakland A's
1993	Frank Thomas, Chicago White Sox
1994	Frank Thomas, Chicago White Sox

AMERICAN LEAGUE
Batting Champions

Year	Player, Club	Avg.
1901	Napoleon Lajoie, Philadelphia Athletics	.422
1902	Ed Delahanty, Washington Senators	.376
1903	Napoleon Lajoie, Cleveland Indians	.355
1904	Napoleon Lajoie, Cleveland Indians	.381
1905	Elmer Flick, Cleveland Indians	.306
1906	George Stone, St. Louis Browns	.358
1907	Ty Cobb, Detroit Tigers	.350
1908	Ty Cobb, Detroit Tigers	.324
1909	Ty Cobb, Detroit Tigers	.377
1910	Ty Cobb, Detroit Tigers	.385
1911	Ty Cobb, Detroit Tigers	.420
1912	Ty Cobb, Detroit Tigers	.410
1913	Ty Cobb, Detroit Tigers	.390
1914	Ty Cobb, Detroit Tigers	.368
1915	Ty Cobb, Detroit Tigers	.370
1916	Tris Speaker, Cleveland Indians	.386
1917	Ty Cobb, Detroit Tigers	.383
1918	Ty Cobb, Detroit Tigers	.382
1919	Ty Cobb, Detroit Tigers	.384
1920	George Sisler, St. Louis Browns	.407
1921	Harry Heilmann, Detroit Tigers	.393

Year	Player, Club	Avg.
1922	George Sisler, St. Louis Browns	.420
1923	Harry Heilmann, Detroit Tigers	.398
1924	Babe Ruth, New York Yankees	.378
1925	Harry Heilmann, Detroit Tigers	.393
1926	Heinie Manush, Detroit Tigers	.377
1927	Harry Heilmann, Detroit Tigers	.398
1928	Goose Goslin, Washington Senators	.379
1929	Lew Fonseca, Cleveland Indians	.369
1930	Al Simmons, Philadelphia Athletics	.381
1931	Al Simmons, Philadelphia Athletics	.390
1932	David Alexander, Detroit Tigers-Boston Red Sox	.367
1933	Jimmy Foxx, Philadelphia Athletics	.356
1934	Lou Gehrig, New York Yankees	.365
1935	Buddy Myer, Washington Senators	.349
1936	Lou Appling, Chicago White Sox	.388
1937	Charlie Gehringer, Detroit Tigers	.371
1938	Jimmy Foxx, Boston Red Sox	.349
1939	Joe DiMaggio, New York Yankees	.381
1940	Joe DiMaggio, New York Yankees	.352
1941	Ted Williams, Boston Red Sox	.406
1942	Ted Williams, Boston Red Sox	.356
1943	Luke Appling, Chicago White Sox	.328
1944	Lou Boudreau, Cleveland Indians	.327
1945	Snuffy Stirnweiss, New York Yankees	.309
1946	Mickey Vernon, Washington Senators	.353
1947	Ted Williams, Boston Red Sox	.343
1948	Ted Williams, Boston Red Sox	.369
1949	George Kell, Detroit Tigers	.343
1950	Billy Goodman, Boston Red Sox	.354
1951	Ferris Fain, Philadelphia Athletics	.344
1952	Ferris Fain, Philadelphia Athletics	.327
1953	Mickey Vernon, Washington Senators	.337
1954	Bobby Avila, Cleveland Indians	.341
1955	Al Kaline, Detroit Tigers	.340
1956	Mickey Mantle, New York Yankees	.353
1957	Ted Williams, Boston Red Sox	.388
1958	Ted Williams, Boston Red Sox	.328
1959	Harvey Kuenn, Detroit Tigers	.353
1960	Pete Runnels, Boston Red Sox	.320
1961	Norm Cash, Detroit Tigers	.361
1962	Pete Runnels, Boston Red Sox	.326
1963	Carl Yastrzemski, Boston Red Sox	.321
1964	Tony Oliva, Minnesota Twins	.323

Year	Player, Club	Avg.
1965	Tony Oliva, Minnesota Twins	.321
1966	Frank Robinson, Baltimore Orioles	.316
1967	Carl Yastrzemski, Boston Red Sox	.326
1968	Carl Yastrzemski, Boston Red Sox	.301
1969	Rod Carew, Minnesota Twins	.332
1970	Alex Johnson, California Angels	.329
1971	Tony Oliva, Minnesota Twins	.337
1972	Rod Carew, Minnesota Twins	.318
1973	Rod Carew, Minnesota Twins	.350
1974	Rod Carew, Minnesota Twins	.364
1975	Rod Carew, Minnesota Twins	.359
1976	George Brett, Kansas City Royals	.333
1977	Rod Carew, Minnesota Twins	.388
1978	Rod Carew, Minnesota Twins	.333
1979	Fred Lynn, Boston Red Sox	.333
1980	George Brett, Kansas City Royals	.390
1981	Carney Lansford, Boston Red Sox	.336
1982	Willie Wilson, Kansas City Royals	.332
1983	Wade Boggs, Boston Red Sox	.361
1984	Don Mattingly, New York Yankees	.343
1985	Wade Boggs, Boston Red Sox	.368
1986	Wade Boggs, Boston Red Sox	.357
1987	Wade Boggs, Boston Red Sox	.363
1988	Wade Boggs, Boston Red Sox	.366
1989	Kirby Puckett, Minnesota Twins	.339
1990	George Brett, Kansas City Royals	.329
1991	Julio Franco, Texas Rangers	.341
1992	Edgar Martinez, Seattle Mariners	.343
1993	John Olerud, Toronto Blue Jays	.363
1994	Paul O'Neill, New York Yankees	.359

NATIONAL LEAGUE
Batting Champions

Year	Player, Club	Avg.
1876	Roscoe Barnes, Chicago	.403
1877	James White, Boston	.385
1878	Abner Dalrymple, Milwaukee	.356
1879	Cap Anson, Chicago	.407
1880	George Gore, Chicago	.365
1881	Cap Anson, Chicago	.399
1882	Dan Brouthers, Buffalo	.367

Year	Player, Club	Avg.
1883	Dan Brouthers, Buffalo	.371
1884	Jim O'Rourke, Buffalo	.350
1885	Roger Connor, New York	.371
1886	Mike Kelly, Chicago	.388
1887	Cap Anson, Chicago	.421
1888	Cap Anson, Chicago	.343
1889	Dan Brouthers, Boston	.373
1890	Jack Glassock, New York	.336
1891	Billy Hamilton, Philadelphia	.338
1892	Cupid Childs, Cleveland	.335
	Dan Brouthers, Brooklyn	.335
1893	Hugh Duffy, Boston	.378
1894	Hugh Duffy, Boston	.438
1895	Jesse Burkett, Cleveland	.423
1896	Jesse Burkett, Cleveland	.410
1897	Willie Keeler, Baltimore	.432
1898	Willie Keeler, Baltimore	.379
1899	Ed Delahanty, Philadelphia	.408
1900	Honus Wagner, Pittsburgh	.380
1901	Jesse Burkett, St. Louis Cardinals	.382
1902	C.H. Beaumont, Pittsburgh Pirates	.357
1903	Honus Wagner, Pittsburgh Pirates	.355
1904	Honus Wagner, Pittsburgh Pirates	.349
1905	J. Bentley Seymour, Cincinnati Reds	.377
1906	Honus Wagner, Pittsburgh Pirates	.339
1907	Honus Wagner, Pittsburgh Pirates	.350
1908	Honus Wagner, Pittsburgh Pirates	.354
1909	Honus Wagner, Pittsburgh Pirates	.339
1910	Sherwood Magee, Philadelphia Phillies	.331
1911	Honus Wagner, Pittsburgh Pirates	.334
1912	Heinie Zimmerman, Chicago Cubs	.372
1913	Jake Daubert, Brooklyn Dodgers	.350
1914	Jake Daubert, Brooklyn Dodgers	.329
1915	Larry Doyle, New York Giants	.320
1916	Hal Chase, Cincinnati Reds	.339
1917	Edd Roush, Cincinnati Reds	.341
1918	Zack Wheat, Brooklyn Dodgers	.335
1919	Edd Roush, Cincinnati Reds	.321
1920	Rogers Hornsby, St. Louis Cardinals	.370
1921	Rogers Hornsby, St. Louis Cardinals	.397
1922	Rogers Hornsby, St. Louis Cardinals	.401
1923	Rogers Hornsby, St. Louis Cardinals	.384
1924	Rogers Hornsby, St. Louis Cardinals	.424

Year	Player, Club	Avg.
1925	Rogers Hornsby, St. Louis Cardinals	.403
1926	Bubbles Hargrave, Cincinnati Reds	.353
1927	Paul Waner, Pittsburgh Pirates	.380
1928	Rogers Hornsby, Boston Braves	.387
1929	Lefty O'Doul, Philadelphia Phillies	.398
1930	Bill Terry, New York Giants	.401
1931	Chick Hafey, St. Louis Cardinals	.349
1932	Lefty O'Doul, Brooklyn Dodgers	.368
1933	Chuck Klein, Philadelphia Phillies	.368
1934	Paul Waner, Pittsburgh Pirates	.362
1935	Arky Vaughan, Pittsburgh Pirates	.385
1936	Paul Waner, Pittsburgh Pirates	.373
1937	Joe Medwick, St. Louis Cardinals	.374
1938	Ernie Lombardi, Cincinnati Reds	.342
1939	Johnny Mize, St. Louis Cardinals	.349
1940	Debs Garms, Pittsburgh Pirates	.355
1941	Pete Reiser, Brooklyn Dodgers	.343
1942	Ernie Lombardi, Boston Braves	.330
1943	Stan Musial, St. Louis Cardinals	.330
1944	Dixie Walker, Brooklyn Dodgers	.357
1945	Phil Cavarretta, Chicago Cubs	.355
1946	Stan Musial, St. Louis Cardinals	.376
1947	Harry Walker, St. L. Cardinals-Phila. Phillies	.363
1948	Stan Musial, St. Louis Cardinals	.376
1949	Jackie Robinson, Brooklyn Dodgers	.342
1950	Stan Musial, St. Louis Cardinals	.346
1951	Stan Musial, St. Louis Cardinals	.355
1952	Stan Musial, St. Louis Cardinals	.336
1953	Carl Furillo, Brooklyn Dodgers	.344
1954	Willie Mays, New York Giants	.345
1955	Richie Ashburn, Philadelphia Phillies	.338
1956	Hank Aaron, Milwaukee Braves	.328
1957	Stan Musial, St. Louis Cardinals	.351
1958	Richie Ashburn, Philadelphia Phillies	.350
1959	Hank Aaron, Milwaukee Braves	.328
1960	Dick Groat, Pittsburgh Pirates	.325
1961	Roberto Clemente, Pittsburgh Pirates	.351
1962	Tommy Davis, Los Angeles Dodgers	.346
1963	Tommy Davis, Los Angeles Dodgers	.326
1964	Roberto Clemente, Pittsburgh Pirates	.339
1965	Roberto Clemente, Pittsburgh Pirates	.329
1966	Matty Alou, Pittsburgh Pirates	.342
1967	Roberto Clemente, Pittsburgh Pirates	.357

Year	Player, Club	HRs
1945	Tommy Holmes, Boston Braves	28
1946	Ralph Kiner, Pittsburgh Pirates	23
1947	Ralph Kiner, Pittsburgh Pirates	51
	Johnny Mize, New York Giants	51
1948	Ralph Kiner, Pittsburgh Pirates	40
	Johnny Mize, New York Giants	40
1949	Ralph Kiner, Pittsburgh Pirates	54
1950	Ralph Kiner, Pittsburgh Pirates	47
1951	Ralph Kiner, Pittsburgh Pirates	42
1952	Ralph Kiner, Pittsburgh Pirates	37
	Hank Sauer, Chicago Cubs	37
1953	Eddie Mathews, Milwaukee Braves	47
1954	Ted Kluszewski, Cincinnati Reds	49
1955	Willie Mays, New York Giants	51
1956	Duke Snider, Brooklyn Dodgers	43
1957	Hank Aaron, Milwaukee Braves	44
1958	Ernie Banks, Chicago Cubs	47
1959	Eddie Mathews, Milwaukee Braves	46
1960	Ernie Banks, Chicago Cubs	41
1961	Orlando Cepeda, San Francisco Giants	46
1962	Willie Mays, San Francisco Giants	49
1963	Hank Aaron, Milwaukee Braves	44
	Willie McCovey, San Francisco Giants	44
1964	Willie Mays, San Francisco Giants	47
1965	Willie Mays, San Francisco Giants	52
1966	Hank Aaron, Atlanta Braves	44
1967	Hank Aaron, Atlanta Braves	39
1968	Willie McCovey, San Francisco Giants	36
1969	Willie McCovey, San Francisco Giants	45
1970	Johnny Bench, Cincinnati Reds	45
1971	Willie Stargell, Pittsburgh Pirates	48
1972	Johnny Bench, Cincinnati Reds	40
1973	Willie Stargell, Pittsburgh Pirates	44
1974	Mike Schmidt, Philadelphia Phillies	36
1975	Mike Schmidt, Philadelphia Phillies	38
1976	Mike Schmidt, Philadelphia Phillies	38
1977	George Foster, Cincinnati Reds	52
1978	George Foster, Cincinnati Reds	40
1979	Dave Kingman, Chicago Cubs	48
1980	Mike Schmidt, Philadelphia Phillies	48
1981	Mike Schmidt, Philadelphia Phillies	31
1982	Dave Kingman, New York Mets	37
1983	Mike Schmidt, Philadelphia Phillies	40

Year	Player, Club	HRs
1984	Mike Schmidt, Philadelphia Phillies	36
1984	Dale Murphy, Atlanta Braves	36
1985	Dale Murphy, Atlanta Braves	37
1986	Mike Schmidt, Philadelphia Phillies	37
1987	Andre Dawson, Chicaco Cubs	49
1988	Darryl Strawberry, New York Mets	39
1989	Kevin Mitchell, San Francisco Giants	47
1990	Ryne Sandberg, Chicago Cubs	40
1991	Howard Johnson, New York Mets	38
1992	Fred McGriff, San Diego Padres	35
1993	Bobby Bonds, San Francisco Giants	46
1994	Matt Williams, San Francisco Giants	43

AMERICAN LEAGUE
Home Run Leaders

Year	Player, Club	HRs
1901	Napoleon Lajoie, Philadelphia Athletics	13
1902	Ralph Seybold, Philadelphia Athletics	16
1903	John Freeman, Boston Pilgrims	13
1904	Harry Davis, Philadelphia Athletics	10
1905	Harry Davis, Philadelphia Athletics	8
1906	Harry Davis, Philadelphia Athletics	12
1907	Harry Davis, Philadelphia Athletics	8
1908	Sam Crawford, Detroit Tigers	7
1909	Ty Cobb, Detroit Tigers	9
1910	Garland Stahl, Boston Red Sox	10
1911	Frank (Home Run) Baker, Philadelphia Athletics	9
1912	Frank (Home Run) Baker, Philadelphia Athletics	10
1913	Frank (Home Run) Baker, Philadelphia Athletics	12
1914	Frank (Home Run) Baker, Philadelphia Athletics	8
	Sam Crawford, Detroit Tigers	8
1915	Bob Roth, Cleveland Indians	7
1916	Wally Pipp, New York Yankees	12
1917	Wally Pipp, New York Yankees	9
1918	Babe Ruth, Boston Red Sox	11
	Clarence Walker, Philadelphia Athletics	11
1919	Babe Ruth, Boston Red Sox	29
1920	Babe Ruth, New York Yankees	54
1921	Babe Ruth, New York Yankees	59
1922	Ken Williams, St. Louis Browns	39
1923	Babe Ruth, New York Yankees	41

Year	Player, Club	Avg.
1968	Pete Rose, Cincinnati Reds	.335
1969	Pete Rose, Cincinnati Reds	.348
1970	Rico Carty, Atlanta Braves	.366
1971	Joe Torre, St. Louis Cardinals	.363
1972	Billy Williams, Chicago Cubs	.333
1973	Pete Rose, Cincinnati Reds	.338
1974	Ralph Garr, Atlanta Braves	.353
1975	Bill Madlock, Chicago Cubs	.354
1976	Bill Madlock, Chicago Cubs	.339
1977	Dave Parker, Pittsburgh Pirates	.338
1978	Dave Parker, Pittsburgh Pirates	.334
1979	Keith Hernandez, St. Louis Cardinals	.344
1980	Bill Buckner, Chicago Cubs	.324
1981	Bill Madlock, Pittsburgh Pirates	.341
1982	Al Oliver, Montreal Expos	.331
1983	Bill Madlock, Pittsburgh Pirates	.323
1984	Tony Gwynn, San Diego Padres	.351
1985	Willie McGee, St. Louis Cardinals	.353
1986	Tim Raines, Montreal Expos	.334
1987	Tony Gwynn, San Diego Padres	.370
1988	Tony Gwynn, San Diego Padres	.313
1989	Tony Gwynn, San Diego Padres	.336
1990	Willie McGee, St. Louis Cardinals	.335
1991	Terry Pendleton, Atlanta Braves	.319
1992	Gary Sheffield, San Diego Padres	.330
1993	Andres Galarraga, Colorado Rockies	.370
1994	Tony Gwynn, San Diego Padres	.394

NATIONAL LEAGUE
Home Run Leaders

Year	Player, Club	HRs
1900	Herman Long, Boston Nationals	12
1901	Sam Crawford, Cincinnati Reds	16
1902	Tom Leach, Pittsburgh Pirates	6
1903	Jim Sheckard, Brooklyn Dodgers	9
1904	Harry Lumley, Brooklyn Dodgers	9
1905	Fred Odwell, Cincinnati Reds	9
1906	Tim Jordan, Brooklyn Dodgers	12
1907	Dave Brain, Boston Nationals	10
1908	Tim Jordan, Brooklyn Dodgers	12
1909	Jim Murray, New York Giants	7

YEAR-BY-YEAR LEADERS

Year	Player, Club	HRs
1910	Fred Beck, Boston Nationals	10
	Frank Schulte, Chicago Cubs	10
1911	Frank Schulte, Chicago Cubs	21
1912	Heinie Zimmerman, Chicago Cubs	14
1913	Gavvy Cravath, Philadelphia Phillies	19
1914	Gavvy Cravath, Philadelphia Phillies	19
1915	Gavvy Cravath, Philadelphia Phillies	24
1916	Dave Robertson, New York Giants	12
	Cy Williams, Chicago Cubs	12
1917	Gavvy Cravath, Philadelphia Phillies	12
	Dave Robertson, New York Giants	12
1918	Gavvy Cravath, Philadelphia Phillies	8
1919	Gavvy Cravath, Philadelphia Phillies	12
1920	Cy Williams, Philadelphia Phillies	15
1921	George Kelly, New York Giants	23
1922	Rogers Hornsby, St. Louis Cardinals	42
1923	Cy Williams, Philadelphia Phillies	41
1924	Jack Fournier, Brooklyn Dodgers	27
1925	Rogers Hornsby, St. Louis Cardinals	39
1926	Hack Wilson, Chicago Cubs	21
1927	Cy Williams, Philadelphia Phillies	30
	Hack Wilson, Chicaco Cubs	30
1928	Jim Bottomley, St. Louis Cardinals	31
	Hack Wilson, Chicago Cubs	31
1929	Chuck Klein, Philadelphia Phillies	43
1930	Hack Wilson, Chicago Cubs	56
1931	Chuck Klein, Philadelphia Phillies	31
1932	Chuck Klein, Philadelphia Phillies	38
	Mel Ott, New York Giants	38
1933	Chuck Klein, Philadelphia Phillies	28
1934	Rip Collins, St. Louis Cardinals	35
	Mel Ott, New York Giants	35
1935	Wally Berger, Boston Braves	34
1936	Mel Ott, New York Giants	33
1937	Joe Medwick, St. Louis Cardinals	31
	Mel Ott, New York Giants	31
1938	Mel Ott, New York Giants	36
1939	Johnny Mize, St. Louis Cardinals	28
1940	Johnny Mize, St. Louis Cardinals	43
1941	Dolph Camilli, Brooklyn Dodgers	34
1942	Mel Ott, New York Giants	30
1943	Bill Nicholson, Chicago Cubs	29
1944	Bill Nicholson, Chicago Cubs	33

Year	Player, Club	HRs
1924	Babe Ruth, New York Yankees	46
1925	Bob Meusel, New York Yankees	33
1926	Babe Ruth, New York Yankees	47
1927	Babe Ruth, New York Yankees	60
1928	Babe Ruth, New York Yankees	54
1929	Babe Ruth, New York Yankees	46
1930	Babe Ruth, New York Yankees	49
1931	Babe Ruth, New York Yankees	46
	Lou Gehrig, New York Yankees	46
1932	Jimmie Foxx, Philadelphia Athletics	58
1933	Jimmie Foxx, Philadelphia Athletics	48
1934	Lou Gehrig, New York Yankees	49
1935	Hank Greenberg, Detroit Tigers	36
	Jimmie Foxx, Philadelphia Athletics	36
1936	Lou Gehrig, New York Yankees	49
1937	Joe DiMaggio, New York Yankees	46
1938	Hank Greenberg, Detroit Tigers	58
1939	Jimmy Foxx, Boston Red Sox	35
1940	Hank Greenberg, Detroit Tigers	41
1941	Ted Williams, Boston Red Sox	37
1942	Ted Williams, Boston Red Sox	36
1943	Rudy York, Detroit Tigers	34
1944	Nick Etten, New York Yankees	22
1945	Vern Stephens, St. Louis Browns	24
1946	Hank Greenberg, Detroit Tigers	44
1947	Ted Williams, Boston Red Sox	32
1948	Joe DiMaggio, New York Yankees	39
1949	Ted Williams, Boston Red Sox	43
1950	Al Rosen, Cleveland Indians	37
1951	Gus Zernial, Philadelphia Athletics	33
1952	Larry Doby, Cleveland Indians	32
1953	Al Rosen, Cleveland Indians	43
1954	Larry Doby, Cleveland Indians	32
1955	Mickey Mantle, New York Yankees	37
1956	Mickey Mantle, New York Yankees	52
1957	Roy Sievers, Washington Senators	42
1958	Mickey Mantle, New York Yankees	42
1959	Rocky Colavito, Cleveland Indians	42
	Harmon Killebrew, Washington Senators	42
1960	Mickey Mantle, New York Yankees	40
1961	Roger Maris, New York Yankees	61
1962	Harmon Killebrew, Minnesota Twins	48
1963	Harmon Killebrew, Minnesota Twins	45

YEAR-BY-YEAR LEADERS

Year	Player, Club	HRs
1964	Harmon Killebrew, Minnesota Twins	49
1965	Tony Conigliaro, Boston Red Sox	32
1966	Frank Robinson, Baltimore Orioles	49
1967	Carl Yastrzemski, Boston Red Sox	44
	Harmon Killebrew, Minnesota Twins	44
1968	Frank Howard, Washington Senators	44
1969	Harmon Killebrew, Minnesota Twins	49
1970	Frank Howard, Washington Senators	44
1971	Bill Melton, Chicago White Sox	33
1972	Dick Allen, Chicago White Sox	37
1973	Reggie Jackson, Oakland A's	32
1974	Dick Allen, Chicago White Sox	32
1975	George Scott, Milwaukee Brewers	36
	Reggie Jackson, Oakland A's	36
1976	Graig Nettles, New York Yankees	32
1977	Jim Rice, Boston Red Sox	39
1978	Jim Rice, Boston Red Sox	46
1979	Gorman Thomas, Milwaukee Brewers	45
1980	Ben Oglivie, Milwaukee Brewers	41
	Reggie Jackson, New York Yankees	41
1981	Bobby Grich, California Angels	22
	Eddie Murray, Baltimore Orioles	22
	Dwight Evans, Boston Red Sox	22
	Tony Armas, Oakland A's	22
1982	Reggie Jackson, California Angels	39
	Gorman Thomas, Milwaukee Brewers	39
1983	Jim Rice, Boston Red Sox	39
1984	Tony Armas, Boston Red Sox	43
1985	Darrell Evans, Detroit Tigers	40
1986	Jesse Barfield, Toronto Blue Jays	40
1987	Mark McGwire, Oakland A's	49
1988	Jose Canseco, Oakland A's	42
1989	Fred McGriff, Toronto Blue Jays	36
1990	Cecil Fielder, Detroit Tigers	51
1991	Jose Canseco, Oakland A's	44
	Cecil Fielder, Detroit Tigers	44
1992	Juan Gonzalez, Texas Rangers	43
1993	Juan Gonzalez, Texas Rangers	46
1994	Ken Griffey, Seattle Mariners	40

CY YOUNG AWARD WINNERS
(Prior to 1967 there was a single overall major league award.)

Year Player, Club
1956 Don Newcombe, Brooklyn Dodgers
1957 Warren Spahn, Milwaukee Braves
1958 Bob Turley, New York Yankees
1959 Early Wynn, Chicago White Sox
1960 Vernon Law, Pittsburgh Pirates
1961 Whitey Ford, New York Yankees
1962 Don Drysdale, Los Angeles Dodgers
1963 Sandy Koufax, Los Angeles Dodgers
1964 Dean Chance, Los Angeles Angels
1965 Sandy Koufax, Los Angeles Dodgers
1966 Sandy Koufax, Los Angeles Dodgers

AL CY YOUNG

Year Player, Club
1967 Jim Lonborg, Boston Red Sox
1968 Dennis McLain, Detroit Tigers
1969 Mike Cuellar, Baltimore Orioles
     Dennis McLain, Detroit Tigers
1970 Jim Perry, Minnesota Twins
1971 Vida Blue, Oakland A's
1972 Gaylord Perry, Cleveland Indians
1973 Jim Palmer, Baltimore Orioles
1974 Jim Hunter, Oakland A's
1975 Jim Palmer, Baltimore Orioles
1976 Jim Palmer, Baltimore Orioles
1977 Sparky Lyle, New York Yankees
1978 Ron Guidry, New York Yankees
1979 Mike Flanagan, Baltimore Orioles
1980 Steve Stone, Baltimore Orioles
1981 Rollie Fingers, Milwaukee Brewers
1982 Pete Vuckovich, Milwaukee Brewers
1983 LaMarr Hoyt, Chicago White Sox
1984 Willie Hernandez, Detroit Tigers
1985 Bret Saberhagen, Kansas City Royals
1986 Roger Clemens, Boston Red Sox
1987 Roger Clemens, Boston Red Sox
1988 Frank Viola, Minnesota Twins
1989 Bret Saberhagen, Kansas City Royals

Year	Player, Club
1990	Bob Welch, Oakland A's
1991	Roger Clemens, Boston Red Sox
1992	Dennis Eckersley, Oakland A's
1993	Jack McDowell, Chicago White Sox
1994	David Cone, Kansas City Royals

NL CY YOUNG

Year	Player, Club
1967	Mike McCormick, San Francisco Giants
1968	Bob Gibson, St. Louis Cardinals
1969	Tom Seaver, New York Mets
1970	Bob Gibson, St. Louis Cardinals
1971	Ferguson Jenkins, Chicago Cubs
1972	Steve Carlton, Philadelphia Phillies
1973	Tom Seaver, New York Mets
1974	Mike Marshall, Los Angeles Dodgers
1975	Tom Seaver, New York Mets
1976	Randy Jones, San Diego Padres
1977	Steve Carlton, Philadelphia Phillies
1978	Gaylord Perry, San Diego Padres
1979	Bruce Sutter, Chicago Cubs
1980	Steve Carlton, Philadelphia Phillies
1981	Fernando Valenzuela, Los Angeles Dodgers
1982	Steve Carlton, Philadelphia Phillies
1983	John Denny, Philadelphia Phillies
1984	Rick Sutcliffe, Chicaco Cubs
1985	Dwight Gooden, New York Mets
1986	Mike Scott, Houston Astros
1987	Steve Bedrosian, Philadelphia Phillies
1988	Orel Hershiser, Los Angeles Dodgers
1989	Mark Davis, San Diego Padres
1990	Doug Drabek, Pittsburgh Pirates
1991	Tom Glavine, Atlanta Braves
1992	Greg Maddux, Chicago Cubs
1993	Greg Maddux, Atlanta Braves
1994	Greg Maddux, Atlanta Braves

NATIONAL LEAGUE
Rookie of Year

Year	Player, Club
1947	Jackie Robinson, Brooklyn Dodgers

Year	Player, Club
1948	Al Dark, Boston Braves
1949	Don Newcombe, Brooklyn Dodgers
1950	Sam Jethroe, Boston Braves
1951	Willie Mays, New York Giants
1952	Joe Black, Brooklyn Dodgers
1953	Junior Gilliam, Brooklyn Dodgers
1954	Wally Moon, St. Louis Cardinals
1955	Bill Virdon, St. Louis Cardinals
1956	Frank Robinson, Cincinnati Reds
1957	Jack Sanford, Philadelphia Phillies
1958	Orlando Cepeda, San Francisco Giants
1959	Willie McCovey, San Francisco Giants
1960	Frank Howard, Los Angeles Dodgers
1961	Billy Williams, Chicago Cubs
1962	Kenny Hubbs, Chicago Cubs
1963	Pete Rose, Cincinnati Reds
1964	Richie Allen, Philadelphia Phillies
1965	Jim Lefebvre, Los Angeles Dodgers
1966	Tommy Helms, Cincinnati Reds
1967	Tom Seaver, New York Mets
1968	Johnny Bench, Cincinnati Reds
1969	Ted Sizemore, Los Angeles Dodgers
1970	Carl Morton, Montreal Expos
1971	Earl Williams, Atlanta Braves
1972	Jon Matlack, New York Mets
1973	Gary Matthews, San Francisco Giants
1974	Bake McBride, St. Louis Cardinals
1975	John Montefusco, San Francisco Giants
1976	Pat Zachry, Cincinnati Reds
	Butch Metzger, San Diego Padres
1977	Andre Dawson, Montreal Expos
1978	Bob Horner, Atlanta Braves
1979	Rick Sutcliffe, Los Angeles Dodgers
1980	Steve Howe, Los Angeles Dodgers
1981	Fernando Valenzuela, Los Angeles Dodgers
1982	Steve Sax, Los Angeles Dodgers
1983	Darryl Strawberry, New York Mets
1984	Dwight Gooden, New York Mets
1985	Vince Coleman, St. Louis Cardinals
1986	Todd Worrell, St. Louis Cardinals
1987	Benito Santiago, San Diego Padres
1988	Chris Sabo, Cincinnati Reds
1989	Jerome Walton, Chicago Cubs

Year Player, Club
1990 Dave Justice, Atlanta Braves
1991 Jeff Bagwell, Houston Astros
1992 Eric Karros, Los Angeles Dodgers
1993 Mike Piazza, Los Angeles Dodgers
1994 Raul Mondesi, Los Angeles Dodgers

AMERICAN LEAGUE
Rookie of Year

Year Player, Club
1949 Roy Sievers, St. Louis Browns
1950 Walt Dropo, Boston Red Sox
1951 Gil McDougald, New York Yankees
1952 Harry Byrd, Philadelphia Athletics
1953 Harvey Kuenn, Detroit Tigers
1954 Bob Grim, New York Yankees
1955 Herb Score, Cleveland Indians
1956 Luis Aparicio, Chicago White Sox
1957 Tony Kubek, New York Yankees
1958 Albie Pearson, Washington Senators
1959 Bob Allison, Washington Senators
1960 Ron Hansen, Baltimore Orioles
1961 Don Schwall, Boston Red Sox
1962 Tom Tresh, New York Yankees
1963 Gary Peters, Chicago White Sox
1964 Tony Oliva, Minnesota Twins
1965 Curt Blefary, Baltimore Orioles
1966 Tommie Agee, Chicago White Sox
1967 Rod Carew, Minnesota Twins
1968 Stan Bahnsen, New York Yankees
1969 Lou Piniella, Kansas City Royals
1970 Thurman Munson, New York Yankees
1971 Chris Chambliss, Cleveland Indians
1972 Carlton Fisk, Boston Red Sox
1973 Al Bumbry, Baltimore Orioles
1974 Mike Hargrove, Texas Rangers
1975 Fred Lynn, Boston Red Sox
1976 Mark Fidrych, Detroit Tigers
1977 Eddie Murray, Baltimore Orioles
1978 Lou Whitaker, Detroit Tigers
1979 John Castino, Minnesota Twins
     Alfredo Griffin, Toronto Blue Jays

Year	Player, Club
1980	Joe Charboneau, Cleveland Indians
1981	Dave Righetti, New York Yankees
1982	Cal Ripken Jr., Baltimore Orioles
1983	Ron Kittle, Chicago White Sox
1984	Alvin Davis, Seattle Mariners
1985	Ozzie Guillen, Chicago White Sox
1986	Jose Canseco, Oakland A's
1987	Mark McGwire, Oakland A's
1988	Walt Weiss, Oakland A's
1989	Gregg Olson, Baltimore Orioles
1990	Sandy Alomar Jr., Cleveland Indians
1991	Chuck Knoblauch, Minnesota Twins
1992	Pat Listach, Milwaukee Brewers
1993	Tim Salmon, California Angels
1994	Bob Hamelin, Kansas City

ALL-TIME MAJOR LEAGUE RECORDS

National	American
\multicolumn{2}{c}{**Batting (Season)**}	

National	American
.438 Hugh Duffy, Boston, 1894 .424 Rogers Hornsby, St. Louis, 1924	.422 Napoleon Lajoie, Phila. 1901
At Bat	
701 Juan Samuel, Phila., 1984	705 Willie Wilson, Kansas City, 1980
Runs	
196 William Hamilton, Phila., 1894 158 Chuck Klein, Phila., 1930	177 Babe Ruth, NewYork, 1921
Hits	
254 Frank J. O'Doul, Phila., 1929 254 Bill Terry, New York, 1930	257 George Sisler, St.Louis, 1920
Doubles	
64 Joseph M. Medwick, St. L., 1936	67 Earl W. Webb, Boston, 1931
Triples	
36 J. Owen Wilson, Pitts., 1912	26 Joseph Jackson, Cleve.,1912 26 Samuel Crawford, Detroit, 1914
Home Runs	
56 Hack Wilson, Chicago, 1930	61 Roger Maris, New York,1961
Runs Batted In	
190 Hack Wilson, Chicago, 1930	184 Lou Gehrig, New York,1931
Stolen Bases	
118 Lou Brock, St. Louis, 1974	130 Rickey Henderson, Oakland, 1982
Bases on Balls	
148 Eddie Stanky, Brooklyn, 1945 148 Jim Wynn, Houston, 1969	170 Babe Ruth, New York,1923
Strikeouts	
189 Bobby Bonds, S.F., 1970	186 Rob Deer, Milwaukee,1987

Sandy Koufax owns season K mark for southpaws.

Pitching (Season)
Games
106 Mike Marshall, L.A., 1974   88 Wilbur Wood, Chicago, 1968
Innings Pitched
434 Joseph J. McGinnity, N.Y., 1903   464 Edward Walsh, Chicago, 1908
Victories
37 Christy Mathewson, N.Y., 1908   41 Jack Chesbro, New York, 1904
Losses
29 Victor Willis, Boston, 1905   26 John Townsend, Wash., 1904
   26 Robert Groom, Wash., 1909
Strikeouts
(Left-hander)
382 Sandy Koufax, Los Angeles, 1965   343 Rube Waddell, Phila., 1904
(Right-hander)
313 J.R. Richard, Houston, 1979   383 Nolan Ryan, Cal., 1973
Bases on Balls
185 Sam Jones, Chicago, 1955   208 Bob Feller, Cleveland, 1938
Earned-Run Average
(Minimum 300 Innings)
1.12 Bob Gibson, St. L., 1968   1.09 Walter Johnson, Washington, 1913
Shutouts
16 Grover C. Alexander, Phila., 1916   13 John W. Coombs, Phila., 1910

WORLD SERIES WINNERS

Year	A. L. Champion	N. L. Champion	World Series Winner
1903	Boston Red Sox	Pittsburgh Pirates	Boston, 5-3
1905	Philadelphia Athletics	New York Giants	New York, 4-1
1906	Chicago White Sox	Chicago Cubs	Chicago (AL), 4-2
1907	Detroit Tigers	Chicago Cubs	Chicago, 4-0-1
1908	Detroit Tigers	Chicago Cubs	Chicago, 4-1
1909	Detroit Tigers	Pittsburgh Pirates	Pittsburgh, 4-3
1910	Philadelphia Athletics	Chicago Cubs	Philadelphia, 4-1
1911	Philadelphia Athletics	New York Giants	Philadelphia, 4-2
1912	Boston Red Sox	New York Giants	Boston, 4-3-1
1913	Philadelphia Athletics	New York Giants	Philadelphia, 4-1
1914	Philadelphia Athletics	Boston Braves	Boston, 4-0
1915	Boston Red Sox	Philadelphia Phillies	Boston, 4-1
1916	Boston Red Sox	Brooklyn Dodgers	Boston, 4-1
1917	Chicago White Sox	New York Giants	Chicago, 4-2
1918	Boston Red Sox	Chicago Cubs	Boston, 4-2
1919	Chicago White Sox	Cincinnati Reds	Cincinnati, 5-3
1920	Cleveland Indians	Brooklyn Dodgers	Cleveland, 5-2
1921	New York Yankees	New York Giants	New York (NL), 5-3
1922	New York Yankees	New York Giants	New York (NL), 4-0-1
1923	New York Yankees	New York Giants	New York (AL), 4-2
1924	Washington Senators	New York Giants	Washington, 4-2
1925	Washington Senators	Pittsburgh Pirates	Pittsburgh, 4-3
1926	New York Yankees	St. Louis Cardinals	St. Louis, 4-3
1927	New York Yankees	Pittsburgh Pirates	New York, 4-0
1928	New York Yankees	St. Louis Cardinals	New York, 4-0
1929	Philadelphia Athletics	Chicago Cubs	Philadelphia, 4-2
1930	Philadelphia Athletics	St. Louis Cardinals	Philadelphia, 4-2
1931	Philadelphia Athletics	St. Louis Cardinals	St. Louis, 4-3
1932	New York Yankees	Chicago Cubs	New York, 4-0
1933	Washington Senators	New York Giants	New York, 4-1
1934	Detroit Tigers	St. Louis Cardinals	St. Louis, 4-3
1935	Detroit Tigers	Chicago Cubs	Detroit, 4-2
1936	New York Yankees	New York Giants	New York (AL), 4-2
1937	New York Yankees	New York Giants	New York (AL), 4-1
1938	New York Yankees	Chicago Cubs	New York, 4-0
1939	New York Yankees	Cincinnati Reds	New York, 4-0
1940	Detroit Tigers	Cincinnati Reds	Cincinnati, 4-3
1941	New York Yankees	Brooklyn Dodgers	New York, 4-1
1942	New York Yankees	St. Louis Cardinals	St. Louis, 4-1
1943	New York Yankees	St. Louis Cardinals	New York, 4-1
1944	St. Louis Browns	St. Louis Cardinals	St. Louis (NL), 4-2
1945	Detroit Tigers	Chicago Cubs	Detroit, 4-3
1946	Boston Red Sox	St. Louis Cardinals	St. Louis, 4-3
1947	New York Yankees	Brooklyn Dodgers	New York, 4-3
1948	Cleveland Indians	Boston Braves	Cleveland, 4-2
1949	New York Yankees	Brooklyn Dodgers	New York, 4-1
1950	New York Yankees	Philadelphia Phillies	New York, 4-0
1951	New York Yankees	New York Giants	New York (AL), 4-2
1952	New York Yankees	Brooklyn Dodgers	New York, 4-3

WORLD SERIES WINNERS

Year	A. L. Champion	N. L. Champion	World Series Winner
1953	New York Yankees	Brooklyn Dodgers	New York, 4-2
1954	Cleveland Indians	New York Giants	New York, 4-0
1955	New York Yankees	Brooklyn Dodgers	Brooklyn, 4-3
1956	New York Yankees	Brooklyn Dodgers	New York, 4-3
1957	New York Yankees	Milwaukee Braves	Milwaukee, 4-3
1958	New York Yankees	Milwaukee Braves	New York, 4-3
1959	Chicago White Sox	Los Angeles Dodgers	Los Angeles, 4-2
1960	New York Yankees	Pittsburgh Pirates	Pittsburgh, 4-3
1961	New York Yankees	Cincinnati Reds	New York, 4-1
1962	New York Yankees	San Francisco Giants	New York, 4-3
1963	New York Yankees	Los Angeles Dodgers	Los Angeles, 4-0
1964	New York Yankees	St. Louis Cardinals	St. Louis, 4-3
1965	Minnesota Twins	Los Angeles Dodgers	Los Angeles, 4-0
1966	Baltimore Orioles	Los Angeles Dodgers	Baltimore, 4-0
1967	Boston Red Sox	St. Louis Cardinals	St. Louis, 4-3
1968	Detroit Tigers	St. Louis Cardinals	Detroit, 4-3
1969	Baltimore Orioles	New York Mets	New York, 4-1
1970	Baltimore Orioles	Cincinnati Reds	Baltimore, 4-1
1971	Baltimore Orioles	Pittsburgh Pirates	Pittsburgh, 4-3
1972	Oakland A's	Cincinnati Reds	Oakland, 4-3
1973	Oakland A's	New York Mets	Oakland, 4-3
1974	Oakland A's	Los Angeles Dodgers	Oakland, 4-1
1975	Boston Red Sox	Cincinnati Reds	Cincinnati, 4-3
1976	New York Yankees	Cincinnati Reds	Cincinnati, 4-0
1977	New York Yankees	Los Angeles Dodgers	New York, 4-2
1978	New York Yankees	Los Angeles Dodgers	New York, 4-2
1979	Baltimore Orioles	Pittsburgh Pirates	Pittsburgh, 4-3
1980	Kansas City Royals	Philadelphia Phillies	Philadelphia, 4-3
1981	New York Yankees	Los Angeles Dodgers	Los Angeles, 4-2
1982	Milwaukee Brewers	St. Louis Cardinals	St. Louis, 4-3
1983	Baltimore Orioles	Philadelphia Phillies	Baltimore, 4-1
1984	Detroit Tigers	San Diego Padres	Detroit, 4-1
1985	Kansas City Royals	St. Louis Cardinals	Kansas City, 4-3
1986	Boston Red Sox	New York Mets	New York, 4-3
1987	Minnesota Twins	St. Louis Cardinals	Minnesota, 4-3
1988	Oakland A's	Los Angeles Dodgers	Los Angeles, 4-1
1989	Oakland A's	San Francisco Giants	Oakland, 4-0
1990	Oakland A's	Cincinnati Reds	Cincinnati, 4-0
1991	Minnesota Twins	Atlanta Braves	Minnesota, 4-3
1992	Toronto Blue Jays	Atlanta Braves	Toronto, 4-2
1993	Toronto Blue Jays	Philadelphia Phillies	Toronto, 4-2

OFFICIAL 1994
NATIONAL LEAGUE RECORDS

COMPILED BY MLB-IBM BASEBALL INFORMATION SYSTEM
Official Statistician: ELIAS SPORTS BUREAU

FINAL STANDINGS

EASTERN DIVISION	W	L	PCT.	GB
MONTREAL	74	40	.649	-
ATLANTA	68	46	.596	6.0
NEW YORK	55	58	.487	18.5
PHILADELPHIA	54	61	.470	20.5
FLORIDA	51	64	.443	23.5

CENTRAL DIVISION	W	L	PCT.	GB
CINCINNATI	66	48	.579	-
HOUSTON	66	49	.574	.5
ST. LOUIS	53	61	.465	13.0
PITTSBURGH	53	61	.465	13.0
CHICAGO	49	64	.434	16.5

WESTERN DIVISION	W	L	PCT.	GB
LOS ANGELES	58	56	.509	-
SAN FRANCISCO	55	60	.478	3.5
COLORADO	53	64	.453	6.5
SAN DIEGO	47	70	.402	12.5

Batting

Individual Batting Leaders

Batting Average	.394	Gwynn	S.D.
Games	116	Bichette	Col.
At Bats	484	Bichette	Col.
Runs	104	Bagwell	Hou.
Hits	165	Gwynn	S.D.
Total Bases	300	Bagwell	Hou.
Singles	117	Gwynn	S.D.
Doubles	44	Biggio	Hou.
Triples	9	Butler	L.A.
		Lewis	S.F.
Home Runs	43	Williams	S.F.
Runs Batted In	116	Bagwell	Hou.
Sacrifice Hits	16	Hill	Mon.
Sacrifice Flies	12	Fletcher	Mon.
Hit by Pitch	12	Vina	N.Y.
Bases on Balls	74	Bonds	S.F.
Intentional Bases on Balls	18	Bonds	S.F.
Strikeouts	114	R. Sanders	Cin.
Stolen Bases	39	Biggio	Hou.
Caught Stealing	16	D. Sanders	Atl.-Cin.
Grounded Into Double Play	20	Gwynn	S.D.
Slugging Percentage	.750	Bagwell	Hou.
On-Base Percentage	.454	Gwynn	S.D.
Longest Batting Streak	23	Roberts	S.D. (May 26-June 20)

TOP 15 QUALIFIERS FOR BATTING CHAMPIONSHIP

BATTER	TEAM	B	AVG	G	AB	R	H	TB	2B	3B	HR	RBI	SH	SF	HP	BB	IBB	SO	SB	CS	GI DP	SLG	OBP	E
Gwynn, T	SD	L	.394	110	419	79	165	238	35	1	12	64	1	5	2	48	16	19	5	0	20	.568	.454	3
Bagwell, J	HOU	R	.368	110	400	104	147	300	32	2	39	116	0	10	4	65	14	65	15	4	12	.750	.451	9
Alou, M	MON	R	.339	107	422	81	143	250	31	5	22	78	0	5	6	42	10	63	7	6	7	.592	.397	3
Morris, H	CIN	L	.335	112	436	60	146	214	30	4	10	78	2	6	5	34	8	62	6	2	16	.491	.385	6
Mitchell, K	CIN	R	.326	95	310	57	101	211	18	1	30	77	0	6	5	59	15	62	6	1	12	.681	.429	4
Jefferies, G	STL	S	.325	103	397	52	129	194	27	1	12	55	0	4	1	45	12	26	12	2	8	.489	.391	7
Walker, L	MON	L	.322	103	395	76	127	232	44	2	19	86	0	6	4	47	5	74	15	5	8	.587	.394	9
Boone, B	CIN	R	.320	108	381	59	122	187	25	2	12	68	5	8	8	24	1	74	3	1	10	.491	.368	12
Roberts, B	SD	S	.320	105	403	52	129	160	15	8	0	31	2	2	3	39	1	57	21	7	7	.397	.383	9
Conine, J	FLA	R	.319	115	451	60	144	237	27	6	18	82	0	4	1	40	4	92	1	2	8	.525	.373	6
Galarraga, A	COL	R	.319	103	417	77	133	247	21	0	31	85	0	5	8	19	8	93	8	3	10	.592	.356	8
Piazza, M	LA	R	.319	107	405	64	129	219	18	0	24	92	0	3	1	33	0	65	1	0	11	.541	.370	10
McGriff, F	ATL	L	.318	113	424	81	135	264	25	1	34	94	0	3	1	50	8	76	7	3	8	.623	.389	7
Biggio, C	HOU	R	.318	114	437	88	139	211	44	5	6	56	1	2	8	62	1	58	39	4	5	.483	.411	7
Butler, B	LA	L	.314	111	417	79	131	186	13	9	8	33	7	2	2	68	0	52	27	8	2	.446	.411	2

INDIVIDUAL BATTING

BATTER	TEAM	B	AVG	G	AB	R	H	TB	2B	3B	HR	RBI	SH	SF	HP	BB	IBB	SO	SB	CS	GI DP	SLG	OBP	E
Abbott, K	FLA	R	.249	101	345	41	86	136	17	3	9	33	3	1	2	16	1	98	3	0	5	.394	.291	15
Alicea, L	STL	S	.278	88	205	32	57	94	12	5	1	29	0	3	5	30	4	38	6	5	2	.459	.373	4
Alou, M	MON	R	.339	107	422	81	143	250	31	5	22	78	0	5	6	42	10	63	7	6	7	.592	.397	3
Andersen, L	PHI	R	.000	29	0	0	0	0	0	0	0	0	0	0	0	0	0	0	0	0	0	.000	1.000	1
Aquino, L	FLA	R	.167	29	6	0	1	1	0	0	0	0	1	0	0	0	0	0	0	0	0	.167	.167	0
Arias, A	FLA	R	.239	59	113	4	27	32	5	0	0	15	1	0	1	9	0	19	0	0	5	.283	.298	2
Arocha, R	STL	R	.111	45	9	0	1	2	1	0	0	0	6	0	0	0	0	5	0	0	0	.222	.200	0
Ashby, A	SD	R	.163	24	49	2	8	8	0	0	0	0	9	0	0	1	0	19	0	0	2	.163	.180	0
Ashley, B	LA	R	.333	2	6	0	2	3	1	0	0	0	0	0	0	0	0	2	0	0	0	.500	.333	0
Astacio, P	LA	R	.064	23	47	2	3	3	0	0	0	0	4	0	0	0	0	22	0	0	0	.064	.064	0

OFFICIAL NATIONAL LEAGUE STATS • 379

Player	Team	B	AVG	G	AB	R	H	TB	2B	3B	HR	RBI	SH	SF	HBP	GDP	BB	IBB	SO	SB	CS	E	OBP	SLG	GW
Ausmus, B.	SD	R	.251	101	327	45	82	117	12	1	7	24	7	6	2	1	30	2	12	63	5	1	8	.358	.314	7
Avery, S.	ATL	L	.102	24	49	4	5	7	2	0	0	5	0	6	2	0	1	0	1	16	0	0	0	.143	.115	1
Bagwell, J.	HOU	R	.368	110	400	104	147	300	32	2	39	116	0	10	4	0	65	4	65	15	14	0	12	.750	.451	9
Ballard, J.	PIT	L	.500	28	2	3	1	0	0	0	0	0	0	0	0	0	0	0	0	0	0	0	0	.500	.500	0
Banks, W.	CHI	R	.122	23	41	3	5	6	1	0	0	0	7	0	0	0	0	0	1	13	0	0	4	.146	.163	0
Barberie, B.	FLA	S	.301	107	372	40	112	151	20	2	5	31	2	2	0	9	23	3	30	65	2	0	4	.406	.356	14
Bass, K.	HOU	R	.310	82	203	37	63	98	15	1	6	35	1	2	0	1	28	6	0	24	2	3	5	.483	.393	2
Batiste, K.	PHI	R	.234	64	209	17	49	58	6	0	1	13	0	2	1	2	3	0	6	32	2	0	11	.278	.239	12
Bautista, J.	CHI	R	.000	58	2	0	0	0	0	0	0	0	0	3	0	0	0	0	0	0	0	0	0	.000	.000	0
Bean, B.	SD	L	.215	84	135	7	29	36	0	0	0	14	0	0	0	0	7	0	0	25	1	0	4	.267	.248	0
Beck, R.	SF	R	.000	48	3	0	0	2	5	0	0	0	0	3	0	0	0	0	0	2	0	0	0	.000	.000	0
Bedrosian, S.	ATL	R	.500	46	2	0	1	0	0	0	0	0	0	0	0	0	0	0	1	1	0	0	0	.500	.500	0
Bell, D.	SD	R	.311	108	434	54	135	197	20	4	8	54	8	3	1	3	29	2	5	88	24	8	14	.454	.353	10
Bell, J.	PIT	R	.276	110	424	68	117	187	35	1	9	45	0	1	1	2	49	4	0	82	2	2	15	.441	.354	15
Belliard, R.	ATL	S	.278	38	97	12	27	37	4	0	2	10	0	0	0	0	15	0	2	21	0	0	1	.381	.372	2
Benavides, F.	MON	R	.242	46	120	9	29	38	7	1	0	9	1	2	2	2	2	0	4	29	2	2	4	.317	.264	1
Benes, A.	SD	R	.188	47	85	8	16	23	2	1	1	6	7	0	0	0	1	0	1	15	0	0	1	.271	.222	2
Benjamin, M.	SF	R	.163	25	49	2	8	9	1	0	0	0	13	0	0	0	0	0	0	22	0	0	0	.184	.180	0
Benzinger, T.	SF	S	.258	38	62	9	16	26	0	0	1	9	0	5	3	3	2	1	4	16	0	0	3	.419	.343	3
Berry, S.	MON	R	.265	107	328	32	87	131	13	2	9	31	1	5	3	2	17	0	2	84	5	1	1	.399	.304	5
Bichette, D.	COL	R	.278	103	320	43	89	145	19	2	11	41	0	2	2	2	32	3	3	50	14	7	3	.453	.347	14
Bielecki, M.	ATL	R	.304	116	484	74	147	265	33	2	27	95	1	4	2	4	19	0	7	70	21	8	17	.548	.334	2
Biggio, C.	HOU	R	.000	19	3	0	0	0	0	0	0	0	0	0	0	0	0	0	0	3	0	0	0	.000	.000	0
Black, B.	SF	R	.318	114	437	88	139	211	44	0	0	56	6	1	2	8	62	2	0	58	39	4	5	.483	.411	7
Blair, W.	COL	L	.059	10	17	0	1	1	0	0	0	0	6	0	0	0	0	0	1	5	0	0	0	.059	.059	0
Blauser, J.	ATL	R	.000	47	6	0	0	0	0	0	0	0	0	0	0	0	0	0	0	5	0	0	0	.000	.000	1
Bogar, T.	NY	R	.258	96	380	56	98	145	21	4	6	45	5	2	2	6	38	0	5	64	1	1	11	.382	.329	13
Bonds, B.	SF	L	.154	50	52	5	8	14	0	0	2	5	2	0	0	1	0	0	2	11	1	0	1	.269	.211	1
Bonilla, B.	NY	L	.312	112	391	89	122	253	18	1	37	81	0	6	3	6	74	18	0	43	29	3	3	.647	.426	3
Boone, B.	CIN	S	.290	108	403	60	117	203	24	1	20	67	1	0	0	2	55	9	3	101	1	3	10	.504	.374	18
Borland, T.	PHI	R	.320	108	381	59	122	187	25	2	12	68	1	0	0	5	24	1	4	74	3	4	0	.491	.368	12
		R	.000	24	3	0	0	0	0	0	0	1	0	0	0	0	0	0	0	0	0	0	0	.000	.000	0

BATTER	TEAM	B	AVG	G	AB	R	H	TB	2B	3B	HR	RBI	SH	SF	HP	BB	IBB	SO	SB	CS	GI DP	SLG	OBP	E
Boskie, S	CHI-PHI	R	.115	21	26	2	3	6	0	0	1	2	0	0	0	0	0	7	0	0	0	.231	.207	1
Bottenfield, K	COL-SF	R	.000	16	1	0	0	0	0	0	0	0	1	0	0	0	0	0	0	0	0	.000	.000	1
Boucher, D	MON	R	.333	10	3	1	1	1	0	0	0	0	0	0	0	0	0	0	0	0	0	.333	.333	0
Bournigal, R	LA	R	.224	40	116	4	26	31	3	1	0	11	5	0	0	9	0	5	0	0	4	.267	.291	3
Bowen, R	FLA	R	.357	8	14	2	5	7	2	0	0	0	0	0	0	0	0	4	0	0	0	.500	.400	0
Branson, J	CIN	L	.284	58	109	18	31	55	4	1	6	16	2	0	0	5	2	16	0	0	4	.505	.316	1
Brantley, J	CIN	R	.000	50	3	0	0	0	0	0	0	0	0	0	0	0	0	1	0	0	0	.000	.250	0
Bream, S	HOU	L	.344	46	61	7	21	26	0	0	1	7	0	0	0	9	2	9	0	1	2	.426	.429	1
Brink, B	SF	R	.000	4	1	0	0	0	0	0	0	0	0	0	0	0	0	0	0	0	0	.000	.000	0
Brocail, D	SD	L	.000	14	2	2	0	0	0	0	0	0	1	0	0	0	0	1	0	0	0	.000	.000	1
Brogna, R	NY	L	.351	39	131	16	46	82	11	2	7	20	1	0	0	6	0	29	0	0	2	.626	.380	0
Brown, J	ATL	R	.133	17	15	3	2	6	1	0	1	1	1	0	0	0	0	6	0	0	0	.400	.133	0
Browne, J	FLA	S	.295	101	329	42	97	131	17	4	3	30	3	2	2	52	0	23	3	1	5	.398	.392	15
Browning, T	CIN	L	.143	7	14	1	2	3	1	0	0	0	2	0	0	0	0	6	0	0	0	.214	.143	0
Brumfield, J	CIN	R	.311	68	122	36	38	64	10	2	4	11	2	0	2	15	0	18	6	3	3	.525	.381	1
Buckels, G	STL	S	.000	10	1	0	0	0	0	0	0	0	0	0	0	0	0	0	0	0	0	.000	.000	0
Buechele, S	CHI	R	.242	104	339	33	82	137	11	1	14	52	2	4	3	39	2	80	1	0	8	.404	.325	5
Bullinger, J	CHI	R	.136	33	22	0	3	5	2	0	0	2	5	0	0	2	0	8	0	0	0	.227	.208	0
Burba, D	SF	R	.000	57	3	0	0	0	0	0	0	0	0	0	0	0	0	0	0	0	0	.000	.000	0
Burkett, J	SF	R	.059	25	51	1	3	3	0	0	0	0	3	0	0	1	0	21	0	0	1	.059	.077	3
Burks, E	COL	R	.322	42	149	33	48	101	8	3	13	24	0	1	0	16	3	39	3	1	3	.678	.388	2
Burnitz, J	NY	L	.238	45	143	26	34	47	3	2	3	15	1	2	0	23	0	45	6	0	1	.329	.347	2
Butler, B	LA	L	.314	111	417	79	131	186	13	9	8	33	7	2	2	68	3	52	27	8	2	.446	.411	2
Caminiti, K	HOU	S	.283	111	406	63	115	201	28	2	18	75	0	3	2	43	13	71	4	3	8	.495	.352	9
Campbell, M	SD	R	.333	3	3	0	1	1	0	0	0	0	0	0	0	0	0	1	0	0	0	.333	.333	0
Candiotti, T	LA	R	.140	23	50	2	7	8	1	0	0	2	3	0	0	0	0	9	0	0	0	.160	.157	0
Cangelosi, J	NY	S	.252	62	111	14	28	32	1	0	1	4	3	0	2	19	1	20	5	1	1	.288	.371	0
Carr, C	FLA	S	.263	106	433	61	114	143	19	2	2	30	6	2	5	22	1	71	32	8	5	.330	.305	0
Carrasco, H	CIN	R	.000	45	6	0	0	0	0	0	0	0	0	0	0	0	0	4	0	0	0	.000	.000	6
Carreon, M	SF	R	.270	51	100	8	27	40	4	0	3	20	0	2	2	7	0	20	0	0	1	.400	.324	1

OFFICIAL NATIONAL LEAGUE STATS • 381

Player	Team	B	AVG	G	AB	R	H	2B	3B	HR	RBI	SH	SF	HP	BB	SO	SB	CS	GDP	SLG	OBP	E
Carrillo, M.	FLA	L	.250	80	136	13	34	7	0	0	9	0	0	1	0	31	3	3	5	.301	.295	1
Carter, A.	PHI	L	.000	20	6	0	0	0	0	0	0	0	0	0	0	3	0	0	0	.000	.000	0
Castilla, V.	COL	R	.331	52	130	16	43	11	1	3	18	0	0	0	7	23	2	1	3	.500	.357	2
Castillo, F.	CHI	R	.000	4	9	0	0	0	0	0	0	1	0	0	0	4	0	0	0	.000	.100	2
Castillo, J.	NY	R	.200	2	5	0	1	0	0	0	1	0	0	0	0	1	0	0	0	.200	.200	0
Cedeno, A.	HOU	R	.263	98	342	38	90	26	0	2	49	0	1	0	8	79	1	1	5	.418	.334	23
Chamberlain, W.	PHI	R	.275	24	69	4	19	5	0	2	6	0	0	0	9	12	0	0	1	.435	.306	0
Cianfrocco, A.	SD	R	.219	59	146	9	32	8	0	4	13	0	1	2	4	36	0	2	2	.356	.252	7
Cimorelli, F.	STL	R	.000	11	2	0	0	0	0	0	0	1	0	0	0	0	0	0	0	.000	.000	2
Clark, D.	PIT	L	.296	86	223	37	66	11	1	10	46	1	3	0	22	48	0	2	5	.489	.355	2
Clark, P.	SD	R	.215	61	149	14	32	6	0	5	20	3	0	3	5	17	1	1	3	.356	.250	3
Clayton, R.	SF	R	.236	108	385	38	91	14	6	3	30	3	3	2	30	74	23	3	7	.327	.295	14
Colbrunn, G.	FLA	R	.303	47	155	17	47	10	0	6	31	0	2	2	9	27	1	1	3	.484	.345	4
Conine, J.	FLA	R	.319	115	451	60	144	27	6	18	82	0	4	4	40	92	2	2	8	.525	.373	6
Cooke, S.	PIT	R	.190	25	42	2	8	0	1	0	6	5	0	0	0	12	0	0	0	.214	.190	1
Coolbaugh, S.	STL	R	.190	15	21	4	4	0	0	0	2	0	0	0	1	4	0	0	3	.476	.217	0
Cordero, W.	MON	R	.294	110	415	65	122	30	3	15	63	3	2	3	41	62	16	8	8	.489	.363	22
Cormier, R.	STL	L	.286	8	14	2	4	0	0	0	1	6	0	0	0	2	0	0	0	.286	.375	0
Crim, C.	CHI	R	.000	49	2	0	0	0	0	0	0	0	0	0	0	0	0	0	0	.000	.000	1
Cromer, T.	STL	R	.000	2	0	1	0	0	0	0	0	0	0	0	0	0	0	0	0	.000	.000	2
Cummings, M.	PIT	L	.244	24	86	11	21	4	1	2	12	0	0	0	4	18	0	1	2	.326	.283	3
Daulton, D.	PHI	L	.300	69	257	43	77	17	3	15	56	0	2	1	33	43	4	1	9	.549	.380	7
DeShields, D.	LA	S	.250	89	320	51	103	11	3	2	33	2	0	0	54	53	27	7	2	.322	.357	5
Destrade, O.	FLA	R	.208	39	130	12	27	4	0	5	15	0	0	0	19	32	1	0	2	.354	.316	1
Dewey, M.	PIT	R	1.000	45	1	1	1	0	0	0	0	0	0	0	0	0	0	0	0	1.000	1.000	1
Diaz, M.	FLA	R	.325	32	77	10	25	4	0	2	11	1	0	0	6	6	0	0	1	.429	.376	4
Donnels, C.	HOU	L	.267	54	86	12	23	7	0	0	5	1	0	0	13	18	1	0	1	.430	.364	0
Dorsett, B.	CIN	R	.245	76	216	23	53	8	0	5	26	2	1	2	21	33	0	0	10	.352	.313	4
Drabek, D.	HOU	R	.241	24	58	21	14	4	0	0	6	6	0	0	2	10	0	0	0	.276	.262	3
Dreifort, D.	LA	R	1.000	28	1	0	1	0	0	0	1	0	0	0	0	0	0	0	0	1.000	1.000	0
Duncan, M.	PHI	R	.268	88	347	49	93	22	1	8	48	2	4	1	17	72	10	4	2	.406	.306	12
Dunston, S.	CHI	R	.278	88	331	38	92	19	0	11	35	5	2	3	16	48	3	8	4	.435	.313	12

BATTER	TEAM	B	AVG	G	AB	R	H	TB	2B	3B	HR	RBI	SH	SF	HP	BB	IBB	SO	SB	CS	GI DP	SLG	OBP	E
Dyer, M.	PIT	R	.000	14	1	0	0	0	0	0	0	0	0	0	0	0	0	0	0	0	0	.000	.000	0
Dykstra, L.	PHI	L	.273	84	315	68	86	137	26	5	5	24	0	1	2	68	11	44	15	4	3	.435	.404	4
Edens, T.	HOU-PHI	L	.000	42	2	0	0	0	0	0	0	0	1	0	0	0	0	1	0	0	0	.000	.000	0
Eisenreich, J.	PHI	L	.300	104	290	42	87	122	15	4	4	43	3	2	1	33	3	31	6	2	8	.421	.371	2
Elliott, D.	SD	R	.000	30	0	0	0	0	0	0	0	0	0	0	0	0	0	0	0	0	0	.000	.000	0
Eusebio, T.	HOU	R	.296	55	159	18	47	73	9	1	5	30	2	5	0	8	0	33	0	1	4	.459	.320	2
Everett, C.	FLA	S	.216	16	51	7	11	18	1	0	2	6	0	0	0	3	0	15	0	0	0	.353	.259	0
Eversgerd, B.	STL	S	.000	40	6	0	0	0	0	0	0	0	6	0	0	0	0	3	0	0	0	.000	.000	2
Faneyte, R.	SF	R	.115	19	26	0	3	6	0	0	1	4	2	0	0	3	0	11	0	0	0	.231	.207	0
Fassero, J.	MON	L	.068	21	44	1	3	5	0	1	0	0	9	0	0	2	0	27	0	0	1	.114	.109	1
Felder, M.	HOU	S	.239	58	117	16	28	34	3	0	1	13	2	0	0	4	0	12	3	0	1	.291	.264	0
Fernandez, T.	CIN	S	.279	104	366	50	102	156	18	6	8	50	4	3	5	44	8	40	12	7	5	.426	.361	4
Finley, S.	HOU	L	.276	94	373	64	103	162	16	5	11	33	13	1	2	28	0	52	13	7	3	.434	.329	4
Fletcher, D.	MON	L	.260	94	285	28	74	124	18	1	10	57	0	12	3	25	4	23	0	0	6	.435	.314	2
Floyd, C.	MON	L	.281	100	334	43	94	133	19	4	4	41	2	3	3	24	2	63	10	3	6	.398	.332	6
Foley, T.	PIT	L	.236	89	123	13	29	45	7	0	3	15	3	0	0	13	0	18	0	0	3	.366	.307	3
Fortugno, T.	CIN	L	.333	25	3	0	1	1	0	0	0	0	0	0	0	0	0	2	0	0	0	.333	.333	0
Foster, K.	CHI	R	.074	13	27	2	2	2	0	0	0	0	3	0	0	0	0	12	0	0	1	.074	.107	0
Franco, J.	NY	L	.000	47	3	0	0	0	0	0	0	0	0	0	0	0	0	3	0	0	0	.000	.000	0
Frascatore, J.	STL	R	.000	1	0	0	0	0	0	0	0	0	0	0	0	0	0	0	0	0	0	.000	.000	1
Frazier, L.	MON	S	.271	76	140	25	38	43	3	1	0	10	1	0	2	18	0	23	20	4	1	.307	.358	0
Freeman, M.	COL	R	.111	19	36	5	4	8	1	0	1	3	3	0	0	2	1	21	0	0	0	.222	.179	0
Galarraga, A.	COL	R	.319	103	417	77	133	247	21	0	31	85	0	5	8	19	8	93	8	3	10	.592	.356	8
Gallagher, D.	ATL	R	.224	89	152	27	34	45	2	0	3	14	2	1	1	22	0	17	0	2	5	.296	.326	0
Garcia, C.	PIT	R	.277	98	412	49	114	151	15	5	2	28	1	1	4	16	2	67	18	9	6	.367	.309	8
Gardner, J.	MON	L	.219	18	32	4	7	9	0	1	0	1	0	0	0	3	0	5	0	0	1	.281	.286	1
Gardner, M.	FLA	R	.040	20	25	0	1	1	0	0	0	0	4	0	0	1	0	10	0	0	0	.040	.077	2
Gilkey, B.	STL	R	.253	105	380	52	96	138	22	1	6	45	0	2	10	39	0	65	15	8	6	.363	.336	2
Girardi, J.	COL	R	.276	93	330	47	91	120	9	4	4	34	6	2	2	21	2	48	3	3	13	.364	.321	5
Glavine, T.	ATL	L	.179	26	56	4	10	11	1	0	0	3	9	0	0	5	0	15	0	0	0	.196	.246	1

OFFICIAL NATIONAL LEAGUE STATS • 383

Player	Tm	B	AVG	G	AB	R	H	2B	3B	HR	RBI	BB	SO	SB	CS	GDP	OBP	SLG	E
Goff, J	PIT	L	.080	8	25	0	2	0	0	0	0	1	11	0	0	0	0	1	.080	.080	2
Gomez, P	SF	L	.000	26	2	0	0	0	0	0	0	0	0	0	0	0	0	.000	.000	1
Gonzalez, L	HOU	L	.273	112	392	57	107	29	8	8	67	45	57	15	13	10	.353	.429	2
Gooden, D	NY	R	.167	7	12	1	2	0	0	0	0	2	1	0	0	0	0	.167	.167	1
Gozzo, M	NY	R	.250	23	16	1	4	2	0	0	3	0	3	0	0	0	0	.313	.294	0
Grace, M	CHI	L	.298	106	403	55	120	23	4	6	44	48	41	0	4	10	.370	.414	7
Greene, T	PHI	L	.385	7	13	2	5	0	0	0	0	0	4	0	0	0	2	.429	.462	0
Greene, W	CIN	L	.216	16	37	5	8	3	0	0	3	1	14	0	1	0	0	.270	.318	3
Grissom, M	MON	L	.288	110	475	96	137	25	4	11	45	6	66	36	6	6	.427	.344	5
Gross, K	LA	R	.149	25	47	2	7	2	0	0	1	1	18	0	0	1	.213	.200	1
Gutierrez, R	SD	R	.240	90	275	27	66	11	2	1	28	2	32	3	0	2	6	.305	.321	22
Guzman, J	CHI	R	.000	8	8	0	0	0	0	0	0	0	4	0	0	0	0	.000	.111	0
Gwynn, C	LA	L	.268	58	71	9	19	3	0	3	13	5	7	0	2	0	1	.333	.394	0
Gwynn, T	SD	L	.394	110	419	79	165	35	1	12	64	48	19	0	0	5	0	.454	.568	3
Habyan, J	STL	R	.000	52	0	0	0	0	0	0	0	0	0	16	0	0	0	.000	1.000	1
Hamilton, J	SD	L	.000	16	40	0	0	0	0	0	0	1	24	0	0	0	0	.000	.047	1
Hammond, C	FLA	L	.136	13	22	1	3	0	1	0	0	0	12	0	0	0	0	.182	.208	1
Hampton, M	HOU	R	.000	44	1	0	0	0	0	0	0	0	1	0	0	0	0	.000	.000	0
Haney, T	CHI	R	.162	17	37	6	6	0	0	0	1	2	3	2	2	1	0	.243	.238	0
Hansen, D	LA	R	.341	40	44	3	15	3	0	1	5	4	5	0	0	0	0	.409	.408	6
Hanson, E	CIN	R	.154	22	39	6	6	1	0	0	1	2	17	0	0	2	.179	.154	0
Hare, S	NY	R	.225	22	40	7	9	1	1	0	2	3	11	0	0	0	4	.300	.295	0
Harkey, M	COL	R	.182	24	22	1	4	0	0	0	3	2	8	0	0	0	2	.182	.182	6
Harnisch, P	HOU	R	.171	18	35	5	6	3	0	0	2	0	10	0	0	0	4	.257	.171	0
Harris, G	COL	R	.175	29	40	2	7	0	0	0	2	0	15	0	0	0	1	.225	.214	17
Harris, G	SD	R	.000	13	0	0	0	0	0	0	0	0	0	0	0	0	0	.000	.000	0
Harris, L	CIN	L	.310	66	100	13	31	3	0	1	14	5	13	0	2	2	0	.360	.340	6
Hatcher, B	PHI	R	.246	43	134	15	33	5	1	2	13	6	14	7	1	1	4	.343	.271	0
Hayes, C	COL	R	.288	113	423	46	122	23	4	10	50	5	36	71	3	6	0	.433	.348	17
Henderson, R	MON	R	.000	3	1	0	0	0	0	0	0	0	0	1	0	0	0	.000	.000	0
Henry, B	MON	L	.290	24	31	0	9	1	0	0	2	0	6	0	0	0	1	.323	.353	0
Heredia, G	MON	R	.313	39	16	5	5	0	0	0	1	0	2	0	0	0	0	.313	.313	1

BATTER	TEAM	B	AVG	G	AB	R	H	TB	2B	3B	HR	RBI	SH	SF	HP	BB	IBB	SO	SB	CS	GIDP	SLG	OBP	E
Hernandez, C	LA	R	.219	32	64	6	14	22	2	0	2	6	0	0	0	0	0	14	0	0	0	.344	.231	0
Hernandez, J	FLA	R	.000	21	1	0	0	0	0	0	0	0	0	0	0	0	0	0	0	0	0	.000	.000	4
Hernandez, J	CHI	R	.242	56	132	18	32	43	3	0	2	9	5	2	1	8	0	29	2	2	4	.326	.291	2
Hershiser, O	LA	R	.205	22	44	4	9	9	0	0	0	4	3	2	0	2	0	10	1	0	0	.205	.245	2
Hickerson, B	SF	L	.185	28	27	1	5	6	1	0	0	0	2	0	0	1	0	9	0	0	0	.222	.241	0
Hill, G	CHI	R	.297	89	269	48	80	124	12	1	10	38	0	1	0	29	0	57	19	6	5	.461	.365	2
Hill, K	MON	R	.146	24	48	1	7	7	0	0	0	2	16	0	0	3	0	17	0	0	0	.146	.196	2
Hillman, E	NY	L	.000	11	8	0	0	0	0	0	0	0	0	0	0	0	0	4	0	0	0	.000	.000	0
Hoffman, T	SD	R	.000	47	3	0	0	0	0	0	0	0	1	0	0	0	0	0	0	0	0	.000	.000	0
Holbert, R	SD	R	.200	5	5	0	1	1	0	0	0	0	0	0	0	0	0	4	0	0	0	.200	.200	0
Hollins, D	PHI	S	.222	44	162	28	36	57	7	1	4	26	0	3	4	23	0	32	1	2	6	.352	.328	11
Holmes, D	COL	R	.000	29	1	0	0	0	0	0	0	0	0	0	0	0	0	1	0	0	0	.000	.000	1
Hope, J	PIT	R	.333	9	3	0	1	1	0	0	0	0	0	0	0	0	0	1	0	0	0	.333	.333	0
Hough, C	FLA	R	.121	21	33	1	4	4	0	0	0	0	4	0	0	1	0	9	0	0	3	.121	.147	0
Howard, T	CIN	S	.264	83	178	24	47	73	11	0	5	24	3	0	0	10	1	30	4	0	3	.410	.302	0
Hubbard, T	COL	R	.280	18	25	3	7	13	1	1	1	3	0	0	0	3	0	4	0	2	0	.520	.357	0
Hundley, T	NY	S	.237	91	291	45	69	129	10	1	16	42	0	3	1	25	4	73	2	1	1	.443	.303	5
Hunter, B	HOU	R	.250	6	24	2	6	7	1	0	0	0	0	0	0	1	0	6	2	0	0	.292	.280	1
Hunter, B	PIT-CIN	R	.234	85	256	34	60	123	16	1	15	57	1	0	0	17	2	56	0	0	3	.480	.277	5
Hyers, T	SD	L	.254	52	118	13	30	33	3	0	0	7	2	0	0	9	0	15	3	0	1	.280	.307	4
Ilsley, B	CHI	L	.000	10	1	0	0	0	0	0	0	0	0	0	0	0	0	0	0	0	0	.000	.000	0
Incaviglia, P	PHI	R	.230	80	244	28	56	107	10	1	13	32	0	2	1	16	3	71	1	0	3	.439	.278	2
Ingram, G	LA	R	.282	26	78	10	22	32	2	1	2	8	8	1	0	7	3	22	3	2	3	.410	.341	2
Jackson, D	PHI	R	.158	26	57	2	9	13	2	1	0	3	7	2	0	2	0	24	0	0	1	.228	.186	0
Jackson, M	SF	R	.000	36	1	0	0	0	0	0	0	0	0	0	0	0	0	0	0	0	0	.000	.000	2
Jacome, J	NY	R	.063	8	16	0	1	1	0	0	0	0	5	0	0	0	0	9	0	0	0	.063	.063	0
Jarvis, K	CIN	L	.250	6	4	0	1	1	0	0	0	1	0	0	0	0	0	1	0	0	0	.250	.250	0
Jefferies, G	STL	S	.325	103	397	52	129	194	27	1	12	55	1	4	1	45	12	26	12	5	9	.489	.391	7
Johnson, B	SD	R	.247	36	93	7	23	38	4	1	3	16	2	1	0	5	0	21	0	0	4	.409	.283	0
Johnson, C	FLA	R	.455	4	11	5	5	9	1	0	1	4	0	1	1	1	0	4	0	0	1	.818	.462	0

OFFICIAL NATIONAL LEAGUE STATS • 385

Player	Team	B	AVG	G	AB	R	H	2B	3B	HR	RBI	SH	SF	HBP	BB	SO	SB	CS	OBP	SLG	E
Johnson, E	SF	R	.154	5	13	0	2	0	0	0	0	0	0	0	0	4	0	0	.154	.154	0
Johnson, H	COL	S	.211	93	227	30	48	9	2	2	10	2	0	2	39	73	11	3	.405	.323	2
Johnstone, J	FLA	R	.000	17	0	0	0	0	0	0	0	0	0	0	0	0	0	0	.000	.000	0
Jones, B	NY	R	.109	24	46	3	5	1	0	0	2	1	0	1	8	19	0	3	.130	.109	1
Jones, C	COL	R	.300	21	40	6	12	2	1	0	3	0	0	0	2	14	0	1	.400	.333	0
Jones, D	PHI	R	1.000	1	1	0	1	0	0	0	0	0	0	0	0	0	0	0	1.000	1.000	0
Jones, T	HOU	L	.400	48	5	0	2	0	0	0	0	0	0	0	0	0	0	0	.400	.400	0
Jordan, B	STL	R	.258	53	178	14	46	8	2	2	15	2	1	0	16	40	4	3	.410	.320	6
Jordan, R	PHI	R	.282	72	220	29	62	10	1	1	37	2	2	1	6	32	2	0	.473	.303	7
Juden, J	PHI	S	.111	6	9	0	1	0	0	0	0	2	0	0	1	6	0	0	.111	.111	3
Justice, D	ATL	L	.313	104	352	61	110	19	0	16	59	0	2	3	69	45	5	2	.531	.427	8
Karros, E	LA	R	.266	111	406	51	108	21	1	11	46	0	1	11	29	53	0	2	.426	.310	13
Kelly, M	ATL	R	.273	30	77	14	21	2	1	0	9	1	1	0	2	17	0	1	.506	.300	9
Kelly, R	CIN-ATL	R	.293	110	434	73	127	23	3	9	45	3	3	3	35	71	19	8	.422	.347	8
Kent, J	NY	R	.292	107	415	53	121	24	5	14	68	5	1	1	23	84	1	0	.475	.341	7
Kile, D	HOU	R	.149	24	47	3	7	1	2	0	2	9	0	0	0	28	0	0	.234	.167	0
King, J	PIT	R	.263	94	339	36	89	23	0	5	42	0	2	7	30	38	3	5	.375	.316	13
Kingery, M	COL	R	.349	105	301	56	105	27	8	4	41	8	1	0	30	26	5	1	.532	.402	4
Klesko, R	ATL	L	.278	92	245	42	68	13	3	23	47	0	2	8	26	48	1	0	.563	.344	7
Krueger, B	SD	L	.500	8	12	1	6	1	0	0	2	3	0	0	0	3	0	0	.583	.500	0
Kruk, J	PHI	L	.302	75	255	35	77	17	0	6	38	0	4	4	42	51	4	1	.427	.395	3
Lankford, R	STL	L	.267	109	416	89	111	25	5	21	57	5	4	7	58	113	11	10	.488	.359	6
Lansing, M	MON	R	.266	106	394	44	105	21	2	3	30	9	2	5	30	37	12	8	.368	.328	10
Larkin, B	CIN	R	.279	110	427	78	119	24	5	12	52	5	5	0	64	58	26	6	.419	.369	10
Lemke, M	ATL	S	.294	104	350	40	103	15	0	0	31	6	3	3	38	37	0	11	.363	.363	3
Leonard, M	SF	L	.364	14	11	2	4	1	0	0	0	0	1	0	0	2	0	0	.636	.500	0
Leskanic, C	COL	R	.167	8	6	0	1	0	0	0	0	1	0	0	0	2	0	0	.333	.167	0
Lewis, D	SF	R	.257	114	451	70	116	15	9	4	29	9	4	1	53	50	30	13	.357	.340	6
Lewis, R	FLA	R	.000	45	5	1	0	0	0	0	0	0	0	0	0	1	0	0	.000	.000	3
Lieber, J	PIT	R	.103	17	39	3	4	0	0	0	0	2	0	0	0	14	0	0	.128	.125	2
Lieberthal, M	PHI	R	.266	24	79	6	21	0	3	1	7	0	0	1	5	5	0	3	.367	.301	2
Lindeman, J	NY	R	.270	52	137	18	37	8	1	7	20	1	1	1	6	35	0	0	.496	.303	4

BATTER	TEAM	B	AVG	G	AB	R	H	TB	2B	3B	HR	RBI	SH	SF	HP	BB	IBB	SO	SB	CS	GI DP	SLG	OBP	E
Linton, D	NY	R	.000	32	7	0	0	0	0	0	0	0	2	0	0	0	0	3	0	0	0	.000	.000	1
Liriano, N	COL	S	.255	87	255	39	65	101	17	5	3	31	3	3	0	42	5	44	0	2	4	.396	.357	10
Livingstone, S	SD	L	.272	57	180	11	49	69	12	1	2	10	0	1	0	6	0	22	2	0	5	.383	.294	6
Lockhart, K	SD	L	.209	27	43	4	9	15	0	0	2	6	1	1	0	4	0	10	2	1	2	.349	.286	1
Longmire, T	PHI	L	.237	69	139	10	33	44	11	0	0	17	1	2	1	10	1	27	2	1	5	.317	.289	3
Lopez, J	ATL	R	.245	80	277	27	68	116	9	0	13	35	2	2	5	17	2	61	0	0	12	.419	.299	3
Lopez, L	SD	S	.277	77	235	29	65	89	16	1	2	20	2	2	3	15	0	39	3	0	7	.379	.325	14
Mabry, J	STL	L	.304	6	23	2	7	10	3	0	0	3	0	0	0	2	0	4	0	0	0	.435	.360	0
Maddux, G	ATL	R	.222	25	63	5	14	16	2	0	0	2	9	0	0	0	0	19	0	0	2	.254	.234	4
Maddux, M	NY	L	.000	27	3	0	0	0	0	0	0	0	3	0	0	0	0	2	0	0	0	.000	.000	1
Magadan, D	FLA	L	.275	74	211	30	58	68	7	0	1	17	0	3	1	39	6	25	0	0	8	.322	.386	4
Maksudian, M	CHI	L	.269	26	26	6	7	9	2	0	0	4	0	0	0	10	0	4	0	1	0	.346	.472	0
Manwaring, K	SF	R	.250	97	316	30	79	101	17	0	1	29	4	3	3	25	3	50	1	1	10	.320	.308	4
Manzanillo, J	NY	R	.000	37	4	0	0	0	0	0	0	0	0	0	0	0	0	2	0	0	0	.000	.000	0
Manzanillo, R	PIT	R	.667	46	3	0	2	3	1	0	0	0	0	0	0	0	0	0	0	0	0	1.000	.667	1
Marsh, T	PHI	L	.278	8	18	3	5	8	0	0	1	3	0	0	0	1	0	1	0	0	0	.444	.316	1
Martin, A	PIT	L	.286	82	276	48	79	126	12	4	9	33	2	1	2	34	3	56	15	6	3	.457	.367	3
Martinez, D	SF	L	.247	97	235	23	58	85	9	3	4	27	0	2	2	21	1	22	3	4	6	.362	.314	3
Martinez, J	SD	R	.000	4	2	0	0	0	0	0	0	0	0	0	0	0	0	1	0	0	0	.000	.000	0
Martinez, P	SD	R	.000	48	5	0	0	0	0	0	0	0	5	0	0	0	0	2	0	0	0	.000	.000	0
Martinez, P	MON	R	.091	24	44	1	4	6	0	1	0	0	5	1	0	3	0	21	0	0	1	.136	.146	4
Martinez, R	LA	L	.273	24	66	4	18	21	0	0	1	5	0	0	0	0	0	18	0	2	0	.318	.284	4
Mathews, T	FLA	L	.500	24	6	1	3	4	1	0	0	3	5	0	0	0	0	2	0	0	1	.667	.500	3
Mauser, T	SD	R	.250	35	4	0	1	1	0	0	0	0	1	0	0	1	0	3	0	0	0	.250	.400	0
May, D	CHI	L	.284	100	345	43	98	145	19	2	8	51	1	2	0	30	4	34	3	2	11	.420	.340	1
McClendon, L	PIT	R	.239	51	92	9	22	38	4	0	4	12	0	1	1	4	1	11	3	0	1	.413	.278	0
McDavid, R	SD	L	.250	9	28	2	7	8	1	0	0	2	0	0	0	0	0	8	1	0	0	.286	.276	1
McDowell, R	LA	R	.000	32	6	0	0	0	0	0	0	0	0	0	0	0	0	1	0	0	0	.000	.000	0
McElroy, C	CIN	L	.167	52	6	0	1	1	0	0	0	1	0	0	0	0	0	3	0	0	0	.167	.167	0
McGee, W	SF	S	.282	45	156	19	44	62	3	0	5	23	0	1	4	15	2	24	3	0	8	.397	.337	1

OFFICIAL NATIONAL LEAGUE STATS

Player	Team	B	AVG	G	AB	R	H	TB	2B	3B	HR	RBI	SH	SF	HP	BB	IBB	SO	GDP	SB	CS	SLG	OBP	E
McGriff, F	ATL	L	.318	113	424	81	135	264	25	1	34	94	0	3	1	50	8	76	7	3	8	.623	.389	7
McGriff, T	STL	R	.219	42	114	10	25	31	6	0	0	13	1	1	1	2	13	11	0	0	0	.272	.308	2
McKnight, J	NY	S	.148	31	27	1	4	5	1	0	0	0	0	1	0	0	2	12	0	0	0	.185	.250	0
McMichael, G	ATL	R	.000	51	0	0	0	0	0	0	0	0	0	0	0	0	0	0	0	0	0	.000	.000	2
McReynolds, K	NY	R	.256	51	180	23	46	73	11	0	4	21	0	2	1	20	0	34	2	0	2	.406	.328	0
Mejia, R	COL	R	.241	38	116	11	28	50	8	1	0	14	1	2	1	15	0	33	3	0	2	.431	.326	7
Merced, O	PIT	L	.272	108	386	48	105	159	21	3	9	51	1	5	1	42	5	58	4	0	17	.412	.343	5
Mercker, K	ATL	L	.054	20	37	0	2	2	0	0	0	0	3	0	0	2	0	15	0	0	0	.054	.100	0
Miceli, D	PIT	R	.000	28	0	0	0	0	0	0	0	0	0	0	0	0	0	0	0	0	0	.000	.000	0
Miller, K	FLA	R	.167	4	6	0	1	1	0	0	0	0	0	0	0	0	0	2	0	0	1	.167	.167	0
Miller, O	HOU	R	.325	16	40	3	13	21	2	0	2	9	0	1	0	2	0	2	0	2	0	.525	.386	4
Milligan, R	MON	R	.232	47	82	10	19	27	2	0	2	12	0	1	0	14	0	21	1	0	0	.329	.337	0
Minor, B	PIT	R	.000	17	0	0	0	0	0	0	0	0	0	0	0	0	0	0	0	0	0	.000	.000	0
Mitchell, K	CIN	R	.326	95	310	57	101	211	18	2	30	77	0	3	0	8	2	62	2	0	12	.681	.429	4
Mondesi, R	LA	R	.306	112	434	63	133	224	27	8	16	56	0	6	0	26	2	78	11	5	9	.516	.333	8
Monteleone, R	SF	R	.000	39	3	0	0	0	0	0	0	0	0	0	0	0	0	0	0	0	0	.000	.000	0
Moore, M	COL	S	.000	29	1	0	0	0	0	0	0	0	0	0	0	0	0	1	0	0	0	.000	.000	0
Morandini, M	PHI	L	.292	87	274	40	80	112	16	6	0	26	5	2	1	34	0	33	10	0	4	.409	.378	6
Mordecai, M	ATL	R	.250	4	4	1	1	3	1	0	0	2	0	0	0	1	0	0	0	0	0	1.000	.400	0
Morgan, M	CHI	R	.125	15	24	1	3	3	0	0	0	0	4	0	0	4	0	10	0	0	1	.125	.160	0
Morman, R	FLA	R	.212	13	33	2	7	12	2	0	1	2	0	0	0	1	0	4	0	0	1	.364	.278	3
Morris, H	CIN	L	.335	112	436	60	146	214	30	4	10	78	0	2	2	46	8	62	6	0	16	.491	.385	8
Mouton, J	HOU	R	.245	99	310	43	76	93	11	2	0	16	2	1	0	1	0	69	24	0	6	.300	.315	3
Munoz, B	PHI	R	.206	21	34	3	7	10	0	0	1	6	0	1	1	0	0	11	0	0	0	.294	.229	1
Mutis, J	FLA	L	.000	35	0	0	0	0	0	0	0	0	0	0	0	0	0	0	0	0	0	.000	.000	1
Myers, R	CHI	L	.000	38	1	0	0	0	0	0	0	0	0	0	0	0	0	1	0	0	0	.000	.000	1
Natal, R	FLA	R	.276	11	29	0	8	10	2	0	0	2	0	0	0	5	0	5	0	0	1	.345	.382	0
Neagle, D	PIT	L	.190	24	42	2	8	11	0	0	1	7	5	0	0	0	0	13	0	0	0	.262	.190	0
Nen, R	FLA	R	.000	44	3	0	0	0	0	0	0	0	0	0	0	0	0	1	0	0	0	.000	.000	2
Nied, D	COL	R	.100	22	40	0	4	4	0	0	0	2	4	0	0	1	0	15	0	0	0	.100	.122	0
Nieves, M	SD	S	.263	10	19	2	5	9	0	0	1	3	0	0	0	0	0	10	0	0	0	.474	.364	0
Noboa, J	PIT	R	.000	2	2	0	0	0	0	0	0	0	0	0	0	0	0	0	0	0	0	.000	.000	0

388 • THE COMPLETE HANDBOOK OF BASEBALL

BATTER	TEAM	B	AVG	G	AB	R	H	TB	2B	3B	HR	RBI	SH	SF	HP	BB	IBB	SO	SB	CS	GI DP	SLG	OBP	E
O'Brien, C	ATL	R	.243	51	152	24	37	72	11	0	8	28	1	1	3	15	2	24	0	0	5	.474	.322	3
Offerman, J	LA	S	.210	72	243	27	51	70	8	4	1	25	6	2	0	38	4	38	2	1	6	.288	.314	11
O'Halloran, G	FLA	L	.182	12	11	1	2	2	0	0	0	1	0	0	0	0	0	1	0	0	0	.182	.167	0
Oliva, J	ATL	R	.288	19	59	9	17	40	5	0	6	11	0	0	0	7	0	10	0	0	2	.678	.364	3
Olivares, O	STL	R	.214	15	28	4	6	9	0	0	1	3	2	0	0	0	0	8	0	0	0	.321	.241	0
Oliver, J	CIN	R	.211	6	19	1	4	7	0	0	1	5	0	0	0	2	1	3	0	0	0	.368	.286	1
Olson, G	ATL	R	.000	1	1	0	0	0	0	0	0	0	0	0	0	0	0	1	0	0	0	.000	.000	0
Oquendo, J	STL	S	.264	55	129	13	34	40	2	2	0	9	1	1	0	21	4	16	1	1	6	.310	.364	4
Orsulak, J	NY	L	.260	96	292	39	76	103	3	0	8	42	0	3	3	16	2	21	4	2	11	.353	.364	3
Otto, D	CHI	L	.000	36	2	0	0	0	0	0	0	0	6	0	0	0	0	1	0	0	0	.000	.000	1
Owens, J	COL	L	.250	6	12	4	3	5	0	1	0	1	0	0	0	3	0	3	0	0	1	.417	.400	0
Pagnozzi, T	STL	R	.272	70	243	21	66	101	12	1	7	40	0	2	0	21	5	39	0	1	3	.416	.327	3
Painter, L	COL	L	.143	15	21	3	3	4	1	0	0	2	3	0	0	0	0	10	0	0	1	.190	.130	1
Palacios, V	STL	R	.000	31	33	0	0	0	0	0	0	0	2	0	0	0	0	15	0	0	0	.000	.000	0
Pappas, E	CHI	R	.091	15	44	3	4	5	1	0	0	5	2	0	1	10	1	13	0	0	1	.114	.259	2
Parent, M	CHI	R	.263	44	99	8	26	39	4	0	3	16	1	0	0	12	3	24	0	1	5	.394	.348	4
Parker, R	NY	R	.063	8	16	1	1	1	0	0	0	0	0	0	1	1	0	2	0	1	0	.063	.063	5
Parrish, L	PIT	R	.270	40	126	10	34	48	5	0	3	16	1	1	1	18	1	28	0	0	5	.381	.363	0
Patterson, J	SF	S	.238	85	240	36	57	78	10	1	3	32	7	1	1	16	1	43	13	3	4	.325	.315	4
Pecota, B	ATL	R	.214	64	112	11	24	35	5	0	2	16	2	1	0	16	0	16	5	1	3	.313	.310	6
Pegues, S	CIN-PIT	R	.361	18	36	2	13	15	2	0	0	2	0	0	0	2	0	5	1	0	3	.417	.395	2
Pena, A	PIT	R	.000	22	1	0	0	0	0	0	0	0	0	0	0	0	0	1	0	0	0	.000	.000	1
Pena, G	STL	S	.254	83	213	33	54	102	13	1	11	34	4	0	6	24	0	54	9	1	3	.479	.344	6
Pendleton, T	ATL	S	.252	77	309	25	78	123	18	3	7	30	3	0	0	12	3	57	2	0	8	.398	.280	2
Pennyfeather, W	PIT	R	.000	4	3	0	0	0	0	0	0	0	0	0	0	0	0	0	0	0	0	.000	.000	0
Perez, Y	FLA	L	.000	44	2	0	0	0	0	0	0	0	0	0	0	0	0	2	0	0	0	.000	.000	0
Perry, G	STL	L	.325	60	77	12	25	41	7	0	3	18	0	0	1	15	0	12	1	0	4	.532	.435	0
Petagine, S	HOU	L	.000	8	7	0	0	0	0	0	0	0	0	0	0	0	0	3	0	0	0	.000	.125	1
Phillips, J	SF	R	.132	15	38	1	5	8	0	0	1	3	0	0	0	1	0	13	0	0	1	.211	.150	0
Piazza, M	LA	R	.319	107	405	64	129	219	18	0	24	92	0	2	1	33	10	65	1	3	11	.541	.370	10

OFFICIAL NATIONAL LEAGUE STATS · 389

Player	B	AVG	G	AB	R	H	2B	3B	HR	RBI	BB	IBB	SO	SB	CS	SLG	OBP
Plesac, D..........CHI	L	.000	54	4	0	0	0	0	0	0	0	0	3	0	0	.000	.000
Portugal, M........SF	R	.354	21	48	4	17	2	0	0	8	4	0	3	0	0	.500	.360
Pratt, T...........PHI	R	.196	28	102	10	20	2	0	5	6	9	1	29	0	1	.333	.281
Prince, T...........LA	R	.333	3	6	2	2	2	0	0	1	2	0	3	0	0	.333	.429
Pugh, T...........CIN	R	.357	10	14	2	5	1	0	0	0	0	0	2	0	0	.429	.438
Pye, E.............LA	R	.100	7	10	2	1	0	0	0	2	1	0	4	0	0	.100	.182
Quantrill, P.......PHI	L	.000	18	3	0	0	0	0	0	0	0	0	1	0	0	.000	.000
Quinlan, T........PHI	R	.200	24	35	6	7	1	2	0	3	3	1	13	0	0	.343	.263
Rapp, P............FLA	R	.122	25	41	1	5	1	0	0	0	0	0	13	0	0	.146	.122
Ready, R...........PHI	R	.381	17	42	5	16	6	0	0	8	4	1	6	1	1	.476	.480
Reed, J.............SF	L	.175	50	103	11	18	6	0	1	7	3	4	21	0	3	.233	.254
Reed, S...........COL	L	.000	61	2	0	0	0	0	0	0	0	0	1	0	0	.000	.000
Reminger, M........NY	L	.000	10	16	1	0	0	0	0	0	0	0	6	0	0	.000	.059
Renteria, R.......FLA	R	.224	28	49	5	11	2	0	2	3	2	1	4	1	0	.347	.269
Reynolds, S.......HOU	R	.091	33	33	0	3	0	0	0	2	2	0	15	0	0	.091	.118
Reynoso, A........COL	R	.176	9	17	0	3	0	0	0	0	0	0	4	0	0	.176	.222
Rhodes, K.........CHI	L	.234	95	269	39	63	17	2	8	19	33	2	64	6	4	.387	.318
Rijo, J.............CIN	R	.204	26	49	4	10	0	0	0	3	1	0	7	0	0	.286	.204
Ritz, K.............COL	R	.000	15	20	0	0	0	0	0	0	0	0	13	0	2	.000	.000
Rivera, B..........PHI	R	.000	9	9	0	0	0	0	0	0	0	0	5	0	0	.000	.100
Rivera, L...........NY	R	.279	32	43	11	12	2	0	1	5	2	0	14	0	1	.581	.367
Roberson, S.......CHI	S	.218	44	55	8	12	2	0	4	9	2	0	14	3	0	.509	.271
Roberts, B..........SD	S	.320	105	403	52	129	15	2	0	31	2	2	57	21	7	.397	.383
Robertson, R......PIT	L	.250	8	4	0	1	0	0	0	0	0	0	3	0	0	.250	.250
Rodriguez, H........LA	L	.268	104	306	33	82	14	0	8	49	17	4	58	0	0	.405	.307
Rodriguez, R......STL	L	.000	56	0	0	0	0	0	0	0	0	0	0	0	0	.000	.000
Rojas, M..........MON	R	.200	58	10	1	2	0	0	0	0	0	0	5	0	0	.200	.200
Roper, J...........CIN	R	.182	16	33	3	6	2	0	0	2	2	0	12	0	1	.316	.212
Royer, S...........STL	R	.175	33	57	3	10	3	0	1	5	2	0	18	0	2	.316	.206
Rueter, K.........MON	L	.118	20	34	1	4	1	0	0	1	2	0	8	0	0	.118	.175
Ruffin, B..........COL	S	.250	56	4	0	1	0	0	0	1	0	0	2	0	0	.250	.400

390 · THE COMPLETE HANDBOOK OF BASEBALL

BATTER	TEAM	B	AVG	G	AB	R	H	TB	2B	3B	HR	RBI	SH	SF	HP	BB	IBB	SO	SB	CS	GI DP	SLG	OBP	E
Ruffin, J	CIN	R	.000	51	8	1	0	0	0	0	0	0	0	0	0	0	0	3	1	0	0	.000	.000	0
Saberhagen, B	NY	R	.172	24	58	7	10	12	2	0	0	1	8	0	0	4	0	14	0	0	0	.207	.226	2
Sager, A	SD	R	.100	22	10	0	1	3	0	1	0	2	1	0	0	0	0	5	0	0	0	.300	.100	0
Sanchez, R	CHI	R	.285	96	291	26	83	98	13	1	0	24	4	1	0	20	4	29	2	5	9	.337	.345	9
Sandberg, R	CHI	R	.238	57	223	36	53	87	9	5	5	24	0	1	7	23	0	40	2	3	6	.390	.312	4
Sanders, D	ATL-CIN	L	.283	92	375	58	106	143	17	4	4	28	2	3	0	32	1	63	38	16	5	.381	.342	2
Sanders, R	CIN	R	.263	107	400	66	105	192	20	8	17	62	1	3	2	41	1	114	21	9	0	.480	.332	6
Sanders, S	SD	R	.125	23	32	0	4	4	0	0	0	0	0	0	0	3	0	16	1	1	2	.125	.200	0
Santiago, B	FLA	R	.273	101	337	35	92	143	14	2	11	41	6	2	1	25	0	57	0	1	11	.424	.322	5
Scarsone, S	SF	R	.272	52	103	21	28	42	8	0	2	13	2	4	0	10	1	20	0	2	1	.408	.330	2
Scheid, R	FLA	L	.000	8	7	0	0	0	0	0	0	0	0	0	0	0	0	2	0	0	0	.000	.000	1
Schilling, C	PHI	R	.107	13	28	0	3	3	0	0	0	1	5	0	0	1	0	10	0	0	1	.107	.138	0
Schourek, P	CIN	L	.174	22	23	1	4	7	0	0	1	1	6	0	0	0	0	3	0	0	0	.304	.208	0
Scott, T	MON	R	.000	40	2	0	0	0	0	0	0	0	0	0	0	0	0	0	0	0	0	.000	.000	0
Seanez, R	LA	R	.000	17	1	0	0	0	0	0	0	0	0	0	0	0	0	1	0	0	0	.000	.000	0
Segui, D	NY	S	.241	92	336	46	81	130	17	1	10	43	0	3	1	33	6	43	0	0	6	.387	.308	5
Seminara, F	NY	R	.000	10	3	0	0	0	0	0	0	0	1	0	0	0	0	1	0	0	0	.000	.000	2
Servais, S	HOU	R	.195	78	251	27	49	93	15	1	9	41	7	3	4	10	0	44	0	0	6	.371	.235	2
Shaw, J	MON	R	.286	46	7	1	2	2	0	0	0	0	3	0	0	0	0	2	0	0	0	.286	.375	0
Sheaffer, D	COL	R	.218	44	110	12	24	31	4	0	1	12	0	0	0	10	2	11	0	0	2	.282	.283	1
Sheffield, G	FLA	R	.276	87	322	61	89	188	16	1	27	78	0	5	6	51	11	50	12	6	6	.584	.380	5
Shipley, C	SD	R	.333	81	240	32	80	114	14	4	4	30	4	2	3	9	1	28	6	6	3	.475	.362	9
Simms, M	HOU	R	.083	6	12	1	1	2	0	0	0	0	0	0	0	0	0	5	1	0	0	.167	.083	0
Slaught, D	PIT	R	.288	76	240	21	69	82	7	0	2	21	1	1	3	34	2	31	0	0	5	.342	.381	1
Slocumb, H	PHI	R	.250	52	4	0	1	1	0	0	0	0	0	0	0	0	0	2	0	0	0	.250	.250	3
Smiley, J	CIN	L	.200	24	55	5	11	14	3	0	0	2	5	0	0	4	0	26	0	0	1	.255	.254	3
Smith, O	STL	S	.262	98	381	51	100	133	18	3	3	30	10	4	0	38	3	26	6	3	3	.349	.326	2
Smith, P	NY	R	.135	21	37	2	5	6	1	0	0	1	6	0	0	0	0	9	0	0	0	.162	.220	8
Smith, Z	PIT	L	.211	26	57	2	12	13	1	0	0	2	2	0	0	0	0	11	0	0	0	.228	.211	0
Smoltz, J	ATL	R	.162	21	37	9	6	10	1	0	1	1	6	0	0	4	0	14	0	0	1	.270	.244	1

OFFICIAL NATIONAL LEAGUE STATS

Player	B	AVG																							
Sosa, S ....CHI	R	.300	105	426	59	128	232	17	6	25	70	1	4	2	25	—	2	92	22	13	7	.545	.389	7	.339
Spehr, T ....MON	R	.250	52	36	8	9	14	3	0	1	5	0	0	0	4	0	1	11	2	1	0	.389	.325	0	—
Stankiewicz, A ....HOU	R	.259	37	54	10	14	20	3	0	0	1	5	2	0	0	12	—	0	12	0	1	0	.370	.313	0
Stanton, D ....ATL	L	.667	49	3	0	2	2	0	0	0	0	1	0	0	0	0	0	0	0	0	0	.667	.667	0	.403
Staton, D ....SD	R	.182	30	66	6	12	26	2	0	4	6	0	1	0	10	0	0	18	0	3	3	.394	.289	0	.667
Stinnett, K ....NY	R	.253	47	150	20	38	54	6	2	2	14	4	2	1	11	0	1	28	2	0	3	.360	.323	3	.289
Stocker, K ....PHI	S	.273	82	271	38	74	95	11	2	2	28	4	4	0	44	0	8	41	2	3	3	.351	.383	3	.323
Strawberry, D ....SF	L	.239	29	92	13	22	39	3	1	4	17	0	2	0	19	0	4	22	0	2	2	.424	.363	2	.383
Sutcliffe, R ....STL	L	.130	16	23	0	3	4	1	0	0	1	3	0	0	0	0	8	6	0	0	1	.174	.130	1	.363
Swift, B ....SF	R	.188	18	32	0	6	9	3	0	0	0	5	0	0	0	0	4	5	0	3	0	.281	.257	0	.130
Swindell, G ....HOU	R	.250	24	44	5	11	14	3	0	0	2	12	0	0	3	0	0	14	0	0	0	.318	.250	0	.257
Tabaka, J ....PIT-SD	R	1.000	39	1	1	1	2	1	0	0	0	0	0	0	0	0	0	0	0	0	0	2.000	1.000	0	.250
Tarasco, J ....ATL	L	.273	87	132	16	36	57	6	0	5	19	0	3	0	9	1	2	17	5	5	0	.432	.313	5	1.000
Taubensee, E ....HOU-CIN	L	.283	66	187	29	53	89	8	2	8	21	1	2	0	15	2	1	31	2	3	5	.476	.333	3	.313
Tavarez, J ....FLA	R	.179	17	39	4	7	7	0	0	0	4	6	0	0	1	0	0	5	0	0	0	.179	.200	0	.333
Taylor, K ....SD	R	.000	1	2	0	0	0	0	0	0	0	1	0	0	0	0	0	1	0	0	0	.000	.000	0	.200
Tewksbury, B ....STL	R	.185	24	54	4	10	12	2	0	0	3	10	0	0	2	0	0	19	0	1	1	.222	.214	1	.000
Thompson, M ....PHI-HOU	L	.274	96	241	34	66	85	7	0	4	33	1	1	0	24	4	0	30	9	0	6	.353	.346	0	.214
Thompson, M ....COL	R	.000	2	4	0	0	0	0	0	0	0	0	0	0	0	0	0	4	0	0	0	.000	.000	0	.346
Thompson, R ....SF	R	.209	35	129	13	27	45	8	2	2	7	0	1	1	15	0	1	32	3	0	2	.349	.290	0	.000
Thompson, R ....NY	R	.225	98	334	39	75	145	14	4	16	59	5	5	3	28	0	4	94	1	1	3	.434	.301	1	.290
Tingley, R ....FLA	R	.173	19	52	4	9	17	3	0	0	2	3	0	0	5	0	0	18	0	0	0	.327	.246	0	.301
Tomlin, R ....PIT	L	.500	10	6	0	3	3	0	0	0	0	2	0	0	0	0	0	2	0	0	0	.500	.500	0	.246
Torres, S ....SF	R	.154	16	26	0	4	4	0	0	0	2	8	0	0	1	0	0	12	0	1	0	.154	.154	0	.500
Trachsel, S ....CHI	R	.186	22	43	3	8	9	1	0	0	5	4	0	0	2	0	0	9	0	0	2	.209	.205	2	.154
Treadway, J ....LA	L	.299	52	67	14	20	23	3	0	0	5	3	0	0	1	0	0	8	0	0	1	.343	.351	1	.205
Urbani, T ....STL	L	.250	20	24	1	6	6	0	0	0	1	4	0	0	0	0	0	5	0	0	0	.250	.308	0	.351
Valdes, I ....LA	R	.000	21	2	0	0	0	0	0	0	0	3	0	0	0	0	0	1	0	0	0	.000	.000	0	.308
Valenzuela, F ....PHI	L	.250	8	12	0	3	4	1	0	0	0	4	0	0	0	0	0	2	0	0	0	.333	.250	0	.000
Van Burkleo, T ....COL	L	.000	2	5	0	0	0	0	0	0	0	0	0	0	0	0	0	1	0	0	0	.000	.000	0	.250
Vander Wal, J ....COL	L	.245	91	110	12	27	47	3	1	5	15	0	0	1	16	0	0	31	2	0	1	.427	.339	4	—

BATTER	TEAM	B	AVG	G	AB	R	H	TB	2B	3B	HR	RBI	SH	SF	HP	BB	IBB	SO	SB	CS	GIDP	SLG	OBP	E
VanLandingham, B	SF	R	.065	16	31	2	2	2	0	0	0	1	4	0	0	0	0	17	0	0	0	.065	.065	0
Van Slyke, A	PIT	L	.246	105	374	41	92	134	18	0	8	30	0	2	2	52	7	72	7	1	9	.358	.340	2
Varsho, G	PIT	L	.256	67	82	15	21	33	6	3	0	5	2	0	2	4	1	19	0	0	1	.402	.307	2
Veres, D	HOU	R	.500	32	2	0	1	1	0	0	0	0	1	0	0	0	0	1	0	0	0	.500	.667	0
Veres, R	CHI	R	.000	10	1	0	0	0	0	0	0	0	2	0	0	0	0	0	0	0	0	.000	.000	0
Vina, F	NY	L	.250	79	124	20	31	37	6	0	0	6	2	0	12	12	0	11	3	1	4	.298	.372	4
Vizcaino, J	NY	S	.256	103	410	47	105	133	13	3	3	33	5	6	2	33	3	62	1	11	5	.324	.310	13
Wagner, P	PIT	R	.162	29	37	1	6	7	1	0	0	2	2	0	0	0	0	10	0	0	0	.189	.162	0
Walker, L	MON	L	.322	103	395	76	127	232	44	2	19	86	5	6	4	47	5	74	15	5	8	.587	.394	9
Wallach, T	LA	R	.280	113	414	68	116	208	21	1	23	78	0	2	4	46	2	80	0	0	12	.502	.356	11
Walton, J	CIN	R	.309	46	68	10	21	28	4	0	1	9	1	0	0	4	0	12	2	1	2	.412	.347	1
Watson, A	STL	L	.158	22	38	3	6	10	2	1	0	5	7	0	0	0	0	4	0	0	0	.263	.179	1
Wayne, G	LA	L	.000	19	1	0	0	0	0	0	0	0	4	0	0	0	0	0	0	0	0	.000	.000	0
Weathers, D	FLA	R	.068	26	44	2	3	3	0	0	0	0	6	0	0	3	0	25	0	0	0	.068	.128	1
Webster, L	MON	R	.273	57	143	13	39	64	10	0	5	23	0	2	6	16	1	24	0	0	7	.448	.370	1
Webster, M	LA	S	.274	82	84	16	23	39	4	0	4	12	4	0	0	8	0	13	1	2	2	.464	.344	1
Wehner, J	PIT	R	.250	2	4	1	1	2	1	0	0	3	0	0	0	0	0	1	0	0	0	.500	.250	0
Weiss, W	COL	S	.251	110	423	58	106	128	11	4	1	32	4	3	0	56	0	58	12	7	6	.303	.336	13
Wendell, T	CHI	L	.000	6	2	0	0	0	0	0	0	0	1	0	0	0	0	0	0	0	0	.000	.000	0
West, D	PHI	L	.071	31	28	2	2	2	0	0	0	0	5	0	0	0	0	12	0	0	1	.071	.071	0
Wetteland, J	MON	R	.250	52	4	0	1	1	0	0	0	0	0	0	0	0	0	1	0	0	0	.250	.250	0
White, G	MON	L	.000	9	7	0	0	0	0	0	0	0	0	0	0	1	0	1	0	0	0	.000	.200	0
White, R	PIT	R	.077	43	13	0	1	1	0	0	0	0	0	0	1	0	0	4	0	0	0	.077	.143	2
White, R	MON	R	.278	40	97	16	27	45	10	1	2	13	0	0	3	9	0	18	1	1	1	.464	.358	2
Whitehurst, W	SD	R	.105	13	19	0	2	2	0	0	0	0	3	0	0	3	0	8	0	0	1	.105	.227	1
Whiten, M	STL	S	.293	92	334	57	98	162	18	2	14	53	0	2	1	37	9	75	10	5	8	.485	.364	9
Whitmore, D	FLA	L	.227	9	22	1	5	6	1	0	0	0	0	0	0	3	0	5	0	1	0	.273	.320	0
Wilkins, R	CHI	L	.227	100	313	44	71	121	25	2	7	39	1	2	2	40	5	86	4	3	3	.387	.317	4
Williams, B	HOU	R	.261	20	23	0	6	6	0	0	0	3	5	0	0	0	0	4	0	0	0	.261	.261	4
Williams, E	SD	R	.331	49	175	32	58	104	11	1	11	42	2	1	3	15	1	26	0	1	10	.594	.392	5

OFFICIAL NATIONAL LEAGUE STATS

		AVG	G	AB	R	OR	H	TB	2B	3B	HR	GS	RBI	SH	SF	HP	BB	IBB	SO	SB	CS	GIDP	LOB	SHO	SLG	OBP
Williams, M.	SF	.267		445	112		74	119	270	16	3	43		96	0	0	3			33	87	1	0	11	.607	.319	12
Williams, M.	PHI	.167		12	12		1	2	3	1	0	0		0	3	5	0			0	0	0	0	0	.250	.167	0
Wilson, W.	CHI	.238		21	17		4	4	5	1	0	0		0	0	1	0			0	7	0	0	0	.429	.273	0
Wohlers, M.	ATL	1.000		1	1		1	1	1	0	0	0		0	0	0	0			0	0	6	0	0	1.000	1.000	1
Womack, T.	PIT	.333		12	5		4	4	4	0	0	0		1	0	1	0			2	0	1	0	0	.333	.429	2
Woodall, B.	ATL	.500		2	1		1	1	1	0	0	0		0	1	0	0			0	0	0	0	0	.500	.500	0
Worrell, T.	SD	.500		2	1		1	1	1	0	0	0		0	0	0	0			0	0	0	0	0	.500	.667	0
Young, A.	CHI	.176		34	3		6	6	7	1	0	0		0	4	0	0			2	0	11	0	0	.206	.176	1
Young, E.	COL	.272		228	37		62	98	13	1	3	1		7	30	5	2			38	0	17	18	7	3	.430	.378	2
Young, G.	STL	.317		41	5		13	20	2	0	0	0		0	0	2	0			0	0	8	2	1	1	.488	.364	0
Young, K.	PIT	.205		122	15		25	39	5	0	3	0		11	20	2	1			8	1	34	2	3	2	.320	.258	3
Zambrano, E.	CHI	.259		116	17		30	55	7	0	6	0		18	75	0	2			16	0	29	2	1	3	.474	.353	2
Zeile, T.	STL	.267		415	113		62	111	195	25	1	19				0	7			52	3	56	1	3	13	.470	.348	12

CLUB BATTING

CLUB	AVG	G	AB	R	OR	H	TB	2B	3B	HR	GS	RBI	SH	SF	HP	BB	IBB	SO	SB	CS	GIDP	LOB	SHO	SLG	OBP
CINCINNATI	.286	115	3999	609	490	1142	1797	211	36	124	2	569	53	42	29	388	51	738	119	51	83	816	4	.449	.350
HOUSTON	.278	115	3955	602	503	1099	1761	252	25	120	8	573	73	35	43	394	58	718	124	44	73	834	4	.445	.347
MONTREAL	.278	114	4000	585	454	1111	1741	246	30	108	1	542	53	42	40	379	39	669	137	36	77	859	5	.435	.343
SAN DIEGO	.275	117	4068	479	531	1117	1631	200	19	92	4	445	67	33	31	319	47	762	79	37	112	867	7	.401	.330
COLORADO	.274	117	4006	573	638	1098	1757	206	39	125	5	540	50	36	23	378	33	761	96	53	96	805	4	.439	.337
LOS ANGELES	.270	114	3904	532	509	1055	1618	160	29	115	2	505	51	31	19	366	33	687	74	57	89	789	7	.414	.333
ATLANTA	.267	114	3861	542	448	1031	1676	198	18	137	0	510	60	29	22	377	39	668	48	31	104	761	7	.434	.333
FLORIDA	.266	115	3926	468	576	1043	1553	180	24	94	2	451	42	30	40	349	25	746	65	26	85	856	6	.396	.330
ST. LOUIS	.263	115	3902	535	621	1026	1617	213	27	108	5	506	44	37	33	434	48	686	76	46	80	845	7	.414	.339
PHILADELPHIA	.262	115	3927	521	497	1028	1532	208	28	80	1	484	51	37	31	396	44	711	67	24	95	841	4	.390	.332
CHICAGO	.259	113	3918	500	549	1015	1583	189	26	109	0	464	54	23	27	364	26	750	69	53	83	802	4	.404	.325
PITTSBURGH	.259	114	3864	466	580	1001	1485	198	23	80	3	435	38	28	22	364	29	725	53	25	90	819	11	.384	.322
NEW YORK	.250	113	3869	506	526	966	1523	164	21	117	6	477	39	31	52	336	40	807	25	36	70	761	3	.394	.316
SAN FRANCISCO	.249	115	3869	504	500	963	1555	159	32	123	3	472	65	27	39	364	47	719	114	40	72	783	2	.402	.318
TOTALS	.267	803	55068	7422	7422	14695	22829	2784	377	1532	31	6973	758	455	451	5193	559	10147	1141	529	1206	11438	78	.415	.333

Pitching

Individual Pitching Leaders

Games Won	16	Hill	Mon.
		Maddux	Atl.
Games Lost	14	Benés	S.D.
Won-Lost Percentage	833	Freeman	Col. (10-2)
Earned Run Average	1.56	Maddux	Atl.
Games	61	Reed	Col.
Games Started	26	Rijo	Cin.
Complete Games	10	Maddux	Atl.
Games Finished	47	Beck	S.F.
Shutouts	3	Maddux	Atl.
		Martinez	L.A.
Saves	30	Franco	N.Y.
Innings	202.0	Maddux	Atl.
Hits	190	Tewksbury	St.L.
Batsmen Faced	744	Maddux	Atl.
Runs	99	Harris	Col.
Earned Runs	96	Harris	Col.
Home Runs	25	Smith	N.Y.
Sacrifice Hits	16	Smiley	Cin.
Sacrifice Flies	9	Hough	Fla.
Hit Batsmen	11	Martinez	Mon.
Bases on Balls	82	Kile	Hou.
Intentional Bases on Balls	12	Ashby	S.D.
Strikeouts	289	Benés	S.D.
Wild Pitches	10	Kile	Hou.
		Lewis	Fla.
		Sanders	S.D.
Balks	5	Manzanillo	Pit.
Games Won, Consecutive	7	Tewksbury	St.L. (April 3-May 11)
		Drabek	Hou. (April 10-May 24)
		Saberhagen	N.Y. (June 30-Aug. 10)
Games Lost, Consecutive	8	Harris	Col. (June 10-Aug. 7)

TOP 15 QUALIFIERS FOR EARNED RUN AVERAGE CHAMPIONSHIP

PITCHER	TEAM	T	W	L	ERA	G	GS	CG	SHO	GF	SV	IP	H	TBF	R	ER	HR	SH	SF	HB	BB	IBB	SO	WP	BK	OPP AVG
Maddux, G.	ATL	R	16	6	1.56	25	25	10	3	0	0	202.0	150	774	44	35	4	6	5	6	31	3	156	3	1	.207
Saberhagen, B.	NY	R	14	4	2.74	24	24	4	4	0	0	177.1	169	696	58	54	13	9	5	4	13	0	143	0	0	.254
Drabek, D.	HOU	R	12	6	2.84	23	23	6	2	0	0	164.2	132	657	58	52	14	5	6	2	45	0	121	2	0	.220
Fassero, J.	MON	L	8	6	2.99	21	21	1	1	0	0	138.2	119	569	54	46	13	7	2	1	40	4	119	6	6	.229
Reynolds, S.	HOU	R	8	9	3.05	33	14	1	0	5	0	124.0	128	517	46	42	10	4	0	6	21	3	110	3	1	.263
Rijo, J.	CIN	R	9	6	3.08	26	26	2	0	0	0	172.1	177	733	73	59	16	4	4	7	52	1	171	0	2	.265
Jones, B.	NY	R	12	7	3.15	24	24	1	0	0	0	160.0	157	685	75	56	10	11	4	9	56	4	80	1	3	.257
Trachsel, S.	CHI	R	9	7	3.21	22	22	1	0	0	0	146.0	133	612	57	52	15	3	3	3	54	3	108	6	0	.242
Jackson, D.	PHI	L	14	6	3.26	25	25	4	1	0	0	179.1	183	755	71	65	13	13	4	2	46	1	129	2	2	.266
Smith, Z.	PIT	L	10	8	3.27	25	24	2	0	0	0	157.0	162	645	67	57	18	7	6	0	34	7	57	2	0	.270
Hill, K.	MON	R	16	5	3.32	23	23	2	2	0	0	154.2	145	647	61	57	12	6	6	6	44	7	85	2	0	.248
Ashby, A.	SD	R	6	11	3.40	24	24	4	4	0	0	164.1	145	682	75	62	16	11	3	3	43	12	121	3	0	.233
Martinez, P.	MON	R	11	5	3.42	24	23	1	1	0	1	144.2	115	584	58	55	11	1	3	11	45	3	142	6	0	.220
Gross, K.	LA	R	9	7	3.60	25	23	1	0	2	0	157.1	162	665	64	63	11	4	1	2	43	2	124	4	1	.263
Burkett, J.	SF	R	6	8	3.62	25	25	3	1	0	0	159.1	176	676	72	64	14	12	5	7	36	7	85	2	0	.286

INDIVIDUAL PITCHING

PITCHER	TEAM	T	W	L	ERA	G	GS	CG	SHO	GF	SV	IP	H	TBF	R	ER	HR	SH	SF	HB	BB	IBB	SO	WP	BK	OPP AVG
Andersen, L.	PHI	R	1	2	4.41	29	0	0	0	11	0	32.2	33	147	20	16	2	3	0	0	15	3	27	0	0	.256
Aquino, L.	FLA	R	2	1	3.73	29	1	0	0	3	0	50.2	39	214	22	21	3	1	2	3	22	4	22	2	0	.210
Arocha, R.	STL	R	4	4	4.01	45	7	1	1	25	11	83.0	94	360	42	37	9	5	1	4	21	4	62	2	0	.287
Ashby, A.	SD	R	6	11	3.40	24	24	4	4	0	0	164.1	145	682	75	62	16	11	3	3	43	12	121	5	0	.233
Astacio, P.	LA	R	6	8	4.29	23	23	3	1	0	0	149.0	142	625	77	71	18	6	3	4	47	4	108	4	2	.252
Avery, S.	ATL	L	8	3	4.04	24	24	0	0	0	0	151.2	127	628	71	68	15	4	6	4	55	4	122	5	0	.227
Ballard, J.	PIT	L	1	1	6.66	28	0	0	0	11	2	24.1	32	112	19	18	5	1	1	1	10	3	11	1	0	.323
Banks, W.	CHI	R	8	12	5.40	23	23	1	0	0	0	138.1	139	598	88	83	16	3	2	2	56	3	91	8	1	.261
Barnes, B.	LA	L	0	0	7.20	5	0	0	0	1	0	5.0	10	29	4	4	1	0	0	0	4	1	5	2	0	.400
Bautista, J.	CHI	R	4	5	3.89	58	0	0	0	24	1	69.1	75	293	30	30	10	5	4	3	17	7	45	2	1	.284
Beck, R.	SF	R	2	4	2.77	48	0	0	0	47	28	48.2	49	207	17	15	10	3	0	0	13	2	39	0	0	.261

396 • THE COMPLETE HANDBOOK OF BASEBALL

PITCHER	TEAM	T	W	L	ERA	G	GS	CG	SHO	SV	IP	H	TBF	R	ER	HR	SH	SF	HB	BB	IBB	SO	WP	BK	OPP AVG
Bedrosian, S.	ATL	R	0	2	3.33	46	0	0	0	0	46.0	41	169	20	17	4	5	2	1	18	5	43	1	0	.243
Benes, A.	SD	R	6	14	3.86	25	25	2	2	0	172.1	155	717	82	74	20	11	1	1	51	2	189	4	0	.237
Bielecki, M.	ATL	R	2	0	4.00	19	1	0	0	0	27.0	28	115	12	12	2	2	1	0	12	1	18	0	1	.277
Black, B.	SF	L	4	2	4.47	10	10	0	0	0	54.1	50	227	31	27	9	3	2	3	16	3	28	1	0	.245
Blair, W.	COL	R	0	5	5.79	47	1	0	0	0	77.2	98	365	57	50	9	2	1	4	39	4	68	4	0	.308
Borland, T.	PHI	R	1	0	2.36	24	0	0	0	1	34.1	31	144	10	9	3	3	1	0	14	3	26	4	0	.248
Boskie, S.	CHI-PHI	R	4	6	5.01	20	14	0	0	0	88.0	88	381	56	49	14	2	3	3	29	1	61	7	0	.257
Bottalico, R.	PHI	R	0	0	0.00	3	0	0	0	0	3.0	3	13	0	0	0	0	0	0	1	0	3	0	0	.250
Bottenfield, K.	COL-SF	R	3	1	6.15	16	1	0	0	0	26.1	33	121	18	18	2	1	2	0	10	0	15	0	2	.306
Boucher, D.	MON	L	0	1	6.75	10	2	0	0	0	18.2	24	84	16	14	6	2	0	0	3	0	17	1	0	.324
Bowen, R.	FLA	R	1	5	4.94	8	8	1	0	0	47.1	50	208	28	26	9	2	2	2	19	0	32	2	0	.273
Brantley, J.	CIN	R	6	6	2.48	50	0	0	0	15	65.1	46	262	20	18	6	5	1	0	28	5	63	1	0	.202
Brink, B.	SF	R	0	0	1.08	6	0	0	0	0	8.1	4	32	1	1	1	0	0	1	2	0	3	1	0	.143
Brocail, D.	SD	R	0	0	5.82	12	0	0	0	0	17.0	21	78	13	11	1	0	2	2	5	3	11	1	1	.304
Browning, T.	CIN	L	3	1	4.20	7	7	0	0	0	40.2	34	169	20	19	8	0	2	0	13	0	22	1	0	.222
Buckels, G.	STL	R	0	1	2.25	10	0	0	0	0	12.0	8	51	5	3	2	2	0	1	7	0	9	0	0	.186
Bullinger, J.	CHI	R	6	6	3.60	33	10	0	0	1	100.0	87	412	43	40	6	3	3	1	34	4	72	4	1	.235
Burba, D.	SF	R	3	6	4.38	57	0	0	0	0	74.0	59	322	39	36	5	5	3	6	45	3	84	3	0	.221
Burkett, J.	SF	R	6	8	3.62	25	25	0	0	0	159.1	176	676	72	64	14	12	5	7	36	7	85	2	0	.286
Campbell, M.	SD	R	1	1	12.96	3	2	0	0	0	8.1	13	43	12	12	5	0	0	0	5	0	10	0	0	.351
Candiotti, T.	LA	R	7	7	4.12	23	22	5	0	0	153.0	149	652	77	70	9	9	8	5	54	2	102	9	0	.259
Carrasco, H.	CIN	R	5	6	2.24	45	0	0	0	6	56.1	42	237	17	14	3	9	5	2	30	1	41	3	1	.210
Carter, A.	PHI	L	0	2	4.46	20	0	0	0	0	34.1	34	149	18	17	5	3	6	2	18	2	18	0	0	.268
Castillo, F.	CHI	R	2	1	4.30	4	4	1	0	0	23.0	25	96	13	11	3	0	0	0	5	0	19	0	0	.278
Castillo, J.	NY	R	0	0	6.94	12	2	0	0	0	11.2	17	54	9	9	2	2	0	1	5	0	1	0	0	.362
Cimorelli, F.	STL	R	0	0	8.78	11	0	0	0	0	13.1	20	73	14	13	0	0	0	0	11	2	1	2	0	.345
Cooke, S.	PIT	L	4	11	5.02	25	23	0	0	0	134.1	157	590	75	75	21	9	3	5	46	7	74	5	2	.298
Cormier, R.	STL	L	3	2	5.45	7	7	1	0	0	39.2	40	169	24	24	6	1	3	1	7	0	26	2	0	.256
Crim, C.	CHI	R	5	4	4.48	49	1	0	0	2	64.1	69	283	36	32	9	6	3	3	24	6	43	2	1	.272
Czajkowski, J.	COL	R	0	0	4.15	5	0	0	0	0	8.2	9	42	4	4	2	0	0	0	8	1	2	1	0	.281

OFFICIAL NATIONAL LEAGUE STATS • 397

Name	T	W	L	ERA	G	GS	CG	SV	IP	H	R	ER	HR	HB	BB	IBB	SO	WP	BK	AVG
Daal, O. .... LA	L	0	0	3.29	24	0	0	0	13.2	12	5	5	1	1	0	0	9	1	1	.245
Davis, M. .... SD	L	1	0	8.82	20	0	0	3	16.1	20	18	16	4	0	1	0	15	0	0	.299
DeLucia, R. ..... CIN	R	0	0	4.22	8	0	0	1	10.2	9	6	5	4	0	0	0	15	1	0	.214
Dewey, M. .... PIT	R	2	0	3.68	45	0	0	1	51.1	61	22	21	4	1	2	1	30	0	0	.303
Dixon, S. .... STL	L	0	0	23.14	2	0	0	0	2.1	3	6	6	0	0	0	0	1	0	0	.333
Drabek, D. ...... HOU	R	12	6	2.84	23	23	0	0	164.2	132	58	52	14	5	6	3	121	2	0	.220
Drahman, B. ... FLA	R	0	0	6.23	9	0	2	0	13.0	15	9	9	2	1	1	0	7	2	0	.300
Dreifort, D. ..... LA	R	0	1	6.21	27	0	0	0	29.0	45	21	20	0	0	2	4	22	2	1	.357
Dyer, M. .... PIT	R	1	0	5.87	14	0	0	0	15.1	15	12	10	1	3	3	3	13	0	1	.268
Edens, T. .... HOU-PHI	R	5	1	4.33	42	0	0	0	54.0	59	26	26	3	4	3	2	39	5	0	.288
Eischen, J. ..... MON	L	0	0	54.00	1	0	0	0	0.2	4	7	4	0	0	0	0	1	0	0	.667
Elliott, D. .... SD	R	0	0	3.27	30	0	1	0	33.0	31	12	12	4	1	0	2	24	0	1	.250
Eversgerd, B. ... STL	L	2	3	4.52	40	0	0	1	67.2	75	32	34	0	3	5	1	47	3	1	.295
Fassero, J. ..... MON	L	8	6	2.99	21	21	0	0	138.2	119	54	46	13	8	5	2	119	6	0	.229
Florie, B. .... SD	R	0	0	0.96	9	0	0	0	9.1	8	1	1	2	0	0	2	8	1	0	.242
Fortugno, T. ... CIN	L	0	0	4.20	25	0	4	0	30.0	32	14	14	0	0	3	1	29	4	2	.288
Foster, K. .... CHI	R	3	4	2.89	13	13	0	0	81.0	70	37	31	6	3	1	3	75	1	0	.234
Franco, J. ...... NY	L	1	4	2.70	47	0	0	30	50.0	47	20	20	7	2	2	0	42	1	0	.244
Frascatore, J. ... STL	R	0	1	16.20	1	1	0	0	3.1	7	6	6	1	2	2	0	2	0	0	.438
Fraser, W. ...... FLA	R	2	0	5.84	29	0	4	0	12.1	20	8	8	2	0	4	5	7	2	2	.370
Freeman, M. ... COL	R	10	2	2.80	19	18	0	0	112.2	113	39	35	10	7	1	3	67	4	4	.262
Frey, S. .... SF	L	1	0	4.94	44	0	0	12	31.0	37	17	17	6	6	1	5	20	4	0	.322
Gardner, M. .... FLA	R	4	4	4.87	20	14	0	3	92.1	97	53	50	14	2	4	1	57	3	1	.276
Glavine, T. ..... ATL	L	13	9	3.97	25	25	2	0	165.1	173	76	73	10	4	5	0	140	8	0	.268
Gomez, P. ...... SF	L	0	0	3.78	26	0	0	0	33.1	23	14	14	2	5	2	0	14	5	0	.211
Gooden, D. .... NY	R	3	4	6.31	7	7	0	0	41.0	46	32	29	9	3	0	3	40	2	0	.282
Gott, J. .... LA	R	5	5	5.94	37	0	17	2	36.1	46	24	24	3	5	3	1	29	4	0	.322
Gozzo, M. ...... NY	R	3	0	4.83	23	8	0	5	69.0	86	48	37	2	0	1	3	28	5	2	.304
Greene, T. ..... PHI	R	2	0	4.54	8	7	0	0	35.2	37	18	18	7	0	6	1	33	5	0	.272
Gross, K. .... LA	R	9	7	3.60	25	23	1	0	157.1	162	65	64	11	1	5	2	124	4	1	.263
Gunderson, E. ... NY	L	0	0	0.00	14	0	0	0	9.0	5	0	0	4	0	2	0	4	0	0	.185
Guzman, J. .... CHI	R	2	2	9.15	4	4	0	0	19.2	22	20	20	3	1	1	2	11	1	0	.289

THE COMPLETE HANDBOOK OF BASEBALL

PITCHER	TEAM	T	W	L	ERA	G	GS	CG	SHO	GF	SV	IP	H	TBF	R	ER	HR	SH	SF	HB	BB	IBB	SO	WP	BK	OPP AVG
Habyan, J	STL	R	2	2	3.23	52	0	0	0	10	0	47.1	50	204	17	17	2	2	0	0	20	8	46	4	0	.275
Hamilton, J	SD	R	9	6	2.98	16	16	1	1	0	0	108.2	98	447	40	36	5	4	2	6	29	3	61	6	0	.241
Hammond, C	FLA	L	4	4	3.07	13	13	0	0	0	0	73.1	79	312	30	25	5	5	2	1	23	1	40	5	1	.281
Hampton, M	HOU	L	2	1	3.70	44	0	0	0	7	0	41.1	46	181	19	17	4	5	0	2	16	1	24	0	1	.282
Hanson, E	CIN	R	5	5	4.11	22	21	0	0	0	0	122.2	137	519	60	56	10	4	3	3	23	4	101	8	1	.283
Harkey, M	COL	R	1	6	5.79	24	13	0	0	3	0	91.2	125	415	61	59	10	5	2	1	35	1	39	0	2	.336
Harnisch, P	HOU	R	8	5	5.40	17	17	1	0	0	0	95.0	100	419	59	57	13	3	3	3	39	1	62	0	0	.269
Harris, G	COL	R	3	12	6.65	29	19	0	0	2	1	130.0	154	588	99	96	22	12	6	5	52	4	82	5	1	.300
Harris, G	SD	R	1	1	8.03	13	0	0	0	3	0	12.1	21	64	11	11	2	2	0	0	8	0	9	3	0	.389
Harvey, B	FLA	R	0	0	5.23	12	0	0	0	10	6	10.1	12	47	7	6	0	0	0	0	3	0	10	0	0	.279
Haynes, H	MON	R	0	0	0.00	4	0	0	0	2	0	3.2	3	17	1	0	0	0	0	0	3	0	1	0	0	.231
Henderson, R	MON	R	0	1	9.45	3	2	0	0	1	0	6.2	9	37	9	7	1	3	0	0	7	0	3	0	0	.333
Henry, B	MON	L	8	3	2.43	24	15	0	0	1	1	107.1	97	433	30	29	10	5	3	2	20	3	70	1	0	.241
Heredia, G	MON	R	6	3	3.46	39	3	0	0	8	0	75.1	85	325	34	29	7	3	4	1	13	3	62	4	1	.281
Hernandez, J	FLA	R	3	6	2.70	21	0	0	0	17	9	23.1	16	97	9	7	1	3	2	1	14	2	13	1	0	.205
Hershiser, O	LA	R	6	6	3.79	21	21	0	0	0	0	135.1	146	575	67	57	15	4	3	1	42	6	72	6	2	.279
Hickerson, B	SF	L	4	8	5.40	28	14	0	0	1	0	98.1	118	436	60	59	20	4	6	1	38	6	59	2	1	.301
Hill, K	MON	R	16	5	3.32	23	23	2	1	0	0	154.2	145	647	61	57	12	6	6	6	44	7	85	3	1	.248
Hill, M	ATL	R	0	0	7.94	10	0	0	0	5	0	11.1	18	64	10	10	2	1	0	0	11	3	10	1	1	.367
Hillman, E	NY	L	0	3	7.79	11	6	0	0	0	0	34.2	45	156	30	30	9	2	1	2	20	1	20	1	1	.321
Hoffman, T	SD	R	4	4	2.57	47	0	0	0	41	20	56.0	39	225	16	16	4	4	2	1	20	6	68	3	2	.193
Holmes, D	COL	R	0	3	6.35	29	0	0	0	14	3	28.1	35	142	25	20	5	2	1	1	24	0	33	2	0	.313
Hope, J	PIT	R	0	2	5.79	8	4	0	0	1	0	14.0	18	64	12	9	2	0	2	4	6	0	6	0	1	.310
Hough, C	FLA	R	5	9	5.15	21	21	0	0	0	0	113.2	118	515	74	65	17	14	4	10	52	1	65	9	4	.274
Hudek, J	HOU	R	0	2	2.97	42	0	0	0	33	16	39.1	24	159	14	13	5	0	9	2	18	2	39	0	0	.174
Hurst, J	CHI	R	0	1	12.60	7	0	0	0	5	0	10.0	15	50	14	14	5	0	2	1	6	0	6	0	0	.341
Ilsley, B	CHI	L	0	0	7.80	10	0	0	0	2	0	15.0	25	74	13	13	5	4	0	0	5	0	9	1	0	.385
Jackson, D	PHI	L	14	6	3.26	25	25	4	1	0	0	179.1	183	755	71	65	13	13	8	2	46	1	129	6	1	.266
Jackson, M	SF	R	3	2	1.49	36	0	0	0	12	4	42.1	23	158	8	7	4	4	1	0	11	0	51	0	0	.164
Jacome, J	NY	L	4	3	2.67	8	8	1	0	0	0	54.0	54	222	17	16	3	3	1	0	17	2	30	2	0	.269

OFFICIAL NATIONAL LEAGUE STATS • 399

Player																				
Jarvis, K ....CIN	R	1	1	7.13	6	3	0	0	0	17.2	22	14	14	4	14	0	5	0	10	1	0	.301
Jeffcoat, M ....FLA	L	0	0	10.13	4	0	0	0	0	2.2	4	3	3	2	3	0	0	0	0	1	0	.364
Johnston, J ....PIT	R	0	0	29.70	4	0	0	0	0	3.1	14	12	11	0	4	0	2	0	1	1	0	.583
Johnstone, J ......FLA	R	1	2	5.91	17	0	0	0	0	21.0	23	20	14	4	14	1	4	0	5	0	0	.264
Jones, B ....PHI	R	12	7	3.15	24	24	1	1	0	160.0	157	105	56	10	56	11	16	0	23	0	3	.257
Jones, D ....PHI	R	2	4	2.17	47	0	0	42	27	54.0	55	75	13	2	14	4	56	4	9	1	0	.255
Jones, T ....HOU	R	5	2	2.72	48	0	0	20	5	72.2	52	14	22	3	22	3	6	0	38	1	0	.202
Juden, J ....PHI	R	1	0	6.18	6	5	0	0	0	27.2	29	23	19	2	19	1	1	1	26	1	2	.276
Kile, D ....HOU	R	9	6	4.57	24	24	0	0	0	147.2	153	84	75	13	75	2	2	1	22	0	0	.275
Krueger, B ....SD	L	3	2	4.83	8	7	1	0	0	41.0	42	25	22	5	13	0	9	0	6	10	1	.259
Leskanic, C ....COL	R	6	3	5.64	44	8	0	2	0	98.0	172	24	14	5	14	1	7	1	30	2	0	.314
Lewis, R ....FLA	R	1	0	5.67	45	0	0	9	0	54.0	27	44	34	2	34	1	10	1	17	0	1	.284
Lieber, J ....PIT	R	6	7	3.73	17	17	0	0	0	108.2	62	44	45	7	45	3	38	1	45	2	3	.271
Linton, D ....NY	R	6	2	4.47	32	3	0	8	0	50.1	116	27	12	3	12	1	25	0	71	2	0	.341
Looney, B ....MON	L	0	0	22.50	1	0	0	0	0	2.0	74	5	3	0	5	0	20	0	29	0	3	.400
Maddux, G ....ATL	R	16	6	1.56	25	25	10	3	0	202.0	4	11	35	5	35	4	0	1	2	0	1	.207
Maddux, M ....NY	R	2	2	5.11	27	0	0	12	2	44.0	150	44	25	4	25	6	31	0	156	3	1	.263
Manzanillo, J .....NY	R	3	2	2.66	37	0	0	14	2	47.1	45	25	25	7	25	5	13	3	32	2	0	.200
Manzanillo, R .....PIT	L	4	2	4.14	46	0	0	11	0	50.0	34	186	24	4	23	2	13	0	48	2	0	.249
Martinez, J ....SD	R	0	2	6.75	4	1	0	0	0	12.0	45	15	9	1	9	0	13	3	39	5	5	.245
Martinez, P ......SD	L	3	2	2.90	48	0	0	18	3	68.1	18	30	22	5	22	5	42	0	7	2	0	.375
Martinez, P ......MON	R	11	5	3.42	24	23	1	1	0	144.2	52	54	31	9	31	0	5	1	52	0	1	.210
Martinez, R ....LA	R	12	7	3.97	24	24	4	0	0	170.0	115	9	55	2	55	11	49	1	3	6	0	.220
Mason, R .....PHI-NY	R	3	5	3.75	47	0	0	12	1	60.0	160	308	58	2	58	2	45	11	142	2	2	.243
Mathews, T ....FLA	R	2	1	3.35	24	2	0	5	0	43.0	55	718	83	6	75	18	56	8	119	6	6	.268
Mauser, T ....SD	R	2	4	3.49	35	0	0	12	0	49.0	45	256	29	8	25	8	25	6	33	0	0	.269
McDowell, R ....LA	R	0	3	5.23	32	0	0	11	0	41.1	50	179	16	3	16	4	9	2	21	1	0	.303
McElroy, C ....CIN	L	1	2	2.34	52	0	0	13	5	57.2	211	21	19	2	19	3	19	1	32	5	3	.244
McMichael, G ....ATL	R	4	6	3.84	51	0	0	41	21	58.2	52	193	25	3	24	3	22	3	29	3	0	.280
Menendez, T ....SF	R	0	0	21.60	6	0	0	0	0	3.1	66	230	15	2	15	5	15	2	38	4	0	.471
Mercker, K ......ATL	L	9	4	3.45	20	17	2	1	0	112.1	8	259	29	8	25	2	19	0	47	3	0	.220
Miceli, D ....PIT	R	2	1	5.93	28	0	0	9	2	27.1	90	19	8	2	8	2	0	0	2	0	1	.220

400 • THE COMPLETE HANDBOOK OF BASEBALL

PITCHER	TEAM	T	W	L	ERA	G	GS	CG	SHO	GF	SV	IP	H	TBF	R	ER	HR	SH	SF	HB	BB	IBB	SO	WP	BK	OPP AVG
Miller, K.	FLA	R	1	3	8.10	8	4	0	0	0	0	20.0	26	92	19	18	3	2	0	1	7	2	11	0	0	.317
Minor, B.	PIT	R	0	3	8.05	17	0	0	0	2	1	19.0	27	90	17	17	4	0	1	2	9	5	17	0	0	.351
Monteleone, R.	SF	R	4	3	3.18	39	0	0	0	8	0	45.1	43	189	18	16	6	2	4	0	13	2	16	2	2	.253
Moore, M.	COL	R	1	1	6.15	29	0	0	0	13	0	33.2	33	158	26	23	4	1	0	5	21	4	33	4	0	.252
Morgan, M.	CHI	R	2	10	6.69	15	15	1	0	0	0	80.2	111	380	65	60	12	7	6	5	35	0	57	5	1	.338
Munoz, B.	PHI	R	7	5	2.67	57	0	0	0	18	1	104.1	101	447	40	31	8	8	5	6	25	5	59	5	0	.252
Munoz, M.	COL	L	4	4	3.74	50	0	0	0	8	1	45.2	37	200	22	19	7	5	1	0	31	5	32	2	0	.223
Murphy, R.	STL	L	4	3	3.79	50	0	0	0	15	2	40.1	35	166	18	17	1	2	1	0	13	4	25	2	0	.230
Mutis, J.	FLA	L	1	0	5.40	35	0	0	0	7	0	38.1	51	177	25	23	6	6	3	1	15	1	30	0	1	.331
Myers, R.	CHI	L	5	2	3.79	38	0	0	0	34	21	40.1	40	177	25	17	3	7	2	0	16	3	32	2	0	.260
Neagle, D.	PIT	L	9	10	5.12	44	24	0	0	0	0	137.0	135	587	80	78	18	7	6	3	49	2	122	3	2	.259
Nen, R.	FLA	R	5	5	2.95	44	0	0	0	28	15	58.0	46	228	20	19	6	3	3	4	17	5	60	3	2	.222
Nied, D.	COL	R	9	7	4.80	22	22	2	1	0	0	122.0	137	538	70	65	15	5	4	4	47	4	74	7	0	.287
Olivares, O.	STL	R	3	4	5.74	14	12	0	0	2	0	73.2	84	333	53	47	10	1	3	3	37	5	26	0	2	.294
Olson, G.	ATL	R	0	2	9.20	16	0	0	0	6	1	14.2	19	84	17	15	1	2	1	1	13	3	10	0	0	.317
Osuna, A.	LA	L	2	0	4.50	15	0	0	0	4	0	8.2	13	43	6	6	0	0	0	0	4	0	7	0	1	.333
Otto, D.	CHI	L	2	0	3.80	36	0	0	0	7	0	45.0	49	200	20	19	4	4	3	1	22	2	19	3	0	.283
Painter, L.	COL	L	4	6	6.11	15	14	0	0	0	0	73.2	91	336	51	50	9	0	3	1	26	4	41	3	0	.302
Palacios, V.	STL	R	3	8	4.44	31	17	1	1	5	1	117.2	104	484	60	58	16	9	7	7	43	2	95	4	3	.246
Pall, D.	CHI	R	0	0	4.50	2	0	0	0	0	0	4.0	8	19	2	2	0	1	0	0	1	0	2	0	0	.444
Park, C.	LA	R	0	0	11.25	2	0	0	0	1	0	4.0	5	23	5	5	1	0	0	0	5	0	6	0	0	.294
Pena, A.	PIT	R	3	2	5.02	22	0	0	0	15	7	28.2	22	118	16	16	5	1	3	0	10	2	27	2	0	.206
Perez, C.	STL	R	2	3	8.71	8	7	0	0	18	12	31.0	52	155	32	30	5	1	5	3	10	1	20	0	0	.391
Perez, Y.	FLA	L	3	0	3.54	44	0	0	0	11	0	40.2	33	167	18	16	4	4	5	0	14	3	41	4	1	.220
Plesac, D.	CHI	L	2	3	4.61	54	0	0	0	14	1	54.2	61	235	30	28	9	6	3	1	13	2	53	0	0	.279
Portugal, M.	SF	R	10	8	3.93	21	21	0	0	0	0	137.1	135	580	68	60	17	6	4	6	45	3	87	5	0	.260
Powell, R.	HOU	L	0	0	1.23	12	0	0	0	2	0	7.1	6	32	1	1	0	0	0	1	5	0	5	0	0	.240
Pugh, T.	CIN	R	0	3	6.04	10	9	0	0	0	0	47.2	60	227	37	32	5	2	5	3	26	0	24	4	0	.314
Quantrill, P.	PHI	R	2	2	6.00	18	1	0	0	5	1	30.0	39	135	21	20	3	2	3	1	10	2	13	2	3	.331
Rapp, P.	FLA	R	7	8	3.85	24	23	2	1	1	0	133.1	132	584	67	57	13	8	4	7	69	3	75	5	1	.266

OFFICIAL NATIONAL LEAGUE STATS

Player	Team				ERA						IP											
Reed, S.	COL	R	3	2	3.94	61	0	0	0	11	64.0	79	33	28	9	0	7	6	26	3	51	1	0	.306
Remlinger, M.	NY	L	1	1	4.61	10	9	0	0	0	54.2	55	30	28	9	2	3	1	35	4	33	3	0	.261
Reynolds, S.	HOU	R	8	5	3.05	33	14	1	1	0	124.0	128	46	42	10	4	0	6	26	3	110	3	2	.263
Reynoso, A.	COL	R	3	4	4.82	9	9	0	0	0	52.1	54	30	28	5	2	2	2	21	1	25	2	2	.278
Rijo, J.	CIN	R	9	6	3.08	26	26	2	0	0	172.1	177	73	59	16	7	2	4	52	1	171	2	2	.265
Ritz, K.	COL	R	5	6	5.62	15	15	0	0	0	73.2	88	49	46	5	2	2	4	35	4	53	6	1	.303
Rivera, B.	PHI	R	3	0	6.87	9	7	0	0	1	38.0	40	29	29	7	6	1	4	22	0	19	3	0	.274
Robertson, R.	PIT	L	0	0	6.89	8	0	0	0	1	15.2	20	12	12	2	1	1	0	10	1	8	0	0	.313
Rodriguez, R.	STL	L	3	5	4.03	56	0	0	0	15	60.1	62	30	27	6	2	1	1	26	0	43	4	0	.270
Rogers, K.	SF	L	0	0	3.48	9	0	0	0	2	10.1	10	4	4	1	0	0	0	6	0	7	0	0	.250
Rojas, M.	MON	R	3	2	3.32	58	0	0	0	27	84.0	71	35	31	11	2	2	4	21	4	84	3	0	.227
Roper, J.	CIN	R	6	2	4.50	16	15	0	0	0	92.0	90	49	46	16	0	3	2	30	0	51	4	1	.255
Rueter, K.	MON	L	7	3	5.17	20	20	0	0	0	92.1	106	60	53	11	3	6	1	23	2	50	2	0	.294
Ruffin, B.	COL	R	4	5	4.04	56	0	0	0	39	55.2	55	28	25	6	6	3	1	30	4	65	5	0	.253
Ruffin, J.	CIN	R	7	4	3.09	51	0	0	0	13	70.0	57	26	24	7	1	2	2	27	2	44	0	0	.223
Saberhagen, B.	NY	R	14	4	2.74	24	24	4	0	0	177.1	169	62	54	13	2	1	9	13	0	143	5	1	.254
Sager, A.	SD	R	1	4	5.98	22	3	0	0	0	46.2	62	34	31	4	0	5	2	16	3	26	1	0	.325
Sanders, S.	SD	R	4	8	4.78	23	20	0	0	1	111.0	103	63	59	10	1	6	6	48	5	109	10	1	.245
Scheid, R.	FLA	L	1	3	3.34	8	5	0	0	0	32.1	35	18	12	2	0	6	0	8	2	17	2	1	.269
Schilling, C.	PHI	R	2	8	4.48	13	13	0	0	0	82.1	87	46	41	10	3	6	6	28	3	58	3	0	.270
Schourek, P.	CIN	L	7	2	4.09	22	12	0	0	3	81.1	90	42	37	11	1	6	2	29	3	69	2	0	.287
Scott, T.	MON	R	5	2	2.70	40	0	0	0	8	53.1	51	17	16	0	2	5	0	18	2	37	1	0	.251
Seanez, R.	LA	R	1	1	2.66	17	0	0	0	6	23.2	24	7	7	2	0	4	0	9	0	18	1	1	.273
Seminara, F.	NY	R	0	2	5.82	10	1	0	0	0	17.0	20	12	11	2	0	0	2	9	1	7	1	0	.303
Service, S.	CIN	R	1	2	7.36	6	0	0	0	0	7.1	8	6	6	2	0	2	2	3	0	5	1	0	.267
Shaw, J.	MON	R	5	2	3.88	46	0	0	0	15	67.1	67	32	29	8	2	2	2	15	2	47	0	0	.254
Slocumb, H.	PHI	R	5	1	2.86	52	0	0	0	16	72.1	75	32	23	2	0	4	4	28	2	58	0	0	.262
Smiley, J.	CIN	L	11	10	3.86	24	24	1	0	0	158.2	169	80	68	18	7	0	2	37	4	112	9	0	.275
Smith, P.	NY	R	4	10	5.55	21	21	0	0	0	131.1	145	83	81	18	5	7	2	42	3	62	4	1	.285
Smith, W.	STL	R	1	1	9.00	8	0	0	0	0	7.0	9	7	7	1	0	0	0	3	0	4	3	0	.300
Smith, Z.	PIT	L	10	8	3.27	25	24	2	1	0	157.0	162	67	57	18	3	7	3	34	2	57	2	0	.270
Smoltz, J.	ATL	R	6	10	4.14	21	21	1	0	0	134.2	120	69	62	15	6	7	6	48	4	113	7	0	.239

PITCHER	TEAM	T	W	L	ERA	G	GS	CG	SHO	GF	SV	IP	H	TBF	R	ER	HR	SH	SF	HB	BB	IBB	SO	WP	BK	OPP AVG
Spradlin, J	FLA	R	0	0	10.13	6	0	0	0	2	0	8.0	12	38	11	9	2	0	2	0	2	0	4	0	0	.353
Stanton, M	ATL	L	3	3	3.55	49	0	0	0	15	1	45.2	41	197	18	18	2	2	1	3	26	3	35	1	0	.248
Sutcliffe, R	STL	R	6	4	6.52	16	14	0	0	0	0	67.2	93	319	53	49	11	3	1	2	32	2	26	4	0	.331
Swift, B	SF	R	8	7	3.38	17	17	1	0	0	0	109.1	109	457	49	41	10	0	2	1	31	6	62	2	0	.262
Swindell, G	HOU	L	8	9	4.37	24	24	1	0	0	0	148.1	175	623	80	72	20	7	2	1	26	2	74	1	1	.302
Tabaka, J	PIT-SD	L	3	0	5.27	39	0	0	0	10	0	41.0	32	181	29	24	4	1	0	0	27	3	32	1	0	.213
Taylor, K	SD	R	0	0	8.31	5	1	0	0	0	0	4.1	9	24	4	4	1	0	0	0	3	0	3	0	0	.409
Telgheder, D	NY	R	0	1	7.20	6	0	0	0	4	0	10.0	11	48	8	8	2	1	0	0	8	2	4	0	0	.282
Tewksbury, B	STL	R	12	10	5.32	24	24	4	1	0	0	155.2	190	667	97	92	19	3	4	3	22	8	79	1	0	.304
Thompson, M	COL	R	1	1	9.00	2	2	0	0	0	0	9.0	16	49	9	9	2	1	0	0	8	0	5	0	0	.400
Tomlin, R	PIT	L	0	3	3.92	10	4	0	0	1	0	20.2	23	89	9	9	2	0	1	0	10	0	17	0	0	.291
Torres, S	SF	R	2	8	5.44	16	14	0	0	0	0	84.1	95	378	55	51	10	4	3	2	42	2	42	4	1	.292
Trachsel, S	CHI	R	9	7	3.21	22	22	1	0	0	0	146.0	133	612	57	52	19	3	3	5	54	4	108	6	1	.242
Urbani, T	STL	L	3	7	5.15	20	10	0	0	2	0	80.1	98	354	48	46	12	3	2	0	21	3	43	0	1	.302
Valdes, I	LA	R	1	1	3.18	21	1	0	0	7	0	28.1	21	115	10	10	2	2	0	0	10	2	28	1	0	.206
Valenzuela, F	PHI	L	1	2	3.00	8	7	0	0	0	0	45.0	42	182	16	15	8	4	0	1	19	1	19	2	0	.247
VanLandingham, B	SF	R	8	2	3.54	16	14	0	0	1	0	84.0	70	363	37	33	4	3	1	2	43	4	56	3	3	.223
Veres, D	HOU	R	3	3	2.41	32	0	0	0	7	1	41.0	39	168	13	11	4	0	2	1	7	2	28	3	0	.247
Veres, R	CHI	R	0	0	5.59	10	0	0	0	1	0	9.2	12	43	6	6	3	1	0	0	5	0	5	0	0	.308
Wagner, P	PIT	R	7	8	4.59	29	17	1	0	4	0	119.2	136	534	69	61	7	8	4	8	50	4	86	4	0	.293
Walton, B	COL	R	1	0	8.44	4	0	0	0	1	0	5.1	6	26	5	5	1	0	0	1	3	1	1	0	1	.273
Watson, A	STL	L	6	5	5.52	22	22	0	0	0	0	115.2	130	523	73	71	15	7	0	0	53	2	74	2	2	.286
Wayne, G	LA	L	1	2	4.67	19	0	0	0	4	0	17.1	19	79	13	9	3	2	1	3	6	2	10	0	1	.279
Weathers, D	FLA	R	8	12	5.27	24	24	0	0	0	0	135.0	166	621	87	79	13	1	4	2	59	9	72	2	1	.306
Wells, B	PHI	R	1	0	1.80	6	2	0	0	2	0	5.0	4	21	1	1	0	0	0	0	3	0	3	0	0	.235
Wendell, T	CHI	R	0	1	11.93	6	0	0	0	1	0	14.1	22	76	20	19	3	0	2	1	10	0	9	0	1	.349
West, D	PHI	L	4	10	3.55	31	14	0	0	7	0	99.0	74	429	44	39	5	4	2	1	61	1	83	9	0	.205
Wetteland, J	MON	R	4	6	2.83	52	0	0	0	43	25	63.2	46	261	22	20	5	4	3	3	21	3	68	0	0	.202
White, G	MON	L	1	1	6.08	7	0	0	0	2	1	23.2	24	106	16	16	4	1	1	1	11	0	17	0	0	.261
White, R	PIT	R	4	5	3.82	43	5	0	0	6	0	75.1	79	317	35	32	9	7	6	1	38	3	38	0	2	.280

OFFICIAL NATIONAL LEAGUE STATS • 403

		W	L	ERA	G	CG	SHO	REL	SV	IP	H	R	ER	HR	HB	BB	IBB	SO	WP	BK	OPP AVG
Whitehurst, W	SD	R	4	7	4.92	13	0	0	13	0	64.0	84	37	35	8	4	26	0	43	4	2	.319
Williams, B	HOU	R	6	5	5.74	20	1	0	13	0	78.1	112	64	50	9	7	41	5	49	4	3	.343
Williams, M	HOU	L	1	4	7.65	25	0	0	0	0	20.0	21	17	17	4	2	24	2	21	4	1	.269
Williams, M	PHI	R	2	4	5.01	12	0	0	8	0	50.1	61	31	28	7	2	15	1	29	2	0	.310
Wohlers, M	ATL	R	7	2	4.59	51	0	0	0	0	51.0	51	35	26	3	1	33	1	58	9	0	.264
Woodall, B	ATL	L	0	1	4.50	1	1	0	0	0	6.0	5	3	3	2	0	2	0	2	0	0	.227
Worrell, T	SD	R	0	0	3.68	3	0	0	0	0	14.2	9	7	6	1	0	5	1	14	0	0	.170
Worrell, T	LA	R	6	5	4.29	38	0	0	27	11	42.0	37	21	20	6	4	12	2	44	1	0	.236
Young, A	CHI	R	4	6	3.92	20	0	0	19	0	114.2	103	57	50	12	6	46	3	65	2	1	.246

CLUB PITCHING

CLUB	W	L	ERA	G	CG	SHO	REL	SV	IP	H	R	ER	HR	HB	BB	IBB	SO	WP	BK	OPP AVG
MONTREAL	74	40	3.56	114	4	8	259	46	1036.2	970	454	410	100	38	288	28	805	32	2	.247
ATLANTA	68	46	3.57	114	16	8	244	26	1026.1	929	448	384	50	38	378	52	865	49	10	.242
CINCINNATI	66	48	3.78	115	6	6	261	27	1038.1	1037	490	436	117	22	339	23	799	35	10	.262
PHILADELPHIA	54	61	3.85	115	7	6	243	30	1024.1	1028	497	438	98	27	377	28	699	41	6	.261
HOUSTON	66	49	3.97	115	9	6	268	29	1029.2	1043	503	454	102	28	367	28	739	45	8	.265
SAN FRANCISCO	55	60	3.99	115	2	4	273	33	1025.1	1014	500	454	122	34	372	40	655	35	6	.262
SAN DIEGO	47	70	4.08	117	8	3	238	35	1045.2	1008	531	474	99	37	393	62	862	32	8	.252
NEW YORK	55	58	4.13	114	7	3	239	27	1023.0	1069	526	470	117	25	332	48	640	48	5	.271
LOS ANGELES	58	56	4.17	115	14	5	286	28	1014.0	1054	549	470	90	21	354	36	732	26	6	.267
CHICAGO	49	64	4.47	113	5	5	239	20	1023.2	1041	508	508	120	33	392	35	717	42	7	.268
FLORIDA	51	64	4.50	115	5	7	300	30	1015.0	1069	576	507	120	19	428	41	649	57	6	.274
PITTSBURGH	53	61	4.64	114	8	2	285	24	1005.2	1094	580	518	117	39	370	52	650	45	13	.281
ST. LOUIS	53	61	5.14	115	7	7	330	29	1018.0	1154	621	581	134	41	355	28	632	24	11	.289
COLORADO	53	64	5.15	117	4	5	329	28	1031.0	1185	638	590	120	49	448	43	703	50	5	.292
TOTALS	802	802	4.21	803	102	78	3843	411	14356.2	14695	7422	6717	1532	451	5193	559	10147	548	106	.267

OFFICIAL 1994 AMERICAN LEAGUE RECORDS

COMPILED BY MLB-IBM BASEBALL INFORMATION SYSTEM
Official Statistician: ELIAS SPORTS BUREAU

FINAL STANDINGS

AMERICAN LEAGUE EAST

CLUB	W.	L.	PCT.	GB
NEW YORK	70	43	.619	-
BALTIMORE	63	49	.563	6.5
TORONTO	55	60	.478	16.0
BOSTON	54	61	.470	17.0
DETROIT	53	62	.461	18.0

AMERICAN LEAGUE CENTRAL

CLUB	W.	L.	PCT.	GB
CHICAGO	67	46	.593	-
CLEVELAND	66	47	.584	1.0
KANSAS CITY	64	51	.557	4.0
MINNESOTA	53	60	.469	14.0
MILWAUKEE	53	62	.461	15.0

AMERICAN LEAGUE WEST

CLUB	W.	L.	PCT.	GB
TEXAS	52	62	.456	-
OAKLAND	51	63	.447	1.0
SEATTLE	49	63	.438	2.0
CALIFORNIA	47	68	.409	5.5

Batting

Individual Batting Leaders

Batting Average	.359	O'Neill	N.Y.
Games	115	Molitor	Tor.
At Bats	464	Fryman	Det.
Runs	106	Thomas	Chi.
Hits	160	Lofton	Cle.
Total Bases	294	Belle	Cle.
Singles	107	Lofton	Cle.
		Molitor	Tor.
Doubles	45	Knoblauch	Min.
Triples	14	Johnson	Chi.
Home Runs	40	Griffey	Sea.
Runs Batted In	112	Puckett	Min.
Sacrifice Hits	14	Kelly	N.Y.
Sacrifice Flies	13	Carter	Tor.
		Fryman	Det.
Hit by Pitch	18	MacFarlane	K.C.
Bases on Balls	109	Thomas	Chi.
Intentional Bases on Balls	20	Vaughn	Bos.
Strikeouts	128	Fryman	Det.
Stolen Bases	60	Lofton	Cle.
Caught Stealing	17	Gagne	K.C.
Grounded Into Double Play	20	Canseco	Tex.
Slugging Percentage	.729	Thomas	Chi.
On-Base Percentage	.487	Thomas	Chi.
Longest Batting Streak	24	Palmeiro	Bal. (April 23-May 22)

TOP 15 QUALIFIERS FOR BATTING CHAMPIONSHIP

BATTER	TEAM	B	AVG	G	AB	R	OR	H	TB	2B	3B	HR	RBI	SH	SF	HP	BB	IBB	SO	SB	CS	GIDP	SLG	OBP	E
O'Neill, P	NY	L	.359	103	368	68		132	222	25	1	21	83	0	3	0	72	13	56	5	5	16	.603	.460	1
Belle, A	CLE	R	.357	106	412	90		147	294	35	2	36	101	1	4	5	58	9	71	9	6	5	.714	.438	6
Thomas, F	CHI	R	.353	113	399	106		141	291	34	1	38	101	0	7	2	109	12	61	2	3	15	.729	.487	7
Lofton, K	CLE	L	.349	112	459	105		160	246	32	9	12	57	4	6	4	52	5	56	60	12	5	.536	.412	2
Boggs, W	NY	L	.342	97	366	61		125	179	19	1	11	55	2	5	0	61	6	29	2	0	10	.489	.433	10
Molitor, P	TOR	R	.341	115	454	86		155	235	30	4	14	75	0	5	1	55	4	48	20	3	13	.518	.410	0
Clark, W	TEX	L	.329	110	389	73		128	195	30	2	13	80	0	6	3	71	11	59	5	1	5	.501	.431	10
Griffey, K	SEA	L	.323	111	433	94		140	292	24	4	40	90	0	6	2	56	19	73	11	3	5	.674	.402	4
Palmeiro, R	BAL	L	.319	111	436	82		139	240	32	2	23	76	0	6	2	54	7	63	7	3	11	.550	.392	4
Franco, J	CHI	R	.319	112	433	72		138	221	19	2	20	98	0	5	5	62	4	75	8	1	14	.510	.406	3
Puckett, K	MIN	R	.317	108	439	79		139	237	32	3	20	112	1	7	7	28	7	47	6	3	11	.540	.362	4
Fermin, F	SEA	R	.317	101	379	52		120	144	21	0	1	35	12	5	4	11	0	22	4	4	9	.380	.338	10
Ripken, C	BAL	R	.315	112	444	71		140	204	19	3	13	75	0	4	4	32	2	41	1	1	17	.459	.364	7
Baerga, C	CLE	S	.314	103	442	81		139	232	32	2	19	80	3	8	6	10	1	45	8	2	10	.525	.333	15
Knoblauch, C	MIN	R	.312	109	445	85		139	205	45	3	5	51	3	3	10	41	2	56	35	6	13	.461	.381	3

CLUB BATTING

CLUB	AVG	G	AB	R	OR	H	TB	2B	3B	HR	GS	RBI	SH	SF	HP	BB	IBB	SO	SB	CS	GIDP	LOB	SHO	SLG	OBP
NEW YORK	.290	113	3986	670	534	1155	1842	238	16	139	5	632	27	37	31	530	34	660	55	40	112	918	4	.462	.374
CLEVELAND	.290	113	4022	679	562	1165	1946	240	20	167	3	647	33	38	18	382	40	629	131	48	80	762	5	.484	.351
CHICAGO	.287	113	3942	633	498	1133	1749	175	39	121	6	602	51	46	20	497	47	568	77	27	91	906	2	.444	.366
TEXAS	.280	114	3983	613	697	1114	1738	198	29	124	7	582	45	34	36	437	37	730	82	35	95	863	3	.436	.353
MINNESOTA	.276	113	3952	594	688	1092	1686	239	23	103	3	556	22	34	41	359	26	635	94	30	89	796	7	.427	.340
BALTIMORE	.272	112	3856	589	497	1047	1689	185	20	139	1	557	15	35	39	438	23	655	69	13	83	833	3	.438	.349
SEATTLE	.269	112	3883	569	616	1045	1751	211	20	153	6	549	48	32	26	372	42	652	48	21	87	784	3	.451	.335
KANSAS CITY	.269	115	3911	574	532	1051	1638	211	38	100	4	538	32	38	33	376	23	698	140	62	72	747	6	.419	.335

OFFICIAL AMERICAN LEAGUE STATS

	AVG	G	AB	R	H	TB	2B	3B	HR	RBI	SH	SF	HP	BB	IBB	SO	SB	CS	GIDP	SLG	OBP	E
TORONTO	.269	115	3962	566	1064	1679	210	30	115	534	30	44	38	387	34	691	79	26	96	.424	.336	4
DETROIT	.265	115	3955	652	1048	1797	216	25	161	622	17	48	34	520	28	897	46	33	86	.454	.352	4
CALIFORNIA	.264	115	3943	543	1042	1612	178	16	120	518	42	29	27	402	24	715	65	54	84	.409	.334	7
BOSTON	.263	115	3940	552	1038	1658	222	19	120	523	38	33	31	404	40	723	81	38	87	.421	.334	5
MILWAUKEE	.263	115	3978	547	1045	1622	238	21	99	510	38	38	33	417	30	680	59	37	85	.408	.335	9
OAKLAND	.260	114	3885	549	1009	1552	178	13	113	515	24	18	21	417	21	686	91	39	79	.399	.330	7
TOTALS	.273	797	55198	8330	15048	23959	2939	325	1774	7885	449	537	425	5938	449	9619	1117	503	1236	.434	.345	65

INDIVIDUAL BATTING

BATTER	TEAM	B	AVG	G	AB	R	H	TB	2B	3B	HR	RBI	SH	SF	HP	BB	IBB	SO	SB	CS	GIDP	SLG	OBP	E
Aldrete, M	OAK	L	.242	76	178	23	43	60	5	0	4	18	2	0	3	20	1	35	2	0	2	.337	.313	1
Alomar, R	TOR	S	.306	107	392	78	120	177	25	4	8	38	7	3	2	51	2	41	19	8	14	.452	.386	4
Alomar, S	CLE	R	.288	80	292	44	84	143	15	1	14	43	0	1	2	25	2	31	8	4	7	.490	.347	4
Amaral, R	SEA	R	.263	77	228	37	60	86	10	2	4	18	7	2	1	24	1	28	5	1	3	.377	.333	2
Amaro, R	CLE	S	.217	26	23	5	5	12	1	0	2	5	0	0	0	2	0	3	0	0	0	.522	.280	15
Anderson, B	BAL	L	.263	111	453	78	119	190	25	5	12	48	3	2	10	57	3	75	31	1	7	.419	.356	1
Anderson, G	CAL	L	.385	5	13	0	5	5	0	0	0	1	0	0	0	0	0	2	0	0	0	.385	.385	0
Anthony, E	SEA	L	.237	79	262	31	62	108	14	1	10	30	2	3	0	23	4	66	6	2	7	.412	.297	2
Baerga, C	CLE	S	.314	103	442	81	139	232	32	2	19	80	3	8	6	10	1	45	8	2	10	.525	.333	15
Baines, H	BAL	L	.294	94	326	44	96	158	12	1	16	54	0	4	0	30	6	49	0	1	9	.485	.356	0
Barnes, S	DET	R	.286	24	21	4	6	9	0	0	1	4	0	0	0	0	0	2	0	0	1	.429	.286	0
Bautista, D	DET	R	.232	31	99	12	23	41	4	0	4	15	0	1	0	3	0	18	0	1	2	.414	.255	1
Becker, R	MIN	S	.265	28	98	12	26	32	3	0	1	8	1	0	0	13	0	25	6	1	2	.327	.351	0
Belle, A	CLE	R	.357	106	412	90	147	294	35	2	36	101	0	4	5	58	9	71	9	6	5	.714	.438	6
Beltre, E	TEX	R	.282	48	131	12	37	42	5	0	0	12	1	0	1	6	0	25	2	5	3	.321	.358	9
Berroa, G	OAK	R	.306	96	340	55	104	165	18	2	13	65	0	7	3	41	0	62	2	7	2	.485	.379	1
Berryhill, D	BOS	S	.263	82	255	30	67	106	17	2	6	34	0	2	0	19	0	59	0	1	6	.416	.312	2

BATTER	TEAM	B	AVG	G	AB	R	H	TB	2B	3B	HR	RBI	SH	SF	HP	BB	IBB	SO	SB	CS	GI DP	SLG	OBP	E
Blosser, G.	BOS	L	.091	5	11	2	1	1	0	0	0	1	0	0	0	4	0	4	0	0	0	.091	.333	3
Blowers, M.	SEA	R	.289	85	270	37	78	118	13	0	9	49	1	3	1	25	2	60	2	2	12	.437	.348	9
Boggs, W.	NY	L	.342	97	366	61	125	179	19	1	11	55	2	4	0	61	3	29	2	1	10	.489	.433	8
Borders, P.	TOR	R	.247	85	295	24	73	97	13	1	3	26	7	2	0	15	0	50	1	1	7	.329	.284	8
Bordick, M.	OAK	R	.253	114	391	38	99	131	18	4	2	37	3	5	3	38	1	44	7	2	9	.335	.320	14
Boston, D.	NY	L	.182	52	77	11	14	28	2	0	4	14	0	0	0	6	0	20	0	1	3	.364	.250	0
Bowie, J.	OAK	L	.214	6	14	0	3	3	0	0	0	0	0	0	0	2	0	2	0	0	0	.214	.214	0
Bragg, D.	SEA	L	.158	8	19	4	3	4	1	0	0	2	0	0	0	2	0	5	0	1	0	.211	.238	0
Brooks, H.	KC	R	.230	34	61	5	14	19	2	0	1	14	0	0	0	2	0	10	2	0	2	.311	.239	0
Brosius, S.	OAK	R	.238	96	324	31	77	135	14	1	14	49	4	6	2	24	0	57	2	6	7	.417	.289	13
Brumley, M.	OAK	S	.240	11	25	0	6	6	0	0	0	2	0	0	0	1	0	8	0	0	0	.240	.269	2
Brunansky, T.	MIL-BOS	R	.234	64	205	24	48	92	12	1	10	34	0	4	0	24	1	57	0	2	3	.449	.309	1
Buford, D.	BAL	S	.500	4	2	2	1	1	0	0	0	0	0	0	0	1	0	0	1	0	0	.500	.500	0
Buhner, J.	SEA	R	.279	101	358	74	100	194	23	4	21	68	2	5	5	66	3	63	0	0	7	.542	.394	2
Butler, R.	TOR	L	.176	41	74	13	13	15	0	1	0	5	4	1	1	7	0	8	0	1	3	.203	.250	1
Canseco, J.	TEX	R	.282	111	429	88	121	237	19	2	31	90	0	2	5	69	8	114	15	8	20	.552	.386	0
Carter, J.	TOR	R	.271	111	435	70	118	228	25	2	27	103	0	6	3	33	6	64	11	0	6	.524	.317	2
Cedeno, D.	TOR	S	.196	47	97	14	19	27	2	3	0	10	3	4	0	10	0	31	1	2	0	.278	.261	8
Chamberlain, W.	BOS	R	.256	51	164	13	42	65	9	1	4	20	0	0	2	12	0	38	0	2	6	.396	.307	0
Cirillo, J.	MIL	R	.238	39	126	17	30	48	9	0	3	12	0	2	1	11	0	16	0	1	4	.381	.309	3
Clark, W.	TEX	L	.329	110	389	73	128	195	24	2	13	80	0	3	6	71	11	59	5	1	5	.501	.431	10
Cole, A.	MIN	L	.296	105	345	68	102	139	15	5	4	23	6	2	1	44	2	60	29	8	3	.403	.375	8
Coleman, V.	KC	S	.240	104	438	61	105	149	14	12	2	33	4	5	1	29	0	72	50	8	0	.340	.285	7
Coles, D.	TOR	R	.210	48	143	15	30	50	6	1	4	15	0	1	2	10	0	25	0	0	2	.350	.263	4
Cooper, S.	BOS	L	.282	104	369	49	104	167	16	4	13	53	1	5	1	30	2	65	0	3	6	.453	.333	16
Cora, J.	CHI	S	.276	90	312	55	86	113	13	4	2	30	11	5	2	38	0	32	8	4	8	.362	.353	6
Correia, R.	CAL	R	.235	6	17	4	4	5	1	0	0	0	0	0	0	0	0	0	0	0	0	.294	.316	0
Cruz, F.	OAK	R	.107	17	28	2	3	3	0	0	0	0	0	0	0	4	0	6	0	0	0	.107	.219	2

OFFICIAL AMERICAN LEAGUE STATS

Player	Team	B	AVG	G	AB	R	H																	
Curtis, C.	CAL	R	.256	114	453	67	116	180	23	4	11	50	7	4	5	37	0	69	25	11	10	.397	.317	4
Cuyler, M.	DET	S	.241	48	116	20	28	36	3	1	0	11	1	1	2	13	0	21	5	3	3	.310	.318	2
Dalesandro, M.	CAL	R	.200	19	25	5	5	9	1	0	1	1	2	0	1	2	0	4	0	0	2	.360	.259	1
Darling, R.	OAK	R	.000	27	1	0	0	0	0	0	0	0	0	0	0	0	0	0	0	0	0	.000	.000	2
Davis, B.	TEX	R	.235	4	17	2	4	7	3	0	0	0	0	0	0	2	0	3	1	0	0	.412	.235	0
Davis, C.	CAL	S	.311	108	392	72	122	220	18	1	26	84	0	0	6	69	11	84	3	2	12	.561	.410	1
Davis, E.	DET	R	.183	37	120	19	22	35	4	0	3	13	0	0	0	18	0	45	5	2	4	.292	.290	0
Davis, R.	NY	R	.143	4	14	0	2	2	0	0	0	1	0	0	0	0	0	4	0	0	0	.143	.143	1
Dawson, A.	BOS	R	.240	75	292	34	70	136	18	0	16	48	0	0	4	9	3	53	2	0	15	.466	.271	0
Delgado, C.	TOR	L	.215	43	130	17	28	57	2	0	9	24	0	0	3	25	4	46	0	1	5	.438	.352	0
Devereaux, M.	BAL	R	.203	85	301	35	61	100	8	2	9	33	0	2	4	22	0	72	1	2	6	.332	.256	2
Diaz, A.	MIL	S	.251	79	187	17	47	69	8	5	1	17	3	3	3	10	1	19	2	5	5	.369	.285	1
DiSarcina, G.	CAL	R	.260	112	389	53	101	128	14	2	3	33	10	4	2	18	0	28	5	7	10	.329	.294	9
Ducey, R.	TEX	L	.172	11	29	2	5	6	1	0	0	1	0	0	0	2	0	12	1	0	0	.207	.226	0
Dunn, S.	MIN	L	.229	14	35	2	8	13	5	0	0	4	0	0	0	1	0	12	0	0	1	.250	.250	1
Easley, D.	CAL	R	.215	88	316	41	68	104	16	1	6	30	4	0	4	29	0	48	5	5	8	.329	.288	7
Edmonds, J.	CAL	L	.273	94	289	35	79	109	13	1	5	37	1	0	1	30	3	72	4	2	3	.377	.343	3
Eenhoorn, R.	NY	R	.500	3	4	0	2	3	1	0	0	0	0	0	0	0	0	0	0	0	0	.750	.500	0
Elster, K.	NY	R	.000	7	20	0	0	0	0	0	0	0	0	1	0	0	0	6	0	0	0	.000	.048	0
Espinoza, A.	CLE	R	.238	90	231	27	55	71	13	0	1	19	4	4	2	1	0	33	1	0	7	.307	.258	10
Fabregas, J.	CAL	L	.283	43	127	12	36	39	3	0	0	16	0	0	1	6	1	18	2	1	5	.307	.321	3
Felix, J.	DET	S	.306	86	301	54	92	158	25	1	13	49	0	4	8	26	2	76	1	6	6	.525	.372	4
Fermin, F.	SEA	R	.317	101	379	52	120	144	21	0	1	35	12	5	4	11	0	22	4	4	9	.380	.338	10
Fielder, C.	DET	R	.259	109	425	67	110	214	16	2	28	90	0	0	4	50	4	110	0	0	17	.504	.337	7
Flaherty, J.	DET	R	.150	34	40	2	6	9	1	0	0	4	0	2	0	1	0	11	0	1	1	.175	.167	1
Fletcher, S.	BOS	R	.227	63	185	31	42	62	9	1	3	11	0	3	2	16	0	14	8	1	7	.335	.296	0
Fox, E.	OAK	S	.205	26	44	7	9	14	2	0	1	1	0	0	0	6	0	8	2	0	0	.318	.255	0
Franco, J.	CHI	R	.319	112	433	72	138	221	19	2	20	98	0	5	5	62	0	75	8	1	14	.510	.406	3
Frye, J.	TEX	R	.327	57	205	37	67	93	20	3	0	18	5	3	1	29	0	23	6	1	1	.454	.408	4
Fryman, T.	DET	R	.263	114	464	66	122	220	34	5	18	85	1	13	5	45	1	128	2	2	6	.474	.326	14

BATTER	TEAM	B	AVG	G	AB	R	H	TB	2B	3B	HR	RBI	SH	SF	HP	BB	IBB	SO	SB	CS	GI DP	SLG	OBP	E
Gaetti, G	KC	R	.287	90	327	53	94	151	15	3	12	57	1	3	2	19	3	63	0	2	9	.462	.328	4
Gagne, G	KC	R	.259	107	375	39	97	147	23	3	7	51	2	1	4	27	0	79	10	17	8	.392	.314	12
Gallego, M	NY	R	.239	89	306	39	73	110	17	1	6	41	5	4	1	38	1	46	0	1	4	.359	.327	11
Gates, B	OAK	S	.283	98	233	29	66	85	11	1	2	24	4	6	1	21	1	32	3	3	8	.365	.337	8
Gibson, K	DET	L	.276	98	330	71	91	181	17	2	23	72	3	2	5	42	3	69	4	5	2	.548	.358	1
Gomez, C	DET	R	.257	84	296	32	76	119	19	0	8	53	2	5	3	33	0	64	0	0	8	.402	.336	8
Gomez, L	BAL	R	.274	84	285	46	78	143	20	1	15	56	3	1	3	41	0	55	0	0	5	.502	.366	5
Gonzales, R	CLE	R	.348	22	23	6	8	14	1	1	1	5	1	1	0	5	0	3	0	0	0	.609	.448	1
Gonzalez, A	TOR	R	.151	15	53	7	8	13	3	1	0	5	1	0	0	4	0	17	2	0	2	.245	.224	6
Gonzalez, J	TEX	R	.275	107	422	57	116	199	18	4	19	85	0	0	4	30	10	66	6	4	18	.472	.330	2
Goodwin, T	KC	L	.000	2	2	0	0	0	0	0	0	0	0	0	0	0	0	1	0	0	0	.000	.000	0
Grebeck, C	CHI	R	.309	35	97	17	30	35	5	0	1	5	3	0	0	12	0	5	0	0	0	.361	.391	2
Green, S	TOR	L	.091	14	33	3	3	4	1	0	0	0	0	0	0	0	0	8	0	0	1	.121	.118	0
Greenwell, M	BOS	L	.269	95	327	60	88	148	25	1	11	45	0	5	4	38	6	26	2	2	12	.453	.348	1
Greer, R	TEX	L	.314	80	277	36	87	135	16	1	10	46	0	4	2	46	2	46	0	2	3	.487	.410	6
Griffey, K	SEA	L	.323	111	433	94	140	292	24	4	40	90	0	2	2	56	19	73	11	3	9	.674	.402	4
Guillen, O	CHI	L	.288	100	365	46	105	127	9	5	1	39	7	4	0	14	2	35	5	4	5	.348	.311	16
Hale, C	MIN	L	.263	67	118	13	31	43	9	0	1	11	1	1	1	16	1	14	1	2	2	.364	.350	3
Hall, J	CHI	R	.393	17	28	6	11	17	3	0	1	5	0	0	1	2	0	4	0	0	2	.607	.452	1
Hamelin, B	KC	L	.282	101	312	64	88	187	25	1	24	65	0	5	3	56	3	62	4	0	4	.599	.388	2
Hamilton, D	MIL	L	.262	36	141	23	37	52	10	1	1	13	2	1	0	15	1	17	3	3	2	.369	.331	0
Hammonds, J	BAL	R	.296	68	250	45	74	120	18	2	8	31	0	5	0	17	1	39	5	0	3	.480	.339	6
Harper, B	MIL	R	.291	64	251	23	73	100	15	0	4	32	0	4	3	9	1	18	0	1	8	.398	.318	0
Haselman, B	SEA	R	.193	38	83	11	16	28	7	1	1	8	1	0	1	3	0	11	1	0	2	.337	.230	3
Hatcher, B	BOS	R	.244	44	164	24	40	54	9	1	1	18	3	0	0	11	0	14	4	5	3	.329	.292	3
Helfand, E	OAK	L	.167	7	6	1	1	1	0	0	0	0	0	0	0	0	0	1	0	0	0	.167	.167	0
Hemond, S	OAK	R	.222	91	198	23	44	64	11	0	3	20	2	0	0	16	0	51	7	6	5	.323	.280	6
Henderson, D	KC	R	.247	56	198	27	49	80	14	1	5	31	1	2	1	16	1	28	2	0	3	.404	.304	3

OFFICIAL AMERICAN LEAGUE STATS

Player		AVG	AB	R	H	2B	3B	HR	RBI	BB	SO	SB	CS			
Henderson, R......OAK	R	.260	87	66	77	13	0	6	20	1	5	45	22	7	0	.365	.411	4
Henry, D.............MIL	R	.000	25	1	0	0	0	0	0	0	0	1	0	0	0	.000	.000	0
Hocking, D........MIN	S	.323	31	3	10	3	0	0	2	0	0	4	2	0	1	.419	.323	0
Hoiles, C............BAL	R	.247	99	45	82	10	0	19	53	0	5	73	2	2	6	.449	.371	0
Howard, C.........SEA	R	.200	9	2	5	0	0	0	0	0	0	6	2	0	0	.240	.250	7
Howard, D..........KC	S	.229	46	9	19	4	1	0	2	1	1	23	3	2	1	.313	.309	0
Howitt, D...........CHI	L	.357	10	4	5	3	0	0	1	0	0	7	0	0	1	.571	.400	1
Hrbek, K...........MIN	L	.270	81	34	74	11	0	10	53	0	1	28	0	0	8	.420	.353	0
Hudler, R...........CAL	R	.298	56	17	37	8	0	8	20	4	0	28	2	2	7	.556	.326	2
Huff, M..............TOR	R	.304	80	31	63	15	3	3	25	0	3	27	2	1	6	.449	.392	5
Hulett, T...........BAL	R	.228	36	11	21	2	1	2	15	0	0	24	1	0	2	.337	.314	1
Hulse, D...........TEX	L	.255	77	58	79	8	4	1	19	7	1	53	18	2	1	.316	.305	3
Ingram, R...........DET	R	.217	12	23	5	5	1	0	2	0	0	2	1	0	0	.217	.240	4
Jackson, B........CAL	R	.279	75	23	56	7	0	13	43	2	2	72	0	0	2	.507	.344	0
Jackson, C........TEX	R	.000	1	2	0	0	0	0	0	0	1	0	0	0	0	.000	.000	3
Jackson, D.........CHI	R	.312	104	43	115	17	3	10	51	1	4	56	7	1	5	.455	.362	0
Jaha, J..............MIL	R	.241	84	45	70	14	4	12	39	1	10	75	3	0	8	.412	.332	1
James, D...........TEX	R	.256	52	28	34	8	4	7	19	2	3	38	3	0	3	.534	.361	8
Javier, S...........OAK	S	.272	109	75	114	23	0	10	44	7	2	76	24	7	7	.399	.349	0
Jefferson, R.....SEA	S	.327	63	24	53	11	0	8	32	0	1	32	0	0	6	.543	.392	4
Johnson, L..........CHI	L	.277	106	56	114	14	14	3	54	0	5	23	26	6	8	.393	.321	2
Jose, F................KC	R	.303	99	56	111	28	2	11	55	0	2	75	10	9	8	.475	.362	0
Joyner, W............KC	L	.311	97	57	174	28	0	8	57	2	5	43	3	12	12	.449	.386	4
Karkovice, R.....CHI	R	.213	77	33	113	20	3	11	29	2	3	68	0	2	0	.425	.325	8
Kelly, P..............NY	R	.280	93	35	44	9	1	2	41	14	5	51	6	5	3	.399	.330	3
Kirby, W...........CLE	L	.293	78	33	80	21	2	3	23	0	1	30	11	4	10	.403	.341	10
Knoblauch, C....MIN	R	.312	109	85	139	6	5	5	51	0	0	56	35	6	4	.461	.381	4
Knorr, R.............TOR	R	.242	40	20	205	45	3	7	19	3	10	35	6	13	3	.427	.301	3
Koslofski, K........KC	L	.250	2	30	53	0	0	0	0	1	1	1	0	7	2	.250	.500	2
Kreuter, C.........DET	S	.224	65	17	38	8	0	1	19	0	4	36	0	0	3	.288	.327	4

412 • THE COMPLETE HANDBOOK OF BASEBALL

BATTER	TEAM	B	AVG	G	AB	R	H	TB	2B	3B	HR	RBI	SH	SF	HP	BB	IBB	SO	SB	CS	GIDP	SLG	OBP	E
LaValliere, M	CHI	L	.281	59	139	6	39	46	4	0	1	24	9	3	1	20	0	15	0	2	4	.331	.368	3
Lee, M	TEX	S	.278	95	335	41	93	121	18	2	2	38	6	1	0	21	0	66	3	4	8	.361	.319	13
Leius, S	MIN	R	.246	97	350	57	86	146	16	1	14	49	1	2	1	37	0	58	2	0	9	.417	.318	8
Lewis, J	CLE	L	1.000	1	1	0	1	1	0	0	0	0	0	0	0	0	0	0	0	0	0	1.000	1.000	0
Lewis, M	CLE	R	.205	20	73	6	15	23	5	0	1	8	0	0	0	2	0	13	0	0	2	.315	.227	0
Leyritz, J	NY	R	.265	75	249	47	66	129	12	0	17	58	0	3	6	35	1	61	0	0	9	.518	.365	6
Lind, J	KC	R	.269	85	290	34	78	101	16	2	1	31	8	1	0	16	1	34	9	5	7	.348	.306	5
Listach, P	MIL	S	.296	16	54	8	16	19	3	0	0	2	1	0	0	3	0	8	2	1	1	.352	.333	3
Litton, G	BOS	R	.095	11	21	2	2	2	0	0	0	0	1	0	0	0	0	5	0	0	0	.095	.091	0
Livingstone, S	DET	L	.217	15	23	0	5	6	1	0	0	1	0	0	0	1	0	4	0	0	0	.261	.250	0
Lofton, K	CLE	L	.349	112	459	105	160	246	32	9	12	57	4	6	2	52	5	56	60	12	5	.536	.412	2
Lovullo, T	SEA	S	.222	36	72	9	16	27	5	0	2	7	0	0	0	9	0	13	1	0	2	.375	.309	1
Macfarlane, M	KC	R	.255	92	314	53	80	145	17	3	14	47	0	3	18	35	1	71	1	0	9	.462	.359	4
Mack, Q	SEA	L	.238	5	21	1	5	8	3	0	0	2	0	0	0	1	0	3	2	1	0	.381	.273	0
Mack, S	MIN	R	.333	81	303	55	101	171	21	2	15	61	1	5	6	32	1	51	4	1	2	.564	.402	2
Mahomes, P	MIN	R	.000	22	0	0	0	0	0	0	0	0	0	0	0	0	0	0	0	0	0	.000	.000	1
Maldonado, C	CLE	R	.196	42	92	14	18	40	5	1	5	12	0	2	0	19	0	31	0	1	1	.435	.333	0
Martin, N	CHI	R	.275	45	131	19	36	48	7	1	1	16	3	2	0	9	0	16	4	2	2	.366	.317	2
Martinez, E	SEA	R	.285	89	326	47	93	157	23	1	13	51	0	1	3	53	3	42	6	4	2	.482	.387	9
Martinez, T	SEA	L	.261	97	329	42	86	167	21	1	20	61	0	4	3	29	2	52	1	2	9	.508	.320	2
Matheny, M	MIL	R	.226	28	53	2	12	18	3	0	1	2	2	0	2	3	0	13	0	0	1	.340	.293	1
Matos, F	OAK	R	.250	14	28	3	7	8	1	0	0	2	1	0	0	0	0	2	1	0	0	.286	.267	3
Mattingly, D	NY	L	.304	97	372	62	113	153	20	1	6	51	0	4	0	60	7	24	0	0	8	.411	.397	2
Mayne, B	KC	L	.257	46	144	19	37	50	5	1	2	20	0	0	0	14	0	27	1	0	3	.347	.323	1
McCarty, D	MIN	R	.260	44	131	21	34	49	8	2	1	12	0	0	5	7	1	32	2	1	3	.374	.322	5
McDowell, O	TEX	L	.262	59	183	34	48	58	5	1	1	15	6	3	0	28	0	39	14	2	3	.317	.355	2
McGwire, M	OAK	R	.252	47	135	26	34	64	3	0	9	25	0	0	0	37	3	40	0	0	3	.474	.413	4
McLemore, M	BAL	S	.257	104	343	44	88	110	11	1	3	29	4	1	1	51	3	50	20	5	7	.321	.354	9

OFFICIAL AMERICAN LEAGUE STATS · 413

Player	Team	B	AVG	G	AB	R	H	TB	2B	3B	HR	RBI	BB	SO	SB	CS	SH	SF	HP	SLG	OBP	GDP
McRae, B	KC	S	.273	114	436	71	119	165	22	6	4	40	6	3	6	54	3	67	28	8	3	.378	.359	3
Meares, P	MIN	R	.266	80	229	29	61	81	12	1	2	24	6	3	2	14	0	50	5	1	3	.354	.310	13
Melvin, B	NY-CHI	R	.212	20	33	5	7	10	0	0	1	4	1	0	0	0	1	7	0	0	2	.303	.235	0
Merullo, M	CLE	L	.100	4	10	1	1	1	0	0	0	0	0	0	0	2	0	1	0	0	0	.100	.250	1
Mieske, M	MIL	R	.259	84	259	39	67	112	13	1	10	38	2	1	0	21	0	62	3	5	6	.432	.320	4
Miller, K	KC	R	.133	5	15	1	2	2	0	0	0	0	0	0	0	0	0	3	0	0	0	.133	.133	0
Mitchell, K	SEA	R	.227	46	128	21	29	46	2	0	5	15	2	1	1	18	0	22	0	0	2	.359	.324	1
Molitor, P	TOR	R	.341	115	454	86	155	235	30	4	14	75	0	1	5	55	4	48	20	0	13	.518	.410	4
Munoz, P	MIN	S	.295	75	244	35	72	124	15	2	11	36	0	1	1	19	1	67	0	0	0	.508	.348	3
Murray, E	CLE	S	.254	108	433	57	110	184	21	1	17	76	2	5	2	31	0	53	8	4	8	.425	.302	3
Myers, G	CAL	L	.246	45	126	10	31	43	6	0	2	8	3	3	3	10	6	27	1	1	3	.341	.299	2
Naehring, T	BOS	R	.276	80	297	41	82	123	18	0	7	42	5	7	1	30	3	56	2	3	11	.414	.349	6
Neel, T	OAK	R	.266	83	278	43	74	132	13	0	15	48	7	1	4	38	5	61	0	3	4	.475	.357	2
Newfield, M	SEA	R	.184	12	38	3	7	11	1	0	1	4	1	0	0	2	1	4	0	0	2	.289	.225	0
Newson, W	CHI	L	.255	63	102	16	26	37	5	0	2	7	2	0	0	0	1	23	0	0	3	.363	.345	1
Nilsson, D	MIL	L	.275	109	397	51	109	179	25	3	12	69	8	1	1	14	0	61	1	0	7	.451	.326	2
Nixon, O	BOS	S	.274	103	398	60	109	126	15	1	0	25	6	8	0	34	9	65	42	1	0	.317	.360	3
Noboa, J	OAK	R	.325	17	40	3	13	16	1	1	0	6	2	2	1	0	1	5	10	0	0	.400	.357	3
Nokes, M	NY	L	.291	28	79	11	23	47	3	0	7	19	1	0	0	55	0	16	1	0	1	.595	.329	3
O'Leary, T	MIL	L	.273	27	66	9	18	27	1	1	2	7	0	0	0	2	0	12	0	1	0	.409	.329	0
Olerud, J	TOR	L	.297	108	384	47	114	183	29	2	12	67	2	5	5	5	0	53	1	2	11	.477	.393	6
O'Neill, P	NY	L	.359	103	368	68	132	222	25	1	21	83	1	3	3	61	12	56	5	4	16	.603	.460	1
Ortiz, J	TEX	L	.276	29	76	3	21	23	2	0	0	9	1	4	0	0	13	11	0	0	0	.303	.329	0
Ortiz, L	BOS	R.	.167	7	18	3	3	5	2	0	0	0	1	0	3	1	0	5	0	0	0	.278	.182	0
Owen, S	CAL	S	.310	82	268	30	83	113	17	2	3	37	3	1	0	49	0	17	2	8	4	.422	.418	8
Palmeiro, R	BAL	L	.319	111	436	82	139	240	32	2	23	76	0	1	6	54	1	63	7	3	11	.550	.392	4
Palmer, D	TEX	R	.246	93	342	50	84	159	14	2	19	59	6	1	2	26	1	89	3	4	7	.465	.302	22
Paquette, C	OAK	R	.143	14	49	4	7	9	2	0	0	0	1	1	0	0	0	14	0	1	0	.184	.143	0
Parks, D	MIN	R	.191	31	89	8	17	26	6	0	1	9	1	0	1	2	0	20	2	0	2	.292	.242	1
Pasqua, D	CHI	L	.217	23	11	2	5	13	2	0	2	4	0	0	0	4	0	9	0	0	1	.565	.217	4

BATTER	TEAM	B	AVG	G	AB	R	H	TB	2B	3B	HR	RBI	SH	SF	HP	BB	IBB	SO	SB	CS	GI DP	SLG	OBP	E
Pena, T.	CLE	R	.295	40	112	18	33	49	8	1	2	10	3	2	0	9	0	11	0	1	6	.438	.341	1
Perez, E.	CAL	R	.209	38	129	10	27	49	7	0	5	16	1	1	0	12	1	29	3	0	5	.380	.275	1
Perry, R.	TOR	R	.125	4	8	0	1	1	0	0	0	0	0	0	0	0	0	1	0	0	0	.125	.125	0
Perry, H.	CLE	R	.111	4	9	0	1	1	0	0	0	1	0	0	0	3	1	1	0	0	1	.111	.357	6
Phillips, T.	DET	S	.281	114	438	91	123	205	19	3	19	61	0	0	3	95	1	105	13	5	8	.468	.409	11
Pirkl, G.	SEA	R	.264	19	53	7	14	35	3	0	6	11	0	0	0	1	0	12	0	0	0	.660	.286	1
Polonia, L.	NY	L	.311	95	350	62	109	145	21	6	1	36	2	1	4	37	3	36	20	12	7	.414	.383	4
Puckett, K.	MIN	R	.317	108	439	79	139	237	32	3	20	112	1	7	7	28	7	47	6	3	11	.540	.362	3
Raines, T.	CHI	S	.266	101	384	80	102	157	15	5	10	52	4	3	1	61	3	43	13	0	10	.409	.365	4
Ramirez, M.	CLE	R	.269	91	290	51	78	151	22	1	17	60	0	4	3	42	4	72	4	0	6	.521	.357	1
Reboulet, J.	MIN	R	.259	74	189	28	49	71	11	1	3	23	2	0	0	18	0	23	0	0	6	.376	.327	7
Redus, G.	TEX	R	.273	18	33	2	9	10	1	0	0	1	0	0	0	4	1	6	0	0	3	.303	.351	0
Reed, J.	MIL	R	.271	108	399	48	108	136	22	0	2	37	4	3	2	57	1	34	5	4	8	.341	.362	3
Reynolds, H.	CAL	S	.232	74	207	33	48	60	10	1	0	11	3	1	1	23	0	18	10	7	5	.290	.310	2
Ripken, B.	TEX	R	.309	32	81	9	25	30	5	0	0	6	1	0	0	3	0	11	2	0	2	.370	.333	2
Ripken, C.	BAL	R	.315	112	444	71	140	204	19	3	13	75	0	4	4	32	3	41	1	0	17	.459	.364	7
Rodriguez, A.	SEA	R	.204	17	54	4	11	11	0	0	0	2	1	0	0	3	0	20	3	0	0	.204	.241	6
Rodriguez, C.	BOS	S	.287	57	174	15	50	69	14	1	1	13	2	1	0	11	0	13	0	0	3	.397	.330	6
Rodriguez, I.	TEX	R	.298	99	363	56	108	177	19	1	16	57	1	7	4	31	0	42	6	3	10	.488	.360	6
Rowland, R.	BOS	R	.229	46	118	14	27	57	3	0	9	20	0	0	0	11	5	35	0	0	2	.483	.295	5
Royer, S.	BOS	R	.111	4	9	0	1	1	1	0	0	0	0	0	0	0	0	3	0	0	0	.111	.111	1
Sabo, C.	BAL	R	.256	68	258	41	66	120	15	3	11	42	4	1	5	20	2	38	1	1	8	.465	.320	4
Saenz, O.	CHI	R	.143	5	14	2	2	4	0	0	0	0	0	0	0	0	0	5	0	0	1	.286	.143	0
Salmon, T.	CAL	R	.287	100	373	67	107	198	18	2	23	70	0	3	5	54	2	102	0	1	3	.531	.382	8
Samuel, J.	DET	R	.309	59	136	32	42	76	9	5	5	21	0	2	3	10	0	26	5	2	4	.559	.364	1
Sasser, M.	SEA	L	.000	3	4	0	0	0	0	0	0	0	0	0	0	0	0	0	0	0	0	.000	.000	0
Sax, S.	OAK	R	.250	7	24	2	6	8	0	0	0	1	0	0	0	0	0	2	0	0	0	.333	.250	0
Schaefer, J.	OAK	R	.125	6	8	0	1	1	0	0	0	0	0	0	0	0	0	1	0	0	0	.125	.125	1

OFFICIAL AMERICAN LEAGUE STATS

Player	Team	B	AVG																		
Schofield, D	TOR	R	.255	95	325	38	83	111	14	1	4	32	8	2	0	4	34	62	7	7	2	.342	.332	11
Seitzer, K	MIL	R	.314	80	309	44	97	140	24	2	5	49	4	3	2	2	30	38	18	2	1	7	.453	.375	11
Shumpert, T	KC	R	.240	64	183	28	44	78	6	2	8	24	5	1	1	0	13	39	8	1	3	0	.426	.289	8
Sierra, R	OAK	S	.268	110	426	71	114	206	21	1	23	92	0	11	0	23	64	8	5	3	15	.484	.298	9
Silvestri, D	NY	R	.111	12	18	3	2	7	0	1	0	1	0	0	0	0	4	9	0	1	0	0	.389	.261	1
Smith, D	CAL-BAL	L	.281	73	196	31	55	90	7	2	8	30	0	0	1	1	12	37	2	4	4	3	.459	.324	7
Smith, Lo	BAL	R	.203	35	59	13	12	15	3	0	0	0	0	0	1	1	11	18	1	0	0	2	.254	.333	0
Smith, M	BAL	R	.143	3	7	0	1	1	0	0	0	2	0	0	0	0	0	2	0	0	0	0	.143	.143	0
Snow, J	CAL	S	.220	61	223	22	49	77	4	0	8	30	2	1	0	1	19	48	2	0	1	2	.345	.289	2
Sojo, L	SEA	R	.277	63	213	32	59	90	9	2	6	22	3	3	0	3	8	25	2	0	2	2	.423	.308	7
Sorrento, P	CLE	L	.280	95	322	43	90	146	14	0	14	62	1	0	0	0	34	68	2	1	7	2	.453	.345	2
Spiers, B	MIL	L	.252	73	214	27	54	66	10	1	0	17	3	3	1	1	19	42	7	1	1	5	.308	.316	4
Sprague, E	TOR	R	.240	109	405	38	97	151	19	0	11	44	2	4	1	11	23	95	1	1	0	11	.373	.296	8
Stanley, M	NY	R	.300	82	290	54	87	158	20	1	17	57	1	0	2	2	39	56	0	1	0	10	.545	.384	14
Steinbach, T	OAK	R	.285	103	369	51	105	163	21	2	11	57	0	6	1	6	26	62	0	2	1	10	.442	.327	5
Strange, D	TEX	S	.212	73	226	26	48	77	12	1	5	26	4	4	2	3	15	38	2	1	3	6	.341	.268	1
Surhoff, B	MIL	L	.261	40	134	20	35	65	15	1	2	22	2	2	2	0	16	14	0	1	1	5	.485	.336	11
Sveum, D	SEA	S	.185	10	27	3	5	8	0	0	1	2	2	0	0	0	2	10	0	0	0	4	.296	.241	4
Tackett, J	BAL	R	.226	26	53	5	12	23	3	1	2	9	0	0	0	0	5	13	0	0	0	1	.434	.317	1
Tartabull, D	NY	R	.256	104	399	68	102	185	24	1	19	67	0	0	1	4	66	111	1	1	0	11	.464	.360	2
Tettleton, M	DET	S	.248	107	339	57	84	157	18	2	17	51	0	0	0	3	5	97	0	1	1	4	.463	.419	0
Thomas, F	CHI	R	.353	113	399	106	141	291	34	1	38	101	0	0	0	7	2	98	0	2	3	15	.729	.487	5
Thome, J	CLE	L	.268	98	321	58	86	168	20	1	20	52	1	0	0	1	2 109	61	0	2	3	11	.523	.359	7
Tingley, R	CHI	R	.000	5	5	0	0	0	0	0	0	0	0	0	0	0	0	46	2	0	0	0	.000	.000	15
Tinsley, L	BOS	S	.222	78	144	27	32	42	4	0	2	14	3	0	3	0	19	2	5	3	0	0	.292	.315	0
Tomberlin, A	BOS	L	.194	18	36	1	7	12	0	1	1	1	0	0	0	0	6	36	0	2	0	2	.333	.310	1
Trammell, A	DET	R	.267	76	292	38	78	121	17	1	8	28	2	0	0	1	16	12	13	1	8	0	.414	.307	10
Turang, B	SEA	R	.188	38	112	9	21	31	5	1	1	8	3	3	0	0	7	35	3	0	1	8	.277	.242	2
Turner, C	CAL	R	.242	58	149	23	36	48	7	1	1	12	2	0	1	2	10	25	3	1	0	2	.322	.290	1
Valentin, J	BOS	R	.316	84	301	53	95	152	26	2	9	49	4	5	0	4	3	42	29	38	3	1	3	.505	.400	8

BATTER	TEAM	B	AVG	G	AB	R	H	TB	2B	3B	HR	RBI	SH	SF	HP	BB	IBB	SO	SB	CS	GI DP	SLG	OBP	E
Valentin, J	MIL	S	.239	97	285	47	68	120	19	0	11	46	4	2	2	38	1	75	12	3	3	.421	.330	20
Valle, D	BOS-MIL	R	.232	46	112	14	26	42	8	1	2	10	2	0	1	9	0	22	0	2	6	.375	.348	3
Vaughn, G	MIL	R	.254	95	370	59	94	177	24	1	19	55	0	2	1	33	6	93	9	5	3	.478	.345	3
Vaughn, M	BOS	L	.310	111	394	65	122	227	25	1	26	82	0	2	10	57	20	112	4	4	6	.576	.408	10
Velarde, R	NY	R	.279	77	280	47	78	123	16	1	9	34	2	2	4	22	0	61	4	2	7	.439	.338	19
Ventura, R	CHI	L	.282	109	401	57	113	184	15	1	18	78	2	8	2	61	15	69	3	1	8	.459	.373	20
Vizquel, O	CLE	S	.273	69	286	39	78	93	10	1	0	33	11	2	0	23	0	23	13	4	3	.325	.325	6
Voigt, J	BAL	R	.241	59	141	15	34	48	5	0	3	20	1	1	2	18	1	25	0	1	4	.340	.327	2
Walbeck, M	MIN	S	.204	97	338	31	69	96	12	0	5	35	1	1	2	17	1	37	1	0	7	.284	.246	4
Ward, T	MIL	S	.232	102	367	55	85	131	15	2	9	45	0	5	3	52	4	68	6	2	9	.357	.328	4
Wedge, E	BOS	R	.000	2	6	0	0	0	0	0	0	0	0	0	0	0	0	3	0	0	1	.000	.143	0
Welch, B	OAK	R	.000	28	1	0	0	0	0	0	0	0	0	0	0	0	0	0	0	0	0	.000	.000	1
Whitaker, L	DET	L	.301	92	322	67	97	158	21	2	12	43	0	4	4	41	4	47	2	0	8	.491	.377	12
White, D	TOR	S	.270	100	403	67	109	184	24	6	13	49	3	5	1	21	3	80	11	3	4	.457	.313	6
Willard, J	SEA	L	.200	6	5	1	1	4	0	0	1	3	0	0	0	1	0	1	0	0	0	.800	.333	0
Williams, B	NY	S	.289	108	408	80	118	185	29	1	12	57	1	2	3	61	2	54	16	9	11	.453	.384	3
Williams, G	NY	R	.291	57	86	19	25	45	8	0	4	13	0	2	0	4	0	17	1	1	6	.523	.319	2
Wilson, D	SEA	R	.216	91	282	24	61	88	14	2	3	27	8	2	1	10	0	57	1	3	11	.312	.244	9
Winfield, D	MIN	R	.252	77	294	35	74	125	15	2	10	43	1	2	0	31	5	51	2	0	7	.425	.321	0
Wrona, R	MIL	R	.500	6	10	2	5	12	4	0	1	3	0	0	0	1	0	8	0	0	0	1.200	.545	1
Young, E	OAK	R	.067	11	30	2	2	3	1	0	0	3	3	0	0	0	0	8	0	0	1	.100	.097	1
Zupcic, R	BOS-CHI	R	.196	36	92	10	18	27	4	1	1	8	4	1	0	4	0	17	0	0	2	.293	.227	0

TOP 15 DESIGNATED HITTERS
(Minimum: 100 At-Bats)

BATTER	TEAM	B	AVG	G	AB	R	H	TB	2B	3B	HR	RBI	SH	SF	HP	BB	IBB	SO	SB	CS	GIDP	SLG	OBP
Molitor, P.	TOR	R	.339	110	436	81	148	223	30	3	13	70	0	4	1	52	4	46	17	0	11	.511	.408
Jefferson, R.	SEA	S	.333	32	102	15	34	55	6	0	5	14	0	0	0	12	1	23	0	0	3	.539	.409
Davis, C.	CAL	S	.314	106	385	71	121	219	18	1	26	84	0	6	1	69	11	81	3	2	12	.569	.414
Franco, J.	CHI	R	.306	99	385	62	118	185	15	2	16	85	0	4	5	53	3	71	7	1	13	.481	.394
Harper, B.	MIL	R	.299	36	147	12	44	55	8	0	1	11	0	2	1	4	1	11	0	0	4	.374	.318
Baines, H.	BAL	L	.296	91	324	44	96	158	12	1	16	54	0	1	1	29	5	47	0	0	9	.488	.356
Gibson, K.	DET	L	.293	56	205	43	60	125	10	2	17	50	1	3	2	24	2	45	3	4	2	.610	.368
Neel, T.	OAK	L	.292	35	130	19	38	66	7	0	7	21	1	1	1	13	1	33	1	1	2	.508	.359
Berroa, G.	OAK	R	.287	44	174	32	50	84	6	2	8	35	0	5	1	20	0	25	3	1	0	.483	.355
Canseco, J.	TEX	R	.282	111	429	88	121	237	19	2	31	90	0	2	5	69	8	114	15	8	20	.552	.386
Hamelin, B.	KC	L	.269	70	216	47	58	125	16	0	17	48	0	4	1	47	3	46	4	2	3	.579	.396
Nilsson, D.	MIL	L	.268	43	164	21	44	78	14	1	6	34	0	5	0	15	6	32	1	0	1	.476	.321
Murray, E.	CLE	S	.255	82	329	46	84	140	15	1	13	61	0	2	0	26	5	40	6	2	8	.426	.308
Winfield, D.	MIN	R	.254	76	291	35	74	125	15	3	10	43	1	2	0	30	5	49	2	1	7	.430	.322
Dawson, A.	BOS	R	.237	74	291	34	69	134	17	0	16	47	0	1	4	9	3	53	2	2	15	.460	.269

Pitching

Individual Pitching Leaders

Games Won	17	Key	N.Y.
Games Lost	15	Belcher	Det.
Won-Lost Percentage	.857	Bere	Chi. (12-2)
Earned Run Average	2.65	Ontiveros	Oak.
Games	53	Wickman	N.Y.
Games Started	25	Belcher	Det.
		Brown	Tex.
		Darling	Oak.
		Deshaies	Min.
		Eldred	Mil.
		Finley	Cal.
		Guzman	Tor.
		Key	N.Y.
		McDowell	Chi.
		Moore	Det.
Complete Games	9	Johnson	Sea.
Games Finished	43	Hernandez	Chi.
Shutouts	4	Johnson	Sea.
Saves	33	Smith	Bal.
Innings	183.1	Finley	Cal.
Hits	218	Brown	Tex.
Batsmen Faced	774	Finley	Cal.
Runs	124	Belcher	Det.
Earned Runs	107	Deshaies	Min.
Home Runs	30	Deshaies	Min.
Sacrifice Hits	9	Abbott	N.Y.
		Appier	K.C.
		Finley	Cal.
Sacrifice Flies	9	Mussina	Bal.
Hit Batsmen	9	Erickson	Min.
		Leiter	Cal.
		Sele	Bos.
Bases on Balls	89	Moore	Det.
		Van Poppel	Oak.
Intentional Bases on Balls	12	Boever	Det.
Strikeouts	204	Johnson	Sea.
Wild Pitches	13	Guzman	Tor.
		Morris	Cle.
Balks	5	Anderson	Cal.
		Leiter	Tor.
Games Won, Consecutive	11	Key	N.Y. (April 14-June 27)
Games Lost, Consecutive	7	Belcher	Det. (April 7-May 13)

TOP 15 QUALIFIERS FOR EARNED RUN AVERAGE CHAMPIONSHIP

PITCHER	TEAM	T	W	L	ERA	G	GS	CG	SHO	GF	SV	IP	H	TBF	R	ER	HR	SH	SF	HB	BB	IBB	SO	WP	BK	OPP AVG
Ontiveros, S.	OAK	R	6	4	2.65	27	13	2	0	5	5	115.1	93	463	39	34	7	2	1	6	26	1	56	5	0	.217
Clemens, R.	BOS	R	9	7	2.85	24	24	3	1	0	0	170.2	124	692	62	54	15	2	5	4	71	1	168	4	0	.204
Cone, D.	KC	R	16	5	2.94	23	23	4	3	0	0	171.2	130	690	60	56	15	1	5	7	54	0	132	5	0	.209
Mussina, M.	BAL	R	16	5	3.06	24	24	4	3	0	0	176.1	163	712	63	60	19	3	9	1	42	1	99	0	0	.248
Johnson, R.	SEA	L	13	6	3.19	23	23	9	4	0	0	172.0	132	694	65	61	14	3	1	6	72	2	204	5	0	.216
Key, J.	NY	L	17	4	3.27	25	25	1	0	0	0	168.0	177	710	68	61	10	4	2	3	52	0	97	8	1	.273
Hentgen, P.	TOR	R	13	8	3.40	24	24	6	3	0	0	174.2	158	728	74	66	21	6	3	3	59	1	147	5	1	.240
Bones, R.	MIL	R	10	9	3.43	24	24	2	1	0	0	170.2	166	708	76	65	17	4	4	5	45	1	57	0	0	.255
Alvarez, W.	CHI	L	12	8	3.45	24	24	2	1	0	0	161.2	147	682	72	62	16	6	5	3	62	1	108	3	0	.241
Nagy, C.	CLE	R	10	8	3.46	23	23	3	0	0	0	169.1	175	717	76	65	15	6	3	2	48	1	108	5	1	.265
Martinez, D.	CLE	R	11	6	3.52	24	24	7	3	1	0	176.2	166	730	75	69	14	3	5	7	44	2	92	4	3	.247
McDowell, J.	CHI	R	10	9	3.73	25	25	6	2	0	0	181.0	186	755	82	75	12	4	4	4	55	2	127	4	0	.266
Kamieniecki, S.	NY	R	8	6	3.76	22	16	1	0	2	0	117.1	115	509	53	49	13	4	3	3	59	5	71	4	0	.261
Bere, J.	CHI	R	12	2	3.81	24	24	0	0	0	0	141.2	119	608	65	60	17	4	4	1	80	0	127	2	0	.229
Clark, M.	CLE	R	11	3	3.82	20	20	4	1	0	0	127.1	133	540	61	54	14	2	7	4	40	0	60	9	1	.273

INDIVIDUAL PITCHING

PITCHER	TEAM	T	W	L	ERA	G	GS	CG	SHO	GF	SV	IP	H	TBF	R	ER	HR	SH	SF	HB	BB	IBB	SO	WP	BK	OPP AVG
Abbott, J.	NY	L	9	8	4.55	24	24	2	0	0	0	160.1	167	692	88	81	24	9	5	2	64	3	90	8	1	.273
Acre, M.	OAK	R	5	1	3.41	34	0	0	0	6	0	34.1	24	147	13	13	4	3	1	0	23	3	21	1	0	.202
Aguilera, R.	MIN	R	1	4	3.63	44	0	0	0	40	23	44.2	57	201	28	18	7	1	1	0	10	3	46	3	0	.306
Alvarez, W.	CHI	L	12	8	3.45	24	24	2	1	0	0	161.2	147	682	72	62	16	6	3	0	62	1	108	3	0	.241
Anderson, B.	CAL	L	7	5	5.22	18	18	1	0	0	0	101.2	120	441	63	59	13	3	6	5	27	0	47	5	5	.300
Appier, K.	KC	R	7	6	3.83	23	23	2	1	0	0	155.0	137	653	68	66	11	9	7	4	63	7	145	11	1	.240
Armstrong, J.	TEX	R	0	1	3.60	2	2	0	0	0	0	10.0	9	41	4	4	3	0	0	2	2	0	7	1	0	.231

THE COMPLETE HANDBOOK OF BASEBALL

PITCHER	TEAM	T	W	L	ERA	G	GS	CG	SHO	GF	SV	IP	H	TBF	R	ER	HR	SH	SF	HB	BB	IBB	SO	WP	BK	OPP AVG
Assenmacher, P.	CHI	L	1	2	3.55	44	0	0	0	11	0	33.0	26	134	13	13	2	1	3	1	13	2	29	1	0	.224
Ausanio, J.	NY	R	2	1	5.17	13	0	0	0	5	0	15.2	16	69	9	9	3	0	0	0	6	0	15	0	0	.254
Ayala, B.	SEA	R	4	3	2.86	46	0	0	0	40	18	56.2	42	236	25	18	2	1	2	0	26	3	76	2	0	.203
Bailey, P.	BOS	R	0	1	12.46	5	0	0	0	2	0	4.1	10	24	6	6	2	0	0	0	3	0	4	0	0	.476
Bankhead, S.	BOS	R	3	0	4.54	27	0	0	0	3	0	37.2	34	156	21	19	5	0	2	0	12	0	25	7	0	.239
Barnes, B.	CLE	L	0	1	5.40	6	0	0	0	2	0	13.1	12	67	10	8	0	3	1	0	15	0	5	0	0	.235
Belcher, T.	DET	R	7	15	5.89	25	25	0	0	0	0	162.0	192	750	124	106	21	2	5	4	78	10	76	6	1	.290
Belinda, S.	KC	R	2	2	5.14	37	0	0	0	10	1	49.0	47	220	36	28	6	0	3	1	24	3	37	1	0	.250
Benitez, A.	BAL	R	0	0	0.90	3	0	0	0	1	0	10.0	8	42	1	1	0	0	0	0	4	0	14	0	1	.216
Bere, J.	CHI	R	12	2	3.81	24	24	0	0	0	0	141.2	119	608	65	60	17	4	4	1	80	0	127	2	0	.229
Bergman, S.	DET	R	2	1	5.60	3	3	0	0	0	0	17.2	22	82	11	11	2	0	1	2	7	0	12	1	0	.301
Boever, J.	DET	R	2	9	3.98	46	0	0	0	27	3	81.1	80	349	40	36	12	4	2	1	37	12	49	2	0	.263
Bohanon, B.	TEX	L	2	2	7.23	11	5	0	0	1	0	37.1	51	169	31	30	6	2	0	1	8	1	26	1	0	.321
Bolton, T.	BAL	L	1	2	5.40	22	0	0	0	3	0	23.1	29	109	15	14	3	1	1	0	13	1	12	1	0	.309
Bones, R.	MIL	R	10	9	3.43	24	24	0	1	0	0	170.2	166	708	76	65	17	4	5	1	45	1	57	3	0	.255
Bosio, C.	SEA	R	4	10	4.32	19	19	4	0	0	0	125.0	137	546	72	60	15	3	6	0	40	1	67	1	0	.277
Boskie, S.	SEA	R	0	1	6.75	2	0	0	0	0	0	2.2	4	13	2	2	1	0	0	0	1	0	0	0	0	.333
Brewer, B.	KC	L	4	1	2.56	50	0	0	0	17	8	38.2	28	157	11	11	4	0	2	0	16	2	25	0	0	.207
Briscoe, J.	OAK	R	4	2	4.01	37	0	0	0	8	1	49.1	31	210	24	22	7	0	1	1	39	0	45	2	0	.185
Bronkey, J.	MIL	R	1	0	4.35	16	0	0	0	9	0	20.2	20	93	10	10	3	0	1	0	12	4	13	1	0	.247
Brow, S.	TOR	R	0	3	5.90	18	0	0	0	9	2	29.0	34	141	27	19	4	0	0	1	19	2	15	6	0	.288
Brown, K.	TEX	R	10	9	4.82	26	25	3	0	0	0	170.0	218	760	109	91	18	2	7	6	50	3	123	7	0	.314
Brumley, D.	TEX	R	0	0	16.20	2	0	0	0	1	0	3.1	6	22	6	6	1	0	0	0	5	0	4	0	0	.400
Burrows, T.	TEX	L	0	0	9.00	1	0	0	0	0	0	1.0	1	5	1	1	0	0	0	0	1	0	0	0	0	.250
Butcher, M.	CAL	R	2	1	6.67	33	0	0	0	12	0	29.2	31	140	24	22	2	1	3	0	23	5	19	2	0	.274
Cadaret, G.	TOR-DET	L	1	1	4.73	38	0	0	0	17	0	40.0	41	191	24	21	4	2	2	1	33	5	29	9	0	.259
Campbell, K.	MIN	R	1	0	2.92	14	0	0	0	0	0	24.2	20	97	8	8	2	2	0	3	5	0	9	2	0	.233
Carpenter, C.	TEX	R	2	5	5.03	47	0	0	0	16	5	59.0	69	263	35	33	7	3	1	1	20	7	39	1	0	.291
Casian, L.	MIN-CLE	L	1	1	7.35	40	0	0	0	10	1	49.0	73	231	43	40	12	7	2	0	16	3	20	0	0	.358
Castillo, F.	TOR	L	5	2	2.51	41	0	0	0	8	1	68.0	66	291	22	19	7	2	3	2	28	1	43	1	0	.260
Clark, M.	CLE	R	11	3	3.82	20	20	4	1	0	0	127.1	133	540	61	54	14	2	7	4	40	0	60	9	1	.273

OFFICIAL AMERICAN LEAGUE STATS · 421

Player		W	L	ERA	G	GS	CG	SV	IP	H	R	ER	BB	SO						AVG
Clemens, R	BOS	R	9	7	2.85	24	24	3	1	0	170.2	124	62	54	15	2	5	4	1	168	0	.204
Cone, D	KC	R	16	5	2.94	23	23	4	0	0	171.2	130	60	56	15	1	5	7	5	132	1	.209
Converse, J	SEA	R	0	0	8.69	13	0	0	0	1	48.2	73	49	47	5	2	3	1	4	39	0	.353
Cook, D	CHI	L	3	1	3.55	38	0	0	0	8	33.0	29	17	13	4	3	0	0	3	26	1	.230
Cornett, B	TOR	R	1	1	6.68	9	0	0	0	0	18.2	40	25	23	5	2	2	1	2	22	0	.331
Cox, D	TOR	R	1	1	1.45	17	0	0	3	0	18.2	7	3	3	3	4	0	3	1	14	0	.113
Cummings, J	SEA	L	2	4	5.63	10	8	0	2	5	64.0	66	43	40	3	1	1	1	3	33	1	.270
Darling, R	OAK	R	10	11	4.50	25	25	0	2	0	160.0	162	89	80	7	5	3	1	6	108	0	.267
Darwin, D	BOS	R	7	5	6.30	13	13	0	0	0	75.2	101	54	53	18	1	5	0	3	54	1	.317
Darwin, J	SEA	R	0	0	13.50	2	0	0	0	0	4.0	7	6	6	13	0	1	0	0	1	0	.389
Davis, S	DET	R	2	4	3.56	35	0	0	0	10	48.0	36	22	19	3	3	1	0	2	38	0	.207
Davis, T	SEA	L	2	2	4.01	42	0	0	0	12	49.1	57	25	22	4	0	3	0	6	28	0	.295
DeJesus, S	KC	R	3	1	4.73	5	4	0	0	0	26.2	27	14	14	2	3	1	0	0	12	0	.276
DeLeon, J	CHI	R	3	2	3.36	42	0	0	0	11	67.0	48	28	25	5	2	1	0	3	67	0	.200
Deshaies, J	MIN	L	6	12	7.39	25	25	0	0	0	130.1	170	109	107	30	6	7	1	3	78	1	.321
Dettmer, J	TEX	R	0	6	4.33	11	9	0	0	0	54.0	63	40	26	10	5	3	0	0	27	0	.286
DiPoto, J	CLE	R	0	0	8.04	7	0	0	0	0	15.2	26	14	14	8	4	0	2	1	9	0	.406
Doherty, J	DET	R	6	6	6.48	18	17	2	0	0	101.1	139	75	73	13	7	4	1	3	28	0	.337
Dopson, J	CAL	R	1	4	6.14	21	5	1	0	4	58.2	67	41	40	6	1	2	0	0	33	1	.288
Dreyer, S	TEX	R	0	0	5.71	3	0	0	0	0	17.1	19	11	11	5	0	1	1	0	11	0	.271
Eckersley, D	OAK	R	5	4	4.26	45	0	0	19	0	44.1	49	26	21	13	3	0	0	2	47	0	.275
Eichhorn, M	BAL	R	6	5	2.15	43	0	0	1	1	71.0	79	26	17	19	2	0	1	0	35	0	.240
Eldred, C	MIL	R	11	11	4.68	25	25	0	0	0	179.0	158	96	93	23	4	7	5	4	98	2	.236
Erickson, S	MIN	R	8	11	5.44	25	25	0	2	0	144.0	173	95	87	15	5	4	4	2	104	0	.299
Fajardo, H	TEX	R	5	5	6.91	18	12	0	0	0	83.1	95	67	64	15	4	9	2	4	45	4	.284
Farr, S	CLE-BOS	R	2	1	5.72	30	0	0	16	4	28.1	41	21	18	5	2	1	2	2	20	2	.345
Farrell, J	CAL	R	1	2	9.00	3	3	0	0	0	13.0	16	14	13	2	0	1	0	0	10	0	.308
Fernandez, A	CHI	R	11	7	3.86	24	24	3	0	0	170.1	163	83	73	25	4	7	3	1	122	3	.250
Fernandez, S	BAL	R	6	4	5.15	19	19	2	0	0	115.1	109	66	66	27	2	5	2	2	95	0	.248
Fetters, M	MIL	R	1	4	2.54	42	0	0	0	10	46.0	41	20	13	4	2	3	1	5	31	3	.243
Finley, C	CAL	L	10	10	4.32	25	25	0	2	0	183.1	178	95	88	21	9	6	3	10	148	0	.260
Finnvold, A	BOS	R	0	4	5.94	8	8	0	0	0	36.1	45	27	24	0	6	3	0	0	17	0	.304
Fleming, D	SEA	L	7	11	6.46	23	23	0	0	0	117.0	152	93	84	17	4	3	1	4	65	4	.311

PITCHER	TEAM	T	W	L	ERA	G	GS	CG	SHO	GF	SV	IP	H	TBF	R	ER	HR	SH	SF	HB	BB	IBB	SO	WP	BK	OPP AVG
Fossas, T.	BOS	L	2	2	4.76	44	0	0	0	14	1	34.0	35	151	18	18	6	2	0	1	15	2	31	1	0	.263
Frohwirth, T.	BOS	R	0	3	10.80	22	0	0	0	8	1	26.2	40	141	36	32	3	4	1	2	17	1	13	1	0	.339
Garagozzo, K.	MIN	L	0	0	9.64	7	0	0	0	0	0	9.1	9	48	10	10	3	1	2	0	7	2	3	2	0	.273
Gardiner, M.	DET	R	2	2	4.14	38	1	0	0	14	5	58.2	53	254	35	27	10	1	2	1	23	5	31	1	0	.233
Gibson, P.	NY	L	1	1	4.97	30	0	0	0	15	0	29.0	26	130	17	16	5	2	1	0	17	3	21	1	0	.236
Glinatsis, G.	SEA	R	0	0	13.50	2	0	0	0	0	0	5.1	9	28	8	8	1	0	0	0	6	0	3	0	0	.429
Gohr, G.	DET	R	0	2	4.50	8	2	0	0	1	0	34.0	36	159	19	17	3	1	0	1	21	1	21	1	1	.263
Gordon, T.	KC	R	11	7	4.35	24	24	0	0	0	0	155.1	136	675	79	75	15	3	8	3	87	3	126	12	1	.237
Gossage, R.	SEA	R	3	0	4.18	36	0	0	0	21	1	47.1	44	197	23	22	6	2	3	3	15	1	29	2	1	.251
Grahe, J.	CAL	R	2	5	6.65	40	0	0	0	32	13	43.1	68	218	33	32	5	3	6	0	18	4	26	4	0	.362
Granger, J.	KC	L	0	1	6.75	2	0	0	0	0	0	9.1	13	47	8	7	2	0	0	1	6	0	3	0	0	.325
Grimsley, J.	CLE	R	5	2	4.57	14	13	0	0	0	0	82.2	91	368	47	42	7	4	2	2	34	1	59	6	0	.283
Groom, B.	DET	L	0	0	3.94	40	0	0	0	10	0	32.0	31	139	14	14	4	0	3	1	13	2	27	0	0	.256
Guardado, E.	MIN	L	0	2	8.47	4	4	0	0	0	0	17.0	26	81	16	16	3	1	2	0	4	0	8	0	0	.351
Gubicza, M.	KC	R	7	9	4.50	22	22	0	0	0	0	130.0	158	561	74	65	11	5	5	0	26	0	59	9	0	.301
Gullickson, B.	DET	R	4	5	5.93	21	19	1	0	0	0	115.1	156	521	79	76	24	7	5	4	25	2	65	4	0	.322
Guthrie, M.	MIN	L	4	2	6.14	50	0	0	0	13	1	51.1	65	234	43	35	8	6	1	0	26	5	38	7	0	.316
Guzman, J.	TOR	R	12	11	5.68	25	25	0	0	0	0	147.1	165	671	102	93	20	1	6	3	76	2	124	13	1	.282
Hall, D.	TOR	R	2	3	3.41	30	0	0	0	28	17	31.2	26	131	12	12	3	2	2	0	14	1	28	1	0	.226
Hammaker, A.	CHI	L	0	0	0.00	2	0	0	0	0	0	1.1	1	5	0	0	0	1	0	0	1	0	1	0	0	.200
Haney, C.	KC	L	2	2	7.31	6	6	0	0	0	0	28.1	36	127	25	23	9	0	2	0	11	0	18	1	0	.333
Harris, G.	BOS-NY	R	3	5	7.99	38	0	0	0	10	2	50.2	64	240	49	45	9	4	3	2	26	4	48	6	0	.312
Harris, G.	DET	R	0	0	7.15	11	0	0	0	3	1	11.1	13	53	10	9	1	0	0	0	4	1	10	1	0	.271
Helling, R.	TEX	R	3	2	5.88	9	9	0	0	0	0	52.0	62	228	34	34	14	2	5	0	18	0	25	0	0	.295
Henke, T.	TEX	R	3	6	3.79	37	0	0	0	31	15	38.0	33	156	16	16	6	0	1	1	12	0	39	3	0	.232
Henneman, M.	DET	R	1	3	5.19	30	0	0	0	23	8	34.2	43	167	20	20	5	2	1	0	17	7	27	3	0	.297
Henry, D.	MIL	R	2	3	4.60	25	0	0	0	7	0	31.1	32	143	17	16	7	1	1	0	23	1	27	0	0	.271
Hentgen, P.	TOR	R	13	8	3.40	34	32	6	3	0	0	174.2	158	728	74	66	21	6	3	1	59	1	147	5	1	.240
Hernandez, R.	CHI	R	4	4	4.91	45	0	0	0	43	14	40.2	44	206	29	26	5	3	1	1	19	0	50	7	0	.238
Hernandez, X.	NY	R	4	4	5.85	31	0	0	0	14	6	40.0	48	187	30	27	5	0	2	2	21	3	37	3	0	.300
Hesketh, J.	BOS	L	8	5	4.26	25	20	0	0	1	0	114.0	117	495	70	54	9	1	2	8	46	3	83	6	1	.267

OFFICIAL AMERICAN LEAGUE STATS · 423

Player	Team	T	W	L	ERA	G	GS	CG	ShO	GF	SV	IP	H	R	ER	HR	SH	SF	HB	BB	IBB	SO	WP	BK	AVG
Hibbard, G.	SEA	L	1	5	6.69	15	0	0	0	0	0	80.2	115	78	60	11	6	2	2	31	1	39	5	0	.328
Higuera, T.	MIL	L	1	5	7.06	17	12	0	0	4	0	58.2	74	55	46	13	2	2	2	36	0	35	0	0	.311
Hill, M.	SEA	R	0	0	6.46	17	0	0	0	2	0	23.2	30	19	17	4	1	1	1	11	3	16	5	0	.306
Hitchcock, S.	NY	L	1	2	4.20	13	6	0	0	2	0	49.1	48	24	23	3	7	0	2	29	0	37	0	0	.265
Honeycutt, R.	TEX	L	1	4	7.20	23	0	0	0	9	2	25.0	37	21	20	4	0	0	1	9	1	18	0	0	.349
Horsman, V.	OAK	L	0	1	4.91	42	0	0	0	6	1	29.1	27	17	16	3	1	0	0	11	2	20	1	0	.266
Howard, C.	BOS	L	1	2	3.63	33	0	0	0	6	0	39.2	35	22	16	0	3	1	0	12	2	22	2	0	.266
Howard, D.	KC	L	0	0	4.50	1	0	0	0	0	0	2.0	4	1	1	0	0	0	0	0	0	0	0	0	.233
Howe, S.	NY	R	3	0	1.80	40	0	0	0	25	15	40.0	28	8	8	2	3	0	0	5	1	18	0	0	.194
Howell, J.	TEX	R	4	1	5.44	40	8	0	0	17	2	43.0	44	29	26	10	0	1	3	16	2	22	4	0	.286
Hurst, B.	TEX	L	2	2	7.11	8	8	0	0	0	0	38.0	53	30	30	8	0	1	4	16	0	24	0	0	.362
Hurst, J.	TEX	L	1	1	10.13	8	0	0	0	3	0	10.2	17	12	12	1	0	0	0	8	0	5	2	0	.342
Hutton, M.	NY	R	0	0	4.91	2	0	0	0	1	0	3.2	4	2	2	0	0	0	0	0	0	1	0	0	.250
Ignasiak, M.	MIL	R	3	0	4.53	23	0	0	0	5	0	47.2	51	25	24	5	1	1	1	13	1	24	3	0	.276
Jimenez, M.	OAK	R	1	4	7.41	8	7	0	0	0	0	34.0	38	33	28	9	1	1	1	32	0	22	0	0	.275
Johnson, D.	CHI	R	2	1	6.57	15	0	0	0	4	0	12.1	16	9	9	2	0	1	0	11	0	7	0	0	.327
Johnson, R.	SEA	L	13	6	3.19	23	23	9	4	0	0	172.0	132	65	61	14	3	0	6	72	1	204	5	0	.216
Kamieniecki, S.	NY	R	8	6	3.76	22	16	1	1	2	0	117.1	115	53	49	13	4	3	3	59	1	71	4	0	.261
Karsay, S.	OAK	R	8	1	2.57	4	4	1	0	0	0	28.0	26	8	8	1	1	0	1	8	0	15	0	0	.252
Key, J.	NY	L	17	4	3.27	25	25	4	2	0	0	168.0	177	68	61	10	6	2	3	52	1	97	8	0	.273
Kiefer, M.	MIL	R	1	0	8.44	7	0	0	0	1	0	10.2	15	12	10	4	3	0	0	8	0	8	0	0	.357
King, K.	SEA	L	0	2	7.04	19	0	0	0	7	1	15.1	21	13	12	4	1	0	0	17	2	6	0	0	.333
Klingenbeck, S.	BAL	R	1	0	3.86	1	1	0	0	0	0	7.0	6	4	3	1	0	0	0	4	0	5	0	0	.240
Knudsen, K.	DET	R	0	1	13.50	4	0	0	0	1	0	5.1	7	8	8	2	0	2	2	3	0	0	0	0	.304
Krueger, B.	DET	L	2	2	9.61	16	0	0	0	2	0	19.2	26	21	21	3	2	0	2	11	2	8	2	0	.321
Langston, M.	CAL	L	7	8	4.68	18	18	2	1	0	0	119.1	121	67	62	13	3	8	3	54	0	109	6	0	.268
Leary, T.	TEX	R	1	1	8.14	6	3	0	0	1	0	21.0	26	19	19	4	0	1	0	11	1	9	1	0	.306
Lefferts, C.	CAL	L	1	1	4.67	30	0	0	0	10	0	34.2	50	20	18	7	3	0	3	12	1	27	3	0	.350
Lettwich, P.	CAL	R	5	0	5.68	20	20	0	0	0	0	114.0	127	75	72	16	4	4	0	42	0	67	3	0	.283
Leiper, D.	OAK	L	0	0	1.93	26	0	0	0	8	0	18.2	13	4	4	2	2	2	0	6	2	14	1	0	.206
Leiter, A.	TOR	L	1	6	5.08	20	20	0	0	15	0	111.2	125	68	63	6	8	9	4	65	3	100	7	5	.285
Leiter, M.	CAL	R	6	7	4.72	40	7	0	0	6	0	95.1	99	56	50	13	3	2	0	35	6	71	2	0	.265
Lewis, S.	CAL	R	0	1	6.10	20	0	0	0	6	0	31.0	46	23	21	5	4	0	3	10	2	10	0	0	.359

PITCHER	TEAM	T	W	L	ERA	G	GS	CG	SHO	GF	SV	IP	H	TBF	R	ER	HR	SH	SF	HB	BB	IBB	SO	WP	BK	OPP AVG
Lilliquist, D	CLE	L	1	3	4.91	36	0	0	0	12	1	29.1	34	127	17	16	6	3	3	1	8	1	15	0	0	.304
Lima, J	DET	R	1	0	13.50	3	1	0	0	0	0	6.2	11	34	10	10	2	0	0	0	3	0	7	1	0	.355
Lloyd, G	MIL	L	2	3	5.17	43	0	0	0	21	3	47.0	49	203	28	27	4	1	2	3	15	6	31	2	0	.269
Lopez, A	CLE	R	2	2	4.24	4	4	0	0	0	0	17.0	20	76	11	8	3	0	0	1	6	0	18	0	0	.290
Lorraine, A	CAL	L	0	2	10.61	4	3	0	0	1	0	18.2	30	96	23	22	7	2	1	0	11	0	10	2	0	.366
Magnante, M	KC	L	2	3	4.60	36	1	0	0	10	0	47.0	55	211	23	24	4	2	1	0	16	1	21	0	0	.289
Mahomes, P	MIN	R	2	4	7.30	12	11	0	0	0	0	37.0	89	357	63	60	18	0	3	6	51	0	33	3	0	.300
Magrane, J	CAL	L	2	9	4.73	21	21	1	1	0	0	74.0	121	517	68	63	22	1	6	7	62	1	53	7	3	.269
Martinez, D	CLE	R	11	6	3.52	24	24	0	0	0	0	120.0	166	730	75	69	14	3	5	4	44	1	53	3	3	.247
McCaskill, K	CHI	R	1	4	3.42	40	0	7	2	18	3	176.2	51	228	22	20	6	1	0	2	22	4	92	3	0	.252
McDonald, B	BAL	R	14	7	4.06	24	24	5	0	0	0	52.1	151	655	75	71	14	6	2	2	54	2	94	3	1	.255
McDowell, J	CHI	R	10	9	3.73	25	25	6	1	0	0	157.1	186	755	82	75	12	4	5	4	42	1	127	4	0	.266
Meacham, R	KC	R	3	3	3.73	36	0	0	0	15	4	181.0	51	213	21	21	6	4	1	2	12	1	36	0	0	.263
Melendez, J	BOS	R	0	1	6.06	10	0	0	0	3	0	50.2	20	76	11	11	3	0	2	2	8	2	9	0	0	.323
Mercedes, J	MIL	R	0	2	2.32	19	0	0	0	5	0	16.1	22	120	9	8	4	2	2	4	16	2	11	1	0	.216
Merriman, B	MIN	R	0	1	6.35	15	0	0	0	4	0	31.0	18	87	13	12	0	0	4	3	14	0	10	0	0	.269
Mesa, J	CLE	R	7	5	3.82	51	0	0	0	22	2	17.0	81	315	33	31	6	3	2	3	26	7	63	3	0	.254
Milacki, B	KC	R	0	0	6.14	10	10	0	0	0	0	73.0	68	254	43	38	3	1	4	1	20	3	17	2	0	.298
Mills, A	BAL	R	3	3	5.16	47	0	0	0	16	0	55.2	43	199	26	26	6	0	4	2	24	4	44	4	0	.251
Minchey, N	BOS	R	2	3	8.61	6	5	1	0	0	0	45.1	44	121	26	22	5	1	0	2	14	2	15	2	1	.427
Miranda, A	MIL	R	2	5	5.28	8	8	0	0	0	0	23.0	39	196	28	27	7	3	0	0	27	0	24	3	1	.234
Mohler, M	OAK	L	1	1	7.71	1	1	0	0	0	0	46.0	3	14	3	2	0	1	0	0	2	0	1	0	0	.167
Montgomery, J	KC	R	2	3	4.03	42	0	0	0	38	27	2.1	48	193	21	20	5	1	1	3	15	8	50	0	0	.276
Moore, M	DET	R	11	10	5.42	25	25	4	1	0	0	44.2	152	679	97	93	27	4	4	4	89	2	62	10	0	.263
Morris, J	CLE	R	10	6	5.60	23	23	1	0	0	0	154.1	163	636	96	88	14	5	4	3	67	1	100	13	0	.292
Moyer, J	BAL	L	5	7	4.77	23	23	2	0	0	0	141.1	158	631	81	79	23	2	4	2	38	0	87	5	0	.271
Mulholland, T	NY	L	6	7	6.49	24	19	2	0	4	0	149.0	163	542	94	87	24	3	2	4	37	3	72	0	0	.303
Murphy, R	NY	L	0	0	16.20	3	0	0	0	1	0	120.2	3	8	3	3	2	0	0	0	0	0	0	0	0	.375
Mussina, M	BAL	R	16	5	3.06	24	24	3	0	0	0	1.2	163	712	63	60	19	3	0	4	42	1	99	0	0	.248
Nabholz, C	CLE-BOS	L	3	5	7.64	14	12	0	0	1	0	176.1	67	254	48	45	6	0	1	3	38	1	28	0	0	.318
Nagy, C	CLE	R	10	8	3.45	23	23	3	0	0	0	53.0	175	717	76	65	15	2	5	5	48	8	108	5	1	.265

OFFICIAL AMERICAN LEAGUE STATS

Player	Team	T	W	L	ERA	G	GS	CG	ShO	Sv	IP	H	R	ER	HR	BB	SO	2B	3B	HR	SB	CS	AVG
Navarro, J	MIL	R	4	9	6.62	29	10	0	0	0	89.2	115	71	66	10	2	4	4	35	4	2	3	.314
Nelson, J	SEA	R	0	0	2.76	28	0	0	0	0	42.1	35	18	13	3	1	1	1	20	8	0	2	.226
Nunez, E	OAK	R	0	0	12.00	15	0	0	0	0	15.0	26	20	20	2	0	2	1	10	10	1	2	.382
Ogea, C	CLE	R	0	1	6.06	4	4	1	0	0	16.1	21	11	11	2	0	0	0	10	1	0	0	.304
Ojeda, B	NY	L	0	0	24.00	2	0	0	0	0	3.0	11	8	8	1	0	0	1	6	0	0	0	.611
Oliver, D	TEX	L	4	0	3.42	43	0	0	2	0	50.0	40	24	19	4	1	6	1	50	6	0	3	.223
Ontiveros, S	OAK	R	6	4	2.65	27	13	0	3	2	115.1	93	39	34	7	6	2	2	56	6	2	5	.217
Oquist, M	BAL	R	3	3	6.17	15	9	0	0	0	58.1	75	41	40	7	1	6	1	39	6	4	0	.319
Orosco, J	BAL	L	3	1	5.08	40	0	0	2	4	39.0	32	26	22	4	4	6	4	36	6	2	2	.222
Pall, D	NY	R	1	2	3.60	26	0	0	0	0	35.0	43	18	14	3	2	3	2	21	1	0	0	.295
Patterson, B	CAL	L	2	3	4.07	47	0	0	0	1	42.0	43	21	19	6	0	0	1	30	2	0	2	.229
Patterson, K	CAL	L	0	0	0.00	1	0	0	0	0	0.2	0	0	0	0	0	0	0	0	0	0	0	.000
Pavlik, R	TEX	R	2	5	7.69	11	11	0	0	0	50.1	61	45	43	8	1	4	4	31	0	0	5	.300
Pennington, B	BAL	L	0	1	12.00	8	0	0	0	0	6.0	9	8	8	2	0	0	0	7	0	0	2	.346
Perez, M	NY	R	9	4	4.10	22	22	0	3	0	151.1	134	74	69	16	5	3	3	109	58	4	7	.238
Phoenix, S	OAK	R	0	0	6.23	2	0	0	0	0	4.1	4	3	3	0	0	0	0	3	2	0	0	.235
Pichardo, H	KC	R	5	3	4.92	45	0	0	0	3	67.2	82	42	37	4	4	3	7	36	24	3	3	.309
Plantenberg, E	SEA	L	0	0	0.00	6	0	0	0	0	7.0	8	0	0	0	0	0	0	7	1	0	0	.174
Plunk, E	CLE	R	7	2	2.54	41	0	0	2	3	71.0	61	25	20	3	2	4	5	73	37	0	7	.231
Poole, J	BAL	L	2	0	6.64	38	0	0	2	0	20.1	32	15	15	2	1	2	1	18	11	2	0	.372
Pulido, C	MIN	L	3	7	5.98	19	14	0	0	0	84.1	87	56	56	17	0	1	0	32	40	3	7	.273
Quantrill, P	BOS	R	1	1	3.52	17	0	0	0	0	23.0	25	10	9	4	2	1	1	15	5	3	3	.278
Reardon, J	NY	R	0	1	8.38	11	0	0	0	2	9.2	17	9	9	3	2	2	0	0	3	0	0	.386
Reed, R	TEX	R	1	1	5.94	4	3	0	0	0	16.2	17	11	11	3	1	0	0	7	7	0	0	.254
Reyes, C	OAK	R	0	3	4.15	27	9	0	0	0	78.0	71	38	36	10	2	3	3	44	12	3	0	.242
Rhodes, A	BAL	L	3	5	5.81	10	10	0	2	0	52.2	51	34	34	8	2	2	1	30	57	0	3	.254
Righetti, D	OAK-TOR	L	0	1	10.18	20	0	0	0	0	20.1	22	23	23	5	2	1	1	19	47	0	0	.278
Risley, B	SEA	R	0	0	3.44	37	0	0	0	0	52.1	22	31	20	7	2	2	0	14	0	1	0	.170
Rogers, K	TEX	L	11	8	4.46	24	24	2	7	0	167.1	169	93	83	24	6	3	4	61	120	0	3	.260
Ruffcorn, S	CHI	R	0	1	12.79	2	2	0	0	0	6.1	15	11	9	1	0	3	1	1	0	0	1	.455
Russell, J	BOS-CLE	R	1	6	5.09	42	0	0	0	0	40.2	43	23	23	9	0	2	2	28	16	2	0	.269
Ryan, K	BOS	R	2	3	2.44	42	0	0	0	0	48.0	46	14	13	5	4	3	1	32	17	3	2	.256
St. Claire, R	TOR	R	0	0	9.00	2	0	0	0	0	2.0	4	2	2	1	0	0	0	2	2	1	0	.444

PITCHER	TEAM	T	W	L	ERA	G	GS	CG	SHO	GF	SV	IP	H	TBF	R	ER	HR	SH	SF	HB	BB	IBB	SO	WP	BK	OPP AVG
Salkeld, R.	SEA	R	2	5	7.17	13	13	0	0	0	0	59.0	76	291	47	47	7	0	3	1	45	1	46	2	0	.314
Sampen, B.	CAL	R	1	1	6.46	10	0	0	0	4	0	15.1	22	75	11	11	1	3	1	3	13	0	9	0	0	.241
Sanderson, S.	CHI	R	8	4	5.09	18	14	0	0	0	0	92.0	110	389	57	52	20	1	2	2	12	1	36	3	0	.296
Scanlan, B.	MIL	R	2	6	4.11	30	12	0	0	9	2	103.0	117	441	53	47	11	1	2	4	28	2	65	0	0	.288
Schullstrom, E.	MIN	R	0	0	2.77	9	0	0	0	5	0	13.0	13	57	7	4	0	1	0	0	5	0	13	3	0	.260
Schwarz, J.	CHI-CAL	R	0	0	5.50	13	0	0	0	5	0	18.0	14	88	13	11	2	0	0	0	22	0	8	0	0	.219
Sele, A.	BOS	R	8	7	3.83	22	22	0	0	0	0	143.1	140	615	68	61	13	1	5	2	60	2	105	4	0	.261
Shuey, P.	CLE	R	0	1	8.49	14	0	0	0	11	5	11.2	14	62	11	11	1	0	0	1	12	0	16	0	0	.280
Small, A.	TOR	R	0	0	9.00	3	0	0	0	0	0	2.0	5	13	2	2	1	0	0	0	0	0	0	0	0	.500
Smith, D.	TEX	L	1	1	4.30	13	0	0	0	2	0	14.2	18	76	11	7	2	1	1	0	12	5	9	0	0	.281
Smith, Le	BAL	R	4	4	3.29	41	0	0	0	39	33	38.1	34	160	16	14	6	5	2	0	11	2	42	0	0	.239
Smithberg, R.	OAK	R	0	0	15.43	2	0	0	0	2	0	2.1	6	13	4	4	1	0	0	0	1	0	3	0	0	.500
Spoljaric, P.	TOR	L	0	1	38.57	1	1	0	0	0	0	2.1	6	21	10	10	3	0	0	0	9	0	2	0	0	.417
Springer, R.	CAL	R	2	2	5.52	18	5	0	0	6	0	45.2	53	198	28	28	9	1	1	0	14	0	28	3	0	.291
Stevens, D.	MIN	R	5	5	6.80	24	0	0	0	6	0	45.0	55	208	35	34	6	2	4	0	23	2	24	0	0	.302
Stewart, D.	TOR	R	7	8	5.87	22	22	1	0	0	0	133.1	151	602	89	87	26	3	0	4	62	4	111	6	0	.285
Stidham, P.	DET	R	0	0	24.92	3	0	0	0	1	0	4.1	12	26	12	12	0	0	1	0	4	1	4	2	0	.571
Stottlemyre, T.	TOR	R	7	7	4.22	26	19	3	1	5	1	140.2	149	605	67	66	19	4	5	7	48	1	105	2	0	.276
Swan, R.	CLE	L	1	1	11.25	12	0	0	0	2	0	8.0	13	43	11	10	2	2	0	0	7	0	2	0	0	.382
Tapani, K.	MIN	R	11	7	4.62	24	24	4	1	0	0	156.0	181	672	86	80	13	1	4	0	39	1	91	0	1	.291
Tavarez, J.	CLE	R	0	1	21.60	1	1	0	0	0	0	1.2	6	14	8	4	0	0	0	0	1	0	0	0	0	.500
Taylor, B.	OAK	R	3	1	3.50	41	0	0	0	11	1	46.1	38	195	24	18	4	1	1	0	18	5	48	0	0	.220
Thigpen, B.	SEA	R	0	2	9.39	12	0	0	0	3	0	7.2	12	40	9	8	3	1	0	0	5	0	3	3	0	.353
Timlin, M.	TOR	R	0	1	5.18	34	0	0	0	16	2	40.0	41	179	25	23	5	0	2	0	20	0	38	0	0	.261
Tomberlin, A.	BOS	L	0	0	0.00	1	0	0	0	1	0	2.0	1	8	0	0	0	0	0	0	0	0	1	0	0	.143
Tricek, R.	BOS	R	1	1	8.06	12	0	0	0	2	0	22.1	32	113	21	20	5	2	0	0	16	2	7	3	0	.330
Trombley, M.	MIN	R	2	0	6.33	24	0	0	0	8	0	48.1	56	219	36	34	10	0	3	3	18	2	32	3	0	.287
Turner, M.	CLE	R	1	0	2.13	24	0	0	0	2	0	12.2	13	65	6	3	0	1	3	0	7	1	5	0	0	.241
Valdez, S.	BOS	R	0	1	8.16	12	1	0	0	2	0	14.1	25	72	14	13	4	0	0	0	8	0	4	1	0	.391
Vanegmond, T.	BOS	R	2	3	6.34	7	7	0	0	0	0	38.1	38	173	27	27	7	0	0	3	21	1	22	0	0	.255
Van Poppel, T.	OAK	R	7	10	6.09	23	23	0	0	0	0	116.2	108	532	80	79	20	4	3	4	89	3	83	3	1	.250

OFFICIAL AMERICAN LEAGUE STATS

Player	Team	L			ERA	G	CG	SHO	REL	SV	IP	H	R	ER	HR	HB	BB	IBB	SO	WP	BK	OPP AVG
Viola, F.	BOS	L	1	1	4.65					0	31.0	34		17	16	2	2	0	0	9	2	.296
Vosberg, E.	OAK	L	0	2	3.95	16		6		0	13.2	16		7	6	2	1	0	0	12	1	.320
Wegman, B.	MIL	R	0	4	4.51	19		19		0	115.2	140		64	58	14	6	2	2	59	3	.303
Welch, B.	OAK	R	3	6	7.08	25		8		0	68.2	79		56	54	10	6	6	2	44	3	.290
Wells, B.	SEA	R	1	0	2.25	5		1		0	4.0	4		1	1	0	4	1	0	3	0	.250
Wells, D.	DET	L	5	7	3.96	16		16		0	111.1	113		54	49	5	0	2	2	71	0	.260
Wertz, B.	CLE	R	0	0	10.38	1				0	4.1	9		5	5	0	0	1	0	1	0	.409
Whiteside, M.	TEX	R	2	2	5.02	47				16	61.0	68		40	34	6	3	5	2	37	1	.286
Wickman, B.	NY	R	5	4	3.09	53				19	70.0	54		26	24	3	0	2	1	56	1	.213
Williams, W.	TOR	R	1	3	3.64	38				14	59.1	44		26	24	2	5	2	2	56	0	.205
Williamson, M.	BAL	R	3	1	4.01	28				0	67.1	75		33	30	9	0	2	3	28	4	.278
Willis, C.	MIN	R	2	4	5.92	49				3	59.1	89		48	39	6	1	3	1	37	0	.335
Witt, B.	OAK	R	8	10	5.04	24		24		0	135.2	151		88	76	22	2	7	5	111	6	.283

CLUB PITCHING

CLUB	W	L	ERA	G	CG	SHO	REL	SV	IP	H	R	ER	HR	HB	BB	IBB	SO	WP	BK	OPP AVG
CHICAGO	67	46	3.96	113	13	9	239	20	1011.1	964	498	445	115	17	377	28	754	19	3	.250
KANSAS CITY	64	51	4.23	115	5	6	247	38	1031.2	1018	532	485	95	33	392	31	717	10	5	.260
BALTIMORE	63	49	4.31	112	13	4	234	37	997.2	1005	497	478	131	26	351	25	666	18	1	.263
NEW YORK	70	43	4.34	113	8	2	241	31	1019.2	1045	534	492	120	21	398	24	656	46	4	.267
CLEVELAND	66	47	4.36	113	17	5	222	21	1018.2	1097	562	494	94	41	404	28	666	58	6	.275
MILWAUKEE	53	62	4.62	115	11	3	252	23	1036.0	1071	586	532	127	29	421	28	577	30	6	.269
TORONTO	55	60	4.70	115	13	4	221	26	1025.0	1053	579	535	127	32	482	23	832	54	7	.266
OAKLAND	51	63	4.80	114	12	9	308	23	1003.1	979	589	535	128	34	510	30	732	42	12	.257
BOSTON	54	61	4.93	115	6	3	308	30	1029.1	1104	621	564	120	31	450	46	729	46	4	.276
SEATTLE	49	63	4.99	112	13	7	252	21	984.0	1051	616	546	109	28	486	39	763	41	1	.274
DETROIT	53	62	5.38	115	15	1	246	20	1018.0	1139	671	609	148	25	449	74	560	59	2	.282
CALIFORNIA	47	68	5.42	115	11	4	257	21	1027.0	1149	660	618	150	45	436	28	682	48	8	.287
TEXAS	52	62	5.45	114	10	4	301	26	1023.0	1176	697	620	157	32	394	29	683	50	5	.288
MINNESOTA	53	60	5.68	113	6	4	272	29	1005.0	1197	688	634	153	31	388	20	602	43	1	.299
TOTALS	797	797	4.80	797	153	65	3600	366	14229.2	15048	8330	7587	1774	425	5938	449	9619	614	68	.273

ALL-TIME LEADERS

BATTING AVERAGE
(4,000 at-bats minimum)

1. Ty Cobb	.367	11. Pete Browning	.341
2. Rogers Hornsby	.358	12. Willie Keeler	.341
3. Joe Jackson	.356	13. Bill Terry	.341
4. Ed Delahanty	.346	14. George Sisler	.340
5. Tris Speaker	.345	15. Lou Gehrig	.340
6. Ted Williams	.344	16. Jesse Burkett	.338
7. Billy Hamilton	.344	17. Nap Lajoie	.338
8. Dan Brouthers	.342	18. Riggs Stephenson	.336
9. Babe Ruth	.342	19. Wade Boggs	.335
10. Harry Heilmann	.342	20. Al Simmons	.334

HITS

1. Pete Rose	4,256	11. Nap Lajoie	3,242
2. Ty Cobb	4,189	12. George Brett	3,154
3. Hank Aaron	3,771	13. Paul Waner	3,152
4. Stan Musial	3,630	14. Robin Yount	3,142
5. Tris Speaker	3,514	15. Dave Winfield	3,088
6. Carl Yastrzemski	3,419	16. Rod Carew	3,053
7. Cap Anson	3,415	17. Lou Brock	3,023
Honus Wagner	3,415	18. Al Kaline	3,007
9. Eddie Collins	3,312	19. Roberto Clemente	3,000
10. Willie Mays	3,283	20. Sam Rice	2,987

DOUBLES

1. Tris Speaker	792	11. Robin Yount	583
2. Pete Rose	746	12. Cap Anson	582
3. Stan Musial	725	13. Charlie Gehringer	574
4. Ty Cobb	724	14. Harry Heilmann	542
5. George Brett	665	15. Rogers Hornsby	541
6. Nap Lajoie	657	16. Joe Medwick	540
7. Carl Yastrzemski	646	17. Al Simmons	539
8. Honus Wagner	640	18. Dave Winfield	535
9. Hank Aaron	624	19. Lou Gehrig	534
10. Paul Waner	605	20. Al Oliver	529

Ty Cobb spiked his batting average to all-time .367.

TRIPLES

1. Sam Crawford — 309
2. Ty Cobb — 295
3. Honus Wagner — 252
4. Jake Beckley — 243
5. Roger Connor — 233
6. Tris Speaker — 222
7. Fred Clarke — 220
8. Dan Brouthers — 205
9. Joe Kelley — 194
10. Paul Waner — 191
11. Bid McPhee — 188
12. Eddie Collins — 186
13. Ed Delahanty — 185
14. Sam Rice — 184
15. Jesse Burkett — 182
16. Edd Roush — 182
17. Ed Konetchy — 181
18. Buck Ewing — 178
19. Stan Musial — 177
  Rabbit Maranville — 177

HOME RUNS

1. Hank Aaron — 755
2. Babe Ruth — 714
3. Willie Mays — 660
4. Frank Robinson — 586
5. Harmon Killebrew — 573
6. Reggie Jackson — 563
7. Mike Schmidt — 548
8. Mickey Mantle — 536
9. Jimmie Foxx — 534
10. Ted Williams — 521
  Willie McCovey — 521
12. Ernie Banks — 512
  Eddie Mathews — 512
14. Mel Ott — 511
15. Lou Gehrig — 493
16. Stan Musial — 475
  Willie Stargell — 475
18. Dave Winfield — 463
19. Eddie Murray — 458
20. Carl Yastrzemski — 452

RUNS BATTED IN

1. Hank Aaron — 2,297
2. Babe Ruth — 2,213
3. Lou Gehrig — 1,995
4. Cap Anson — 1,981
5. Stan Musial — 1,951
6. Ty Cobb — 1,937
7. Jimmie Foxx — 1,922
8. Willie Mays — 1,903
9. Mel Ott — 1,860
10. Carl Yastrzemski — 1,844
11. Ted Williams — 1,839
12. Dave Winfield — 1,829
13. Al Simmons — 1,827
14. Frank Robinson — 1,812
15. Eddie Murray — 1,738
16. Honus Wagner — 1,732
17. Reggie Jackson — 1,702
18. Tony Perez — 1,652
19. Ernie Banks — 1,636
20. Goose Goslin — 1,609

Hank Aaron went from historic 715th to 755 home runs.

SLUGGING AVERAGE
(4,000 at-bats minimum)

1.	Babe Ruth	.690		Mickey Mantle	.557
2.	Ted Williams	.634	12.	Hank Aaron	.555
3.	Lou Gehrig	.632	13.	Ralph Kiner	.548
4.	Jimmie Foxx	.609	14.	Hack Wilson	.545
5.	Hank Greenberg	.605	15.	Chuck Klein	.543
6.	Joe DiMaggio	.579	17.	Duke Snider	.540
7.	Rogers Hornsby	.577	18.	Frank Robinson	.537
8.	Johnny Mize	.562	19.	Al Simmons	.535
9.	Stan Musial	.559	20.	Dick Allen	.534
10.	Willie Mays	.557		Earl Averill	.534

ON-BASE PERCENTAGE
(4,000 at-bats minimum)

1.	Ted Williams	.483	11.	Ferris Fain	.425
2.	Babe Ruth	.474	12.	Eddie Collins	.424
3.	John McGraw	.465	13.	Joe Jackson	.423
4.	Billy Hamilton	.455		Mickey Mantle	.423
5.	Lou Gehrig	.447		Dan Brouthers	.423
6.	Rogers Hornsby	.434		Max Bishop	.423
7.	Ty Cobb	.433	17.	Mickey Cochrane	.419
8.	Jimmie Foxx	.428	18.	Stan Musial	.418
	Tris Speaker	.428	19.	Cupid Childs	.416
	Wade Boggs	.428	20.	Jesse Burkett	.415

STOLEN BASES

1.	Rickey Henderson	1,117	11.	Joe Morgan	689
2.	Lou Brock	938	12.	Willie Wilson	668
3.	Billy Hamilton	912	13.	Tom Brown	657
4.	Ty Cobb	891	14.	Bert Campaneris	649
5.	Tim Raines	764	15.	George Davis	616
6.	Eddie Collins	744	16.	Dummy Hoy	594
7.	Arlie Latham	739	17.	Maury Wills	586
8.	Max Carey	738	18.	George Van Haltren	583
9.	Honus Wagner	722	19.	Hugh Duffy	574
10.	Vince Coleman	698	20.	Ozzie Smith	569

Rickey Henderson keeps adding to his stolen-base mark.

RUNS SCORED

1. Ty Cobb 2,246
2. Babe Ruth 2,174
   Hank Aaron 2,174
4. Pete Rose 2,165
5. Willie Mays 2,062
6. Cap Anson 1,996
7. Stan Musial 1,949
8. Lou Gehrig 1,888
9. Tris Speaker 1,882
10. Mel Ott 1,859
11. Frank Robinson 1,829
12. Eddie Collins 1,821
13. Carl Yastrzemski 1,816
14. Ted Williams 1,798
15. Charlie Gehringer 1,774
16. Jimmie Foxx 1,751
17. Honus Wagner 1,736
18. Jim O'Rourke 1,732
19. Jesse Burkett 1,720
20. Willie Keeler 1,719

WALKS

1. Babe Ruth 2,056
2. Ted Williams 2,019
3. Joe Morgan 1,865
4. Carl Yastrzemski 1,845
5. Mickey Mantle 1,733
6. Mel Ott 1,708
7. Eddie Yost 1,614
8. Darrell Evans 1,605
9. Stan Musial 1,599
10. Pete Rose 1,566
11. Harmon Killebrew 1,559
12. Lou Gehrig 1,508
13. Mike Schmidt 1,507
14. Eddie Collins 1,499
15. Rickey Henderson 1,478
16. Willie Mays 1,464
17. Jimmie Foxx 1,452
18. Eddie Mathews 1,444
19. Frank Robinson 1,420
20. Hank Aaron 1,402

GAMES

1. Pete Rose 3,562
2. Carl Yastrzemski 3,308
3. Hank Aaron 3,298
4. Ty Cobb 3,035
5. Stan Musial 3,026
6. Willie Mays 2,992
7. Rusty Staub 2,951
8. Dave Winfield 2,927
9. Brooks Robinson 2,896
10. Robin Yount 2,856
11. Al Kaline 2,834
12. Eddie Collins 2,826
13. Reggie Jackson 2,820
14. Frank Robinson 2,808
15. Honus Wagner 2,792
16. Tris Speaker 2,789
17. Tony Perez 2,777
18. Mel Ott 2,730
19. George Brett 2,707
20. Eddie Murray 2,706

Babe Ruth didn't draw a walk here, but he was walk champ.

WINS

1. Cy Young 511
2. Walter Johnson 417
3. Pete Alexander 373
   Christy Mathewson 373
5. Jim Galvin 364
6. Warren Spahn 363
7. Kid Nichols 361
8. Tim Keefe 342
9. Steve Carlton 329
10. John Clarkson 328
11. Eddie Plank 326
12. Nolan Ryan 324
    Don Sutton 324
14. Phil Niekro 318
15. Gaylord Perry 314
16. Tom Seaver 311
17. Charley Radbourn 309
18. Mickey Welch 307
19. Early Wynn 300
    Lefty Grove 300

WINNING PERCENTAGE
(1,500 innings minimum)

1. Al Spalding .796
2. Dave Foutz .690
3. Whitey Ford .690
4. Bob Caruthers .688
5. Lefty Grove .680
6. Vic Raschi .667
7. Larry Corcoran .665
   Christy Mathewson .665
9. Sam Leever .660
10. Sal Maglie .657
11. Dick McBride .656
12. Sandy Koufax .655
13. Johnny Allen .654
14. Ron Guidry .651
15. Lefty Gomez .649
    Roger Clemens .649
    Dwight Gooden .649
18. John Clarkson .648
    Mordecai Brown .648
20. Dizzy Dean .644

EARNED-RUN AVERAGE

1. Ed Walsh 1.82
2. Addie Joss 1.89
3. Mordecai Brown 2.06
4. John Ward 2.10
5. Christy Mathewson 2.13
6. Al Spalding 2.14
7. Rube Waddell 2.16
8. Walter Johnson 2.17
9. Orval Overall 2.23
10. Will White 2.28
    Ed Reulbach 2.28
12. Jim Scott 2.30
13. Tommy Bond 2.31
14. Eddie Plank 2.35
15. Larry Corcoran 2.36
16. Ed Killian 2.38
    Eddie Cicotte 2.38
    George McQuillan 2.38
19. Doc White 2.39
20. George Bradley 2.42

Cy Young's 511 wins were achieved in a 22-year career.

STRIKEOUTS

1. Nolan Ryan   5,714
2. Steve Carlton   4,136
3. Bert Blyleven   3,701
4. Tom Seaver   3,640
5. Don Sutton   3,574
6. Gaylord Perry   3,534
7. Walter Johnson   3,509
8. Phil Niekro   3,342
9. Fergie Jenkins   3,192
10. Bob Gibson   3,117
11. Jim Bunning   2,855
12. Mickey Lolich   2,832
13. Cy Young   2,803
14. Frank Tanana   2,773
15. Warren Spahn   2,583
16. Bob Feller   2,581
17. Jerry Koosman   2,556
18. Tim Keefe   2,545
19. Christy Mathewson 2,502
20. Don Drysdale   2,486

SHUTOUTS

1. Walter Johnson   110
2. Pete Alexander   90
3. Christy Mathewson 79
4. Cy Young   76
5. Eddie Plank   69
6. Warren Spahn   63
7. Nolan Ryan   61
   Tom Seaver   61
9. Bert Blyleven   60
10. Don Sutton   58
11. Ed Walsh   57
    Jim Galvin   57
13. Bob Gibson   56
14. Mordecai Brown   55
    Steve Carlton   55
16. Gaylord Perry   53
    Jim Palmer   53
18. Juan Marichal   52
19. Rube Waddell   50
    Vic Willis   50

SAVES

1. Lee Smith   434
2. Jeff Reardon   367
3. Rollie Fingers   341
4. Rich Gossage   310
5. Bruce Sutter   300
6. Dennis Eckersley 294
7. Tom Henke   275
8. John Franco   266
9. Dave Righetti   252
10. Dan Quisenberry 244
11. Sparky Lyle   238
12. Hoyt Wilhelm   227
13. Gene Garber   218
14. Doug Jones   217
15. Dave Smith   216
16. Randy Myers   205
17. Bobby Thigpen   201
18. Roy Face   193
19. Mitch Williams   192
20. Mike Marshall   188

ALL-TIME LEADERS • 439

Can anyone ever top Nolan Ryan's 5,714 strikeouts?

COMPLETE GAMES

1. Cy Young	749		11. Jim McCormick	466
2. Jim Galvin	646		12. Gus Weyhing	448
3. Tim Keefe	554		13. Pete Alexander	437
4. Kid Nichols	531		14. Christy Mathewson	434
Walter Johnson	531		15. Jack Powell	422
6. Bobby Mathews	525		16. Eddie Plank	410
Mickey Welch	525		17. Will White	394
8. Charley Radbourn	489		18. Amos Rusie	392
9. John Clarkson	485		19. Vic Willis	388
10. Tony Mullane	468		20. Tommy Bond	386

GAMES PITCHED

1. Hoyt Wilhelm	1,070		11. Jeff Reardon	880
2. Kent Tekulve	1,050		12. Don McMahon	874
3. Rich Gossage	1,002		13. Phil Niekro	864
4. Lindy McDaniel	987		14. Charlie Hough	858
5. Rollie Fingers	944		15. Dennis Eckersley	849
6. Gene Garber	931		16. Roy Face	848
7. Cy Young	906		17. Tug McGraw	824
8. Sparky Lyle	899		18. Nolan Ryan	807
9. Jim Kaat	898		19. Walter Johnson	802
10. Lee Smith	891		20. Gaylord Perry	777

FEWEST WALKS PER NINE INNINGS
(Minimum 1,500 innings)

1. Al Spalding	0.49		11. Jim Whitney	1.06
Candy Cummings	0.49		12. Jim Galvin	1.12
Tommy Bond	0.49		13. Deacon Phillippe	1.25
4. George Bradley	0.60		14. Will White	1.26
5. George Zettlein	0.61		15. Babe Adams	1.29
6. Terry Larkin	0.71		16. Jack Lynch	1.38
7. Dick McBride	0.74		17. Addie Joss	1.41
8. John Ward	0.92		18. Cy Young	1.49
9. Fred Goldsmith	0.96		19. Guy Hecker	1.51
10. Bobby Mathews	0.97		20. Lee Richmond	1.53

One of Hoyt Wilhelm's 1,070 games was no-hitter in '58.

GAMES STARTED

1. Cy Young	815		11. Warren Spahn	665
2. Nolan Ryan	773		12. Tom Seaver	647
3. Don Sutton	756		13. Jim Kaat	625
4. Phil Niekro	716		14. Frank Tanana	616
5. Steve Carlton	709		15. Early Wynn	612
6. Tommy John	700		16. Robin Roberts	609
7. Gaylord Perry	690		17. Pete Alexander	599
8. Jim Galvin	689		18. Fergie Jenkins	594
9. Bert Blyleven	685		19. Tim Keefe	593
10. Walter Johnson	666		20. Bobby Mathews	568

INNINGS PITCHED

1. Cy Young	7,355.1		11. Kid Nichols	5,056.1
2. Jim Galvin	6,003.1		12. Tim Keefe	5,047.1
3. Walter Johnson	5,915.0		13. Bert Blyleven	4,970.0
4. Phil Niekro	5,404.1		14. Bobby Mathews	4,956.1
5. Nolan Ryan	5,386.0		15. Mickey Welch	4,802.0
6. Gaylord Perry	5,350.1		16. Tom Seaver	4,782.2
7. Don Sutton	5,282.1		17. Christy Mathewson	4,780.2
8. Warren Spahn	5,243.2		18. Tommy John	4,710.1
9. Steve Carlton	5,217.1		19. Robin Roberts	4,688.2
10. Pete Alexander	5,190.0		20. Early Wynn	4,564.0

ACTIVE LEADERS

HITS

1. Dave Winfield 3,088
2. Eddie Murray 2,930
3. Andre Dawson 2,700
4. Paul Molitor 2,647
5. Wade Boggs 2,392
6. Ozzie Smith 2,365
7. Lou Whitaker 2,296
8. Alan Trammell 2,260
9. Cal Ripken 2,227
10. Rickey Henderson 2,216

HOME RUNS

1. Dave Winfield 463
2. Eddie Murray 458
3. Andre Dawson 428
4. Cal Ripken 310
5. Joe Carter 302
6. Darryl Strawberry 294
7. Kent Hrbek 293
8. Harold Baines 277
9. Jose Canseco 276
10. Tom Brunansky 271

Dave Winfield got his first hits with San Diego in '73.

RUNS BATTED IN

1. Dave Winfield 1,829
2. Eddie Murray 1,738
3. Andre Dawson 1,540
4. Harold Baines 1,198
5. Cal Ripken 1,179
6. Joe Carter 1,097
7. Kent Hrbek 1,086
8. Don Mattingly 1,050
9. Tim Wallach 1,045
10. Lou Whitaker 1,040

GAMES

1. Dave Winfield 2,927
2. Eddie Murray 2,706
3. Andre Dawson 2,506
4. Ozzie Smith 2,447
5. Lou Whitaker 2,306
6. Willie Wilson 2,154
7. Alan Trammell 2,153
8. Paul Molitor 2,131
9. Rickey Henderson 2,080
10. Cal Ripken 2,074

WINS

1. Jack Morris 254
2. Dennis Martinez 219
3. Charlie Hough 216
4. Bob Welch 211
5. Dennis Eckersley 188
6. Frank Viola 175
7. Roger Clemens 172
8. Rick Sutcliffe 171
9. Dave Stewart 165
10. Scott Sanderson 162
    Bill Gullickson 162

STRIKEOUTS

1. Jack Morris 2,478
2. Charlie Hough 2,362
3. Dennis Eckersley 2,245
4. Roger Clemens 2,201
5. Mark Langston 2,110
6. Bob Welch 1,969
7. Dennis Martinez 1,923
8. Dwight Gooden 1,875
9. F. Valenzuela 1,861
10. Frank Viola 1,822

SAVES

1. Lee Smith 434
2. Jeff Reardon 367
3. Rich Gossage 310
4. Dennis Eckersley 294
5. Tom Henke 275
6. John Franco 266
7. Dave Righetti 252
8. Doug Jones 217
9. Randy Myers 205
10. Bobby Thigpen 201

GAMES PITCHED

1. Rich Gossage 1,002
2. Lee Smith 891
3. Jeff Reardon 880
4. Charlie Hough 858
5. Dennis Eckersley 849
6. Jesse Orosco 754
7. Dave Righetti 708
8. Steve Bedrosian 703
9. Larry Andersen 699
10. Craig Lefferts 696

Jack Morris reigns as active leader in wins and strikeouts.

Chili Davis' red-hot bat is improving with age.

Paul O'Neill was splendid splinter en route to .359.

Revised and updated third edition!

THE ILLUSTRATED SPORTS RECORD BOOK
Zander Hollander and David Schulz

Here, in a single book, are more than 400 all-time—and current—sports records with 50 new stories and 125 action photos so vivid, it's like "being there." Featured is an all-star cast that includes Martina Navratilova, Joe DiMaggio, Joe Montana, Michael Jordan, Jack Nicklaus, Mark Spitz, Wayne Gretzky, Nolan Ryan, Muhammad Ali, Greg LeMond, Hank Aaron, Carl Lewis and Magic Johnson. This is *the* authoritative book that sets the record straight and recreates the feats at the time of achievement!

Buy them at your local bookstore or use this convenient coupon for ordering.

PENGUIN USA
P.O. Box 999 — Dept. #17109
Bergenfield, New Jersey 07621

Please send me _____ paperback copies of THE ILLUSTRATED SPORTS RECORD BOOK 0-451-17117-9 at $5.99 ($6.99 in Canada) each. Please enclose $2.00 per order to cover postage and handling. I enclose ☐ check ☐ money order.

Name_____

Address_____

City _____ State _____ Zip Code _____

Allow a minimum of 4-6 weeks for delivery.
This offer prices and numbers are subject to change without notice.